Moving Media Storage Technologies
Applications & Workflows for Video and Media Server Platforms

Karl Paulsen

AMSTERDAM • BOSTON • HEIDELBERG • LONDON • NEW YORK • OXFORD • PARIS
SAN DIEGO • SAN FRANCISCO • SINGAPORE • SYDNEY • TOKYO

Focal Press is an imprint of Elsevier

Focal Press is an imprint of Elsevier
30 Corporate Drive, Suite 400, Burlington, MA 01803, USA
The Boulevard, Langford Lane, Kidlington, Oxford, OX5 1GB, UK

Library of Congress Cataloging-in-Publication Data
Paulsen, Karl, 1952-
  Moving media storage technologies : applications & workflows for video and media server platforms / Karl Paulsen.
     p. cm.
  Includes bibliographical references and index.
  ISBN 978-0-240-81448-3 (hardback)
  1. Computer storage devices. 2. Multimedia systems. 3. Digital video. 4. Client/server computing. I. Title.
  TK7895.M4P38 2011
  006.7–dc22

                                                                                          2011003092

British Library Cataloguing-in-Publication Data
A catalogue record for this book is available from the British Library.

ISBN: 978-0-240-81448-3

For information on all Focal Press publications
visit our website at *www.elsevierdirect.com*

Printed in the United States of America
11 12 13 14 15   5 4 3 2 1

Typeset by: diacriTech, Chennai, India

CONTENTS

Companion website: www.elsevierdirect.com/companions/9780240814483

Acknowledgments

Books like these cannot be brought forth without an enormous amount of support from colleagues, friends, and professionals who devote their lives and careers to the betterment of the industry as a whole. I have been fortunate over my career spanning some 35 years in broadcasting and systems engineering to have worked with and been surrounded by the best of the best. Through a continued involvement with the Society of Motion Picture and Television Engineers (SMPTE) since the early 1980s, it has been an ambition of mine to convey the knowledge gained to the up-and-comers of this profession.

Purpose of this book: to help inform and extend value to my colleagues and all those who read this book is this author's greatest hope.

I would like to thank some particularly influential people who have helped make this book, and my previous books, successful and those who have supported my writing and made it possible for me to convey the knowledge I have accrued. First, it is important to recognize my editor at *TV Technology*, Tom Butts, who has supported the longest running column about video and media server technologies, which I have anchored for more than 15 years. The feature column of "Media Server Technologies" has appeared monthly in the magazine and on the Web for well over 150 installments. The title has now changed to "INSIGHT: Storage Technology" to more appropriately represent the next generation of topics. The second person I must thank is Debra McAdams, author and editor, who has provided the wisdom, humor, and faith to see that the column remains a success.

Third are those who are equally influential from the technology and the business sides. These individuals are my silent (and yet sometimes quite active) mentors; they most assuredly include John Luff, S. Merrill Weiss, Clyde Smith, and Al Kovalick. My thanks to them for being there when the questions needed to be answered.

Finally, at the top of the list is my family, my wife and partner, Jenny, and our children, Melissa and Kevin, to whom this book is dedicated because without their support, it would not have been possible.

INTRODUCTION

Storage technologies have fundamentally changed the landscape of digital media in a profound way. Gone are the days of using a single hard disk drive on a workstation as the sole means to store digital content. Nearly vanished is the practice of capturing video and audio only on videotape. The practice of transferring videotape recordings into an edit station and then manipulating sequences of images and sound has matured to the point that the content now goes straight from a file captured in a camcorder to a storage system where any number of other activities will happen. This is what the industry has coined "digital" or "file-based workflows."

Videotape as we know it is close to the end of its practical life. The fledgling domain of storing images as files is well onto its way toward becoming the default means to capture, store, and work; driving digital workflows forward on an almost incomprehensible schedule. As a consequence of this new generation of digital workflows, the volumes of unstructured data are growing to staggering proportions at unprecedented rates. Managing these files has become a science, taking the IT world and placing it into another dimension.

In the not-too-distant past, data would simply be stored on disk or on tape with those peripheral devices simply connected to a server or a local workstation. The storage platform, be that as it may, was considered a peripheral entity to the computer. Issues surrounding security, permissions, access rights, and protection were handled by the server; the duty of editing or producing was left to the workstation or PC. Storage management was rather straightforward; but that is no longer the case.

Storage is now an entity unto its own, detached and independent from the computers and workstations, especially in the media content, production, and editorial world. Storage is now just a segment of the overall system of tools that users employ to do their work. For this new storage environment, the term "storage network" was conceived. It started out simple: attach a self-contained box with a disk drive or two to a network port or a bus (e.g., SCSI, Firewire, USB, etc). Begin working. Simple enough, yes. Add more workstations, attach the storage to Ethernet, add more connections, start sharing files among the workstations, and soon you ran out of storage. No problem, add another network-attached storage (NAS) box.

This practice continues today, almost everywhere. It works until it no longer does; or it can no longer grow; or the system slows to a crawl because too many users who are all facing a deadline need access to too little storage. Trying to find the data is a whole other issue, one we are just beginning to discover.

This is the state of the industry in all too many corners of the production, postproduction, and media entertainment content creation world. To the rescue comes the storage network, whether it is a storage area network (SAN), a NAS, or a cluster. This is where the industry will be tomorrow. And this is what this book addresses—the future of the storage industry for moving media.

Who Is This Book for?

This book was written for those who want to know more about the evolving world of networked storage solutions for moving media than what you can find by searching for topics on SANs, LANs, and NASs. The book is aimed at the media professional, the IT administrator, the broadcaster, and the managers who are faced with making choices that are driven as much by revenue generation as practicality and functionality. The topics inside this cover should be looked upon as both reference guides and as plain language explanations about the subject matter important to the selection and implementation of storage systems, networked or otherwise. In the context of the technology, the book continually applies explanations and examples in support of collaborative workflows for an all-digital moving image environment.

By moving images, we of course mean video. And video can only be so interesting without sound, so we collectively associated sound and video to the moving image. Then, there is that additional "information" about the moving images that allows users to catalog, locate, and annotate the video and audio so that it provides better value to the next user who needs access to it. The terms "metadata" and "media asset management" are covered in Chapter 13 as they pertain to the storage environment. Both of these are essential to the successful management of any storage solution at any scale.

The reader may be a user, a technician, or someone who just needs a book that "covers it all." The book will not get into how Final Cut Pro works on a MacBook Pro, nor will it look at precisely how to build up a video/media server farm that produces content for video on demand. It will let the user be exposed to and become familiar with many of the architectures and storage subsystem topologies in use today so as to help them make informed decisions before trusting the word of a storage solution provider without even a question or a reason to doubt.

About This Book

One cannot just leap into the middle of storage technologies without some background and some perspective. The pages ahead start out by covering the historical development of digital recording and disk technologies that serve as the foundation of where we are today. The first chapters look at the perspectives of information as data, especially in its video form. Included are topics about the forms and formats of digital disk recording, and the video/media servers that placed the footprint in the sand for this new era of digital recording and file management.

The next group of chapters takes a look under the hood of those components and pieces that make up a storage environment. We go under the cover of the hard drive, and take a look at the buses, ports, and interfaces that support the storage platforms both internally and externally. Then, we move on to the various kinds of storage, from drives and arrays to optical and solid state media.

At the next juncture, the book starts to get deeper into the technologies that make up and support storage networks. This is where we get into the specifics of media-centric environments. How the files are interchanged, transcoded, and manipulated are key elements in making all digital file-based workflows happen. The chapters that follow explore forms of IP storage, clustering, archives, and backups.

With sufficient introductions to the terminologies, the book then covers the real crux of storage: networks, intelligent high-performance and shared storage, and how these systems can scale in terms of extensibility and interoperability to provide the resources needed for the activities that depend upon the networked storage environments we now live in. Toward the end of this book, we look at storage management and how to build resilient, fault-tolerant virtual systems that are usable, serviceable, and functional.

Recording Moving Media

The 1980s and 1990s saw a continual progression of advancements in videotape recording formats. Disk storage technologies were barely infants during the development of a maturing digital videotape era. Manufacturers continued to add new products that used the emerging compression technologies and placed them into linear tape formats, knowing that eventually the deployment of disk-based storage, production, and editing was on the horizon and would ultimately be the replacement storage medium for those formats they created.

Once the disc or disk (the former being the optical form, the latter being the magnetic form) became the formidable solution that it is today, the recording processes began to move away from linear tape and on to solid state media, removable disc media, and transportable/removable hard disk media. With mobile and wireless technologies where they are today, many have not even a clue about what recording a "video" to a VHS tape is. To this generation there are no moving parts, just screens and the ether (wired or otherwise).

This is where we are headed: any image, anywhere, anytime. Yet, managing that data becomes the 64 million dollar question both technically and virtually. This is where this book helps the user and the technologist to better understand how the pieces fit together into a cohesive workspace that functions in a productive and efficient manner.

Why This Book?

There are dozens of books about network storage, resilient storage systems, IP-based storage systems, and the list goes on. These are all valuable and important references from which to draw upon. In researching for this writing and in looking for the deep dives on the subject matter, the author found the research and knowledge that these renowned books on storage provided offered excellent value and a much greater understanding of the interior structures of network-based storage systems. However, they are quite technical, focused on IT or database management, and in some cases provided only a marginal connection to applications for media and motion imaging.

It is the goal of this book to add some common sense relationships between storage technologies and the applications upon which those production and distribution activities depend upon. Much of what the moving media industry has learned about came from the IT world. Many of the processes and standards used by the storage industry were developed and ratified by the IT industry, which includes the IETF, ISO, IEC, SNIA, and others. Without these organizations development would remain bogged down in endless debate about being sure that legacy or backward capabilities be maintained forever. In reality, that just is not possible. To slow down progress by insisting that inappropriate or no longer implemented technologies remain the lowest common denominator does nothing to help advancement.

So this is what change is about; it is about a future that can be as extensible as it is practical. Inside these covers, you will get a glimpse at the past, a look at the present, and a view to the future.

The connections in the media and entertainment world that this author has enjoyed over the past 20 years of writing about disk-based storage media for video and production have been invaluable in helping to understand, explain, and pontificate about the directions that storage has taken. The professionals at companies including Avid, Grass Valley (in all its iterations), Omneon (now a part of Harmonic), SeaChange, Evertz, and Harris/Leitch have all provided the support and wisdom necessary to find, understand, and then compile the subject matter in this book.

In another corner of the universe are those storage system providers that take on a different position with regard to high-performance and high-availability storage that is centered not only on media and entertainment but also for the oil and gas industry, medical imaging and data, geotechnical exploration, and computing industries of today and tomorrow. These companies provide storage solutions at a different level from those just previously mentioned. They are the makers of SANs and NASs that you see in enterprise-class installations for structured and unstructured data, but you also see them in the animation shops, production houses, and even in the network distribution centers for CBS, Fox, and others.

The storage specialists at NetApp, Isilon/EMC, Data Direct Networks, IBM, HP, Hitachi Data Systems, Quantum/StorNext, BlueArc, and many others have helped the industry to grow and to answer the calls for innovative storage systems in atmospheres unlike any others. Without the storage solution providers mentioned already, such motion picture projects as Avatar, Tron, and Thor could not happen. These are the kinds of endeavors that would not be possible without the likes of the products that these companies have developed often under duress, and certainly under a time constraint.

There are many noted professionals in the industry where this author works that are the visionaries and directors who have instilled the drive and ambition to assemble the content you will see between Chapter 1 and the back cover. It would be impossible to recognize all of them and do even a few the justice that they all deserve. The value and wisdom that these individuals, their companies, and the marketplace have conveyed is immeasurable. So the author would again like to thank them all and hope their contributions to the development of the industry as a whole continues.

INFORMATION, DATA, AND VIDEO

The process of digitally storing moving images and sound begins by converting once analog video and audio signals into a stream of discrete representations of binary numbers corresponding to sampled levels of chroma and luminance (for video) or for audio, correlating the changes in dynamic air pressure, which have already been converted into electrical signals as they were captured by transducers over time. In the digital media world, this string of binary information is represented as data and is often referred to as bits and bytes.

The recording function collects, organizes, and retains this data in a format that can be recovered for reproduction as visual information on a display or audible information on a loudspeaker-like transducer. In between the collection and the reproduction phases, the data is retained on a media form. The retention platform is referred to as storage, which can be both a process (i.e., the process of actually capturing or placing the data onto a recordable media) and the physical media itself (e.g., a magnetic hard disk, a lineal videotape, or an optical disc such as a CD-ROM or a Blu-ray Disc).

KEY CHAPTER POINTS

- When does data become information
- Qualifying structured versus unstructured data
- Requirements for the storage of moving images
- Identifying analog composite and component video signal sets
- Digital video recording explained in terms of its components
- Elements of digital video (bit depth, colorimetry, and formats)

Data Structure

In general, data may be classified as either unstructured or structured. The factor for classification is determined by how the data is stored and how it is managed. Rigidly defined data is much easier to access and manage than random sets or elements that are arranged in nondiscriminate structures.

Rigidly structured data is traditionally relegated to databases that are built and maintained by a fully fledged database management system (DBMS). Unstructured data is considered "everything else"; however, there is an area in between, which is neither rigidly structured nor completely unstructured. This gray area is called semistructured because it has a reasonable amount of order or grouping but is clearly not consistent across an enterprise, a department, or even an individual.

In business, more than 80% of an enterprise's data that is typically used for non-media-related purposes is unstructured. This raises huge concerns for the enterprise as unstructured or semistructured data consumes an enormous amount of storage and is extremely difficult to manage.

Taking an ad hoc approach to data structures for media-related data extends the complexities well beyond what the traditional business space has had to face—with the issues and concerns growing even larger. From this, the business and technologies of storage have become a science.

Information

Data that is created either by individuals or by enterprises needs to be stored so that it can be accessed and easily recovered for processing at a later time. There is no reasonable purpose for data unless it is capable of being presented in a meaningful form. In the business world, the knowledge and intelligence derived from this data are called information.

Before the current digital age, data were collected on printed paper and stored in filing cabinets or placed on library shelves as books or periodicals. Information could be gathered from this format because there was a structure for accessing the data that could be configured in a repeatable and definable classification. The Dewey Decimal Classification (DDC), also known as the Dewey Decimal System, was developed by Melvil Dewey in 1876, and is an example of a proprietary system that is used for library classification. The DDC is one methodology for arranging data in a structured classification.

Today, information is categorized by myriad methods each tailored to a product, an application, a location, or a service. Much of the information presented is dependent on a form of indexing. The indexing uses the concepts of tagging to put the data into a structure that is usable by others. Search engines have become the foremost means of discovering that information.

Given the enormous and growing amounts of media-related information, the value of intelligent storage and the systems associated with searching and retrieval are being elevated to new proportions. Managing the storage systems, and complimentary distribution paths such as networks and transmission devices, is becoming a significant part of what was once an area dedicated to the information technology (IT) sectors only.

For the media and entertainment industries and the public and private business sectors, these concepts are rapidly changing, resulting in a new paradigm for those systems associated with the storage of media-centric data and information.

Storing the Moving Image

Film was and remains one of the most notable forms of storing visual information either as a single static format (as in a photograph) or a series of discrete images on a continuous linear medium (as in a motion picture film).

For at least the past three decades, moving images and sound recordings have been stored on various media including wires, plastics and vinyl materials, rigid metallics, or other polymers, but primarily these recordings have been captured on the most well-known magnetic media, simply referred to as "tape."

The information contained on this lineal magnetic recording media is often segregated by the type of recorded information contained on the media, that is, sound on audiotape, visual images with sound on videotape, and for the computer industry bits representing binary information on data tape. Over the course of time, the format of these audio-, video- and data-recording processes has moved steadily away from the analog recordings domain toward the digital domain. This migration from analog to digital recording was made possible by a multitude of technological innovations that when combined into varying structures, some standardized and others not, formulate the means by which most of the audio, visual, and data are currently retained (see Fig 1.1).

However, these are all changing, as will be seen and identified in the upcoming portions of this book. Videotape as a recording and playback medium is gradually, but finally, moving away from the traditional formats of the past nearly half century.

History of recording and media

1877—Edison makes the first recording of a human voice on the first tinfoil cylinder phonograph.	**1984**—Digital Equipment Corporation (DEC) introduces Digital Linear Tape (DLT), which was formerly called CompacTape, and the TK50 drive for the MicroVAX II and PDP-11.
1898—Valdemar Poulsen (Denmark) patents the "telegraphone," the first magnetic recorder that uses steel wire.	**1985**—Magneto-optical (MO) disc drive is introduced.
1925—The first electrically recorded discs and Orthophonic phonographs go on sale.	**1985**—The standard for compact disc read-only memory (CD-ROM) computer discs (produced by Sony and Philips) that use the same laser technology as the audio CD is introduced.
1928—Dr. Fritz Pfleumer receives a patent in Germany for application of magnetic powders to strip off paper or film.	**1987**—Digital audio tape (DAT) players are introduced.
1944—The Minnesota Mining and Manufacturing (3M Company) begins coating experiments for tape under Ralph J. Oace.	**1991**—First ADAT (Alesis Digital Audio Tape) recorders are shipped in March.
1948—The first Ampex Model 200 tape recorders are employed for The Bing Crosby Show #27, which is recorded on 3M Scotch 111 gamma ferric-oxide-coated acetate tape.	**1992**—Digital compact cassette (DCC) created by Philips and Matsushita (Panasonic). Sony develops the MiniDisc as a rival.
1951—The Ampex team, led by Charles Ginsburg, begins work on a videotape recorder in October. Bing Crosby Enterprises demonstrates its experimental 100 in./second, 12-head VTR.	**1996**—DVD players are first introduced and only available in Japan.
1953—Vladimir K. Zworykin and RCA Labs demonstrate a longitudinal three-head VTR running at 360 in./second that uses amplitude-modulated (AM) sound.	**1997**—The first DVD players available in the United States.
	1998—The first DVD players are available in Europe.
1956—Ampex demonstrates the first practical quadruplex VTR at the Chicago National Association of Broadcasters (NAB) exhibition on April 14. The "quad" uses 2-in.-wide 3M tape running at 15 ips over a rotating head assembly recording at a slant on the tape surface with AM sound. Over the next 4 years, 600 units at $75,000 each are sold, mostly to the television network stations.	**2000**—Sony introduces the Playstation 2 console in Japan, which has the capability to play DVD movies.
	2000—September, first commercial LTO-1 tape format with 100-Gbyte storage and 20 Mbytes/second data transfer speeds introduced.
1959—Toshiba demonstrates a prototype single head helical scan VTR using 2-in. tape running at 15 ips. Following the demonstration, Sony begins to develop its helical scan VTR.	**2002**—The Blu-ray Disc Association is founded. Sony, on February 19, 2002, in partnership with nine companies, unveil the plans.
1963—Sony markets the first open-reel 1/2-in. helical scan VTR for home use at a retail price of $995.	**2002**—On August 29, Toshiba and NEC propose to the DVD Forum a next-generation optical disc format that will become the HD DVD.
1967—The first instant replay is shown using the Ampex HS-100 color video disk recorder for ABC's "World Series of Skiing" in Vail, Colorado.	**2004**—January, Sony introduces the Hi-MD, a further development of the MiniDisc format, which would later support MP3, as well as other computer data formats.
1969—Sony introduces the first 3/4-in. U-matic 1-hour videocassette, which is available in the United States in 1971.	**2004**—Toshiba unveils first prototype HD DVD player at the Consumer Electronics Show, to be backward compatible with the DVD.
1975—Sony introduces the Betamax consumer VCR. The console sold for $2295, with a 1-hour 1/2-in.-tape cassette sold for $15.95.	**2005**—Sony and Toshiba begin discussions of a possible single-format HD version of the DVD, which end up nowhere.
1976—JVC introduces to Japan the "Video Home System" (VHS) format videocassette recorder (VCR) for US$885.	**2006**—The first Blu-ray players are sold, with the first title released on June 20, 2006. Microsoft announces it will support the HD DVD for the Xbox 360 gaming platform, including movie playback.
	2007—Combination HD DVD and Blu-ray players are introduced. It is almost too late as the studios are starting to announce they are stopping support for HD DVD in favor of Blu-ray Disc.
1978—Pioneer develops the laser disc, first used by General Motors to train its Cadillac sales staff. Pioneer begins selling home version laser disc players in 1980.	**2008**—Throughout the year, HD DVD production ceases and retailers stop carrying or producing content—Blu-ray Disc wins the format battle.
	2010—January, first LTO-5 specification is announced, products become available in Q2-2010.

Figure 1.1 A selected history of recording and physical media development.

Digital Video Recording

Digital video recording is a generalization in terminology that has come to mean anything that is not expressly an analog recording. These much belabored references have worked their way into every facet of the industry, compounded even more by the widespread introduction of high definition and the transition from analog over-the-air transmission to digital terrestrial television (DTT) broadcasting.

Clarifying 601 Digital Video

It goes without saying that digital video brought new dimensions to the media and entertainment industry. For the video segment of the industry, this began in earnest with the development of standardized video encoding in the 1980s whereby interchange and formalized products could store, in high quality, the video characterized by its original description as CCIR 601, which later became known as ITU-R BT.601 when the CCIR, International Radio Consultative Committee (French name: Comité consultatif international pour la radio), merged with others, and in 1992 became the ITU-R, International Telecommunication Union-Radiocommunications Sector.

As with many emerging technologies, technical jargon is generated that is filled with marketing hype that makes the concept "sound good" regardless of the appropriateness or accuracy of the terminology. Digital video recording was no different. With its roots embedded in analog (NTSC and PAL) structures, digital video terminology has become easy to misinterpret. In the hope that the readers of this book will be given the opportunity to "get it right," we will use the terminology that is standards based, or at least as close to the industry accepted syntax as possible. To that end, we'll start by describing the migration from analog component video through to compressed digital video storage.

Analog Component Video

Prior to digital video-encoding technologies being used for the capture and storage of moving media, videotape transport manufacturers recognized that the image quality of moving video could be better maintained if it was carried in its component video structure as opposed to the single-channel composite video format used throughout studios and transmission systems prior to digital (e.g., as composite NTSC or PAL video). Not unlike the early days of color television signal distribution in the studio, where video would be transported as discrete components throughout portions of the signal chain, the process of video interchange between analog tape recorders was pioneered by the early use of "dubbing" connector interfaces between component analog transports.

Analog Component Signals

In the era of early color television broadcasting, the impact of the legacy monochrome (black and white) signal sets remained as facilities moved from hybrid monochrome and color systems to an all color analog television plant. Those component video signals that comprised the technical elements of video signal systems consisted of both composite signals and discrete sets of signals including the primary red-green-blue (RGB) triplet set of color signals. Depending on the makeup of the video processing chains, additional horizontal and vertical synchronization (H and V) signals, composite sync (S), and color subcarrier (3.58 MHz color burst) might have been distributed throughout the facility.

Often, these signals were carried on individual coaxial cables throughout the television plant. As color television systems developed further, the number of individual discrete signals diminished, except for specialty functions such as chroma keys. The concept of component video signal technologies reemerged in the early 1980s, enabled by the desire to carry other sets of individual channels of component analog video on either pairs or triplets of coaxial cabling.

Two fundamental signal groups make up the so-called component analog video signal set. The signal set described by the three primary colors red-green-blue, better known as simply RGB, may be considered the purest form of the full bandwidth set of video signals. In a three-channel color television imaging system, a set of signals is generated from the light focused in the camera's lens and is passed to the prismatic optic block (see Fig 1.2). When the field image passes through the prism and is optically divided into three images, each corresponds to one of the elements of the RGB color set. Depending on the electrical makeup of the image, which may be a CCD or a CMOS imager, the electrical signals generated by the imager are amplified and their components are applied to electrical systems in which they are eventually scaled and combined according to the signal standard to form a television video signal.

Analog component video signal sets found in video systems may include more than just the primary RGB triplet of signals. These additional component signal sets, designated as RGBS, RGBHV, or RG&SB signals, are often used when connecting computer-generated video graphic signals to displays configured for video graphics array (VGA) signals and beyond.

In its "pure" format, RGB signals should be considered full-bandwidth representations of optic-to-electrical energy. In this format, full-bandwidth RGB signals are rarely used in video processing or video production. RGB signals generally do not use compression and in turn do not impose real limits on color depth or resolution. As a result, they require a huge

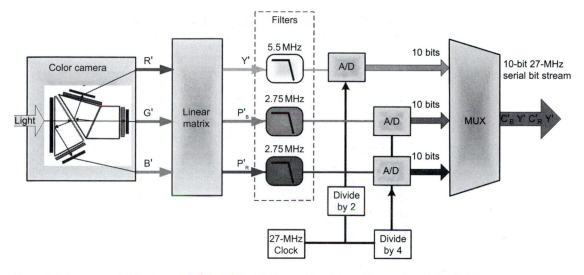

Figure 1.2 Component video to serial digital video bit stream signal flow, filter, and multiplex (MUX).

amount of bandwidth to carry the signal and contain significant amounts of redundant data since each color channel will typically include the same black-and-white image associated with the percentages of color information for the RGB channel they represent. Recording this type of RGB signal onto analog lineal videotape would be impractical, though not necessarily unimplemented. While the digitization of the "pure RGB signals" would offer the cleanest preservation or integrity of the image, it is fraught with a myriad of issues far beyond the topics of this section.

Typically, when component signals are used in analog or digital video recording, the RGB components are not used but instead a different scaling and combination referred to as color difference signals or sometimes just component video signals are used. Component video signals are scaled differently than the straight pure RGB signals, given that video displays must account for both the human visual system and the physical properties of the display system. Because of these issues, we alter the scaling of the RGB signals to produce a nonlinear set of video component signals that are used in displays, digitized videos, and compression systems. When these nonlinear signal sets are derived, they are referenced with prime (') marks that follow each of the alpha characters. Then, the three primary colors are designated as R'G'B'.

Color Difference Designations

When referring to color difference signal sets, the term luma is established to reference the colorless video channel. Luma should not be confused with luminance, which is confined to color science. Luma is derived from the properly scaled combinations of the red-blue-green channels. Luma is designated by Y' (pronounced as "why" + "prime") and is specifically and directly used in the video system terminologies to distinguish it from the color science–related Y ("without prime") luminance.

This luma (Y') signal is derived from the scaled set of the original full-bandwidth RGB-triplet color set that is used in video applications, referred to as R'G'B'. The Y' component is computed as a weighted sum of these nonlinear R'G'B' primary components using coefficients calculated from the reference primaries according to the method given in SMPTE RP 177 Recommended Practice. The derivation of the Y' signal commonly used for analog encoding is

$$Y' = 0.2126R' + 0.7152G' + 0.0722B'$$

The associated video signal set that contains the color information component is referred to as chroma and is designated by the letter C. You may see differing variants of the Y and C combinations throughout video signal technologies (refer to Table 1.1 for more information).

Digital from Its Components

When applying analog component video to digital video applications, the three nonlinear video signal information sets are transformed into one luma signal and two chroma signals. These signals are subjected to nonlinear processing, with the chroma signals scaled and band limited. For digital video applications, the luma and chroma sets are designated as Y', C'_R, and C'_B. This digital signal format is described in ITU-R BT.601, the convention stating that the C'_R and C'_B pair will represent color difference signals with values from 16 to 240 (in 8-bit quantization).

For applications in which the analog video signal representations are used in color encoding and analog interfaces, the three nonlinear video signal information sets are transformed into a different set of three color difference signals, containing one luma and two chroma channels. As with the digital set, each of these signals has been subjected to nonlinear processing, with the chroma signals band limited. They are designated as Y', P'_R, and P'_B. By convention, P'_R and P'_B represent color difference signals in the analog video signal domain whereby the typical voltage excursion is between −350 mV and +350 mV. The luma (Y')

Table 1.1 Component Analog and Digital Recording Levels

Luma and Chroma Components Used in Analog Video Encoding

Format	1125/60/2:1 720/60/1:1	525/59.94/2:1 625/50/2:1 1250/50/2:1
Y'	$0.2126R' + 0.7152G' + 0.0722B'$	$0.299R' + 0.587G' + 0.114B'$
R' − Y'	$0.7874R' − 0.7152G' + 0.0722B'$	$0.701R' + 0.587G' + 0.114B'$
B' − Y'	$−0.2126R' − 0.7152G' + 0.9278B'$	$−0.299R' + 0.587G' + 0.886B'$

Luma and Chroma Components for Analog Component Video

Format	1125/60/2:1 SMPTE 240M	1920 × 1080 SMPTE 274M 1280 × 720 SMPTE 296M	525/59.94/2:1 625/50/2:1 1250/50/2:1
Y'	$0.2126R' + 0.701G' + 0.087B'$	$0.2126R' + 0.7152G' + 0.0722B'$	$0.299R' + 0.587G' + 0.114B'$
P'_B	$(B' − Y')/1.826$	$[0.5/(1 − 0.0722)] (B' − Y')$	$0.564 (B' − Y')$
P'_R	$(R' − Y')/1.576$	$[0.5/(1 − 0.2126)] (R' − Y')$	$0.713 (R' − Y')$

Luma and Chroma Components, Offset and Scaled for Digital Quantization

Format	1920 × 1080 SMPTE 274M 1280 × 720 SMPTE 296M	525/59.94/2:1 625/50/2:1 1250/50/2:1
Y'	$0.2126R' + 0.7152G' + 0.0722B'$	$0.299R' + 0.587G' + 0.114B'$
C'_B	$0.5389 (B' − Y') + 350\ mV$	$0.564 (B' − Y') + 350\ mV$
C'_R	$0.6350 (R' − Y') + 350\ mV$	$0.713 (R' − Y') + 350\ mV$

signal has a voltage excursion (i.e., a dynamic range) of 700 mV. Figure 1.3 shows how the color difference matrix generates the Y', R − Y' and B − Y' signals from the original RGB signals.

Auxiliary Signals

An auxiliary component, sometimes called the alpha channel, is designated by the letter A. This component may optionally accompany R'G'B' and $Y'C'_B C'_R$ signal sets. The interfaces denoted as R'G'B'A and $Y'C'_B C'_R A$ include this auxiliary component that, when present, has the same signal characteristics as the Y' or G' channel, that is, a colorless signal prescribing the luminance level of the video signal.

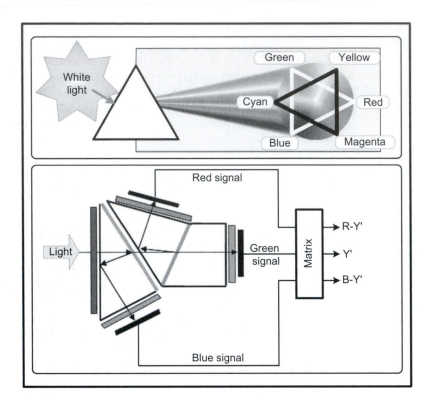

Figure 1.3 Component video signals derived from captured light, separated by a prism, and presented to a matrix to produce the color difference signals used in analog component and digital component video signals.

YUV Confusion

Another derivation of component analog video is used by those areas using the 625-line 25-frame-per-second PAL (Phase Alternating Line) standard, as opposed to the 525-line 30-frame-per-second NTSC (National Television Systems Committee) standard. This signal set, called YUV, has a similar structure with the luma channel (Y) derived from scaled nonlinear red-green-blue (R'G'B') signals:

$$Y = 0.299R' + 0.587G' + 0.114B'$$

The PAL system refers to its color difference signals as U and V, which like NTSC, are used to carry the chroma information. For composite signal encoding, each has a typical bandwidth of 1.3 MHz:

$$U = 0.493(B' - Y)$$

$$V = 0.877(R' - Y)$$

Note that some documents may show that the U signal equals 0.492(B' − Y).

Although the terminology is widespread, when the application involves conversion to component digital video, these Y'UV color difference components are almost never used. The improper association of YC_BC_R with YUV has remained for some time, the latter being a different color space that is not used in digital media, and that should only be applied in composite analog PAL-based signals (i.e., in non-NTSC analog TV transmission or videotapes).

Bit Depth

To fully describe digital video signal systems, especially when addressing digitally encoded formats, additional information is necessary. Digital video specifications must state whether the digital representation employs uniform quantization (linear), PCM, 8-bit, 10-bit, or 12-bit video encoding. The importance of this becomes much more obvious when considering the formats and structures of the capture (ingest) processes, the transport, and the storage of the digital video. The bit depth can play a significant role in the metrics related to file sizes and thus storage capacity, plus the ability to retain a greater signal quality when used in video production, special effects, cross or film conversion, and archive.

Additional considerations having to do with digital image processing are also impacted as the numerical calculation requirements are increased as well.

Colorimetry and Conversion

Another important metric related to colorimetric analysis and opto-electronic transfer functions of the signal is the defining of the proper color space parameters. These parameters are of particular importance whenever signals are transcoded or repurposed from one format to another, e.g., when converting from a standard definition to high-definition format. The standard that defines these parameters is ITU-R BT.709.

Legacy material created on systems before the acceptance of SMPTE and ITU-R standards may contain different or improper colorimetry parameters. Although the differences are small and most likely noticed only with precision test materials, designers and users should be aware that some of this legacy material in this format was originally created using the SMPTE 240M standard, which prescribed a different colorimetry relationship.

When converting between digital and analog representations of signals, for both displays and production equipment, it is important to recognize that the colorimetry can be affected. Most of the available professional video signal processing hardware provides the proper scaling and conversion software, but systems employed in the early 1990s and even some flavors of software-only codecs may not properly apply all of the conversion parameters. Only modern test signal and measurement systems can detect these colorimetry discrepancies.

Typical groupings of component video may be comprised of two signals (Y and C) as is used in S-Video or a triplet of luminance and color difference signals (YP_BP_R), commonly found in analog videotape formats or the signal outputs of consumer devices such as gaming consoles or DVD players.

A Digital Media World: Going Forward

The developments in digital media recording took several steps and paths to get to where it is today. The formats that are commonplace today evolved through a combination of various moving media technologies, extraordinary improvements in computing capabilities, and adjustments to production and information technology workflow, as well as a gradual industry acceptance.

There are dozens of excellent books and thousands of citations online that describe the overwhelming number of digital media formats and their terminologies. It is sometimes complicated and often difficult to understand completely just how these various flavors of media interoperate, due in part to some of the confusion raised by the vernacular that came out of the industry needing to identify the previously undiscovered forms of content and program production. In many situations, marketing buzzwords were created to describe the functionality of the services and the systems. Many of today's file formats for digital recording came directly from the manufacturers, who created their own means and methods for the digital capturing and retention of these moving images.

These myriad variations in compression formats, bit rates, coding structures, wrappers, containers, and nomenclatures are aimed at encouraging the acceptance and the widespread use of digital video and file-based workflows that abound throughout the public and private sectors of the industry.

We have seen the evolutionary paths of videotape recording from analog to digital. Videotape is still with us, albeit not nearly as prominent as it was at the conclusion of the previous millennium. The legacy content in vaults, on shelves, and in the basements of homes and businesses all tell a story that needs to be preserved for future generations. The means and methods of that preservation hinge on how that material is stored and how it can be recovered much later in history.

Going forward, it is evident that the storage medium of choice will eventually drive videotape recording away from its current linear magnetic media format. The future, at least for the present, appears to be centered on solid state, magnetic- or optical-based disk storage, with a continued dependence on linear magnetic digital tape recordings for archive and preservation. The next major task then must clearly focus on managing that media for the long term.

Further Readings

Society of Motion Picture and Television Engineers Standards.
    http://www.smpte.org/home/

International Telecommunication Union - Radiocommunications Sector (ITU-R)
    standards.
    http://www.itu.int/

Advanced Media Workflow Association.
    http://www.aafassociation.org/

Watkinson, J. (2008). *The art of digital video* (4th ed.).

2

DIGITAL DISK RECORDING

Videotape has remained the predominant form of recording and storage for moving images dating back to the 1950s when Ampex Corporation developed what would be the first commercial form of television recording. Within a decade following that introduction, alternative means of capturing and playing back media on formats other than videotape and film would start to emerge.

Those who worked in the broadcast industry during the late 1960s may remember the earliest form of commercial disk recorders—camouflaged under the hood as the "instant replay" device. Like what the analog videotape recorder of its day did for television programming and broadcasting, this analog video disk recorder with its stunt features of forward, backward, still, and other non-real-time capabilities would prove to be the catalyst that single handedly changed the viewing experience for televised live sports forever.

Another 20 years would pass before development of nonlinear recording and playback would again have a serious commercial and professional impact. For disk-based recording to succeed, a new set of core technologies plus a paradigm shift in workflow would be necessary in order for the ideas, concepts, and practicalities of today's digital disk–based recording to occur.

Many of the digital disk recorder (DDR) developments have made their way well into the consumer space, changing the way we view television and moving media forever.

KEY CHAPTER POINTS

- A historical development of analog recording on videotape and disk
- The impact from analog instant replay, and how disk recording technologies evolved
- The core technologies responsible for advancements in moving media storage and applications
- Digital disk recorders as clip stores, still stores, and media recorders

- The JPEG and MPEG picture compression formats, with an introduction to the video and image compression technologies used in the DDR/DVR and early nonlinear editing systems
- DDRs and DVRs in the marketplace, professional and home media recorders, and server platforms, including audio

Recording Moving Images

Recording video images onto both magnetic linear tape and spinning magnetic storage surfaces had similar and parallel developments. Alongside, the development of magnetic recording tape, random-access video-on-demand, which had been predicted in 1921, was demonstrated in principle as early as 1950.

The concept of recording video onto a spinning platter would be shown just shortly before the 1951 John Mullin (Bing Crosby Enterprises) demonstration of an experimental 12-head videotape recorder (VTR) that ran at 100 in. per second. To put this into perspective, this development occurred about the same time as the first disk drive and the provisions for color NTSC (in 1953) were being introduced.

A rudimentary plastic video disk was demonstrated at the Salone Internazionale della Tecnica in 1957 by Antonio Rubbiani, and a few years later, technologists at CBS developed a procedure for a video disk recorder.

Origins of Videotape Recording

Recording video onto linear magnetic media (as videotape) was developed by a team of engineers at Ampex Corporation led by Charles Ginsburg, who began work on the videotape recorder (VTR) in 1951. Ampex would eventually manufacture both the magnetic tape and the recording systems that would support the process, but not at first.

Ampex demonstrated its first three-head system in November 1952 and, in March 1953, a second system, using four heads, was shown. However, problems continued with the "Venetian blinds" effect due to discontinuous recording from one head to the next. In 1954, Charles Anderson and the Ampex team, including Shelby Henderson, Fred Pfost, and Alex Maxey, were working on an FM circuit that debuted in February 1955. Later, Ray Dolby designed a multivibrator modulator, Maxey discovered how to vary tape tension, and Pfost developed a new sandwich-type magnetic head. The product's technology would be dubbed the quadruplex (quad) videotape recorder.

A half-century later, in 2005, the original team would be awarded, some posthumously, the Lifetime Achievement in Technology Emmy for their contributions of what would be remembered as the "quad" VTR.

In preparation for the first public demonstration of video recording at the Chicago convention of the National Association of Radio and Television Broadcasters (NARTB) in April 16, 1956, an improved VTR, later to become the Ampex Mark IV, was shown to Bill Lodge of CBS and other TV people. The Mark IV, later renamed the VRX-1000, used 2-in. wide tape, which ran at 15 in. per second past a transverse track, rotating head assembly, and employed FM video and AM sound recording. Ampex took out a trademark on the name videotape for its recorder. In 1959, color videotape was debuted during the Nixon–Khrushchev Kitchen Debate in Moscow.

Dawn of the Video Disk

The Minnesota Mining and Manufacturing Company (3M Company), which produced the first 2-in. wide videotape for the VRX-1000, showed a 1964 noise-plagued video disk, publicly demonstrating that this new disk format had a future. Although less than a year before the first demonstration of a random access, still-image generating, recording, and playback device, the demonstration utilized disk-drive recording technologies and changed the future of recording in a profound way. Some 20 years later, the concept of a "video serving device" would emerge, a breakthrough that took its roots from television sports, and began in the form of the instant replay.

Television Instant Replay

At the July 1965 SMPTE conference in San Francisco, MVR Corporation showed a 600-frame (20 second), black-and-white video recorder, the VDR-210CF model, that would record individual video frames. CBS used the device as a freeze-action video disk around August of that year. The MVR, with its shiny aluminum, nickel-cobalt-coated magnetic disk, was used in football telecasts to instantly play back short-action sequences in normal motion or freeze the motion on a single frame.

Ampex took a different approach creating an 1800 RPM spinning metal disk with a series of stepper motor-driven recording heads that moved radially across the platters, creating 30 seconds of normal video using analog recording technologies. The disk-based system recorded 30 video tracks per second, with each track holding one NTSC frame, giving a total of 1800 NTSC fields.

The heads could be rapidly moved to any location on the disk for replay at normal speed, or when the heads were slowed down and the same frame was repeated in multiple sets, a slow-motion playback stunt feature could be created. When the playback stepper heads were paused and the platters continued to spin, the same frames were repeated with a freeze frame continuously displayed.

In March 1967, the first commercially available video magnetic disk recorder with appropriate slow and stop motion, the Ampex HS-100, was placed into service. Effects included rapid playback at normal speed, forward and reverse slow motion, and stop action (freeze frames). The first commercial use of the Ampex HS-100 was at the World Series of Skiing program for the US Ski Championships in Vail, Colorado; it marked the dawn of the disk recorder for instant replay in live television broadcasting.

Digital Recording Supplants the Analog Disk Recorder

The analog video disk recorder had a long and productive life. It would find use in video editing under computer control, in special effects creation, as a substitute for another VTR transport, and in other creative endeavors. Ultimately, this disk-based recording device proved to be not just profitable but expensive and marginally unreliable with highly specialized maintenance skills and a high cost of ownership. The disk recorder would be confined mostly to sports but did find its way into editorial and special effects in commercial postproduction.

As the dawn of digital technologies emerged, takeoffs of the disk recorder took on other aspects. The devices would find themselves embedded in special effects systems used for video graphics and compositing in the mid-1980s. By the end of the 1980s, there was sufficient demand and experimentation with digital video disk recording that true product lines would emerge. As hard disk drive technologies for the emerging computer data industry took off, the disk recorder would be used in the products for graphics and still images. Ultimately, the concepts of dedicated disk recorders would pave the way to the infancy of the videoserver and the era of digital media storage technologies.

Fundamentals of Digital Disk Recording

The broadcast and postproduction industry have seen the migration from transport-based linear tape recording to professional videoserver and nonlinear digital disk recording. Workflow, technology, and operational costs have all contributed to this paradigm shift. The transition from videotape to magnetic disk storage and server-based production is now well into its third decade. Along the way, we've seemed to have lost the developmental evolution of the mainstream disk recorder and the nonlinear editing (NLE) platform. We find that historically the concepts of the professional video disk recorder had been around long before NLEs and videoservers.

The videoserver is a descendent of the digital disk recorder (DDR). The earliest DDRs would use similar recording principles to those used in the D-1 videotape format that recorded video sampled as 8-bit (ITU-R BT.601) data as individual paired sets of Y-frames (luminance) and C_B/C_R frames (based on R-Y and B-Y color difference signals) onto predetermined track locations stored progressively and continuously around the magnetic surface of each respective Y and C_B/C_R disk drive pair.

In these early digital video disk recorders, paired sets of hard disk drives (from two to many) would be configured such that the component elements of the individual video frames were recorded to dedicated tracks so that when played back there would be minimal latency when searching for frames and almost no need for buffering of the video data for synchronization purposes.

If one looked at the track mapping on the drives, you would find that the real estate allocated for a given frame would be consistent each time the frame was recorded or played out. For example, frame 39's Y component always could be found in the thirty-ninth position of the Y drive, with the corresponding C_B/C_R color difference frame always mapped to the thirty-ninth position on the C_B/C_R drive. The two sets of disk drives, running in exact synchronization, were either written to (during record) or read from (during playout) one frame at a time. This concept allowed for repetitive stop motion, frame-specific replacement for editing, or precise sequential playback as video clips without necessarily recording time code or other counter information from the original video sources.

One early DDR recorded precisely 750 frames of luminance data on one drive and 750 frames of color difference data on the other, for a total of 25 seconds of NTSC (at 30 frames per second) or 30 seconds of PAL (at 25 frames per second). Using external or integrated frame buffer technologies, a frame could be read into memory, manipulated (e.g., painted or layered onto another image) externally, and then written back to the same position on the same disk drives. The result was frame-by-frame graphic image manipulation, the concept leading to the early days of digital or computer animation.

Purpose-Built Applications

Products would be introduced that used multiple sets of hard drives purposely configured as digital disk recorder drive sets and combined internally or with other external devices, such as compositors and digital video effects units. Disk recorders were first devised to record still images that could be used in live and post-production graphics. Most of the applications were dedicated to the platform they were created on. Evolution led to the exchange of the data on removable spinning media. These types of DDR devices would eventually acquire extended capabilities that allowed a series of frames to be played back, thus generating what would be called the (short) clip, a term coined to represent a sequence of video frames assembled as either an animation or a string of video. In almost every case, the systems were proprietary although some companies devised a means to move the "files" between comparable devices over a network transport such as 10base2 and 10base5 ("thicknet") Ethernet at rates well below 10 Mbits/second.

These innovations triggered the age of digital video graphics and animation on professional video platforms. In parallel with these video-specific applications, the emerging growth of personal computers and higher end computer graphics workstations would again change the working way of television production.

Professional video producers would utilize these high-quality, full-bandwidth video disk recorders and integrate them into editing systems or computer graphics imaging (CGI) systems. Broadcasters would still use the store devices for live news telecasts. However, it wouldn't be until video compression technologies began to develop that there would be a significant deployment of disk drive storage technologies for nonlinear video editing systems. Any widespread adoption of disk recording systems for motion video would have to wait for motion-JPEG and MPEG compressions.

First String Players

Products from companies such as Quantel (*Paintbox* and *Harry*) and Abekas Video Systems (*A42, A60, A62* and *A64*) would become commercially available in the 1980s. Abekas's first product, introduced in 1982, was the A42 Digital Video Still Store. The product, generically called just a "still store," recorded and played back still video images with an associated key signal for use in live broadcast operations. The A62 Digital Disk Recorder was dubbed the world's first digital video recording machine with a built-in real-time digital video keyer.

Various other digital tape–based and disk-based products were introduced in both component digital (the D-1 format described through ITU-R BT.601) and composite digital (D-2) format. These devices gained acceptance within the broadcast production marketplace around the beginning of the 1990s.

However, the industry faced a problem. People needed more storage capacity. Moving video consumed a lot of data in D-1 or D-2 forms. Reliable, large-capacity hard disk drives in the mid-1980s were still rare and very expensive. Modern storage systems even remotely similar to today's storage area networks (SAN) or network-attached storage (NAS) were still years away. Large-scale video playout systems with record or playout times in excess of 200 seconds were far too costly to implement. Thus, to increase the amount of video storage, video compression technology would have to come to the rescue. The high-performance, high–bit rate compression technologies taken for granted today were still in the laboratory stage and slowly making their way through the standardization processes.

Core Technologies for Digital Disk Recording

Three core technologies have aided in the development of the digital disk recording platforms used throughout the media and entertainment industry.

Spinning Magnetic Disks: The First Core Technology

The development of the spinning magnetic disk drive (and ultimately disk arrays) would be paramount to the success of digital video recording and storage. Although digital linear tape for professional video recording was available before disk drives of comparable storage capacities, the disk drive made possible nonlinear storage and retrieval—the "emerging technology" that promoted the successful development of digital media overall.

The spinning disk would, and still today, prove essential to the development of modern compressed and digital video recording. Even though there have been great successes with optical disc platforms, solid state and flash memory, and even to a lesser degree, holographic recording, the hard disk drive still remains the predominant storage media for moving images.

With that said, the early development of compressed digital images was governed by the storage capacity of the hard disk and by the processing technologies available during these early times. Much like the software that didn't enter into widespread usage until the code could be stored reliably and

Half-century of spinning disk drives

1956	**First disk drive** IBM model 350 "RAMAC" 5-MB capacity, consisting of fifty 24-in. disks		1981	**First personal computer** IBM model 5150 "IBM PC" with floppy or cassette only [First IBM desktop model 5100, introduced in 1975]
1961	**First use of zoned recording** BRYANT model 4240 90-MB capacity, consisting of twenty-four 39-in. disks		1981	**First 10.5 in. rigid disk drive** FUJITSU model F6421 "Eagle" 446-MB capacity, consisting of six 10.5-in. disks
1962	**First drive to use air-bearing heads** IBM model 1301 "Advanced disk file" 28-MB capacity, consisting of twenty-five 24-in. disks		1981	**First 3.5 in. flexible disk** Sony model OA-D30V 0.4375-MB capacity, single 3.5-in. disks
1963	**First removable disk pack** IBM model 1311 "Low cost file" 2.69-MB capacity, consisting of six 14-in. disks		1982	**First 9 in. rigid disk drive** Control data model 9715-160 "FSD" 150-MB capacity, consisting of six 9-in. disks
1965	**First drive to use voice coil actuator** IBM model 2310 "RAMKIT"—Single disk cartridge 1.04-MB capacity, single 14-in. disk		1983	**First 3.5 in. rigid disk drive** RODIME model RO 352 10-MB capacity, consisting of two 3.5-in. disks
1966	**First drive with ferrite core heads** IBM model 2314 29.17-MB capacity, consisting of eleven 14-in. disks		1985	**First card mounted disk drive** Quantum model "Plus hardcard" 10-MB capacity, single 3.5-in. disk [Disk plus controller]
1971	**First track following servo system** IBM model 3330-1 "Merlin" 100-MB capacity, consisting of eleven 14-in. disks		1988	**First 1 in. form factor 3.5 in. disk** Connor peripherals model CP3022 21-MB capacity, single 3.5-in. disks
1971	**First flexible disk media (read only)** IBM model 23FD "Minnow" 0.0816-MB capacity, single 8-in. disks		1990	**First disk drive with PRML encoding** IBM model 0681 "Redwing" 857-MB capacity, consisting of twelve 5.25-in. disks
1973	**First flexible disk media (read-write)** IBM model 33FD "IGAR" [Sets industry standard for 8"] 0.156-MB capacity, single 8-in. disk		1991	**First use of thin film magnetoresistive heads** IBM model 0663 "1.043" 1.043-GB capacity, consisting of eight 3.5-in. disks
1973	**First low mass heads, lubricated disk** IBM model 3340 "Winchester" [First sealed assembly] 35- or 70-MB capacity, two or four 14-in. disks		1993	**First 7200 RPM disk drive** Seagate technology model ST 12550 "Barracuda" 2.139-GB capacity, consisting of ten 3.5-in. disks
1976	**First 5.25 in. flexible disk drive** Shugart associations model SA400 0.2188-MB capacity, single 5.25-in. disks		1997	**First 10,000 RPM disk drive** Seagate technology model ST19101 "Cheetah 9" 9.1-GB capacity, consisting of eight 3.25-in. disks
1979	**First 8 in. rigid disk drive** IBM model 62PC "Piccolo" 64.5-MB capacity, consisting of six 8-in. disks		1999	**First 1 in. disk drive** IBM "Microdrive" 340-MB capacity, single 1-in. disks
1980	**First 5.25 in. rigid disk drive** Seagate model ST506 5-MB capacity, consisting of four 5.25-in. disks		2000	**First 15,000 RPM disk drive** Seagate technology model ST318451 "Cheetah X15" 18.350-GB capacity, consisting of three 2.5-in. disks

Figure 2.1 Chronological evolution of spinning magnetic disk drives from 1956 through 2000.

efficiently, media would remain on videotape for many years while technology developed and market usage grew.

Digital Image Compression: The Second Core Technology

The technology that leads to the success of digital media recoding and storage development began with those standards developed out of the Joint Photographic Experts Group (JPEG) who, in 1992, standardized a tool kit of image processing based on a lossy compression format used in the capture and storage of photographic images. The JPEG standard specifies how an image is compressed into a stream of bytes and subsequently decompressed back into an image. The JPEG standard specifies only the codec and not the file format used to contain the stream.

Table 2.1 ISO/IEC Standards for JPEG and JPEG-LS

	Part	ISO/IEC Standard Number	ITU-T REC. (Public Release Date)	Document Title	Description
JPEG	Part 1	ISO/IEC 10918-1: 1994	T.81 (1992)	Requirements and guidelines	
	Part 2	ISO/IEC 10918-2: 1995	T.83 (1994)	Compliance testing	Rules, checks for software conformance, per Part 1
	Part 3	ISO/IEC 10918-3: 1997	T.84 (07/96)	Extensions	Extensions to improve Part 1 including SPIFF file format
	Part 4	ISO/IEC 10918-4: 1999	T.86 (1998)	JPEG registration profiles; SPIFF: profiles, tags, color spaces, compression types; APPn markers; and registration authority	Methods to register parameters used to extend JPEG
	Part 5	ISO/IEC FCD 10918-5	Under development	JPEG file interchange format [JIFF]	2009, JPEG committee establishes Ad Hoc Group to standardize JIFF as JPEG Part 5
JPEG-LS	Part 1	ISO/IEC 14495-1	T.87 (1998)	Baseline JPEG-LS	Lossless and near-lossless compression of continuous-tone still images
	Part 2	ISO/IEC 14495-2	T.870 (2002)	Extensions JPEG-LS	Rules, checks for software conformance, per Part 1

Following the JPEG (lossy) standards development, the committee later revisited the lossless coding mode within JPEG. The JPEG-LS mode was a late addition to the standard, and in the baseline form of JPEG (not using arithmetic coding) the algorithm used was not a 'state of the art' technique. However, this eventually led to the discussions from which came the JPEG 2000 standard prominently used today. Table 2.1 shows the JPEG and JPEG-LS development phases. Table 2.2 shows the JPEG 2000 standard.

Motion JPEG

The principles of the JPEG codec were independently adapted such that a series or string of individually captured frames from a moving video image could be stored to a disk drive, linked as a single group of pictures, and then played back sequentially to reform the original moving image. This notion was dubbed "motion-JPEG" (a nonstandardized implementation) and was widely used by non-linear editing manufacturers, most notably Avid Technologies, which was founded in 1987 by William J. Warner. The use of MJPEG during these early years of product deployment was well before the formal approval of MPEG encoding, which was developed by the Motion Picture Experts Group and standardized under the International Organization for Standardization (ISO). Motion-JPEG is still used in many types of imaging systems including surveillance and some video editing or graphics systems.

Extensions of these proprietary implementations of JPEG formats continued and were applied in many products including still stores, clip stores, videoservers, and surveillance recorders, with many still being used today.

JPEG 2000

The development of JPEG 2000, a wavelet-based image compression standard and coding system, also created by the Joint Photographic Experts Group committee in 2000, was intended to supersede their original discrete cosine transform-based JPEG standard. The JPEG 2000 codec is one of the founding compression formats for scalable, high-resolution imaging such as that used in digital cinema applications, as well as high-quality security systems, where analysis of the captured images as still frames is extremely important. (see Table 2.2)

As requirements for extended recording capabilities continued, a trade-off would be necessary. Either disk drives would have to get a lot larger in order to store the files or motion-JPEG codec technologies would need to be fine-tuned so that the images could be stored on the hard disk drives available at that time. While this requirement was being contemplated, MPEG compression technologies were being developed that would address the growing needs of standard video and audio formats, streaming video applications, and lower bit rates.

MPEG-1

Video applications eventually begin to use a new compression format designed for moving image applications. MPEG would be that new compression format. The standards process began with the formation of a subcommittee in the International Standards Organization (ISO) which would be called the Moving Pictures Experts Group (MPEG). The first meeting was held in May 1988 and was attended by 25 participants. The first MPEG-1 codec would be built on H.261, the ITU-T video coding standard originally designed in 1990 for the transmission of video and audio over ISDN lines.

Table 2.2 ISO/IEC Standards for the JPEG 2000 Image Coding System

Part	ISO/IEC Standard Number	ITU-T REC. (Public Release Date)	Document Title	Description
Part 1	ISO/IEC 15444-1	T.800 (2000)	Core coding systems	Lossless, bit-preserving, and lossy compression methods for coding bi-level, continuous'-tone gray-scale, palletized color, or continuous-tone color digital still images
Part 2	ISO/IEC 15444-2	T.801 (2004)	Extensions	Lossless, bit-preserving, and lossy compression methods for coding continuous-tone, bi-level gray-scale, color digital still images or multicomponent images
Part 3	ISO/IEC 15444-3	T.802 (2002)	Motion JPEG 2000	Wavelet-based JPEG 2000 codec for coding and display of timed sequences of images (motion sequences), possibly combined with audio, and composed into an overall presentation. this specification defines a file format and guidelines for using the codec for motion sequences
Part 4	ISO/IEC 15444-4	T.303 (2002)	Conformance testing	Specifies framework, concepts, methodology for testing, and criteria to claim compliance with ISO/IEC 15444-1; provides framework for specifying abstract test suites and for defining procedures for compliance testing
Part 5	ISO/IEC 15444-5	T.804 (2003)	Reference software	Provides two independently created software reference implementations; the software reference is informative only
Part 6	ISO/IEC 15444-6		Compound image file format	Defines a normative, but optional, file format for storing compound images using the JPEG 2000 file format family
Part 8	ISO/IEC 15444-8	T.807 (2007)	Secure JPEG 2000	Specifies the framework, concepts, and methodology for securing JPEG 2000 code streams
Part 9	ISO/IEC 15444-9	T.808 (2005)	Interactivity tools, APIs and protocols	Defines, in an extensible manner, syntaxes and methods for the remote interrogation and optional modification of JPEG 2000 code streams

Continued

Table 2.2 ISO/IEC Standards for the JPEG 2000 Image Coding System *(Continued)*

Part	ISO/IEC Standard Number	ITU-T REC. (Public Release Date)	Document Title	Description
Part 10	ISO/IEC 15444-10	T.809 (2008)	Extensions for three-dimensional data	Set of methods that extends the elements in the core coding system; extensions that may be used in combinations of encoding and decoding; support for variable DC offset; arbitrary wavelet transform kernels; multicompoent transformations; nonlinear transformations; region of interest
Part 11	ISO/IEC 15444-11	T .810 (2007)	Wireless	Provides syntax allowing JPEG 2000 coded image data to be protected for transmission over wireless channels and networks
Part 12	ISO/IEC 15444-12	(2004)	ISO base media file format	Specifies the ISO base media file format, a general format for a number of other specific file formats; contains timing, structure, and media information for timed sequences of media data, such as audio/visual presentations
Part 13	ISO/IEC 15444-13	T.812 (2008)	Entry level JPEG 2000 encoder	Defines a normative entry level JPEG 2000 encoder providing one or more optional complete encoding paths that use various features per ISO/IEC 15444
Part 14	ISO/IEC AWI 15444-14	JT1/SC29	XML structural representation and reference	Part 14 remained in committee with a target publication date of May 2011

The MPEG target goals included specifying a codec that produced moving video that could be carried at a low 1.5 Mbits/second bit rate (i.e., T-1/E-1 data circuits) and at a data rate that would be similar to those used on audio compaq discs. The MPEG-1 standard strictly defines the bit stream and the decoder functionality. Neither MPEG-1 nor its successor MPEG-2 defines the encoding process or how encoding is to be performed.

Drawbacks to MPEG-1 would become evident as the development of MPEG-2 began.

MPEG-1 Weaknesses

• Limitation of audio compression to two channels (stereo)
• No standardized support for interlaced video

- Poor compression quality when used for interlaced video
- Only a single standardized profile (Constrained Parameters Bitstream)
- Unsuitable for higher resolution video
- Only a single color space of 4:2:0

The limitations of MPEG-1 made it impractical for many professional video applications. Hence, another solution was necessary, which could provide better processing for higher resolution images and enable higher data rates.

MPEG-2

Recognizing that compressed video and audio systems would be the enabling technology for high-quality moving images and that the broadcast industry would be facing the development of a digital transmission system, the MPEG committees went back to work on an improved implementation of the discrete cosine transfer and their associated systems.

The MPEG-2 system, formally known as ISO/IEC 13818-1 and as ITU-T Rec. H.222.0, is widely used as the format for digital signals used by terrestrial (over-the-air) television broadcasting, cable, and direct broadcast satellite TV systems. It also specifies the format of movies and other programs that are distributed on DVD and similar discs. As such, TV stations, TV receivers, DVD players, and other equipment are often designed to this standard.

MPEG-2 was the second of several standards developed by the Moving Pictures Experts Group (MPEG). The entire standard consists of multiple parts. Part 1 (systems) and Part 2 (video) of MPEG-2 were developed in a joint collaborative team with ITU-T, and they have a respective catalog number in the ITU-T Recommendation Series.

While MPEG-2 is the core of the most digital television and DVD formats, it does not completely specify them. The ITU-T Recommendations provide the study groups and ongoing work related to most of the currently employed, and industry accepted, coding formats. Extensive technical information and descriptions related to implementations using MPEG-2 and MPEG-4 coding systems, as well as applications of JPEG and its moving image extension, are available from a number of sources.

Networked Services: The Third Core Technology

Along with many other systems, digital video technologies, storage systems, and their interfaces tend to depend on the principle and structures of networked systems. The components of networking contribute to real-time and non-real-time operating systems, file transport and interchange, and content management or distribution. Most of the IT-based networking technologies developed for data-centric and computer systems are applied in the structure and feature sets found in today's videoservers, their storage subsystems, and the intelligent management of media and associated metadata.

Networked services are the key to workflow collaboration, to high-speed interconnects, to content delivery mechanisms, and to the internal architectures of secured and protected data storage systems. Even as the world evolves through the 1- and 2-Gb Ethernet topologies, to the 4-, 6-, and 8-Gb Fibre Channel systems, and on toward 10-, 40-, and 100-Gb technologies, media storage infrastructures will keep pace with these developments in order to support the continually growing demands on video, audio, and data.

DDR, DVR, or Videoserver

The question on the minds those who saw digital disk recording rise in acceptance would become "Is videotape dead?" That question may never fully be answered, but while the volume of videotape diminishes, the growth in linear data tape storage (e.g., Linear Tape-Open or LTO) continues.

The 1990s saw a gradual and steady shift to disk-based recording as the requirements for faster access increased and as the dependencies on robotic videotape libraries decreased. Today, there is reluctance by some to use tape drives for archive, based on a combination of the cost basis for the library slots and on the continually evolving capabilities of disk drives as a substitute for tape.

At first introduction, disk recording technologies did not become a mainstream component, at least for the broadcaster, until the development of the professional videoserver began in the mid-1990s. Disk recorders saw most of their uses as storage platforms for still images. Once the images could be recovered fast enough from a disk to be "frame sequential," that is, they could be assembled at 30 frames per second (and interlaced), the value of disk storage became evident.

Beginning with the purpose-built digital disk recorders (DDRs) and the move to nonlinear editing with its compressed video systems that stored video (as files) on internal disk drives, there were only a few applications that made practical and economical sense. Those applications were mainly in the postproduction industry where special effects or high-end graphics with multilayer compositing was a thriving business for those with the right hardware (see Fig 2.2).

The disk recorder inside a nonlinear editor was seen by many as the up-and-coming alternative to linear-based videotape editing.

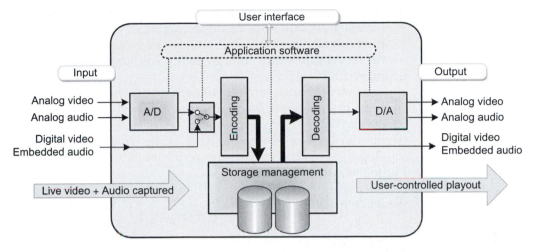

Figure 2.2 Basic input and output flows for a digital disk recorder.

Bit Buckets

When the device that stores the image files from a video and the sound in an audio stream is used principally as a bit bucket, it is simply a repository for the bits that make up the audio/video or transport stream file. One would not necessarily call that kind of a device a digital disk recorder (DDR).

For a device to function as a DDR, it must be configured to accept a real-time live video stream, as analog video or as digital video per SMPTE 259M (standard definition) signal, or per SMPTE 292M (high definition) signal. The device must process the signals, formulate them into data elements that can be stored on a disk platform, and then reassemble at playback in real time.

For definition purposes, we'll make the repeated distinction that a DDR (sometimes known as a "digital video recorder" or DVR) must be capable of capturing real-time video and audio signals, storing them, and then playing them back as video and audio in at least a linear fashion. In doing this, the quality of the audio and video should not suffer any appreciable degradation.

Basic Functionality of a DDR

To be considered a DDR (or DVR), there would be certain minimal functions that the device must be consistently capable of doing:

- Ingesting the moving media through conventional input ports, in real time

- Recording while playing
- Browsing of and indexing or cataloging of the files (clips) on the system
- Accessing the clips in any order for near instantaneous playback
- Sequencing and controlling of playout and record by either its own applications or by external control, such as from a protocol like VDCP
- Playing back of synchronization audio, video, and ancillary data (closed captions or time code) on demand and without degradation

Secondary Capabilities of a DDR

Generally accepted features that are inherent in a videotape transport plus additional functionality including:
- Audio and video splitting for separate playback
- Video and audio synchronization to a house reference signal (i.e., be able to genlock)
- Jog/shuttle features for video or audio locations
- Ability to accept multiple audio- and video-source configurations including, but not limited to,
  - analog and digital video inputs and outputs
  - standard-definition and high-definition video inputs and outputs
  - embedded or discrete AES audio
- Stunt features including reverse, slow motion, and freeze frame/stills playout
- Protection of the storage subsystem data elements through RAID-based architectures

Remote control and addressable catalogs through protocols or by third-party interfaces, such as VDCP, are recommended in order for the DDR to function in a production environment.

Additional Functions and Capabilities of a DDR

Through networking and file transfer services, a DDR should allow for the interchange of data files over a network connection, plus optional feature sets such as follows:
- A second alpha (luminance) channel used for key channel information
- External storage in a mathematically protected (RAID) system, or the equivalent
- Protective features such as redundant power supplies, fans, system disks, or control systems
- Ability to specify differing recording and/or compression formats
- Ability to record and play back transport streams

How the actual video and audio data is stored on the device is irrelevant to the baseline functionality of a DDR. What is the most important is that the video and audio elements are as easy to access and use as its linear videotape equivalent.

Comparing DDRs to Videoservers

When the DDR adds some or all of those items identified previously as "additional features or capabilities," especially the ability to function in a file-based domain (network connected, multiple records or playback channels, or the interchange of files with other devices), the DDR has gone beyond a simple VTR-replacement mode and has become essentially a videoserver.

When speaking strictly of a recording device that primarily accepts linear serial digital video inputs (SMPTE 259M or SMPTE 292M), the videoserver has a very similar media structure to that of the videotape recorder, with certain exceptions:
- Physically, the media is of a disk-based or solid state memory format.
- The recorder/server has nonlinear or random access playout capabilities.
- Reproduction of the video slip is nearly instantaneous.
- There are starting, stopping, cueing, and still capabilities from any segment or video clip.
- There is random on demand access to video clips.
- Images are stored as files and may be shuffled, moved, or transported by means of other than a conventional baseband video/audio interface.

A DDR or DVR is a close cousin to a videoserver, but the server has much more sophistication and may be its own platform that calls the media content from ancillary storage. The DDR will intrinsically be self-contained, with the exception that it may have storage that can be externally attached or moved.

DDR Storage

At a higher level, the media storage properties for a disk recorder will most likely be in a protected architecture, typically using conventional spinning hard disk drives in a RAID-based (mathematically protected) configuration or a duplicative structure such as mirroring or replication. The content may be stored in a native (full-bandwidth) format, using the coding structures of the baseband video. Such an example would be the D-1 component digital format, whereby the bit stream of a $Y'C_RC_B$ digital video signal is recorded to the disk drive and when played back does not suffer from lossy compression properties.

The moving images on a DDR may be stored in an entirely proprietary manner if it is in a closed system. The DDR may take files created by another application or from other PC-like work-stations (e.g., finished clips from Adobe After Effects) and then reformat them for playout on their particular platform.

Another, more familiar, and today highly common means of digital video storage will compress the incoming serial digital bit stream (video and audio, independently or otherwise) by means that are standardized per industry recognized and accepted encoding practices, such as MPEG or similar formats. In this example, after compressing the video, the DDR now saves data as, for example, MPEG video and audio files to the hard disk and on play-out decodes those files to baseband digital video and AES audio for presentation to other video productions or signal systems.

Clip Servers

The DDR/DVR and its successor the videoserver in their sim-pler forms may be configured into scaled-down versions that are designed for the recording and playing back of short segments of video as "clips." There are now dozens of various products that, since the early years of digital or analog still store devices, capture both still images and short-segment clips for use in news, sports, and video loops for displays. This market space is being extended to other storage and coding platforms that are deeply integrated into peripheral or mainstream video production equipment.

The evolution of the DDR, as the videoserver took off as a more complete platform for moving video, began to take on the forms called clip or image servers. In the consumer space, the DVR has appeared by the millions as part of set-top boxes for cable or satellite broadcasting. PCs and workstations have included the capabilities of these DVR feature sets, as have iPods and other sim-ilar video recording and playback systems and mobile devices.

Clip servers may be as simple as the DDR or may take on much more sophistication such as those used in sports replay systems (e.g., the EVS [XT]2 + and the Grass Valley K2 Solo Media Server). High-performance replay systems are built around those concepts that are found in the video/media server platform but include specialized user interfaces that allow rapid recue, segment collection and repackaging, exportation of the media as files to dedicated or other third-party systems, and highly networked,

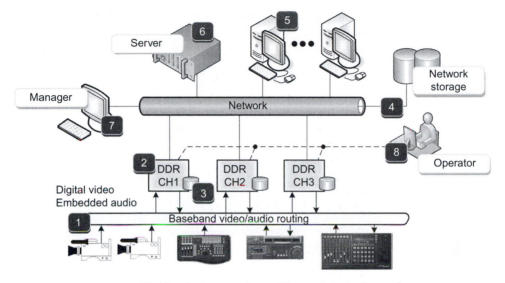

Workflow for live recording, editing, and playback

[1] Real-time baseband digital video from cameras, live production, audio, VTRs is routed to DDR channels [2], where clips are recorded and stored to local DDR storage [3].

Operator [8] controls recording and replay/playback of DDR channels.

Files ingested on DDRs are replicated onto network storage [4], allowing for editing of program segments on workstations [5], which are attached to the network storage [4].

Files created during the edit process are migrated from storage [4] back to DDR storage [3] where they are played back from DDRs [2] to the baseband audio/video router [1].

Server [6] and manager [7] control other processes associated with asset management, file transfers, and configurations.

Figure 2.3 Workflow for disk-based replay and playout system typical for a combined live and postproduction operation for sports or other live venues.

user programmable systems aimed at professional and broadcast applications. An example of a complete workflow with replay DDRs, editing, and network storage is shown in Fig. 2.3.

Clip servers, as image storage devices, have found their way into video production switchers integrated with playout and effects channels that can store from a few frames to hundreds of seconds of high-definition video. Usually, this form of clip server uses some form of solid state- or flash memory–based storage and is built into the video production switcher directly. The feature sets for these forms of video clip servers may be limited to the functionalities of the production systems and may lack export capabilities or external streaming playout unless as a part of the video production switchers, mix effects, or program buses.

Clip Server File Formats

Highly compact clip servers, for example, compact (1 RU) off-the-shelf IT-like servers, are not uncommon platforms for clip servers. When equipped with HD/SD-SDI inputs and outputs, solid state drives (SSD), or integral disks for storage, these devices may record and play MXF-wrapped video files in profiles that are compatible with prominent manufacturers of video production and recording equipment such as the Panasonic P2/P2 HD (as DVCPro) or Sony XDCAM formats.

For other than live, baseband ingest, clips may be transferred into the server and/or saved over gigabit Ethernet to external storage devices, or interconnections to other serving platforms, including PC or Mac workstations. These servers can be highly versatile and reliable and may be used in a variety of applications for image ingest, synchronized playback, and even full-length program playout using a third-party playout control system.

Applications for these devices run the gamut from digital signage for theme parks, broadcasters, news organizations, production companies, and arena or stadium replay control rooms. On a much broader scale, streaming media servers (a related type of clip server) may be utilized for video on demand or similar applications where the number of streams is not on the order of those required for services such as YouTube.

The architecture of these more dedicated forms of clip servers allow, even during video recording or playback, for clips to be added to the local storage via a network connection. Provided there is sufficient local storage on board, there is no time lost because of the switching disks or because of external media such as tape, memory cards, USB sticks, and so on.

Most applications will use the file formats for video and audio that are used by many of the industry accepted standard encoding schemes, both for professional video and (depending on the coding software of the clip server) possibly other "nonbroadcast" formats or wrappers. The listing of available file formats for clip servers and DDRs is dependent on what the particular manufacturer of the devices has selected for their usually software-based codecs. Dedicated platforms that do not offer or have a requirement for external interfaces or file exchanges may effectively utilize any form of encoding that makes their platforms perform, which could include wavelet compression or even conventional PC/MAC-based formats.

Clip Server Storage

When using commodity-based server and storage systems for these clip servers or DDR applications, the manufacturer may select to use disk drives or solid state memory systems (including

SSD) that are integrated with the hardware platform they have built their systems on. Given that the purpose of these devices is aimed at short-term, limited duration media files, the likelihood of requiring costly high bandwidth, resilient storage platforms is minimal. As such, a vendor may select to use low-cost SATA drives that can be easily interchanged should a drive fail. The drives employed in these applications could be commodity off the shelf plug-and-play drives or third party disk arrays.

Drive bandwidth requirements will probably not be a limiting performance factor. With today's disk drives, most of the purpose-built systems are able to support single or dual streams of 50–100 Mbits/second files (such as DVCPRO50 or DVCPRO HD) without too much difficulty. However, once there becomes a requirement for the recording of two or more streams combined with FTP network transfers between devices and simultaneous multistream playouts, most users will find they need a server-based system rather than a standalone single disk recorder platform.

Videoserver platforms may generally be used as clip or image servers, with the caveat that the ability to access multiple frames or very short-duration clips based on a continual "back to back" may be encumbered. In such applications, a professional videoserver may need some additional buffering time (varying from a few frames to a second or two) to charge the video playback coding engines and to make ready the next clip for a seamless transition between the last frame of one clip and the first frame of the next. For this, and other cost-related factors, videoservers that are designed for mission critical program or commercial length playback may not be advised for use in this application.

DVR Marketplaces

The consumer and home viewing sector has come to realize the impact of the digital video recorder (DVR). Albeit the DVR has been branded almost universally as a "TiVo," and the word has almost become a verb, the functionality of the DVR as built into the platforms ranging from satellite receiver systems to cable set-top boxes (STBs) and more recently into the home PC or television display itself is not unlike that of the professional digital disk recorder or clip server.

In STB configurations, most DVRs will record the incoming signal not as files but as transport streams. The signals from the cable and satellite systems are generally delivered as MPEG-2 or MPEG-4 streams. Seldom will these STB devices allow the recording of discrete video and audio signals, unless equipped with selected video and audio input cards. For the carrier-based DVR, this practice reduces the component count and in turn makes them less costly when produced in mass proportions for cable system and satellite uses.

The impact of DDRs and video-media servers has produced paradigm changes in all aspects of life—from television production workflow to home television viewing. The significance is that these devices and their associated counterparts have taken what was once a dominant videotape-based marketplace and shifted it away from linear functionality, not unlike what the DVD has done to the home VHS recorder. Even as we've entered the second decade of the new millennium, videotape continues to have a significant place in the capture and retention of the moving image—but that too is beginning to fade as solid state devices capable of holding more data than a lineal videotape are being incorporated into cameras, mobile devices, and other media delivery platforms. All of these next-generation systems have functionality not unlike that found in the home DVR.

Home Media Network Disk Recorders

The dividing line between a dedicated DDR/DVR, and when DDR functionality is integrated into alternative platforms (e.g., a home media network), is a fine line segmented by cost, performance, scalability, and feature sets. Limiting factors that differentiate the groups include resolution, performance, storage capabilities, and media format awareness.

One benefit of this new era of digital media distribution is that users can store all of their music, movies, TV shows, and videos as data on hard drives rather than have them stacked on shelves or in the basement box collection. However, with high-definition television, and higher quality files, added to the ever-growing larger collections of media, this can still add up to a lot of storage.

Finding an appropriate storage solution suited for the users' needs can be complicated, especially as one tries to balance expandability with performance. Not to mention, there is still a need for backup, network-wide access, permissions, security of the assets, and more.

For example, Microsoft, as well as others, have developed home media server platforms that have the sophistication of professional media content servers, yet are focused on what the consumer needs to organize, back up, protect and secure, plus exchange those files over local and Internet network services. This, of course, raises the same level of questions and concerns as the users of professional serving products—insufficient storage and issues with storage management complexities. Faced with this dilemma, but on a much wider scale, Microsoft looked at these issues and over time developed a new storage technology that enables users to use both internal and external hard drives of any size. This takes away the dedicated platform approach that other makers of home media networking systems have taken.

Protection, scalability, and extensibility are important requirements for the sustainability of media asset platforms. Microsoft found this and developed their Windows Home Server Drive Extender. This product, as a concept, has a built-in protection application as one of its prime features, enabled by folder duplication that is set up for specific user-specified shared folders on home servers. It functionally works by maintaining two copies of a shared folder on separate hard drives, protecting against the failure of a single hard drive on a single device. This not only improves content management but also adds elements of protection and security heretofore not easily available at a consumer level on PC platforms.

This is just one of the many enabling technologies integrated into a moving media storage that is extensible to DVR systems coupled with home networking, and in turn, we are seeing similar kinds of functionality in the professional and industrial market spaces at far less cost.

Audio

Not to be left out, the radio and the news industries rely heavily on closed or purpose-built systems for the recording and playing back of commercial content, reporter stories, music, and other audio media. These devices, although less complex in terms of handling video, offer precisely the same capabilities as the DDR or videoserver, but for audio only.

Instant start or stop capabilities and repeatability are the two main functional requirements for an audio clip server implementation. In studios where on-air operations are closely coupled with various other radio production requirements, these systems will be networked or directly interfaced with digital audio workstations (DAWs), audio consoles, amplifiers, and other control surfaces to allow for a complete production workflow.

Radio has been using forms of audio clip serving devices long before the popularity of video or media serving systems. Television sound effects that follow video animation clips all use these clip players during live productions to enhance their graphics or the start of an instant replay sequence. Clip servers or audio disk recorders have essentially replaced the older legacy audio carts by the hundreds in news operations and production studios.

Further Readings

Joint Photographic Experts Group (JPEG)

A working group of the International Organization for Standardization or International Electrotechnical Commission (ISO/IEC), (ISO/IEC JTC 1/ SC29/WG 1), and of the International Telecommunication Union (ITU-T SG16) responsible for the popular JPEG, JPEG 2000, and more recently, the JPSearch and JPEG XR families of imaging standards.

The WG 1 group meets nominally three times a year, in Europe, North America, and Asia.

http://www.jpeg.org

Joint Bi-level Image Experts Group (JBIG)

A group of experts nominated by national standards bodies and major companies to work to produce standards for bi-level image coding. The "joint" refers to its status as a committee working on both ISO and ITU-T standards. The official title of the committee is ISO/IEC JTC1 SC29 Working Group 1 and it is responsible for both the JPEG and JBIG standards.

JBIG have developed IS 11544 (ITU-T T.82) for the lossless compression of a bi-level image, which can also be used for coding gray scale and color images with limited numbers of bits per pixel. As of late 2010, work is nearing technical completion on a new standard known as JBIG2 offering significant technical advantages over both MMR and JBIG1 coding.

http://www.jpeg.org/jbig/

Liaison organizations for JPEG and JBIG include IPTC, NATO, W3C, IMTC, CCSDS, Dicom, I3A, and JPEG 2000 Group (www.j2g.org)

Microsoft Home Server

Applications for consumer and other uses related to the sharing, storage, and distribution of media content on personal and other public or private networks.

http://www.microsoft.com/windows/products/winfamily/ windowshomeserver/

Moving Pictures Experts Group (MPEG)

A working group of ISO/IEC in charge of the development of international standards for compression, decompression, processing, and coded representation of moving pictures, audio, and their combinations.

http://mpeg.chiariglione.org

3

VIDEO MEDIA SERVERS

In August 1994, station KOLD-TV (Tucson, Arizona) installed an HP (Hewlett-Packard) Broadcast Videoserver as a key part of its strategic upgrade to the station's broadcast technology and a replacement for its current robotics-based videotape commercial delivery platform. It was the first commercial broadcast installation of a videoserver platform although cable was using similar technologies for movie delivery and ad insertion in a similar time perspective.

The HP videoserver product, and others that would be announced in the next several months, would begin an era that would change the course of broadcast television forever.

This chapter outlines the videoserver for those unfamiliar with its physical systems, signal sets, control protocols, and basic storage systems.

KEY CHAPTER POINTS

- Distinguishing video and media server platforms from disk recorders, and their processors, the tape-based robotics controlled library management systems
- A historical overview of early videoserver systems for broadcast transmission and video media production
- Descriptions of videoserver components, their input and output interfaces, standard- and high-definition transport formats for videoservers, AES-embedded and Dolby-compressed digital audio, and serial data transport interface (SDTI) as SMPTE 305M-2005
- Descriptions of machine control protocols, such as VDCP and others, along with time code and ancillary data sets commonly found on videoservers

Carrying Over from the DDR

The logical extension of the digital disk recorder, for professional applications, was to provide more computer-like serving capabilities. This required an increase in performance (bandwidth or through-put). It further required the capabilities inherent in computer server platforms such as shared and protected high-performance storage, hot-swappable easily maintained drive systems, expansion capabilities for storage growth, and a host of other features (which will be discussed later in this chapter) be made available such that the services provided by these new devices, called video or file servers, would be reliable enough for broadcast users to purchase them and really put them into service.

Sony Betacart

The broadcast marketplace had been using cassette-based robotic "cart machines," from the Sony Betacart BVC-10 (see Fig. 3.1) through the Sony LMS (a later digital version called the "Library Management Systems") and others included Lake Systems "LaCart," Odetics, and Panasonic flavors since the 1985 time frame. The author of this book was fortunate enough to place one of the first Sony Betacarts into service on June 22, 1985, at the new Seattle television station—KTZZ-TV 22. At that time, a complete Betacart package consisted of the following:

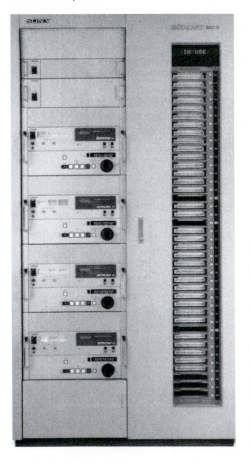

Figure 3.1 Sony Betacart model BVC-10 from 1986. Reprinted from *SMPTE* journal, *95(10)*, October 1986, 1066.

Sony Audio matrix switcher—BVS-A10
Sony Video matrix switcher—BVS-V10
Sony Remote control box—BVR-20
Sony Betacam playback decks—4 ea. BVW-11 (oxide-based transports)
Sony remote control keyboard (programmers keyboard)—BVR-11
Sony barcode label printer—BVBP-11
Sony barcode writer (programming keyboard for printer)—BVBC-10
Sony operating system software disks—BZC-xx (uses 720K 3.5" disks)
VDU—a 12" monochrome video monitor (used as the display CRT for programmers)

The weight without decks was about 1000 pounds, and the power was 13 A at 120VAC single phase. The system was used to play both commercials and full-length programs.

Over time, many similar competitive robotics-based videocart machine products were introduced to the marketplace (see Fig. 3.2 for a depiction of the Sony Betacart workflow). These incredibly expensive devices remained in sustained operations throughout the development of the videoservers that ultimately pushed them into retirement.

The first implementation of videoservers for those facilities with videotape-based cart machines was to provide a disk-based cache between the tape library

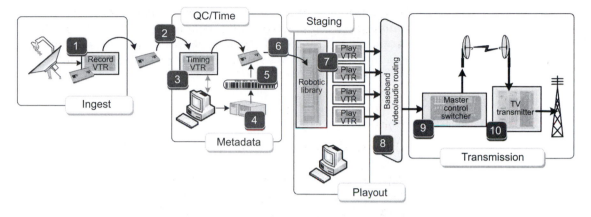

Workflow for Ingest – Preparation – Scheduling – Playback – Transmission

[1] Videotape loaded into VTR for program record

[2] Videotape shelved, reloaded to timing VTR[3], manually cued, start of message (SOM), end of message (EOM), metadata logged and label printed [4], label applied to tape cassette, tape then shelved until needed for air

[6] Tape is retrieved, loaded into robot [7], at scheduled time robot loads cassette to play VTR automatically, upon trigger from master control, content plays out to routing switcher [8].

[9] Master control switches program into playout stream, signal links to television transmitter [10] and program plays to air

Figure 3.2 Workflow of early automated videotape-based robotic library play to air.

and the final air chain. Tapes would be loaded from the tape library to the videoserver cache and then played to air. Intelligent software would request tapes not already on the server to be loaded, where the automation system would then transfer the tapes into the server based on the SOM (start of message) and EOM (end of message) metadata held in the tape library's database.

Since the robot controllers and the tape transports were the "weakest links" in the systems, the disk-based cache system provided a level of protection and redundancy that stations heretofore had to create secondary dub reels (as backups) to achieve in order to protect the on-air integrity. Worse yet, in very high-profile markets, the stations used two Betacarts (or other robotic libraries) in main and protect modes—an enormous cost that was supplanted by the introduction of the videoserver cache.

Universal Server Approach

Influenced by the emergence of multimedia, including early ventures into interactive television, manufacturers of computer and data-centric systems endeavored to find a means to exchange video and audio media between clients on their network.

Companies sought to develop and offer a complete information management solution for users who looked to capitalize on the economic advantages of accessing any form of data, for example, relational, spatial, text, images, audio, and video over any network or from any location.

Oracle was an early player in this particular domain—linking video with business applications. In 1995, as an extension to their existing Oracle7 relational database management system (RDBMS) applications, the company developed the Oracle Videoserver. The product extended the company's lead as the "first and only provider of a 'universal server,'" video-enabled existing applications, and allowed for the creation of a new class of enterprise multimedia applications such as training on demand, multimedia kiosks, and online video help.

These "videoservers" were not aimed at the professional or broadcast video marketplace as they lacked the deterministic and visual quality properties necessary for real-time record and playback of audio and video in an isochronous fashion. Nonetheless, they did provide the catalyst for what would in less than a decade become a paradigm shift in how audio or video media would be distributed.

Videoserver Differentials

The professional or broadcast videoserver, in contrast to a DDR or the "data-centric" Oracle model described previously, takes the features of the single-channel digital disk recorder (DDR) and multiplies them across one-to-many inputs and/or outputs. Depending on the architecture that the server manufacturer employs, a server channel will usually be at least a single input (for recording) and single output (for playback). The ratio of the number of inputs and outputs varies but in most cases is at least a pair or multiples of inputs and/or outputs.

Videoservers nearly always share media data from a common storage platform. Functionally, a videoserver performs more than one operation, that is, it needs the ability to record (ingest) and play out (playback) simultaneously.

Tektronix PDR100

The Tektronix PDR100, produced in February 1995, was one of the early videoservers that took the concepts of a DDR and coupled them into a four-channel video recording and four-channel video playback system sharing a common storage system integral to the product.

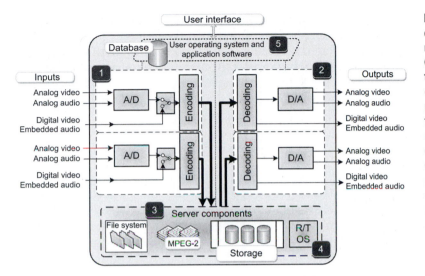

Figure 3.3 Basic functional diagram of 2-input by 2-output real-time videoserver. (1) Conversion and encoding to files; (2) decoding and conversion from files for playout; (3) server system with file system, file management, and storage; (4) real-time operating system (R/TOS); (5) user interface, record, playout, metadata and database, control interfaces between user or automation and videoserver.

The Profile series videoservers were designed to emulate the quality of the Sony Betacam SP (metal oxide) videotape format. The compression format was motion-JPEG, with its storage platform either internal to the chassis or with an optional disk expansion unit. The integral storage system was capable of incorporating 4, 8, or 12 4-Gbytes SCSI hard drives (considered "large" for that time period).

The optional PDX103 disk expansion unit had its own power supply and as many as 16 additional hard disks in a unit that was four-rack high, 25.5 in. deep, and 19 in. wide. The expansion unit came with either eight drives (two banks of four drives supporting two disk recorder boards in the PDR100), a single bank of eight drives to support one disk recorder board, or 16 drives that would fully utilize the capacity of two disk recorder boards.

Tektronix saw the potential of the videoserver early. They quickly offered peripheral products, such as the PLS-200 Exabyte-based tape library for archive, and a series of drive expansion chassis that allowed the user to scale the system to their own requirements.

Within two years, Tektronix introduced the Profile PDR200, also a two- or four-channel unit using 9-Gbytes Ultra-SCSI disk drives. The updates included 24-bit AES/EBU digital or analog audio, a 30 Mbits/second internal bandwidth, and a Fibre Channel networking interface. For its 20% increase in price over the PDR100, you doubled the storage, added digital audio, and increased the bandwidth.

Other manufacturers and products, including ASC Audio Video Corporation (which was acquired by Leitch in September 1997),

Hewlett-Packard's MediaStream Server Broadcast Series (later Pinnacle Systems and eventually Avid Technology), and SeaChange Technology (later SeaChange International), began their entry into this emerging marketplace in the same time frame or very shortly thereafter. By 1998, there were at least five significant players building some form of videoserver for broadcast use. The start of the era of tapeless operations was emerging.

Applications of the Early Server

Other professional videoserver products began appearing in the marketplace once the acceptance, and the operational under-standings, were firmly in place. Broadcast videoservers were used initially in two basic operating modes. For those broadcasters using aging cassette-based or videotape-based commercial and interstitial playback systems, for example, an Odetics, Panasonic MARC, or Sony Betacart/LMS, the videoserver would become the on-air playback device and the cassette system would become the backup. This workflow found tapes being made for the cart machine and those same tapes being dubbed into the videoserver, a process not unlike the backup protection reel that was common in the early days of the cart machine for major mar-kets or for those with apprehensions about having only a single commercial playback device.

Cart machine manufacturers would begin incorporating the videoserver platform into the cart machine system, using it as a cache for playout instead of relying on multiple discrete individ-ual tapes that were prone to failure (see Fig. 3.4). Tapes would be

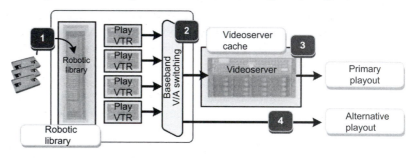

Combination videoserver cache and robotic library

[1] Videotape loaded into robotic library.

[2] Under integrated control with robotic library and videoserver, clips or entire breaks are cached to the videoserver [3].

Upon playout from the videoserver [3], the same cassettes would playout from the robotic library, providing parallel paths for redundancy. Should the server fail to play, or if a last minute change was made for material not cached to the videoserver, the alternative playout path [4] would be used.

Figure 3.4 Videoserver imple-mentation model with robotic library and videoserver acting as a cache—providing redun-dancy with parallel operating modes and ability for last-minute changes.

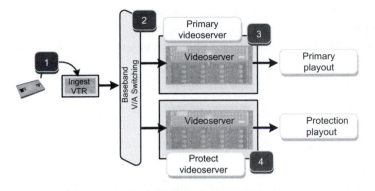

Primary and protection (mirrored) videoserver model

[1] Videotapes, or other sources, are dual ingested [2] to two videoservers, with the same mirrored databases, and identical files (content) on both.

[3] Main or primary air playout comes from this server. The identical files are loaded and played out from the protect videoserver [4], in synchronization with each other.

Figure 3.5 Mirrored videoserver implementation model in which two identical servers contain the same material (content), and each play back in synchronization with each other, in a "primary" and an alternative "protect" mode.

kept in the cart library and then dubbed via an automation controller into the server for playout. Last-minute changes that were not previously dubbed into the server could be played back from the cart machine.

In many systems, especially where the videoserver was the only ingest and playout device, users would install two systems that ran in mirrored AIR and PROTECT configurations (see Fig. 3.5).

Servers for Movies and Digital Ad Insertion

Preparing to capitalize on the cable industry's aggressive deployments, another form of server would be necessary, which could deliver audio or video content without the stringent requirements of the baseband videoserver. Television ad sales operations were looking for an option other than the (conventional) videoserver. Cable operators (MSOs) looked toward that "single-channel integrity" platform from which to deploy their digital ad insertion systems.

In November 1995, SeaChange—already a major player in the cable industry—introduced its second-generation Videoserver 100 platform, bringing to the world a new avenue in (digital) ad insertion. The platform supported a variety of wide-area networks such as T1, Ethernet, FDDI, ATM, and SONET. It enabled the cable operators to quickly transmit ads and infomercials from their business office to multiple headends.

In this same time frame, the delivery of long-form videos of any length would become yet another requirement for digital videoservers. These systems would support a wide range of video on demand applications including near video on demand (NVOD) and time delay, provide for extensive storage capability, and utilize high-quality MPEG-2 compressed digital video for delivery.

Added Functionality in the NLE

Nonlinear editing systems (NLEs), in their early days (ca. late 1980s), combined the functionality of a DDR, the operational interfaces of an edit decision list (EDL), and a relatively new introduction called a timeline editor. The NLE, dominated by Avid Technologies, Inc., which was founded in 1987 by William J. Warner and introduced its first product the Media Composer in 1989, would become the benchmark and de facto standard until the era of direct desktop editing. The NLE in general was at first a proprietary purpose-built system that captured individual program segments, manipulated and processed the video and audio, and then output a completed program. The user interface was a computer display, mouse, and keyboard. The feature sets found in a professional broadcast videoserver were unnecessary for these dedicated, single-purpose units that were used primarily for off-line "work prints" and edit decision list generation. In this kind of workflow, a time code print would be approved, and then, the full bandwidth video would be conformed in a linear online edit bay. This would work for quite some time until the image quality was equaled to that of the original material, and then, collaborative and file-based workflows were introduced.

After years of development, NLE devices have become as complex and sophisticated as the videoserver. Entire platforms consist now of mixed ingest, compression, editing, storage, and playout for many sets of user applications including on-set production, dailies, postproduction, effects, and television news. NLEs are sold as software-only versions, which can run on PCs, Macs, laptops, and full-fledged workstations. As dedicated complete systems, these advanced NLE systems are now using complex sophisticated networking solutions at gigabit speeds.

Videoservers as Media Servers

The industry has managed to name these video-based serving platforms with a number of varying and appropriate, in most cases, names. Typically, we see the words "videoserver" intermixed with "file servers" and "media servers." There is probably no one correct answer. Essentially, a video serving platform is a system of hardware and software that can capture, store, and deliver files that contain moving images and sound. It is further enabled through the use of storage networking (SAN or NAS) for shared storage and heightened bandwidth, so as to deliver multiple streams of real-time, uninterrupted video.

Videoserver Operations

Placing a videoserver into service involves more than connecting video and audio inputs and outputs to the rear panel and turning it on. To effectively utilize the server, a thorough understanding of the underlying architecture is necessary. We'll begin by discussing the ground-level basics of the videoserver as it applies in the environments used by broadcasters and multichannel video program distributors (MVPDs).

Each manufacturer has its own particular way of configuring its videoserver's functionality. Some will offer a basic one- or two-channel device that is intended for the simpler functions such as record, library, cache, and playback. These simple servers have limited expansion and are marked for a price niche rather than from an expansion or enterprise-wide performance perspective. This is not to say that this level of videoserver is any less capable of producing images from disks; it was most like designed for limited operations and without a heavy initial price point.

Basic Configurations

Space does not allow us to delve into specific manufacturer configurations for videoservers for many reasons. To do so would mean we'd leave several servers off the list, which wouldn't be justified. The permutations of server product lines have grown by orders of magnitude since their early introductions in the 1990s, and this would become an oversized book that would read like a catalog, which would become obsolete in less than a year or two. However, we will look into some of the concepts developed by manufacturers simply because they have taken either a unique or a more common approach to building their storage subsystems.

Videoservers at the high end run the gamut from full-bandwidth disk recorders for high-definition video that is used mainly in high-end production environments and digital cinema production and are capable of capturing and storing uncompressed video at high resolutions of SMPTE 292 up through 2K and 4K images; to the lower end, standard definition or streaming media servers for mobile distribution where compression is high, image resolution is moderate, and performance degradation is minimal. In the middle range, there are off-line editors, seldom with less than D-1 quality with MPEG-2 long GOP encoding, which are used strictly for rough cutting with no intention of airing the resultant product.

Impractical Storage

To provide even the most basic understanding about how much drive storage is nominally required, a full-bandwidth standard-definition video disk recorder is going to cut into storage capacity at around the rate of 22.5 Mbits/second for just the uncompressed 8-bit video data only. If you recorded everything, including 10-bit video, embedded audio, and ancillary data, the server would consume 33.75 Mbits/second at even standard-definition (SMPTE 259) video resolution.

An ancient 4-Gbytes computer disk drive is capable of recording about 120 seconds of video at the full 10 bits of ITU-R BT.601, 4:2:2 component digital sampling, and eight channels of AES audio. For broadcast operations, this hasn't been practical for over 15 years, and now with high-definition content such as SMPTE 292 video, it would be grossly impractical to use discrete, conventional hard disk storage space for any level of daily commercial operations. Furthermore, it becomes pointless to stack multiple hundreds of disk drives, even with the new terabyte drives, into several array chassis and put only a few minutes or seconds of video on each drive, unless you are doing 4K resolution, film transferred imagery for digital cinema mastering.

For these reasons and more, compressed video technology has become the standard for videoserver applications, providing additional storage space with no sacrifices in visual image quality.

Main Videoserver Components

Videoserver systems are fundamentally comprised of two main components. The first is a record/play unit that interfaces to and from the second component, the storage array. In a modular videoserver system, these components are provided with some levels of expansion. Figure 3.6 shows a detailed block diagram of a typical videoserver system.

The record/play unit, essentially a combination of a video coding engine and serving components, consists of several elements, which are described below.

Selectable Baseband Video Inputs

For standard definition in digital or analog formats, either a SMPTE 259M serial digital interface (SDI) or analog flavors in composite and component are presented to the input codec. For a high-definition format, generally both SMPTE 259M and SMPTE 292 baseband SD and HD inputs are presented to the same input port. Professional videoservers, especially those with HD capabilities for broadcast applications, have essentially

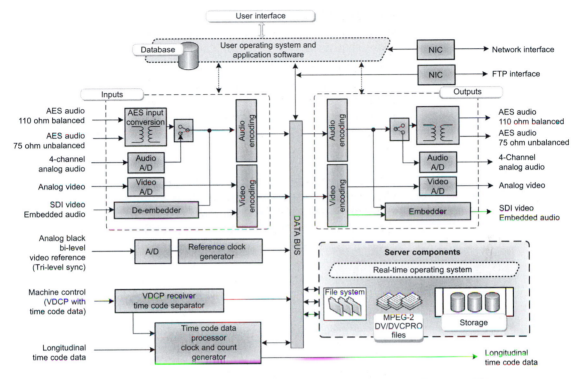

Figure 3.6 Videoserver internal signal flow diagrams, components typical to conventional video serving systems with AES audio in four forms: analog, AES unbalanced (75 ohm on coax), AES balanced (110 ohm twisted pair media), and embedded into the serial digital bit stream (SD, HD, or 3 Gbytes/second).

moved away from any analog composite or component I/O (or would offer them only as options). The inputs may encode the input to either 8 bits or 10 bits, allowing the user to select the depth during server setup/maintenance modes.

Selectable Audio Inputs

In similar arrangement to the video inputs, audio may either be analog or AES3 standard digital audio. Physical connector (and electrical) options include the 75 ohm BNC (unbalanced) input as AES3id, or as 110 ohm AES3 (balanced) using twisted pair cabling presented to 3-pin XLR connectors. Most servers accept only 48 kHz sampling (20-bit resolution) in at least two sets of AES inputs, yielding four tracks of audio as two stereo pairs. With surround sound and multilingual requirements, many video-servers are providing at least four AES streams providing eight tracks of audio on two groups of AES.

AES-3id-2001

The unbalanced version of the AES implementation is usually carried on coaxial cable with a line driver source impedance of 75 ohms and a return loss of better than 15 dB over the frequency band of 0.1–6 MHz. This form of carriage, usually found in broadcast facilities with discrete (AES) audio, became prevalent in the mid-1990s as AES on digital video transports—and eventually videoservers—came into being.

Sampling

Most of the professional servers will deal mainly with 48 kHz AES sampling (with at least 20-bit resolution) in at least two sets of AES inputs, yielding four channels of audio, generally identified as two stereo pairs. The advent of surround sound and multilingual audio has forced the requirements for at least four sets of AES inputs (eight channels of audio) to fulfill six-channel surround and at least one additional stereo pair of audio for second languages.

Sony/Philips Digital Interconnect Format

The more familiar name for the Sony/Philips Digital Interconnect Format is S/PDIF, which is sometimes simply called the "Sony Philips Digital Interface." S/PDIF is a digital audio interface method designed primarily by Sony and Philips and later standardized as IEC 60958 Type II (prior to 1998, it was known as IEC 958). S/PDIF is seldom found in the broadcast or professional videoserver domain. There is more likelihood of finding such implementations in an audio server although that would be confined mainly to digital audio workstation (DAW) systems.

An electrical comparison of the variations in AES3 and S/PDIF is summarized in Table 3.1 and in Fig. 3.7.

Table 3.1 Industry Standard Digital Audio Interfaces

Parameter	AES3	AES3	AES3id	S/PDIF
Interface	Balanced	Balanced	Unbalanced	Unbalanced
Connector	XLR-3	CAT-5$_E$	BNC	RCA
Impedance	110 ohm	110 ohm	75 ohm	75 ohm
Output level	2–7 V-pp	2–7 V-pp	1.0 V-pp	0.5 V-pp
Maximum output	7 V-pp	7 V-pp	1.2 V-pp	0.6 V-pp
Maximum current	64 mA	64 mA	1.6 mA	8 mA
Minimum input	0.2 V	0.2 V	0.32 V	0.2 V
Cable	STP	CAT-5	COAX	COAX
Maximum distance	100 m	400 m	1000 m	10 m

Conversion Between AES3id and S/PDIF

Translating the signal levels between the variances in AES and S/PDIF requires that passive circuitry be added between one format and another. These additional components are sometimes embedded in the front and back end I/O circuitry or may be packaged in discrete interface devices—often called "baluns"—which are frequently found in broadcast infrastructures (see Fig. 3.8).

Embedded Audio

Embedded AES audio, which used to be an option, is now very common on SMPTE 259M or SMPTE 292 inputs and outputs, that is, when devices provide serial digital interfaces (HD/SD-SDI). Embedded I/O saves significantly on connector count and internal conversion. Typically, videoserver products may place as many as 16 or more tracks of audio, which can now be carried on the embedded SDI transport per industry standard grouping specifications.

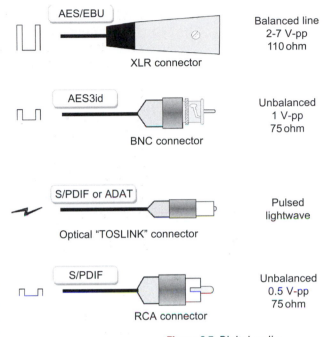

Figure 3.7 Digital audio interface connectors, signal levels, impedance, and signal waveforms.

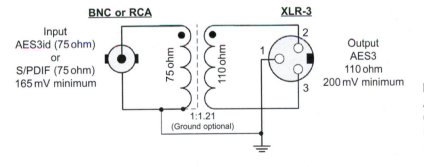

Figure 3.8 Unbalanced 75 ohm AES3id balanced to balanced (balun) 110 ohm AES3 adaptor using passive transformer coupling.

Most of the videoservers generally have the capability to use embedded audio on the output SDI signal even if it had been presented as discrete inputs. Devices with the physical real estate on the chassis may provide both discrete AES and embedded signals on their I/O ports, providing flexibility and negating the need for external embedding or disembedding components.

They may also offer shuffling of the audio tracks on playout. These are manufacturer's feature choices, and if uncertain the user is cautioned to investigate the specifications prior to implementation.

Dolby Compressed Audio

High definition video drove the requirements for 5.1 channel sound, which is employed in most broadcast television programming. The individual surround sound channels are usually carried as a grouping of PCM AES audio streams, combined and compressed using Dolby E, and presented to the videoserver as a single AES stream. Dolby E allows for as many as eight discrete audio tracks to be encoded and carried on this transport. The signal may be embedded into the SD/HD-SDI transport. At least 20 bits of AES audio must be available in order to carry Dolby E (noting that 16-bit audio reduces that track count from eight to six, still sufficient for surround, but is not generally used).

Dolby Digital (AC3) is the standard for ATSC broadcast emission. However, carrying highly compressed multichannel audio on the video signal presents complications to the videoserver (and some video signal distribution components). First, AC3 is a data set that spans the digital space of both the audio tracks on a single AES stream. Second, the AC3 signal is not frame bound, that is, its data footprint covers more than the area of a single field of video and cannot be properly (cleanly) switched at the video frame boundary points. Third, as a data signal, some servers will not recognize that this is something other than an AES signal and not properly separate it from the video stream or incorrectly slice it for storage on the disk systems. Finally, as videoservers have improved in technical architectures, and the transmission side of broadcast seldom stores AC3 on other than a transport stream server, it has become unnecessary to go through the complicated efforts of insuring that the AC3 signal is properly treated as it is routed (distributed) throughout the facility, except just before emission.

For comparison, Dolby E was designed quite differently from AC3 and presents none of the problems that AC3 does for servers. Nonetheless, the user is wise to validate his or her uses and the specifications of the videoserver audio and video technologies before implementation.

Audio/Video Delay

Components that process the video stream but don't delay the audio stream to match the video processing delay will result in video frames that will no longer be synchronously aligned to the Dolby E frames. Further processing actions could cause the corruption of Dolby E frames and consequently create artifacts such as audio pops and clicks, once decoded.

Data Processing in Audio Equipment

Dolby E is designed to pass through existing audio equipment. However, care must be taken as Dolby E can no longer be classed as purely audio due to its compressed nature. Equipment used in a system must also be Dolby E aware. This means the equipment may not apply the same audio functions that are familiar with normal audio processing such as gain, phase inversion, audio sample rate conversion, and transitioning or mixing. If this kind of processing is applied to Dolby E data, the stream will be corrupted and may become unrecoverable Dolby E data yielding no ability to decode the Dolby E stream downstream.

MADI

MADI, more formally known as Serial Multichannel Audio Digital Interface, is a standard describing the data organization for a multichannel audio digital interface. MADI is a standard described in AES10-2008 where details include a bit-level description, features in common with the AES3 two-channel format, and the data rates required for its utilization. The specification provides for the serial digital transmission of 32, 56, or 64 channels of linearly represented digital audio data at a common sampling frequency within the range 32–96 kHz, having a resolution of up to 24 bits per channel. MADI makes possible the transmission and reception of the complete 28-bit channel word (excluding the preamble) as specified in AES3, providing for the validity, user, channel status, and parity information allowable under that standard. The transmission format is of the asynchronous simplex type and is specified for a single 75-ohm coaxial cable point-to-point interconnection or the use of fiber-optic cables. The AES10-2008 revision includes minor changes to conform to those revisions of AES3 and AES5-2008, the AES recommended practice for professional digital audio describing preferred sampling frequencies for those applications using pulse-code modulation (PCM), providing clarification of sync reference signals and link transmission-rate tolerance and references for the nonreturn-to-zero-inverted (NRZI) and the 4B5B coding schemes.

Serial Data Transfer Interface

Serial data transfer interface (SDT), standardized as SMPTE 305M and extended as SDTI-CP (content package), is a means to interface packetized compressed digital bit streams between devices. This optional interface method has been used on DVCPro videotape transports, some codecs for satellite or other transport platforms, and may be found on some server products such as the EVS XT[2] video replay platforms (http://www.evs.tv).

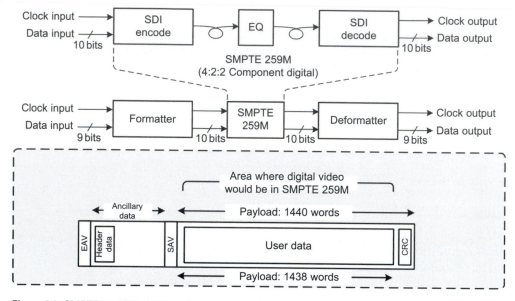

Figure 3.9 SMPTE 305M Serial Data Transport Interface (SDTI).

The SMPTE 305M interface is only defined for the SDI signal transport per SMPTE 259M. A high-definition version, HD-SDTI, is described in SMPTE 348M (see Fig. 3.9 for SD-SDTI and Fig. 3.10 for HD-SDTI).

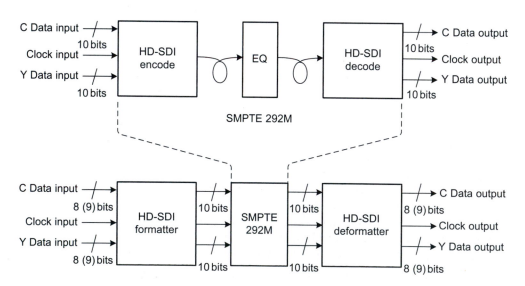

Figure 3.10 Arrangements of HD-SDTI wrapped around SMPTE 292M.

Baseband Video Outputs

Most videoserver platforms will provide a matched set of inputs and outputs, generally in the same formats as the inputs. The exceptions are rare, but it is possible to find products that only accept embedded audio or may only output embedded audio.

Reference Signals

In the majority of implementations, video black burst from the facility's house reference generator is applied to a dedicated input port on the videoserver. Users may select among this external reference, an internal reference (referred to as "free-run" mode), or one of the digital video inputs or analog (if provided) in a mode referred to as "self-run" mode.

When a videoserver is integrated exclusively into a digital environment, an external reference signal is used essentially only for video signal timing purposes, which allows for the alignment of the playback outputs to the other video signals in the broadcast plant. This reference may be unnecessary if the videoserver functions purely as a file-generation device and has no real-time video output for signal distribution.

Control

Videoservers may be controlled under a variety of interfaces ranging from simple start, stop, and cue from a general-purpose input/output (GPIO) trigger, to a serial control on a balanced differential (RS422) or unbalanced (RS485 or RS232) interface, to a network IP control over an Ethernet carrier.

VDCP

Most videoservers provide at least one RS422 machine control port per channel of the videoserver. The terminology "channel" has no standard definition and may vary depending on the manufacturer's implementation. Using the common RS422 (or occasionally the RS485 method) of the machine control, emulation of common VTR modes is provided usually as VDCP (video disk control protocol) and is known by a variety of names including the Sony 9-pin protocol, and for extended modes, the BVW-75 extended protocol.

Time code data may be carried between devices over this interface, as well as clip identification or simple asset management information (house number, clip number, etc.)

An example communications protocol (as used by Probel) is:

RS485/RS422, 8-Bit DATA, 1 STOP Bit, EVEN Parity, and 38.4K Baud.

Network IP Control

Some videoserver platforms offer a native control interface over an Ethernet port that communicates directly with either an automation system or other control mechanism.

A goal for a universal control protocol, despite significant advances in the areas of networking, has never been achieved. Attempts to divine such a control code would require a normalization of all the various control interface parameters (e.g., Sony, Ampex, CMX, Odetics) between devices, to one common set of protocols. Unfortunately, such a protocol would presume that all specialized functions, some specific to the videoserver and some to the controlling system, would require a formal standardization process and might result in a reduction of manufacturer-specific performance and capabilities for disk-based systems.

General-Purpose Input/Output (GPIO)

Most of the devices provide at least one external "closure–type" trigger for each channel. GPIO functions may be dedicated to functions such as start, stop, cue, recue, and advance or may be set into software that is assigned during initial setup configurations by the user.

Further descriptions of the control interface protocols are included at the conclusion of this chapter.

Time Code

Videoservers used in broadcast facilities generally find it is necessary to employ some method to catalog or frame count the media being ingested or played back. Digital time and control code, as referenced by the ubiquitous SMPTE 12M standard and for use in systems at 30, 30/1.001, 25, and 24 frames per second, are the commonly accepted means for establishing a time coincident marking of the video frames and runtime in a videoserver. For most of the broadcast facilities, time code will be referenced to a master house clock slaved to the master sync and reference system.

Time code data, specific to the video clip recording, is most often carried to the videoserver from the source VTR over the RS422 serial control interface. Many servers will provide a single linear time code port that applies time code to the server for recording or time synchronization purposes.

The 32 bits used for time code account for eight digits that represent hours:minutes:seconds:frames (HH:MM:SS:FF). There are at least three options for the carrying of time code either to or from linear videotape.

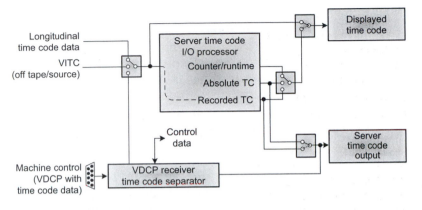

Figure 3.11 Time code flow within a videoserver.

Vertical Interval Time Code (VITC)

In an analog signal, VITC is carried in the vertical blanking interval (VBI) on one or two scan lines, usually on line 14 (line 277) for 525/59.94 systems. For analog videotape, VITC should be carried on two nonconsecutive lines. Tradition has placed VITC on line 16 (279) and line 18 (281), with a field mark bit added for field 2 (even). VITC can be ingested into the server via the conventional analog composite signal input. The VITC data is usually automatically detected, extracted from the baseband signal (often ahead of digitization), and saved so that it can be recovered once the respective clips are returned to their native condition at the output of the server. Figure 3.11 shows some of the methods that videoservers employ for time code processing.

Longitudinal Time Code (LTC)

On both analog and still in some digital formats, LTC is recorded on a longitudinal track on the original videotape. Each frame carries 80-bit cells and results at a bit rate of 1.2 Kbits/second. The LTC signal is brought into the server as an analog signal (0 dBm into 600 mW) in the same fashion as a conventional videotape transport. Depending on the architecture of the server, LTC is saved in a similar manner to that of VITC. LTC is then regenerated and output at the time the specific clip is played back.

The third way that SMPTE time code can be delivered to the server is in similar fashion to how it might be delivered to an external device—such as the computer-assisted edit controller—in a conventional editing environment. This time code data is embedded in the control data stream and transported into or out of the server, in the data stream transmitted using the RS422 serial data protocol on 9-pin D connectors. The control protocol (such as in most Sony video recorders) will determine where that data is placed in the serial control bit stream.

Time code is an important element in machine control and in automation systems. Many transport functions, such as recording into the server, play, cue, stop, and reverse, rely heavily on existing established tape transport controls. A machine control interface that includes carrying time code information, similar to a tape transport control stream, is almost a necessity.

Most broadcast facility automation systems rely on time code information for addressing videotape segment locations. Once the program is transferred into a server for delay broadcasting, time shifting, or other purposes, the timing relationship between tape and clip should be preserved. Some servers may not preserve the original time code but simply begin a new count sequence at the start of each clip. However, in most cases, the server will recreate the time code sequence on the RS422 machine control line when playback is initiated.

User Bits

In addition to the 32 bits used for time code, an additional 32 bits per frame are designated as user bits. User bits, a form of metadata seldom used in broadcast any longer, were used for separate purposes specific to the controller or controlling device for which they were generated. There may be a second time code stream as a real-time offset from an original recording or a set of characters (such as ASCII/ISO). Some legacy automation or control systems built their cueing and tape-identification structure around a dependence on user bits. The user and the vendor would need to be aware of what the server does or might do to this information that is important to be saved for other uses.

Drop- or Nondrop-Frame Time Code

Time code may be conveyed as either drop frame or nondrop frame. In 525/59.94 systems, the number of frames per second is no longer an integer number and an adjustment must be made for the extra frame numbers that would be generated as time moves linearly forward. The prescribed pattern, which occurs every 66 2/3 seconds, is the frequency that the extra frame numbers must be dropped, in pairs, in order for time code to stay in synchronization with real clock time over the course of several minutes or more. The "drop-frame" time code version was created to combat this.

In order for the sequences to even out over long time periods, frame numbers 00:00 and 00:01 must be dropped at the start of every minute, except at the tenth minute, when the frame numbers are all retained.

Clips stored in a videoserver are not necessarily recorded in a "one frame to one time code number" fashion, especially with compressed video. Data representing the number of frames is attached to the clip, and then, the appropriate time code is regenerated as the video stream plays back. This method is employed against the actual time code data, which is being retained individually linked in a one-to-one relationship with every frame of video.

As video and audio signals are compressed, timing relationships are no longer retained on a frame-like basis. The concept of compression uses the elimination of redundant data (image and audio wise), thus elements of some "frames," per se, are not retained (except in the case of I-frame-only compression). With MPEG-2, time stamping takes on a different meaning altogether, given that the presentation order of the compressed frames is no longer the same as a linear frame–based video stream (the profound details of the various time stamps and other elements of MPEG-2 or other compression coding syntax are beyond the scope of this discussion).

Network Connections

For most of the early videoserver applications, a 10/100 Mbit Ethernet port was provided, which enabled operational services used during setup or for live monitoring. Generally, this interface used Ethernet and was configured for anything the manufacturer intended it for.

Today, the use of network interfaces are for a much broader set of uses, including FTP, broadband connections to WAN/LAN, and more specifically as the means to exchange files or other data between servers and other file transfer mechanisms.

Any other available physical connections to a videoserver will be manufacturer specific.

SCSI

Depending on the storage architecture of the manufacturer, physical drives may be mounted internally or may be in external enclosures, usually in a RAID configuration. With the increased requirements for high-speed or high-bandwidth data interfaces, including NAS and SAN, discrete SCSI connections have all but vanished from modern videoserver systems. When the storage drives are internally mounted, then you probably won't find a usable external SCSI connection. Should the server use an external SCSI drive configuration, the number of SCSI ports on the videoserver's primary enclosure will depend on the number of SCSI buses that the system supports.

Fibre Channel

Early videoservers manufactured in the first- or second-generation era were using FC over twisted copper pairs. Optical fiber connection had not provided a cost-effective solution throughout the 1990s. Once network storage systems, such as SANs, found their way into video storage applications, the entire videoserver architecture would be changed.

Fibre Channel drives, until at least the later part of the 2000s, remained the mainstream high-performance storage platform of choice. Most of the videoservers, even today, will continue to use them although alternative solutions are continuing to be developed and deployed.

Depending on the specific server and storage architecture, Fibre Channel would be used to connect a server and its Fibre Channel disk drives or arrays, either internally or externally. Interfacing multiple sets of FC drives and chassis to the main serving elements would require a managed FC switch that controlled the distribution of data between devices at the bandwidths necessary to move data between storage and server in real time.

Alarms and Diagnostics

Critical alarms may be triggered via either GPO contact closures or other independent ports, allowing users to configure signaling as they desire. The signals that trigger alarms might include primary power supply failure, fan or airflow failure, over temperature, or a fault in the computer or compression engines themselves.

Today, most of these functions are carried on the Ethernet port to an external software application that can be managed by the user, the automation system, a control platform (for example via SNMP), or even remotely monitored via a VLAN or tunnel into the server from an outside entity such as the videoserver manufacturer.

Graphical User Interface

When the videoserver is built around a PC-based board set, it will most likely have its own PC-like I/Os: generally, a VGA output for display, a keyboard, and a mouse port. These three items together are termed GUI (or graphical user interface). In many systems, a KVM (keyboard-video-mouse) router is used to communicate between a central set of user workstations and the videoservers.

Peripheral Ports

These port interfaces, consisting of 9-pin serial ports (or in older systems a 25-pin parallel port), may still be found on some platforms. Some servers now make use of a USB port instead of the legacy 25-pin ports for such devices as boot drives or external optical drives that would have been used for loading software. Most of the videoservers manufactured since the later 1990s and early 2000s now include at least a single DVD drive as part of the "PC-like" operating platform.

Modular Expansion

Videoservers are available in many form factors and chassis configurations as there are storage arrays. For dedicated chassis-based systems, only a modest amount of expansion can be expected either internally or externally to the server. Inside the crate, one may still find additional slots destined for new or additional codecs or channels. Outside, modular access to breakout panels, control panels, or other interface devices may be available if the server does not currently populate all its input and output ports.

Videoserver Storage

The storage systems for a videoserver may be composed of either internal sets of hard disk drives or solid state memory (SSD or flash) integrated with the server's chassis or as external drive sets that are often configured in sets of modular chassis with plug-in drives. These may be direct-attached storage (DAS) or in some cases small network-attached storage (NAS) systems. External drive storage systems, also referred to as arrays or RAID sets, may be configured as NAS or as elements in a storage area network (SAN).

Storage capacity is based on the number of physical drives in a given array, the number of arrays in the overall system, and the configuration of those drives as RAID sets. Arrays may be directly connected via copper or fiber-optic cabling to the server chassis, or they may be connected via a network switch. The network switch (or simply "switch") choice is based on the types of drives used and may be Fibre Channel or gigabit Ethernet.

Built-in storage, as when the drives are confined to a manufacturer's particular chassis, will generally only provide for a fixed amount of storage. If the user wishes to expand that storage, his or her choices may be limited unless the server was provisioned so as to attach external storage as NAS or SAN.

As storage requirements increase, the accepted approach for nonnetworked storage-based videoservers has been to add one or more drive expansion chassis, usually in a RAID configuration. How these arrays are configured and how the bandwidth of the system is kept sufficiently high for the service requirements of the videoserver will be based on the server and drive capabilities designed into the product.

The following chapters will discuss the various elements of RAID, arrays, and other forms of storage systems.

Codecs in Videoservers

Compression engines that may be used in video-based media servers include a family of motion-JPEG, one or more of the prominent MPEG-2 profiles, MPEG-4 including Part 2 and Part 10 as H.264/AVC, JPEG 2000, and others. Most compression uses some form of discrete cosine transform (DCT) methods for spatial compression of each image although MPEG uses both spatial and temporal compressions consisting of I, B, and P frames, except in I-frame-only implementations (such as Sony IMX), whereby spatial compression of each individual frame is used.

Codecs often allow for the use of multiple data or compression rates, giving users the flexibility in the grade or degree of image quality they want and in the size of the files they wish to store.

Videoservers allow profiles to be set such that the user can select the data rate on a file-by-file (clip-by-clip) basis. This is valuable when considering the quality of the image the user wishes to maintain during the encoding process, as the bit rate (and the GOP structure in MPEG) determines the volume of storage required for a given unit of recording runtime.

Ancillary Data Sets

The devices discussed in this chapter are categorized according to the "video" servers definition because they deal essentially with video and audio (analog and digital), they include broadcast centric signal sets such as vertical blanking interval (VBI) and other ancillary data spaces that are in the digital domain, and they use time code (or frame location identification) as a means to catalog the frame numbers in relation to real time.

Beyond Analog

With the oncoming sunset of analog over the air broadcasting, and the adoption of digital terrestrial television (DTV), the industry began to deal with entities beyond 525/59.94 standard-definition video. Yesterday's concerns took on new dimensions as the recording and storage of higher bit rate signals (such as HDTV) became a reality. Signals with data rates greater than 270 Mbits/second added to a fledgling host of other compressed signals at less than 100 Mbits/second emerged as the implementation of DTV moved forward. Digital signals for videoservers would be presented as SMPTE 259M (270/360 Mbits/second) or SMPTE 292 (1.485 Gb/second) for high-definition SDI video.

The introduction of (MPEG-2) video compression would place new demands on the user and the server. When other codecs, such as DV, were introduced, the manufacturers had to address them. It would not be long before the file sharing between a videoserver and a production class nonlinear editing platform would emerge.

By the time of US analog television decline and the move to ATSC over the air digital television (which the US Senate moved from 2006 to February 17, 2009 and then again to June 12, 2009), many broadcast facilities would be using video serving platforms, file-based workflow and file interchanges, nonlinear editing platforms and servers for production and news, and have very little videotape in their systems (for capture or final mastering and archive).

Videoserver products from various manufacturers offer multiple video format I/O options. First- and second-generation videoserver I/O options conformed to serial component digital on an SMPTE 259M transport for 8- or 10-bit 4:2:0 (or higher quality 4:2:2) sampling, and on rare occasion, one might find an I/O and an encoder at $4f_{SC}$ as NTSC (pr $8f_{SC}$ as PAL) composite digital interface. Later generations have added high-definition (SMPTE 292) signals, and now 3D (stereoscopic) in HD and 3 Gbits/second as input signals on SDI bit streams.

Filtering and Preprocessing

For broadcast applications, those servers including analog composite inputs would preprocess and filter the incoming signal for a variety of image-related purposes. Filtering is necessary prior to digitization so that aliasing does not occur in the digital signal. Noise reduction, another element of the analog-to-digital process, should also happen ahead of compression in both a dynamic and an adaptive nature.

Composite analog decoders generally use four possible forms of filtering. A notch filter will tailor a signal to separate, remove, or otherwise suppress portions of the signal that might otherwise overextend the amount of work necessary to compress the signal for little or no improvement to the image itself. Notch filters, when improperly applied, can introduce artifacts into pictures that have luma (Y) details at frequencies near the color subcarrier.

A temporal filtering process is used for still images but not for motion images. The filtering templates detailed in ITU-R BT.601-x have been standardized for studio digital video systems and define both a passband and a stopband insertion gain that shapes the signal so that the signal can be digitized properly and without overshoot or aliasing.

The third, spatial-adaptive filtering, is added for motion-related images but not for stills. The fourth filtering process uses a combination of spatial and temporal adaptive filtering that offers a compromise between the two.

When the real-time linear input signal is an SDI (component digital) signal, much of the filtering previously described for analog inputs is less critical or unnecessary. In broadcast facilities that are still essentially analog based, wider bandwidth component digital videos are only "island" based and still may use NTSC (or PAL) as the interconnect signal format between devices. Analog signals may be converted to digital before feeding the input to an SDI-only-based videoserver, unless that videoserver has its own analog-input converters integrated internally.

When a composite analog signal contains vertical interval information, such as closed caption data (e.g., on line 21), the server should preserve that data in its storage system. Depending on the codec or processing of the videoserver, this data may be stripped from the analog signal and distributed as a form of ancillary data over the videoserver's internal bus architecture. Whether as an analog or digital signal, any ancillary data presented at the input should be reinserted on the output stream or available for use as ancillary or metadata of some form.

In the Digital Domain

The input and output linear signal sets in videoservers may be in either the analog or the digital domain. The files that are generated or read by the videoserver's codec contain data sets comprised of video and audio essence, and metadata. This metadata may be structural or descriptive in nature. It may be constrained to only the videoserver platform, or the metadata may be exchanged with outside asset management systems.

In their earliest implementations, videoservers were justified as a means to reduce the issues impacting the cost and maintenance of tape transports, linear videotape inflexibility, complexities in automation and tracking systems, physical media costs, reliability of the transport, and the preservation of image quality over time. For those broadcast facilities using these early platforms (in the period around 1995–1997), a professional videoserver seemed to be confined principally to video-based uses. It was a device detached from the infant nonlinear editor, with a different purpose and a completely different set of associated workflows.

Early adopters found the videoserver (also known as "file server") as a "VTR replacement." This was a benefit to designers because it has essentially constrained the timing and the resolution of the video data to a defined and understood realm. However, the elements found in today's videoservers are more feature rich, don't deal with analog I/O constraints as much, and carry significantly more ancillary data than in the late 1990s.

Videoservers as Editing Platforms

As the development of both videoservers and nonlinear editing systems continued, some videoserver manufacturers began to target editing functionality beyond simple "tops-and-tails" trimming for automated play to air activities. While constrained more to video disk recorders, the edit functionality of a videoserver was capable of assembling segments into a composite group of images and rendering them to a single file. Over time, those requirements diminished as dedicated nonlinear editing (NLE) platforms gained momentum.

As NLEs became more focused on editing functionality, videoservers began to focus on more specialized uses, such as mission critical play-to-air or transmission platforms. This change limited the videoserver's editing functionality to only a handful of simplified tasks such as clip trimming of the tops and tails of recorded segments. As true file-based workflows developed, differing practices emerged. NLE editors became craft editors and servers became service devices that supported the end products produced by the NLE.

Throughout the previous decade, great strides have been made in integrating third-party applications, such as in editing and media asset management, so that users would not necessarily be required to depend on isolated, individual islands of storage to support their file-based workflow ambitions.

Manufacturers of video serving platforms have seen their products flourish into an atmosphere where NLEs and transmission servers (those designated for play to air) can live harmoniously. Storage product vendors and server manufacturers have rigorously developed the capabilities that allow for "edit-in-place" activities on their storage platforms. Such systems now enable third-party platforms to mount the storage systems of these video or media server platforms, and treat them as essentially their own centralized storage repository, eliminating the requirements for separate storage systems that must be managed and supported. Once heretofore proprietary platforms for editing are now embracing open APIs, shared file interchange, and collaborative working environments.

In the world of television viewing and entertainment, systems that can manage hundreds of video streams (channels) simultaneously have been operating at several of the major content aggregation and distribution enterprises. Video on demand and digital ad insertion on transport stream–based platforms for cable and satellite providers have evolved in all dimensions. IPTV serving platforms now use stream servers that utilize similar architectures to those previously described videoservers, but for delivery of contiguous file sets over a WAN/MAN to headends and homes in many of the major markets.

The Future of Videoservers

Professional production and broadcast servers are available with myriad storage configurations, various input–output configurations, and sophisticated capabilities for the storage and presentation of video and audio. The video serving platform is no longer a proprietary or vendor-limited product. Video disk recorders have developed into high-performance multipurpose video delivery systems by combining fundamental core technologies with modern-day network technologies to produce flexible, extensible, scalable, and interoperable platforms.

The video serving platform with its ancillary set of storage solutions has caused a paradigm shift in workflow for the media and entertainment industry, as well as for all forms of media management from the home to the global enterprise. Broadcasters, communications companies, telcos, and corporations have recognized that intelligent storage may now be utilized in every aspect and in all forms of information conveyance.

The concepts that have grown out of those infant videoservers have successfully changed the way media will be captured, stored, and managed forever.

Communications Protocols Used in Video Serving Platforms

For reference purposes, the next section outlines some of the more preferred and industry accepted means of communication and control videoserver systems.

Sony 9-pin Protocol

The fundamental interface uses a serial RS422 connection between videotape transports and control devices. Applications for this pinout/protocol include broadcast automation, linear and nonlinear editing platforms, and other discrete devices such as DNF controllers or shot boxes.

Several extensions and adaptations have been created to serve the functionalities of other devices and then the emerging videoserver marketplace. Some of those control extensions are summarized in the following sections.

Some of the industry names for the Sony control protocol include the following:

Sony 9-pin
Sony P2
Sony VTR protocol

Sony RS422
Sony Serial
BVW75

Network Device Control Protocol

Laurent Grumbach, first as an employee of Louth Automation, which was acquired by Harris Broadcast, designed and developed a network-based protocol, which Harris called Network Device Control Protocol (NDCP), a TCP/IP-based alternative to the traditional serial connection protocols to broadcast devices built around the video disk control protocol or VDCP. NDCP is an XML compliant protocol, based loosely on the concepts found in SOAP. The hope was that vendors would standardize their broadcast devices to use this protocol instead of the more common practice of offering proprietary control and interface protocols for their devices. By using a network-based protocol, device control would be insulated from the controlling application, have a standardized set of control terms (using XML), not be constrained to the limited cable lengths of an RS422 serial line, and allow for network-centric fanout or communications instead of fixed physical connections built around a differential receive/transmit implementation on shielded twisted pairs.

Video Disk Control Protocol

VDCP is a proprietary, de facto communications protocol developed primarily to control videoservers for broadcast television. VDCP, originally developed by Louth Automation, is often called the "Louth Protocol." At the time it was developed, an extension was needed to how videotape transports were controlled that reflected the uniqueness to videoservers. Hewlett-Packard (later sold to Pinnacle Systems and eventually to Avid) and Tektronix (who later acquired the Grass Valley Group that then spun off GVG to Thomson) were both bringing to market the first of the platforms (HP MediaStream and Tektronix Profile) to be used in the broadcast industry. Louth Automation designed the protocol based on the Sony VTR protocols, which leveraged the Sony Library Management System (LMS) and the Sony videotape transports. The principal design work was carried out by Kenneth Louth and Stan Becker.

VDCP uses a tightly coupled master-slave methodology. The controlling device takes the initiative in communications between the controlling automation system device and the controlled video disk device.

As videoserver systems have become more complex, clips are ingested from a variety of sources. The VDCP playout controller cannot assume that a clip was ingested from a VDCP recorder with the same assumptions about time code. The VDCP time code model is limited and will not work for clips from all sources, which results in a cueing error.

VDCP has also been implemented over IP (Ethernet).

Video Archive Communications Protocol

VACP, developed and employed by the former Louth Automation, uses a tightly coupled master-slave serial communication model between the controlling device (automation system) and the controlled device (video archive system). The controlling device will take the initiative in communications. The topology will be point to point.

VACP conforms to the Open System Interconnection (OSI) reference model. Layer 1 is the physical layer, which consists of the electrical and mechanical specifications. Layer 2, the data link layer, covers the synchronization and error detection and recovery for the information transmitted over the physical link. Layers 3 and 4 provide network functionality and are not applicable. Layer 5, the session layer, provides the control structure for communications between applications: it establishes, manages, and terminates connections (sessions) between cooperating applications. Level 6, the presentation layer, contains the control language (dialect). The command table and command description of this VACP document provides the functionality of Layer 6.

Serial Communications

Control and information transfer between equipment have been defined by serial communications standards for decades. The best known is RS232, which defines the communication between data terminal equipment (DTE) and data communication equipment (DCE). At relatively short distances and low-speed data transfer, the RS232 serial interface is the simplest and easiest to implement from at least the physical transport perspective. More demanding communications at higher data rates will use more current, nonnetwork-based standards such as RS422, RS423, and RS485. Serial RS422, the most common machine control interface for video and media server systems, will be discussed in this section, compared with other protocols where appropriate.

Serial, balanced, and differential are the keywords for the RS422 interface standard. Serial means that the information is sent bit by bit on a single transmission line, like those sent over RS232. Balanced and differential signaling is what distinguishes RS422 from RS232. When using RS232 interfaces, signals are sent on lines that share a common zero-level or ground point. With RS422, each signal line consists of two wires, preferably twisted and shielded to reduce noise. The voltage difference between the two lines is an indication of the signal value rather than the voltage level. Looking at the voltage differences with RS422, rather than the voltage levels, mitigates the influence of noise that is induced by external sources and allows for higher data rates and cable lengths compared with those of RS232.

Table 3.2 shows the differences in speed and cable length for RS422 versus other serial interfaces that may be used to interconnect devices including hosts, computers, and other terminal equipment typically found in media, television, and other broadcast facilities.

Table 3.2 Characteristics of Commonly Used Machine Control and Data Communications Interfaces

Parameter	RS232	RS423	RS422	RS485
Differential	No	No	Yes	Yes
Maximum number of drivers	1	1	1	32
Maximum number of receivers	1	10	10	32
Modes of operation	Half duplex or full duplex	Half duplex	Half duplex	Half duplex
Network topology	Point to point	Multidrop	Multidrop	Multipoint
Maximum distance (standard)	15 m	1200 m	1200 m	1200 m
Maximum speed at 12 m	20 Kbits/second	100 Kbits/second	10 Mbits/second	35 Mbits/second
Maximum speed at 1200 m	1 Kbits/second*	1 Kbits/second	100 Kbits/second	100 Kbits/second
Maximum slew rate	30 V/μs	Adjustable	N/A	N/A
Receiver input resistance	3.7 KΩ	≥4 KΩ	≥4 KΩ	≥12 KΩ
Driver load impedance	3.7 KΩ	≥450 Ω	100 Ω	54 Ω
Receiver input sensitivity	±3 V	±200 mV	±200 mV	±200 mV
Receiver input range	±15 V	±12 V	±10 V	±7.12 V
Maximum driver output voltage	±25 V	±6 V	±6 V	±7.12 V
Minimum driver output voltage (loaded)	±5 V	±3.6 V	±2.0 V	±1.5 V

*RS232 should not be run for 1200 m

Noise in the signals carried on the cable is reduced by twisting the signal lines and providing an overall shield around the pairs of cables. External sources will induce noise currents that are then reversed at each twist of the wire pairs. This approach cancels the induced noise and improves the integrity of the data signals on the end-to-end run of the cable.

There are additional improvements when using RS422 over RS232 besides just the maximum data speed and overall cable length. RS232 was specifically defined as an interface between computers, printers, and terminals with modems. Modems would translate the communication signals to protocol acceptable for long-distance communication (i.e., a device was located on the other side of the control room or building). RS422 allows the direct connection of intelligent devices, without the need of modems. Where an RS232 line driver is only designed to serve one receiver, a RS422 line driver can serve up to 10 receivers in parallel, allowing one central control unit to send commands in parallel to as many as 10 slave devices. However, those slave devices are unable to send return information over a shared interface line.

RS422 allows a multidrop network topology rather than a multipoint network where all nodes are considered equal and every node has send and receive capabilities over the same line. Should a multipoint communication network be required rather than a multidrop, then implementation over RS485 is the better choice because it offers a maximum of 32 parallel send and 32 receive units on one communication channel.

Video Disk Recorder: Command and Control Specification

This specification was developed by Odetics Broadcast Corporation as a set of commands for the control videoserver and video disk devices. Grass Valley later extended the specification with a list of new and extended commands and called this new extended protocol Advanced Media Protocol (AMP).

Advanced Media Protocol

Advanced Media Protocol is an extension of the Odetics protocol, which is supported by videoserver manufacturers as a client application through external control devices connected via RS422 serial connectors or Ethernet network connections.

Control protocol support for clip and file names has been limited to 8 bytes, restricting users from creating realistic and practical names. AMP supports variable-length clip names, allowing lengths up to 64 Kbytes. The size of the clip name is, thus, limited only by the capabilities of the videoserver platform. In a networked environment, commands can be issued through the network using protocols such as TCP/IP, IPX, RPC, etc.

Ethernet access is possible using DCOM or sockets on the Profile XP platform. Interfacing with sockets is similar to interfacing with DCOM, requiring only that the send and receive functionality be changed from DCOM send/receive units to sockets send/receive units.

AMP Client applications run in modes such as protocol control-only mode (where a Grass Valley Profile XP channel is controlled by a remote third-party application and the local AMP Client application only monitors activities on the channel); local and protocol control mode (where a channel can be controlled by either the local AMP Client application or the third-party applications such as a hardware controller or a software application); active clip (where the AMP "preset id" is considered the active clip that controls channel resources); or preview clip (where the AMP "preview preset id" is considered the preview clip).

EVS AVSP

EVS AVSP is a protocol developed by EVS Broadcast Equipment of Belgium for the control of their suite of videoserver and video disk replay systems. The data rate is 115.2 Kbits/second via a serial control over RS422, with Ethernet control in its future.

Thomson DD35

Thomson DD35 is a serial control protocol utilized in Thomson production switchers for interfacing with clip stores, replay systems, and video disks.

Further Readings

SMPTE 305M-2005 (Revision of SMPTE 305.2M-2000)
A standard that specifies a data stream protocol used to transport packetized data. The data packets and synchronizing signals are only compatible with 10-bit operation of SMPTE 259M and are generally carried over a coaxial cable physical material using BNC connectors. The protocol parameters are compatible with the 4:2:2 component SDI format. The data stream uses the digital television active line for the payload. Ancillary data packets, defined by SMPTE 291M and set in the horizontal blanking interval are used to identify the payload application. The payload data may be organized in fixed-length blocks or variable-length blocks.

SMPTE 338M-2005 (Revision of SMPTE 305.2M-2000)

The High Data Rate Serial Data Transport Interface (HD-SDTI) is a compatible (with SMPTE 305M) standard that provides the mechanisms necessary to facilitate the transport of packetized data over a synchronous data carrier. The HD-SDTI data packets and synchronizing signals provide a data transport interface compatible with SMPTE 292M (HD-SDI) and can readily be used by a coaxial cable–based infrastructure.

The SMPTE 338M standard uses a dual-channel operation with each line carrying two data channels each forming an independent HD-SDTI data transport mechanism. The two channels are word multiplexed onto a single HD-SDI stream with one line channel occupying the C (chroma) data space and the other line channel occupying the Y (luminance) data space that would be applicable in the carriage of baseband high-definition video. It should be understood that users may only carry one form of information at a time. If transporting as data, video may not also be carried at the same time.

This implementation provides for a baseline operation that supports a constant payload length per line channel with a maximum payload data rate up to approximately 1 Gbits/second.

4

HARD DRIVE ANATOMY

The single most important electromechanical device in the entire set of components of a storage system is its media—the spinning hard disk drive—which is written to and read from on a nearly continuous basis. The achievements obtained from the earliest IBM drives of the 1950s to the present modern area of storage are remarkable. Through the development and combination of mechanical systems, magnetic materials, and electronic control interfaces, the digital age has moved well into the information age almost in similar fashion to how the invention of the transistor and its extreme counterpart the microprocessor helped mold the computer and electronics industries we've grown to depend on.

To put this into a perspective, International Data Corporation reports that the hard drive industry is expected to sell more than 300,000 petabytes worth of products over the next 5 years (2010–2015), which is an increase of 40.5 million units in 2009 to 52.6 million units in 2014 for the enterprise market.

This chapter focuses on the origination and the development of the physical hard disk drive from RAMAC to the Minnow, from 24-in. to 2.5-in. form factors, and from a few kilobytes to multiple terabytes of data. It includes the components of the disk drive, the subjects of drive scheduling, areal density and performance, and head construction. It concludes with a look at the future techniques being used by drive manufacturers who are pushing capacities beyond 3 Tbytes and putting areal densities at the half-terabyte per square inch dimension.

KEY CHAPTER POINTS

- A brief history of the development of the magnetic spinning disk drive from 1893 through modern times
- Outline of the fundamental components of the hard disk drive
- Disk optimization parameters, latency, seek time, and scheduling elements
- Areal density and the makeup of the read–write heads from ferromagnetic to giant magnetoresistance to heat-assisted magnetic recording (HAMR), thermally assisted recording (TAR), and bit-patterned recording (BPR)

Magnetic Recording History

Magnetic recording history portrays that Valdemar Poulsen, a Danish telephone engineer who started his work at the Copenhagen Telephone Company in 1893, began his experimentation with magnetism so as to record telephone messages. Poulsen built and patented the first working magnetic recorder called the telegraphone. It would not be until the early 1950s before there was any potential commercial development for storing data in a semipermanent format.

Disk drive development has continued nonstop from the 1950s to the present. A historical summary of that development process for disk drives and flexible media (Fig. 4.1) shows the

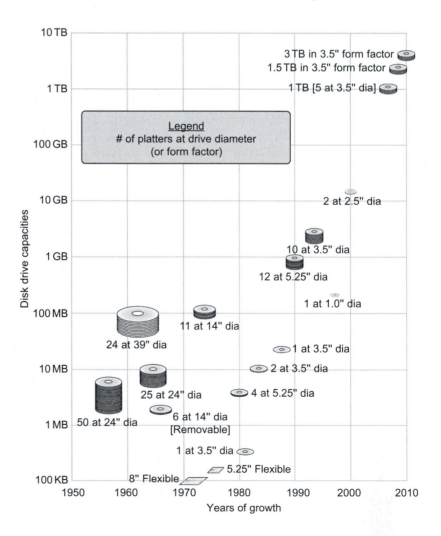

Figure 4.1 Development of spinning disk–based media since 1956.

steady advancement in capacity versus physical size that has led to the proliferation of data storage for all forms of information and in all sectors of modern life.

Storing Bits on Drums

The first method for the storage of bits used magnetic patterns that were deposited on cylindrical drums. The bits were then recovered by a device that would later become the magnetic head. First-generation hard disk drives had their recording heads physically contacting the surface, which severely limited the life of the disk drive. IBM engineers later developed a mechanism that floated the head above the magnetic surface on a cushion of air, a fundamental principle that would become the major piece of physical technology for magnetic disk recording for decades to come.

First Commercial HDD

The first commercially manufactured hard disk drive was introduced on September 13, 1956, as the IBM 305 RAMAC, which was the acronym for "Random Access Method of Accounting and Control." With a storage capacity of 5 million characters, it required fifty 24-in.-diameter disks, with an areal density of 2 Kbits per square inch (drives today have specs in the hundreds of gigabits per square inch). The transfer rate of the first drive was only 8.8 Kbits/second.

The IBM model 355-2 single-head drive, at that time, cost $74,800, which is equivalent to $6233/Mbyte. Once developed, the IBM engineers determined that a need for removable storage was required. IBM assigned David I. Noble a job to design a cheap and simple device to load operating code into large computers. Using the typical terminology of that era, IBM called it the initial control program load, and it was supposed to cost only $5 and have a capacity of 256 Kbits.

During 1968, Noble experimented with tape cartridges, RCA 45 RPM records, dictating belts, and a magnetic disk with grooves developed by Telefunken. He finally created his own solution, which was later known as the floppy disk. At the time, they called it the "Minnow." As the first floppy, the Minnow was a plastic disk 8 in. in diameter, 1.5 mm thick, coated on one side with iron oxide, attached to a foam pad, and designed to rotate on a turntable driven by an idler wheel. The disk had a capacity of 81.6 Kbytes. A read-only magnetic head was moved over the disk by solenoids that read data from tracks prerecorded on the disk at a density of 1100 bits per inch.

The first "floppy" disk was hard sectored, that is, the disk was punched with eight holes around the center marking the beginning of the data sectors. By February 1969, the floppy disk was coated on both sides and had doubled in thickness to a plastic base of 3 mm. In June 1969, the Minnow was added to the IBM System 370 and used by other IBM divisions. In 1970, the name was changed to Igar, and in 1971, it became the 360 RPM model 33FD, the first commercial 8-in. floppy disk. With an access time of 50 ms, the 33FD was later dubbed the Type 1 diskette. Its eight hard sector holes were later replaced by a single index hole, making it the first soft sector diskette. The Type 1 floppy disk would contain 77 tracks and the format for indexing of the drive data was referred to as IBM sectoring.

A double-density, frequency-modulated 1200-Kbit model 53FD floppy, introduced in 1976, followed the previous 43FD dual-head disk drive, which permitted read and write capability on both sides of the diskette. Coincidentally, the floppy disk emerged from IBM at the same time the microprocessor emerged from Intel. Disk-based recording technology had actually arrived some 20–25 years prior to the August 1981 debut of IBM's first personal computer, the PC.

Hard Disk Contrast

By contrast in 1962, IBM had introduced its model 1301, the first commercially available 28 MB disk drive with air-bearing flying heads. The 1301's heads rode above the surface at 250 micro-inches, a decrease from the previous spacing of 800 micro-inches. A removable disk pack came into production in 1965 and remained popular through the mid-1970s. A year later, ferrite core heads became available in IBM's model 2314, to be followed by the first personal computers (PCs).

The IBM Winchester drive, introduced in 1973, bore the internal project name of the 30-30 Winchester rifle and used the first sealed internal mechanics. The IBM model 3340 Winchester drive had both a removable and a permanent spindle version, each with a capacity of 30 Mbytes. The height of the drive's flying head had now been reduced from its original 800 microinches to 17 microinches.

Seagate would introduce its 5.25-in. form factor ST-506 in 1980, the drive featuring four heads and a 5-Mbyte capacity.

Personal Computing

IBM introduced the PC/XT, which would use a 10-Mbyte model ST-412 drive. This model would set the standard for the PC-compatible future. A few years later, the 3.5-in. form factor

RO352, introduced in 1983 by Rodime, would become and remain the universal size for modern hard disk drives through the early development of modern personal computers until the 2.5-in. was introduced for portable applications in 1988.

Drive Components

The internal components of a typical Integrated Drive Electronics (IDE) magnetic hard disk drive are shown schematically in Fig. 4.2.

Hard Drive Components

The hard disk storage device has been called a Direct Access Storage Device (DASD) or disk. Physically, and internally, the drive consists of one or more magnetic disks mounted to a single central spindle. Traditionally, moving head disks, also called spinning disks, use this center spindle, which is somewhat like an axle, to attach a series of disk platters. As the spindle rotates, the platters are also caused to spin. Platters are often double sided allowing data to be stored and retrieved from each side of each platter.

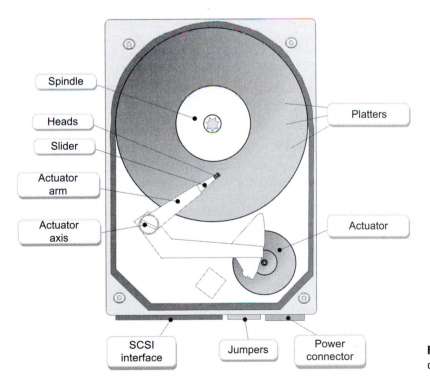

Figure 4.2 Internal components of a hard disk drive.

A boom or moveable arm, called an actuator arm, has a series of read–write heads attached to it—one for each platter. The head is attached to the tip of the boom arm. As the boom arm moves from the outer edge to the inner spindle side of the platter, it can align itself over the tracks on each platter.

Commands given from the disk controller, which reacts to requests from the host device (e.g., a computer), cause the actuator and boom arm assembly to move to a position that allows the drive to read or write data from or to the disk.

Disk drives are inherently mechanical devices, as such they impose certain physical and electromechanical obstacles to achieving perfect performance. One of these obstacles is the time it requires to obtain data once a request to obtain the data is received by the hard drive controller from the host computing device.

The platter surface is divided into regions: tracks, track sectors, geometrical sectors, and clusters. Figure 4.3 shows how these regions are laid out, and the details of the sector consisting of a header (containing synchronization information), the data area, and a trailer (containing the error correction code [ECC] for each data sector).

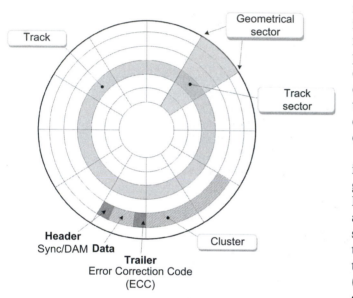

Figure 4.3 Layout of the surface of a disk drive, its regions (clusters, sectors, and tracks), and the components of one sector (header, data, and trailer).

Rotational Access Time

The surface of the platter has tracks, which are circular concentric rings of data that will cover one complete revolution of the disk's platter. The cylinder of a disk is that set of the same concentric tracks located on all the disk platters, usually on the top and the bottom of each. Access time, a limiting parameter of the tracks, is a major concern of rotational disks, burdened by the sum of these electrical and mechanical time constraints:

1. Rotational delay (latency)—the time taken by the platter to rotate to the proper location where the data is to be read from or written to
2. Seek time—the time taken by the boom arm with the heads attached to move to the proper cylinder

3. Transmission time—the time taken to read and/or write the data from and/or to the drive platter surface

When compared to a processor's speed or the time to access solid state memory, disk access time is exceedingly slow. This makes the disk drive the single-most time-restrictive device in a system.

Spinning Platters

The "Winchester" disk drive, well-known over a few decades, consists of magnetically coated platters made from a nonmagnetic material, usually aluminum alloy or glass, which are coated with a thin layer of magnetic material, typically 10–20 nm in thickness. An outer layer of carbon is added for protection. Older disks used iron oxide as the magnetic material, but current disks use a cobalt-based alloy.

The magnetic surfaces of the platters are divided into multiple submicrometer-sized magnetic regions. In each of these areas, a single binary unit of information is contained. Originally, each of the magnetic regions is horizontally oriented, but after 2005, the orientation was changed to be perpendicular for reasons discussed later.

Each of these magnetic regions is composed of a few hundred magnetic grains, arranged in a polycrystalline structure and typically about 10 nm in dimension (10 times less than the thickness of a very thin coat of paint). Each group of these grains are formed into a single magnetic domain. Each group of magnetic regions then form a magnetic dipole. The dipole creates a nearby, highly localized magnetic field, which the pickup heads of the drive use to determine the status of the data in that region.

Attached to the end of each actuator arm is a write head that when precisely positioned over the top of the region can magnetize that region by generating an extremely focused, strong magnetic field. Initially, disk drives used an electromagnet both to magnetize the region and then to read its magnetic field by electromagnetic induction. More recent versions of inductive heads would include "metal in gap" (MIG) heads and thin film (TF) heads, also called thin film inductive (TFI). TF heads are made through a photolithographic process that is similar to the fabrication process of silicon-based microprocessors. The TF/TFI manufacturing process uses the same technique to make modern thin film platter media, which bears the same name.

The evolution of disk drives brought with it increases in data density. The technology eventually found read heads that were made based on the principles of magnetoresistance (MR)

ferromagnetics. In MR heads, the electrical resistance of the head changes according to the magnetic strength obtained from the platter. Later developments made use of spintronics, known also as spin electronics and magnetoelectronics. This technology, which is also used to make magnetic semiconductors, exploits the intrinsic spin of the electron and its associated magnetic moment, in concert with its fundamental electronic charge. The magnetoresistive effect in the MR head is much greater than in earlier forms. More about MR and its relative, giant magnetore-sistance (GMR) is covered later in this chapter.

The areal density now present in drives that reach multiple-terabyte proportions have overcome some incredible complications in magnetic science and physics. As these drives continue to develop, effects where the small size of the magnetic regions create risks that their magnetic state could be changed due to thermal effects have had to be addressed and engineered for. One of the countermeasures to this impending effect is mitigated by having the platters coated with two parallel magnetic layers. The layers are separated by a 3-atom-thick layer of a nonmagnetic rare element, ruthenium (Ru). The two layers are magnetized in opposite orientations, which reinforces each other. A process called "ruthenium chemical vapor deposition" (CVD) is used to create thin films of pure ruthenium on substrates whose properties can be used for the giant magnetoresistive read (GMR) elements in disk drives, among other microelectronic chip manufacturing processes.

Additional technology used to overcome thermal effects, as well as greater recording densities, takes its name from how the magnetic grains are oriented on the platter surface. The technology, called perpendicular magnetic recording (PM), was first proved advantageous in 1976, and applied commercially in 2005. Within only a couple more years, the PMR technology was being used in many hard disk drives and continues to be used today.

Spin Control

Drives are characteristically classified by the number of revolutions per minute (RPM) of their platters, with common numbers being from 5,400 up to 15,000. The spindle is driven by an electric motor that spins the platters at a constant speed.

In today's disk drives, the read–write head elements are separate, but in proximity to each other. The heads are mounted on a block called a slider, which is set at the end point of a boom arm, or actuator arm, which is positioned by a step-like motor. The read element is typically magnetoresistive while the write element is typically thin-film inductive. A printed circuit board receives commands from the disk drive's controller software, which is managed by the host operating system and the basic input–output system. A head actuator mechanism pushes and pulls the boom arm containing the read–write head assemblies across the platters. The heads do not actually contact the platters but "fly" over the surface on a cushion of air generated by the air turbulence surrounding the spinning disk platters.

The distance between the heads and the platter surface are tens of nanometers, which is as much as 5000 times smaller than the diameter of a human hair.

Writing and Reading the Disk

The write process of recording data to a hard disk drive happens by directionally magnetizing ferromagnetic material deposited on the surface of the drive platter to represent either a binary 0 or a binary 1 digit. The data is read back by detecting the magnetization of the material when a pickup device (a head) is passed over the top of the tracks where that data is stored.

Disk Drive Form Factors

Disk drives are characterized into groups of "form factors," which are represented by dimensions, usually expressed in inches. Some believe these numbers relate to the diameters of the physical spinning media (the platters) but in actuality they are rooted in the size of the bay (or slot) that they originally were placed into during the early years of disk drive growth for the PC workstation.

8-in. Form Factor Floppy

The 8-in. format, which started with flexible media around 1971, a decade before the PC, set the stage for the form factor sizing that has sustained the terminology till at least the proliferation of the laptop. The 8-in. drives, introduced by IBM (1972) and DEC, included both single-sided single-density (SSSD) and double-sided double-density (DSDD) versions. The marketed capacities ranged from 1.5 Mbits to 6.2 Mbits unformatted. In these early days, formatting consumed much of the available actual bit storage.

The 8-in floppy could be found in broadcast equipment (e.g., the Quantel PaintBox and others) and continued in use through the 1980s. The last production versions released by IBM (model 53FD) and Shugart (model 850) were introduced in 1977.

5.25-in. Form Factor

The 5.25-in. form factor is the oldest of the drives used in the personal computer world, and it debuted first on the original IBM PC/XT. In the early 1980s, this form factor had been used for most of the IBM PC's life span but is now most definitely obsolete. The root of the form factor was that it was slotted into the 5.25-in.-wide drive bay that was used first to house the 5.25-in. floppy disk drives found in PCs. The bay size designation has sustained through existing modern PCs and workstations but are now primarily for CD-ROM or DVD/Blu-ray drives or similar devices.

The 5.25-in. hard drive has not been in production for these applications since the late-1980s, although high end drives used in servers were still available through sometime in the mid-1990s. The 5.25-in. form factor was essentially replaced by the 3.5-in. form factor for both physical space reasons and performance improvements.

Internal Components

Generally, the 5.25-in. drives used 5.12-in.-diameter platters. The exterior dimensions are 5.75 in. wide by 8.0 in. deep. The drives were available in only two different height profiles: a full-height version that was the same height as the floppy drive on the original PC and half-height. Other nonstandard heights for 5.25-in. drives were typically 1 in. high or less. Quantum would dub these drives as "low profile" or "ultra-low-profile." Table 4.1 shows the specifications used in the 5.25-in. form factor family.

Table 4.1 Profiles and Dimensions of the 5.25-in. Form Factor Hard Drives

| Form Factor | Bay/Housing Dimensions | | | Life Cycle/Applications |
	Width (in.)	Depth (in.)	Height (in.)	
5.25" Full-height	5.75	8.0	3.25	Drives of the 1980s, large-capacity drives with multiple platters through the mid-1990s
5.25" Half-height	5.75	8.0	1.63	Early 1980s through early 1990s
5.25" Low-profile	5.75	8.0	1.0	Middle to late 1990s
5.25" Ultra-low-profile	5.75	8.0	0.75–0.80	Middle to late 1990s

3.5-in. Form Factor

For over a decade, the 3.5-in. form factor has maintained its place as "the standard" in the desktop PC world although many other high-capacity storage implementations also use this in their multidrive arrays and storage product lines. Like the earlier 5.25-in. form factor, the 3.5-in. form factor is named not for the dimensions of the drive components themselves but rather for the way they fit into the same footprint of the drive bay originally created for the 3.5-in. floppy disk drives.

A 3.5-in. form factor drive will traditionally use 3.74-in. platters with an overall housing width of 4.0 in. and depth of approximately 5.75-in.

Higher speed 10,000 RPM spindle speed drives reduced their platter size to 3 in., with 15,000 RPM (Seagate) drives using 2.5-in. diameter platters. The 3.5-in. form factor has been maintained for compatibility, but the reduction in size of the physical media is for performance purposes.

3.5-in. Profiles

The 3.5-in. form factor drives come in the two profiles shown in Table 4.2. The larger profile half-height drive, which is 1.63 in. in height, uses this name because the drives are of the same height as the older half-height 5.25-in. form factor drives. Half-height 3.5-in. form factor drives may still be found in servers and other higher end storage systems.

The "slimline" or "low-profile" drive found in the 3.5-in. form factor family is only 1 in. in height. Some drives have reduced their height from the 1-in. standard and are now available in 0.75-in. high versions.

Table 4.2 Profiles and Dimensions of the 3.5-in. Form Factor Hard Drives

| Form Factor | Bay/Housing Dimensions | | | Life Cycle/Applications |
	Width (in.)	Depth (in.)	Height (in.)	
3.5" Half-height	4.0	5.75	1.63	High-end, high-capacity drives
3.5" Low-profile	4.9	5.75	1.0	Common to most PC drives, industry recognized standard

Table 4.3 Small Form Factor 2.5-in. Drives

| Form Factor | Bay/Housing Dimensions | | | Life Cycle/Applications |
	Width (in.)	Depth (in.)	Height (in.)	
2.5"/19 mm height	2.75	3.94	0.75	High-capacity drives used in larger laptops
2.5"/17 mm height	2.75	3.94	0.67	Midrange capacity drives, used in some laptops
2.5"/12.5 mm height	2.75	3.94	0.49	Low capacity drives, used in smaller laptops (and in some notebooks)
2.5"/9.5 mm height	2.75	3.94	0.37	Low-capacity drives used in mobility platforms, very small laptops, mininotebooks/notebooks

2.5-in. Form Factor Drives

The introduction of 2.5-in. form factor drives made notebook computers much more popular, with mobility being the driving factor. Many laptop or notebook computers have used 2.5-in. form factor hard drives (or less) for the following reasons:

- Size reduction—the drives take up less space, allowing laptops and notebooks to be reduced in overall size.
- Power reduction—the smaller drives consume less power and in turn extend battery life.
- Rigidity and durability—smaller platters reduce the susceptibility to shock damage.

Other Form Factors

The first 1.8-in. form factor drives were introduced in 1991. Integral Peripherals' 1820 model was the first hard disk with 1.8-in. platters. After the introduction of this model, and the 2.5-in. form factor drives, the previous "mold" for designating drive form factors was broken. The newer technologies would not be used as much in bays or slots but were now being placed into sleds, holders, or as PC Card disk drives.

The first 1.3-in. form factor was introduced in 1992 by Hewlett-Packard as the model C3013A. The drive capacities reached in the 30–40 Gbytes domain during early 2008.

Disk Performance Optimization

To maximize disk drive performance, many elements must work together to achieve the highest efficiencies. Such elements include the optimization of the mechanical systems, best use of the available bandwidth, management of the number of devices being accessed on the bus, and the application of best approach algorithms taking into account the usage and purpose that the disk drives will be deployed in.

To mitigate problems with delays, requests for data read and writes must be serviced in a logical order based on several factors. Some of these are mechanically dependent and others algorithm dependent. To optimize disk drive performance, service requests should be administered with the least amount of mechanical motion.

Latency

Any delay in getting a command started or the overall time involved between issuing a command and having it (fully) executed is considered latency. Latency can be impacted by several factors, which will be discussed in the following sections.

Bandwidth

A disk's bandwidth is defined as the total number of bytes transferred, then divided by the total time between the first request for service and the completion of the last transfer. Controlling the bandwidth allocation requires scheduling of requests for service.

Disk Scheduling

In the early years of disk drive development, disk scheduling algorithms concentrated mostly on minimizing the seek time, that is, the time from when the host request is issued to when the request is fulfilled. The majority of the time required to fulfill a request involves positioning the head over the data track itself. This includes getting the actuator arm that carries the heads to the proper position ahead of when the track actually appears beneath the head and without having to wait another rotational period for the track to realign under the head. The length of time these actions take becomes the single highest contribution to disk access latency.

With the continuous development of disk drives came an abundance of improvements in rotational optimization that included the control of when the various read-write requests were actually executed, along with variations in the algorithms that make up how the disk performs. Such improvements were covered under a set of terminologies and types of actions referred to as "scheduling."

First-Come First-Served Scheduling

This mode is almost primitive given the changes in drive technologies over the past two decades. As the name suggests, the first-come first-served (FCFS) mode acts on the first instruction it receives and completes it before accepting the next one. This form of scheduling, also known as "first-in first-out" (FIFO) in some circles, results in significant wait times for the head or arm assembly to get from any one location to another. Moreover, under heavy request loads, the system can be inundated to the point it can lose track of the processing order.

This unregulated scheduling mode has at least one major consequence. Principally, FCFS has the potential for extremely low system throughput, typically resulting in a random seek pattern caused by the controller's inability to organize requests. This disorganization induces serious service delays.

FCFS has some advantages. First, the access time for the servicing of requests is fair. FCFS prevents the indefinite postponement of requests for services, something other scheduling modes have to their disadvantage. Second, there is low overhead in the execution time for service requests, that is, no additional processing is considered. This is essentially "brute force" action at its highest.

Shortest Seek Time First Scheduling

This scheduling mode, as its name implies, uses the shortest seek time first (SSTF) concept to recognize where the head and actuator assembly is related to the particular cylinder it is positioned over, then ties that position to the execution of the next request.

SSTF is a direct improvement over the FCFS algorithm. It works by a process whereby the hard drive maintains an incoming buffer to hold its continually changing set of requests. A cylinder number is associated with each incoming request. A lower cylinder number indicates that the cylinder is closer to the spindle. A higher number indicates that the cylinder is further away, that is, closer to the edge of the disk platter. Of course, the rotational speed is greater at the edge, and the distance that point at the edge must travel to complete a full rotation is much farther than near the spindle center. There is more data on the outer edge and thus more places to locate at the same amount of time.

Because this variance cannot be substantiated and depending on how the numbers are generated, most specifications will average the number from each end of the platter or use statistics that come from the middle part of the disk as their reference point.

The SSTF algorithm resolves which request is nearest to the current head position, and then it places that request next in its queue. Compared with FCFS, SSTF results in a higher level of throughput, with lower response time, and produces a sensible solution for batch processing on a system-wide basis.

The SSTF disadvantages stem from unfair access times in the servicing of requests. Activities are now dependent on the previous data access. Situations where the data is more randomly scattered about the drive increases the access time latency. Contiguously laid down sequential data, such as in the recording or playout of a lengthy video segment, will not see an increase in access times. However, randomly distributed data laid down inconsistently during the write process, and then randomly recalled by a different application, may see extensive increases in the access time.

The SSTF also creates the possibility for an indefinite postponement of requests for services. If all the data reading activities were near the same region that the heads were currently positioned in, a potentially lengthy period could result before data located in another region of the platters might be accessed. SSTF produces a high variance in overall response times, which is generally seen as unacceptable for interactive systems.

Access Time Components

Access time is the greatest contributor to the high side of the latency equation. The time that it takes to access data on a drive is impacted by two major components, both mechanical in nature.

Rotational Delays

Rotational delay (or latency) is the additional time required for the spindle to rotate to the desired sector of a cylinder such that the appropriate data is positioned below the read–write head itself. When the rotational speed is faster, as expressed in revolutions per minute (RPM), there is less rotational delay because the period required to reach that position is shorter.

Delay is further affected by the number of cylinders and whether those cylinders are at the edge (i.e., a greater distance to rotate for positioning) as opposed to near the spindle (thus, a lesser distance to rotate for positioning).

Seek Time

This is the time required for the disk to move the heads to the cylinder containing the desired sector, that is, the time required for the head and actuator arm to move from its previous (or current) position to its next position such that it is ready to actually perform the requested read or write function.

Seek time can have a bigger impact on the overall latency than the rotational delay. This is why disk optimization and scheduling algorithms concentrate more on reducing seek times.

Servicing and Scheduling Criteria

The policies used in the processes associated with servicing and scheduling requests for access (both read and write) are categorized according to certain criteria.

- Throughput—the volume of data accessed and that is actually retrieved from the disk or written to the disk, in a given time period.
- Mean response time—the sum of the wait time and the service time in accessing the data.
- Predictability—calculated as the variance of response times as a standard deviation from a mean. If the variance from the mean is high, there is less predictability. If the variance from the mean is low, there is more predictability.

Whenever a policy can keep these variances low, there will be a tendency to stabilize the servicing of those requests. How those optimizations are fulfilled is the job of the microcode that is written into the drive's controller. There are proven strategies used in optimizing seek times, which are discussed in the next section.

Optimization Strategies for Seek Times

Improvements that have been made from the previous FCFS and SSFT algorithms include SCAN and C-SCAN. Each of these descriptions are much deeper looks under the hood than the general user would probably need to know, but these approaches show how disk drive technologies have been combined to provide us all with greater capabilities than back in the days of floppies and 5.25-in. hard drives.

SCAN

One advancement over SSFT is called SCAN. To minimize seek time, the disk controller code will first serve all its requests in one direction until there are no more in that direction. Then, the head movement is reversed, and the service is continued. SCAN enables a better servicing of requests and, in turn, provides a very good seek time because the edge tracks will receive better service times. However, one should note that the middle tracks will get even better service than the edge tracks.

When the head movement is reversed, the drive will first service those tracks that have recently been serviced, where the heaviest density of requests, assuming a uniform distribution, are presumed to be at the other end of the disk. The SCAN algorithms will utilize principles that consider directional preferences and then service newly arriving requests only if they are ahead of the direction of the current SCAN.

The direction of the head/actuator assembly is called a sweep. The sweep generally continues from the spindle toward the outermost track until the targeted track is reached or until there are no further requests in that particular direction. Once the target or the edge is reached, the direction is reversed until the sweep reaches the innermost track or again, until there are no more requests in that direction.

Elevator Algorithm

In order to optimize efficiency, the sectors on a hard drive and the requests for data access should not be based on the order in which requests were received. The action order should be set by where the current head position of the drive is at the instance the request is received. Since a hard drive will continually receive new requests, each of them is placed into a queuing system whose operational requirement is to fulfill the current requests and then remove the older requests. Sometimes these requests are delayed, especially since the queuing system will continually re-order those requests based on specific controller algorithms and the physical functionality of the drive.

The SCAN algorithm acts like and is sometimes referred to as "elevator seeking" because it is constantly scanning the disk using the motion of the disk's actuator arm and the head positioning associated with that arm to determine which requests it should act on. The "elevator algorithm" is essentially a scheduling routine that, in principle, works like a building elevator: it moves only in the direction of a request from passengers and stops only on the floor that people wish to get on or off.

When a drive is idle and a new request arrives, the initial head and actuator assembly movement will be either inward or outward in the direction of the cylinder where the data is stored. Additional requests will be received into the queue, but only those requests in the current direction of arm movement will be serviced until the actuator arm reaches the edge or the center spindle side of the disk, depending on the direction it was travelling at that time. This is just like the SCAN principle described previously.

SCAN Variations

SCAN has developed into subsets that use other algorithms that are specific to the drive and controller microcode instructions written into firmware. Each of these variations offers differing tactics to handle the servicing of requests. Some of the following SCAN alternatives may still be found in various hard drive applications.

C-SCAN

This variation, also known as the Circular Elevator Algorithm, provides a more uniform wait time than the straightforward SCAN methodology. C-SCAN ensures that a scheduling request for service will only occur in a single direction, treating the cylinders as a circular list that wraps around from the last cylinder to the first cylinder.

In C-SCAN mode, the head and actuator arm assembly travels from one side of the disk to the opposite side using a "shortest seek mode" for the next request in the queue. The seek direction begins at the center (spindle side) and advances outward to the edge. Once the arm reaches the edge of the disk, it then rapidly returns to the spindle side of the disk and continues servicing the queued requests in a single direction. The arm essentially only scans in a "center to edge" only direction, and then retraces (like analog television CRT raster scanning) back to the center. C-SCAN optimizes performance by ensuring that the expected distance from the head to the next data sector is always less than half the maximum distance that the arm must travel.

FSCAN

Another alternative disk scheduling algorithm is called FSCAN. This mode uses two subqueues. As the scan is in process, all the current requests are placed in the first queue and all new (incoming) requests are placed into the second queue. The servicing of any new requests, stored in the second queue, is deferred until all current (i.e., "old") requests have been processed. Once the current scan is completed, which may take several passes from center to edge, all the first-queue requests are flushed, the arm is taken to the new queue entries, and the process is resumed all over again.

LOOK

This mode is similar to SCAN, with a twist. Instead of continuing the sweep to one side and returning, the head and actuator arm assembly will stop moving in its current direction, either inwards or outwards, when there are no further requests that reside in that particular direction.

C-LOOK

A version of C-SCAN, this C-LOOK mode has the head and actuator arm assembly tracking only from the first to the last request in one of the directions. The actuator arm then reverses direction immediately and without tracking the disk fully again from the first to the last.

N-Step-SCAN

With SSTF, SCAN, and C-SCAN, there is the possibility that the arm may not move for a considerable period of time. This probability is more evident in high-density disks that are likely to be affected the most. Low-density disks and/or disks with only one or two surfaces are likely candidates for N-Step-SCAN, also known as N-Step LOOK. The primary feature of this mode is aimed at avoiding "arm stickiness."

N-Step-SCAN uses directional preferences and a disk scheduling algorithm that segments the request queue into subqueues of length N. Breaking the queue into segments of N requests makes service guarantees possible. Subqueues are processed one at a time. While a queue is being processed, new requests must be added to some other queue. If fewer than N requests are available at the end of a scan, then all of them are processed with the next scan.

When the values of N are large, the performance of N-step-SCAN approaches that of SCAN. When the value of N equals 1, then a FIFO policy is adopted. N-Step-SCAN works like SCAN, except that after a directional sweep has commenced, any newly arriving requests are then queued for the next sweep. Therefore, this algorithm will service only N requests at a time. Subsequent requests entering the request queue will not get pushed into N-sized subqueues, which are already full per the "elevator algorithm." Thus, request starvation is eliminated, and guarantees of service within N requests is made possible.

The N-Step-SCAN mode provides for good overall throughput. Of all the modes discussed earlier, it has the lowest variances because it works by reordering the service request queue for optimum performance and throughput.

EDF

Earliest Deadline First, or EDF strategy, is a mode where the block of the stream with the nearest deadline would be read first. EDF is utilized when there is a real-time guarantee requirement for the data access, as in streaming video.

EDF in its precise sense results in poor throughput and excessive seek time. EDF is most often applied as a preemptive scheduling scheme. The cost penalties for preemption of a task and scheduling of another task are considerably high. The overhead caused by task preemption is on the same order of magnitude as the time incurred for at least one disk seek. Thus, EDF needs to be adapted or combined with file-system strategies.

You may also see EDF augmented with the JIT designation, as in EDF/JIT, referring to the extension "just in time."

SCAN-EDF

This strategy combines both SCAN and EDF methods using the seek optimization benefits of SCAN and the real-time guarantees of EDF. Like in EDF, the service request with the earliest deadline is always served first, among those requests with the same deadline. The request that is first, according to the scan direction, is served first. Among the remaining requests, this mode is repeated until there are no requests with this deadline left.

The hybrid SCAN-EDF variation of the SCAN disk scheduling access algorithm is intended for use in a real-time environment where, in general, the requests are served according to an "Earliest Deadline First" (EDF) mode. When two requests share the same deadline, they may be reorganized according to SCAN.

An appropriate example of how to apply SCAN-EDF is when a videoserver retrieves file data from a hard disk during the play-out function. In this process, video that streams from a system will impose tight real-time constraints on data delivery from the storage system. One cannot simply "wait" for the actions of the disk scheduling to preempt a file being read. In a simpler sense, if a videoserver retrieves data once every second for each video channel, then SCAN-EDF can be applied and the goal of reducing the effects of seek overhead can be better met.

Deadline Sensitive SCAN

Usually written as "DS-SCAN," Deadline Sensitive SCAN is an algorithm for the scheduling of real-time disk I/O requests. DS-SCAN is a simple, yet powerful hybrid of traditional EDF and SCAN algorithms. Fundamentally, the feature of DS-SCAN is that it closely imitates the behavior of the SCAN algorithm so as to increase the effective throughput of disk, but subject to the deadlines of real-time request constraints so that the services are not missed.

Functionally this algorithm attempts to schedule the disk servicing requests (i.e., the "I/O requests") without impacting the deadlines of the real-time requests. Traditional SCAN does not take this into account. DS-SCAN does not have a fixed service schedule, which provides it with the flexibility to deal with real-time request streams that prescribe finely tuned deadlines. Its framework allows for the support of periodic real-time, aperiodic real-time, and best-effort requests, in whole or as a mixed set.

DS-SCAN will dynamically track how tight the request deadlines are using the idea of reserving "spare deadlines" that can be implemented when they are in demand. This concept basically follows the SCAN order until it needs to defend the real-time requests, during which time it shifts to EDF order.

Best Effort

This classification, one of two types in DS-SCAN, has no deadlines associated with it. Best effort requests could be considered against the disk scheduling model when compared with real-time scheduling. This is not to say it is detrimental to the DS-SCAN model; it might be considered as a relaxation mode, when the disk request algorithm can do what it is best suited to do given the previous mode it was in.

Real-Time Disk Scheduling

Virtually all disk devices will utilize an intelligent disk scheduling algorithm that incorporates "positional awareness." Many disks themselves may have more intelligence and efficient scheduling capabilities than those found in external schedulers. Today's storage systems may find many, sometimes varying, instances of disk scheduling methodologies present in multiple locations of the hardware, such as in the disk itself or in the RAID controller.

With today's emphasis on real-time content delivery, a real-time disk scheduling algorithm is essential. However, the bar must be raised when there are continual and concurrent requests to provide service access from multiple sources. This kind of activity is referred to as "concurrent access requests." It is becoming more important to address these issues as single drives are now exceeding 2 Tbytes and will approach the domain of 5 Tbytes or so before too long.

To address these growing activities in concurrent access requests, researchers have been exploring ways to maximize the throughput for modern storage devices by allowing concurrent I/O requests at the device whenever possible. Real-time disk scheduling algorithms of the past were modeled around a storage device receiving a single request at a time. This model dramatically reduced utilization and slowed the throughput in modern storage devices.

Today, RAID arrays and most disks already have an efficient positional-awareness scheduling algorithm built into firmware or software controllers. The controls are optimized for the proficiencies of the drive and per the kinds of activities requested through the host in concert with the file system. DS-SCAN is utilized as needed, but it can suffer from conditions where multiple requests arrive at the same time.

The DS-SCAN algorithm can be extended so as to properly account for multiple outstanding service requests and in turn guarantee those real-time constraints for both outstanding and pending real-time requests. The name that is associated with the research and proposals from HP Labs is "Concurrent DS SCAN" (CDS SCAN). For a more detailed look at the research proposal from HP Labs please refer to the "Further Readings" section at the conclusion of this chapter.

Group Sweeping Scheduling

Group Sweeping Scheduling (GSS) is aimed at reducing the number of disk actuator arm movements thus reducing access time and latency. In this model, requests for services are served in cycles (i.e., a "round-robin- like" manner), with the set of N streams being divided into G groups. These groups are then served in a fixed order.

The individual streams within a group are served according to SCAN, that is, there will not be a fixed time or order by which the individual streams within a group are served. In other words, in one cycle, a specific stream may be the first to be served and then in another cycle it may be the last.

A variable smoothing buffer, sized according to the cycle time and data rate of the stream, is used to assure continuity. If the SCAN scheduling strategy is applied to all streams of a cycle without any grouping, the playout of a stream cannot be started until the end of the cycle of its first retrieval where all requests are served once because the next service may be in the last slot of the following cycle. As the data must be buffered in GSS, the playout can be started at the end of the group in which the first retrieval takes place. As SCAN requires buffers for all streams, in GSS, the buffer can be reused for each group. Further optimizations of this scheme are proposed.

In this method, each stream is served once in each cycle. GSS is a trade-off between the optimization of buffer space and arm movements. To provide the requested guarantees for continuous media data, a "joint deadline" mechanism is introduced whereby each group of streams is assigned one deadline, that is, the joint deadline. This deadline is specified as being the earliest one out of the deadlines of all streams in the respective group. Streams are grouped such that all within the group are comprised of similar deadlines.

Capacity Factors, Transfer Time and Obstacles

Besides the various algorithms and mechanical controls, disk drives are generally specified according to their storage capacity. The factors affecting storage capacity include areal density, track density and recording density. These, along with transfer time impacts and other obstacles impacting hard drive performance are discussed in the next sections.

Areal Density

The volume of data capable of being stored in a given amount of hard disk platter space is called the "areal density" of that specific disk drive. Over the years, areal density has been equated, improperly, to bit density or sometimes just "density." In actuality, areal density is a two-dimensional metric calculated by multiplying two linear measures: recording density (bit density) and track density. The result is measured in bits per square inch (BPSI or bits/in.^{2}).

Track Density

This is the measure of how tightly the concentric tracks on the disk are packed. That is, the number of tracks that can be placed down per inch of radius on the platters. If there is a usable storage space along a radius equal to 1.0 in. of length, and in that amount of space the hard disk has 20,000 tracks, then the track density of that drive would be approximately 20,000 tracks per inch (TPI).

Linear or Recording Density

The linear or recording density is defined as the measure of how tightly the bits are packed per unit length of track. If a 1-in. track can hold 225,000 bits of information, then the linear density for that track is 225 Kbits per inch per track (BPI).

Nonuniformity

The tracks are concentric circles, so every track on the platter's surface will be of different length. Not every track can be written with the same density. So, the numbers are rather nebulous, and you will find that manufacturers usually quote the maximum usable linear record density capacity for each drive.

Densities on modern drives can be in the upwards of billions of bits per square inch. The usual metric is expressed as "gigabits per square inch" (Gbits/in.²). The product of the track density and linear or record density yields the areal density of the drive. You will find that in some cases, the two measures that encompass areal density are specified separately. You will further note that there will be data sheets that do not show the two components individually. Thus, the expression is difficult to evaluate and leads engineers into looking at each of the numbers separately, especially since they are quite different in terms of how they reflect the aspects of disk drive performance.

Transfer Time

Transfer time is another variable that is associated with disk drive specifications. This metric ties together rotational speed, the number of bytes to be transferred, and the seek time.

Transfer time is directly linked to access time. Access time is calculated as a summation of the "command overhead time" (the time from when a command is issued to when the command is fulfilled) plus the "seek time" added to the "settling time" of the head and actuator arm assembly, and then any additional rotational latency or other latencies that are accumulated due to head and platter positioning within the system. Transfer time also includes the number of bytes to be transferred, the number of bytes on a track and the rotation speed of the drive platter assembly.

Obstacles

Areal density is strongly correlated to the transfer rate specifications of the disk drive. In general, the higher the drive's areal density, the higher its transfer rates will be. Most of the improvements in transfer rate are due not to track density but by the ability to increase bit density.

The main obstacle to increasing track density is assuring that the tracks are not so close that erroneous data would be read. This is exacerbated when the reading of one track causes the heads to pick up data from adjacent tracks. To prevent this anomaly, the magnetic fields are made weaker to prevent interference. This has lead engineers to develop much better designs in read–write head technologies, perpendicular recordings, and the use of Partial Response Maximum Likelihood (PRML) methods to improve signal detection and processing.

Balancing performance with the parameters of bit density and transfer rates creates foggy understanding of what these ratios really mean. For example, if drive "0" has an areal density 5% lower than that of drive "1," but its bit density is 10% higher, it will have a higher transfer rate than drive "1." Bit density and track density impact positioning performance. An increase in either one will allow data on the hard disk to be stored physically closer together on the disk. The effect is that it reduces the distance that the read–write heads must seek to find different magnetic segments of data stored on the disk; this slightly improves seek time.

Again, the linear density of a disk is not constant over the drive's entire surface. Also, remember that when reading density specifications, the cut sheets usually list only the maximum density of the disk.

Current high-end hard disks are exceeding 100 Gbits/in.^{2} in areal density, and it has been only a few years since 1 Gbits/in.^{2} was state of the art. For example, in March 2010, Toshiba Corporation announced additions to its 5400 RPM line of 2.5-in. HDDs. One of its features is an areal density of 839.1 Mbits/mm^2 (~542 Gbits/in.^{2}). This is an incredible piece of science, given that as the bit size drops and the bits are packed closer together, the magnetic fields must become weaker. This then requires more sensitive head electronics to properly detect and interpret the data signals. Achieving these increased bit packing densities was possible by developments in head technologies and associated algorithms such as PRML, which are discussed shortly.

Read–Write Heads

Disk drive read–write heads are functionally tiny electromagnets that transform electrical signals to magnetic signals and magnetic signals back into electrical signals. Each bit of data stored on the hard disk is encoded using a special method that translates zeros and ones into patterns of magnetic flux reversals.

Originally, the heads were composed of ferrite, metal-in-gap, and thin-film materials, made to work by the use of two main principles of electromagnetic force. The first (write process) applies an electrical current through a coil, which produces a magnetic field. The direction of the magnetic field produced depends on the direction of the current that is flowing through the magnetic coil. The second (read process) is opposite, whereby applying a magnetic field to a coil causes an electrical current to flow, which is detected by the coil and then records the direction of the magnetically charged particles on the disk.

The direction that the current flows depends on the direction of the magnetic field applied to the coil.

Magnetoresistance (MR)

Newer magnetoresistive (MR) heads use a different principle to read the disk. The complete technical name for the first-generation MR heads is anisotropic magnetoresistive (AMR), yet they have traditionally been called just "magnetoresistive." However, with "giant magnetoresistive" (GMR) heads on the market, there is the possibility for confusion between the terms "magnetoresistive" and "giant magnetoresistive," so some companies have reverted to calling the older MR heads "AMR" heads to distinguish them from GMR.

An MR head uses a conductive material that changes its resistance in the presence of a magnetic field. As the head flies over the surface of the disk, the head significantly changes the resistance as the magnetic fields change in correspondence to the stored patterns on the disk. A sensor in the assembly detects these resistive changes and the bits on the platter are read.

MR heads have allowed significantly higher areal densities to be used on the platters, increasing the storage capacity and, to a lesser extent, the speed of the disk drive. The MR head is several times more sensitive to magnetic flux changes in the media, which allows the use of weaker written signals, and lets the magnetic bits (grains) be closer spaced without causing interference to each other. This higher packing density, that is, the "areal density," has contributed significantly to large improvements in overall storage capacities.

Read Only

MR technology is available only for the read process. For the write process, a separate standard thin-film head is used. By splitting the duties between the two types of heads, additional advantages are gained. The traditional ferrite-based heads that did both reading and writing are an exercise in trade-offs. Efficiencies were hard to come by, and balancing those improvements that would make the head read more efficiently would make it write less efficiently. Furthermore, for the best results, a wider data track was written to ensure the media was properly magnetized, but the heads would prefer to read a narrower track to insure signals from adjacent bits were not accidentally picked up.

These dual head combinations are sometimes referred to as "merged heads."

Giant Magnetoresistance (GMR)

Several years ago (predating its 1997 introduction), IBM introduced the "giant magnetoresistive" (GMR) read head. These heads work on the same fundamental principles as the original anisotropic magnetoresistive (AMR or MR) heads but use a different design that results in better performance.

GMR heads are not named "giant" because of their size; in fact, they are actually smaller than the regular AMR (or MR) heads developed by IBM many years ago. Rather, GMR heads are named after the giant magnetoresistive effect, first discovered in the late 1980s by two European researchers, Peter Gruenberg and Albert Fert, working independently. The researchers found when working with large magnetic fields and thin layers of various magnetic materials, they noticed there were very large resistance changes when these materials were subjected to magnetic fields. Although their experiments used techniques and materials not suitable for manufacturing, the discoveries provided the basis for the GMR technology.

GMR Effect

Engineers and scientists at IBM's Almaden Research Center developed GMR, turning their discovery into a commercial product after experimenting with many different materials. The GMR effect would work when materials were deposited onto multiple layers of materials through sputtering, which is the same technique used in making thin-film media and thin-film read–write heads.

By December 1997, IBM had introduced its first hard disk product using GMR heads, which today are comprised of four layers of thin material sandwiched together into a single structure (as shown in Fig. 4.4).

When the GMR head passes over a magnetic field of one polarity (e.g., "0" on the disk), the free layer has its electrons turn to be aligned with those of the pinned layer. This creates a lower resistance in the entire head structure. When the head passes over a magnetic field of the opposite polarity ("1"), the electrons in the free layer rotate, so they no longer are aligned with those of the pinned layer. This effect increases the resistance of the overall structure, which is caused by changes to the spin characteristics of electrons in the free layer. IBM named these structures "spin valves," like the rotatable shut-off valve found in a plumbing fixture.

Highly Resistive

GMR heads are superior to conventional MR heads because they are more sensitive. The older MR heads would exhibit a resistance change when passing from one magnetic polarity to another of typically about 2%. In GMR heads, this range is increased to between 5% and 8%. This lets the GMR heads detect much smaller, weaker signals. GMR heads are typically fitted with a shroud to protect against stray magnetic fields that are made much smaller and lighter than MR heads. This makes the GMR heads much less subject to interference and noise due to their increased sensitivity.

Figure 4.4 GMR head construction.

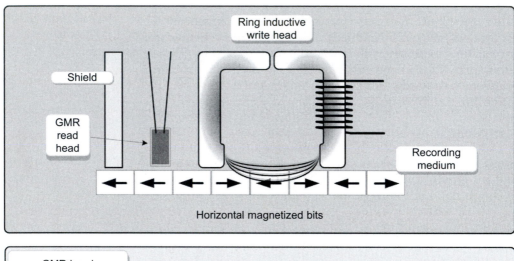

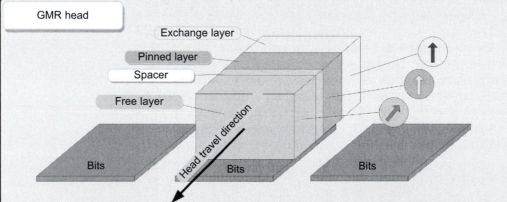

Free layer: A sensing layer, made of a nickel–iron alloy, passes over the surface of the data bits to be read. This layer is free to rotate and so responds to the magnetic patterns on the disk.

Spacer: A nonmagnetic material, typically made of copper, is placed between the free and pinned layers to insulate them magnetically.

Pinned layer: A layer of cobalt material held in a fixed magnetic orientation by virtue of its adjacency to the exchange layer.

Exchange layer: Comprised of an "anti-ferromagnetic" material, typically of iron and manganese, which fixes the pinned layer's magnetic orientation.

Special amplification circuits convert the weak electrical pulses from the head into digital signals representing the data read from the hard disk. Error detection and correction circuitry compensate for the increased likelihood of errors as the signals get weaker on the hard disk.

Partial Response Maximum Likelihood

Coupled with magnetoresistive (MR) head technology is another principle known as Partial Response Maximum Likelihood (PRML). Together with the read channel technologies, these have become two of the most significant solutions in drive head technologies. Alone, each delivers substantial improvements in certain areas over legacy drive technologies with inductive heads and peak detection read channels. MR and PRML reduce the necessity for many of the capacity and performance trade-offs inherent to disk drive design while continuing to decrease the costs per gigabyte of magnetic spinning disk storage.

PRML Read Channels

PRML read channels further provide another means of obtaining areal density improvements while also aiming to improve performance through increased data transfer rates. As bit densities increase, so do the possibilities of intersymbol interference (ISI). ISI results from the overlap of analog signal "peaks" now streaming through the read–write head at higher rates. ISI has traditionally been combated by encoding the data as a stream of "symbols" as it is written, which separates the peaks during read operations. The problem was that the encoding process requires more than one symbol per bit, which produces a negative impact on both performance and disk capacity.

With PRML, read channels separating the peaks during read operations is unnecessary. Instead, advanced digital filtering techniques are used to manage intersymbol interference. The process uses digital signal processing and "maximum likelihood" data detection to determine the sequence of bits that were "most likely" written on the disk.

Drives using PRML read channels can use a far more efficient coding scheme that obtains its value proposition by its ability to now facilitate the accuracy of the data during read back. For example, drives using traditional peak detection typically experience a ratio of user data to stored symbols of 2–3. Third-generation PRML development for drive manufacturers are now using an encoding scheme that increases that ratio to 16–17. This simple relationship "predicts" 40% more capacity on the disk for actual user data and in turn has a positive impact on the internal data transfer rate for the drive system.

Complementary Advantages

Both these technologies (MR and PRML) are capable of delivering substantial advantages over traditional disk drive technologies. As the development of PRML has increased, inductive head (MR) drives were delivering a 20%–30% increase in areal density for a similar price point to the older technologies. When implemented together, MR heads and PRML read channels provide for faster data transfers, fewer soft errors per unit of storage, and the ability to filter the signal from the disk, which in turn provides a cleaner signal recovery during the read process.

These forms of disk drive head implementations and recording processes have increased areal density by record amounts. Since combining them with the application of the GMR technology, collectively, these types of disk heads been leading the race to better drive performance.

No-ID Recording

One further discussion about disk drive performance increase relates to the header that is typically recorded at the start of each sector on a disk. Usually, disks will have a prefix portion, or header, that is used to identify the start of the sector. The header contains the sector number and a suffix portion (a trailer or footer), which contains a checksum that is used to ensure the integrity of the data contents. Newer drives are now omitting this header and use a No-ID recording, a process whereby the start and end points of each sector are located via predetermined clock timing. No-ID recording allows more space for actual data.

Yet that is not the end of the advances in creating higher volume and greater densities in recording, as will be seen in the next section.

Advanced Format Sector Technology

This new technology increases the capacity of the hard drive while still maintaining data integrity. Drive manufacturers as early as 2009 have begun to use this new technology as a means to effectively increase the bits stored on the drives. Advanced Format drives have incorporated several changes that seek to optimize the data structure on the hard drive. Fundamentally, the technology increases the physical sector size from the traditional 512 bytes to a more efficient 4096 (4K) byte sector size.

Because this is transitory technology, an inordinate amount of existing drives would be impacted, so as to ease the transition, the current Advanced Format drives will provide "512-byte emulation" (also written 512e) located at the drive interface. The intent of 512e is to maintain backward compatibility with legacy applications.

Impacts to Operating Systems

Most modern operating systems have been designed to work efficiently with Advanced Format (AF) drives. For optimum performance, it is important to ensure that the drive is partitioned correctly and that data is written in 4K blocks by both the operating system and the application. Recent operating systems handle this automatically, and legacy systems would need to be looked at on a case-by-case basis.

Legacy Limitation

Hard drive technology from 30 or more years ago set the basis for most of the "storage constraints" by limiting the amount of user data that could be stored in the traditional 512-byte sectors. The storage industry has sought to improve this stale architecture by changing the size of the sectors on the media so that they can store 4096 bytes (4Kbytes) of data per sector as opposed to legacy devices with their 512-byte limit.

Advanced Format drives use larger sectors, now 4K bytes, which is the equivalent of putting the eight legacy (512-byte) sectors into one new single 4K sector. The Advanced Format approach yields two benefits (see Fig. 4.5). First, by eliminating the repetitive portions that would be found if using the legacy 512-byte methodology, the amount of space available for actual data increases in proportion to the removal of the seven extra sets of fields in the logical block. Notice that each legacy 512-byte sector had to include a Sync Field/DAM section and an ECC section, plus a gap. The Advanced Format technology reduces this to just one set for each larger 4K sector.

By optimizing the eight sets of overhead associated with each smaller sector, the drive overall will use less space to store the same amount of information resulting in a format efficiency improvement almost equivalent to one block for every eight.

The second benefit is that the AF uses a larger and more powerful error correction code (ECC), which provides for better integrity of user data. These benefits improve overall system performance by adding capacity and reducing overhead.

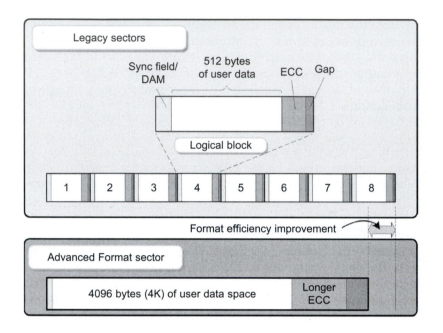

Figure 4.5 Comparison of legacy and Advanced Format sectors.

Reducing Overhead

In the legacy format, each sector of the track contained a gap, a Sync/DAM (lead-in), and error correction information. The current (legacy) architecture is quite inefficient for Error Correction Code (ECC), so there is a significant overhead component required to support multiple blocks of ECC.

Eliminating the extra Sync/DAM blocks, intersector gaps, and the eight individual blocks of ECC improves error rates within the same capacity of storage. It increases data integrity through a more robust error correction scheme that uses a longer set of ECC code words. A 50% increase in burst error correction is obtained when using AF, again through the use of the larger ECC code word.

Compatibility

Increased sector sizes are already employed by many disk drive interface technologies; however, many systems including PCs, digital video recorders, mobile devices, and servers are inflexible and will only work with 512-byte sectors. To retain compatibility with existing devices, Advanced Format media includes an emulation mode, whereby the 512-byte sector device is modeled at the drive interface (see Fig. 4.6).

By mapping logic sectors to physical sectors, compatibility at the interface is maintained.

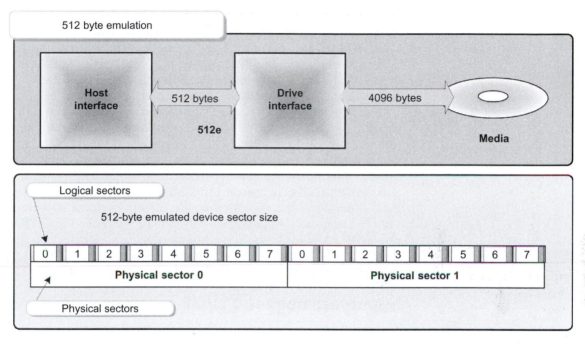

Figure 4.6 Emulation mode for 512-byte hosts uses "512e" to interface Advanced Format media with legacy systems.

Advanced Format Standards

Provisions for the Advanced Format technology are included in the efforts of the American National Standard of Accredited Standards Committee INCITS working group, which drafted the "AT Attachment 8-ATA/ATAPI Command Set (ATA8-ACS)" document in 2007, and in the "SCSI Block Commands (SBC-3)" standards, which allow for a disk drive to report Advanced Format sector sizes and other performance optimization information. These standards are used for SATA, SAS, USB, and IEEE 1394 interface technologies.

The Advanced Format technology is designed to work on most of the current operating systems including Windows Vista, Windows 7, and Mac OS X. It is not optimized for legacy OSs such as Windows XP, but utilities are available that allow Advanced Format drives to run at full performance on Windows XP.

Next-Generation Applications

Next-generation notebooks have more storage than ever before. Cellular phones and mobility devices, such as iPads, are using solid state storage, but the hard drive technologies continue to push the limits of drive heads, storage, and areal density and the physics of keeping the devices cool and stable. Manufacturers continue to push the areal density and capacity envelopes of 2.5-in. SATA drives. For example, in 2010, Toshiba debuted a 750-Gbyte, two platter design, and a 1-Tbyte three-platter design, running at 5400 RPM, with a six-head version seek time of around 12 ms. The transfer rate of this drive is 3 Gbits/second to the host, and it features a 5.55 ms average latency.

The new drive uses 4K sectoring with Advanced Format technology, and along with this improved error-correcting code functionality and enhanced data integrity, this seems to be the next benchmark in modern, small form factor drives. However, at what point will the limits be reached? Some believe we are already there. Like the current multicore CPU technologies, it is indeed possible that the brick wall is being approached where today's magnetic technologies will not be improved on. That potential problem is being addressed in laboratories as the "superparamagnetic limit" keeps getting closer.

Superparamagnetic Limit

The predicted rate of increase for hard drive areal density has reached just about 40% per year based on the advances in capacities witnessed over the course of the previous two decades. However, the growth in how data is stored and then read back from spinning magnetic platters is its own Achilles heel. Some believe that areal density has its own limit factor on just how much manufactures can shrink the recording process to stuff more data on the drive. One of those factors that points to this limit is called the superparamagnetic limitation in magnetic recording.

This effect is believed to be the point beyond which data could not be written reliably due to the phenomena referred to as "bit flipping," a problem where the magnetic polarity of the bit on the disk platter changes, turning the data into meaningless noise. The amount of space on a hard drive platter is typically measured in gigabytes per square inch (ca. 2009). To obtain the full capacity of a drive, one multiplies this number times the number of platters contained within a drive, which is also a high-level way to assess the drive's likely performance.

Over time, however, this limit has been pushed out to beyond 400–500 Gbits/in.^{2} as evidenced by some of the highest areal densities ever created in recent times.

TAR and BPR

Modern methods used for recording data to hard disk drive platters use two conventional methods: thermally assisted recording

(TAR) and bit-patterned recording (BPR). Both methods allow conventional hard drives to hit areal densities in the hundreds of gigabytes-per-square-inch range, but each method suffers from its own drawbacks.

BPR relies on segregating the disk sectors with lithographed "islands," while TAR relies on heating and cooling techniques that preserve the data in nearby sectors. The underlying issue is the process behind magnetizing the grains on a platter, which changes their magnetic polarization to indicate a binary 1 or 0 state. When this is uncontrolled, the effects of bit flipping become evident.

As these bits get closer together, the areal density increases, which subjects the surface of neighboring clusters of bits to interference during the magnetization process. If a cluster of bits gets flipped due to the interference issue, data accuracy vanishes.

TAR attempts to push beyond this issue by briefly heating and cooling bits during the recording process, which allows a manufacturer to use small-sized bits that are more resistant to the magnetization of neighboring bits.

On the flip side, bit-patterned recording (BPR) isolates grains into varying islands on the drive platter, which are demarcated by molecular patterns on the platter itself. The BPR process could, in theory, shrink down to one bit per isolated grain; yet in order to work, the actual write head on the drive itself would need to match the size of these clusters of grains.

When combining the features of BPR and TAR, each solves the other's problem. With BPR's magnetic islands, small-grain media is no longer needed; and with TAR, it ensures that only the bit that is heated is written, eliminating the need for a specific size of write head. Collectively, they form a writing system that can limit bits to microareas on inexpensive surfaces, without the impacts on surrounding data bits.

Heat-Assisted Magnetic Recording

Around 2002, development turned toward a new process called heat-assisted magnetic recording (HAMR). At the time, it was believed the technology would require another 5–6 years before being brought to market. The process is based on the principle of optically assisted or "near-field recording," a technology that uses lasers to heat the recording medium. HMAR was pioneered by the now-defunct TeraStor Corporation and Quinta, which was later acquired by Seagate.

By using light to assist in the recording process, hard disk drive capacity could potentially be increased by two orders of magnitude. The concept heats the magnetic medium locally, which in turn temporarily lowers its resistance to magnetic polarization. The research suggests that the process might allow us to reach the era of terabytes-per-square-inch areal densities, opening up capacities beyond the current limit of 2-Tbyte products.

HAMR is a technology that magnetically records data onto a highly stable media by first heating the material through the use of laser thermal assistance. These high-stability magnetic compounds, such as iron platinum alloy, can store single bits on to a much smaller area without the superparamagnetic constraints that have limited current hard disk drive storage technology. HAMR was further developed by Fujitsu in 2006 so that it could achieve 1-Tbit/in.^{2} densities, and Seagate has stated that as much as a 37.5-Tbyte drive could be produced using HAMR.

Of course, the drawback to using HAMR is that the materials must be heated to apply the changes in magnetic orientation; and laser-powered disk drives are only one side of the coin. To achieve this gargantuan scale of storage capacity, it will also take so-called bit-pattern media to make the ends meet.

Together, HAMR helps with the writing process and bit patterning allows for the creation of the media. In current magnetics technologies for disk drives, each bit is represented by an island of about 50 magnetic grains. These patches are irregularly shaped, similar to felt pen dots on paper or the half-tone ink printing found on newsprint. In printing, each dot needs to cover only a certain area if it is to remain distinct and legible. In magnetics, this is the same. Through a chemical encoding process, an organized molecular pattern can be put onto the platter's substrate at the moment of creation. Through this, HAMR can then put a single bit on every grain.

If this technology is successful and it can be mass produced, today's disk sectors could become a distant dust cloud, to be replaced by magnetic arrays that are self-organizing, produced as lithographic patterns along a platter's circumferential tracks. The future of storage technologies, at the mechanical or magnetic level, hinges on developmental research like that being done by Seagate, Fujtisu, and others. HAMR and bit patterning are just two of the technologies still under development.

Further Reading

"Real-time disk scheduling algorithm allowing concurrent I/O requests." Carl Staelin, Gidi Amir, David Ben-Ovadia, Ram Dagan, Michael Melamed, Dave Staas. HP Laboratories, 2009. File name: HPL-2009-344.pdf

5

BUSES, PORTS, AND INTERFACES

Storage and memory, when referring to computer data storage, are those components, devices, and the recording media that perform storage and memory functions and allow for the retention of digital data for a period or duration. Storage of the data, as one of the core functions of the modern computing system, may be thought of as "information retention."

Memory is often referred to as a form of semiconductor-based storage. Semiconductor memory is usually fast, but may often only be utilized as temporary storage. This form of memory is known principally as random-access memory (RAM).

Mass storage is the nomenclature generally associated to more permanent forms of memory, such as optical discs, forms of magnetic storage like hard disk drives, and other types, which would be slower than RAM or flash memory. Mass storage also refers to huge amounts of data often stored in centralized libraries that are accessible by the masses.

History will reveal that memory and storage were originally defined by the terms "main memory" and "secondary storage," respectively. Further discussion will find that those terms also make reference to "internal memory" and "external memory," which in turn led to the evolution of network-based storage, that is, NAS and SANs. As comparatively large amounts of RAM are now found even in the simplest of netbooks, personal computers and workstations continue to grow; the lines dividing one form of storage from another have been blurred due in part to the advances and requirements for memory in all forms.

KEY CHAPTER POINTS

- Parallel and serial buses used for the functioning of storage and peripheral devices
- An exploration of the internal computer buses, such as PCI, EISA, and PCI-X

- Ports and storage bus standards comprising of SMD, ESDI, SSA, HIPPI, ATA and PATA, IDE, IPI, and SASI
- SCSI basics including command sets, identification schemes, arbitration, and bus bandwidth
- SCSI implementation generations from SCSI-1 to Ultra-640

Carrying and Transferring Data

In computer architectures, the subsystem that is the carrier or transfer medium between those components inside a computer or between computer subsystems is called a bus. The bus should not be confused with a network, especially when describing the transfer of data or information between computers per se.

The name came from electrical systems that called these buses (or busbars) after those physical highways that carried services such as power supply voltages, signaling services, and eventually instructional controls for external systems. Early computer systems utilized physical wiring bundles often arranged as parallel sets of insulated strands called ribbon cables (see Fig. 5.1), which interconnected memory components and peripherals together.

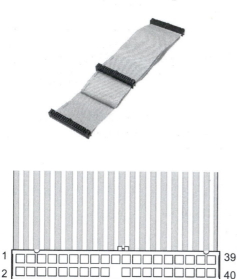

Figure 5.1 Layout of a 40-pin parallel ATA (PATA) ribbon cable that interconnects various parallel bus components, such as disk drives, inside the computer or server chassis.

Bus Types

In its most generic distinction, buses will generally carry data either in a parallel (bit per wire) mode or in a serial mode (single string on a differential or single-ended wire). In the early days of computer implementation, parallel interfaces were common at both the chip and peripheral connectivity levels. Over a period of time, as high speed requirements increased in frequency, interfaces migrated to serial architectures that are most prevalent today on devices such as USB, FireWire (IEEE 1394), the Serial Advanced Technology Attachment (SATA) interface, and other network-like interfaces.

Parallel Buses

Buses that carry data words in parallel, on multiple wires, are called parallel buses. Early disk drive interfaces were always parallel because serial technology had not been sufficiently developed, and a parallel bus could be easily implemented with the technologies, receivers, and transmitters of the early pre-1980s era.

Parallel SCSI, formally called the SCSI Parallel Interface (SPI), is an example for implementation of both the SCSI family and parallel interfaces or connections. The cable utilized to connect these devices was known as the Centronics 50-pin SCSI (see Fig. 5.2).

Serial Buses

When the data is carried sequentially on a single wire, with a data rate that is much higher than a parallel bus, the signals are carried on a serial bus. A serial bus will inherently mitigate skew errors (i.e., the difference between signal timing) or cross talk (i.e., when signals appear in the adjacent wires of a parallel path).

Peripheral or Storage Buses

Distinctions between buses continue to evolve as storage, memory, and interface technologies advance. Storage buses have generally been segmented from other buses and are intended to address the connectivity protocols and formats for carrying information between host computer and storage-based systems. Storage buses originally came to fruition because the storage devices in the early days of mainframes and minicomputers were physically isolated due in part to their size. As data transfer demands increased, higher speed parallel buses improved and eventually migrated to serial formats.

As storage became more "detached" from the inner workings of the small frame workstation or PC, the portability of storage (and other related) devices for a computer evolved. The peripheral interface bus emerged with implementations such as Universal Serial Bus (USB), IEEE 1391 (as Apple's FireWire or Sony's i.LINK), Camera Link, EIA/RS422 and RS485, Apple Desktop Bus, MIDI, and even Fibre Channel.

Internal Computer Slot Interfaces

In addition to peripheral and storage buses, internal computer buses are used to carry data internally between slot-type cards and the central processing unit (CPU). Created in 1981 by IBM, the 8-bit Industry Standard Architecture (ISA) was the first motherboard slot type used on PCs. The ISA bus was updated to 16 bits

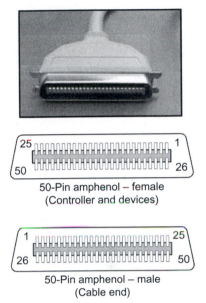

50-Pin amphenol – female
(Controller and devices)

50-Pin amphenol – male
(Cable end)

Figure 5.2 Centronics 50-pin SCSI connector.

in 1984 at the time when the PC AT was released. The 16-bit version operated at 8 MHz, with a maximum theoretical transfer rate of 8 Mbytes/second. This data transfer rate would be unacceptable for performance-demanding applications such as video and networking. This level of application required a migration to faster slot types, all with a target goal of increasing the performance of peripheral devices.

Selected examples of interconnect and computer buses include the following:

- Peripheral Component Interconnect (PCI) from Intel
- Peripheral Component Interconnect Extended (PCI-X), a high-performance motherboard slot type created by HP, IBM, and Compaq for use on servers, available in two speeds in PCI-X 1.0 and four speeds in PCI-X 2.0
- Extended Industry Standard Architecture (EISA) created by Compaq (now HP)

Storage Bus Standards

To better understand how storage technologies for moving media applications have evolved, the following sections will discuss some of the storage bus standards and their implementations. Not all these buses can be addressed in great detail; however, one can see that by virtue of the increased speeds and performance requirements in computer and media systems, the consistent evolution of storage buses marched forward while disk drive capacities and CPU speeds increased in lock step with Moore's Law.

Moore's Law

Intel cofounder, retired chairman, and CEO Gordon Moore predicted, in 1965, that the number of components the industry would be able to place on a computer chip would double every year. Moore updated his prediction in 1975 to once every two years. Nonetheless, what has become known as Moore's Law remains a guiding principle for the semiconductor industry to deliver ever more powerful chips while further decreasing the cost of electronics.

Storage Module Device

The family of hard disk drive storage devices first shipped by Control Data Corporation (CDC) in December 1973 as the model CDC 9760 offered an unformatted 40-Mbytes capacity as a "storage module device" (SMD) disk drive. Future variants of the CDC product line were announced in June 1974 through 1975 and included an 80-MB, a 150-MB, and a 300-MB version.

By definition, the SMD interface required two flat interface cables: an "A-cable" for carrying control commands and information, and a "B-cable" for carrying data. Each cable had to run from the physical disk drive to a controller and then to a host device (e.g., a computer). The interface's transfer bandwidth was limited at 9.6 Mbits/second.

The SMD interface was supported mostly by 8-in. and 14-in. removable and nonremovable disk drives. SMD was mainly implemented on disk drives utilized in mainframes and minicomputers.

Future developments in the SCSI interface eventually replaced SMD around the mid-1980s.

The First 5.25-in. Hard Disk Drive

Called the ST-506, this 5.25-in. hard disk drive was introduced in 1980 by Seagate Technology (then called Shugart Technology). The ST-506 stored up to 5 Mbytes of formatted data. It was the drive used by IBM in its first generation PC/XT products. The drive was connected to a controller with three cables: a 34-pin common control cable, a 20-pin data channel cable, and a third that provided power for each device. A disk controller would be the interface between the drive and the computer.

A second generation drive, the ST-412, added a buffered seek capability and an onboard microcontroller that would move the head arm to the desired location without waiting for the mechanics to settle. The ST-506 had an average seek time of 170 ms with the ST-412 improving that by 50% to 85 ms. Seek times for the ST-412 would eventually get down to 15–30 ms by the late 1980s.

Enhanced Small Disk Interface

As a follow on to the first 5.25-in. hard drive (Shugart's model ST-506), Maxtor Corporation developed an Enhanced Small Disk Interface (ESDI) in the early 1980s. ESDI improved on the ST-506 by moving certain parts that were traditionally kept on the controller (such as the data separator) into the drives themselves. The control bus was more generalized such that other devices, such as removable disks and tape drives, could also be connected. ESDI would use the same cabling as the ST-506.

ESDI could handle data rates of 10, 15, or 20 Mbits/second, whereas the top speed for the ST-506 was only around 7.5

Mbits/second. ESDI would remain popular through the mid-to-late 1980s, with many high-end SCSI drives (of that era) that were actually high-end ESDI drives with SCSI bridges integrated on the drive.

By 1990, SCSI had matured enough to handle high data rates and multiple types of drives. ATA was quickly overtaking ST-506 in the desktop market. These events made ESDI less and less important over time, and by the mid-1990s, ESDI was no longer in common use.

Serial Storage Architecture

Designed as a peripheral interconnect interface (ca. early-1990s) for all forms of storage or computer-related devices (e.g., CD-ROMs, tape drives, printers, workstations, servers, and storage subsystems), the Serial Storage Architecture (SSA) was pioneered by IBM's storage subsystem development group along with other vendors/partners. When SSA development began, the stated goal was: "…to achieve high performance for a majority of applications and to provide a road map to growth in device data rates".

SSA claimed high reliability with comprehensive error detection and recovery. It was implemented in low-cost CMOS requiring relatively little power. SSA did not require expensive and fragile cabling like SCSI interfaces.

SSA opened the door to a new storage interface standard (through the ANSI standard group X3T10.1). Intended as a replacement for parallel SCSI, one of the features of SSA was its ability to independently address different devices without being affected by other devices on the network link. To accomplish this, each SSA fundamental building block would be made up of a single port with a capacity to carry two 20 Mbytes/second conversations simultaneously (see Fig. 5.3).

By design, data protection for critical applications was guaranteed because a single cable failure would not prevent access to data. All the components in a typical SSA subsystem were connected via bidirectional cabling. Ring-based link architectures in the SSA network also had a built-in feature called "spatial reuse," which permitted each link to operate independently.

As many as 192 hot-swappable disk drives could be supported per system with up to 32 separate RAID arrays supported per adapter. When SSA was deployed in a server/RAID environment, it was capable of providing up to 80 Mbytes/second of

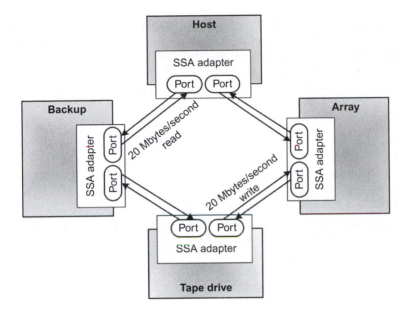

Figure 5.3 Serial Storage Architecture (SSA) connectivity with nodes and ports.

data throughput; with sustained data rates as high as 60 Mbytes/ second in non-RAID mode and 35 Mbytes/second in RAID mode.

High-Performance Parallel Interface

HIPPI, a standardized point-to-point protocol popular in the late 1980s through the mid-to-late 1990s, is used in the attachment of high-speed/high-performance storage devices to supercomputers.

Initially (ca. 1987) the HIPPI implementation was defined for a 50-wire twisted pair cable, running at 800 Mbits/second (100 Mbytes/second) on a 32-bit data bus. HIPPI was later upgraded to a 1600 Mbits/second (200 Mbytes/second) with a 64-bit data bus running on optical fiber cable. In an effort to further improve the speed, the HIPPI-6400 standard, which was later renamed the Gigabyte System Network (GSN), offered a full-duplex bandwidth of 6400 Mbits/second (800 Mbytes/second) in each direction.

In November 1991, three years after the initial draft was delivered to ANSI, HIPPI became the first national standard for Gbits/ second data transmission.

HIPPI is no longer used considering that the widely available Ultra3 SCSI provided transfer rates of 160 Mbytes/second, and Fibre Channel continued its development offering a simpler interconnect for both HIPPI and SCSI with speeds of up to

400 Mbytes/second on optical fiber and 100 Mbytes/second on a single pair of twisted copper wires.

Many of the concepts and features developed for HIPPI are integrated into technologies such as InfiniBand.

IDE

The Integrated Drive Electronics (IDE) port is probably the most common and popular interface used by middle era (ca. 1990–2000) hard disk drives. During that period, IDE and ATA were the competitive lower cost alternative to SCSI drives (SCSI is discussed later in this chapter). Although the Advanced Technology Attachment (ATA) name is associated as a general purpose disk drive interface, the correct representation of IDE is actually ATA, which was reflected from the first IBM PC to use the original 16-bit Industry Standard Architecture (ISA) bus.

The IDE (or ATA) port is responsible for connecting IDE devices to the host computer. This port does not control the hard disk; therefore, it should not be represented as a controller.

The port/interface was popularized through the integration of the logic controller placed directly onto the hard disk drive chassis. With control of the IDE drivers resident to the disk drive itself, this implementation corrected many physically generated anomalies such as complexity, independence of the controller, and poor signal integrity.

Parallel ATA

Developed as an interface standard for the connection of storage devices (e.g., hard disks, solid state drives, floppy drives, and CD-ROM drives) in computers, this standard is maintained by the X3/INCITS committee. PATA uses the underlying AT Attachment (ATA) and AT Attachment Packet Interface (ATAPI) standards.

Following the market introduction of Serial ATA (2003), the original ATA was retroactively renamed Parallel ATA (PATA). Parallel ATA is restricted to cable lengths of up to 18 in. (0.457 m), limiting the technology as an internal computer storage interface. By the beginning of 2007, PATA had largely been replaced by Serial ATA (SATA) in new computer systems.

The ATA and subsequent PATA standards evolved to include several transfer rates (see Table 5.1). Achieving these transfer rates requires special cables and that the port must support the transfer rate, the hard disk drive must support the respective

Table 5.1 Advanced Technology Attachment (ATA) Standards

Standard	Mode	Maximum Theoretical Transfer Rate (Mbytes/second)
ATA	Mode 0, single word	2.1
ATA	Mode 0, multiword	4.2
ATA	Mode 1, single word	4.2
ATA	Mode 2, single word	8.3
ATA-2	Mode 1, multiword	13.3
ATA-3	Mode 2, multiword	16.6
ATA-4	UMDA Mode 1	25
ATA-4 [ATA/33]	UMDA Mode 2/Mode 3	33.3
ATA-5	UMDA Mode 3	44.4
ATA-5 [ATA/66]	UMDA Mode 4	66.6
ATA-6 [ATA/100]	UMDA Mode 5	100
ATA-7 [ATA/133]	UMDA Mode 6	133

transfer rate, and the operating system (OS) must be properly configured (e.g., bus mastering drivers and direct memory access [DMA] mode enabled).

SCSI

SCSI (pronounced "scuzzy"), more properly called the Small Computer Systems Interface, is the computer systems interface that is one of the most widely adopted and utilized storage buses in modern history. SCSI improved upon the IDE/ATA interfaces and has its root beginnings between 1979 and 1981 when Shugart, working with NCR, developed the Shugart Associates Systems Interface (SASI) as a scheme that would address devices logically rather than physically. The SCSI addressing scheme would be parallel in structure and byte-based.

IPI over SASI

To place disk drive development in perspective, recall that in 1975 the personal computer was only a hobbyist's dream. Any incorporation of a floppy disk or a hard disk drive into the yet to be invented IBM PC was still several years away. By 1980, the IBM PC was still only a white board concept. The American

National Standards Institute (ANSI), in 1980, had rejected standardization of the proposed Shugart Associates SASI standard and preferred Intelligent Peripheral Interface (IPI), a server-centric storage interface used in the 1980s and early 1990s (standardized as ISO-9318), which ANSI thought would be more sophisticated than SASI.

Arguments among developers included controversial topics such as using a differential versus a single-ended interface, a 10-byte versus 6-byte commands, and a serial versus parallel argument, which was technologically too far advanced for productive implementation.

As is typical in the realm of advancing technologies, product development continued whereas the standardization process stalled. By 1982, ANSI committee X3T9.2 was formed, and the basis of SCSI, as it would eventually be known, was developed. In 1984, the draft proposal was completed and submitted to ANSI for approval. Subsequently, by this time, device controllers and host adapters were already in the market. Apple Computer had introduced the Macintosh, which used the yet to be standardized SCSI principles for its storage and peripheral interconnects.

Common Command Sets

ANSI X3.131-1986 was finally published in its approved form as SCSI-1, but not without a rash of headaches that had surfaced as a result of nonstandard products already in service throughout the marketplace. Between 1984 and 1986, as more SCSI drives came in the market, it was discovered that a separate driver had to be written for nearly each type of drive. Finally, as a means to clarify and quantify the many variations that were being identified, the evolutionary development of a Common Command Set (CCS) for hard disk drives was begun.

The CCS was essentially a means within a protocol that described how host devices would access and communicate with other devices (e.g., drives, scanners, printers, etc.) The early CCS proposals were not mandatory, and each manufacturer figured they could interpret them as they needed.

SCSI Evolution

As with any emerging technology, SCSI developed from an 8-bit parallel architecture with 6 m cables through its UltraSCSI forms, and eventually moved from a parallel to a serial implementation. With these changes came not only increases in bandwidth but also changes in the physical and logical interfaces.

The remainder of this chapter will deal with the parallel implementations, and the following chapter will discuss the serial versions, including SATA, eSATA, and iSCSI.

SCSI-1

SCSI-1 employed an 8-bit parallel bus and utilized a parity scheme. SCSI-1 ran either asynchronously at 3.5 Mbytes/second or synchronously at 5 Mbytes/second. The maximum permitted bus cable length was 6 m, which was better than the 18-in. (0.45 m) limit of the ATA interface. The electrical interface used was low voltage; however, there were implementations that included a high-voltage differential (HVD) version with a maximum cable length of 25 m.

SCSI-2

Introduced in 1994, this standard provided the roadmap to what would become Fast SCSI and Wide SCSI.

Fast and Wide SCSI Variants

Fast SCSI doubled the maximum transfer rate to 10 Mbytes/second, and Wide SCSI doubled the bus width to 16 bits. These increases allowed Wide SCSI to reach a maximum transfer rate of 20 Mbytes/second. These improvements suffered the penalty of reducing the maximum cable length to 3 m, so utilization was limited to very short connections between host computers and external disks.

SCSI-2 further specified a 32-bit version of Wide SCSI, employing two 16-bit cables per bus. This implementation was not widely accepted by SCSI device vendors due to its cost and the close-on-the-heels development of SCSI-3.

SCSI-3

The first parallel SCSI devices that exceeded the SCSI-2 Fast and Wide capabilities were simply designated SCSI-3. SCSI-3 was called the third generation of the SCSI parallel interface and was also known as SPI-3 for SCSI parallel interface number three.

Ultra and Fast-20 SCSI

Introduced in 1996, these variants doubled the bus speed to 20 Mbytes/second for the 8-bit (narrow) systems and 40 Mbytes/second for 16-bit (wide) systems. Although the 3 m maximum cable length remained, the single-ended Ultra SCSI development suffered from an undeserved reputation of unstable or extreme sensitivity to cable length and other fault conditions. The cheap manufacturing of the connectors and terminators triggered the blame for the failure, and ultimately the demise of this era of Ultra and Fast-20 SCSI development.

Ultra-2

Sometimes referred to as LVD SCSI, Ultra-2 SCSI was introduced around 1997, and its implementation featured a low-voltage differential (LVD) bus. LVD provided a much greater resistance to noise, which in turn allowed for a maximum bus cable length of 12 m.

Despite the data transfer rates, which increased to 80 Mbytes/ second, technology was now advancing much faster than wide-spread implementation, and the Ultra-2 SCSI lifespan was relatively short. It was not long before Ultra-2 SCSI was superseded by Ultra-3 (also known as Ultra-160) SCSI.

Ultra-3

Known also as Ultra-160 SCSI, this version was introduced around the end of 1999. Ultra-3 was a basic overall improvement on the Ultra-2 SCSI standard, whereby the transfer rate was again doubled to 160 Mbytes/second through the deployment of double transition clocking.

Ultra-160 SCSI further offered other new data related features including an error correction process called cyclic redundancy check (CRC) and domain validation (and negotiation), a feature that improves the robustness of the process by which different SCSI devices determine an optimal data transfer rate.

Ultra-320

Another working draft (Revision 10) came forth on May 6, 2002, doubling the transfer rate of Ultra-160 (to 320 Mbytes/second). By the end of 2003, nearly all SCSI hard drives being manufactured were of the Ultra-320 family.

Ultra-640

Known also as Fast-320, Ultra-640 was promulgated by INCITS as a standard (367-2003 or SPI-5) in early 2003. Doubling the interface speed from Ultra-320, to 640 Mbytes/second, the Ultra-640 standard pushed the limits of LVD signaling and further deteriorated the cable lengths making it nearly infeasible to chain more than one or two devices on the bus. By this time, most manufacturers left the parallel-SCSI architecture and looked forward to the development of Serial Attached SCSI (SAS) for their future.

Table 5.2 Disk Drive Storage Bandwidth

Storage Device (Abbreviation)	Additional Description	Rate (Mbits/ second)	Rate (Mbytes/ second)
PC floppy disk dontroller (1.2 Mbytes/ 1.44 Mbytes capacity)		0.5	0.062
CD Controller	1x speed	1.17188	0.1465
Modified Frequency Modification (MFM)	Early 5.25-in. HDD	5	0.625
Run Length Limited (RLR)		7.5	0.9375
DVD controller	1x speed	11.1	1.32
Enhanced Small Disk Interface (ESDI)		24	3
ATA programmed input/output	Mode 0	26.4	3.3
HD DVD controller	1x speed	36	4.5
SCSI	Narrow 5 MHz	40	5
ATA programmed input/output	Mode 1	41.6	5.2
ATA programmed input/output	Mode 2	66.4	8.3
Fast SCSI	8 bits/10 MHz	80	10
ATA programmed input/output	Mode 3	89.8	11.1
ATA over Ethernet (AoE)—Fast	per path	100	12.5
SCSI over fast Ethernet		100	12.5
ATA programmed input/output	Mode 4	133.3	16.7
Fast, wide SCSI	16 bits/10 MHz	160	20
Ultra SCSI (Fast-20 SCSI)	8 bits/20 MHz	160	20
Ultra Direct Memory Address (DMA) ATA 33		264	33
Ultra wide SCSI	16 bits/20 MHz	320	40
Ultra-2 SCSI (Fast-40 SCSI)	8 bits/40 MHz	320	40
Ultra Direct Memory Address (DMA) ATA 65		528	66
Ultra-2 Wide SCSI	16 bits/40 MHz	640	80
Serial Storage Architecture (SSA)		640	80
Ultra Direct Memory Address (DMA) ATA 100		800	100
Fibre Channel 1GFC	1.0625 GHz	850	106.25
AoE over Gigabit Ethernet	per path	1000	125
SCSI over Gigabit Ethernet		1000	125
Ultra Direct Memory Address (DMA) ATA 133		1064	133
Ultra-3 SCSI (Ultra 160 SCSI, Fast-80 Wide SCSI)	16 bits/40 MHz DDR	1200	160
Serial ATA (SATA-150)		1200	150
Fibre Channel 2GFC	2.125 GHz	1700	212.5
Serial ATA 2 (SATA-300)		2400	300
Serial Attached SCSI (SAS)		2400	300

Continued

Table 5.2 Disk Drive Storage Bandwidth *(Continued)*

Storage Device (Abbreviation)	Additional Description	Rate (Mbits/ second)	Rate (Mbytes/ second)
Ultra-320 SCSI (Ultra4 SCSI)	16 bits/80 MHz DDR	2560	320
Fibre Channel 4GFC	4.25 GHz	3400	425
Serial ATA 3 (SATA-600)		4000	600
Serial Attached SCSI (SAS) 2		4000	600
Ultra-640 SCSI	16 bits/160 MHz DDR	5120	640
Fibre Channel 8GFC	8.5 GHz	6800	850
AoE over 10 Gbit Ethernet (10 GbitE)	per path	10,000	1250
SCSI over 10 Gbit Ethernet (10 GbitE)		10,000	1250
Fibre Channel over 10 Gbit Ethernet (FCoE 10 GbitE)		10,000	1250
SCSI over InfiniBand 4x		40,000	5000
SCSI over 100G Ethernet (theoretical)		100,000	12,500

SCSI Command Sets

The organization of data on the drive or associated peripherals is of little concern to the host computer as the interface presents the data to and from the host in a uniform or standardized method. Peripherals can manage their own housekeeping without bothering the computer host itself. Housekeeping functions such as control of media flaws, file allocation table structures, spindle and head/arm control, and others are performed as device-specific background tasks.

SCSI Identification Number

SCSI devices identify themselves using what is called a SCSI ID, a unique number that addresses each unique device on the bus. The SCSI bus can address up to eight logical units (LUNs). Typically, the numerical ordering for the LUNs is from 0 to 7, and each LUN can play the role of either a target or an initiator.

Initiator or Target

The device that originates the signal, pole, or inquiry is referred to as the initiator. The SCSI ID of the initiator is generally set to the highest priority value (e.g., "7" in an eight device implementation). Should there be two initiators, their SCSI IDs are usually set to 7 and 6. The remaining SCSI IDs would be used for disk drives or other target devices.

The target will be the device that the initiator intends to reach. This concept is extended throughout data peripheral interfacing technologies.

The "initiator" will generally issue a command or request, and the "target" will execute that request. SCSI, by design, must consist of at least one initiator and one target device. Some SCSI devices can act as both initiator and target.

The initiator is considered by most to be the host adapter and is generally awarded the highest number, 7, as its SCSI ID. The first device, usually the system drive, is then given 0, and for the most part, these are the only two IDs that need to be in the system.

Generally, SCSI ID 0 has the lowest priority, and 7 has the highest priority. Devices with SCSI ID 1 through 6 are typically ordered such that the next number, 1, is the second hard disk drive, followed by any removable media, scanners, printers, etc.

The computer may have more than one SCSI bus, usually referred to by letters (i.e., bus A or bus B). In this case, the buses must be "balanced," that is each side must contain the same amount of SCSI devices on each bus. SCSI buses can effectively increase the number of devices on the bus. When 32-bit SCSI-3 was implemented, up to 32 devices would be supported.

A single SCSI ID can apply to an entire set of drives, such as in a single RAID array. By definition, the RAID array appears as a single drive, although it may consist of dozens of drives in a single enclosure or group of enclosures.

Arbitration

SCSI is both a logical and a physical scheme. At the high level, it contains a logical protocol used to communicate between computers and peripherals. At the low level, it defines the wiring scheme to connect a variety of physical peripherals.

All SCSI commands start with a process called "arbitration," which is initiated because when one or more devices attempt to access the bus, something must decide (i.e., arbitrate) which signal gets which level of attention. During this arbitration phase, 8- or 16-bit data bus signals will be used to identify which device(s) is requesting access. To ensure proper arbitration, all SCSI devices on the bus must implement the same arbitration algorithm so that the resultant pole result is always unanimous.

Priorities

The priority sequence for an 8-bit-wide parallel SCSI bus is relatively simple; yet the priority sequence for a 16-bit-wide parallel SCSI bus must meet legacy requirements, which complicates the arbitration phase.

Bus Bandwidth Limitations

The arbitration process induces a considerable degree of overhead. During the time when arbitration occurs, no data is transferred on the bus, which can use up a lot of bus bandwidth. To this end, the SCSI-3 Parallel Interface (SPI-3) standard defined a feature that reduced the overhead experienced during arbitration. A simplified protocol, one of the five optional features of Ultra-3 SCSI, is called Quick Arbitration and Selection (QAS), which is also known as "quick arbitration and select" or by IBM's name "arbitration select," or by Adaptec's name, "quick arbitrate."

QAS reduces the number of times that arbitration must occur on the bus. When employed, a device waiting for the bus can access data more quickly after the device on the bus sends its completion signal and without having to initiate a new arbitration process. Although this could lead to domination of the bus, a provision in the specification mitigates the unfair blocking of other devices that may be of a lower priority, or may not implement the QAS processes.

Further Readings

Serial ATA International Organization (SATA-IO).
   http://www.serialata.org/

Peripheral Component Interconnect Special Interest Group (PCI-SIG).
   http://www.pcisig.com/

Serial Storage Architectures (SSA) - Chapter 36 (pp. 443–458)
   "Video and Media Server Technologies," Karl Paulsen (Focal Press)

"HIPPI—the first standard for high-performance networking,"
   Stephen C. Tenbrink and Donald E. Tolmie, Los Alamos Science,
   Number 22 (1994)

1394 Trade Association and Whitepapers.
   http://www.1394ta.org/index.html
   http://www.1394ta.org/press/WhitePapers/
      Firewire%20Reference%20Tutorial.pdf

Universal Serial Bus and USB Implementers Forum, Inc. (USB-IF).
   http://www.usb.org/home

6

SATA, SAS, AND RAID

As disk drive technologies continued their growth through the late 1990s, the parallel interfaces used by these storage devices could no longer support any further increases in data transfer rates and thus became impractical as a means of connectivity between hosts and disk storage components. The generational expansion of SCSI was fueled by quantum leaps in the development of higher capacity, higher speed, and higher performance storage in the form of spinning disks.

Parallel SCSI interfaces, formally called the SCSI Parallel Interface (SPI), as used in external drive connectivity would fade as the technical landscape was dramatically and radically transformed. As parallel SCSI approached its practical performance limits, serial interfaces gained new ground as high-speed serial transceivers and very large-scale integration (VLSI) technology reached breakthroughs.

The fundamental SCSI protocols, in theory, have endured. The transports have developed from parallel SCSI through Serial Attached SCSI, to Serial ATA (SATA), and to external SATA (eSATA). This chapter discusses serial technologies in detail and why RAID is important to both data protection and bandwidth or throughput (performance) improvement.

KEY CHAPTER POINTS

- Serially connected storage technologies that have evolved out of the original parallel SCSI protocols: SAS, SATA, eSATA, and eSATAp
- Redundant Array of Independent Disks (RAID)
- How data is protected using RAID, how bandwidth and performance are affected at each RAID level, the differences and applications of RAID levels, and an explanation of hybrid RAID sets and why they are utilized

Transitioning from Parallel to Serial Technologies

Moving from parallel to serial data transfer technologies was inevitable. The original appeal brought by SCSI included

- a shared bus enabling easy connections among multiple SCSI devices
- multiple data paths for increased throughput
- understandable and relative ease in implementation

However, these features were gradually displaced by the demands for increased performance and a greater degree of scalability. Figure 6.1 depicts the parallel versus serial carriage of data between a host and a device. Several collective disadvantages forced the change from parallel to serial data transfer technologies.

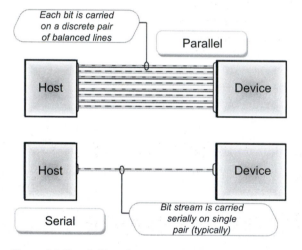

Figure 6.1 Parallel interface versus serial interface between the host and the device.

Reduced Performance

As faster throughputs forced clock speeds to increase, mitigating skew errors became an increasingly more difficult task. Increasing the data and clock rates required shorter cable lengths between SCSI devices, and the cross talk radiating between close-spaced signal lines, which was being generated by the high-frequency electromagnetic interference (EMI) radiation, caused significant distortion and losses in data integrity. In many cases, poorly fabricated cables failed to perform at these high data rates, and eventually, the unreliability of the parallel SCSI peripherals gave the overall technology a bad name in the industry.

Scalability

Theoretically, parallel SCSI allowed for a maximum of 15 devices per 16-bit bus (seven devices for the early 8-bit bus). As more devices are added, the shared bus architecture reduces the available bus access per device. This results in a lower number of usable devices, often well below the specified 15.

Crippling Issues

Parallel SCSI and parallel ATA (PATA) were not designed to be compatible. The expense and bulkiness of the cables complicated the costs and flexibility of implementation. Interchanging devices with bus activity was not possible, so devices could never be "hot pluggable." SCSI ID addresses needed to be manually assigned to each device on the bus, and each string of devices on the bus had to be properly terminated.

Serial technology would become the solution to all the above-mentioned consistently annoying issues.

Serial Attached SCSI (SAS)

At a high level, Serial Attached SCSI (SAS) is defined as a computer bus that moves data to and from storage devices over a serial data communications transfer technology. Parallel SCSI carries several data bits together on a link composed of multiparallel channels on paired wires, whereas serial communications send data one bit at a time, sequentially and usually in a scrambled format, over a single wire bus, a precise twisted pair of wires, or communications channel. Table 6.1 compares the differences in their two technologies.

Table 6.1 Comparison of Parallel SCSI to Serial Attached SCSI (SAS)

	Parallel SCSI	Serial Attached SCSI (SATA)
Architecture	Parallel—all devices connected to a shared bus	Serial—point-to-point, discrete signal paths
Performance	320 Mbytes/second—performance degrades as devices are added to the shared bus	3 Gbytes/second—road map to 12 Gbytes/second, performance does not degrade with added devices
Scalability	15 drives (devices)	Greater than 16,000 drives
Compatibility	SCSI only, not compatible with other drive interfaces	Compatible with serial ATA (SATA)
Cable length (max)	12 m in total, includes the sum of all cable lengths on the bus	8 m per discrete connection—total domain cabling in thousands of feet
Cable form factor	Multitude of conductors, bulky, costly, complicated connections	Compact connectors
Hot-plug capable	No	Yes
Device ID	Manually set—may not duplicate ID numbers, creates bus conflicts	Worldwide unique ID set at time of manufacture—no user involvement
Termination	Manually set—must properly terminate with special terminators per bus interface	Discrete signal paths—termination by default—no user involvement

SAS is specified in the American National Standard Institute (ANSI) standard called "Serial Attached SCSI (Small Computer System Interface)," also known as ANSIINCITS 376-2003. The complete specification is contained in a 465-page document from the InterNational Committee for Information Technology Standards (INCITS), the standards community organization formerly known as NCITS.

SAS drives were initially available in a 3.5-in. form factor up to 72 Gbytes (10K RPM) and up to 146 Gbytes (15K RPM). They were introduced in 2004 in a new, small 2.5-in. form factor at up to 36 Gbytes at 10K RPM, with 15,000 RPM drives on the road map.

At the end of 2010, SAS drives had reached into the 6-Gbits/second SCSI data rate, and between 2011 and 2014, that rate is expected to double to 12 Gbits/second, according to the SCSI Trade Association (SCSITA) road map.

Advantages

SAS is especially of interest for accessing mass storage devices, especially external and portable hard drives. SAS offers advantages over the older parallel technologies, including
- thinner cables
- less bulky connectors
- longer cable lengths
- less cross talk (due to fewer conductors in the cables)
- low-cost serial interfaces (vs. the hardware for parallel interfaces)

SAS technology addressed the evolving storage interconnect requirements of the enterprise class-computing environment. SAS technology drew from several aspects of Fibre Channel, SCSI, and SATA—combining them to create an enterprise class interface for the replacement of parallel SCSI.

Applications and Features

The logical evolution of SCSI, that is, SAS, includes the long-established software advantage and multichannel, dual-port connection interfaces found in SCSI. SAS was defined (in late 2003) to be the next generation of SCSI after Ultra 310. SAS would evolve to include and feature the following key points:
- Mainstream production began in 2004
- Features of the SCSI base command set
- Preempts and bypasses Ultra 640
- Offered as a cost-sensitive or high-reliability choice
- Targeted for mid-range to high-end servers
- Multilane tiering
- Universally supports SATA devices

Transfer Rates and Transitions

The current implementations of SAS offer data transfer rates in excess of 3 Gbits/second, and products with 6-Gbit/second adapters have been available since January 2009. The second generation of Serial Attached SCSI (SAS 2.0) increases the speed of the interface up to 6 Gbits/second.

A second update, referred to as SAS 2.1, further improves SAS device connectivity through two important updates. The first is a change in the interconnection; now, there is a small form factor high-density (HD) connector, often referred to as the mini-SAS HD connector. This new interconnect allows for greater storage device density in enclosures, especially when using 2.5-in. enterprise-class disk drives or the similar form factor solid state drives (SSDs). SAS 2.1 also reduces electrical signal cross talk to provide a better signal-to-noise ratio over connections. This provides economic incentives for storage systems that will be making the transition from a Fibre Channel to an SAS architecture.

The potential for SAS is rates in excess of 10–12 Gbits/second.

Compatibility

Devices using SAS are compatible with Serial ATA (Serial Advanced Technology Attachment; SATA) devices and are therefore compatible with devices that use earlier SCSI technologies. SAS uses the standard SCSI command set and provides backward compatibility with second-generation legacy SATA drives.

Point-to-Point Architecture

SAS is a point-to-point serial architecture that is simpler than its parallel predecessor SCSI. SAS is better suited to scalability than parallel SCSI and offers significantly higher throughput, currently at 6 Gbits/second.

SAS Architecture

The SAS architecture consists of six layers, like other layered architectures (e.g., the OSI model).

Figure 6.2 shows that the SAS architecture starts from the lowest level called the SAS Physical Layer where the electrical specs for the cable and connectors are defined. Above the Physical Layer is the SAS PHY Layer where data encoding, link speed, link negotiation, and link capabilities (in SAS-2) are found. The SAS Link Layer describes the frame transmission, which sits atop the connection management primitives.

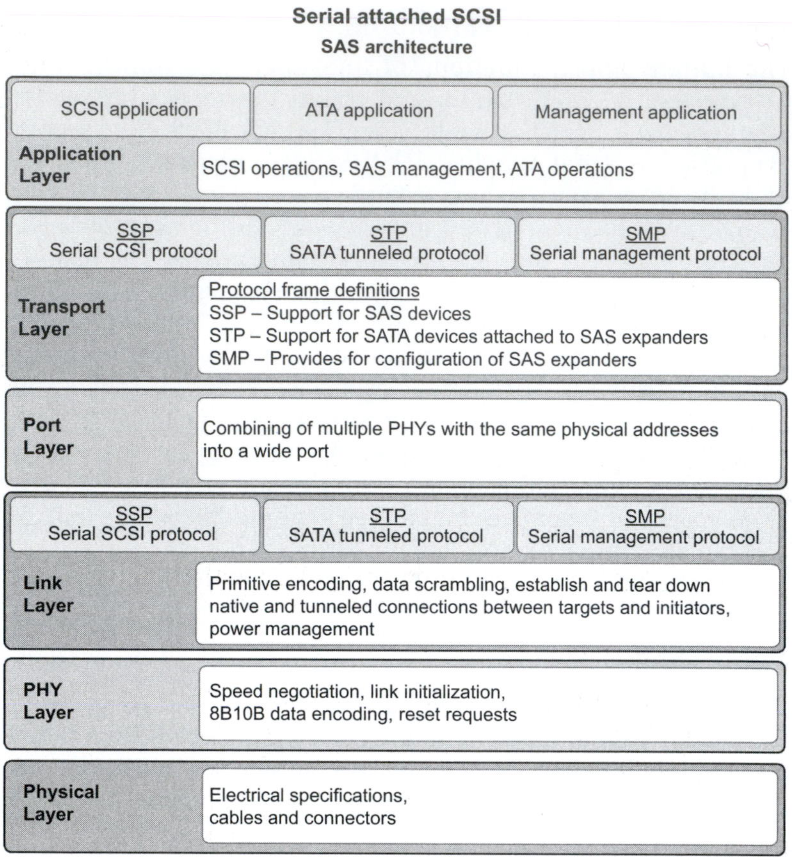

Serial attached SCSI

SAS architecture

SCSI application	ATA application	Management application

Application Layer	SCSI operations, SAS management, ATA operations

SSP\nSerial SCSI protocol	STP\nSATA tunneled protocol	SMP\nSerial management protocol

Transport Layer	Protocol frame definitions\nSSP – Support for SAS devices\nSTP – Support for SATA devices attached to SAS expanders\nSMP – Provides for configuration of SAS expanders

Port Layer	Combining of multiple PHYs with the same physical addresses into a wide port

SSP\nSerial SCSI protocol	STP\nSATA tunneled protocol	SMP\nSerial management protocol

Link Layer	Primitive encoding, data scrambling, establish and tear down native and tunneled connections between targets and initiators, power management

PHY Layer	Speed negotiation, link initialization, 8B10B data encoding, reset requests

Physical Layer	Electrical specifications, cables and connectors

Figure 6.2 Serial Attached SCSI (SAS) architecture.

On top of the SAS Link Layer is the SAS Port Layer where the wide port handling is set. Next is the SAS Transport Layer where the protocol frame definitions are placed, which consists of the Serial SCSI Protocol (SSP) transport, the Serial ATA Tunneled Protocol (STP) transport, and the Serial Management Protocol (SMP) transport. Finally, in much the same fashion as the OSI model is the Application Layer where the SCSI and ATA mode and log pages, and the spin up management for SMP functions are placed.

SAS System Components

The basic components of a typical SAS system will consist of four parts: initiator, target, service delivery system, and expanders.

The network topology, showing the components described next, is shown in Fig. 6.3.

Initiator

The entity or the device that originates or begins the operation, and sends device service and task management requests for processing to a target device, and receives responses for the same requests from other target devices. Initiators may be provided as an on-board component on the motherboard (as is the case with many server-oriented motherboards) or as an add-on host bus adapter.

Target

A device containing logical units and target ports that receives device service and task management requests for processing and sends responses for the same requests to initiator devices. A target device could be a hard disk or a disk array system.

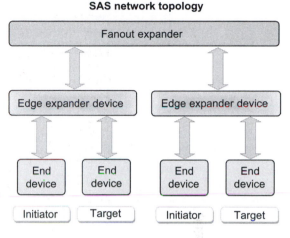

Figure 6.3 SAS network topology.

Service Delivery Subsystem

The part of an I/O system that transmits information between an initiator and a target. Typically, cables connecting an initiator and the target with or without expanders and backplanes constitute a service delivery subsystem.

Expanders

These are devices that form part of a service delivery subsystem and facilitate communication between SAS devices. Expanders facilitate the connection of multiple SAS end devices to a single initiator port.

Wide and Narrow Ports

Each SAS port has a worldwide unique 64-bit SAS address, enabling the designation of a 24-bit company ID by IEEE and a 36-bit vendor-specific ID assigned by the organization associated with the company ID. The SAS port contains one or more PHYs and may be grouped: an SAS port with a group of PHYs having the same physical addresses is called a wide port and an SAS port with only one PHY is called a narrow port (see Fig. 6.4).

SAS Applications

SAS has become a widespread data storage interface in servers that is on target to becoming a viable contender for external

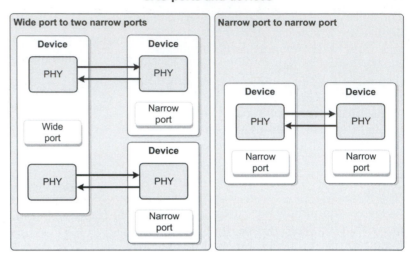

Figure 6.4 Ports and devices showing the wide port with more than one PHY and the narrow port with only one PHY.

storage systems. Today, those systems remain primarily Fibre Channel (FC) and serial ATA (SATA) disk drives; yet next-generation SAS-2 (and SAS-2.1) components, available since early 2009, are creating a renewed interest that is promoting this transition.

Sitting squarely in the 6-Gbit/second transfer rate domain and coupled with the added enhancements beyond SAS 1.1, the newer SAS-2/2.1 appears to be taking command over FC as a faster and more advanced disk interface. With only 4-Gbit/second transfer rates for FC drives and the 3.5-in. form factor drives nearing the end of their prowess, SAS appears to be the high-end drive interface of the future for servers and storage systems alike.

SAS Impacts on FC and SATA Drives

For FC and SATA drives, certain camps believe that the continuous deployment of FC as a disk interface will have a finite life span. Unable to extend beyond high-end servers and storage arrays, the costs of Fibre Channel disks remained high. For comparison, a SAS host bus adapter (HBA) will cost only about a third of the price of an FC HBA.

FC has routinely been chosen for high performance with SATA selected for large-capacity storage. The drawback is that FC and SATA require support from two different interface chip sets. Deciding early in the product development phase which format of disk interface to use or requiring conversion chips for the two to coexist in a single-storage system becomes a cost position negative for manufacturers who want to offer the benefits and performance capability of the two.

On the flip side, SAS and SATA can be supported by a single chip, thus reducing interface costs, power levels, and complexity. Promoters believe that enterprise-class SAS drives are comparable with high-end FC drives, the exception being that SAS will present a smaller cooling and power footprint and will enable a single back-end interconnect technology for both SAS and SATA.

SAS Standards

The T10 technical committee of the InterNational Committee for Information Technology Standards (INCITS) develops and maintains the SAS protocol. The SCSI Trade Association (SCSITA) promotes the technology.

SATA

Introduced in 2001, Serial ATA (SATA) has become a primary internal storage interconnect for workstations, desktops, and mobile PCs. Since May 2009, more than one billion SATA hard disk drives had been shipped. SATA has achieved a significant presence in enterprise applications through the enabling of integration in higher capacity, more cost-effective storage.

SATA is a 1.5-Gbit/second serial point-to-point architecture aimed at low-cost implementations. Initially, SATA desktop disk drives were available up to 250 Gbytes on 7200 RPM platters.
- The first production units were released in the second half of 2003.
- It evolved from parallel ATA (PATA) with a minimal feature set.
- It is extremely cost point sensitive.
- It is used in non-mission-critical applications for internal boot drives or near-line tape staging (cache).

eSATA

External SATA (eSATA) extends the SATA technology outside the PC and offers the highest performance of any mainstream external storage interface. An external interface for SATA technologies, formally called External Serial Advanced Technology Attachment, it competes with FireWire 400 and universal serial bus (USB) 2.0 with a focus on providing fast data transfer speeds for external storage devices.

As the next-generation (NexGen) internal bus interface for hard drives, SATA replaced ATA legacy technology. With a more streamlined interface compared with ATA, the SATA interface provides for a serial architecture with much greater data transfer speeds than the older parallel technology.

eSATA cables are narrow, up to 2 m (6.56 ft) in length, whereas parallel cables are considerably wider and are limited to 45.7 cm (18 in.) in total length. By using the extensions of eSATA, the SATA technologies are now expanded to encompass external storage solutions.

eSATA Transfer Rates

Even with eSATA reaching transfer rates of between three and six times that of USB 2.0, IEEE 1394, or FireWire 400 (800), eSATA does have at least one drawback. Implementing eSATA requires a separate power connector to be provided, but this also changed with the most update called eSATAp (Power over eSATA).

eSATA remains an excellent choice for external disk storage, and unlike USB and FireWire interfaces, eSATA is not required to translate data between the client interface and the host computer, which in turn enhances data transfer speeds while reducing computer CPU cycles and stress on other resources. Furthermore, with eSATA, the need for an extra off-load chip is also eliminated.

Port Multipliers

Devices that provide the capability for a single SATA port to communicate with multiple drives are called "port multipliers." These devices are transparent to hard drives, yet the host remains aware that it is communicating with multiple drives. The SATA port multipliers (PM) are simple unidirectional splitting mechanisms that allow for a single active host connection to communicate with up to 15 drives. The link bandwidth to the controller regulates the overall available bandwidth, which as of the current SATA-IO Revision 3 is 1.5, 3, or 6 Gbits/second.

Port multipliers will typically reside on an enclosure's backplane and support all standard SATA drives. PMs allow for significantly higher performance for external storage over either FireWire or USB (see Fig. 6.5).

Point-to-Point Connections

SATA connectivity is typically implemented on a point-to-point (P2P) basis, consisting of a single drive connected to a single

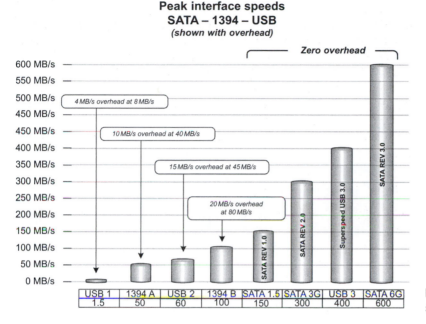

Figure 6.5 SATA peak interface speeds.

controller port via a single cable. The maximum number of drives in an array is predicated on the controller's port count. SATA port multipliers permit a change to that point-to-point relationship via port multiplication technology. Thus, port multipliers are a cost-effective and easy storage expansion methodology that enables the aggregation of multiple drives and improved performance.

Port Multiplier Switching

There are two ways that the SATA port multiplier (PM) may be driven: command-based switching and frame information structure (FIS)-based switching, each explained in the following sections (see Figs. 6.6 and 6.7).

Command-Based Switching

Conceptually similar in functionality to a mechanical A/B switch, command-based switching is one of the two port multiplier technologies for SATA. In this mode, the controller is only able to issue commands to a single disk at a time. It cannot issue commands to another disk until the command queue for the current transaction has been completed for the disk that it currently communicates with.

This single-disk-at-a-time mode gets in the way of Native Command Queuing (NCQ) and will reduce the ability to utilize

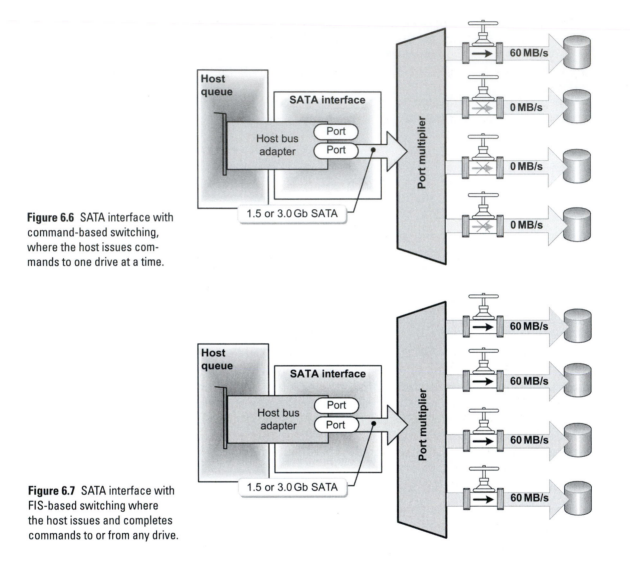

Figure 6.6 SATA interface with command-based switching, where the host issues commands to one drive at a time.

Figure 6.7 SATA interface with FIS-based switching where the host issues and completes commands to or from any drive.

the full bandwidth of the link. Because command-based switching cannot take advantage of the higher speed host link, it is used mostly for simple drive expansion where storage capacity (and not performance) is the principle concern.

Frame Information Structure (FIS)

An FIS is a mechanism to transfer information between host and device application layers. FIS-based switching provides for simultaneous connections to high-performance multiple storage drives. Functionally, the host issues and completes commands to drives at any time. Through a port multiplier, the data is directed to any drive that is ready for the I/O operation. An arbitration algorithm ensures a balanced data flow between the host and the storage device(s).

Unlike command-based switching, FIS-based switching allows for the aggregation of reads so as to make full use of the potentially higher bandwidth of the host link. FIS switching takes full advantage of the performance benefits of Native Command Queuing (NCQ) on the port multiplier, resulting in aggregated throughput of up to the total bandwidth of the host band link.

Tagged and Native Command Queuing

Parallel ATA (PATA) used a version of Tagged Command Queuing (TCQ) that allowed the operating system (OS) to send multiple read-write requests to certain ATA drives. Native Command Queuing (NCQ) was preceded by PATA's version of Tagged Command Queuing. ATA's attempt at integrating TCQ was constrained by the requirement that ATA host bus adapters needed to use ISA bus device protocols to interact with the operating system. The resulting high CPU overhead and negligible performance gain contributed to poor market acceptance for TCQ.

NCQ differs from ATA TCQ. In NCQ, the host bus adapter programs its own first-party DMA (direct memory access) engine with the DMA parameters that the CPU gave when it issued the command. In ATA TCQ, the CPU has to be interrupted by the ATA device so that the CPU can ask the ATA device which command is ready to be executed and then program the ATA host bus adapter's third-party DMA engine. Each command is of equal importance in NCQ. This is preferable since the drive itself is the most aware of its own performance characteristics.

To enable NCQ, it must be supported and enabled in the SATA host bus adapter and in the disk drive as well. An appropriate driver must be loaded into the operating system so as to enable NCQ on the host bus adapter. Newer chipsets will support the Advanced Host Controller Interface (AHCI), which should allow a generic driver supplied by the operating system to control and enable NCQ. The mainstream Linux kernels produced at the time of Windows XP supported AHCI natively, but Windows XP required the installation of a vendor-specific driver even if AHCI was present on the host bus adapter. Windows Vista natively supports both AHCI and NCQ.

NCQ technology is designed as an aid to increasing SATA drive performance and, under certain conditions, allows an individual SATA drive to optimize the order in which the read and write commands are executed. This intelligence is handled internally by the drive and in turn reduces latency resulting in increased performance.

eSATA Peripheral Interfaces

Motherboards that are without an eSATA connector can be accommodated by a peripheral component interconnect (PCI) card that can be installed in an available PCI slot. Notebook computers could use an external eSATA device made for the PCMCIA, PC Card, or ExpressCard slot, depending on the model and implementation.

eSATAp

eSATAp, known as "Power over eSATA" or "eSATA/USB Combo," combines the strength of high-speed eSATA capabilities with the compatibility of USB into a single port. eSATAp devices are now capable of being self-powered. A desktop workstation with an eSATAp port can supply 12-V power for a 3.5-in. form factor hard disk drive or a 5.25-in. DVD-RW without the need for a separate external power source. On a typical notebook with the eSATAp port, the 5-V power supply is capable of driving a 2.5-in. HDD or solid state drive (SSD).

eSATAp can be implemented in machines with a spare SATA port, which includes PC notebooks, desktops, Apple Mac Pro, and Linux or Unix servers.

Fast SATA

eSATA enables the use of fast SATA drives for external disk arrays, not only expanding valuable storage real estate but also enabling truly fast portable storage. Hot-plug and hot-swappable features in SATA promote portability for users or for those that exchange large volumes of media on a frequent basis.

When looking to acquire an eSATA controller or bus card, be certain it supports the SATA standard required by the particular SATA hard drive you will be using. Hardware support for newer standards is usually backward compatible, but the reverse does not hold. For example, an eSATA controller made for SATA 150 would not support the faster transfer speeds of a SATA 300 hard drive.

6-Gbits/second SATA

SATA-IO released the Serial ATA Revision 3.0 specification that allows developers, manufacturers, and end users of SATA equipment to look forward to substantially increasing through-put to 6 Gbits/second over a wide variety of storage, enterprise, and workstation/PC applications.

The same cables and connectors used for current SATA implementations can also be used to connect 6-Gbit/second SATA devices. With any of these next-generation high-speed interfaces, SATA-IO recommends utilizing good-quality components (wire, connectors, etc.) to ensure data integrity and robust operation at the fast 6-Gbit/second transfer rate.

Cables that are already at the threshold of 3-Gbits/second operating margins will probably experience lower performance than the expected threshold of 6 Gbits/second due to an increased number of resends. The SATA Revision 3.0 specification addresses this issue by defining the Compliance Interconnect Channel (CIC), outlined as a mathematical model of a compliant channel, as well as an insertion/return loss plot defining the most extreme losses the system can sustain and still be compliant. Like most standards, the CIC specification does not state the components that are to be used in a system, but rather it defines the overall performance and quality the system must exhibit.

End users should consult an Integrators List, available to the public, before buying new cabling.

RAID

Protecting data stored on disk systems has been a highly relevant activity that continues to be improved as technologies advance. There are a number of choices and methodologies for data protection, many of which are explored throughout this book. For disk-based storage, the choices available may be divided into two fundamental groups: the mathematical protection of the data using parity-based methods and the replication of that data whereby it is repeated on other sets of disks or disk volumes.

Both of these methods are used by manufacturers of storage systems for moving media applications. Both technologies are well proved and accepted and both provide additional value to the host systems that they support.

We will begin by looking at the mathematical protection methods as they are applied to a technology commonly known as "RAID."

Origin and Historical Perspective

In 1988, researchers presented a landmark paper "A Case for Redundant Arrays of Inexpensive Disks," which described the concepts for five methods of data protection on disk arrays. David Patterson, Randy Katz, and Garth Gibson at the University of California at Berkeley had studied methods aimed at guarding against data destruction due to failure of drives, and in their paper, they described techniques for mapping (designated as "striping") data across drives and their associated arrays for performance benefits. The commercial development of the concepts began in 1989 when the first nonmirrored version with commercial viability was announced by Compaq. By the middle of the 1990s, the concept and its name "RAID" had become a household word although its actual linguistic meaning would change as development moved forward and the technology gained acceptance.

When first introduced, RAID stood for "redundant array of inexpensive disks," but the word "inexpensive" has since been modified to "independent," presumably because the word inexpensive became only relative as storage capacities changed and the marketplace evolved. In reality, influenced by the proliferation and need for storage on a global scale, the cost of *all* storage has become comparatively inexpensive over time.

RAID by the Numbers

The numeric system for RAID was an outgrowth of the first Berkeley publication. The numbers were adopted over time to indicate certain types of protection and data mapping schemes. In the researchers' first publication, only five levels were described, but a sixth form of protection was added a few years later. The principle advantage behind the RAID concept is that data is spread across a number of independent disks in a manner that provides additional security for the data compared to keeping all the data on a single disk. Data protection is provided (in most RAID configurations) by the way that the redundancy data itself is stored separately from the primary data. The redundant data may be a complete copy of the original data (as in mirroring) or it may by simulated by adding extra data known as parity bits. The later method would be used to reconstruct the primary data set through the principles of Exclusive OR (XOR) algorithms should elements of the disk hardware fail.

RAID technology can be applied to stand-alone or independent subsystems for computer data, image storage, media servers, systems designed for video on demand, and most any computer hosted data system. Given the cost-effectiveness of small form factor disk drives, the promoters of RAID claim that there are significant improvements in reliability and maintainability across all storage platforms when using RAID—whether the implementation is in hardware or software.

RAID storage systems themselves provide significantly higher performance than individual disk drives. These improvements may be found not only in mechanical spinning disk systems but also in solid state drives (SSD) or flash memory storage platforms.

Opposing Arguments

Early opposition to RAID stated that RAID can be expensive and unnecessary and that there are alternative methods to similar performance at a better cost point. Those arguments have since subsided now that we have smaller physical hard drives sizes, the storage capacities of the RAID arrays are comparatively enormous, and the costs for the various components are much less than when the principles of RAID were first developed. Thus, the recognized architecture for the storage of data on magnetic spinning disks, including media content, became characterized by its RAID number. This well-recognized, but often misunderstood, term was entrenched in the computer data industry long before it was used for the storage of media on videoservers or other moving media platforms.

RAID terminology, whether used in the professional videoserver context or in home computer applications, is sometimes still confusing due to early marketing hype that exploited a continual "fear of failure" that would result in the loss of unrecoverable data. Decades after its introduction, the arguments continue not only about the value that RAID provides in whole but what RAID number makes best sense for the particular application it will be used in. The reality is that without RAID, or another undefined technology, the bandwidth requirements we've grown accustomed to in arrayed storage systems could not have been realized.

During the introductory periods of professional videoservers for broadcast television transmission, the term RAID was widely used and also abused because of misunderstandings. At the time, long before its current acceptance, RAID numbering was as much a marketing tool as it was a technology—especially when it came to understanding what the RAID numbering system meant. This further resulted in the myth that "the higher the RAID number, the better the performance." Unfortunately, this misconception about RAID numbering continues in some circles even after several years of explanation and implementation. The RAID number can be as misleading to some as the term "digital video" is to others.

Architecture, Subsystems, and RAID

In the context of this discussion, the term "architecture" will be used to describe the physical structure of the elements that make up a RAID storage subsystem. In a broader sense and for these applications, "architecture" is found to be both a process and a product of the planning, designing, and manufacturing of those technical systems that surround or are employed in a particular storage system.

The term "subsystem" is used because, for the most part, the RAID array, which is the grouping of disks, is intended to be an element of an overall system comprised of a host (typically a computer and associated operating system) and an input/output engine (for example, a video encoder or decoder). The RAID subsystem becomes a well-organized, efficient bit bucket that allows large volumes of data to flow in and out so that it supplements the functionality of the entire system overall.

To distinguish between different architectures of RAID, a numbering scheme was developed, which was intended to identify various combinations of drives, the striping methods for spreading that data throughout those drives, the bandwidth performance, the protection level, and the parity scheme that is rigidly associated with the RAID level which it supports.

Artificial Interpretations

During the early development of RAID, concern was expressed that the use of the term RAIDn, also referred to as a "RAID level" (with "n" generally a single- or double-digit number from 0 to 5 and above), was an attempt to capitalize on the incorrect notion that the higher the RAID level, the higher the reliability or performance of the RAID array (also referred to as the "RAID set"). RAID levels that are recognized by the original Berkeley papers and the now dormant RAID Advisory Board (RAB), who helped the industry to standardize the terminology and technology applications, have been categorized from RAID Level 1 to RAID Level 6.

There are additional RAID levels recognized in the Berkeley papers, but not by the RAB that include Level 0, also known as disk striping, where data is organized or mapped in "stripes" across the set of drives. Since the Berkeley papers, and the dissolving of the RAB, additional levels have been added, which include RAID 7 and RAID 1E (enhanced). These are explained further in this section.

A drive array cannot be created by simply connecting a series of SCSI drives to a SCSI interface or controller. Arrays will generally consist of electronics that format, using software or firmware, and then distribute data in some structured form across all of the drives. A RAID system consists of a specialized set of electronics and instructions that operate in conjunction with the various drives to form protective and fault-tolerance functions necessary to meet the level of RAID designated. Some videoserver manufacturers have developed their own RAID architecture in software, thus eliminating the dependence on a physical set of circuitry, known as a "hardware controller," that performs the RAID operations.

By combinations, base RAID levels, sometimes called hybrid RAID levels, additional features, and functions are created. The more familiar hybrids include Level 53, a combination of Level 0 and Level 3 that marries disk striping and the features of Level 3 parity. Level 10 mixes disk striping and mirroring, resulting in improved I/O performance and data reliability. Some suggested that this numbering system would lead to confusion among end users or that it would be contrary to generally accepted industry practice. The arguments may be true, but the practicality of the hybrids has proved their usefulness.

The RAIDbook and the RAB suggested that "RAID levels should be chosen with numbers that impart meaning, not confusion." Despite what the book said, the confusion surrounding RAID nomenclature continued. By 1997, the RAB had recognized nine RAID implementation levels. Of the nine levels, five conformed to the original Berkeley RAID terms developed from the 1988 researcher's efforts, with four other additional RAID terms acknowledged by the RAB. RAID 0, RAID 6, RAID 10, and RAID 53 were developed through committee work anchored by manufacturers, suppliers, and consumers. The techniques used in providing protection, performance, and redundancy in a RAID array become the primary differentiators between the varying RAID levels.

RAID 0

Also referred to as striping, this implementation places the data in a striped format (that is, distributed randomly) across an array of disks without providing any redundant information or parity. The striping of an array, although enhancing performance especially in high–transfer rate environments, has one serious downside. Since there is no redundancy or parity information recorded and there are no redundant disks, the failure of any one drive results in the complete loss of all data on the drive array. Thus, RAID 0 is primarily used for performance applications where bandwidth (throughput) improvements over a single drive become the primary target objective.

Data Striping

The term RAID 0 is seldom used even though the principle is commonly practiced. In earlier times, RAID 0 referred to the absence of any array technology. The RAB states that the term implies data striping, "a means to evenly distribute data so that during the read request, the blocks can be rapidly recovered at random with a minimum of latency." The result is supposed to be faster access, which means more bits are retrieved in a similar time frame, which infers a "higher bandwidth," a result of an increase in throughput.

RAID 1

RAID 1 is the simplest, most reliable, and easiest of the RAID levels to implement and understand. In RAID 1, as data is presented to the storage array, it is immediately duplicated as a redundant copy, residing on at least one separate drive, as shown in Fig. 6.8. RAID 1 is also referred to by terminology such as "disk-mirroring," "shadowing," or "duplexing."

When data is stored on two or more separate drives, 100 percent total redundancy is achieved. The controller system continually matches the data on one drive to the data on another, and should any discrepancy occur, the system then begins a thorough sweep of all the drives' content to ensure there are not other issues with the entire data set. If an error is detected, then a remapping process begins that restores the mirrored integrity of the drives.

This approach provides for a continual backup of all the data, thus improving reliability while further providing a high level of availability, especially when reading the data. If one disk component fails or is replaced, all of the information can be restored without any downtime because it has already been backed up.

RAID 1 writes as fast as a single disk. The systems are typically single I/O and nonscalable, which means that system performance improvements are not increased by simply adding more disk elements to the array. RAID 1 is not prominent in servers designed for video purposes. The term "mirroring," in the world of video, takes on a different meaning—typically addressed by providing two

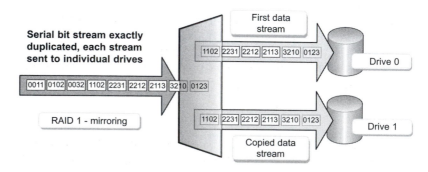

Figure 6.8 RAID 1 mirroring depicts how data is duplicated and exact copies sent to each drive or drive array (Drive 0 and Drive 1).

complete and independent videoserver systems (including I/O, processing engines, controllers, and storage) that operate in parallel under the control of a third-party automation system that monitors the functions and the health of the overall system.

Figure 6.8 shows how RAID 1 works. At the input port, the bit mapping of the data string is sent to Drive 0 and its "mirror" Drive 1. All data is duplicated for total redundancy. RAID 1 provides good reliability for data, does not require a complicated RAID controller (which may be implemented in software), and is relatively inexpensive to implement.

Mirrored professional videoserver systems nearly always run in parallel, with a failure of any component in the primary system resulting in a switch over to the mirrored system until the primary system can be repaired. For highly reliable systems, RAID 1 is sometimes extended to DVD archives, data tape systems, and other spinning disk arrays that store content online, near line, or off-line.

RAID 2

RAID 2 is the only RAID level that does not use one or more of the techniques of mirroring, striping, or parity. RAID 2 was developed for those early, very large diameter disks that needed to operate synchronously. In those early implementations, it was assumed that these large mass storage devices would be prone to constant disk errors, so RAID 2 employed error checking, such as Hamming codes, to produce higher data transfer rates. The technique used solid state, random-access memory (RAM) to detect and correct errors.

RAID 2 interleaves bits or blocks of data, with the drives usually operating in parallel and employing a special form of striping with parity that is similar in principle to error-correction coding and employs a process of scrambling data and recording redundant data onto the disk as it is recorded. This redundant information helps to detect and correct errors that may arise during read cycles. In a RAID 2 system, the drive spindles are fully synchronized. The system will use redundant disks to correct single bit errors and detect double bit errors. Error-correction algorithms determine the number of disks required in the array.

RAID 2 was very expensive, and there were virtually no commercially available implementations of RAID 2. This method has all but evaporated from the traditional storage environments.

RAID 3

RAID 3 is an array of N drives with bit or byte striping across all but one of the drives, as shown in Fig. 6.9. A single dedicated drive

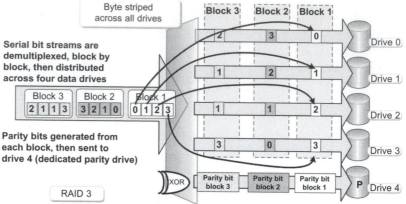

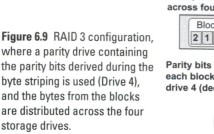

Figure 6.9 RAID 3 configuration, where a parity drive containing the parity bits derived during the byte striping is used (Drive 4), and the bytes from the blocks are distributed across the four storage drives.

contains redundancy data that is used to mathematically reconstruct the total data stream in the event any one member drive fails. The redundancy data is kept separately on a dedicated parity drive.

In a five-drive RAID 3 set, data is distributed across all four primary drives. Parity bits are built from that block data and stored as byte-level parity on the fifth drive.

RAID 3 uses parallel data access and has the advantage of high data rates, which increases performance over single-disk structures. Each disk in the entire array is used for each portion of the read-write operation.

In a RAID 3 array, all of the disks are synchronized so that both read and write performances cannot be hampered. Each logical record from the data stream is broken up and interleaved between all of the data drives except the parity drive. Each time that new data is written to the data drives, a new parity is calculated and then rewritten to the parity drive.

RAID 3 is often a preferred choice when large blocks of sequential transfers are required. Applications in imaging, CAD/CAM, and digital video or media servers may select RAID 3 because of its ability to handle large data block transfers. In streaming video applications, contiguous blocks of data are written to the array so that during playback only a minimal amount of searching is required, increasing efficiency and throughput.

One disadvantage that results, which is common to all striped arrays, is a poorer level of write performance compared with single or duplex/mirrored drives, a drawback that can be controlled by proper buffering and sectoring during the write process. By definition, the entire RAID 3 array can execute only one I/O request at a time, referred to as single-threaded I/O, which may or may not be important, depending on the application. Some controllers and smart arrays have minimized this impact by providing intelligent algorithms and larger disk caches to buffer data temporarily while being written to the drive.

With the use of a discrete byte-level parity drive, if a drive goes down, protection is temporarily lost until that drive is replaced and the parity information is reconstructed. Vendors will often configure mission-critical arrays with two parity drives as a second level of protection. The cost of this implementation must be weighed against the volume of data to be stored per unit dollar and physical space.

RAID 4

RAID 4 is characterized by block-level striping with a dedicated parity drive. RAID 4 improves performance by striping data across many disks in blocks and provides fault tolerance through a dedicated parity disk. The significant difference between RAID 4 and RAID 3 is that it uses blocks instead of bytes for striping. It is similar to RAID 5 except that RAID 4 uses dedicated block-level parity instead of distributed byte-level parity. Block striping improves random-access performance compared to RAID 3, but the dedicated parity disk remains a bottleneck, especially for random write performance.

RAID 4 lets the individual member disks work independently of one another. Advantages include good input and output performance for large data transfers and good read performance, fault tolerance, format efficiency, and other attributes similar to those found in RAID 3 and RAID 5.

As with most striping, write times are extended because the data is dispersed across several drives in segments. With RAID 4, if a block on a disk goes bad, the parity disk can rebuild the data on that drive. If the file system is integrated with the RAID subsystem, then it knows where the blocks of data are placed and a management control scheme can be implemented such that parity is not written to the hot disk.

Another drawback to RAID 4 is extra steps become necessary to update check data and user data. Furthermore, if the parity disk fails, all data protection is lost until it is replaced and the parity drive data is rebuilt. RAID 4 storage systems are uncommon in most storage architectures and almost never implemented in professional videoserver applications.

RAID 5

RAID 5 is characterized by its capabilities of high transaction throughput with support for multiple concurrent accesses to

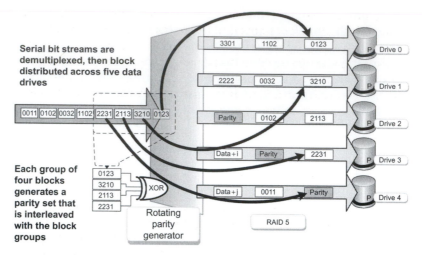

Serial bit streams are
demultiplexed, then block
distributed across five data
drives

| 3301 | 1102 | 0123 | P Drive 0

| 2222 | 0032 | 3210 | P Drive 1

| Parity | 0102 | 2113 | P Drive 2

| Data+i | Parity | 2231 | P Drive 3

| Data+j | 0011 | Parity | P Drive 4

0011 0102 0032 1102 2231 2113 3210 0123

Figure 6.10 The RAID 5 configuration, where a rotating parity generator assembles the bits from each block and interleaves them across the storage drives.

Each group of
four blocks
generates a
parity set that
is interleaved
with the block
groups

0123
3210
2113
2231

XOR

Rotating
parity
generator

RAID 5

data. RAID 5 is employed when independent data access is required. High read-to-write ratios are most suitable for RAID 5. Typically, the more disks in the array, the greater the availability of independent access.

RAID 5 uses block or record striping of the data stream, as shown in Fig. 6.10. The serial digital data word is spread at the block-level across all of the disks in the array. Independent access is available because it is now possible to extract the entire specific data block from any one drive without necessarily accessing any other. Latency and seek times are effectively reduced, resulting in performance increases.

In a RAID 5 configuration, should any single drive fail the read and write operations may still continue. Parity data generated at the block level is interleaved throughout the entire set of disks, allowing for continuous operations and rapid recovery. RAID 5 (and RAID 3) may be used in more high-performance applications.

As each block of data is written to the array, a rotating parity block is calculated and inserted in the serial data stream. The parity block is interleaved throughout all the disks and can be recovered from any of the drives at any time. Because parity information is rotated over all of the drives in the array, the I/O bottleneck of accessing the single parity disk (as in RAID 3) when concurrent accesses are requested is significantly reduced.

When a single drive in a RAID 5 array fails, the read and write operations will continue. Recall that data is block striped across all of the drives, so if the data to be read resides on an operational drive, there are no problems; yet if data is to be written to the array, the controller simply prohibits writing to that particular failed drive.

If data resides on a failed drive, the read process uses the parity information interleaved on the remaining drives to reconstruct the missing data. The algorithms that determine where the data resides are quite sophisticated, statistically tailored to allow nearly transparent operations during failure modes. The host never sees the failed drive and the entire array remains transparent.

RAID 6

In RAID 6, two sets of parity values are calculated for each parcel of information. This information is then stored on two discrete parity-only drives. In mission-critical implementations, especially when a 100% mirror of a system is unachievable, often a second parity drive is added to the structure of a RAID 5 array. This provides the added benefit that two drives may fail without a complete loss of data, provided they are not the two parity drives. In the event one drive fails, the entire array can continue with a second level of protection while a replacement drive is found and installed.

The disadvantage, of course, is that with two parity drives, every write operation requires that two parity blocks be written, thus write performance is lower, yet the read performance of RAID 6 remains equal to RAID 5 implementations.

As disk drive densities continue to increase and organizations continue to adopt SATA disk drives to reduce storage costs, data loss due to concurrent disk drive failure and error in a RAID group has become an increasing risk. Single-parity RAID 5 does not protect against such double-failure events. While RAID 1+0 and conventional RAID 6 do provide sufficient protection, each has serious drawbacks: RAID 1+0 requires nearly twice the number of disk drives, and conventional RAID 6 slows write performance significantly. Table 6.2 shows the various "straight RAID" levels and their feature sets.

Multiple RAID Levels

In some implementations, there is added value when using additional levels of RAID that are combined to improve performance, access time, overall bandwidth, and data throughput.

Multiple RAID levels, when grouped or layered, will provide additional protection, drive redundancy, and reduce the failure modes for those particular combinations—usually at a cost penalty. When bandwidth (throughput) is required, such as when delivering multiple streams of high-definition video while simultaneously

Table 6.2 Comparison of Various RAID Levels

Feature Sets	RAID 0	RAID 1	RAID 1E	RAID 5	RAID 5EE	RAID 6	RAID 10	RAID 50	RAID 60
Minimum drive count	2	2	3	3	4	4	4	6	8
Date protection	None	Single-drive failure	Single-drive failure	Single-drive failure	Single-drive failure	Two-drive failure	Up to one disk per subarray	Up to one disk per subarray	Up to two disks per subarray
Read performance	High	High	High	High	High	High	High	High	High
Write performance	High	Medium	Medium	Low	Low	Low	Medium	Medium	Medium
Read performance (degraded)	N/A	Medium	High	Low	Low	Low	High	Medium	Medium
Write performance (degraded)	N/A	High	High	Low	Low	Low	High	Medium	Low
Utilization capacity (%)	100%	50%	50%	67%–94%	50%–88%	50%–88%	50%	67%–94%	50%–88%
Typical applications	Workstations, data logging, real-time rendering, highly transitory data	Operating systems, transactional databases	Operating systems, transactional databases	Data warehousing, Web serving, archiving	Data warehousing, Web serving, archiving	Data archive, backup to disk, high availability, large-capacity servers	Fast databases, application servers	Large databases, file servers, application servers	Data archive, backup to disk, high availability, large-capacity servers

Table 6.3 Mirroring and Striping Hybrid RAID Sets

Hybrid RAID Nomenclature	Mirror—Stripe—Parity Configuration	Details
RAID 10 RAID 1+0	Stripe (RAID 0) of mirrored (RAID 1) disks	Minimum of two disks, such as RAID 0+1 with stripe reversed
RAID 0+1	Mirror (RAID 1) of striped (RAID 0) disks	Minimum of four disks, such as RAID 1+0 with stripe reversed, not as robust as RAID 10
RAID 100 RAID 1+0+0	Stripe of RAID 10 arrays (also called RAID 10+0)	Load spread across multiple controllers, better random read performance, top-level stripe done in software
RAID 0+3 RAID 3+0	Dedicated parity across striped (RAID 0) disks	Three sets of RAID 0 disks in a RAID 3 grouping
RAID 30	Striping of dedicated parity arrays	Combines two RAID 3 arrays in a RAID 0 mode, striped across both RAID 3 arrays
RAID 50 RAID 5+0	Block-level stripes (RAID 0) combined with distributed parity (RAID 5)	Minimum of six drives required, one drive per RAID 5 stripe may fail before data loss, high fault tolerance
RAID 51 RAID 5+1	Two RAID 5 sets mirrored (RAID 1), "mirroring above single parity"	Each RAID 5 set resides on separate controller, may be implemented as a "layered" RAID
RAID 05 RAID 0+5	Several stripes (RAID 0) of RAID 5 sets	Minimum of three RAID 5 sets, generally not found in production RAID array sets
RAID 53	Typically used interchangeably with RAID 30 and RAID 0+3	Striping of RAID 3 (dedicated parity) sets in a RAID 5 (distributed parity) configuration
RAID 60 RAID 6+0	RAID 0 striped across RAID 6 elements	Combines straight block-level striping of RAID 0 with double distributed parity of RAID 6
RAID 61 RAID 6+1	Mirroring above dual parity	Combines mirroring (RAID 1) with double distributed parity of RAID 6

ingesting (recording) several feeds, these concepts can further provide better storage space per unit drive of utilization.

Table 6.3 summarizes the usual hybrid configurations employed by storage system vendors, with additional information in the following sections.

Mirroring

Mirroring is a process where multiple copies of a given RAID level are employed. RAID levels 0+1 and 1+0 (i.e., RAID 10) represent a layering of the two elementary levels of RAID. In this example, RAID 10 combines data striping (from RAID 0) and equal data splitting (RAID 1) across multiple drive sets. Duplexing is a variant of RAID 1 that includes mirroring of the disk controller, as well as the disk.

Striping with Parity

Striping with parity is when single RAID levels 2 through 5 and multiple RAID levels 0+3 (e.g., RAID 53), 3+0, 0+5, and 5+0 use parity with striping for data redundancy.

Neither Mirroring nor Parity

RAID level 0 is striping without parity and provides no redundancy.

Mirroring and Striping with Parity

When multiple RAID levels, such as 1+5 and 5+1, are employed for redundancy protection, this is referred to as both mirroring and striping with parity. This concept provides better data protection and balances out the inefficiencies sometimes found in certain straight RAID set configurations. Selecting the appropriate hybrid configuration that best suits the application that the storage must support depends on the server or the storage architect.

There are certainly cost penalties for hybrid sets, but when mission-critical applications demand high performance, the cost trade-offs are minimal.

RAID 7

This variation was never an open industry standard, but a trademarked term from now-defunct storage vendor Storage Computer Corporation (ca. 1996). RAID 7 was a term used to market a proprietary RAID design sold into VAX systems and described in a number of inaccurate and inconsistent forms: a hybrid of RAID 3 with a write cache, RAID 4 with a write cache, and an array with an internal CPU plus a combination of striping as a RAID-5-like model. Little has been heard from the company (whose stock ticker was "SOS") since around 2001 when a lawsuit was filed in Texas claiming patent infringement. RAID 7 has not been sold since the company disappeared around the mid-2000s.

Hot Standby Drives

Professional videoserver vendors generally provide a second, hot standby disk drive that is placed into service should more than one primary drive fail or when certain other conditions prevail.

This hot standby is not generally a part of the operating storage environment and may or may not be part of the actual RAID set. Hot standby drives provide another level of protection, minimizing the requirement that a technician be immediately available to replace a failed drive. Servers located in remote environments, or where they are not readily accessible, may employ this additional protection.

Users should be conscious of how this drive is used and why it is provided in a system.

RAID 1E

Depending on the vendor, RAID 1E may also be called striped mirroring, enhanced mirroring, or hybrid mirroring. It is a RAID level that combines RAID 0's striping capabilities with RAID 1's mirroring protection. This RAID configuration appears to be a lot like RAID 10; however, a critical difference between RAID 1E and RAID 10 is that RAID 1E uses an odd number of disks to achieve data protection while RAID 10 requires the use of an even number of disks.

RAID levels 0 and 1 each require a minimum of two disks, but RAID 1E requires a minimum of three disks. Furthermore, RAID 10 requires at least four disks. Similar to a RAID 1 configuration, RAID 1E has a 50% disk capacity overhead, allowing for only half of the total capacity of the array to be available for use.

RAID 1E stripes data across all of the disks in the array as in RAID 0. The advantage to RAID 1E is that a copy of the data is then striped across all of the disks as well. Striping data in the same way that an initial stripe would is a drawback because copies of the data still reside on the same disk as the original copy. RAID 1E shifts the second copy of the data to another physical disk.

In Fig. 6.11, each number refers to a block of data; the number with a suffix M refers to a mirrored block of data.

To see what happens during a drive failure, assume that disk 5 fails, which contains block 3 and block 8, along with the mirrored copies of blocks 5 and 10. The array can sustain this failure because it has mirrored copies of blocks 3 and 8 stored on

RAID 1E - Mirrored data block protection

Figure 6.11 Simplified look at RAID 1E mirrored data block protection.

disk 1. Theoretically, the loss of multiple disks in a RAID 1E array is sustainable, provided the failed disks are not adjacent to one another.

RAID 1E provides potentially more performance than a traditional RAID 1 array, and like RAID 1, RAID 1E's primary disadvantage is its 50% disk capacity overhead. RAID 1E has been found to have relatively low support from the disk-controller manufacturers.

RAID 5E and RAID 5EE

RAID 5EE and RAID 5E are similar. The former employs a more efficiently distributed spare drive and supports faster rebuild times. Both RAID levels stripe data and parity across all of the drives in the array.

RAID 5EE provides both data protection and increased throughput. An array assigned to RAID 5EE has the capacity of the logical drive reduced by the capacity of two physical drives in the array: one for parity and one for the spare.

In RAID 5EE, the spare drive is a part of the array. However, unlike RAID 5E (which utilizes contiguous free space for the spare), a RAID 5EE spare is interleaved with the parity blocks allowing data to be reconstructed rapidly if a physical drive should fail. Under this configuration, sharing the spare drive with other arrays is not permitted. Spare drives for any other array must be dedicated to that particular array.

In RAID 5EE, a minimum of four drives are required and only one logical drive in an array is allowed. Depending on the firmware (this level is firmware specific) and the stripe-unit size, RAID 5EE may use a maximum of either 8 or 16 drives.

RAID 5EE offers 100% data protection and provides more physical drive storage capacity than RAID 1 or RAID 1E. Its disadvantages are lower performance than RAID 1 or RAID 1E and that you may not share a hot spare with another array.

Hardware RAID Arrays

The primary components of an external RAID array consist of an enclosure with power supplies, which are usually redundant, fans (also redundant), and a backplane to interconnect the drive sets that are usually provided on individual removable sleds that can be easily inserted and removed in a hot-plug mode. The RAID controller is usually a hardware device with software logic in ASIC or FPGA. The interface to the system may be parallel SCSI (less common in modern systems), Fibre Channel, or Gigabit Ethernet. There will be several sets of disk drives, mounted onto the sleds or in some configurations on a ruggedized and/or removable chassis designed to isolate the drives from the other components.

RAID in Software

RAID implemented in software is where a computer runs the RAID tasks on its own internal CPU instead of a dedicated, purpose-built RAID-controller board set. Software RAID is implemented in a variety of ways: as a straight software solution on a computer or as a hybrid solution comprised of some hardware that is designed to increase performance and reduce system CPU overhead, or integrated on a server.

This implementation, because it is running on a computer, is subjected to the same kind of risks that any computer might have. Software RAID is limited to the current operating system (OS). It may be vulnerable to viruses and attacks over a network. Software RAID generally will only run in write-through mode (as opposed to hardware RAID that can run in write-back mode).

Hardware-assisted software RAID aids in overcoming some of the deficiencies in pure software-only RAID. These implementations will generally come with hardware such as a host bus adapter (HBA) with a RAID BIOS, or a RAID BIOS embedded on the computer's host motherboard.

In the professional videoserver domain, Harris (Leitch) NEXIO storage platforms run a patented, Emmy® Award-winning RAIDsoft™ (software RAID) management system on a RAID 3 protocol that protects a logical volume form losing content due to a single drive failure. This RAIDsoft implementation continually reads and decodes parity information as opposed to some hardware configurations where the RAID controllers do not begin reading from the parity drive until the failure of a data drive is underway.

The software optimizes a drive rebuild process by harnessing the processing power of every CPU on the SAN in concert, which yields a faster equivalent rebuild time compared to a hardware RAID controller. In a software RAID, a rebuild process will only need to recreate the missing data on that single disk, thus removing the need to rebuild the whole drive, which in turn reduces rebuild time significantly.

Alternative Disk Sets and Configurations

Deep archives are traditionally employed for storing massive amounts of inactive data. This archival data may be kept on linear magnetic data tape (DLT or LTO) or on optical storage, such as DVD-RAM or Blu-ray, although that popularity has decreased significantly following the commercial introductions of Blu-ray and HD-DVD.

MAID as an Archive Alternative

Deep archives are used for off-site storage, backup protection, or disaster recovery. So when access to data is infrequent, yet that data may need to be readily accessible, in whole or in part, another method of near-line storage may be employed. A Massive (or Monolithic) Array of Idle Disks (MAID) is a near-line, short- or long-term storage technology that retains accessible data on spinning disks but allows those disks to be placed in an idle state, in either groups of drives or individually. The acronym was coined in the late 1990s at the University of Colorado in Boulder, where students were working on a research project to build high-density online storage that consumed less power.

COPAN Systems, located in Longmont, Colorado, brought that research to market and is believed to be the first company to ship a system (February 2004). Since that time, COPAN (whose bankrupted assets were acquired by Silicon Graphics Incorporated [SGI] in February of 2010) had installed 300 or more systems worldwide. Since then only a handful of other vendors have joined the market.

MAID disks are arranged in a scalable configuration that literally shuts down the drive spindles when the data on that drive is not being accessed. Combining this configuration with an intelligent, active file system management application will suspend only those drives that are not expected to be used for many hours or days. MAID powers down the head motor and parks the heads until the file system calls for a particular segment of data to be accessed. When access is requested, only those appropriate disks are restarted, and the data is transferred to another higher bandwidth store or sent by FTP to another server for appropriate use.

The benefits claimed by MAID are that it increases longevity, reduces power consumption, and mitigates the negative issues associated with linear tape, robotic libraries, or optical drives. MAID will require a few more seconds to return to an active state, but the principle purpose of MAID is not for online activity.

One of the concerns raised by the MAID opposition is that in this kind of configuration, especially when put into in an archive application, the drives might be sitting idle for too long. At the point where the drives are commanded to spin up again, the possibility that some of the drives might not respond or come up to speed at all is elevated. Drives are designed to run continuously, they are engineered with lubricants or other mechanical systems that do not necessarily remain idle for long periods of time. A similar concern is raised with removable or portable hard drives that effectively become shelved, stored in a nonoperating environment for long periods, and then are suddenly brought back into service.

JBODs

The term "Just a Bunch of Disks (JBOD)" is not an official RAID configuration although RAID configurations could offer it as an option. A JBOD array (see Fig. 6.12) basically takes a bunch of disks and turns them into one large partition. JBOD offers no redundancy, and with some RAIDs, a disk failure in the array will cause the whole JBOD array to fail.

The official term for JBOD is "spanning," and it refers to a set of disks that have not been configured according to a RAID level that store the same data redundantly on multiple disks and still allow the drive set to appear to the operating system as a single disk. JBOD will not deliver any advantages over using separate disks independently, and certainly will not provide any level of fault tolerance or performance benefits versus a RAID configuration.

The JBOD array will read and write at the same speed as a normal disk, unlike a RAID 0 stripe configuration.

SBODs

The Switched Bunch of Disks (SBOD), utilized in some professional media server platforms, have performance advantages over JBOD, allowing as much as a four-fold increase of throughput and a two-time increase of IOP performance. SBOD technology could seriously be considered a replacement or augmentation strategy for current Fibre Channel JBOD implementations.

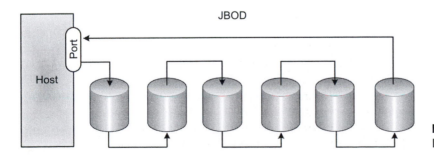

Figure 6.12 Just a Bunch of Disks (JBOD) signal path.

By standard, Fibre Channel Loop Architecture (FC-AL) is limited to 128 devices. As the device count on the FC-AL increases, the ability to provide scalable performance to all the devices on the loop decreases as each of them competes for communication resources. This is referred to as "resource starvation" and the problem grows as array sizes increase to their maximum.

Many SANs have employed FC-AL within the storage arrays to connect the actual storage devices (disks or tapes) to the controllers, essentially allowing the daisy chaining of up to 126 drives on one controller. The drawback in this concept is that it limits performance and complicates diagnosing problems.

Better performance has been achieved by a number of array manufacturers through the adoption of a technology called "Inspeed," developed by the former storage switch company Vixel, which was purchased by Emulex in late 2003. Inspeed technology puts what amounts to an FC-AL switch at the drives and allows the controller to establish point-to-point connections between a storage device and the controller. This technology provides for higher bandwidth and higher overall performance. Vixel called the resulting architecture a Switched Bunch of Disks or simply "SBOD," playing off the name of JBOD storage configurations (see Fig. 6.13).

SBOD may be found in technology employed by Xyratex, whose product is designed as a plug-and-play replacement for Fibre Channel JBOD technologies. Xyratex claims its implementation has a much better RAS and performance than the JBOD equivalent.

In the Xyratex implementation, SBOD devices use an internal crossbar switch to provide device communication while simulating the presentation of those FC-AL devices connected to it. The principle reduces the number of hops required for host-to-device communication. SBOD creates an almost direct host-to-device communication path, with the added feature of being able to

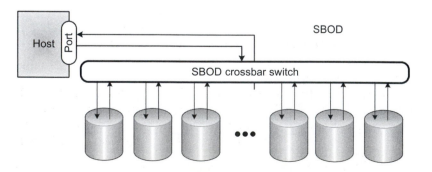

Figure 6.13 Switched Bunch of Disks (SBOD) data path.

trunk two FC links within one simulated FC-AL loop such that interenclosure effective loop bandwidth is doubled.

By eliminating the "physical loop" architecture, each node is connected via a dedicated link, which in turn supports full error management and diagnostics without disruption to other devices in the "logical loop." Together, these concepts vastly improve reliability and serviceability.

The performance improvements experienced by using SBOD devices with this trunking technology show no significant degradation in performance up to the point where loop saturation limits are reached. SBODs further employ nonblocking processes that allow concurrent initiator access to the logical loop with a demonstrated total throughput peaked at 1550 Mbytes/second while the maximum performance in an equivalent JBOD configuration peaks at 384 Mbytes/second.

Error Prevention Methods

In addition to the various methods used in assuring the accuracy of the data and its proper recovery, the rapid growth in both the physical and electronic storage capacities still creates hardships in data integrity. The following sections cover various schemes and technologies that are aimed at improving data integrity at various levels of the storage platforms.

Unrecoverable Error Rates (UER)

With all the preventative measures available in disk storage, the move toward high-capacity, low-cost disks creates a substantial increase in the risks of data loss should a double disk failure occur or if unrecoverable media errors during reconstruction (MEDR) are found. Either of these conditions could occur whenever a drive fails, or when a drive is replaced and a rebuild of the array set is undertaken. The rising fear comes from how to handle any data loss that occurs because of MEDR.

Disk capacities have doubled every 18 months, but the error correction technologies have not improved at these same rates. Drive specifications have noted relatively constant uncorrectable error rates (UERs) across many generations of drives; yet truth be told, there has been little improvement in error handling through disk technology generations.

This has led to adaptations of RAID configurations from SBOD to RAID 1+0, to RAID 5 and RAID 6, and presumably beyond. High-performance drive system providers have handled some of these issues by designing alternatives to these hybrid RAID configurations.

RAID 5 Schemes

RAID 5 uses single parity as its protection scheme against a single disk failure. Traditionally, this implementation offers sufficient protection against not more than a single failure event. The drawback is that no other disk failure or uncorrectable media error can occur while reconstruction is in progress. During normal operation, if there is an unrecoverable error and the event is a read error, then recreating data from parity occurs almost instantaneously, and the array remains online. However, if a disk in a RAID 5 group fails, then all its data has to be recreated and the array remains in a vulnerable degraded mode (without parity protection) until all the data has been reconstructed onto a spare disk. In a high-density situation, for a slow disk, or when the disk is very large (i.e., 1-Tbyte drive or more), this process will take an extremely long time.

RAID 5 does not protect against double disk or media failures, thus without additional protection schemes, employing a single RAID 5 model for mission-critical data can be risky. RAID 5 is not a particularly inexpensive implementation, which is one of the reasons vendors may limit RAID group size to 3+1 or 5+1 (three or five data drives plus one parity drive). This equates to a 17%–33% disk budget allocation just to parity the disk(s).

RAID 1+0 Schemes

RAID 1+0 configurations use mirroring to protect against "double-disk failures." For mission-critical applications, this is not an uncommon implementation but comes with a two-time price impact (drives, space, cooling, power, and applications) as well.

While somewhat of an insurance policy, complete protection against disk or media failure is not guaranteed. With RAID 1+0, while protecting against double disk or media failure scenarios, there are still opportunities for breaches to occur. Should there be a failure of both disks on the same mirror, the result is data loss. That is, should one disk fail in a mirror, there is only one way to recover from that failure, which is to copy all of the data from the mirror onto an spare disk, assuming one is available. While this copying is going on, there is a high-risk time period during which the probability of an unrecoverable error (UE) increases proportionately with the number of bits being transferred.

Some RAID 1+0 configurations do provide an add-on synchronous mirroring product that mitigates the problem of data loss during the copy period; however, such protection adds to the overall cost, with some synchronous mirroring licenses costing multiple hundreds of thousands of dollars depending on the size of the storage subsystem being mirrored. Furthermore, the synchronous mirroring option does require a total separate array to be employed as a destination.

RAID 6 Options

Those who choose RAID 6 implementations will see that dual parity is used to protect against double disk failure. RAID 6 provides an excellent data protection scheme without the higher costs associated with RAID 1+0 solutions. However, a standard RAID 6 implementation will compromise overall system performance, with as much as a 33% performance hit.

Dual Parity (RAID-DP)

Of course, there are companies that offer yet another solution to the dual-parity, RAID 6 offering, with features designed to reduce the performance impact hit previously mentioned. Remember that in dual parity (DP), the parity data is duplicated and stored in two discrete disks.

Methods used to implement RAID 6-DP including dual check data computations (parity and Reed-Solomon), orthogonal dual-parity check data, and diagonal parity. SNIA defines RAID 6-DP as any form of RAID that continues to execute read-write requests to all of a RAID array's virtual disks in the presence of any two concurrent disk failures.

Error Correction and Scrubbing

RAID uses a proactive operation to detect errors, which involves periodically scrubbing all the disks in the array. The process issues the read operations for each physical disk block, computes a checksum over its data, and then compares the computed checksum to the checksum located in its data integrity segment.

Should the checksum comparison fail, called a "checksum mismatch," the data is then reconstructed from other disks in the RAID group, after each of those checksums is verified. If no reconstruction is necessary, the parity of the data blocks is generated and compared with the parity stored in the parity block.

Should the parity not match the verified data, the scrub process proceeds to fix the parity by regenerating those bits from the data blocks. When a system is protected by double parity, it is definitively possible to tell precisely which of the parity or data blocks is corrupt. This mismatch between data and parity is called a "parity inconsistency."

Disk-block corruptions may be caused by either hardware or software errors, or both. Hardware errors can consist of disk drive or disk shelf firmware bugs, bad memory, and even adapter failures. Software bugs may also cause some corruption. In many cases, the source of the corruption is unidentifiable.

The following represents corruption classifications used by some vendors in defining potential risks that may be mitigated through alternative schemes.

Checksum Mismatches (CMs)

Checksum mismatches refer to instances where corruption is detected from mismatched data and checksum calculations, which may be caused by data content corrupted by components within the data path, a torn write wherein only a portion of the data block was successfully written, or a misdirected write where the data was written to either the wrong disk or the wrong location on the disk resulting in an overwriting and corrupting of the data already there or to be written into that location. Checksum mismatches may be detected whenever a disk block is read, such as a file system read, a data scrub, or a RAID reconstruction.

Identity Discrepancies (IDs)

A corruption class that occurs when a mismatch is detected when the disk block identity check is performed during a file system read. Probable causes could include a lost write (typically occurring because a write destined for disk is not written but believed to be written); or a misdirected write, where the original disk location fails to update. This can happen when the disk's firmware replies that a write was successful, but the write never actually occurred. Identity discrepancies can be detected only during file system reads.

Parity Inconsistencies (PIs)

PIs occur when there is a mismatch between the parity computed from data blocks and the parity stored on disk, despite the individual checksums being valid. This error might be caused by software bugs in the disk system or firmware, in-memory corruptions, processor miscalculations, or lost or misdirected writes. Parity inconsistencies are only detectable during data scrubs.

Conclusions

Protecting the myriad sets of data generated while still increasing system performance is made possible through the intelligent use of the original SCSI protocols that were initially developed way back in the late 1970s and early 1980s. Since that time, a family of technology on all fronts has marched along and the needs for storing the data that is being generated by that technology just keep growing as well. This chapter (and Chapter 5) have demonstrated the achievements in storage technologies from consumer through enterprise devices.

Additional topics that delve into the Internet protocol suites of storage will follow later in this book, as will studies of how intelligent storage systems are being used to track and house moving media.

Further Readings

The RAID Advisory Board (RAB) was an organization that organizes the technological harmony of those entities that would produce RAID-based storage systems. The organization has disbanded, but reference to them remains at the Web site http://www.raid-advisory.com, which provides links to more than just RAID storage applications.

Information on SATA, SAS, and other classes of storage technologies can be found at

SATA spec development, meeting notes, presentations, and proposals, http://www.t13.org

SATA working group Web site www.serialata.org

Serial Attached SCSI spec development, presentations, and proposals, http://www.t10.org

Serial Attached SCSI marketing and business information, http://www.scsita.org

SOLID STATE DISKS

The technologies surrounding solid state drives (SSD) have been in use for at least a couple of decades. Until recently, seldom were there mainstream SSD applications for the enterprise or data center, nor were there many practical uses of SSD in storage subsystems for professional moving media applications. As the cost of flash memory began to drop dramatically in the later part of the previous decade (*ca.* 2008–2009), and the storage size of memory modules began to grow, the implementation of SSD systems began to increase.

SSD may stand for either solid state disk or solid state drive. Purists would argue that it cannot be a disk because that would assume it has a form of "disk" media that spins. Perhaps, it is assumed that because SSD is evaluated in competitive terms against the HDD, and depending upon the system, may use the same SAS, SATA, or Fibre Channel storage interfaces, that the SSD really is not just a disk—more appropriately it is a drive.

Regardless, this chapter will look at the SSD as a formidable type of storage, one that offers many advantages to magnetic or optical spinning disk storage systems, not the least of which is power consumption, reduction of access time, and resistance to shock.

Irrespective of SSD's advantages and capabilities, which are covered in this chapter, a looming question still remains: As the storage industry takes a hard look at cost-control and its environmental ecosystems, just how soon will the move to SSD accelerate for enterprise level implementations?

KEY CHAPTER POINTS

- An overview, history, and development of flash memory, which is the media form utilized in solid state disks
- The components, cell structure, and operations of flash memory
- Outlining the values and the limitations of flash memory

- The designations, applications, and differences between NOR and NAND memories
- How data protection and security are handled in solid state disks
- Applications for flash memory and the components in a solid state disk

Solid State Storage Evolution

In an era of increasing file sizes, megalith-like storage requirements, rotational disk drive capacities exceeding terabyte proportions, and an astounding dependence upon storage in dimensions previously unobtainable comes a restoration of a nearly lost technology—solid state memory for mass storage.

The evolution of flash-based memory for consumer and professional applications has helped drive a renewal in solid state, scalable enterprise storage. Various memory technologies have been developed to address differing applications for solid state disk data storage. One of the dividing lines in memory is whether it is volatile or non-volatile in nature. Hard drives are for the most part non-volatile. That is, once the magnetic state is set (i.e., to a one or a zero), that state is maintained unless some significant catastrophic outside force alters that state.

While hard drives solve the majority of the volatility issues, other physical constraints create another level of encumbrance.

Limiting Factor

Since the early days of mechanical storage on magnetic spinning disks, the physical properties associated with the storing and retrieving of data from the disk platters have continued to be a performance-limiting factor. Despite myriad advancements over the years in hard drive technology, the issues of seek time latency that accompany the spindle speeds, armatures, and head assemblies have continued to place restrictions of the accessibility of the data.

Fundamentally, the management of disk-based storage is governed by the physical structural requirements surrounding the depositing and recovering of data bits that lie in a series of lineal concentric tracks around the surface of the platter. This data, organized as blocks, are tracked in a tabled sequence of pointers that are controlled and arranged by a combination of resident firmware and additional third-party software, which is overseen at the application layer by the disk operating system.

Hard disk drive management methodologies differ from the approach utilized in solid state memory.

Dynamic Random Access Memory

The first type of solid state memory technology to gain any note-worthy foothold at the enterprise level was the Dynamic Random Access Memory (DRAM) SSD.

DRAM should be noted as a volatile memory technology. DRAM utilizes capacitors to store data, which are required to be continually refreshed (via electrical power) in order to preserve the data state of each memory element. Thus, a DRAM SSD's drawback is that if power is removed, the capacitor's state cannot be refreshed and the data are lost.

Manufacturers, in their effort to address the volatility issues, will typically build-in an alternate power source such as a back-up internal battery to enable the refresh state and preserve the state of memory. DRAM SSD technologies may employ the movement of data to a secondary HDD, or to another flash-based memory system as a data protection scheme should a power failure event occur.

An advantage of DRAM SSD is that its access is completely random. Each cell is addressed in an X-Y fashion for both read and write operations. In terms of data access speed, DRAM SSDs remain the fastest technology as they performs both reads and writes at approximately the same speed. This makes their principle selling point performance.

The drawback to the DRAM SSD is that it has a greater power requirement, which may be seen as cost prohibitive for most enterprise-level applications. This in turn creates an opening for cheaper flash-based, energy-efficient SSD technology.

Flash Memory

Flash, as a form of non-volatile memory (NVM), can be electrically erased and reprogrammed. Flash memory has recently appeared in products for professional video media serving applications including video on demand, cache, and near term/near line storage. In the NVM category, flash memory is the technology of choice versus DRAM because in flash, the storage cells retain data whether power is applied or not.

Flash memory has become the core element in SSD technologies, replacing the concept of DRAM SSD, which first showed its applicability in the early 1980s.

Development

Flash development began in the mid-1980s when Dr. Fujio Masuoka, working for Toshiba, presented his invention to the

1984 IEEE Integrated Electronics Devices meeting held in San Jose, California, USA. It was not long before Intel recognized the tremendous potential and began production by introducing the first commercial NOR type flash chip in 1988. CompactFlash was originally based on it, though later cards moved to less expensive NAND flash. Toshiba announced NAND flash at a developers meeting in 1987.

The solid state disk (drive) had origins going back as far as the 1950 where two memory technologies (core memory and card capacitor read only store [CCROS]) were being used in vacuum tube-type computers. By 1987, a 16 kilobyte RAM-based solid state drive was introduced by Texas Memory Systems, with others, including StorageTek and Sharp. Showing implementations throughout the early to mid-1980s.

The introduction of flash-based SSD came in 1995, and by 2009 at 1 TB flash SSD was in the production chain offering 654 Mbytes/second (maximum) write speeds and 712 Mbytes/second (maximum) read speeds. The same year saw a 6 Gbits/second SATA interface SSD from Micron Technology.

Flash Memory Functionality

Data are stored in flash memory as an array of floating gate transistors called "cells." Each cell traditionally stores one bit of information. Subsequent generations of flash memory devices, referred to as multi-level cell devices, are capable of storing more than one bit per cell by varying the number of electrons placed on the floating gate of a cell. Manufacturers touted their respective products based upon how their particular versions of flash cell technologies were implemented.

Flash utilizes cell-based floating-gate transistors that will store a charge for an extended period of time, even when no power supply is connected (see Fig. 7.1). These memory cells are similar to an electronically programmable read-only memory (EPROM). The cell technology employs a thin oxide insulation that surrounds the floating gate and traps the charged electrons. This insulation prevents leakage, which is a loss of charge state once power is removed.

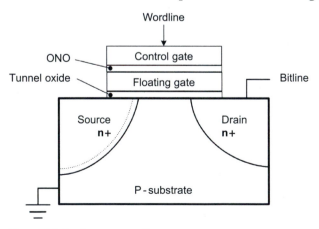

Figure 7.1 Flash memory cell.

Floating Gate Charges

The flash memory cell functions by storing a charge in the floating gate. The presence of charge determines whether the channel will conduct or not. During the read cycle, a logical 1 at the output corresponds to the channel being in its low resistance. This is referred to as its ON state. The control gate is used to charge up the gate capacitance during the write cycle.

Serial Access

Unlike the X-Y addressing in DRAM, flash access must be in serial fashion. Flash further relies on a controller to bring the data out of the chip and correctly present it to the processor.

NAND and NOR

Flash memory will be categorized like conventional logic. It can be either in a NOR-gate like configuration, first available around 1987, or as a NAND-gate model, which was developed in the 1988–1989 timeframe. Fundamentally, the distinctions between NOR and NAND are described by
- speed of access and/or erasure
- how individual memory cells are connected (NOR is parallel, NAND as serial)
- how read-write interfaces (page based versus randomly accessible) are facilitated

NOR-gate Flash

NOR flash memory requires a long time period for both its erase and write cycle operations. A positive attribute for NOR flash is that it provides full addressing to data buses, permitting random access reads and programming to any memory location. Furthermore, its value is that it will endure between 10,000 and 1,000,000 erase cycles.

NOR flash memory's drawback is that complete random access rewrite or erasure operations are inhibited because any individual memory cell's state can only be changed from its native state (as a logical 1) to its opposite state (a logical 0). Successive writes that change a cell's bit from logical 1 to logical 0 are permitted, but returning a single memory bit in a cell to its native state (logical 0) must be accomplished by an erasure of an entire block; that is, all the bits must revert to a logical 1.

Similar to common memory, the NOR read-only mode is provided by address and data bus mapping. Like other address-mapped memory, NOR flash memories can be used as execute-in-place (XiP) memory, behaving as a ROM memory mapped to a certain address. XiP memory is a requirement for most embedded systems.

The unlocking, erasing, and writing processes for NOR memory use special commands that are written to the first page of the mapped memory. As defined by Intel, the commands (called the "common flash interface") provide a list of all available commands to the physical driver. Apart from being used as a read-only memory (ROM), NOR-based flash memory may also be partitioned with a file system and may be further used in almost any solid state storage device.

NAND

NAND flash followed NOR development in 1989, which came principally from Samsung and Toshiba. NAND exhibits both faster erase and write times, higher density, and a lower cost-per-bit compared with NOR flash. NAND flash, also known as NAND-gate flash, endures 10 times the erase and write cycles of NOR flash. The core of most removable USB flash drives use the NAND flash memory format.

NAND flash's disadvantage is in its input/output (I/O) interface, which allows only sequential access to data. While this makes NAND suitable for mass-storage devices such as PC cards and various memory cards, some believe it is less useful for computer memory.

NAND flash uses tunnel injection for writing and tunnel release for erasing. Tunneling is the principle of injecting charge carriers (i.e., the electrons and holes of solid state physics) to an electrical conductor through a thin layer of an electric insulator. The I/O for NAND flash memory cells are not individually random accessible. Thus data, arranged as pages, must be addressed in blocks, much like how hard disk drives are organized. Reading and programming is accomplished on a page basis; however, erasure must occur in complete blocks.

NAND flash memories are incapable of providing execute-in-place (XiP) memory operations due to their physically different construction principles.

When executing software from NAND memory, virtual memory strategies are used. When used in this fashion, memory contents must be paged into memory-mapped RAM and then executed from there. This requirement makes the presence of a memory management unit (MMU) on the system a necessity.

NAND versus NOR

NOR flash has no shared components and is more expensive to produce. It is found mainly in consumer and embedded devices such as cell phones, smart devices, and PDAs.

NOR provides faster read speed and improved random access capabilities. However, NOR technologies, such as write and erase functions, are slow compared to NAND. NOR has a larger memory cell size than NAND, limiting scaling capabilities and therefore achievable bit density compared to NAND. Figure 7.2 shows the structures for NAND, AND, and NOR cells.

NAND offers fast write/erase capability but its sacrifice is that its read speed is slower than NOR. Nonetheless, NAND memory is more than sufficient for most consumer applications such as digital video, music, or data storage. Because of NAND's fast write/erase speed, its higher available densities, and its lower cost-per-bit compare with NOR, many feel that NAND memory makes it a more favorable technology for file storage, consumer applications, and SSD applications.

NAND offers over 5 Mbytes/second of sustained write performance. The block erase times are an impressive 2 ms for NAND versus 750 ms for NOR. While NAND has several significant positive attributes, it is not well-suited for direct random access.

Offering users the ability to rewrite data quickly and repeatedly, NAND is typically used for storing large quantities of information in devices such as flash drives, MP3 players, multifunction cell phones, digital cameras, and USB drives. NAND flash memory continues to increase its inroads into the enterprise storage domain, especially in applications such as SSD.

Cell Structures

An important consideration for enterprise users is whether NAND flash memory is of a single-level cell (SLC) or multi-level cell (MLC) configuration. Although the less-costly MLC flash can store twice, as two or more bits per cell and multiple levels of charge, it does not perform as well and is less reliable than SLC.

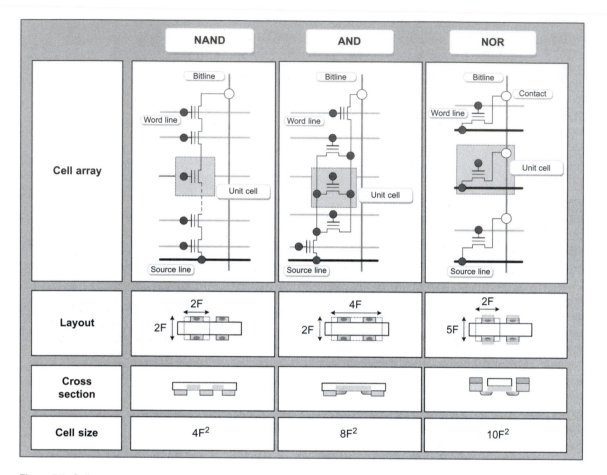

	NAND	AND	NOR
Cell array	Bitline, Word line, Unit cell, Source line	Bitline, Word line, Unit cell, Source line	Bitline, Contact, Word line, Unit cell, Source line
Layout	2F × 2F	4F × 2F	2F × 5F
Cross section			
Cell size	$4F^2$	$8F^2$	$10F^2$

Figure 7.2 Cell structures for NAND, AND, and NOR configurations.

Single-Level Cell

One of the preferred SSD technologies uses flash memory known as single-level cell (SLC). This technology is currently favored by many vendors producing storage systems aimed at enterprise-level data needs. In SLC NAND flash, each memory cell stores an analog representation of the data and two levels of charge.

SLC is said to be the dominant flash memory technology for SSD used in enterprise storage systems today, with estimates stating that SLC factors into more than 80% of enterprise-grade memory applications.

Multi-Level Cell

Multi-level cell (MLC) flash stores multiple bits per cell. MLC NAND, however, requires error correcting codes (ECC) to ensure

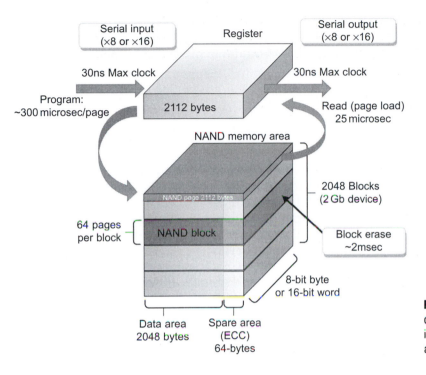

Serial input
(×8 or ×16)

Register

Serial output
(×8 or ×16)

30ns Max clock

30ns Max clock

Program:
~300 microsec/page

2112 bytes

Read (page load)
25 microsec

NAND memory area

2048 Blocks
(2 Gb device)

NAND page 2112 bytes

64 pages
per block

NAND block

Block erase
~2msec

8-bit byte
or 16-bit word

Data area
2048 bytes

Spare area
(ECC)
64-bytes

Figure 7.3 The NAND device's memory structures, input-output paths, and data area allocations.

data integrity. MLC NAND has the benefit of being cheaper due to the denser storage method used, but software complexity can be increased to compensate for a larger bit error ratio (BER).

NAND flash (see Fig. 7.3) includes extra storage on each page, found in a spare area of 64 bytes (16 bytes per 512-byte sector). This area stores the ECC code as well as other information like wear-leveling or logical-to-physical block mapping. ECC can be performed in hardware or software, but hardware implementation provides an obvious performance advantage.

Pages and Blocks

Groups of cells are organized into pages, the smallest structure that is readable/writable in a SSD, with four kilobyte pages standard on SSDs (refer to Figures 7.4 and 7.5).

Pages are grouped together into blocks. It is common to have 128 pages in a block, which is equal to 512 kB in a block. A block is the smallest structure that can be erased in a NAND-flash device, so while you can read from and write to a page, you can only erase a block (i.e., at 128 pages at a time). This is one of the most important parts of understanding SSDs.

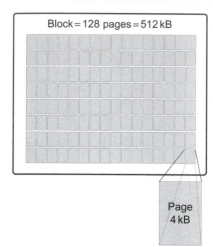

Block = 128 pages = 512 kB

Page 4 kB

Figure 7.4 Page/block arrangement for the NAND cell.

Figure 7.5 NAND cell block and plane arrangement.

Arrays of cells are grouped into a page; arrays of pages are grouped into blocks. Blocks are then grouped into planes. There are multiple planes on a single NAND-flash die. There can be multiple dies in a package (i.e., two or four per package), and multiple packages can be layered atop one another.

Error-Correcting Codes

Error-correcting codes are schemes that allow for the integrity of random data to be retained as the data are recovered from a storage system, transmission, or the like. The principal idea for achieving error detection and correction is to add redundancy in the form of extra data to a message. The device (e.g., a receiver) then uses this redundancy to check for the consistency in a delivered message or bit stream. Error-detection and correction schemes can be either systematic or non-systematic.

In data storage systems, the more common practices use such schemes as repetition codes, parity bits, check sums, cyclic redundancy checks (CRC), and error-correction codes (ECC). Providing schemes like ECC in hardware or software elevates the robustness of the system.

For MLC NAND memory, during a programming operation, the ECC unit calculates the error-correcting code based on the data stored in the sector. The ECC code for the respective data area is then written to the respective spare area. When the data are read out, the ECC code is also read, and the reverse operation is applied to check that the data are correct.

It is possible for the ECC algorithm to correct data errors. The number of errors that can be corrected will depend upon the correction strength of the algorithm used. Simple Hamming codes provide the easiest hardware implementation, but can only correct single-bit errors. Reed-Solomon codes can provide a more robust error correction and are used on many of today's controllers.

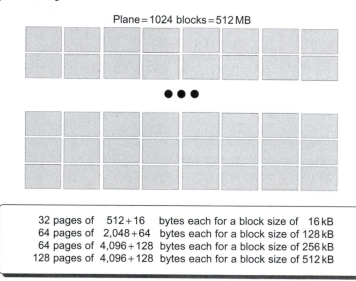

Plane = 1024 blocks = 512 MB

32 pages of	512 + 16	bytes each for a block size of 16 kB
64 pages of	2,048 + 64	bytes each for a block size of 128 kB
64 pages of	4,096 + 128	bytes each for a block size of 256 kB
128 pages of	4,096 + 128	bytes each for a block size of 512 kB

BCH codes (used to correct multiple random error patterns) are also popular due to their improved efficiency over Reed-Solomon.

Block Management

NAND flash's block management is provided by software, which is responsible for wear-leveling or logical-to-physical mapping. This software may also provide the ECC code if the processor does not include ECC hardware.

The large die size used in NAND fabrication results in some NAND devices shipping from the factory with some bad blocks. The software managing the device is responsible for mapping the bad blocks and replacing them with good blocks. These blocks are mapped in such a way that the software can scan all the blocks to determine where the good blocks and bad blocks are located. Initialization software simply scans through all the blocks to determine which are bad and then builds a table of bad blocks for future reference.

Special care must be given not to erase the bad-block marks originated by the factory. Some blocks marked bad at the factory may be functional at certain temperatures or voltages but could in other conditions fail sometime in the future. Once the bad-block information is erased, it cannot be recovered.

Preventing Wear Out

Given that NAND flash memory chips will wear out after successive writes, it is imperative that frequent data accesses do not occur on a single or limited number of flash chips. To mitigate this wearing out, flash SSD manufacturers incorporate solutions that abstract the physical storage layer from the logical layer. Though a computer system will write data to the same logical address every time, the software engineering of the flash controller will move the underlying physical address around to the least written blocks on flash memory chips or least written locations within the chip. This process is known as "wear leveling."

A unique characteristic of flash blocks is that if they are bad, writing to that block will fail. This problem is easily detected by the flash controller, which then will write the data to a different flash block and remove the bad block from any future write or read actions.

NAND Flash Memory Applications

Promoters and analysts say that single-level cell is the dominant flash solid state drive technology in enterprise storage systems. While SLC drives, which only store one bit of data

Table 7.1 SLC and MLC NAND Flash Characteristics

Function	SLC NAND Flash	MLC NAND Flash
Random read	25 µs	50 µs
Erase	2 ms/block	2 ms/block
Programming	250 µs	900 µs

per cell, are benchmarked as being longer-lasting and more reliable than MLC, the MLC drives store multiple pieces of data per cell; thus, they can deliver a higher storage capacity per unit area.

The use of MLC technology can lower the cost of memory storage systems, as was the case for memory cards (per examples in 2005); the final retail price of an MLC flash card was as much as one-third less than SLC cards of the same capacity. For consumer applications in video recording and playback, higher speed SLC flash offers no serious advantage, whereas the lower cost of MLC flash can be a significant asset. Table 7.1 compares the functional distinctions between SLC and MLC NAND flash.

Performance

The performance of flash memory typically considers three parameters:
- read speed
- write speed
- endurance

For consumer audio and video applications, read speed is important during the playback of stored audio and video, and is equally important in the retrieval of data files from mass storage. However, write speed is just as significant a factor in the recording of audio and video signals to ensure bits are not lost and that continuity of the images is consistent.

Endurance, described as the number of write/erase cycles a flash memory cell can tolerate, impacts the useable lifetime of a device. MLC flash memory meets or exceeds the requirements of consumer applications in all three categories.

Real-Time Video

One of the most demanding applications from the standpoint of read and write performance is the recording and playback of video and audio signals, such as in a digital camera or digital video recorder. Performance levels will depend on the video quality desired from the compression format and bit rates selected.

High-definition (HD) video signal recording may use either MPEG-2 or MPEG-4 compression, or other semi-proprietary or standardized compression schemes based on MPEG or other concepts.

MLC flash memory, for example, those made with a 90 nm process and using large-block architecture, achieve a read speed of up to 108 Mbits/second. This is fast enough for four times or faster playback speeds. With a write performance of up to 20 Mbits/second, real-time MPEG-2 video recording at HD quality is obtainable.

While SLC flash systems can have slightly higher read performance (e.g., up to 128 Mbits/second) and typical write performance of up to 45 Mbits/second, the performance differences do not necessarily add significant value in video recording or playback.

Audio Applications

Portable MP3 players fall well within the read and write performance of MLC flash. Even for full CD quality stereo, audio recording and playback will only require approximately 0.124 Mbits/second of storage bandwidth.

Access to Data

In any storage system, data access is a performance criterion that has a direct impact on the return on investment in terms of time, reliability, repeatability, support, and maintenance. SSDs are devices that can clearly change the perspectives regarding access.

Stress Testing

As a benchmark comparison, solid state disk access times can be as much as one hundred times faster than that of the fastest spinning hard disk drive.

To understand how the parameters surrounding data access are quantified, a stress test would be generated that exercises the storage components against known benchmarks from another system. In computer programming, the "Create, Read, Update, and Delete" (CRUD) model is used to test and evaluate persistent storage. This test model is sometimes modified to suit the particulars of the media that is being stressed. Database operations will often use stress test analysis because they will typically search for, retrieve, modify, and then replace data that are located all over the storage system or systems and, at the disk level, all over the surfaces of the drives themselves.

When analyzing performance in a database application, one stress test conducted over a 24-hours period involved both reading and writing in a sequential and random fashion with 4K, 8K, 16K, 32K, and 64K I/O block sizes structured with 25 different workloads. The claimed performance of one SSD was equivalent to the performance of 10–16 Fibre Channel hard disk drives.

SSD Latency

Latency is one of the biggest issues in assessing hard drive performance. Even with the newest forms of 2.5-in. HDD storage, the problem of latency in SSD becomes a non-issue. SSDs, when configured as RAM disks, have incredible IOPS (input–output operations per second) numbers, which fall on the order of 70,000 to upwards of 100,000–250,000 IOPS.

An average enterprise-class 15,000-RPM hard drive achieves between 350 and 400 IOPS. The average enterprise-class SSD pushes 80,000 IOPS, a 200-fold increase. Such performance benefits outweigh the cost differential in certain instances, particularly when factoring in savings from energy costs.

Applications requiring extremely fast location and/or retrieval of data, such as online credit-card transactions, video on demand, or information-heavy Web searches, will benefit from solid state technology.

Block-Locking Protection

Protection of the non-volatile data in a flash device has always been an important consideration. Flash memory products feature dynamic hardware block locking, which keeps critical code secure while non-locked blocks are programmed and erased.

The block-locking scheme offers two levels of protection. First, it allows software-only control of block locking, which is useful for data blocks that are frequently changed. The second protection level requires hardware interaction before locking can be changed. This aids in protecting infrequently changed code blocks.

Locking capabilities may be employed differently depending upon the product family.

Security

At the forefront of many applications is security. As an example, certain flash products may be equipped with two 64-bit one-time pad (OTP) protection registers. OTP registers are used to increase system security. Intel programs a unique, unchangeable 64-bit number into one of the OTP protection registers, and the end user (as desired) can program the other 64-bit register. Once programmed, the end user's segment can be locked to prevent further reprogramming. The OTP information can also be used as a small-encrypted security key for system authentication, or for manufacturing traceability.

Solid State Disk Applications

The use of flash memory and SSD has increased many fold since the period beginning around 2005.

Flash memory has some obvious advantages over DRAM or disk storage. Flash can store orders of magnitude more data in the same physical footprint as DRAM. Its reliability is extremely high, as much as 100 times better than a disk drive. Flash's access time is approaching 250 times that of spinning disks' access times.

RAM-Cache with Flash

When looking at system architectures, a mixture of RAM-cache with flash support is not uncommon. The combination of RAM and flash aids in balancing buffer speeds for an all SSD or flash-based storage subsystem.

Flash SAN

In this RAM-cache form, the application of RAM—with its extremely fast read and write performance—may support between 10% and 15% of the temporary storage cache, with the balance of the SAN utilizing flash only. This model will find that the RAM is used mainly for buffering, with the principle data content residing in non-volatile flash memory. Since flash can be read very fast, compared to its write times, moving assets from "permanent" flash storage to RAM can be managed on a demand basis. Populating the flash storage component can happen directly from the input stages of the storage system, or when demands or vulnerability warrant, by employing a combination of the RAM buffer into the flash memory.

SSD products now provide comparative performance capabilities to that of 15,000 RPM spinning disk SANs. In production as of mid-2009, this showcases how flash SANs compare to traditional spinning disk SANs, which offer sustained I/O rates of only around 300 IOPS.

Houston, Texas based Texas Memory Systems (TMS) offers a 5 TB flash SAN in a 2U chassis that draws less than 230 watts of power. The flash SAN utilizes SLC NAND flash to provide shareable, high-performance storage for IT organizations. TMS's RamSan-620 has extremely low latency, with sustained I/O rates up to 250,000 IOPS (at 4K block sizes) for reads or writes, with random bandwidth up to 3 Gbytes/second. The system employs dual ported 4-Gbit Fibre Channel controllers, or may be equipped with one to four DDR InfiniBand ports. Each flash card in the TMS RamSan-620 includes on-board RAID protection to protect against chip failure.

In addition, an advanced chip-level ECC provides multiple regions of bit correction per block. A more recent product (RamSan-63) features 4–10 TB of flash storage, with 500,000 IOPS and 8 Gbytes/second randomly sustained throughput. This unit consumes only 450 watts making this type of application ideal for lowering the total cost of operations (TCO) and for green data center storage environments.

Flash NAS

USB dongles are one of the more familiar applications of solid state memory technology. A typical implementation may be a USB 2.0 as an FTP server or Secure Digital (SD) card. Data transfer is in the area of 10 Mbytes/second with up to 2 TB of storage using a FAT32 file system.

Flash-Based Protection

Flash-based stores can be protected in similar means to their rotational spinning disk counter parts. RAID techniques, such as RAID-3 or RAID-5, are deployed using specially purposed single or dual controllers that manage the striping in similar fashion to RAID-3 for hard disks.

Video serving applications may employ the same kinds of RAID protection, usually in software, including ECC-parity and secondary hot standby drives or additional second parity drives. While complete mirroring, as in RAID 1, is another alternative, it carries with it double the cost.

Justification

There may still remain some arguments that are difficult to dismiss. Even with 64 Gbyte flash memory, in a single stage environment it may be hard to justify flash versus the cost of a single 1 TB hard disk drive. However, to gain the bandwidth and throughput necessary for a conventional professional or broadcast videoserver storage system, some still feel that other sets of components need to be included in addition to a dedicated or single SSD-array configuration.

Concurrent Users

One further justification is that when implementing solid state storage, one finds that it typically relieves I/O bottlenecks, which allows processors to run closer to maximum throughput. Conventional thinking suggests that adding concurrent users requires adding more servers, but with solid state storage (i.e., with SSD), the number of concurrent users scales as a result of improved server efficiency.

Flash-Only Solution

The "flash-only" solution may not yet be viable for those mission-critical, large file size systems found in broadcast play-out operations. However, new implementations for products using flash are being introduced that could change that landscape. These flash-based servers now make up components including supplemental edge servers, caches, or video on demand (VOD) applications.

Cost

Any time a reference to the cost of storage is printed, it can immediately be presumed as "out-of-date," just because the technology and the cost to manufacturer scale proportionately. That said, despite declining prices, SSDs remain far more expensive when put on a cost-per-gigabyte basis, at about 10 times that of a hard disk drive.

Nonetheless, depending on performance, SSDs can range in cost from $3 to $20 per gigabyte. Comparatively, hard drives range in price from 10 cents per gigabyte on the low end to between $2 and $3 per gigabyte for enterprise-level, 15,000-RPM models. This puts SSD versus HDD pricing at about 20:1 for the bottom end of both technologies. Analysts expect that this will stay in effect for the next several years.

In recent times, the cost of NAND memory has seen a 50% drop, but there is still little cost advantage when comparing bytes of HDD to bytes of SSD. However, the "cost-per-gigabyte" factor is not the most important one when looking at some of the access-heavy data center applications. Here, it is the cost per IOPS that becomes the benchmark to beat.

Portability and Green Perspectives

With operational costs high on the agenda of businesses, utilizing SSD technologies in certain applications will significantly reduce the power consumption for the physical storage system and for the supporting cooling requirements as well. Data centers are recognizing this, and where there are demands for access of data on a repeated basis, or for short-term cache activities, adding SSD RAM-disk devices will help reach these targets.

When portability is required, SSD power consumption becomes an equally important factor (see Table 7.2). SSD will use far less energy than traditional HDDs because there are no motors to drive in a SSD. It is true that the hard disk industry has

Table 7.2 Power Consumption of 2.5-in. SSD versus HDD

Function	SATA SSD Solid state	SATA HDD Standard	PATA HDD Extended Temp
Read	0.41 W	1.9 W	1.9 W
Write	0.41 W	1.9 W	1.7 W
Idle	0.32 W	0.60 W	0.99 W
Standby	0.24 W	0.13 W	0.26 W
Sleep	0.24 W	0.13 W	0.26 W

All power expressed in watts (W)
Source: Data from Samsung, Fujitsu, and Seagate

taken steps to address power requirements by implementing idle drive spin down, and through the development of hybrid HDDs, but even with these implementations, most regular HDDs will consume more power than a SSD.

Applications for SSD

The high-level storage performance, ruggedness, and reliability of MLC NAND flash technology will support the increased mobility and functionality of a wide range of consumer electronics and a growing number of professional video applications.

Online transactional processing, streaming video on demand, and even virtual desktop infrastructures (e.g., netbooks and tablet computers) can make excellent use of SSDs. The devices are available in the popular form factors and capacities exist for a variety of computer and memory applications. The 2.5- and 1.8-in. form factors found for many SSD devices help squeeze these devices into space-starved products.

Blade servers are using SSDs to increase throughput, and to reduce the footprint on a card-by-card basis. The rise in multicore processor blades is increasing the demand, and the viability, for SSD.

Late generation 32 nm NAND flash in mSATA and Half-Slim modules lay claims to providing greater design flexibility, as well as space and cost savings when compared to SSDs with hard disk drive form factors and cases. These kinds of modules are available in 1.8-in. form factors with capacities up to 128 Gbyte, helping to bring the performance advantages of SSDs to notebooks, portable electronics, and embedded systems.

Toshiba's high-performance HG3 series 32 nm solid state drives are available in capacities up to 512 Gbyte with sequential read speeds up to 250 Mbits/second, and these are useful for computing applications and a variety of other storage solutions.

Bitmicro's E-Disk technology offers 800 Mbytes/second full duplex burst rate and storage capacity of up to 1.1 TB in a Fibre Channel (4 Gbit, dual port) interface. A write endurance of over 76 years with 100 Gbytes/day erase/write cycles puts this kind of technology squarely in the face of the future.

Supplementing Video on Demand with SSD

Streaming movies to thousands of users is a daunting task requiring a high number of servers capable of delivering a huge volume of streaming media files. The challenges associated with video on demand (VOD) that related directly to performance problems include the high number of concurrent users and the randomness of content access.

VOD systems are prominent from hotels to cable systems to the Web. These installations are guaranteed to see periods where there will be a very high number of concurrent users, especially with new releases or specials. Streaming video is typically a relatively easy task for hard disk drive videoserver systems where sequential access to contiguous data is the only operation they are doing. Conversely, VOD does not result in sequential disk accesses. VOD allows users to access stunt features such as start, stop, pause, rewind, and fast-forward. Compound these issues with multiple concurrent users and access to the stream becomes completely random. This is the most stressful activity for VOD servers.

Moving the most highly accessed content to a SSD designed for video on demand can significantly reduce access issues. The SSD application, in this case, augments but does not necessarily replace the disk-based VOD system. This high-demand content can be shared across multiple VOD servers without contention. The additional SSD bandwidth provides a good fit for large VOD installations.

Set-Top Box and DVR Functionality

SanDisk and NDS, leading providers of technology solutions for digital pay-TV, announced in September 2010 that NDS successfully combined set-top box software and solid state drives enabling a new range of lower cost set-top boxes (STBs) with DVR-like functionality. The new solutions allow for the deployment of energy-efficient STBs with decreased power consumption, small form factors, and virtually silent operation.

The robust performance needed for video consumption, and the increased implementation of on-demand services, including progressive download and live-pause technologies, has been pushed forward with SSD. Furthermore, to facilitate simpler integration, SSDs are employing an industry standard SATA interface enabling straightforward design and integration for STB manufacturers.

Mobile devices, ultra-thin laptops (for example, the Apple MacBook Air) and numerous consumer and professional computing devices are replacing HDD with SSD. Flash devices are finding their way into data system accelerators. Anywhere where power and size are factors, SSDs are turning up. The trend is not expected to change anytime soon.

Further Readings

Solid State Drive Alliance (SSDA):
A trade organization, an international organization founded jointly by A-DATA,
  Allion, ASMedia, CoreSolid Storage, ITE, ITRI, JMicron, Phison, Silicon
  Motion, Silicon Power, Solid State System and TOSHIBA, whose purpose is to
  define, integrate and promote the SSD Compliance Standard.
  http://www.ssdalliance.org

SSDA Compliance Program
A program designed to give the consumer the confidence to buy SSD products
  with stable and reliable quality. SSDA established an industry known criteria
  for SSD product manufacturers to follow. Products that pass this level of
  acceptability are added to the Integrators List and have the right to license the
  SSDA Certified Logo.

Updated online posting of solid state drives can be found at Storage Search
  http://www.storagesearch.com/ssd.html

8

OPTICAL STORAGE MEDIA

Media that can be recorded to, removed, and then transported to another device has long been a dominant force in most of the entertainment industries, long before the emergence of the Internet, microwave communications, etc. Metallic, shellac–paper–wax-based composites, and polyvinyl chloride records were long considered the only durable (primarily consumer) means to exchange recorded music and voice among users. Analog audio tape became the next formidable method for the common exchange of media, and it was one of the earlier forms for easily recording, playing back, and rerecording data for computers.

Removable form factors used for storing computer data have been around for as long as data storage itself has. Punch cards and paper tape were two of the more prominent forms of media storage that began around the mid-1960s and remained in use in some places through the mid-1980s.

Today there are many more reliable, durable, and higher-density formats in use for the storage of computer data. We find those form factors to be in the shape of solid state memory, transportable spinning hard disk drives, data tape, videotape, holographic devices, and optical mediums. This chapter focuses primarily on the evolution of optical storage, which includes familiar recent developments such as Blu-ray Disc and less familiar forms, such as the early laser disc and holographic recording.

KEY CHAPTER POINTS

- Defining removable optical media along with the development of the compact disc (CD), DVD, laser disc, and Blu-ray Disc followed by the death of HD DVD
- Holographic media for data storage, its development and history, and how holograms are made for moving images and other data using various innovative technologies
- Guidelines for the care, storage, and handling of optical media

Defining Removable Media

Removable media that contains data may be divided into two broad categories: (1) those which are essentially self-contained storage systems (e.g., a USB stick, SSD memory card, a transportable hard disk, or a solid state drive) and (2) those which depend upon a secondary mechanical device that performs the read and/or write functions to and from physical media (e.g., a CD-ROM, DVD, or laser disc). These kinds of media are intended to be easily interchanged and can be stored in an off-line environment usually for indefinite periods of time.

Removable Hard Drives

Although it is certainly possible to remove the spinning hard drive from your personal computer by opening the chassis and disconnecting it from the rest of the computer, this is not a practical approach for most of the common applications for the physical exchange of media. Drive products that can be removed from a chassis and plugged into another chassis, which are actually hard drives and which differ in physical architecture from transportable drives, are still available and employed when high-volume data sets are needed. Such drives usually have no power supplies and cannot be directly connected with USB or eSATA connections. These drives are set into a transportable "sled" configuration and are often found in video or film-transfer production facilities that are not equipped with high-speed data links or in those that require the security of a lockable device that can be removed and then stored off-line in a vault or other secure location.

In this chapter, the storage methods discussed will define "removability" to apply to media that is routinely extracted from the record/playout device with a simple user action that does not involve technician level actions to achieve transportability. These fall principally into the categories of optical media, and potentially the recent offerings in holographic media captured in an optical fashion.

Optical Media Definitions

We are accustomed to using CDs and DVDs for a multitude of purposes, including media storage, gaming, music, and entertainment. They have been the replacement for linear tape for viewing, recording, or listening to music, home movies, or theatrical motion pictures. Optical storage has evolved over the course of the last few decades to become the quintessential formats of choice for the storage of physical data on media that is durable and low cost.

Most users were only familiar with a relatively finite set of optical media types until about the mid-to-late 1990s when significant changes in optical formats allowed for a new generation of recording features and storage options. To begin, we will first look at defining and categorizing these forms of optical media by their technical names and properties.

Terminologies with Misconceptions

DVD, discs, and disks: these are three common terms in the physical media storage universe that are misused or confused on occasion. To set the record straight, as represented by industry accepted terminology, we will now hopefully clarify these terms according to ISO/IEC definitions instead of industry rhetoric.

Disc

Starting with the most common mistake, the usage and spelling of the words "disk" and "disc" are still confusing to many. Essentially, the spelling "disc" (with the ending "c") grew from reference to the CD, a spin-off of Laserdisc technology.

A disc refers to optical media, such as an audio CD, CD-ROM, DVD-ROM, DVD-RAM, or DVD-Video disc. Some discs are read-only (ROM), others allow you to burn content (write files) to the disc once (such as a CD-R or DVD-R, unless you do a multisession burn), and some can be erased and rewritten over many times (such as CD-RW, DVD-RW, and DVD-RAM discs).

All discs are removable, meaning that when you unmount or eject the disc from your desktop or Finder, it physically comes out of your computer. The media can then be shelved, moved to another device, placed into a jukebox, or kept in an archive or library environment for backup or data protection purposes.

Disk

When spelled with the ending letter "k", disk refers to magnetic media, including the outdated floppy disk, a computer's hard disk drive, external hard drives, the components of disk arrays, and the ever familiar term RAID (Redundant Array of Independent Disks). Disks will always be rewritable unless intentionally write-protected, locked, or damaged. Disks may also be partitioned in two or more volumes and may be virtualized for mass storage and collaborative functions.

To protect the fragile nature of the disk's recording surfaces and heads, most disks will be sealed inside a metal or plastic casing that houses most of the mechanisms, electronics, and firmware, collectively making up what is best known as a "hard (disk) drive" (HDD).

CD Technology

Sony demonstrated its first optical digital audio disc in September 1976. By 1979, Sony and Philips Consumer Electronics had established a joint task force to develop and design a new digital audio disc. A year later, the Red Book would be produced, which would become the Compact Disc standard, officially called Compact Disc-Digital Audio (CD-DA) for audio.

Audio CDs have been in commercial or consumer use since October 1982. Standard CDs, whose diameter is 120 mm, can store up to 799 Mbytes of data, essentially up to 80 min of uncompressed audio. A smaller version referred to as the Mini CD will have diameters ranging from 60 to 80 mm. The Mini CD was popular for singles, advertisements, and device drivers, with an audio capacity of up to 24 min. An even smaller business card-sized rectangular CD with sizes ranging from 85×54 mm to 86×64 mm holds about 10–65 Mbytes of CD-ROM data for around 6 min of audio storage.

This disc technology expanded to encompass data storage (CD-ROM), write-once audio and data storage (CD-R), rewritable media (CD-RW), video compact discs (VCDs), super video compact discs (SVCDs), photo CD, picture CD, CD-i, and enhanced CD.

Audio is almost always compressed before recording to a CD, often in formats such as AAC or MP3.

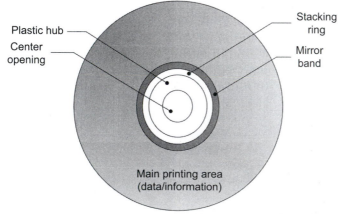

Plastic hub

Center opening

Stacking ring

Mirror band

Main printing area (data/information)

Figure 8.1 Optical compact disc component layout.

CD Components

The physical media is an almost pure polycarbonate plastic 1.2 mm in thickness and 15 to 20 g in weight. Moving from the disc center outward, the components include the following: the center spindle hole, the first-transition area (i.e., the clamping ring), the clamping area (stacking ring), the second-transition area (mirror band), the information (data) area, and the rim (see Fig. 8.1).

A thin layer of aluminum (a silvery white member of the boron group of chemical elements, with symbol Al and atomic number 13) or, more rarely, gold (symbol Au) is applied to the disc surface, making it reflective. The aluminum layer is protected by a film of lacquer that is normally spin-coated directly onto the reflective layer. A label may be printed onto this lacquer layer.

The data storage makeup for the CD is comprised of a series of tiny indentations known as "pits," which are encoded in a spiral track molded into the top of the polycarbonate layer. Each pit is approximately 100 nm deep by 500 nm wide and will vary between 850 nm and 3.5 μm in length. Lands separate the areas between the pits.

The distance between the tracks is called the pitch, which for the CD is 1.6 μm. CDs are read by focusing a 780 nm wavelength (near infrared) from a semiconductor laser through the bottom of the polycarbonate layer. The change in height between pits appears as ridges by the laser, and the lands produce an intensity difference in the reflected laser light. A photodiode pickup sensor measures the intensity changes, producing "read" data from the disc.

NRZI Encoding: Non-return-to-zero inverted (NRZI) encoding is used to produce the binary data representation. The reflection intensity changes that are measured from pit to land or land to pit will indicate a binary one. No change indicates one or more zeros. At least two, but no more than ten, zeros between each one is defined by the length of the pit. In turn, the data is decoded by reversing the eight-to-fourteen modulation used in mastering the disc, and then reversing the Cross-Interleaved Reed-Solomon Coding, which reveals the raw data stored on the disc.

Recordable Compact Disc (CD-R)

This format, which stands for Compact Disc-Recordable, is an extension of the CD format that allows data to be recorded only once on a disc. The process used is called dye sublimation (explained shortly). CD-R is defined in Part II of the Orange Book standard, the set of specifications created by Philips and Sony that define the optical signal characteristics, physical arrangement, writing methods, and testing conditions for CD-R and CD-RW (Orange Book Part III) discs.

Digital Versatile Disc

Digital Versatile Disc is the proper name for the familiar DVD nomenclature, contrary to the belief that the disc was used primarily for video storage and often mistakenly called "digital video disk (disc)." The development of the recordable DVD has progressed to include both single layer (SL) and dual layer (DL) discs. Table 8.1 describes DVD capacities, data rates and rotational speed parameters.

Table 8.1 DVD Capacities and Drive Speeds

	DVD Capacity		
Disc Type	Data Sectors	Capacity (Bytes)	Capacity (Gbytes)
DVD-R SL	2,298,496	4,707,391,808	4.7
DVD+R SL	2,295,104	4,707,372,992	4.7
DVD-R DL	4,171,721	8,543,666,176	8.5
DVD+R DL	4,173,824	8,547,991,552	8.5

	DVD Drive Speeds and Data Rates		
Drive Speed	Data Rate (Mbytes/second)	Data Rate (Mbits/second)	Write Time DVD+R SL
1X	1.32	10.56	60
2X	2.64	21.12	30
4X	5.28	42.24	15
8X	10.56	84.48	7.5
16X	21.12	168.96	3.75
20X	26.40	211.20	3.00
22X	29.04	232.32	2.73
24X	31.68	253.44	2.50

SL, Single layer; DL, Dual layer.

Physical versus Application Formats

One of the things to understand in this technology is the differences between the physical formats (such as DVD-ROM and DVD-R) and the application formats (such as DVD-Video and DVD-Audio). The DVD-ROM is a base format that holds data, whereas DVD-Video (more often simply a DVD) defines how video programs (usually theatrical releases of motion pictures) are stored on disc and played back using a DVD-Video player or a DVD drive in a personal computer.

The difference is similar to that between a CD-ROM and an audio CD. The DVD-ROM (DVD-read only memory) family includes these recordable variations:
• DVD-R/RW
• DVD-RAM
• DVD+R/RW
with the application formats including the following:
• DVD-Video
• DVD-Video Recording (DVD-VR)
• DVD+RW Video Recording (DVD+VR)
• DVD-Audio Recording (DVD-AR)

- DVD-Audio (DVD-A)
- Super Audio CD (SACD).

Other special application formats for gaming have also been created for console devices such as the Sony PlayStation 2 and Microsoft's Xbox.

DVD-R

This is the familiar short name for Digital Versatile Disc-Recordable. A DVD-R allows data to be written to the media once and then read many times. DVD-R uses the dye-sublimation recording technology and conforms to ISO/IEC DIS 23912:2005: Information Technology that specifies the quality of the prerecorded, unrecorded, and recorded signals, the format of the data, the format of the information zone, the format of the unrecorded zone, and the recording method. The 80-mm nominal diameter disc has a capacity of 1.46 Gbytes per side, and the 120-mm version holds 4.71 Gbytes per side. The disc may be manufactured as either single or double sided. A 9.4-Gbyte dual layer (DL) version (DVD-R DL) was introduced in 2005.

The full ISO/IEC 23912:2005 specification for DVD-R provides information about the conditions for conformance, the environments in which the disc is to be operated and stored, the mechanical and physical characteristics of the disc, and the definitions and requirements for the mechanical interchange between data processing systems. The document further defines the physical disposition of the tracks and sectors, the error correcting codes, and the coding method used.

For interchange, ISO/IEC 23912:2005 further defines the characteristics of the signals recorded on the disc, which enables data processing systems to read the data from the disc, the interchange of discs between disc drives, the standard for volume, and file structure. It also provides the specifications for full data interchange between data processing systems.

Dye Sublimation and Manufacturing

The DVD manufacturing and duplication processes use a printing technique called dye sublimation, which employs heat to transfer dye onto a medium such as a plastic card, paper, or fabric. When mass duplicating the DVD, an original master disc is turned into an etched glass master through the use of a laser beam recorder (LBR). The master is used to create molded, stamped, and later lacquered discs. The steps of the manufacturing process include the following: injection molding, dye coating, edge cleaning, drying, sputtering, bonding glue, online scanning, prewriting (for DVD-R only), printing, and packaging.

DVD+R

The short name for Digital Versatile Disc+Recordable, DVD+R is a format for a recordable DVD, which also uses dye-sublimation recording technology. DVD+R conforms to ISO/IEC 17344:2005: Information Technology—Data interchange on 120-mm and 80-mm optical disc using the "+R" format. Data capacities are the same as DVD-R at 4.7 Gbytes (120 mm) and 1.46 Gbytes (80 mm) per side.

The DVD+R format allows data to be written once to the disc, but can be read from many times. The disc is suitable to applications such as non-volatile data storage, audio, or video. A DVD+R disc is incompatible with the older DVD-R standard and can be found in both single layer (SL) and dual layer (DL) variants.

DVD-RW

The rewritable (RW) format of the DVD family, formally called the Digital Versatile Disc-ReWritable. This format uses phase change recording technology conforming to ISO/IEC 17342:2004: Information technology—80 mm (1.46 Gbytes per side) and 120 mm (4.70 Gbytes per side). DVD-RW media allows for data to be written to the disk several hundred times and read many times.

DVD+RW

The RW in the suffix stands for DVD+ReWritable, a format of a rewritable DVD disc that uses phase change recording technology and conforms with ISO/IEC 17341:2005. +RW format has a capacity of 4.70 Gbytes (120 mm) and 1.46 Gbytes (80 mm) per side.

DVD+RW is an erasable format that is based on CD-RW technology. It is not supported by the DVD Forum despite some of the member companies still backing it. The format uses a high-frequency wobbled groove that provides for highly accurate sector alignment during the recording process. There is no embossed addressing information like that found in other recording mediums. For this DVD+RW format, data can be written to and read many times from the disc. Most DVD+RW drives will also write to CD-R and CD-RW media.

Differences between "- or +" RW

The DVD-RW and DVD+RW technologies are similar in nature with the -RW using the wobbled groove and the +RW using the high-frequency wobbled groove. The +RW Version 2.0 will format as either CAV or CLV, whereas the -RW is limited to CLV.

The -RW format is specifically suited for audio and video recording (but not for computer data storage or backup), whereas +RW can be used for both data and audio/video.

"Plus" Formats

The former DVD+RW Alliance was brought together as a group of electronic hardware, optical storage, and software manufacturers who in 1997 created and promoted a format standard of recordable and rewritable DVDs, known as the "plus" format. As of 2004, plus format DVDs were available in three forms: DVD+R, DVD+RW, and DVD+R DL. In late 2005, DVD+RW DL (dual layer) was released. With that and the emergence of Blu-ray Disc and HD DVD, the development of the DVD as an essentially sustainable media has ceased.

The Alliance had two major working groups. The DVD+RW Product Promotions Group was responsible for the promotion work of the Alliance for the plus format products. The DVD+RW Compatibility and Convergence Group was responsible for working on those technical issues related to the compatibility between the various hardware products using the plus format.

At the time of its formation, the alliance members included the following:

Dell Computer Corporation
Hewlett-Packard (HP) Company
Mitsubishi Chemical Corporation
Royal Philips Electronics N.V.
Ricoh Company, Ltd.
Sony Corporation
Thomson SA (RCA)
Yamaha Corporation

The unofficial site that represented this Alliance, http://www.dvdplusrw.org states that it dedicated to the DVD+RW and DVD+R format. Furthermore, the organization states it is "by far the largest independent online source for DVD+RW information."

Blu-ray Disc

Blu-ray Disc (BD) is a high-density physical media format with a capacity of 25 Gbytes per layer, which uses a blue-ultraviolet laser and a 0.1-mm data depth. The much thinner cover layer enables higher bit densities, but its manufacturing processes required that significant changes to production equipment be made.

Initially, Blu-ray was intended for consumer/home recording, professional recording, and data storage. The first release of a Blu-ray disc recorder by Sony (in Japan, April 2003) was designed for home recording only and worked only with Japan's digital HD broadcast system. Later on, the development of a read-only format, called BD-ROM, enabled and promoted the mass market distribution of prerecorded movies.

The principal Blu-ray backers were Dell, Hitachi, HP, LG, Panasonic, Philips, Pioneer, Mitsubishi, Samsung, Sharp, Sony, and Thomson (see Table 8.2 for the various Blu-ray disc formats and drive speeds).

Technical Details for Blu-Ray Disc

The base Blu-ray Disc format has a capacity of 25 Gbytes (per layer) and employs a 0.1-mm recording depth as a method to reduce aberration from disc tilt. The laser is a 405-nm blue-violet semiconductor with 0.85 NA (numerical aperture) lens design to provide 0.32-μm track pitch (which is half of what the pitch of a DVD is)

Table 8.2 Blu-ray Disc Specifications

Blu-ray Disc Capacity				
Disc Type	Disc Diameter (cm)	Capacity (Gbytes)	Capacity (Mebibytes)	Capacity (Bytes)
Standard SL	12	25	23,866	50,050,629,632
Standard DL	12	50	46,742	4,707,372,992
Mini SL	8	7.8	7,430	77,91,181,824
Mini DL	8	15.6	14,860	15,582,363,648

Blu-ray Disc Speed				
Drive Speed	Data Rate (Mbytes/second)	Data Rate (Mbits/second)	Write Time (min) BD SL	BD DL
1X	4.5	36	90	180
2X	9	72	45	90
4X	18	144	22.5	45
6X	27	216	15	30
8X	36	288	11.25	22.5
10X	45	360	9	18
12X	54	432	7.5	15

SL, Single layer; DL, Dual layer.
Write times (in minutes) should be considered theoretical.

and as little as 0.138-μm pit length. Figure 8.2 compares additional technical format differences (such as wavelength, capacity, and ratio of capacity) between the DVD and the Blu-ray disc formats.

Variations include 23.3-Gbyte capacity with 0.160-μm minimum pit length (used by Sony's Professional Disc system) and 25-Gbyte capacity with 0.149-μm minimum pit length. The physical discs use phase-change groove recording on a 12-cm diameter, 1.2-mm thick disc, similar to DVD-RW and DVD+RW. The data transfer rate is 36 Mbits/second. The recording capacity for a single layer is about 2 hours of HD video (at 28 Mbits/second) or about 10 hours of standard definition video (at 4.5 Mbits/second).

The two base formats for Blu-ray are called Blu-ray Disc Rewritable (BD-RE) and Blu-ray Disc Recordable (BD-R).

Increased Capacity Specifications

Sharp promoted a Blu-ray disc type with a recording capacity based on the BDXL specification created by the Blu-ray Disc Association's member companies, which allows for discs with capacities as high as 128 Gbytes.

The current Blu-ray Discs offer a dual-layer format for capacities up to 50 Gbytes. This new technology allows for triple (100 Gbytes) and quadruple (128 Gbytes) layer discs. In an optical disc recording, the storage capacity of the disc is principally determined by the spot size, which is proportional to the light-source wavelength λ and inversely proportional to the numerical aperture (NA) of the objective lens. Thus, capacity is in inverse proportion to the square of spot size.

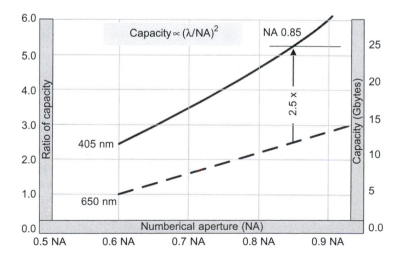

Figure 8.2 Comparison of DVD (= 650 nm) to Blu-ray (= 650 nm) Disc in terms of wavelength, capacity, and ratio of capacity (information provided by the Blu-ray Disc Association).

The latest technology has discs with 100-Gbyte recording capacities (launched only in Japan) as of July 2010 and with a player (from Sharp) that will handle the format also introduced in Japan only. These versions had no other scheduled delivery plans outside of Japan as of October 2010.

Development is expected to continue, with progress made in additional formats and multilayered technologies.

Higher Density Multilayer

In response to meeting the promises of the Blu-ray Disc made when the format was first released in 2003, the Blu-ray Disc Association announced the BDXL and IH-BD formats. Both BDXL and IH-BD are specially designed formats with specific market segments in mind. Newly designed hardware is required to playback or record BDXL or IH-BD media. However, because the new media specifications are extensions of current Blu-ray Disc technology, future BDXL and IH-BD devices can be designed to support existing 25-Gbyte and 50-Gbyte Blu-ray Discs.

Note that for PlayStation users, there is no hope that a firmware update will save the Playstation 3 (PS3) this time.

BDXL

In April 2010, the Blu-ray Disc Association announced a new BDXL (High Capacity Recordable and Rewritable disc) format capable of storing up to 128 Gbytes (write-once) or 100 Gbytes (rewritable). The BDXL format is known also as BD-RE Version 3.0; it also carries the tag "TL" (triple layer). The wavelength of the LD remains 405 nm, with the first two individual cover layer thicknesses (L0 = 100 μm and L1 = 75 μm) also the same as SL and DL BD-RE Version 2.1. The third layer, L2, has a cover layer thickness of 57 μm.

The minimum mark length for BD-RE is 149 nm, and for BDXL it is 112 nm. The data transfer rate is the same as the higher end of BD-RE, at 72 Mbits/second, with the write speed for media at 2×.

The format requires a new player to access these discs since the format goes three or four layers deep and will likely require a more powerful laser. Aimed at mass storage for corporate data uses, who are currently still using other mediums for archiving (e.g., LTO or DLT tape), this disc hopes to be a new permanent archive option, along with the new Intra-Hybrid Blu-ray Discs (IH-BD), designed with one 25-Gbytes read-only layer and one 25-Gbytes rewritable layer on the same platter.

IH-BD

The Intra-Hybrid Blu-ray Disc (IH-BD) incorporates a single BD-ROM layer and a single BD-RE layer so as to enable the user to view, but not overwrite, critical published data while providing the flexibility to include relevant personal data on the same physical disc. This lets consumer specific applications, in which combining published content with related user data on a convenient, single volume is desirable, move forward with these new features.

Both the ROM and the RE layers on IH-BD discs provide 25-Gbytes of capacity.

HD DVD

Blu-ray Disc's format competition was the now defunct HD DVD (High-Definition/Density DVD), developed by Toshiba. HD DVD's first consumer-based release was in Japan on March 31, 2006, with the United States joining on April 28, 2006. Although their product introduction beat Blu-ray by nearly three months, it was not long before HD DVD was found to be rejected by consumers and eventually the studios and others stopped supporting it.

Before 2003, when the DVD Forum had selected Toshiba's Advanced Optical Disc (AOD) format as the successor to DVD, the company promised it would be finished sooner than Sony's Blu-ray. The DVD Forum subsequently renamed the Toshiba format "HD DVD" to associate it with the DVD product. Meanwhile, Sony continued its work on Blu-ray, even though their efforts looked significantly behind. The Blu-ray technologies, which included the blue-ultraviolet laser change, would require extensive retooling of the manufacturing lines. Thus, it was believed that HD DVD would reach the market faster and cheaper in essence because of its similarities to the DVD player assembly, as well as the support that came from Microsoft on the PC desktop, which also added the format in its Xbox 360 game console.

The Walt Disney Company's then CEO Michael Eisner sold HDi (once called "iHD") and the Windows Media Digital Rights Management (DRM), hoping again to gain studio acceptance. On the surface, it looked as though Microsoft now had the time, technology, and studio deals on its side, whereas the Blu-ray technology was falling further behind and was complicated even more by both its new manufacturing requirements for the disc and the player and its floundering support from the studios.

The entire competitive landscape was frequently compared with the Betamax/VHS format battles of the 1980s that created a format war that confused and irritated consumers.

Figure 8.3 Format for Selected Optical Recording Media Globally

FORMAT	BACKERS	DATA DEPTH	VIDEO	AUDIO	CAPACITY (SL)	CAPACITY (DL)	DATA RATE	LASER
Blu-ray (BD)	Blu-ray Disc Association (BDA)	0.1 MM	MPEG-2 HD H.264 VC-1	PCM, Dolby Digital+ DTS HD	27 GB	50 GB	36 Mbits/sec	Blue (405 NM)
HD DVD	DVD Forum	0.6 MM	MPEG-2 SD/HD H.264 VC-1	PCM, Dolby TrueHD (MLP) MPEG-2 HD, H.264, VC-1	15 GB (ROM) 20 GB (RECORD)	30 GB (ROM) 40 GB (RECORD)	36 Mbits/sec	Blue (405 NM)
WMV HD	Microsoft	0.6 MM	WMV9	WMA9	4.7 GB STANDARD DVD	8.5 GB STANDARD DVD	2 Mbits/sec	Red (650 NM)
EVD	eWorld (Gov't of China)	0.6 MM	MPEG-2 HD (Later AVS)	ExAC	N/A	8.5 GB (ROM)	22 Mbits/sec	Red (650 NM)
FVD	AOSR/ITRI (Taiwan)	0.6 MM	WMV9 (1280 x 720)	WMA9	6 GB	11 GB	25.05 Mbits/sec	Red (650 NM)

It became obvious by the end of 2004 that Toshiba would not be delivering their HD DVD a year ahead of Blu-ray as promised. The industry began to view Blu-ray as more credible, despite the DVD Forum's continued commitment to HD DVD. Sony had successfully developed more hardware partnerships than Toshiba, which remained the only significant manufacturer of HD DVD players. The struggle by Toshiba continued, and by 2005, there was speculation that the company was ready to drop HD DVD and join the Blu-ray consortium, but Microsoft pushed to continue with the plan.

The first HD DVD players still were not ready until early 2006. Blu-ray players would debut just a few short weeks after the HD DVD players were launched. However, by year end 2006, Microsoft had begun selling an external HD DVD player (which cost approximately $200) for the Xbox 360 at about the same time Sony introduced its PlayStation 3 with an integrated Blu-ray player.

The Obsoleteness of HD DVD

The industry had heavily backed Blu-ray; but in fairness, Microsoft had worked equally to create the perception that HD DVD was a viable product. The reason, many believe, is that the HD DVD platform would be Microsoft's last effort to gain adoption of its VC-1 (by now a SMPTE Standard) and HDi (formerly iHD) standards, and its implementation of the Advanced Content interactivity layer in the HD DVD, which they used in the Xbox 360 HD DVD add-on, as well as stand-alone HD DVD players.

Microsoft was further unsuccessful in getting WinCE into other embedded markets (ranging from music players to hand-held computers to smart phones) and had similarly failed to establish Windows Media as a download format against ISO's AAC and H.264, popularized by Apple's iTunes.

In a final act of desperation, HD DVD managed to sign up Paramount and DreamWorks as new exclusive movie studios for HD DVD, pitting roughly half of the motion picture studios behind each of the two rival formats. Warner Bros. was unique in that it offered titles in both formats. Right or wrong, Microsoft's efforts to prolong the format war had nothing to do with the players or the media; it was driven by the promotion of its proprietary software for platforms that were already segregated by the marketplace.

Confused by the format uncertainty, there were slow sales across the board. With Microsoft's refusal to cooperate, Warner Bros. then announced a pullout of HD DVD just prior to the Consumer Electronics Show (CES), which destroyed the momentum of

Microsoft's HD DVD marketing push at what is the largest annual consumer electronics showcase for new products. Not long after this, retailers including Wal-Mart withdrew support for HD DVD, putting their support behind Blu-ray.

With the obsoleteness of HD DVD, the strategy behind Microsoft's aspiration to inject its hand strongly into media development was deflated, plus it caused a huge hole in the VC-1 standard despite the fact that it had already been written into the Blu-ray standard along with H.264. Blu-Ray developers were moving toward H.264, which allowed them to master progressive scan HD discs; in addition, in the high stakes of consumer electronics, H.264 would ultimately drive the higher performance 1080p screens, dubbed "true HD" (for marketing purposes only), and change the course of movie watching all over again.

H.264 would become the replacement for MPEG-2 as a compression technology that would allow delivery to mobile devices, as well as downloadable versions using the same codec for playback on devices such as the PSP and iPod. Blu-ray Disc would enable the much desired digital rights management (DRM) needed to satisfy the studios, which along with High-Definition Multimedia Interface (HDMI Version 1.3 and beyond) would add insurance to the copy protection the studios demanded through High-bandwidth Digital Content Protection (HDCP).

Holographic Storage

Holographic storage is truly a form of solid state storage that uses optical technologies and a polycarbonate plastic-like media for containing the data. Employing the same principles as those in producing holograms, laser beams are used to record and read back computer-generated data that is stored in three dimensions. The target for this technology is to store enormous amounts of data in the tiniest amount of space.

Holography breaks through the density limits of conventional storage by recording through the full depth of the storage medium. Unlike other technologies that record one data bit at a time, holography records and reads over a million bits of data with a single flash of laser light. This produces transfer rates significantly higher than current optical storage devices. Holographic storage combines high storage densities and fast transfer rates, with a durable low-cost media at a much lower price point than comparable physical storage materials.

The flexibility of the technology allows for the development of a wide variety of holographic storage products that range from consumer handheld devices to storage products for the enterprise. Holographic storage could offer 50 hours of high-definition video on a single disk, storage of 50,000 songs on media that is the size of a postage stamp, or half a million medical X-rays on a credit card.

Technology for Holographic Data Recording

Light from a single laser beam is split into two beams, the signal beam (which carries the data) and the reference beam. The hologram is formed where these two beams intersect in the recording medium. The diagram in Fig. 8.4 shows the schematic view of both the write and read functions for holographic recording and reproduction.

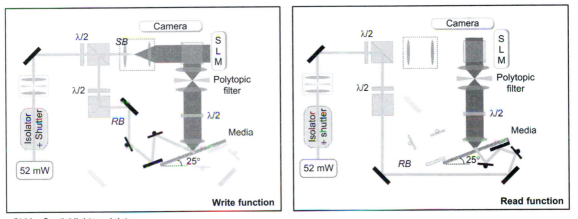

SLM = Spatial light modulator
Reading → Reference beam (RB) only is required for reading
Writing → Reference beam (RB) + signal beam (SB) both used for writing

Figure 8.4 Schematic of holographic storage showing write and read functions.

WORM and Rewritable

Holographic media can be "write once-read many" (WORM), where the storage medium undergoes some irreversible change, and "rewritable" where the change is reversible. Rewritable holographic storage is achieved via the photorefractive effect typically found in crystals. Data that is written to a holographic device occurs with a single flash of the laser, effectively in parallel, which is unlike current storage technologies that must record and read one data bit at a time. The system works through the principles of mutually coherent light that comes from two sources that are blended to create an interference pattern in the media, that is, areas that are light and areas that are dark.

Holograph Recording Physics

In the areas where there is constructive interference, the light is bright. In this region, electrons are promoted from the valence band to the conduction band of the material, given that the light has relinquished the electrons' energy to cross the energy gap. Positively charged vacancies are called holes. The holes must be immobile in rewritable holographic materials.

Where there is destructive interference, the amount of light is far less, thus much fewer electrons are promoted.

Electrons in the conduction band are free to move in the material. Their movements are determined by two opposing forces presented to the electrons. The first force is the Coulomb force between the electrons and the positive holes that they have been promoted from. The force either drives the electrons to stay where they are or it moves them back to their original location. The second force is a pseudo force or diffusion that encourages movement to areas where electrons are less dense. When the Coulomb forces are not too strong, electrons will move into the dark areas.

The strength of the hologram is impacted by the recombination factors deciding whether or not a hole moves back to a valance band. Immediately after being promoted (i.e., a result of the Coulomb forces), there is a possibility that a given electron will be found to recombine with a hole and thus move back into the valence band. The faster the rate of recombination the fewer the number of electrons that have this opportunity to move into the dark areas. After some electrons have moved into the dark areas and recombined with those holes, a permanent space-charge field between the electrons that moved to the dark spots and the holes in the bright spots is left. This electro-optical effect leads to a change in the index of refraction.

Only a reference beam is necessary for the information to be retrieved, which is "read out" from the hologram. The reference beam is sent into the material in a way precisely identical to when the hologram was first written. As a result of the index changes in the material that were created during writing, the beam splits into two parts. One beam part recreates the signal beam where the information is stored, which is not unlike the way a CCD imager converts its information into a more usable form.

Theoretically, holograms are capable of storing one bit per cubic block, equal to the size of the wavelength of light used in writing its data. For example, 632.8-nm wavelength light from a red-laser could store 4 Gbits/mm³. However, in actuality, the data density would be far lower, due in part to the need for adding error-correction, imperfections in the optical systems, costs of producing a "perfect" medium, and other technology and manufacturing limitations.

Write Functions

The process for encoding data onto the signal beam is accomplished by a device called a spatial light modulator (SLM). The SLM translates the electronic data of 0s and 1s into an optical "checkerboard" pattern of light and dark pixels. The data are arranged in an array or page of over one million bits. The exact number of bits is determined by the pixel count of the SLM.

At the point where the reference beam and the data carrying signal beam intersect, the hologram is recorded in the light sensitive storage medium. A chemical reaction occurs causing the hologram to be stored into the media. By varying the reference beam angle or media position with minute slight offsets, layers of hundreds of unique holograms are recorded in the same volume of material (see Fig. 8.5 for the write function in pictorial form).

Reading Data

In order to read back the data, the reference beam deflects off the hologram, in turn reconstructing the stored information. This hologram is projected onto a detector that reads the entire data page of over one million bits all at once. This distinguishing principle of parallel read-out provides holography with its fast transfer rates (see Fig. 8.6 for the read function in pictorial form).

Holographic Innovations

Although no one has successfully mass marketed this technology, vendors have been working on the commercialization of the technologies for well over a decade. The best known, most publicized development and line of products came from InPhase Technologies. Originally founded in December 2000 as a Lucent Technologies venture that spun out of Bell Labs research, InPhase worked on a holographic storage technology capable of storing in excess of

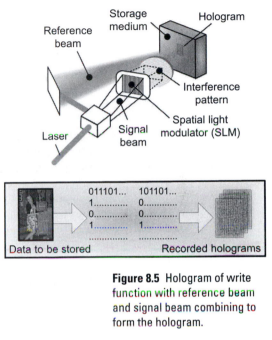

Figure 8.5 Hologram of write function with reference beam and signal beam combining to form the hologram.

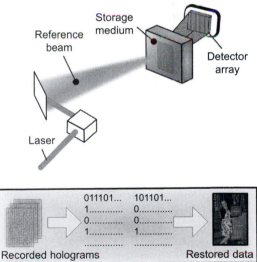

Figure 8.6 Hologram data recovery uses only the single reference beam and the detector array.

200 Gbytes of data, which could be written four times faster than the speed of current DVD drives.

Demonstration

Partners in developing, using, and testing the technology have included Turner Broadcasting System (TBS), who in conjunction with InPhase and the Hitachi Maxell prototyped recording medium, provided for one of the more formidable tests in October 2005 when engineers from InPhase and TBS introduced a promotional advertisement into InPhase's Tapestry holographic disk as a data file.

The content was recorded using InPhase's holographic prototype drive onto a holographic disk manufactured by Hitachi Maxell (an InPhase partner and investor). The file was then played back from the drive, electronically migrated to a videoserver and played back to air.

TBS was investigating the feasibility of using holographic storage for broadcasting television content, especially given the need to store high-quality, high-definition (HD) movies with their extremely large data requirements. The capacity of holographic disks enabled TBS to store broadcast programming as files on media other than spinning magnetic disks (which consume massive amounts of space and power) or physical data tape (e.g., LTO-4). The real value, according to TBS, is that the high data transfer rate allowed TBS to migrate files on and off the videoserver disks and the holographic media quickly.

The InPhase Tapestry holographic system was capable of storing more than 26 hours of HD video on a single 300-Gbyte holographic disk, which was recorded at a 160-Mbit/second data rate. Maxell's holographic removable drive housed one 13-cm optical disk with storage capacity for up to 150 million pages, more than 63 times the capacity of a DVD.

The line of 300-Gbyte InPhase Tapestry products was to commence in 2006, which was to represent the initial offering in the family of InPhase holographic drives and media. According to predictions from Maxell, the product road map would have put capacities ranging up to 1.6 Tbytes and with data rates of 960 Mbits/second by year end 2010.

In a joint demonstration with Ikegami at the IBC 2007 in Amsterdam, an initial product was shown based on an Ikegami-branded 300 Gbytes external holographic drive associated with a PC. The demonstration intended to show a cost-effective, tapeless solution for archiving large video files finished on nonlinear editing systems and acquired with Ikegami Editcam and Editcam HD tapeless camcorders. The external holographic drive enabled users of Ikegami's camcorders to transfer edited or camera-original video content via FireWire or FTP interfaces to highly stable 300-Gbyte holographic cartridges for archiving and retrieval.

The versions shown were not rewritable, although that was expected to change as development continued.

Marketplace

These products were not intended for the consumer, as DVD and Blu-ray Discs were. Due to the high costs of the recording platforms, this marketplace was aimed at broadcasters, among other users such as medical data or other permanent high data concentrations.

Holographic Hiatus

Since these tests, InPhase had ceased business and then reemerged only a month later on March 18, 2010 when Signal Lake, an investor in next-generation technology and a computer communication company, announced that it had acquired the majority stake in InPhase Technologies, Inc. Signal Lake was the original founding lead investor in InPhase that helped it spin out of Bell Laboratories in conjunction with the then Lucent New Ventures Group in December 2000. As of late October 2010, the two principle venture capital investors (Acadia Woods Partners and Signal Lake) were at odds on how to restart the InPhase organization (more information on InPhase and holographic storage for archive purposes is included in Chapter 12).

Collinear Dual Laser Approach

Traditionally, holography will employ two beams, a separate signal (data) and a second reference beam, to create the interference pattern that is then stored onto the holographic material. The methodology requires a precise alignment and is complicated even further when the light must be focused onto rotating media that would be compatible with CD and DVD-like drive designs. An alternative approach uses two laser beams that are concentrated into a single beam of coaxial light. The concept creates a three-dimensional hologram composed of data fringes.

The player system is housed in a ruggedized platform similar to an industrial DVD player. By employing a server system and a single objective pickup system, tracking and focus are better controlled. With a media rotation speed of 300 RPM, such a system will establish 23,000 pulses per second, as the lens floats

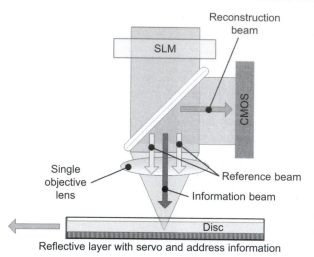

Figure 8.7 Collinear holography with its two laser beam formats.

above the revolving disc. The lens system has an integral microadjustment servo-like system that compensates for flutter or vibration.

Two beams of differing wavelengths are used. For data recording and reading, a 532-nm green solid laser is employed. For the servo tracking control and focus, a red semiconductor laser is used to read a built-in reference track embedded into the media in a pitted aluminum substrate. The red laser is selected so that it will not photosensitize the holographic recording material (refer to Fig. 8.7).

A dichroic mirror is employed to converge the two beams onto the same optical path before entering the objective lens. The disc media is coated with a reflective film, and the objective lens provides for the correct focus of the beam on to the film. Functionally, the recording laser beam is divided by beam splitters into the information beam and the reference beam. The information beam is converted into 2D page data through the employment of a digital micro-mirror device (DMD), similar to that used in DLP displays for television or digital cinema projection. The two beams are then merged back into the same optical axis through beam splitters incident to the objective lens. The holographic medium then captures the data in the form of interference patterns.

To reconstruct the data stored in the hologram, the reference beam is channeled incident to the objective lens. This "reconstruction beam" passes through the objective lens and is returned to a CMOS sensor and decoded using a Fast Fourier Transform (FFT).

Data Security Opportunity

This technology offers new possibilities for data protection. Since the 3D hologram is recorded using the 2D page data and is surrounded by a reference pattern formed collectively through the mirrors of the DMD device, the page data cannot be read back except by reproducing the exact reference pattern that was used to record the data. This essentially becomes a form of encryption, with over a million key combinations for each 2D page. Each page could employ a different reference key. The Holographic Versatile Disc (HVD) system is capable of writing

23,000 pages/second, which could yield a fully encrypted disc that would require 22 gigakeys/second to unlock.

Holographic Versatile Disc

Optware Corporation, in Yokohama, Japan, was established in 1999 as a development venture for holographic recording technology developed from a team of former Sony optical engineers who developed a different method of holographic storage called collinear Holographic Versatile Disc (HVD), which was described previously in this chapter. The technology was designed to enable storage of up to 3.9 Tbytes of data on a CD-sized disc with a data transfer rate exceeding 1 Gbit/second.

In 2005, Optware stated that it planned to release a Holographic Versatile Card (HVC) media product around the end of 2006, with a capacity of around 30 Gbytes. A reader device and a reader/writer device would also be launched as part of their HVC-related products to coincide with the standardization of the technology, which was expected in December 2006 by Ecma International, the organization promoting standardization of information and communication technologies. The card would be almost the same size as a credit card, with the drive system to be the size of a surface-mounted hard disc drive system.

As of 2010, with no further announcements or development in the limelight, and potentially as a result of the proliferation in high capacity Blu-ray Disc (BD) technologies, it is unclear where the product line will go.

Holographic Forums

The Holography System Development Forum (HSD Forum), which was originally formed from the HVD Alliance and the HVD FORUM, is the coalition of corporations with a purpose to provide an industry forum for testing and technical discussion of all aspects of HVD design and manufacturing. As of August 2009, the HSD Forum consisted of over 20 corporations including Apple, Mitsubishi, Fuji Photo Film Company, Optware, Hitachi, and many more.

Holographic Disc Cartridge (HDC) Standards

At its eighty-eighth General Assembly (December 2004), Ecma International, a private membership-based nonprofit SDO, established its Technical Committee 44 (TC44), which was to be dedicated to standardizing HVD formats based on the Optware technology. On June 11, 2007, TC44 published the first two HVD standards: ECMA-377, which would define a 120-mm diameter, 200-Gbyte HVD recordable cartridge; and ECMA-378, defining a 120-mm diameter, 100-Gbyte HVD-ROM disc. The next stated goals are for the 30-Gbyte HVD cards, followed by the submission of these standards to the International Organization for Standardization (ISO) for approval.

Micro-Holographic Storage

April 2009 saw General Electric (GE) Global Research demonstrating a micro-holographic storage material that could eventually result in the capability of storing as much as 500 Gbytes of data on a standard 120-mm Blu-ray/DVD-sized disc.

Unlike the DVD or Blu-ray Disc that store data only in the surface layers of the disk (for Blu-ray Disc, this is single, dual, triple, and potentially quadruple layers), the holographic storage involves storing data throughout the entire disk in multiple layers. The hardware and format of GE's holographic storage technology will be similar to that used in current optical storage technology, allowing micro-holographic players to be backward read-compatible with existing CDs, DVDs, and Blu-ray Discs.

Targets and Worries

Long-term archiving of medical information in a nondestructible format is certainly a target for these forms of optical storage. The hardship is that holographic storage technology research and preliminary product development is now exceeding a full decade or more. Every 5 years, the industry is finding a new storage technology; the issues become not in making the technology work, but in dealing with concern over the support of legacy hardware and apprehension over the adoption of newer technologies. Thus, we ask the question, "Will we need to continually migrate to a new technology that barely has any track record of survival?"

Care and Handling

Optical media should be handled on its edges only, as the materials are subject to physical damage that could render some or all of the data unrecoverable. Compact discs may be prone to damage from both normal use and the effects of environmental exposure. On a CD, the pits are much closer to the label side of a disc, thus enabling defects and contaminants on the clear side to be out of focus during playback. Consequently, CDs are more susceptible to damage occurring on the label side of the disk.

Scratches that appear on the disc's clear side may be repaired by refilling them with similar refractive plastic or by carefully polishing the surface with an optical cleaner.

Some guidelines to caring for physical media include the following:

- Allocate a cool, dry, dark environment where the air is clean for disc storage.
- Only handle discs by the outer edge or the center hole.
- For marking the label side of a disc, only use a nonsolvent-based felt-tip permanent marker; avoid adhesive labels.
- Avoid getting any dirt or other foreign matter to contact the disc; remove any foreign material (including fingerprints, smudges, and liquids) by wiping with a clean cotton fabric in a straight line from the center of the disc toward the outer edge. Never wipe in a direction going around the disc.
- Avoid bending discs, or exposing them to sunlight or extreme temperatures.
- Use plastic cases that are specified for CDs and DVDs, and return them to their cases after use, storing them in upright position, that is, "book style."
- Do not open a recordable disc package until you are ready to record data onto the disc, check the disc before recording, and clean the disc or discard a noncleanable disc.
- Use a CD/DVD cleaning detergent, isopropyl alcohol, or methanol to remove stubborn dirt or material.

Further Readings

Care and Handling of CDs and DVDs—A Guide for Librarians and Archivists. http://www.itl.nist.gov/iad/894.05/papers/CDandDVDCareandHandling-Guide.pdf

Normative References (from ITL/NIST)

ISO 18927:2002 Imaging materials—Recordable compact disc systems—Method for estimating the life expectancy based on the effects of temperature and relative humidity, first edition

IEC 60908 (1999-02): Compact disc digital audio system. This document including amendments approximates the Philips-Sony Red Book

ISO/IEC 10149:1995 Read-Only 120 mm Optical Data Disks (CD-ROM)

EMCA130 2nd Edition—June 1996 Data interchange on read-only120 mm optical data disks (CD-ROM)

Orange Book, part B—Recordable Compact Disc System, November 1990 (SONY and Philips Corp.)

ISO/IEC 16448:2002 Information technology—120 mm DVD Read-only disk

ISO/IEC DIS 23912:2005 Information technology—80 mm (1.46 GBytes per side) and 120 mm (4.70 GBytes per side) DVD Recordable Disk (DVD-R)

ISO/IEC 17344:2005: Information technology—Data interchange on 120 mm and 80 mm optical disk using +R format—Capacity: 4.7 GBytes and 1.46 GBytes per side

ISO/IEC 17342:2004: Information technology—80 mm (1.46 GBytes per side) and 120 mm (4.70 GBytes per side) DVD re-recordable disk (DVD-RW)

ISO/IEC 17341:2005: Information technology—Data interchange on 120 mm and 80 mm optical disk using +RW format—Capacity: 4.7 GBytes and 1.46 GBytes per side

ECMA-267, 2001, 120 mm DVD Read-Only Disk, 3rd edition

ECMA-337, DVD+RW—Rewritable Optical Disks, 4.7 Gbytes

ECMA-338, DVD-RW—Rewritable Optical Disks, 4.7 Gbytes)

9

INTERCHANGE, TRANSCODING, AND WRAPPERS

Until the advent of digital technologies and before file-based workflow, the video industry (as NTSC or PAL) had a common denominator by which it exchanged content (i.e., picture and audio essence). The coaxial cable interface, per the SMPTE 170 standard, was the fundamental real-time interface used to move video content between one device and another. Audio would be carried on a separate interface, and the storage medium of choice was a relatively few different video (or audio) tape formats. The analog successor, SDI (SMPTE 259M and SMPTE 292M), further provided for a common, consistent, and standardized transport between devices regardless of how the original essence was stored on the medium where it was generated or transported.

Only as recently as a couple of decades ago, issues of exchanging file-based media were nonexistent. Beginning with the dawn of nonlinear editing, which emerged in the early 1990s, the transport and manipulation of video and audio (essence) would begin a transformation from a real-time nature to a non–real time domain. Early instances of video content for production purposes being stored as files would appear on purpose-built platforms using proprietary codecs that kept individual frames of video on hard drives, and then under software control would play back the string of individual frame files to reproduce the original or modified moving images.

Content interchange, even among similar devices, was very limited. If the content was to be used on a different system, it would generally be "printed" back to videotape in real time from the original nonlinear workstation, then physically moved ("sneaker netted") to and re-ingested onto the other platform or nonlinear workstation. The interchange of data between devices could only occur if the physical workstation platforms were of the same vintage, version number, and functionality. It would be some time before networking over Ethernet or file-based interchange between these video platforms would become part of any mainstream workflow.

As nonlinear editing, computer-generated imaging (CGI), and effects compositing on computer-based platforms became popular, the issues surrounding the interchange of content on videotape, without degrading its quality, gave rise to a need for what we eventually termed "file-based workflows." The process, except for a few instances, was relegated to only a few platforms and for the most part, content was only exchanged between similar devices from the same manufacturer. "File interchange," and the storage of those files onto separate subsystems, was a workflow that did not occur except when those systems were identical, right down to the specific software, codec, and application version.

This chapter discusses the issues and challenges associated with file interchange and workflow, beginning with the introduction of the platforms and moving through the topics of wrappers, transcoding of files, and the various processes of migrating the essence (audio, video, and data) through the working environment now comprised of servers, networks, and compressed video domains.

KEY CHAPTER POINTS

- Real-time, non-real-time, online, and off-line postproduction processes related to content as files
- Vocabularies and terminologies related to working with file-based workflows as applied to transcoding and essence
- Files, platforms, and formats defined as they apply to media-centric operations in a file-based or streaming environment
- Elements of the Media Exchange Format (MXF) standards, including how MXF came to be from the origins of the EBU and the SMPTE Task Force report of the late 1990s
- Description of Patterns, metafiles, containers, and wrappers in their fundamental forms including how they are applied through items and packages
- Conversion and the steps in transcoding as it relates to both baseband and file formats, transrating, and multiplatform conversion and distribution
- Real-time and off-line transcoding, with the three modes of transfer characteristics

Moving Toward Non–Real Time

Early computer-controlled electronic editing of video content was an almost entirely linear-only process that was governed by the lack of any affordable digital formats, nonlinear or random-access storage platforms, or software-based architectures. While computerized linear videotape editing (e.g., on the CMX editors) was certainly a serious advancement from the days of film editing, it was a far cry from what we consider "normal" in today's thinking with the process of timeline-based, nonlinear video and audio editing.

The transition from real-time, linear workflows to non–real-time, random-access file-based workflows evolved over a period of about 50 years. It began with the first videotape recorders (and continued through the demise of regular film-only editing) then progressed through various videotape and nonvideotape platforms. The ramp up started with off-line editing and moved to timeline-based, graphical user interfaces to almost entirely a nonlinear postproduction world.

Off-line Editing

The development of today's current practices began from the processes referred to as "off-line editing." Off-line, as it became known, evolved out of the need to control the time spent in the online linear editing suite. By predetermining the EDK using off-line systems, the online editing process would then be reserved for the final conforming of a program only. The development of today's nonlinear editing platform most assuredly dated back to the concepts of off-line editing processes.

Initially, off-line editing was performed on less expensive ½-in. VHS or Umatic ¾-in. tape decks where the original material was first copied to this format with a burned-in "window-boxed" image of the time code that would allow the human editor to reference the precise frame of the video segment they would be "clipping" and joining to subsequent clips during the creation of the edit decision list or EDL. The process was usually a cut-only assembly of the sequences, with annotations for transitions, effects, or titling being added externally during the decision process. These off-line tools allowed editors to make decisions, that is, create their EDLs, which would later be used in the online postproduction environment.

The same computer-driven electronic controllers that were used in the online production suite would be utilized in the off-line process but would be connected to these less-expensive transports. The off-line version was frequently used as an approval process but seldom would the off-line version be used as a final production release. This workflow would later be transformed to an electronic tapeless editing process that became the roots of what would be called nonlinear editing (NLE)—a method of rapidly creating the EDL without the intent of delivering a final product from that platform.

Computerized Editing

Early computer-based NLE systems were used in much the same fashion as their tape-based editing system counterparts. The workflow began with an initial step of ingesting each segment of content from a master videotape into the NLE platform, where it was recorded to disk. Since the images to be used in generating the EDL did not need to be of high quality, the earliest NLEs used a format that produced a marginal- to mid-quality reproduction of the video and audio segments. The resultant deliverables from the NLE were a numerical EDL and a "rough-cut" audio and video version of the completed program.

The EDL data would be output to a floppy diskette, which would then be imported to the online computer editing system. The video and audio rough cut could be played out and recorded to a ¾- or ½-in. tape that would be used as a reference for the online edit session. Sometimes the workflow included transferring, in real time, and recording rough-cut content to a crystal master videotape. During the online edit session, the final "conformed cut" would be insert-edited over the top of the rough-cut version already on the master tape, replacing the rough version with a final version of high quality that precisely matched the rough-cut version.

Early NLE implementations might not have employed editing on a graphic display, trick-effect previews, scrub audio, dissolves, keys, or effects—let alone any kind of video simulation of the edit directly to a computer screen. However, it was not long before companies, such as Avid Technology, would pioneer a new concept called "timeline editing" that would cause a paradigm shift in the workflows of first off-line and eventually online editing on a computerized workstation.

Compressed Video

Video compression technologies would become a key component to the development of on-screen visual, electronic nonlinear editing (NLE) workflow. Of the relatively few NLE platforms that were available in the early years, most employed their own proprietary codec that captured each linear frame of video and saved them as a linked string of individual files that when played back produced a reasonable representation of the original images. Again, quality at first was not the motivational force behind the NLE, as a rough version of what the final segments would look like was submitted and then a conformed cut was created in the linear online edit suite.

These NLEs used the JPEG tool kit and tailored it to the architecture of the software-based editing platform. Even though the tool kits used standard JPEG compression properties, the motion-JPEG implementations were nearly always unique to the NLE, by platform, version, and audio/visual "reference" level. This forced the user to buy one or more NLE workstations, all usually configured with proprietary I/O cards, disk drives, and controllers; and software licenses coupled with maintenance or support contracts that ensured the user would remain "locked" into that vendor's system.

All of the activity remained the same for awhile, with the concept of "file-based workflows" still a decade or more away from reality back during this time. Analog video and audio interchange, thus, remained locked to videotape, retaining it as the only true interface between one system and another. Serial digital I/O was unnecessary at the time, yet within a few years of implementation, as compression improved and codec card sets with SDI I/O emerged, we began to see a demand for a completely digital video version, promoted by the advances in codec quality, real-time processing, rendering of dissolves, etc.

Issues with Interchange

The professional audio and video production industry, such as the computer industry, has adapted to the requirements of translating and changing from one platform to another or from one software product to another, for quite some time. For the video and audio industry, the interchange of files between vendor-specific platforms or between standardized or nonstandardized video or audio compression formats occurs through a process called transcoding.

As the professional industry (i.e., broadcast and postproduction) began to accept the notion of digital video, attempts to address the issues associated with interchanging material content, at a file level, between one platform and another gradually paved the way to an infant form of file standardization. Once this foundation was cast, a basis for file-based interchange was enabled and the dependency on real-time, linear transport, and videotape storage began its asymptotic slope toward extinction.

Incompatibilities

Today, video and audio content is used in more ways and on more devices than was ever anticipated during the emergence of nonlinear editing and disk-based storage. In similar fashion, content is captured, produced, and then released for consumption using a plethora of platforms, technologies, and distribution methodologies, which strive to find a common means for interchange.

Unfortunately, the growth of incompatible and competing formats for production and delivery, including broadcast, creates a set of issues that has to be resolved each time a new encoding concept is envisioned or introduced. It goes without saying that no single format can provide all that people require, but that has not stopped the progression of new and improved encoding technologies aimed at addressing both the user's needs and the growing technical issues associated with the digital video era. Continuing the evolution of systems demanded a solution that would provide a suitable means for interchange that could serve as many users, formats, and resources as possible.

The solution is called transcoding and is defined as the process of converting or translating one format of media to another. The process facilitates the requirements necessary for moving video, audio, and associated other data media through the workflows surrounding production, postproduction, replication, archive, and delivery.

Media File Vocabularies and Terminologies

To place the processes of handling media files into perspective, some fundamental terminologies must be established. The industry has prescribed different sets of terminologies that are used in describing the elements that make up files and their associated ancillary elements. Some of these are recognized nomenclatures, others share similar names, and still others use alternative names interchangeably. Often, these nomenclatures convey differing and sometimes incorrect meanings.

File Format Clarification

File formats should not be confused with file systems or operating systems, which are discussed in "Files and Operating Systems" (available on the companion website). File formats are prescribed structures that are created from media that is usually compressed from full-bandwidth audio and video streams during the capture or ingest process. Files are then stored on magnetic, solid state, or optical media or are used in the transmission process between different locations on a network-based topology.

In our ever evolving multimedia, audio and video world we have developed literally shopping carts full of file formats. The variety of files, formats, and media structures creates hardship when trying to assess a consistent vocabulary for describing these files and formats. An even greater issue is raised when dealing with the challenges of interoperability between the makers of equipment that must process and transform these files for use on their systems and for distribution or delivery to and from varying platforms.

For consistency purposes, we would like set parameters and descriptions that are recognized by the industry and a reasonable degree of conformity at a standards level. Throughout this book, that is, not only when discussing the conversion and transcoding processes but also when examining workflow and storage system properties associated with file-based media, we will utilize those terms that are established by recognized standards organizations, such as the Society of Motion Picture and Television Engineers (SMPTE) and the International Telecommunication Union (ITU). When terms have been adopted without a standards body recommendation, perhaps as a de facto representation, those will be identified accordingly.

Platforms and Systems

At the most basic level, a platform is the fundamental technology of a system's (e.g., a computer's) hardware and software, which defines how a system is operated and determines what other kinds of services (e.g., software) can be used. Thus, when looking at how this applies to a workflow built around files, the components that make up the various elements that touch and interact with the workflow can be thought of as the platform.

A moving media file, which might contain video, audio, data, and metadata, is the fundamental element that carries the appropriate sets of bits that when properly interpreted by the system components will produce the visual, aural, and other information including the "bits about those bits" when sent to those components. In order for this set of bits to be properly interpreted by other platforms, certain rules need to be followed and the formats of those bits must be correctly understood by the other platform or platforms.

In a video recording and playback system, the basic technology of the system's hardware and software must be constructed such that it defines how the video and audio are encoded and it must also determine what other kinds of video and audio can be presented to the system for playback. The hardware component definitions might include the size and proportions of the video, the screen size that the video will be presented on, the processing capabilities of the encoder or decoder components, and much more relative information all aimed at describing the relationship of the video data to the system. Each of these elements will have limitations that govern what types of video, audio, data, or metadata can be interpreted. If there is insufficient processing capability, then there will be limitations on what size or dimensions of video can be produced, such as standard definition versus high definition.

The hardware in these systems will be used for specific purposes. It might be an embedded system for mobile applications or it might be highly agile to handle multiple tasks simultaneously, such as in a videoserver with ingest (record), playback (output), and file-transfer capabilities.

In addition, in a system, there will be software that has been designed to address the specific limitations and performance capabilities of the hardware. In essence, the software should match the hardware's design purpose or it will not produce the expected set of results. Hardware and software considerations must also take into account factors such as power, bandwidth, user quality of experience, and other parameters that define the uses and applications for each.

One of the primary reasons why we see so many formats emerging in the video and audio industry is that new platforms are continually developed that make improvements in the quality of experience that the user needs, wants, or hopes to achieve. The result is that new video and audio encoding technologies are produced, which intend to answer the needs or wants of the user. In turn, we find that new formats, created by new encoding methods, produce new platforms on a cyclic nature defined by users, video equipment manufacturers, or combinations of both. Whether a format, platform, or product survives depends on its acceptance by the community who buys or uses these emerging and evolving technologies, for most any reason.

These new platforms are faced with the daunting task of either complying with all the previous legacy formats or ignoring them, and hoping their new platforms will be more profitable and successful than the legacy predecessors. The end result is that for users to enjoy the new added value of this new platform requires that another external element be able to translate or adapt the file so that it can be presented to the new platform, thus making the new platform extensible to users who might need to use it for more than a single dedicated application.

Compressor–Decompressor

A fundamental element that handles the major elements of video (or audio) compression is the codec. By definition, at the simplest level as it applies to the moving media technology space, a codec is the hardware, or software, engine that moves frames of video or audio from the uncompressed domain to the compressed domain (a compressor) or vice versa (a decompressor). Both elements are required in an end-to-end solution that takes video and audio content in real time into a system and stores it for later release (output) as video and audio, once again.

Let's state that again, this time referring to the diagram in Figure 9.1. Video and audio are presented to the input of a device on a physical connector, usually a BNC connector. If the video and audio are carried as a stream in the standard video formats per SMPTE 259M (SD) or 292M (HD) transport (as embedded audio in the serial digital interface, SDI) domain, then the digital stream is considered video "full bandwidth" with a data rate of 270 Mbits/second for SD (SMPTE 259M) or 1.485 Gbits/second for HD (SMPTE 292M).

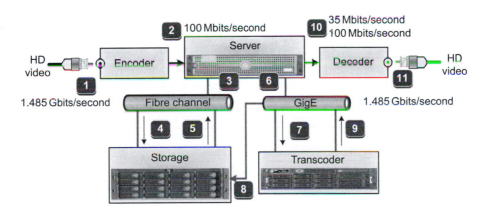

Ingest
(1) Baseband 1.485 Gbit/second HD digital video is input to Encoder through (2). The Encoder creates 100 Mbit/second DVCPRO HD compressed files that are transported through path (3) from the server on Fibre Channel over path (4) to storage.

Transcode
DVCPRO HD 100 Mbit/second files called from storage (5) to server (3), buffered and moved through (6) on GigE network through (7) to transcode engine; files are transcoded to 35 Mbit/second MPEG-2, then through the server they move back into storage through path (9→8).

Playback
Files playback from storage on path (5→3) to server; then through path (10) to decoder. Software codecs in the decoder allow native 100 Mbit/second DVCPRO HD or transcoded 35 Mbit/second MPEG-2 files that are decoded to baseband HD as 1.485 Gbit/second SMPTE 292M high-definition video (11).

Figure 9.1 Functional diagram of the I/O, encoder, server, storage, transcode engine, decoder, and network interface (Fibre Channel and Gigabit Ethernet) for a typical videoserver system.

There are a lot of data to store, and in 90% of the applications that employ file-based workflows, the higher raw bit rates are seldom employed. So, the full-bandwidth data is presented to an encoder that compresses the video and audio into a format—hopefully an open standardized format, and deposits those elements, as a file, to storage.

Figure 9.1 shows elements of a digital video system signal flow: video encode, transcode, storage, and decoder for playback. The signal flow is hypothetical as there are many alternative configurations possible.

The encoder, usually one half of a codec pair, changes that bit stream into a compressed format that is selected from a plethora of available industry accepted formats. The instrument that changes this bit stream from a linear real-time format to a file may be either a hardware-based codec or a software-based codec. Many professional videoserver platforms developed since the mid-1990s have employed hardware-based codecs, but the trend in the past 5 years or so has moved away from hardware-based codecs with embedded software applications that do the compression to a world of software-based codecs. The later, software-based codecs have both advantages and disadvantages, which are arguably marketplace-based advantages depending on the vendor or codec software licensee who promotes the implementation. The flexibility of a software-based system is that as technology is improved, the systems are not as easily painted into a corner they can't escape from. Software codecs can be upgraded without necessarily replacing the hardware underneath them.

Profile and Level

To properly describe and address compression formats, there are two principle terms—profile and level—that are necessary in order to describe the parameters and performance of the particular functionality of the codec. For example, in the MPEG standards, a "profile" defines the specifics of color space resolution and scalability of the bit stream. A "level" describes a specified set of constraints that indicate a degree of required decoder performance for a given profile.

A level of support within a profile will specify the maximum picture resolution, frame rate and size, and bit rate that a decoder may be capable of using. A decoder conforming to a given level is required to be capable of decoding all bit streams that are encoded for that level and for all lower levels.

Of the two more familiar compression formats, MPEG-2 and MPEG-4, used for moving image applications in professional environments, there are several sets of profiles and levels. For MPEG-2, some examples include the following:

- MPEG-2 MP@ML, read as "Main Profile" at "Main Level," describes a standard definition video signal with a maximum bit rate of 15 Mbits/second.
- MPEG-2 MP@HL, read as "Main Profile at High Level," describes a high-definition video signal with a maximum bit rate of 80 Mbits/second (Table 9.1).

For H.264, a derivative of the MPEG-4 Part 10 (or AVC) standard for compression, there are 17 defined sets of capabilities (i.e., Profiles) that are used to target specific classes of applications. Examples of Profiles for nonscalable 2D video applications include the following:

- Constrained Baseline Profile (CBP)—primarily used for low-cost applications such as videoconferencing or mobile.

Table 9.1 MPEG-2 Profiles and Levels Commonly Used in Compressed Digital Video

MPEG-2 Profiles

Name	Abbreviation	Picture Coding	Chroma Format	Scalable Modes
Simple profile	SP	I, P	4:2:0	None
Main profile	MP	I, P, B	4:2:0	None
SNR scalable profile	SNR	I, P, B	4:2:0	SNR scalable
Spatial profile	SPATIAL	I, P, B	4:2:0	SNR or SPATIAL scalable
High profile	HP	I, P, B	4:2:0/4:2:2	SNR or SPATIAL scalable
422 profile	422	I, P, B	4:2:0/4:2:2	None
MVP profile	MVP	I, P, B	4:2:0	Temporal

MPEG-2 Levels

Name	Abbreviation	Frame Rates	Horizontal Resolution (Max)	Vertical Resolution (Max)
Low level	LL	23.976, 24, 25, 29.97, 30	352	288
Main level	ML	23.976, 24, 25, 29.97, 30	720	576
High 1440	H-14	23.976, 24, 25, 29.97, 30, 50, 59.94, 60	1440	1152
High level	HL	23.976, 24, 25, 29.97, 30, 50, 59.94, 60	1920	1152

- Baseline Profile (BP)—used for applications supported in CBP, plus additional features, but still requires only a limited degree of computing power for the decode process.
- High Profile (HiP)—a primary profile used particularly for high-definition disc storage applications, such as Blu-ray and the DVB HDTV broadcast service.
- High 4:2:2 Profile (Hi422P)—for professional applications with 4:2:2 chroma subsampling that is built on top of the High 10 Profile (Hi10P), which supports 10 bits per sample of picture decoding (Table 9.2).

MPEG-4 Visual (Part 2 of ISO/IEC 14496 "Coding of Audio-Visual Objects") covers a very wide range of functionalities and types of data, which includes the following:

- Static textures—as in still images
- Moving video—rectangular frames

Table 9.2 MPEG-4 Part 4 Profiles and Levels Commonly Used in Compressed Digital Video

MPEG-4 Part 4 Profiles and Levels

Name (Abbreviation)	Profile	Level	Resolution	Frame Rate	Application
Constrained Baseline Profile (CBP)	Baseline	1	176 × 144	15	3G
Baseline Profile (BP)	High	2.1	480 × 272	23.976	PSP
Main Profile (MP)	High	2.1	480 × 272	25	PSP
Extended Profile (XP)	High	2.1	480 × 272	29.97	SDTV
High Profile (HiP)	High	3	720 × 480	29.97	SDTV
High 10 Profile (Hi10P)	High	3	720 × 576	25	HDTV
High 4:2:2 Profile (Hi422P)	High	3.1	1280 × 720	25	HDTV
High 4:4:4 Predictive Profile (Hi444P)	High	3.1	1280 × 720	30	HDTV
High 10 Intra Profile	High	3.3	1280 × 720	50	HDTV
High 4:2:2 Intra Profile	High	3.3	1920 × 1080	60	HDTV
High 4:4:4 Intra Profile	High	3.3	1920 × 1080	25	HDTV
Cavlc 4:4:4 Intra Profile	High	3.3	1920 × 1080	30	HDTV
Scalable Baseline Profile	High	4	1920 × 1080	24	Blu-ray
Scalable High Profile	High	4	1920 × 1080	25	Blu-ray/HD DVD
Scalable High Intra Profile	High	4	1920 × 1080	29.97	Blu-ray/HD DVD
Stereo High Profile	High	4	1920 × 1080	30	Blu-ray/HD DVD
Multiview High Profile	Support for two or more views (temporal and MVC interview)				

- Video objects—shapes of an arbitrary nature in regions of moving video
- 2D and 3D mesh objects—shapeable, deformable objects
- Animated human faces and bodies

Metafile

A metafile describes how essence, data, and metadata are stored, but the metafile does not describe how that information is coded. In the context of audio and video, a metafile would also be known as a container. In computer data systems, metafile is a term that is generically used to mean a file format that stores multiple types of data.

Graphics Metafiles

For graphics, metafiles would commonly include the following file formats:

- PICT—originally used on Apple's Macintosh computers as a standard metafile format.
- CGM—defined by ISO/IEC 8632, and known as Computer Graphics Metafile, an open international standard file format for two dimensional (2D) vector graphics, raster graphics, and text.
- EPG—Encapsulated PostScript is a standard format for importing and exporting PostScript language files among applications in a variety of heterogeneous environments. The format is based on and conforms to the Document Structuring Conventions (DSC) detailed in the PostScript Document Structuring Conventions Specification.
- PDF—Portable Document Format is an open standard for document exchange, created in 1993 by Adobe Systems that is used for representing two-dimensional documents (and more latterly 3D) in a manner independent of the application software, hardware, and operating system.
- SVG—Scalable Vector Graphics is a family of specifications of an XML-based file format for describing both static and dynamic 2D vector graphics.
- RTF—Rich Text Format file is a proprietary document file format developed by Microsoft Corporation (1987) that supports Microsoft products and cross-platform document interchange. The current version V 1.1.9-2008 uses XML markup, custom XML tags, SmartTags, and Math elements that follows the Office Open XML (OOXML) specification of ECMA-376, Part 4.
- WMF—In the Windows operating system, the complete term is Windows Metafile (WMF); this is also known as the Enhanced Metafile (EMF).

Generic Metafile

In a more general perspective, the metafile program is enabled to identify and open a container file but might not be able to decode the data contained in that file. Such a program would have lacked the required decoding algorithm, or it could be that the metadata did not provide sufficient information to point to the decoding algorithm. It could also be that there was more than one decoder required: one for audio, one for video, and one that interprets the data inside the container.

By definition, a container format could enfold any type or form of data; however, most of the container formats are specialized for specific data requirements, for example, those that will be discussed in the following contexts of moving media technologies, especially those that are associated with audio and video.

Container or Wrapper

When either of these terms is used in the context of moving media, "container" or "wrapper" is a specialized metafile that describes the grouping of or the set of multiple types of audio, video, data, and metadata, which are associated together as a complete "package" that is delivered to a platform. Examples of wrappers (or containers) include the following:

- QuickTime—developed by Apple, a proprietary multimedia framework that handles video, picture, sound, images, and interactivity
- AVI—Audio Video Interleave or Audio Video Interleaved, part of the video for Windows technology
- ASF—Microsoft's proprietary digital audio/digital video container format called Advanced Systems Format; formerly, yet still known as Advanced Streaming Format or Active Streaming Format (ASF is part of the Windows Media framework)
- MXF—The SMPTE wrapper standard most commonly associated with media files
- M2TS and M2PS— MPEG-2 transport streams (TS) or program streams (PS) that carry the MPEG-2 essence and associated data
- VOB—data in a container called a video object, which is associated with video for DVD videos
- LXF—a proprietary container form for the Leitch/Nexio video-server platform from Harris Broadcast
- GXF—a SMPTE standard (SMPTE 360M) wrapper format developed for the Tektronix/Grass Valley videoserver platform; the first standardized wrapper format; set the tone for what would later be the Material eXchange Format (MXF).

- 3GPP (and 3GPP2)—the 3rd Generation Partnership Project, standards for the creation, delivery, and playback of multimedia over third generation (3G), high-speed wireless networks

The industry has already accepted the notion there will never be a universal file format that would suit all applications in all instances. However, the industry has made great strides in addressing interoperability through the establishment of a universal and standardized professional wrapper format. The wrapper acts like a covering or a bottle that protects its contents from disruption or contamination as those elements are transported (carried) between one place and another.

Wrappers serve two purposes mainly: to gather program material and related information and identify those pieces of information. A wrapper does not add much value but is invaluable in providing a unified way to structure content and to access it.

In the early days of file formats for moving images (audio and video), and prior to the standardization of a wrapper format for moving material, there were some wrapper formats that had already been in use. None of these were widely accepted, or they did not provide sufficient capability in terms of openness, extensibility, performance, etc. The movement to develop a set of wrappers was started to coalesce the requirements and ideas and to prepare a standardization process, which ultimately became the Material eXchange Format (MXF).

Generic Wrapper

A generic wrapper is at the highest level of the food chain, and when associated with media applications, it is categorized between streaming wrappers and storage wrappers.

Streaming Wrappers

Streaming wrappers, when applied through a streaming mechanism, provide the container for moving content over IP, Fibre Channel, and other transports.

Storage Wrappers

Storage wrappers, when applied through a mechanism for storage, allow content to be stored in raw form into specialized storage platforms or on a recognized file system such as NTFS or CIFS.

Format

A particular set of codecs (i.e., encoder and/or decoder sets) and a set of containers (or wrappers) collectively make up a "format." The format may be either platform agnostic (i.e., platform independent) or platform dependent (i.e., platform specific), that is, it must be played back on a platform that is compliant with the format and compatible with the format's applications.

A cross-platform and platform-specific format is one that is compatible with a varietal set of operating systems but is principally intended for playback on a given family of players.

One should not associate a compression format with a wrapper format. Wrappers are not necessarily affected by the contents of the wrapper and are for the most part agnostic to things such as essence, compression formats, line structures, ancillary data, and so on. The wrapper, whether for media applications or simply other collections of data, is best thought of as a specification for a container that describes how essence (data) and metadata are stored and not how they are coded.

An application (or program) that is able to identify and/or open a wrapped container file would not necessarily be able to decode the contents of that container file. The decoding activity is generally provided by another application in either hardware or software.

Files and Streams

To appreciate the differences between file and stream transfers, let's look at the major characteristics of each.

File Transfers

In a network, a file transfer is a packet-based data movement over a reliable interconnect that is usually acknowledged by the receiver, which is then heard by the transmitter. The file transfer may be accomplished using removable media (disc, USB drive, etc.). The transfer is initiated with a known start and usually a known end point. It may be a point-to-point or point-to-multipoint, with limitations, transfer. The file formats are often structured to allow essence data to be widely distributed or random byte positions. The transfers are not normally synchronized to an external clock.

Stream Transfers

System transfers are implemented as a point-to-multipoint or broadcast transfer that is open ended with no predetermined start or end point. The interconnect is over a data-streaming interface that is usually unacknowledged. The formats for streaming are usually structured to allow access to essence data at a sequential byte position using a streaming decoder.

Content

The fundamental base element in a file structure for moving or multimedia applications consists of individual sets of raw audio, video, and data, which are referred to as "essence." Audio generally will consist of individual or paired tracks of sound, including video description tracks or narrative scratch notations. Video could be moving pictures or static images such as graphics or full-screen stills, in resolutions from QCIF through high definition or beyond. Data is information such as time code, closed caption data, descriptions for open captions, etc., but is not considered metadata related to the structures of the files.

When these sets of essence elements are combined with the metadata associated with that essence, they form "content." To aid in the movement of packages of content, as files, throughout a system with some level of association, content is enveloped or surrounded by a "wrapper," which is also known in the industry as a "container." Both terms are confusing and used with much flexibility. Wrappers or containers are often referenced in describing file formats, file extensions, and other descriptors (for example, in the context of a file type as in ".MOV wrapped," from the Apple QuickTime Movie perspective, or as in "MXF wrapped," from the SMPTE MXF standards set).

Material eXchange Format (MXF)

One of the more recognized example references for media-centric file interchange structures is described in the Media eXchange Format (MXF) work efforts of SMPTE. This suite of standards, engineering guidelines, and practices outline, describe, and frame up the methodologies widely used as a foundation for interchange of content as files for multimedia (i.e., audio/video) applications. The specification allows users to take advantage of non–real-time transfers that combine essence and metadata so that it may efficiently be interchanged between servers, storage systems, and businesses.

MXF is a complicated set of SMPTE standards documents that need not be thoroughly understood by many in order for MXF to be effectively implemented. The compliance issues surrounding MXF have been massaged, contorted, and distorted by the confusion among the users, manufacturers, and general community since the adoption of the first specifications in the late 1990s. The following sections of this chapter are meant to skim the top-level descriptions and components that make up the MXF file specifications and frameworks. This section hopefully provides users with a fundamental idea of the terms and top-level requirements for MXF compliance.

Raw Materials

When referring to multimedia (audio/video) applications, the term essence is described by the SMPTE 377-1-2009 standards document for MXF as the fundamental "raw video, audio, and data streams." By including the word "raw," essence is described at its basic state without additives that mention such modifiers as high definition or standard definition (video), analog or AES (audio), and time code or closed captioning (data). While this term is described by MXF, the essence may optionally be contained in an MXF file itself.

An essence container describes that part of an MXF file that carries one or more essence streams. The container may optionally carry metadata that is closely associated with the essence streams. The essence container consists of a stream of bytes that are identified by a unique Stream ID value. Within the scope of a single MXF file, this particular example for the Stream ID is a 32-bit integer that uniquely defines a data stream within that container.

Some formats may include multiple containers. The same compression format (e.g., MPEG-2) may be found in a transport stream (TS) container such as when video, audio, and data are used for broadcast or satellite distribution. The same MPEG-2 may be placed into a program stream (PS) container for storage or delivery, such as in a DVD. Similar scenarios can be applied to codecs such as MPEG-4 Part 2, H.264/AVC or MPEG-4 Part 10, or H.263, which is used as a low-bit-rate codec in older videoconferencing systems.

Task Force for MXF

The origins of MXF can be traced back to the mid-1990s. At that time, the convergence between the IT and the television industries was being taken for granted. Networking, video compression, and video capable storage were in their infancies, with each collectively paving the way to a paradigm shift in production, transmission, and distribution of content. As nonlinear editing was becoming commonplace and videoservers were beginning to be accepted as a reliable replacement for VTRs, the problems with interchange of files between systems and on diverse platforms needed to be addressed.

Impromptu solutions for interchange were being developed and promoted by manufacturers with only a minute amount of standardization backing. This, sadly, resulted in myriad incompatible file formats, ad hoc workflows, and differing terminologies. Where SDI had established itself as a reliable, interoperable link, a completely different scenario was developed, which had little correlation to tape-based workflows or real-time streaming media interchange.

The European Broadcasting Union (EBU) and SMPTE joined forces to produce a blueprint for the implementation of new technologies, which was to look forward a decade or more. The task force produced a pair of documents: a report on user requirements and a detailed collection of the analyses and results obtained from the task force study.

The complete work, published in July 1998, is called the "Task Force for Harmonized Standards for the Exchange of Programme Material as Bitstreams." The work had a major impact on the industry, with the most important disclosure stating the awareness of an obvious need to perform formal standardization work on "wrappers and metadata." Ultimately, metadata was placed on a par with audio and video, with the establishment of a standard wrapper becoming a fundamental component in file-based media interoperability and interchange.

Structure of a Basic MXF File

The fundamental MXF file begins with a File Header, followed by a File Body, and ends with a File Footer. The data structure of the MXF file includes a full definition of the File Header and File Footer. A number of associated documents are required to provide the full specification of an MXF file.

File Header

A File Header must be present at the start of every MXF file. It shall include the Header Partition Pack and the Header Metadata as shown in Figure 9.2; and may also include a Run-In and an optional index table, as shown in Figure 9.3.

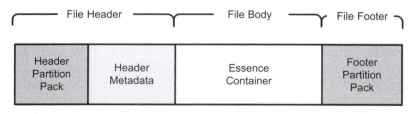

Figure 9.2 Overall data structure of a simple MXF file.

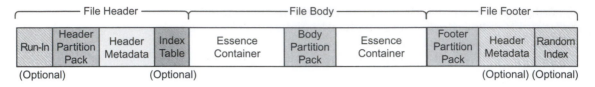

Figure 9.3 Overall data structure of an MXF file with optional components.

File Body

This middle section provides the mechanism for embedding essence data within MXF files and shall contain zero or more essence containers. When there is more than one essence container in the File Body, the essence containers shall be multiplexed together using Partitions.

For an Essence Element, there shall be an associated MXF essence container specification defining how the Essence Element shall be "key-length-value" (KLV) encoded in the essence container, how the Index Table specification shall be applied for indexing the Essence Element, and how to identify the Essence Descriptors that are required to describe the Essence Element.

MXF Metadata

The standard allow for MXF metadata-only files. These files may have no File Body and hence no essence containers.

File Footer

The File Footer is located at the end of the file, and shall include a Footer Partition Pack. The File Footer may also include a repetition of the Header Metadata and a Random Index Pack and may include one or more optional Index Table segments.

The File Footer must be present unless there is a Specialized Operational Pattern used, which defines the footer to be absent or optional, and if so, there are other mechanisms that shall be used to identify that the status of the file is complete and that it is closed.

Partitions

Each MXF file is divided into a number of Partitions that logically divide the file to allow easier parsing, to aid in streaming, and to manage the creation of Index Tables, which ease random access into a storage system. An MXF file may contain zero or many

different essence containers and Partitions, which help to manage them. Partitions shall consist of and be ordered as follows:
- one Header Position (at the front)
- zero or more Body Partitions (or Partitions of other types) in the middle
- zero or one Footer Position (which must follow the last of the Body Partitions)

An open Partition is the one in which the required Header Metadata values have not been finalized, that is, the required values may be incorrect. A closed Partition is the one that has a Partition Pack where all the values have been finalized and are correct, and either contain (a) no Header Metadata or (b) all the proper Header Metadata with required values that are finalized.

Operational Patterns

This portion of the standard defines the specific details of every component in an MXF file together with the framework needed to define the relationships between the components. The MXF-OP structures specify the levels of file complexity. The MXF standards intend that Operational Patterns (OP) be written and standardized as separate documents, giving rise to a dynamic set of documents that can be appended without having to reballot the entire MXF set of standards each time a new OP or another portion is added.

The Operational Pattern of a file is identified via a Universal Label (UL) value in properties that are stored in the Preface and in the Partition Packs.

In the Operational Pattern definitions, there may be constraints placed on the capabilities of the File Body. Most Operational Patterns will be written as a constraint on the axes, either in the item complexity or in the package complexity. These are referred to as Generalized Operational Patterns. Regardless of the Operational Pattern, any MXF decoder should be able to read the Partition Pack of the File Header and include the ability to skip over any Run-In bytes. Any MXF decoder should be able to report the contents of the file. It should report if the file is beyond the decoder's capabilities and why it cannot process the file.

A metadata-only file of an Operational Pattern may be created, which has no essence containers and shall correctly report the complexity of their timeline per the mechanisms defined in the MXF Operational Pattern identification structures and labels.

The most commonly used Operational Patterns are the General Operational Pattern OP1a and the Specialized Operational Pattern OP-Atom.

Specialized Operational Pattern Atom

"OP-Atom," defined in SMPTE 390M-2004, is a specialized Operational Pattern for the storage and exchange of an MXF file with a tightly defined structure. OP-Atom is designated for a single item of essence described by a single essence track. The standard defines the operating restrictions, structural metadata objects, and individual attributes, which shall be applied to the MXF file-format specification to achieve interoperability when exchanging a single item of audiovisual material. It is a simple, predictable, layout with minimum scope for variation, specifically intended for applications where each essence track is held separately.

Some applications may find that OP-Atom's provisions are unsuitable, in which case a Generalized Operational Pattern or a different Specialized Operational Pattern should be used. Regardless of the chosen OP, the suitability of a particular pattern needs to be judged on a per-application basis.

With regard to OP-Atom, some specific areas to consider are as follows:

- Optimization where the record (file creation) process is completed before a playout (file read) process is started. This may make OP-Atom unsuitable for concurrent applications, such as when the record/playout (file creation/file reading) processes happen at the same time.
- OP-Atom places a full index table in the footer. When the encoding uses variable bit rate (VBR) essence, this may make it impossible to use the file as a streaming format, especially where stream delivery requires an advanced knowledge of the frame boundaries. In addition, with VBR essence, a possibly very large index table would need to be stored separately until the file recording ends.
- OP-Atom files only hold a single track of essence data. Where applications need an external mechanism to synchronize essence among multiple files, this standard does not define such a synchronization method. However, OP-Atom does include an annex detailing a method of informatively recording synchronization among files created as a group.

The general constraints for OP-Atom in MXF include the items in Table 9.3; note that the Body Partition constraints refer to additional details found in Section 8 of the SMPTE standard and relate to whether the compression is constant bit rate (CBR) or VBR.

Table 9.3 Operational Constraints of the Simplest Form of an MXF File

Operational Pattern OP-Atom (per SMPTE 390M-2004)	
File Kind	*MXF*
Operational Pattern	OP-Atom
Role	Continuous recording
	Exchange of a single audiovisual item
Essence	Single essence container
	Single essence track
Material package	1
Number of material package source clips per essence track	1 or more
Top-level file packages	1
Number of essence container types	1
Low-level source packages	0 or more
Partition limits	Single closed and complete Header Partition
	Single complete Footer Partition
Body Partitions	Dependent upon either constant bit rate (CBR) or variable bit rate (VBR)
Index tables	Required
Editing support	None (additional options)
Streaming support	Depends solely on the essence container

For OP-Atom files with CBR index tables, the constraints for these Partitions are to be followed:

- Header Partition—including closed and complete Header Metadata and an optional index table, no essence container data
- Body Partition—including the complete essence container
- Footer Partition—including a repeat of the index table, no Header Metadata

For OP-Atom files with VBR index tables, the constraints for these Partitions are to be followed:

- Header Partition—including closed and complete header and an optional "sparse" index table, no essence container data
- Body Partition—including the complete essence container
- Footer Partition—including the complete index table, no Header Metadata

Items and Packages

Figure 9.4 shows the Generalized Operational Patterns described on two axes—the horizontal "Item Complexity" axis, and the vertical "Package Complexity" axis—according to the complexity of the items (playlists or edit lists) and the packages (single, ganged, or alternatives). Operational Pattern qualifiers define file parameters that are common to all Operational Patterns.

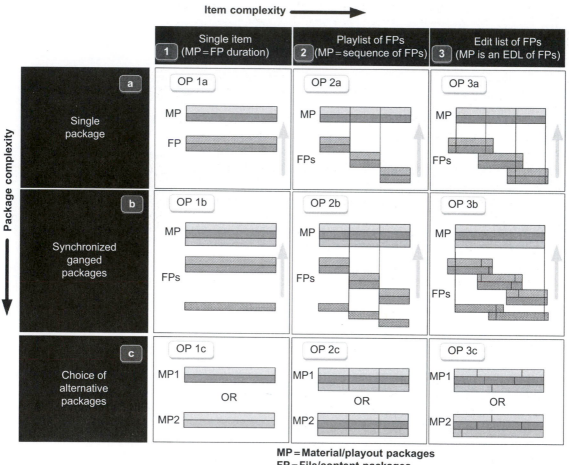

MP = Material/playout packages
FP = File/content packages

Figure 9.4 Generalized Operational Pattern (OP) complexities or "structures" are described in the horizontal (Item Complexity) and vertical (Package Complexity) axes.

The Material Package (MP) is a subclass of the Generic Package with a number defined by an Operation Pattern specification. The tracks of the Material Package shall define the "output timeline" of the file when played. There are constrains, which are detailed in the MXF documents, pertaining to the MP. For example, there can only be one time code component in a time code track of an MP. Furthermore, the number of Picture Tracks, Sound Tracks, and Data Tracks are controlled by the OP specification and by the Top-Level Source Package(s), which are associated with the Material Package.

The Source Package, Top-Level File Packages (which consist of the Source Packages), and the references to a descriptor that describes the essence are subclasses of the Generic Package. In addition, there are Lower Level Source Packages that document the derivation or history of the source clips of the source essence.

Item Complexity

This axis describes that there is more than one File Package (FP) and how on the timeline they are arranged according to the following:

Single Item—when only one item is contained in a file; it will consist of a single MP, or Material Package Source Clip, that will be the same duration as the FP or Top-Level File Package(s).

Playlist Items—when several items are butted against each other; each MP is the same duration as an entire FP.

Edit Items–when the file contains several items with one or more edits; any MP may come from any part of any appropriate FP.

Package Complexity

A Package is the name used for all subclasses of the Generic Package, and in the MXF Operational Pattern axes, is layered (and designated by an alpha character) according to the following:

Single Package—the MP (Material Package) can only access a single FP (Top-Level File Package) at a time.

Ganged Packages—the MP can access one or more FP at a time. Alternate Packages—when there are two or more alternative MPs each of which can access one or more FP at a time. These Alternate Packages may comprise either single packages and/or ganged packages.

Essence Container

The essence container standards provide those specifications for the Picture, Sound, and Data essence containers that are in a File Body. The File Body can contain one or more essence containers. Various other associated MXF essence container specifications describe how these different essence components are placed in the MXF file.

Each essence container specification must meet the needs of program interchange, with each essence container specification written as a stand-alone document or document set that in turn must meet the requirements set out within the master SMPTE MXF document (S377-1-2009c) in order for it to be accepted as a compliant MXF essence container.

All essence and metadata types can be constant data rate or variable data rate.

Descriptive Metadata

Descriptive Metadata standards define optional editorial metadata that enhances the usability of the essence content of an MXF file.

SMPTE Universal Labels

MXF Files include SMPTE Universal Labels (ULs) in the File Header that provide for an early identification of the Operational Pattern (OP), of the existence of Descriptive Metadata plug-ins, and of the essence containers in the File Body.

Dark Metadata

Metadata values that are inserted into a file, which are unknown to a decoder, are called dark metadata. This metadata may be privately defined and generated. The metadata may include new properties that were added to the set, or it may be standard MXF metadata not relevant to the application processing the referenced MXF file.

Rules are set in the MXF standard regarding the use of dark metadata so as to prevent numerical or namespace clashes when private metadata is added to a file already containing dark metadata.

MXF Extensibility

The structures, Operational Patterns, implementations of various coding formats, and the KLV coding structure of MXF consist of several documents. More is added to MXF all the time through

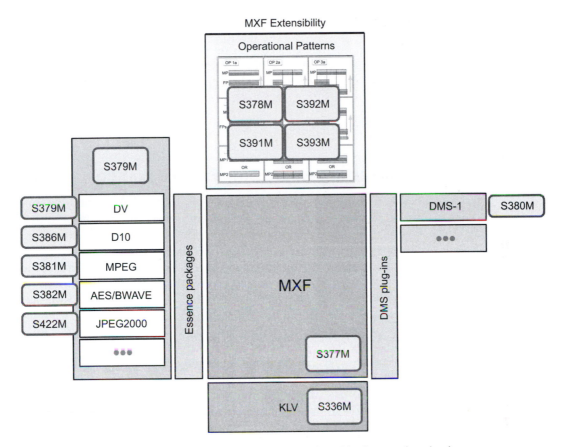

Figure 9.5 Architectural diagram of the MXF suite of standards and implementation plug-ins.

the work of the SMPTE Standards Community, along with the manufacturers of codecs, image capturing systems, and servers. Figure 9.5 shows the relationships and divisions of the MXF documents suite for users with access to the SMPTE standards or for searching on the website for more details.

The extensibility architecture of the SMPTE MXF set of standards has the core SMPTE MXF document (S377M) and the associated essence sets on the left, the Descriptive Metadata Scheme (DMS) plug-ins on the right, and the Operational Patterns on the top. The data encoding protocol, in terms of KLV is described in SMPTE 336M.

Conversion and Transcoding

We begin the second part of this chapter focusing on the conversion of, and the transcoding of, those compliant files that need to interoperate on various platforms used throughout the media industry. To distinguish what occurs in the baseband or linear real-time domain versus the file-based domain where transcoding occurs, let us first look at the basics of conversion for audio and video signals.

First, we will look at conversion whereby traditional analog signals are made into digital or when a digital signal is converted into another form of a digital signal—applicable to when moving from standard definition to high definition or vice versa.

Converting Audio and Video Essence

Raw essence as video or audio will be found with several degrees of variation. For example, at the root level, audio may be either analog or digital. To prepare analog audio essence for use in digital systems, it must be converted from one format (analog) to another format (digital). The original physical transport format for audio, that is, how the signal is carried on a physical medium, may be either as balanced (differential) or as unbalanced signals. The signal level might be high (e.g., 0 db) or low (−20 db). It might have a wide dynamic range (20–20 kHz) or it might have telephone line quality ranging from 400 to 3400 Hz.

Before any conversion, the format of that audio should be known so that it can be converted to another form and then digitally quantized (i.e., sampled), so it can meet the parameters of its new format in the digital world (see Fig. 9.6). A lot of the audio quality issues in a digital audio signal will depend on the sample rate, that is, the "resolution" of the actual digital audio signal. Audio on a CD will have better quality than streaming audio in a YouTube video clip; and a professional digital audio recording using 96 kHz or higher sample rates at 24-bit resolution will produce the highest "mastering" quality. The diagram shows schematically why the differences in sampling rates make such a difference in the final audio. AES digital audio, for a broadcast application, will typically have 48 kHz sample with 16 bits on the low end to 20–24 bits on the high end.

In order for compressed audio to be carried on the AES transport, certain bit rates and sampling rates must be adhered. Those specifications can be found in many of the Dolby Laboratories' or Linear Acoustic's websites (refer to the end of this chapter for additional information and links to these sites).

Videos (as pictures) face a similar discussion. Analog NTSC video has never really had any form of analog audio directly associated with it at baseband levels. The only time that analog audio and video might actually have been coupled was when modulated together for transmission, such as in analog television

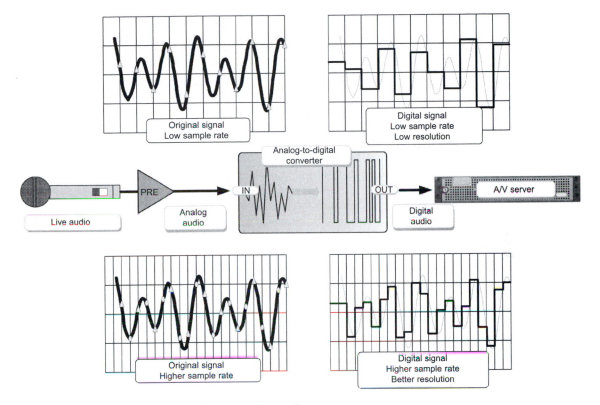

Figure 9.6 Simplified analog-to-digital conversion for audio.

broadcast or in analog cable systems. Depending on the analog system (PAL, NTSC, or SECAM), when preparing for conversion to any digital format, certain other parameters must be considered. For example, if the video carries other ancillary data in the vertical or horizontal blanking areas, one would need to describe the conversion processes necessary to retain that data once it is converted to the digital domain.

When analog high definition was in its infancy, similar effects had to be dealt with; albeit, the relatively short-lived period of analog high definition and its proprietary nature in general caused little industry concern. Nonetheless, if the MUSE high-definition release (with its 1035 active lines) was to work, the content feeding that transport system had to be converted (in the analog domain) to deal with the line scanning issues and bandwidth constraints of the technology available at that time. Even the French during the 1940s, with its 819-line system developed by René Barthélemy, had reached 1015 lines and even 1042 lines before their future French President François Mitterrand (on November 20, 1948) finally decreed a broadcast standard of 819 lines.

First High Definition

As a side note, high-definition analog broadcasting actually did begin at the end of 1949 as a 737-line interlaced format that could not be converted to or from other line or scanning formats. This French TV system was arguably the world's first HDTV system. By today's standards, the French system could be called 737i and possessed a maximum theoretical resolution of 408×368 line pairs (the digital equivalent of 816×737 pixels), but it had only a 4-by-3 aspect ratio (Table 9.4).

Table 9.4 Common Videoconferencing and High-Resolution Computer Display Mappings in Pixels

	Formats	X/Y Pixels
Videoconferencing resolutions	QCIF	176×144
	QSIF	166×120
	SIF	320×240
	CIF	352×288
	NTSC-4SIF	704×480 640×480
	PAL-4CIF	704×576 (H.264 ANNEX D)
	16CIF	1408×1152
High-resolution computer displays	WUXGA	1920×1200 (16:10 aspect ratio)
	QXGA	2048×1536 1024×768
	WQXGA	2560×1600 (16:10 aspect ratio)
	WQSXGA	3200×2048
	QUXGA	3840×2400 ($4 \times 1920 \times 1080$)
	HSXGA	5120×4096 (5:4 aspect ratio)
	WHSXGA	6400×4096 (15.6:10 aspect ratio)
	HUXGA	6400×4800 (4:3 aspect ratio)
	UHDTV	7680×4320 HUDV (33 megapixels)
	WHUXGA	7680×4800

Analog, Digital, and Up/Down Conversions

Conversion from a raster perspective is fundamentally described as when one format is changed to a differing format with more or less video scan lines, a different aspect ratio or a combination of both. The process can be for either audio or video although audio escapes the concept of up- and downconversion—being replaced with mono, stereo, or multichannel/surround modification. Video conversion may be designated as upconversion, generally believed as taking a standard-definition picture and converting it to a high-definition image. Video conversion could also be a downconversion whereby a high-definition image is changed to a standard-definition image or a standard-definition image (SDTV as 720×486) is downconverted to a QSIF (quarter common immediate format) resolution bounded as 176×144 pixels, or to another mobile format for cell phones, smartphones, or apps.

Audio may be converted from analog to digital as AES3 or some other proprietary digital audio format. AES3 is the more common conversion practice, however some systems may also use the Multichannel Audio Digital Interface (known better as MADI), which is an electronic communications protocol defining a data format and an electrical interface for carrying multiple channels of digital audio. The audio could be stereo analog as two discrete channels that when converted becomes a single AES stream with two channels. There may be multiple sets of analog audio that are converted to multiple streams of AES or MADI. The streams may be further combined using industry accepted compression practices offered by Dolby, such as Dolby Digital (AC3) for transmission purposes or Dolby E for contribution purposes.

Depending on the application, external hardware for streaming signals, such as over an SDI transport, may be used or internal software (or hardware) that is integrated into a device, for example, a videoserver, would convert the signal formats on playout. The audio may be carried discretely as AES over an AES-3id transport or it may be embedded into the SDI video transport stream per SMPTE 272M-2004.

If the conversion process only produces a stream of digital bits, such as a high-definition SDI signal, the stream may never been seen as a file and would simply be sent to a real-time digital encoder, as is the case when an ATSC MPEG-2 encoder prepares the signal for over-the-air digital terrestrial broadcasting. Even in this ATSC example, if that same HD program segment were encoded into an MPEG-2 compliant ATSC transport stream (TS) with a fixed program length, this entire TS segment could be made into and stored as a file with all the appropriate syntaxes and elements. A transport stream server, could then release it to a television transmitter's exciter, or transport the file over a network (or satellite link), or for direct playout through an MPEG decoder that converts that signal back into baseband HD video.

Format Conversion

Once an element of video or audio leaves the analog domain, goes through the digital conversion process, and then becomes a file, a number of additional parameters must be addressed. One of those parameters that must be specified is the encoding format. As an example, when the signal of raw essence, such as a 270 Mbit/second serial digital interface (SDI) video stream conforming to the SMPTE 259 standard is presented to the input of a videoserver, it is usually compressed to achieve a much smaller bit rate and then formatted for storage on a disk drive or other storage systems. The file created may or may not conform to a standard that is recognized by the industry. It may also be compressed to a known standard, for example, MPEG-2 MP@ML, but stored on the videoserver's disk arrays in a proprietary format. It may be wrapped to MXF or to MOV when presented as a file to an outside network. If the devices and their files only needed to operate in a completely closed system, the vendor-specified proprietary format may be completely transparent to the outside world.

Hopefully, the user will choose a product that at the very least recognizes and follows a process for creating those files using known and recognized compression formats (e.g., MPEG-2, DV, etc). For interchange and openness, when those files are presented to another system, network, or device, the file should be properly wrapped (e.g., as QuickTime, MXF) as it moves from hard disk storage and onto the network connection, and then is placed onto another platform.

Sometimes, quite frequently now in file-based workflow, a file will use a wrapper or a compression format that is not compatible with the system, which will be discussed next. This could be due to the codecs available on the next server in the chain or because the files were not stored on a platform in a format and with a wrapper that is industry recognized. At this point in the workflow, the file would need to be transcoded in order for it to be recognized by another codec.

Transcode Pipeline

There are effectively two things that need to happen, depending on how the file is originally constructed and what the receiving end needs. If both ends of the chain (source and destination) can accept the same wrapper (or container) formats—as would be the case with an MXF source file format being delivered to an MXF compliant device on the destination end—then perhaps only a transformation of the coding format needs to occur. However, if the original file is QuickTime wrapped (i.e., a MOV QuickTime reference file), encoded as H.264 (AVC-intra), and the receiver expects to see MXF wrapped MPEG-2 422 Profile@ML, then both unwrap/rewrapping and format decode/re-encoding must occur.

The workflow by which this transcode process happens follows the process of receiving a file and first dismantling it into individual audio, video, and data elements (picture, sound, and data essence). This step is called demultiplexing.

The next step then takes each of the demultiplexed elements and decodes them from the incoming compression format to a level where software can then transform those elements and re-encode them to the output compression format required by the receiving (i.e., destination) device. Once properly encoded, the signals are recombined according to the parameters of the file format of the receiving device and then rewrapped into a container format also suitable for the receiving device.

Production-level transcoding requires significant compute horsepower; yet, today there are transcoding products on PCs and Macs that do "flipping" as part of their routine functionality. Early systems used server-class hardware and storage and required time frames usually in excess of real time just to do a simple conversion. Some users found that anything that consistently took longer than real time was better suited to a process where a videoserver just played back the content in real time and it was re-encoded into a different videoserver port or platform. This methodology becomes highly impractical and overly resource intensive when content is delivered only as files or when a high demand of conversion results in provisioning multiple sets of real-time hardware encoders.

Today, modern transcode engines operate with multicore processors or blade servers and can handle dozens of streams simultaneously and render multiple sets of files, each with different wrappers and compression formats. This is the growing trend in media workflow for file-based architectures. Figure 9.7 describes the functions typically found on a transcode engine's user interface. This is the screen where most of the routine setups are made. This instrument becomes the place where the "workflow" is defined that produces finished files corresponding to the output requirements designated. Completed files are published to Web servers, FTP watch folders or to other devices downstream, such as videoservers or video-on-demand platforms.

Inputs include files, FTP watch folders, real-time video capture, Web-based content, etc.

Preview content before transcoding, applying filters or presets, and review the files after transformation

3g2, 3gp, AAC, AC3, AIFF, ASF, AVCHD, AVC-Intra, AVI, DV, FLV, M4A, M4V, MOV, MP3, MP4, MPEG, MPG, MXF, PCM, WAV, WMA, WMV

Inputs

Presets

Filters

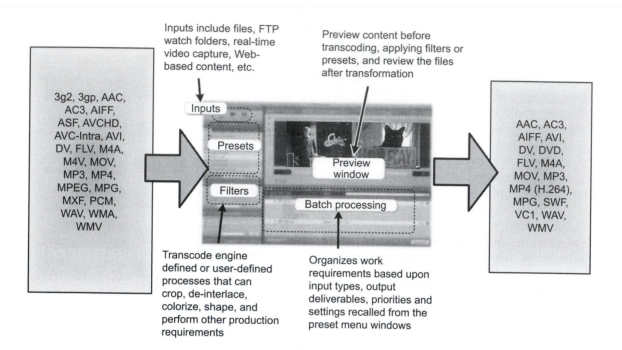

Preview window

Batch processing

AAC, AC3, AIFF, AVI, DV, DVD, FLV, M4A, MOV, MP3, MP4 (H.264), MPG, SWF, VC1, WAV, WMV

Transcode engine defined or user-defined processes that can crop, de-interlace, colorize, shape, and perform other production requirements

Organizes work requirements based upon input types, output deliverables, priorities and settings recalled from the preset menu windows

Figure 9.7 Typical transcode engine user interface where file format profiles, batch processing, and control of the filter and presets are enabled.

Multiplatform Conversion and Distribution

Earlier, we discussed the concept of a platform as being the fundamental technology of a system's (e.g., a computer) hardware and software, which defines how a system is operated and determines what other kinds of services (e.g., software) can be used. In the sense of media files, there are four components that make up the platform (each of these components has been discussed at varying levels throughout this chapter):

• Codec
• Profile
• Level
• Container (wrapper)

When the user intends to deliver his or her video content to more than one platform, such as to an iPhone, to YouTube, for recording to a DVD, or to Blu-ray disc, the content will need to be transcoded. If in the production or asset management processes, there needs to be a master or house format created or a proxy generated so the assets may be found on a search mechanism, the process of transcoding must occur.

The transcoding process is done in software. It avoids "printing to tape" or returning to baseband for transfer as SD or HD video. Instead, transcoding includes the steps of taking the video file and decoding it, scaling it, and encoding it again so that it will work on the desired platform. After the file is prepared, it must be transferred, that is, moved from the source storage platform to the target platform.

Steps in Transcoding

The steps involved in a transcode process are further elaborated in Figure 9.8. Here, the file is first demultiplexed, that is, the file is unwrapped, taken apart, and converted into audio, video, and, depending upon the file, certain data (such as captioning or time code information) components.

Then, each of those components are decoded into their respective elements and then transformed. The transforming process may include something as simple as scaling from standard definition to high definition or it may involve altering the frame rate or scanning rate, cropping of the picture to fit a particular release format, or filtering to prepare it for the bandwidth constraints of the encoding process.

Transrating

The process of converting digital information from one transmission rate to another transmission rate is called "transrating." In case of video, this could be a bit rate change that did

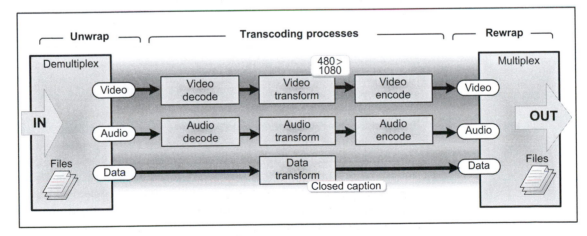

Figure 9.8 Abbreviated flow diagram for the steps involved in transcoding an A/V file, with ancillary data, from one format to another.

not impact the coding of the video image. In audio, this could be a sample rate change. It is also frequently called "bit rate reduction." This technology results in a continued high video quality level by effectively reusing information about the previous encoding while delivering a more cost-effective solution through smaller file sizes or more efficient transmission over the network.

Benefits of transrating include the re-multiplexing of variable bit rate (VBR) streams, which is relevant for both DVB-T (terrestrial) and DVB-S/DVB-S2 (satellite) and for cable environments where the MSO wishes to pack as many programs into a given bandwidth as possible. Single MPEG-2 programs that are encoded as a part of a statistical multiplex (STAT-MUX) may vary in bit rate from 2 to 10 Mbits/second; transrating may be used to ensure that the operator does not have to reserve expensive, mainly unused overhead in the downstream network.

Other transrating features include the reduction of constant bit rate (CBR) streams, and IP streaming of MPEG-2 services where services are rate limited for a single service, enabling a CBR on a specified bit rate, typically significantly lower than both average rates of incoming CBR or VBR programs.

Finally, transrating aids in ensuring compliance with service-level agreements (SLAs) between network operators and content providers by limiting and controlling the rates of single programs that are retransmitted over a DTV network (e.g., a broadcast station that uses the full ATSC that allowed 19 Mbits for a single station may find the cable provider only employing 12–14 Mbits for the retransmitted signal in the same MPEG-2 format).

Transrating may be applied in an open-loop or closed-loop mode. The closed-loop method employs a "learning loop" that takes extra steps to reduce the bits in a stream by learning from what it processed just a few frames previously. These systems are sometimes known as multipass.

Broader Capabilities

Today, further capabilities are included in transforming such as the addition of logos, the concatenation of other files or formats, and even layering or transitional effects. In audio transformations, it may involve shuffling of the tracks in a multichannel stream, compression or band shaping, or changing from one sample rate (e.g., 44.1 kHz) to another (such as 48 kHz), and adjusting the bit rate from 24 bits to 16 bits.

If the conversion is from SD to HD and there is closed captioning data involved, then the data must be conformed from the SD version (as CEA 608) to the HD digital equivalent (as CEA 708). If metadata describes the audio compression format (e.g., Dolby E or dial_norm), then this must also be properly parsed and prepared according to the expectations of the final encoding format.

After the elements are appropriately transformed, then each of them will be presented to encoders before they can be made back into files. Encoding is set according to the MPEG or other encoding scheme, with the appropriate profile and level associated with the essence.

Once encoded, the individual essence components are remultiplexed and wrapped according to the file format requirements for final delivery to the storage platform, network, or editing system, which will next receive the file.

Real-Time Versus Off-line Transcoding

In the early periods when transcoding was mostly associated only with files and because of limitations on computing horsepower, most transcoding occurred in an "off-line transcoding" mode. Today, with the advent of real-time delivery, video-on-demand preparation, and high degrees of compression or software delivery, it is now common practice to segregate the transcoding processes even further.

Real-Time Transcoding

Transcoding in real time is just what it infers; it is the processing of files as streams in hardware that is specifically purposed for live or nearly live delivery or transmission. The files are usually encoded at only fixed or constant bit rates, presented to the transcoding system as linear streams, and often built using hardware-based silicon components. This real-time processing is expensive compared to off-line transcoding systems. They are usually found in mission critical systems whereby a stream might be delivered to an over-the-air broadcast while simultaneously being delivered to the Web, near video on demand, or to a nonlinear editing platform for recutting during a live event such as a sport venue or a live breaking newscast.

From a performance and scalability perspective, two variables come into play: the number of channels or services required to be delivered to how many discrete platforms and the number of differing profiles that those channels must provide. For scalability, the real-time transcoding "farm" needs to identify how many channels will be required at peak times and how many output profiles are produced for those channels. These factors are influenced by the use case of the service level agreement (SLA) that the provider must account for.

Off-line Transcoding

This application hinges on the needs of a production service that is not dependent on a live or real-time delivery constraint. This is often the case when movies are ingested and then prepared for users on a variety of platforms. It is not unusual for a content aggregator or multichannel video programming distributor (MVPD) to end up producing a dozen or more formats from each movie master that is used by the Web, cable, satellite, packaged formats, on demand, etc.

In each of these respective releases, the transcode process may wish to employ VBR encoding, depending on the intended use. They are almost always producing files and not streams (although they could prepare files for streaming applications).

The performance and scalability of off-line transcoding has many variables. Factors that affect the performance of the system include the number of processors, the size of the memory, the bandwidth and amount of disk cache, and, if connected to other subsystems, the network the transcode farm is connected to. In terms of scalability, the system is measured by the number of transcoding tasks that can occur concurrently and in what amount of time. Again, the system must be considered on a use-case basis or according to the SLA the user and the customer has between them. Figure 9.9 compares real-time (i.e., "live") transcoding to off-line (i.e., "faster or slower than real time") transcoding functions.

Transfer Characteristics

Transcoding has helped to enable three modes of transfer, which are applicable, and now quite common, to the media industry regardless of the medium that is being used for the media. The three modes include streaming, download, and adaptive bit rate.

Streaming

Streaming occurs when video is pushed to or pulled from a server to a device that is then immediately, or very shortly thereafter,

	Real-time transcoding	Off-line transcoding
Encoding	Fixed rate	Variable rate
Format	Streams	Files
Platform	Hardware	Software
Applications	Live/streaming	VOD–DVD/Blu-ray motion pictures
Costs	High	Low–high
Quality/value	Low–moderate	Moderate–high

Figure 9.9 Applications and comparative value points in real-time versus off-line transcoding related to performance, hardware, cost, and application.

put into a playback mode. Selected examples of formats that are designed for this application form include the following:

- Flash 7 (Adobe, formerly Macromedia)
- Flash 8 (Adobe, formerly Macromedia)
- Windows Media (Microsoft)
- Real Media (Real Networks)
- QuickTime (Apple)

There are also special cases where the streaming application is intended for a live event.

Download

Downloads are videos that are pulled from a server to a device, stored or buffered on that device, and then played back at a later time. Examples of video download include the following:

- Windows Media (Microsoft)
- QuickTime (Apple)
- iPhone Sideload

The special case for download is called "progressive download" that involves delivering video files using a Web server. Progressive is sometimes referred to as "HTTP streaming," but it is not really streaming at all, only a simplified bulk download of a video file to a computer. Web servers will use the Hypertext Transport Protocol (HTTP) to transfer files over the network. HTTP operates on top of the Transport Control Protocol (TCP), which controls the actual transport of data packets over the network and is optimized for guaranteed delivery of data, regardless of its format or size.

With progressive download, the Web server does not care about the file size or the transfer rate, so the system just waits for the right network bandwidth and the file is delivered using a best effort model. Some WAN optimizers can aid in supporting download speeds, but those applications usually are disassociated with the Web servers that are preparing and submitting those files to the network.

Adaptive Bit Rate

When video is downloaded in small chunks and then played back one at a time, this is generally accomplished through the principles of adaptive bit rate encoding. Examples of adaptive bit rate encoding for streaming applications include the following:
- Dynamic Streaming for Flash (Adobe)
- HTTP Adaptive Streaming for iPhone/iPad (Apple)
- Smooth Streaming for Silverlight (Microsoft)

Examples and Conclusions

The flexibility offered in transcoding and transfer operations is growing more complex and more valuable as each new compression format is introduced and as each new device or delivery platform is marketed. These multiformat, application-targeted models allow users to choose the appropriate configurations for the needs of the organization, customer, or user. Through the deployment of these conversion, transcoding, and transfer models, it has become possible to stream in multiple formats, deliver in multiple resolutions, and produce variations in bit rates simultaneously so as to optimally reach a diverse new set of audiences.

Figure 9.10 shows the integration of a transcoding platform with a decision tree that automatically can properly conform standard-definition or high-definition video files to a prescribed release format based on the user describing how those images should be prepared and in what aspect ratio and image format (SD or HD). This is just one segment of what might comprise a complete workflow model for the ingesting, processing, preparing, and delivery of file-based media and content.

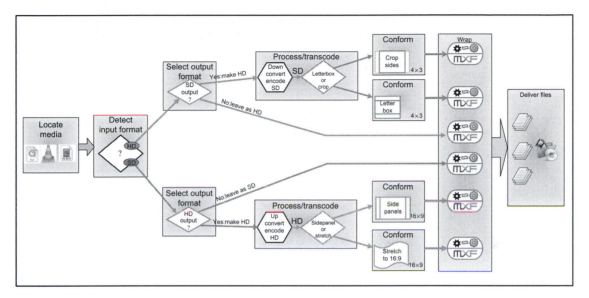

Figure 9.10 Example of a media aware process for delivering SD or HD source files in any of the five different final output formats while staying entirely in the file-based domain.

Further Readings

Useful references to video, audio, and other file formats:
http://www.fileinfo.com/filetypes/video

SMPTE and EBU work and study project that resulted in the foundation for file-based workflows: "Task Force for Harmonized Standards for the Exchange of Program Material as Bitstreams," Final Report: Analyses and Results, July 1998.
The document can be found at
http://www.smpte.org/standards/tf_home/Final_Report_-_Findings.pdf

SMPTE Standards that are informative with respect to the MXF standards include (a) ANSI/SMPTE 298M-1997, Television—Universal Labels for Unique Identification of Digital Data; (b) SMPTE 336M-2001, Television—Data Encoding Protocol using Key-Length-Value; (c) SMPTE EG 42—MXF Descriptive Metadata.
A listing of the MXF Operational Pattern standards that include (a) SMPTE 390M: OP-Atom; (b) SMPTE 378M: OP-1a (the minimal and simple MXF file); (c) SMPTE 391M: OP-1b; (d) SMPTE 392M: OP-2a; (e) SMPTE 393M: OP-2b; (f) SMPTE 407M: OP-3a, OP-3b; (g) SMPTE 408M: OP-1c, OP-2c, OP-3c.
Guides to digital audio practices, conforming files and audio to meet the various industry standards, and practical applications for multichannel sound can be found at

Dolby Laboratories.
http://www.dolby.com/professional/technology/index.html

Linear Acoustic.
http://www.linearacoustic.com/wpapers.htm

10

IP STORAGE

Block data storage has been driven by user demand and the vendors who have continued to find new efficiencies in storage data networking. The goals for developing and implementing IP storage networking are directed by the aim to reduce the costs associated with acquisition, administration, and support.

The migration away from fixed dedicated networking infrastructures that are supported over high speed Gigabit Ethernet is being achieved by employing protocols centered on IP, such as iSCSI, iFCP, and FCIP, to moving block data. This chapter looks at these various types of storage subsystems and devices that define the future of storage on IP networks.

KEY CHAPTER POINTS

- Internet protocol in a connected or connectionless environment, and the basics of IP-addressing, domain naming, and Ethernet
- Storage that is connected over IP networks as IP storage (IPS)
- Defining and detailing IP networking: iSCSI, iFCP, FCIP, iSNS
- QoS for IP storage networks, RSVP, MPLS, InfiniBand
- Security and other considerations for implementing storage over IP networks

Internet Protocol

In complex networks, dynamic routing is enabled by using Internet Protocol (IP). By taking advantage of IP, storage can be extended over the network, and through the use of the protocols we will be discussing, it becomes an alternate means for moving the block data of the network.

We will start the discussion on IP storage with a brief overview and review of the fundamentals, including the protocols, definitions, and standards associated with this technology.

Delivering Packets by IP

Data can be sent between one computer and another over the Internet through IP. The Internet is essentially the interconnection of many individual networks. The Internet Protocol is the governing set of rules that allows one network to communicate with any other network. When configured for broadcast messages, this communication could be sent to all the other networks with like and proper configurations.

In this example model, each host computer on the Internet will have at least one IP address that uniquely identifies it from other computers on the Internet. When data are sent or received using this protocol, the message will be divided into small chunks of data called "packets." The sender's Internet address and the receiver's address are included in each packet.

Each network needs to know its own address on the Internet and the address of any other networks with which it communicates. To be part of the Internet, an organization needs an Internet network number, which can be requested from the Network Information Center (NIC). The unique network number is then included in any packet that is sent out of the network onto the Internet.

Typically, the packet is first sent to a gateway (i.e., a computer) that knows about a small portion of the Internet. The gateway reads the packet, discovers the destination address, and forwards the packet to an adjacent gateway that then reads that destination address and forwards it the next. The process continues across the Internet until one of the gateways recognizes that the packet does belong to a computer within its immediate neighborhood, also known as a domain. At this point, the gateway forwards that packet directly to the computer whose address was specified originally from the host or sending computer.

Messages are usually divided into a number of individual small sizes, the packets, so that if necessary the packets may take different routes to get to the destination domain (neighborhood). This causes the packets to arrive in a different order than they were sent in. In this model, IP's responsibility is to just deliver them to the right address. Transmission Control Protocol (TCP), another very familiar protocol, is charged with reordering and reassembling the randomly delivered packets into the proper order.

Connected or Connectionless

In the Open Systems Interconnection (OSI) communication model, IP is in Layer 3, known as the Networking Layer. IP is called a "connectionless" protocol. There is no continuous connection between any of the points that are communicating. As packets traverse the Internet, each of them is treated as an independent unit of data with no relationship to any other unit of data that is also on this vast highway.

Transmission Control Protocol (TCP), which is a connection-oriented protocol that was standardized in 1981 in RFC 793, is the instrument that keeps track of the packet sequence in a message.

Internet Protocol Version 4 (IPv4) is the most widely used version of IP today. When engineered, IPv4 was thought to possess all the addresses and space ever imagined for use on the Internet. This, however, was not the case, so IP Version 6 (IPv6) was developed to create much longer addresses and in turn, the possibility of many more Internet users. IPv6 includes the capabilities of IPv4. Any server that is capable of supporting IPv6 packets is by definition also able to support IPv4 packets.

IP Address Classes

Since networks will vary in size, four different address formats called "classes" are used. In IPv4, an IP address will usually be expressed as four decimal numbers, each representing eight bits, separated by periods. This is sometimes known as the "dot address" or "dotted quad notation."
- Class A addresses are for large networks with many devices (represented as "network.network.network.local").
- Class B addresses are for medium-sized networks.
- Class C addresses are for small networks (fewer than 256 devices) (represented as "network.network.network.local").
- Class D addresses are multicast addresses.

The number version of the IP address can be (and usually is) represented by a name or series of names called the domain name.

Addresses

In addition to the network address, information is needed about which specific machine or host in a network is sending or receiving a message. Thus, an IP address needs both its unique network address, and a host number, which would be unique within the network. The host number is sometimes referred to as a local or machine address.

Part of the local address can identify a subnetwork (i.e., a subnet address), which allows a network to be subdivided into several physical subnetworks. In this mode, there might be several different local area networks that are configured to handle many devices.

Domain Naming

The system that locates an entity (e.g., a commercial, educational, or non-profit organization) on the Internet is built around the concept of a "domain name." The familiar Web annotation uses three basic segmentations for this system.

When the location is described as

www.mydomainname.com,

this locates an Internet address for "mydomainname.com" at an Internet point 199.0.0.5. It is served by a particular host server that is named "www" (World Wide Web). The last part of the domain name, in our example ".com," reflects the organization or entity's purpose, and is called the "top-level" domain name. For example, ".com" stands for commercial; ".edu" for education; ".org" for organization, etc. This nomenclature is assigned when a user applies for and registers their particular domain name.

The "mydomainname" part of the domain name, together with the top-level portion, is called the "second-level" domain name. This second-level domain name is a human-readable representation of the actual Internet address that it maps to. Second-level domain names must be unique on the Internet. They are registered with one of the ICANN-accredited registrars for the COM, NET, and ORG top-level domains. Additional top-level domains include ".tv", or if they are non-USA based, they may be geographically associated with the country they are registered to, for example, ".ca" is for Canada, ".it" is for Italy, etc.

The third level defines a particular host server at the Internet address. In this example, "www" is the name of the server that handles Internet requests (note that a second server could be annotated as "www2." The third level of domain name is not required; as such a fully qualified domain name could have been simply "mydomainname.com" (the server is then assumed).

The nomenclatures allow for additional "subdomain" levels to be used. If desired, one could employ the domain name

"www.yoursubdomainname.mydomainname.com."

The Uniform Resource Locator (URL), on the Web, is that part of the domain addressing scheme that tells a domain name server using the domain name system (DNS) where (or if) a request for a given Web page is to be forwarded. The domain name is therefore mapped to an IP address representing a physical point on the Internet.

Ethernet

A widely installed local area network (LAN) technology, Ethernet is standardized under the IEEE 802.3 specifications. Gigabit Ethernet is standardized in IEEE 802.3z, with 10 Gbit Ethernet in IEEE 802.3a. The IP-related standards are managed under the auspices of the Internet Engineering Task Force (IETF) through the process of Requests for Comments (RFCs) that handle a growing range of diverse topics, including protocols and management issues.

Ethernet was originally developed by Xerox from an earlier specification called Alohanet (for the Palo Alto Research Center Aloha network) and then developed further by Xerox, DEC, and Intel. Ethernet was named by one of its developers, Robert Metcalfe, for the passive substance called "luminiferous ether," which was once thought to pervade the universe, carrying light throughout. Table 10.1 shows the progress of Ethernet standards from 1972 through the proposed additions (prefaced with the "P") anticipated for adoption in 2011.

Devices, ranging from hosts to switches, are connected to the local area network (LAN) through special grades of twisted pair

Table 10.1 Ethernet Standards and Classifications

Ethernet Communications Standards					
Ethernet Standard (P = Proposed)	*Date*	*Standard*	*Speed (bits)*	*Speed (bytes)*	*Description*
Experimental	1972		2.94 Mbits/second	367 Kbytes/second	Over coax cable, cable bus
Ethernet II (DIX v2.0)	1982		10 Mbits/second	1.25 Mbytes/second	Over thick coax
802.3	1983	10BASE5	10 Mbits/second	1.25 Mbytes/second	Over thick coax
802.3a	1985	10BASE2	10 Mbits/second	1.25 Mbytes/second	Over thin coax (thinnet or cheapernet)
802.2b	1985	10BROAD36			
802.3c	1985		10 Mbits/second	1.25 Mbytes/second	
802.3d	1987	FOIRL			FOIRL = Fiber Optic Inter Repeater Link

Continued

Table 10.1 Ethernet Standards and Classifications *(Continued)*

| Ethernet Communications Standards | | | | | |
Ethernet Standard (P = Proposed)	Date	Standard	Speed (bits)	Speed (bytes)	Description
802.3e	1987	1BASE5			"StarLAN"
802.3i	1990	10BASE-T	10 Mbits/ second	1.25 Mbytes/ second	Over twisted pair
802.3j	1993	10BASE-F	10 Mbits/ second	1.25 Mbytes/ second	Over fiber optic cable
802.3u	1995	100BASE-TX	100 Mbits/ second	12.5 Mbytes/ second	Fast Ethernet with autonegotiation
802.3x	1997				Full duplex and flow control, incorporates DIX framing
802.3y	1998	100BASE-T2	100 Mbits/ second	12.5 Mbytes/ second	Over low quality twisted pair
802.3z	1998	1000BASE-X	1 Gbits/second	125 Mbytes/ second	Ethernet over fiber optic cable
802.3-1998	1998				Revision of the base 802.3 standard
802.3ab	1999	1000BASE-T	1 Gbits/second	125 Mbytes/ second	Gigabit Ethernet over twisted pair
802.3ac	1998				Maximum frame size extended to 1522 bytes (Q-tag)
802.ad	2000				Link aggregateion for parallel links (later IEEE 802.1AX)
802.3-2002	2002				Revision to base 802.3 standard, prior amendments, errata
802.3ae	2003	10GBASE-SR	10 Gbits/ second	1250 Mbytes/ second	Ethernet over fiber (10GBASE-LR; -ER; -SW; -LW; -EW)
802.3af	2003				Power over Ethernet (PoE) power = 12.95 watts
802.3ah	2004				Ethernet in the First Mile
802.3ak	2004	10GBASE-CX4	10 Gbits/ second	1250 Mbytes/ second	Ethernet over twin-axial cable
802.3-2005	2005				Revision to base 802.3 standard, 4 prior amendments, errata

Table 10.1 Ethernet Standards and Classifications *(Continued)*

Ethernet Communications Standards					
Ethernet Standard (P = Proposed)	Date	Standard	Speed (bits)	Speed (bytes)	Description
802.3an	2006	10GBASE-T	10 Gbits/second	1250 Mbytes/second	Ethernet over unshielded twisted pair (UTP)
802.3ap	2007		1 and 10 Gbits/second	125 and 1250 Mbytes/second	Backplane Ethernet on printed circuit boards (PCB)
802.3aq	2006	10GBASE-LRM	10 Gbits/second	1250 Mbytes/second	Ethernet over multimode fiber
P802.3	2006				Frame expansion
802.3at	2009				Power over Ethernet (PoE) power = 25.5 watts
802.3au	2006				Isolation requirements for PoE (802.3-2005/Cor 1)
802.3av	2009		10 Gbits/second		EPON
802.3aw	2007				Equation fix in 10GBASE-T (released as 802.3-2005/Cor 2)
802.3-2008	2008				Revision of base standard, with 802.3an/ap/aq/as amendments
802.3az	2010				Energy efficient Ethernet
802.3ba	2010		40 and 100 Gbits/second		Ethernet over 1 m. Backplane, 10 m. Cu, 100 m MMF/40 m SMF
802.3bb	2009				Increases Pause Reaction Delay (802.3-2008/Cor 1)
802.3bc	2009				Update, move Ethernet TLV (type-length-value)
P802.3bd	~7/2011				Priority-based flow control, IEEE 802.1 Data Center Binding
P802.3be	~2/2011				Creates 802.3.1 MIB definitions for Ethernet
P802.3bf	~6/2011				Provide accurate indication of TX and RX initiation times
P802.3bg	~9/2011				Provide 40 Gbits/second PMD, optically compatible with SMF 40 Gbits/second

cable, syntactically called "category" cabling. Cabling categories are numbered according to the data speed and performance characteristics specified for the bitrates they will carry.

Their host or device signals, when connected, then compete for access to the network using a Carrier Sense Multiple Access with Collision Detection (CSMA/CD) protocol.

Internet Engineering Task Force

The Internet Engineering Task Force (IETF) is the open international community of network designers, operators, vendors, and researchers supporting the evolution and smooth operation of the Internet, whose Mission Statement is documented in RFC 3935.

IETF Working Groups are divided into areas that are managed by area directors (ADs), who are members of the Internet Engineering Steering Group (IESG). Architectural oversight is provided by the Internet Architecture Board (IAB), which also adjudicates appeals when complaints are received that the IESG has failed. The IAB and IESG are chartered by the Internet Society (ISOC).

The Internet Assigned Numbers Authority (IANA), also chartered by the ISOC, is the central coordinator, responsible for the assignment of unique parameter values for Internet protocols. IANA acts as the clearinghouse in the assignment and coordination of the uses for numerous Internet protocol parameters.

The IETF holds meetings three times a year, with the bulk of its work conducted via other electronic means. The IETF has eight functioning areas related to technology development and standards:
- Applications
- Internet
- Operations and Management
- Routing
- Security
- Sub-IP
- Transport
- User Services

Inside this structure, the IETF working group on "Internet Protocol Storage (IPS)," aimed at studying IP storage, was formed.

IP Storage

Significant interest in using IP-based networks to transport block storage traffic began around the end of 2000. The initiatives for IP storage evolved on a foundation of previously established

IEEE 802.3 Ethernet standards and the IP-related standards from the diverse Request for Comments (RFCs) of the IETF. These two industry standards, IP and Ethernet, only describe a part of the equation for network storage on IP.

IP storage needed to accommodate the earlier recognized standards for SCSI and for Fibre Channel storage devices. The principle entities responsible for these standards were under the purview of the INCITS (formerly NCITS) Committees:

- INCITS T10 for SCSI
- INCITS T10 for Fibre Channel Protocol (FCP)
- INCITS T11 for Fibre Channel transport

The IP Storage Working Group was a chartered group tasked with developing a protocol to transport the Small Computer Systems Interface (SCSI) protocol over the Internet. The iSCSI protocol defines a mapping of SCSI transport protocol over TCP/IP so that SCSI storage controllers (principally disk and tape arrays and libraries) can be attached to IP networks (notably Gigabit Ethernet and 10 Gbit Ethernet).

The IP Storage Working Group functioned from September 25, 2000, through November 1, 2007, pursuing a pragmatic approach to the encapsulation of existing protocols, (e.g., SCSI and Fibre Channel), into a set of IP-based transport or transports. The group further focused on related issues (e.g., security, naming, discovery, and configuration), as opposed to modifying existing protocols.

The working group also considered whether a layered architecture providing common transport, security, and/or other functionality for its encapsulations was the best technical approach.

The following sections will begin to focus on the approaches and implementations that emerged from the 7-year efforts of the IP Storage Working Group.

iSCSI

The family of protocols most associated with communicating between I/O devices, especially storage systems, is the Small Computer Systems Interface (SCSI). SCSI is a client-server architecture. The clients of a SCSI interface are called "initiators." Initiators issue SCSI commands to request services from components, and logical units of a server known as "targets."

A "SCSI transport" maps the client-server SCSI protocol to a specific interconnect. An initiator is one endpoint of a SCSI transport and a target is the other endpoint. The SCSI protocol has been mapped over various transports, including parallel SCSI, IPI, IEEE-1394 (FireWire), and Fibre Channel (FC). These transports are I/O specific with limited and designated distance capabilities.

The iSCSI protocol is a means of transporting SCSI packets over TCP/IP, providing for an interoperable solution that can take advantage of existing Internet infrastructure, Internet management facilities, and address distance limitations. The iSCSI protocol aims to be fully compliant with the standardized SCSI Architecture Model (SAM).

iSCSI RFCs

In recent times, study groups inside the IETF have been working towards a consolidation of several RFCs into a single document that combines certain groups and makes additional updates to the specification of others. The iSCSI documents included in this effort include

- RFC 3720, which defined the original iSCSI protocol.
- RFC 3721, which discusses iSCSI naming examples and discovery techniques.
- RFC 3980, which added an additional naming format to iSCSI protocol.
- RFC 4850, which followed up by adding a new public extension key to iSCSI.
- RFC 5048, which offered a number of clarifications and a few improvements and corrections to the original iSCSI protocol.

This consolidation will supersede the text found in RFCs 3720, 3980, 4850, and 5048, placing them into a single document; and it makes additional updates to the consolidated specification, which will include a further update to the naming and discovery techniques cited in RFC 3721.

iSCSI Protocol

The iSCSI protocol is a mapping of the SCSI command, event, and task management model over the TCP protocol. SCSI commands are carried by iSCSI requests. SCSI responses and status are carried by iSCSI responses. iSCSI also uses the request response mechanism for iSCSI protocol mechanisms.

Initiator–Target Messages

The terms "initiator" and "target" refer to "iSCSI initiator node" and "iSCSI target node," respectively, unless otherwise qualified. In keeping with similar protocols, the initiator and target divide their communications into messages. This consolidated document uses the term "iSCSI protocol data unit" (iSCSI PDU) for these messages.

For performance reasons, iSCSI allows a "phase-collapse." A command and its associated data may be shipped together from initiator to target, and data and responses may be shipped together from targets.

Transfer Directions

The iSCSI transfer direction is defined with respect to the initiator. Outbound or outgoing transfers are transfers from an initiator to a target, while inbound or incoming transfers are from a target to an initiator.

An iSCSI task is an iSCSI request for which a response is expected. In the consolidation document "iSCSI request," "iSCSI command," request, or (unqualified) command have the same meaning. Furthermore, unless otherwise specified, status, response, or numbered response have the same meaning.

Network Address Authority (NAA)

The INCITS T11 Framing and Signaling Specification [FC-FS] defines a format called the Network Address Authority (NAA) format for constructing worldwide unique identifiers that use various identifier registration authorities. This identifier format is used by the Fibre Channel and SAS SCSI transport protocols. As FC and SAS constitute a large fraction of networked SCSI ports, the NAA format is a widely used format for SCSI transports. The objective behind iSCSI supporting a direct representation of an NAA-format name is to facilitate construction of a target device name that translates easily across multiple namespaces for a SCSI storage device containing ports served by different transports. More specifically, this format allows implementations wherein one NAA identifier can be assigned as the basis for the SCSI device name for a SCSI target with both SAS ports and iSCSI ports.

The iSCSI NAA naming format is "naa" plus a "." (dot), followed by an NAA identifier represented in ASCII-encoded hexadecimal digits, as shown in Fig. 10.1.

```
naa . 52004567BA64678D
```
iSCSI NAA naming with 64-bit NAA value

```
naa . 62004567BA64678D0123456789ABCDEF
```
iSCSI NAA naming with 128-bit NAA value

Figure 10.1 NAA identifier types in 64-bit and 128-bit ASCII-encoded hexadecimal notation.

iFCP

Fibre Channel is a frame-based, serial technology designed to promote peer-to-peer communication between devices at gigabit speeds with low overhead and minimal latency. To successfully implement and integrate the advantages found in Fibre Channel, especially when the physical or geographic separation between nodes or systems exceeds the distance specifications of the Fibre Channel standards, alternative provisions have been designed to provide a more universal solution for new and existing systems. Some of these alternative and supplemental protocols are described in the following sections of this chapter. Most of these solutions are bundled under the heading of TCP/IP-based networks.

Chapter 6 also provides an extensive look into Fibre Channel and storage area networking.

Gateway Protocol to TCP/IP

Internet Fibre Channel Protocol (iFCP) is a gateway-to-gateway protocol for the implementation of Fibre Channel fabric functionality over a TCP/IP network. The iFCP protocol standard was developed by the IETF per RCC 4172 (September 2005). Its functionality is provided through TCP protocols for Fibre Channel frame transport via the distributed fabric services specified by the Fibre Channel standards. The iFCP architecture enables internetworking of Fibre Channel devices through gateway-accessed regions with the fault isolation properties of autonomous systems and the scalability of the IP network.

Provisions

iFCP uses TCP to provide congestion control, error detection, and recovery. iFCP's primary objective is to allow for the interconnection and networking of existing Fibre Channel devices, at wire speeds, over an IP network. The protocol, and its method of frame address translation, permit the attachment of Fibre Channel storage devices to an IP-based fabric through transparent gateways. The protocol achieves transparency by allowing normal Fibre Channel frame traffic to pass directly through the gateway with provisions (where necessary) for intercepting and emulating the fabric services required by a Fibre Channel device.

Fabric

The iFCP protocol enables the implementation of Fibre Channel fabric functionality on an IP network in which IP components and technology replace the Fibre Channel switching and routing infrastructure. The example of Fig. 10.2 shows a Fibre Channel network with attached devices. Each device accesses the network through an N_PORT (node port) that is connected to an interface whose behavior is specified in FC fabric switch (FC-FS) or FC arbitrated loop (FC-AL2). In this case, the N_PORT represents any of the variants described; with the interface to the fabric able to be an L_PORT, F_PORT, or FL_PORT.

Within the Fibre Channel device domain, addressable entities consist of other N_PORTs and Fibre Channel devices internal to the network that perform the fabric services defined in Fibre Channel General Services-3 (FC-GS3).

One example of an equivalent iFCP fabric is shown in Fig. 10.3. The fabric consists of two gateway regions, each accessed by a single iFCP gateway.

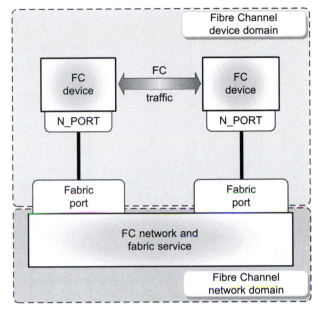

Figure 10.2 An example of a Fibre Channel network.

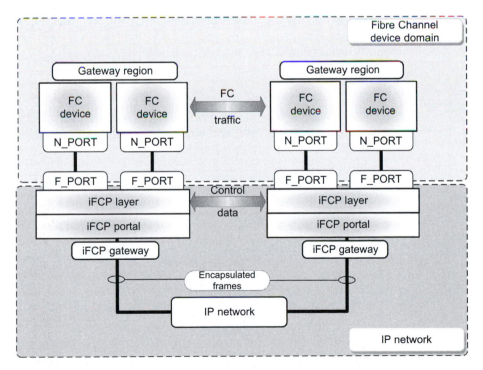

Figure 10.3 Example of an iFCP fabric with its interface to an IP network.

Each gateway contains two standards-compliant F_PORTs and an iFCP Portal for attachment to the IP network. Fibre Channel devices in the region are those locally connected to the iFCP fabric through the gateway fabric ports.

Looking into the fabric port, the gateway appears as a Fibre Channel switch element. At this interface, remote N_PORTs are presented as fabric-attached devices. Conversely, on the IP network side, the gateway presents each locally connected N_PORT as a logical Fibre Channel device.

iFCP Services

The main function of the iFCP protocol layer is to transport Fibre Channel frame images between locally and remotely attached N_PORTs.

Transport Services

When transporting frames to a remote N_PORT, the iFCP layer encapsulates and routes the Fibre Channel frames comprising each Fibre Channel Information Unit via a predetermined TCP connection for transport across the IP network.

When receiving Fibre Channel frame images from the IP network, the iFCP layer de-encapsulates and delivers each frame to the appropriate N_PORT.

Other

The iFCP protocols provide for other services and models, which are detailed in RFC 4172 (Section 5 onwards). Some of those additional services and models include
- iFCP support for link services and messaging
- TCP transport of iFCP frames
- iFCP Session Model
- iFCP Session Management
- Fibre Channel Frame Encapsulation/De-Encapsulation
- Fibre Channel Broadcast and Session Management

Security

The iFCP protocol is designed for use by gateway devices deployed in enterprise-class data centers. These environments characteristically have security gateways aimed at providing network security through a high degree of isolation from public networks. Nonetheless, iFCP data may need to traverse security gateways in order to support SAN-to-SAN connectivity across those public networks.

iFCP relies upon the IPSec protocol suite to provide data confidentiality and authentication services. iFCP relies upon Internet Key Exchange (IKE) as the key management protocol. Detailed considerations for use of IPsec and IKE with the iFCP protocol can be found in [SECIPS].

iFCPs communicate across gateways, and as such are subjected to unwanted attacks. These adversarial threats may include attempts to

- acquire confidential data and identities by snooping data packets,
- modify packets containing iFCP data and control messages,
- inject new packets into the iFCP session,
- hijack the TCP connection carrying the iFCP session,
- launch denial-of-service (DOS) attacks against the iFCP gateway,
- disrupt the security negotiation process,
- impersonate a legitimate security gateway, or
- compromise communication with the iSNS server.

iFCP gateway administration must be prepared to thwart these attacks by implementing and confidentially using (through per-packet encryption) data origin authentication, integrity, and replay protection on a per-datagram basis. Because iFCP is a peer-to-peer protocol, the iFCP gateway must implement bidirectional authentication of the communication endpoints and be prepared to use them. Administrators must implement and enable the use of a scalable approach to key management.

Other security related practices should include

- Authorization or authentication
- Policy control
- iSNS (discussed later in this chapter)
- Other applicable technologies from IPsec and IKE per recommendations in RFC 4171, Section 10.3.1 "Enabling Technologies."

The next section discusses the mechanisms for LAN, WAN, and MAN connectivity useful in interconnecting Fibre Channel SAN islands over an IP network.

Fibre Channel Over IP (FCIP)

Fibre Channel over TCP/IP (FCIP) describes mechanisms that provide for the interconnection of islands of Fibre Channel storage area networks over IP-based networks to form a unified storage area network in a single Fibre Channel fabric. FCIP enables the transmission of Fibre Channel (FC) information by tunneling

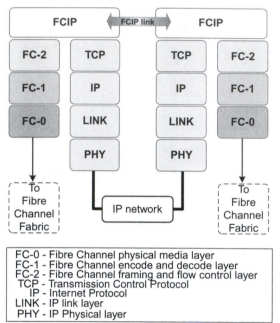

FCIP protocol model

FC-0 - Fibre Channel physical media layer
FC-1 - Fibre Channel encode and decode layer
FC-2 - Fibre Channel framing and flow control layer
TCP - Transmission Control Protocol
IP - Internet Protocol
LINK - IP link layer
PHY - IP Physical layer

Figure 10.4 The "FCIP Protocol Stack Model" showing the relationship between FCIP and other protocols.

data between storage area network (SAN) facilities over IP networks. IP-based network services offer connectivity between the SAN islands over LANs, MANs, or WANs. Figure 10.4 shows the FCIP stack and its relationship to other protocols.

FCIP may be found annotated as FC/IP, while also being called "Fibre Channel tunneling" or "Fibre Channel storage tunneling." This storage networking technology was developed by the IETF and is defined in RFC 3821 (July 2004). These mechanisms are an important technology for linking Fibre Channel SANs.

Complementary

FCIP and iSCSI are complementary solutions that are typically used for different purposes. FCIP transparently interconnects Fibre Channel (FC) SAN islands over IP networks, while iSCSI allows IP-connected hosts to access iSCSI or FC-connected storage.

With FCIP, Fibre Channel frames are encapsulated in IP so that both SCSI and non-SCSI frames can be transported over an IP network. With iSCSI, SCSI commands and data frames are encapsulated in IP to support I/O disk access over an IP network.

By combining FCIP and iSCSI, enterprises are able to:

* Interconnect SAN islands.
* Provide applications including remote backup and replication, while performing Fibre Channel I/O communication.

Nominal Distances

Fibre Channel standards have elected to use nominal distances between switch elements that are less than the distances available in an IP network. Since Fibre Channel and IP-networking technologies are compatible, it is reasonable to turn to IP networking as a medium for extending the allowable distances between Fibre Channel switch elements.

One fundamental assumption made in the FCIP specification is that the Fibre Channel traffic is carried over the IP network in such a manner that the Fibre Channel fabric and all Fibre Channel devices on the fabric are "unaware of the presence of the IP network." As such, FC datagrams need to be delivered in such time as to comply with existing Fibre Channel specifications.

FCIP Link

The FCIP Link (Fig. 10.5) is the basic unit of service provided by the FCIP protocol to an FC fabric. An FCIP link connects two portions of an FC fabric using an IP network as a transport to form a single FC fabric.

Figure 10.5 FCIP Link model.

At the points where the ends of the FCIP Link meet portions of the FC fabric, an FCIP Entity combines with an FC Entity to serve as the interface between FC and IP. In an implementation that tunnels an FC fabric through an IP network, it is necessary to combine an FC Entity with an FCIP Entity in order to form a complete interface between the FC fabric and IP network. An FC Fabric may contain multiple instances of the FC/FCIP Entity pair shown on either side of Fig. 10.6.

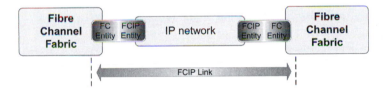

Figure 10.6 Model for two connected FC/FCIP Entity pairs.

An FCIP Link shall contain at least one TCP connection, and it may contain more than one TCP connection. The endpoints of a single TCP connection are FCIP Data Engines (see Fig. 10.7), with the endpoints of a single FCIP Link being FCIP Link Endpoints (FCIP_LEP).

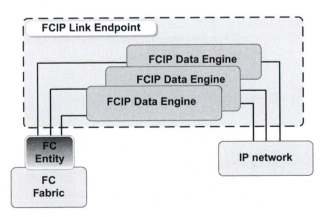

Figure 10.7 Fibre Channel over IP Link Endpoint (FCIP_LEP) model.

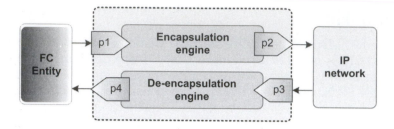

Figure 10.8 Fibre Channel over IP Data Engine (FCIP_DE) model.

An FCIP_LEP is a transparent data translation point between an FC Entity and an IP network. A pair of FCIP_LEPs communicating over one or more TCP connections create an FCIP Link to join two islands of an FC fabric, producing a single FC fabric (Fig. 10.8). The FCIP Data Engine (FCIP_DE) is a combination dual bidirectional encapsulation/de-encapsulation device through which data enter and leave through a set of four portals. The portals are not required to examine or process the data that traverse them.

Clarification

It is easy to get this (FCIP) and the previously described iFCP confused, given the order and similarities of the two acronyms. One should understand that FCIP simply *extends* existing Fibre Channel fabrics through the medium of an IP network. In FCIP, TCP/IP is used only to traverse a metro or wide area distance.

By comparison, iFCP is a migration strategy from current Fibre Channel SANs to future IP-based SANs. The gateways of iFCP can either complement existing FC fabrics, or they may replace them entirely, while still leveraging the substantial investments that had been made in an existing Fibre Channel storage architecture.

Since iFCP enables customers to build IP SAN fabrics, it becomes a convenient means to migrate to a mixed Fibre Channel/iSCSI environment. Furthermore, iFCP will potentially offer users a channel to minimize the Fibre Channel fabric component and maximize the use of their legacy TCP/IP infrastructure.

Internet Storage Name Service (iSNS)

Used for interaction between Internet Storage Name Service (iSNS) servers and iSNS clients, this protocol facilitates automated discovery, management, and configuration of iSCSI and Fibre Channel devices (using iFCP gateways) on a TCP/IP network. iSNS provides for intelligent storage discovery and management of services comparable to those found in Fibre Channel networks. The goal is to allow for a commodity IP network to function in a capacity similar to that of a storage area network (SAN).

iSNS facilitates a seamless integration of IP and Fibre Channel networks through its capabilities of emulating Fibre Channel fabric services, and through the management of both iSCSI and Fibre Channel devices (using iFCP gateways). Internet Storage Name Service provides added merit to any storage network comprised of iSCSI devices and iFCP gateways addressing Fibre Channel devices, or any combination thereof.

Standards-compliant iSNS implementations are required to support the iFCP protocol; however, supporting the iSCSI protocol is optional.

iSNS Architectural Components

The set of components that make up the iSNS architecture, per RFC 4171, adopted in September 2005, include the following components consisting of the iSNS protocol, its client, servers and database.

iSNS Protocol (iSNSP)

A lightweight and flexible protocol that specifies how iSNS clients and servers communicate. The protocol is appropriate for various platforms, including switches, targets, and server hosts.

iSNS Client

These initiate transactions with iSNS servers using the iSNS Protocol (iSNSP). iSNS clients are processes that are co-resident in the storage device. They can register device attribute information, download information about other registered clients in a common discovery domain (DD), and receive asynchronous notification of events that occur in their DD(s). A special type of iSNS client, called a management station, will have access to all DDs stored in the iSNS.

Management Station

A management station will use iSNS to monitor storage devices and to enable or disable storage sessions by configuring discovery domains, usually interacting with the iSNS server as a control node endowed with access to all iSNS database records and with special privileges to configure discovery domains. Through manipulation of the discovery domains, management stations control the extent of device discovery for iSNS clients querying the iSNS server. The management station may use proprietary protocols or SNMP-based solutions to cross reference, report on different segments of the enterprise network, or transfer device records between the iSNS servers.

iSNS servers

These servers will respond to iSNS protocol queries and requests. They will initiate iSNS protocol state change notifications (SCNs). The properly authenticated information submitted by a registration request is stored in an iSNS database.

State Change Notification (SCN)

SCN is a service that allows the iSNS server to issue notifications about network events affecting the operational state of storage nodes. The iSNS client may register for notifications on behalf of its storage nodes for notification of events detected by the iSNS server. SCNs notify iSNS clients of explicit or implicit changes to the iSNS database. The connectivity state of peer storage devices in the network are not necessarily indicated by the service. The storage device's response to receipt of a state change notification is determined by the type of implementation of these services.

SCN Registrations

Two types of SCN registrations are possible: regular registrations and management registrations. A regular SCN registration indicates that the Discovery Domain Service shall be used to control the distribution of SCN messages. Regular SCNs will not contain information about discovery domains.

A management SCN registration can only be requested by control nodes, and are not bound by the Discovery Domain Service. Authorization to request management SCN registrations may be administratively controlled.

Management registrations result in management SCNs, whereas regular registrations result in regular SCNs.

iSNS Database

As the information repository for the iSNS server(s), this database maintains information about iSNS client attributes. A directory-enabled implementation of iSNS may store client attributes in a Lightweight Directory Access Protocol (LDAP) directory infrastructure.

Lightweight Directory Access Protocol (LDAP)

LDAP is an application protocol for querying and modifying directories (a set of objects with attributes organized logically in a hierarchical manner) that are implemented in IP networks.

Mapping FC and iSCSI Devices

The iSNS database will store information about the naming and discovery of both Fibre Channel and iSCSI devices, allowing the iSNS server to store mappings of a Fibre Channel device to a proxy iSCSI device "image" in the IP network. Similarly, mappings of an iSCSI device to a "proxy World Wide Name (WWN)," a unique identifier used to identify a particular Fibre Channel target, can be stored under the WNN Token field for that iSCSI device.

What iSNS Does

iSNS is a scalable information facility for the registration, discovery, and management of networked storage assets. The service provides a unified service framework for topology discovery that integrates iSCSI, iFCP, and is extensible to FCIP and other IP storage protocols, and further integrates with the DNS infrastructure.

iSNS facilitates device discovery and configuration, which in turn enables SANs to scale from smaller, departmental size storage systems to enterprise-wide applications. Normally, in a conventional network environment, all devices that are attached to the network are considered hosts. Hosts must possess sufficient intelligence to discover and communicate with other hosts throughout the network. In the case of the Internet, the domain name system (DNS) enables a host to perform these activities through the name/address resolution process.

For storage devices, there are a unique set of requirements. Storage devices do not initiate transactions; they wait for active hosts (e.g., file servers) to initiate requests. Storage end nodes must first register their presence on the network in order for the discovery process to commence. In the case of SCSI, the bus polling action normally associated with host servers that are directly attached to the SCSI storage devices can automatically discover the storage devices, such as disk arrays, which are connected to the host. This is because in this topology, the server exclusively "owns" the direct attached storage (DAS) and the server determines when it is available for use.

However, in a SAN (or other network attached storage device), polling processes are not feasible as the storage resources may be scattered across an intricate network. Managing who owns the storage at any moment is even more complicated, inferring that at any moment more than one server may discover the same storage target. Initiators must be capable of identifying SAN resources and resolve if they have authorization to access them.

This is where the iSNS specification from IETF RFC 4171 comes into play. The specification establishes the policies and methods for device discovery in Fibre Channel protocol (FCP) and IP storage networks, as well as iSCSI. Implementation of iSNS can occur on any form of network, either individually or simultaneously, depending upon the user configuration.

Unified Discovery and Management

The nature of both Internet and network storage necessitates that a number of solutions be available that address the specifics of the topologies, structures, and other issues that are part of the particular storage device. For Internet storage, we have looked

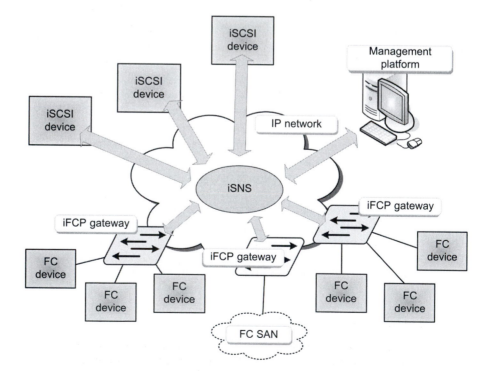

Figure 10.9 A unified discovery and management framework using iSNS.

at iSNS as a means to support discovery and management of the storage platforms that would be addressed.

A unified approach to these methods was the intent of the developers and promoters of iSNS through the various RFC documents. What resulted is a framework that enables a uniform set of parameters applicable to each implementation. The diagram (Fig. 10.9) depicts how iSNS is used to manage and allow for the discovery of these storage resources regardless on which Internet storage protocol the devices are on.

The following sections will explore some of the distinctions and peculiarities that must be addressed when adopting such a unified framework across Internet-based storage systems.

Fiber Channel Discovery

Fiber Channel, which supports both arbitrated loop (FC-AL) and fabric topologies, becomes one of the complicated challenges. In FC-AL, polling the rather limited number of devices (a total of 126 end nodes) is rather straightforward. However, if the storage system is a fabric, there are 15.5 million potential end nodes.

Polling through all possible devices on a FC Fabric is impractical, even at gigabit speeds; thus, the FC Fabric provides for a name service definition to aid in the discovery process. Because every storage device must register with the SNS, an initiator need only query the SNS and ask for a list of all the devices that support FCP.

The SNS only responds to initiator inquiries, so as part of the access control system, another mechanism is employed to restrict discovery only to authorized hosts.

Zoning

In FC switched fabrics, the segregation of devices is accomplished through zoning, which creates groups of authorized devices that communicate with each other through either hard zoning, called "port attachment," or soft zoning through the WWN. The definitions, established manually by an administrator, may restrict initiator inquiries to only those targets that are reported by the SNS and are in the same zone.

Using SCN Functions

In addition to zoning and SNS, Fibre Channel further provides for state change notification (SCN) functionality to notify initiators when storage devices are available or enter the fabric.

Distributed Intelligence

Some of the discovery processes depend upon the distributed intelligence of the fabric. The change notifications and policies are fabric specific; that is, each fabric maintains its own SNS database and thus its own sets of notifications and policies. When scaling these services to an enterprise-class SAN, this creates problems because each fabric must now be enabled to share its data in its own particular SNS database such that any initiator on the network can discover any potentially viable target.

IP Storage Support

iSNS provides for support of iFCP and iSCSI. Given that IP storage solutions are based on so many discrete protocols, each with their own unique requirements and transport protocols, the management problems and discovery processes are faced with similar issues to those encountered in FCP. One cannot assume that all the switches or routers on a network will have discovery mechanisms available to them. Therefore, the iSNS must be portable, flexible, and of a scale that is lightweight enough to be extensible and attachable over multiple IP storage switches.

Quality of Service for IP Storage Networks

All data within the infrastructure of the network will receive the same priority unless there is a means of setting policies for the delivery of that data.

Class of Service (CoS)

In FC SANs, a majority of the applications run over Class 3 services, a connectionless implementation that provides for a best-effort delivery with no acknowledgment. There are classes above this (Class 2 and Class 1), and classes below it, although these are less used in practice. In the section on Fibre Channel in Chapter 6, there is additional discussion of the class structure.

Nonetheless, going to a higher class, which improves service by providing greater feedback and reliability that data were actually transferred, results in a trade-off in overall SAN performance. QoS therefore is a metric whereby a higher level of service such as a guarantee of prescribed bandwidth or expedited delivery results in a slowdown of actual data throughput.

Scaling the service levels requires the addition of more complex and costly network equipment.

Traffic Prioritization

Buffer queues enable class-of-service prioritization. When there is no class designations, packets will by FIFO forwarded (i.e., "first-in/first-out"). Multiple buffer queues are necessary to effectively prioritize traffic flow. Traffic is sorted by a priority tagging method, some of which are self-assigned. Low end switches have fewer buffer queues, while higher quality devices utilize a full complement of queues so as to fulfill all the needed packet priority levels.

The ability to sustain high levels of high-priority traffic forces some starvation of the lower priority queues, and it may result in packets being dropped in order to meet the high sustainability requirements of the system.

TOS Precedence

In the IP datagram header, at the network layer of the stack, is an 8-bit "type of service" (TOS) field that sets the precedence, the type of service, and a must be zero bit. The TOS field uses a 4-bit sequence to set the five classes of service ranging from "minimum delay" through "normal service," which are defined per RFC 1349. As an example, for bulk transfers, such as those using FTP, the "maximum throughput" class would be used so as to enable the most data to be transferred through the network.

Differentiated Services

The 8-bit IP header used for the TOS was redefined in RFC 2474 and RFC 2475 as "differentiated services," more commonly known simply as DiffServ. This implementation now becomes a policy-based system allowing the CoS to be set at each node in the network. DiffServ further allows these forward decisions the ability to let the data hop through the network using rules know as "per-hop-behavior" (PHB). A differentiated services code point (DSCP) specifies the particular per-hop behavior and is applied to each packet. Support for DSCP is still lacking in some network equipment, and DSCP is not compatible with IP precedence.

Service levels can be established by PHB rules that set priority requirements, bandwidth, and packet dropping preferences. The rules can be dynamically changed to address levels of network traffic or congestion, such as one form of data exchange receiving a higher degree of preferential treatment versus another form of data exchange.

Performance Predictability

With the trend of turning to centralized and consolidated storage so as to better support server virtualization and private cloud environments, enterprises are considering implementing SANs based on iSCSI that will generally lack any predictability with regard to performance. This inability to ensure the quality of service for the SAN when it is more than ever necessary to ensure application performance is a subject that has been boiling to the surface for the past several years—especially with the emphasis on "services in the clouds" so prominent.

Traffic Shaping

If networking and storage applications used traditional traffic shaping techniques to better manage and ensure iSCSI SAN traffic, this could change the complexion of QoS for IP-based storage solutions. By using TCP/IP Traffic Shaping to achieve predictability in iSCSI service, one could effectively throttle traffic to iSCSI target servers so as to enable traffic prioritization.

Implementing throttling controls to prioritize workloads and then dynamically changing those priorities depending on need potentially allows one to control resource utilization and ensure the QoS of the SAN.

Theory and Research

From the concept that consolidated storage systems in which virtual disks rely on a shared storage pool of underlying hardware are less dependable than dedicated local storage units, research suggests that a method that introduces throttling on both the read and the write requests, with decision making being orchestrated by a proportional integral derivative (PID) controller, would potentially enable a controlled environment by which LAN traffic could be optimized for the resources that are available at that time.

While throttling outgoing (i.e., read requests) to some extent is simpler than throttling write requests, the most common form of shaping for inbound traffic is ingress policing, which drops packets from a sender when a bandwidth threshold is crossed. By using this method, congestion control mechanisms then adjust the sender rate to a point that can be sustained without any excessive packet dropping. This method is not very satisfactory for establishing a high degree of QoS in the SAN given that packet loss might lead to the inefficient use of the network link when packet retransmits reach too high a level.

Variable Delay

As an alternative, and to address the limitations previously cited, another method of throttling was proposed that introduces a variable additional delay to packets that are sent back to the initiators (or the clients in SCSI terminology). To counter this, read requests are merely throttled by delaying all outbound packets containing any payload. To throttle write request without dropping packets, the outbound ACK packets containing no payload are simply delayed. The actual delay is achieved using NetEm, an enhancement of the traffic control facilities of Linux that permits the adding of delay, of packet loss, and other scenarios as needed to enhance network traffic performance. NetEm is built using the existing QoS and DiffServ facilities in the Linux kernel. To supplement NetEm, a modified PID controller is employed; together, this combination is used to dynamically mark the packets. This efficient bidirectional mechanism is then used to throttle individual iSCSI initiators. Because packet delay throttling is utilized as a means to influence its input value, this becomes a means of predicting the average wait time of those resources that are being controlled.

Throttling Decisions

Deciding when to apply throttling decisions must be made based upon capacity availability, yet the "state of available capacity" never remains constant given that it depends on the rate, direction, and pattern of the workloads. The resource saturation level is determined by the use of consumer response time measurement. By using the basic building blocks found in this research work, it may be possible to create a vast amount of prioritization schemes. The schemes would then become the metric to make these throttling decisions and in turn optimize efficiencies in the flow of packets over the network.

Resource Reservation Protocol (RSVP)

RSVP is another network-control protocol that provides a different QoS strategy from those employed in DiffServ. RSVP is used to establish a level of service for Internet application data flows through a network. Data flows are a stream of packets that originated from a single particular IP address or TCP port number and are sent to one or more fixed destination IP addresses or TCP port numbers. RSVP supports both unicast and multicast simplex sessions.

Unlike routing protocols, RSVP manages flows of data rather than making decisions for each individual datagram (see Fig. 10.10). Data flows consist of discrete sessions between specific source and destination machines. A session is more specifically defined as a simplex flow of datagrams to a particular destination

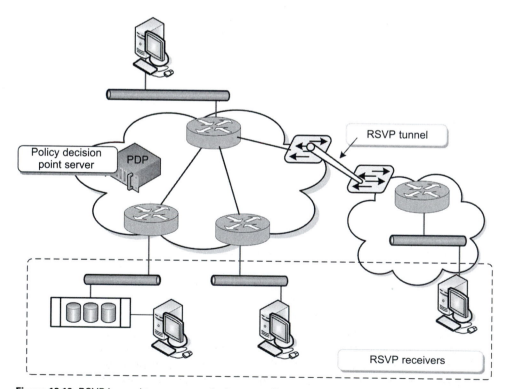

Figure 10.10 RSVP is used to reserve paths between IP networks.

and transport layer protocol. The identification data used in sessions consist of the destination address, a protocol ID, and the destination port.

Storage applications benefit from RSVP through application services such as data replication, mirroring, remote backup, or vaulting.

Post-production block-based content distribution, and storage, also benefit from this practice because RSVP will set and maintain a served bandwidth and a priority service level for the duration of the transaction.

RSVP is used to specify the QoS by both hosts and routers, thus maintaining the router and host state to provide the requested service. Using RSVP, hosts will request a QoS level from the network on behalf of an application data stream. Routers then use RSVP to deliver QoS requests to other routers along the path(s) of the data stream. RSVP is not universally deployed in IP networks. To maintain the data flow through non-RSVP served components, an RSVP tunnel must be established across those non-RSVP segments by the use of two RSVP-enabled IP routers. The portion of the cloud that is not RSVP-capable must have sufficient (excess) bandwidth to fulfill the end-to-end QoS requirements.

Supervision of RSVP requests is centrally administered by the Common Open Policy Services (COPS) protocol specified in RFC 2748, which authenticates permissions for the requests via a centralized "policy decision point" (PDP). The instrument that supports these policies, the "network policy server," enforces the compliance of RSVP-enabled switches or routers within the network.

While RSVP requires policy and decision logic to implement, once the RSVP data path is established, standard IP datagrams can be streamed from source to destination without any additional variation or modification.

Multiprotocol Label Switching (MPLS)

MPLS techniques are applicable to ANY network layer protocol. MPLS is standardized by the IETF in RFC 3031. Principally, MPLS is deployed in high-performance networks to connect from as little as two facilities to very large facilities on the network. It is a highly scalable, protocol agnostic, data-carrying mechanism.

Packet forwarding is the concept used in routers to move packetized payloads of data, including routing instruction headers, throughout a network. As packets (in connectionless IP network layer protocol) travel from one router to another, each router must make its own independent forwarding decision for each packet it encounters. The router will analyze the packet's header and then run a network layer routing algorithm against that header. Each router in the chain then advances the packet to the next hop based on its analysis of the packet's header. This is done independently for each packet and for each router in the network.

Packet headers contain significantly more information than what is needed to select the next hop in the network. To select the next hop, the entire set of possible packets are partitioned into a set of "Forwarding Equivalence Classes (FECs)," and then each FEC is mapped to a next hop. Insofar as the forwarding decision is concerned, different packets that get mapped into the same FEC are indistinguishable. The same path will be followed for all packets belonging to a particular FEC and will travel from a specific node. If multipath routing is in use, they will all follow one of a set of paths associated with the FEC.

In MPLS, packet to FEC assignment is done once at the point where the packet enters the network. Through what is referred to as "labeling," the FEC to which the packet is assigned is encoded as a short fixed length value (the "label"). As packet forwarding continues to the next hop, the label is sent along with it, and there is no further analysis of the packet's network layer header at each hop. This label, which is used as an index into a table, will look up and specify the next hop. At that hop, a new label will replace the old label and the packet is then forwarded to its next hop.

Thus, packet-forwarding decisions are made solely on the contents of this label, without the need to examine the packet itself. This lets one create end-to-end circuits across any type of transport medium, and encapsulates packets using any protocol. A router that supports MPLS is known as a "Label Switching Router" (LSR).

MPLS Transport Profile

As of late, the ITU-T and IETF have been working to harmonize the differences in transport profiles for MPLS. The ITU-T version is called "T-MPLS" and the IETF version is called "MPLS-TP" (transport profile). The efforts of the IETF can be found in RFC 5317 (February 2009). Simply stated, the concern raised by the Joint Working Group of the IETF is that parameters in the ITU-T version may conflict with those in the IETF version, and the incompatibility of IETF MPLS-TP and ITU-T T-MPLS would "represent a mutual danger to both the Internet and the Transport network."

As of the release of RFC 5921 in July 2010, work is continuing on the development of "A Framework for MPLS in Transport Networks," which ties together the requirements of RFC 5654, "Requirements of an MPLS Transport Profile."

InfiniBand

InfiniBand is an I/O architecture originally intended to replace PCI and to address high-performance server interconnectivity, often abbreviated as "IB." InfiniBand originally began as two separate initiatives: one from Intel, called the "Next Generation I/O," and the other from IBM, Compaq, and HP, called "Future I/O." The two efforts were merged into a set of standards driven by the InfiniBand Trade Association (IBTA).

The system architecture was aimed toward replacing the standard bus with a switched matrix that was patterned after Gigabit Ethernet and Fibre Channel switching. It is designed to mitigate the problems in the SCSI bus limitations in terms of device support, distance, and speed.

Architecture

The InfiniBand Architecture (IBA) is designed around a point-to-point, switched I/O fabric, whereby end node devices (ranging from inexpensive I/O devices to very complex host computers) are interconnected by cascaded switch devices. The IBA

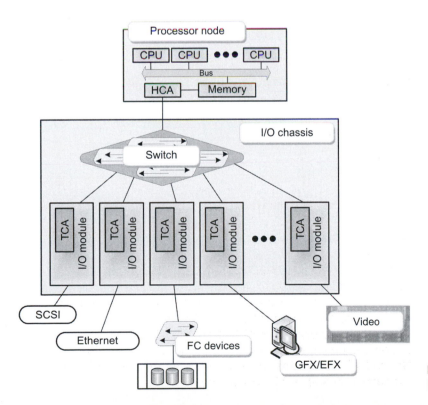

Figure 10.11 Single host InfiniBand Architecture (IBA).

Specification describes a first order interconnect technology for interconnecting processor nodes and I/O nodes to form a system area network. The architecture is independent of the host operating system (OS) and processor platform.

IBA supports a range of applications from being the backplane interconnect of a single host (Fig. 10.11), to a complex system area network (SAN) consisting of multiple independent and clustered hosts and I/O components (Fig. 10.12). The InfiniBand term "SAN" is not related to the term "Storage Area Network," although to some degree they appear similar, sans the Fibre Channel expectations.

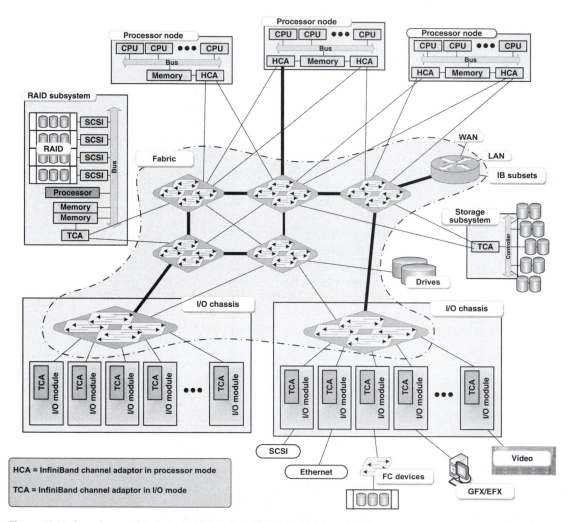

Figure 10.12 Complex multiple host and fabric InfiniBand Architecture (IBA) system area network (from InfiniBand Architecture Specification Volume 1, Release 1.2.1).

System Components

The devices in an IBA system are classified as
- Channel adapters
- Switches
- Routers
- Repeaters
- Links that interconnect switches, routers, repeaters, and channel adapters
  The management infrastructure includes
- Subnet managers
- General Service Agents

Channel Adapters and Verbs

Channel adapters are the IBA devices in the processor nodes and I/O units that generate and consume packets. The channel adapter will also terminate a link and/or execute transport-level functions. It may be either a Host Channel Adapter (HCA), which supports the "verbs interface," or a Target Channel Adapter (TCA), which is typically used to support I/O devices. TCAs are not required to support the verbs interface.

A "verbs interface" is an abstract description of the functionality of an HCA. An operating system may expose some or all of the verb functionality through its programming interface. A "verbs consumer" is a direct user of the verbs.

Switches

Switches primarily pass along packets based on the destination address in the packet's local route header. A switch will consume and source packets that are required for managing the switch proper. A switch port may (optionally) incorporate the properties of a physical TCA port.

Routers

Routers will not generate or consume packets, with the exception of management packets. Routers will only pass, that is, forward packets based on the packet's global route header. The router will replace a packet's local route header as the packet passes from one subnet to the next.

IBA routers are a fundamental routing component in the architecture of inter-subnet routing, which is provided for by IBA switches. Routers promote the interconnection of subnets by relaying packets between the subnets.

Management

IBA provides for a "subnet manager" and an infrastructure that supports a number of general management services. Each node in the management infrastructure requires a subnet management agent, which then defines a general service interface that allows for the addition of general services agents.

The IBA defines a "common management datagram" (MAD) message structure for communicating between managers and management agents.

Subnet Manager (SM)

The subnet manager is an entity attached to a subnet that is responsible for the configuration and management of switches, routers, and channel adapters. The subnet manager can also be implemented on other devices, such as a channel adapter or a switch.

Subnet Management Agent (SMA)

Each node provides a Subnet Management Agent (SMA) that the subnet manager accesses through an interface called the Subnet Management Interface (SMI), which allows for both local identifier (LID) routed packets and directed route packets.

Directed routing provides the means to communicate ahead of switches and end nodes configuration. Only the SMI allows for directed route packets.

Service Agents

Additional management agents, referred to as General Service Agents (GSA), may be added at each node. The GSA may be accessed through the General Service Interface (GSI), which only supports LID routing. There are several general service classes defined in the IBA, the depth of which is beyond this brief overview of InfiniBand.

Performance and Applications for IBA

InfiniBand can be found in various system architectures, wherever there is a requirement for high-speed, low-latency communications. One area where IB is utilized is in accelerating the parallel-processing capabilities of multiple GPUs (graphics processing units) for 3D (stereoscopic) and multidimensional rendering of images in real time. In this application, it is imperative that a GPU talk directly to the memory (storage) system so that efficiencies are maximized both during read and write operations, offloading those activities from the CPUs of the rendering farm or workstation(s).

IB is also found in media data centers as the interface between complex storage systems and compression or transcode engine farms. Given the volume of data that must travel from the store as raw content, through the compressor or transcoder, and back to active storage, it is essential to have the highest performance computer (HPC) backbone available to maximize throughput and improve efficiencies.

IBA provides levels of performance that can be application specific to the needs of storage, workflow, or processing. The roadmap through 2014 is outlined in Fig. 10.13 which shows how multiple lanes of bandwidth can be scaled to meet the objectives of the enterprise.

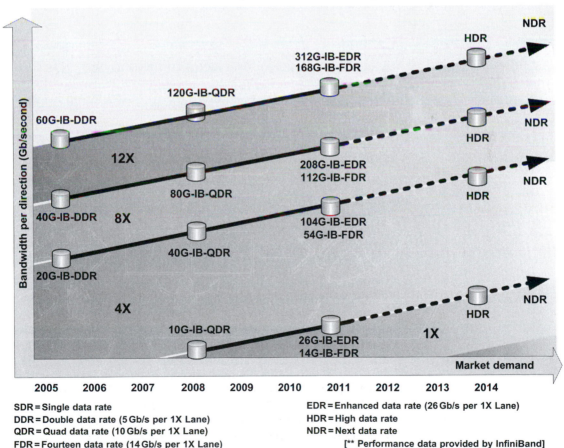

Figure 10.13 InfiniBand performance and roadmap.

Link Performance

Three levels of performance are currently available in the InfiniBand Architecture:

- 10 Gbits/second
- 20 Gbits/second
- 40 Gbits/second

The link speeds provide for low-latency communication within the fabric and enable higher aggregate throughput than other protocols.

Fibre Channel and Gigabit Ethernet

The InfiniBand Architecture is complementary to Fibre Channel and Gigabit Ethernet, enabling those networks to connect into the edge of the InfiniBand fabric, which improves access to InfiniBand Architecture-enabled computing resources.

Cabling

In addition to a board form factor connection integral to the IB fabric architecture, InfiniBand also supports active and passive copper (up to 30 meters pending speeds), and fiber-optic cabling (up to 10 km).

IP Storage Considerations

Enterprise-class networks will routinely employ expensive to deploy, often difficult to manage Fibre Channel technology for their high-performance storage networks. Maintenance of such systems are well beyond the capabilities of most small- or medium-sized IT departments, usually requiring outside resources to monitor, diagnose, and tune up when modifications are needed, capacities are reached, or performance requirements change—such as when a new department is created or a major activity is added.

Less expensive and simpler technology can be found by employing IP network (e.g., Ethernet) technology and components for organizations ranging in size from small (SOHO) to large (corporate) users. Organizations can now deploy inexpensive storage networks capable of transporting storage data anywhere Internet access is available or where there is support for SCSI storage commands across that particular IP network.

Whether the storage area network is Fibre Channel based or is of another breed, switches and routers will play an essential role in establishing sufficient IP storage performance through the segmenting of storage traffic from other regular LAN-user traffic, while also maintaining security throughout the entire network architecture.

IP Switches and Routers

Most current IP switches and routers now provide for the high-end features necessary to support these activities. Such reliability features should include capabilities for active/active clustered failover, failback, and multipathing.

IP storage implementation performance depends heavily on the selection of the appropriate IP storage switch or router, demanding careful consideration of port speed, segmentation, interoperability, security, and application compatibility.

Determining the Need

When looking at implementing an IP storage network, the first consideration should be to evaluate the need for that IP storage network. It may not be practical to add IP storage if the entity has already deployed an all Fibre Channel storage solution. However, by implementing an inexpensive and well-understood IP storage infrastructure, more servers could be cost-effectively interconnected to the fabric, which could noticeably improve the organization's server resource availability.

Consider those applications that will be functional on the IP SAN segment, since certain applications may perform better on an IP SAN, with others requiring the performance obtained only on a Fibre Channel SAN. Never be reluctant to do some thorough testing, on your specific network, as an aid in identifying potential compatibility issues with your applications.

Logical Separation Points

Smaller organizations might find themselves deploying only IP storage networks. Larger IT departments already invested in a Fibre Channel storage solution need to determine how or if IP storage fits into their global storage perspective. In concentrated activities, such as found in media content creation or post-production, it might be more practical to place non-media related user data on IP storage, and dedicate mission-critical applications and its data to the Fibre Channel SAN. Here, the breed of IP switching will make all the difference in performance, and may be specifically required in order to attain the expected throughput necessary for those activities.

IP SANs may be more suitable for remote offices where there is a lesser degree of concentrated activities or when there are smaller staffs attached to that local area network. If local, temporary, or scaled-back data exchanges can be managed across the Internet, then it becomes natural to select the IP switches and routers appropriate to those activities.

Other technical considerations should also be included in the selection of IP switches and routers. These include SAN segmentation support and cross domain inter-fabric routing; mapping of zones across SAN segments; or virtualization used to segregate IP SANs—the term VSAN (from Cisco) comes to mind.

Security Considerations

IP SAN security features are a matter of fact given the ubiquitous nature of IP and how it can impair IP SAN security. IP SANs should remain logically separated from other LAN user traffic in order to prevent sensitive data from unexpectedly leaking out across the LAN and onto the Internet. The selection of a switch or router for the IP SAN necessitates an evaluation of the authorization and authentication capabilities of the IP switch or router.

Ports and Connectivity

If iSCSI is implemented as a supplement to an existing Fibre Channel SAN, then the switch and/or router solution will need to implement both IP and FC ports on the same physical device. The availability and performance requirements in terms of the number of ports and their connectivity parameters for iSCSI must provide for adequate expandability. Some iSCSI gateways will combine multiple Gigabit Ethernet ports and multiple FC ports into a single device, allowing for the linking of servers with both iSCSI and FC storage systems.

These devices need multiple protocol and translation support by and between other protocols that are suitable to the specific needs of your application. If required, select an IP switch or router that is enabled to handle translations between many sets of protocols:

- FCP to FCIP
- FCP to iFCP
- FCP to SRP (Secure Remote Protocol)

- iSCSI to FCP
- FCP to FICON

(FICON is IBM's proprietary name for the ANSI FC-SB-3 Single-Byte Command Code Sets-3 Mapping Protocol of Fibre Channel.)

Other Features

Advanced features like active/active clustered failover, failback, and multipathing capabilities all help to improve the reliability and availability of the IP SAN.

Active/Active Clustering

Active/Active clustering is a means of having two separate instances running in the cluster, that is, one (or more) per machine. Active/Active clustering refers to a two-node cluster, with each node running server instances, but each with a different set of databases. The setup is conceptually the same as having two Active/Passive nodes, except that one node must be a named instance.

Failback

Failback is the process of returning an operation back to its original configuration following a disaster, a failover, or a scheduled maintenance period.

Multipathing

Multipathing is the establishing of alternate paths to prevent issues when a server is attempting input/output operations and the failure of a given path occurs. The system is corrected by the use of another path associated with a given device.

Management Tools

All IP switches and routers will provide for some level of management, almost exclusively as software, and often as a Web-enabled (browser) user interface. The effectiveness and flexibility of these software tools is extremely important when tasked with the management of any scale of storage system (IP or Fiber Channel).

Tools should allow for the straightforward configuration of these devices and for the routine (and diagnostic) maintenance of the systems. Such management tools should allow for certain performance-monitoring capabilities, such as resource utilization analysis and/or service level (i.e., SLA) management. Intelligent health-monitoring features will aid in identifying faults and should provide for a messaging service capable of alerting an administrator or technician. Faults should all be logged, along with performance parameters so that system trending analysis can be routinely performed either in the background or on command.

Other features such as enhanced monitoring for ISL trunking will aid in configuring or analyzing inter-switch performance and port consolidation.

Acceleration and Compression

WAN centric attributes may be desired especially when IP devices are intended to operate over geographically separate connections. These features are designed to optimize bandwidth and more traffic between sites on an accelerated basis.

Fibre Channel over IP (FCIP) compression will reduce the amount of redundant data, significantly decreasing the total amount of data that are passed across the WAN. FCIP write acceleration and FCIP tape acceleration help to improve storage traffic over the WAN by mitigating the latency caused by command acknowledgements.

Security

The Internet, because of its ubiquity, has become notorious for security problems. Data security for IP and for Fibre Channel SANs must now be combined in order to meet regulatory, data protection, and privacy concerns, making storage security now an even more important topic.

The critical issues associated with SAN implementations, and communications defenses, have generated a storage security gap of growing proportions.

Authentication

Most SAN environments do not address the aspects of authentication; in fact, most SANs are designed using the assumption that authentication will or has taken place elsewhere in the system.

Protocols that have emerged to partially address this lack of security in authentication include

- Fibre Channel Authentication Protocol (FCAP)
- Fibre Channel—Security Protocol (FC-SP)
- DH-CHAP (Diffie-Hielman CHAP)

Organizations frequently presume authentication that occurs at the file or record layers (i.e., databases) should be sufficient. This presumption ignores lower network level authentication requirements and would be analogous to requiring authentication of a Web application, yet not commanding authentication for a Web server SSH connection or for an open telnet session—both of which open the door to full data compromises.

At the simplest level, management applications used to administer storage data will usually require a username and password for authentication. Other applications having access to the SAN may provide for indirect authentication. At other levels, authentication modules have been developed for switch-to-switch, node-to-node, and node-to-switch connectivity.

The security protocols that have been introduced as of the mid-2005 to 2010 time frame are aimed at alleviating security concerns that are becoming extended into FC SANs as a result of the introduction of IP-based connectivity and IP storage platforms. The following sections will explore some of those protocols and implementations.

Fibre Channel—Security Protocol (FC-SP)

FC-SP is a specification for Fibre Channel security that features device-to-device authentication, management of authentication passwords (known as shared secrets), data origin authentication, and anti-replay protection was developed around the 2006 time frame as part of the INCITS T11, Project 1570-D. The provisions of this protocol are designed to safeguard SAN traffic against unauthorized access and to aid in preventing accidental or unintentional configuration changes that would interrupt application availability.

FC-SP was drafted as a modular standard to define different levels of compliance. To claim FC-SP Authentication Compliance (AUTH-A), the storage system, storage networking device, or the host bus adapter (HBA) must support switch-to-switch, device-to-switch, and device-to-device authentication using the Diffie-Hellman Challenge Handshake Authentication Protocol (DH-CHAP) with a NULL DH group.

Before allowing communication, per this profile, FC-SP requires that the devices must authenticate to each other using a unique value, known as a "shared secret." To perform the authentication, each fabric component must either know the shared secret associated with other entities with which it is communicating or rely on a third party that knows the secret, such as through the use of a Remote Authentication Dial In User Service (RADIUS) server or a Terminal Access Controller Access-Control System Plus (TACACS+) server.

In turn, each device must also know, or be able to access, its own secret. This process eradicates the possibility of unauthenticated communication. The concept is effective in safeguarding the SAN against a rouge server instigating a network attack or a switch that impersonates a valid device.

Device Identity

Many Fibre Channel-specific access control mechanisms rely upon the device identity known as port World Wide Name (pWWN), a sort of MAC address, but one that is not intended to be secure or hack-proof. Many management tools will legitimately allow the changing of the pWWN for a device relatively easily. However, the upshot of potentially unauthorized changing of a pWWN is that those traditional Fibre Channel access controls are now circumnavigated with the intention of maliciously affecting the network, resulting in damaging outcomes for the enterprise.

Fibre Channel access control functionalities that traditionally depend on the pWWN include the following.

Zoning

Zoning is a basic tool in FC used to restrict communications between given groups of devices.

Port Security

Port security is the binding of a specific device to a specific switch interface with the intent of minimizing connection errors.

Logical Unit Number (LUN) Mapping and Masking

LUN mapping and masking is built into storage devices or servers to functionally limit or profile the data access depending on host access authorization.

The flexibility of FC-SP allows devices that support the protocol to operate in a fabric that includes non-FC-SP compliant devices or resources. The protocol authentication guarantees the effectiveness of those Fibre Channel access control approaches traditionally in use, even if a would-be attacker uses the pWWN of a valid device (see Fig. 10.14).

Other security methods for authentication that utilize FC-SP may be directly implemented by the manufacturers of the switches or routers themselves. Management access using the HBAs is another means to control access to FC storage systems. Bidirectional parameters enable the HBA to authenticate in

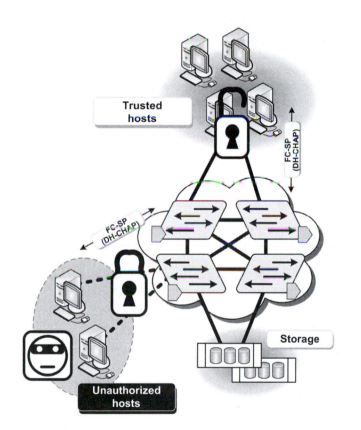

Figure 10.14 By implementing DH-CHAP authentication through the HBA, host threats are prevented.

one direction, such as when a server authenticates a switch, and then bidirectionally when each device authenticates the other. By offering the choice, one-way being easier to deploy, but two-way being more secure, the users have choices that can reflect the overall architecture of the network storage system.

Authorization

Authorization parameters are usually provided with WWNs derived from the Fibre Channel HBAs. WWNs can be port WWNs (pWWNs), which identify the port, or node WWNs (nWWNs), which identify the node on the fabric.

Encryption

In most SAN environments, encryption does not exist unless a third-party at-rest encryption device is used. Encryption at-rest is when data are physically stored in an encrypted manner. From the standpoint of security, this can be appealing. Consider the case of two databases: database A (which has encryption in-flight) and database B (where there is encryption at rest). If someone decides to compromise database A, and assuming the hacker has database A in their hands, the data could then be read like any other file. In other words, if data can be copied or taken to another environment, then none of the security measures put in place to protect the data are enforceable.

Natively, Fibre Channel does not employ encryption in any of layers 0 through 4.

Auditing

For most SANs, any auditing aspects would be enabled only at the device or application level, such as in a Fibre Channel switch or a management application. While there is error management possible via the fabric, there are typically no provisions in most SANs for security auditing.

Integrity Checking

Currently, there are no native methods for checking the integrity of the Fibre Channel frames.

Quality of Service (QoS)

Availability is a level of performance, which in turn signifies a quality of service (QoS) level. When storage data become unavailable, the networks as well as the applications will quickly disintegrate. The aspect of availability, also referred to as QoS, is indirectly available in layer 2 Fibre Channel frames per the error control fields of the FC frame. Nonetheless, there will be more QoS aspects than data availability, although availability is arguably the most important aspect of SAN security.

Further Readings

IETF IP Storage Working Group
> Documents that are archived related to the technologies, and the RFCs
>> discussed in this chapter can be found at:
>>> http://tools.ietf.org/wg/ips/

Fibre Channel, SCSI, and InfiniBand trade associations
> http://www.fibrechannel.org/
> http://www.scsita.org/
> http://www.infinibandta.org/

LISA 2010, San Jose, CA November 2010 Proceedings
> "Using TCP/IP Traffic Shaping to Achieve iSCSI Service Predictability"
> J. Bjørgeengen, University of Oslo; H. Haugerud, Oslo University College

Network Emulation with NetEm
> Stephen Hemminger, Open Source Development Lab, April 2005

11

OBJECT-BASED STORAGE

The concepts of "objects" and how storage devices associate with objects are unique in that they depart from the architectures of traditional file and storage systems. Getting a grasp on objects can help to paint a better picture of what the promoters of MXF and metadata for moving media had in mind when they set out to formalize those standards over 15 years ago.

Object-based storage, unlike block-based storage, encapsulates user data, its attributes, and the information associated with describing that user data together, as opposed to having them linked externally by a separate organizing mechanism. This combination enables object storage to determine data layout and quality of service on a per-object basis, improving flexibility and manageability.

The natural evolution of the block storage interface, object-based storage, is aimed at efficiently and effectively meeting the performance, reliability, security, and service requirements demanded by current and future applications. The storage interface provides an organizational container, the object, into which user data, attributes, permissions, and intelligence about each of them can be kept in a secure manner.

KEY CHAPTER POINTS

- A thorough discussion of objects and relationships that storage systems have in terms of containers, object-based storage (OBS), object-based storage systems (OSS), and object-based storage devices (OSD)
- Block-based versus object-based disk and storage structures
- The OSD command set and its derivation that came from the research at Carnegie Mellon University in the early 1990s on Network-Attached Secure Disks (NASD)
- NFS Version 4.1 and the Parallel Network File System (pNFS), which originated from the research on NASD and is implementing OSD functionality
- Security mechanisms that add data integrity to OSD implementation

Moving Media Storage Technologies

- An application case for OSD, the eXensible Access Method (XAM) storage interface, along with the future of the standards and other related topics

Introduction: Objects

An "object" is a container for data and attributes. Typically, large data files are broken down and stored in one or more objects. The protocol, object-based storage (OBS), specifies the several operations that are performed on objects, and it is based on what is known as an object-based storage device (OSD). Objects can be employed in smaller single computer/server applications or in massively parallel server/processor systems.

Object-based storage offers another improvement in security, accessibility control, and prevention of malicious damage.

Data Access Models

The technology is known as the Object-Based Data Access Model and is similar to the established data access methods like those of parallel SCSI, serial attached SCSI (SAS), Fibre Channel Protocol (FCP) and other block-based methods. The model also relates to file-based methods found in NFS and CIFS.

Analogous to a logical unit, but unlike a traditional block-oriented device providing access to data organized as an array of unrelated blocks, OSD as an object store allows access to data by means of a virtual entity that groups data together as "storage objects," according to needs that are determined by the user.

Objects are typically composed of the following:
- Object identifier (OID)
- Attributes (inferred and user supplied)
- User metadata (structural or descriptive metadata, e.g., date, time or file type)
- Actual data

In this model, unlike that of a host-based file system, storage space is allocated internally by the OSD itself. The OSD will manage all the required low-level storage, the space management, and all necessary security functions. Given there is now no host-based metadata for an object, an application can only retrieve an object by using its object identifier (OID). Figure 11.1 depicts the differences in the traditional block-based disk structure versus the object-based disk storage structure.

In an OSD, a collection of objects forms a flat space of unique OIDs. By rearranging pointers to objects, sets of virtual file hierarchies can be emulated (see Fig. 11.2).

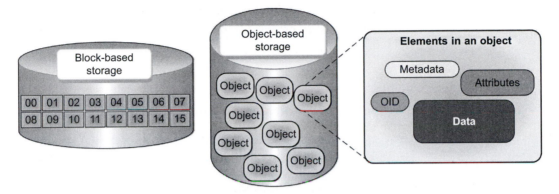

Figure 11.1 Block-based versus object-based disk structures.

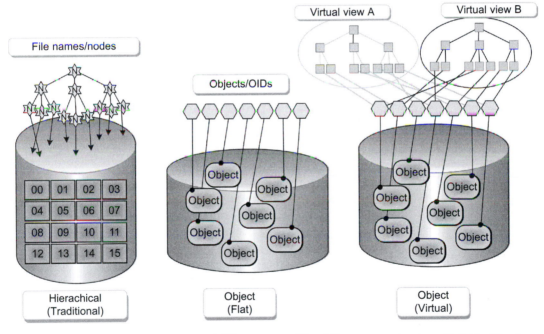

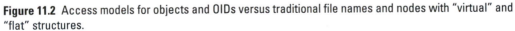

Figure 11.2 Access models for objects and OIDs versus traditional file names and nodes with "virtual" and "flat" structures.

Object-Based Storage Device

An OSD is a computer storage device, similar to disk storage, but it is intended to work at a higher level. An OSD provides the mechanisms to organize data into flexible-sized data containers, called objects, as opposed to a traditional block-oriented (disk) interface that reads and writes fixed-sized blocks of data. The object is the fundamental unit of data storage in an OSD, which contains the elements shown on the right side of Fig. 11.1.

The OSD has the responsibility for managing the storage of objects as a set of data, attributes, OIDs, and associated user metadata.

Object Types

Each object is a self-contained unit, which provides the users with the flexibility they need to encapsulate data and then share it under their complete control. Host-based data management applications and file systems are able to store both user data and metadata. The object attributes in OSD enable associations of applications with any OSD object. Such attributes are contained in the association hierarchy (shown in Fig. 11.3), and they include the following: root objects, partition objects, collection objects, or user objects. Attributes may be used to describe specific characteristics of an OSD object. These attributes are similar in concept to the structural metadata found in the SMPTE metadata definitions, so they fit well into this OSD architecture. The attributes include information such as the OSD object's total amount of bytes occupied, the logical size of the OSD object, or when the OSD object was last modified.

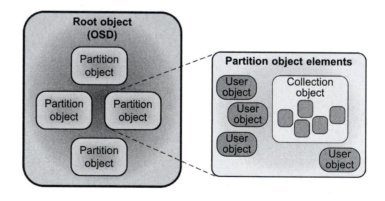

Figure 11.3 Object types with associated attributes.

Object-Based Storage

OBS is a protocol layer that is independent of the underlying storage hardware. OBS can take advantage of commodity hardware economics. As a standard, OBS claims to avoid the high cost of specialized storage servers.

OSDs, coupled with data-aware storage and attribute interpretation, can manipulate objects, thus aiding in search, data mining, and data manipulation applications.

OSD Command Set

The original work began in 1994 at Carnegie Mellon University (Pittsburgh, PA) as a government funded project that essentially developed the concepts of what would be called Network-Attached Secure Disks (NASD). The support continued through an advisory group, the National Storage Industry Consortium, who helped in the drafting of the interface specification that would later be submitted to the International Committee for Information Technology Standards (INCITS) T10, who develops standards and technical reports on I/O interfaces, particularly the series of Small Computer System Interface (SCSI) standards. This work was ratified as the ANSI T10 SCSI OSD V1 command set and subsequently released as INCITS 400-2004. The efforts gained the support of the Storage Networking Industry Association (SNIA), a body that works closely with standards body organizations (SBOs) to promote technical objectives from user- and vendor-supported groups. Work has continued on further extensions to the interface under the heading of a "V2" version.

Like the effects that object-based programming (OBP) has already had on the industry, the movement toward OSD implementation promises to have as an important and similar impact on enterprise wide storage as OBP did on programming well over a decade ago.

Command Interface

The command interface, which became the initial OSD standard, "Object-based Storage Device Commands" (approved for SCSI in 2004), includes the commands to create and delete an object, write and read bytes to and from the individual objects, and set and retrieve the attributes of the object.

By definition, each object has both data (as an uninterpreted sequence of bytes) and metadata (an extensible set of attributes describing the object). The OSD command interface includes commands to do the following:

- Create and delete objects.
- Write and read bytes to and from individual objects.
- Set and get attributes of objects.

The OSD is responsible for managing the storage of objects and their metadata. The OSD standard further implements a security mechanism that provides per-object and per-command access control.

Attributes

A key component of the OSD standard relates to the flexibility and connections of attributes to objects. An enormous number

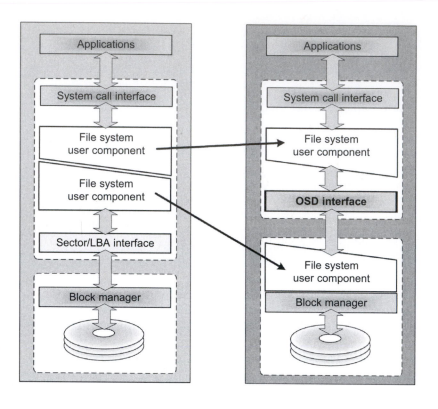

Figure 11.4 Traditional model versus object-based model for access as per the T10 OSD-3 working group of INCITS.

of attribute pages are available, per the ANSI T10 SCSI OSD V1 standard, which defines 2^{32} ($4.295 \times 10^9 = 4{,}294{,}967{,}296$) attribute pages per object, 2^{32} attributes per attribute page.

A comparatively minute range of this attribute name space is predefined by the standard. The application can use (or define) the predominant part of the space, allowing for superior data services and an improved quality of service (QoS).

Attribute Categories

The categories of attributes used in object-based storage systems are as follows:

- Storage attributes that are similar to inodes, that is, data structures on a traditional Unix-style file system (such as UFS), which store basic information about a regular file, directory, or other file system object. These storage attributes are used by the OSD to manage block allocations for data. They include such items as the capacity used, the OID, the logical length, or block pointers.
- User attributes that are used by applications and metadata managers to store higher level information about the object. This information includes capacity, density, performance, cost,

manageability, reliability, availability, serviceability, interoperability, security, power usage, adaptability, capability, and quotas.

System Layers and Devices

Attributes and metadata will be stored directly with the data object. They are automatically passed between layers and across devices. When objects pass through a designated system layer or device, that layer may then react based on the values in the attributes that it interprets. Any other attributes that are not recognized (i.e., not understood) are passed along unmodified and unacted upon. This concept is ideal for media systems where workflows consistently handle data that needs some form of action taken based upon what that data actually is (e.g., transcoding from SD to HD based upon a flag setting in the workflow management).

Another application handles the objects that are marked either as temporary or as high reliability. Because attributes are stored with user data, a service level can be attached to that data, which would manage secondary activities, such as better caching, prefetching, or migration.

OSD Versions

Several research projects have explored object storage and implemented prototype systems with various semantics. The initial OSD standard, Object-based Storage Device Commands (OSD), for SCSI was approved in 2004. A second version of the command set (OSD-2) was finalized in late 2008 yet remains stalled in the standardization process. OSD-3, the latest version, is under development with its current draft T10/2128-D revision 02 published on July 10, 2010.

Storage Categories

Storage technologies can be classified into three major categories as follows: direct-attached storage (DAS), network-attached storage (NAS), and storage area networks (SAN). A brief introduction follows, with much greater detail found in Chapter 15.

Direct-Attached Storage

DAS is computer storage, usually magnetic drives or solid-state drives that are directly attached to a computer workstation or server. DAS is the simplest and easiest to implement form of disk storage.

Network-Attached Storage

NAS is a file-based storage architecture for hosts connected to an IP network or a LAN. Typically, the functionality of a NAS requires that the file servers manage the metadata, which describes how those files are stored on the devices. The advantages to a NAS implementation are in terms of their data sharing and secure access through a server or workstation.

NAS Advantages

Network-attached storage became popular because it uses inexpensive, reliable, and reasonably fast Ethernet topologies and associated protocols. NAS offsets the impacts of a fussy, costly, yet very fast Fibre Channel alternative. The Network Files System (NFS) is highly utilized on NAS as a storage protocol for compute clusters. Unfortunately, as data sets and file sizes have grown exponentially, the relative speed of Ethernet has not quite kept up with that growth, especially when adding in the growth in bandwidth requirements. With 10-Gbit Ethernet (10 GigE) acceptance rising, many of these Ethernet problems are now being solved. Nonetheless, NFS has had a hard time scaling to gigabit Ethernet, which is reason in part why TCP Offload Engines (TOEs), custom hardware pipelines, and other implementations have emerged for gigabit Ethernet storage subsystems.

Further development in a parallel NFS (pNFS), which is sanctioned by the IETF, has helped this situation. pNFS is discussed later in this chapter.

Storage Area Networks

A SAN is a block-based architecture where the client has direct access to disks on a switched fabric network, which is usually Fibre Channel based (although that model has been changing). The SAN's main advantage is in its capability to transfer large amounts of data in units of blocks. The SAN may also be constructed with several sets of parallel data and control paths providing for multiple machine access and data processing, including metadata handling. With this degree of activity, the need for security and access control is essential.

Unfortunately, blocks on a SAN have a poor security model that relies on coarse grain techniques involving zoning and logical unit number (LUN) masking. Object-based storage helps in resolving the security issues, as discussed later in this chapter.

The SAN technology's intent is to replace bus-based architecture with a high-speed, higher bandwidth switched fabric.

Combining SAN and NAS Advantages

An object-based system, when implemented as a SAN technology, combines the advantages of high-speed, direct-access SANs and the data sharing and secure access capabilities of NAS.

Earlier trends (ca. 2006) saw the emergence of NAS head–based file servers that were placed in front of SAN storage. This practice continues today, but the development of parallel NAS (pNAS) at the client side is a change that is expected in the current NAS had/SAN combination.

Network-Attached Secure Disks

In the 1990s, research on NASD examined the opportunities to move additional processing power closer to the actual disk drive when in a NAS environment. As distributed file systems have increased in popularity as a means to access data across LANs, there have been a number of approaches to improve them. The scalability and storage management associated with these exposed file systems has raised security concerns for at least the last two decades. NASD and object-based storage have helped to control this exposure.

Traditionally, a server-attached disk (SAD) storage configuration would transfer data via the server's memory. At the time of the transfer, the server synchronously oversees rights and privileges assigned per the structure of the security scheme set by the administrator. SAD systems would typically have two independent networks: the local area network (LAN) and the storage bus. In this system, all data travels over both networks. Storage subsystems used by SAD generally will implement some level of self-management and extensibility, with both being limited by the SAD file system design. Part of the concept of NASD was to overcome those limitations and in turn provide for greater flexibility and higher performance.

Access Control and Security in OSD

An important aspect of this NASD work related to access control is how data and its associated attributes can be securely accessed by systems and users. NASD researchers from Carnegie Mellon described a security protocol for object storage that allowed a security manager to provide fine-grained access control to a shared storage device on a network. In turn, this work linked into a higher level building block that could be aggregated together to provide large-scale, secure storage.

NASD efficiently supports asynchronous oversight (access control) and secure communications using capabilities that have been cryptographically sealed by the appropriate authority, for example, the file system manager or partition manager. The approach is dependent upon the shared secret between a NASD drive and the authority in order to maintain this long-term relationship. A four-level key hierarchy is used as follows:

- Master key—also called the "top key" that is off-line and only accessible by the drive owner (i.e., the system administrator).
- Drive key—an online key available to the drive administrator used for manipulating partitions, setting partition keys, or for any object-based operation (optional).
- Partition key—an online key used by the file system manager to set working keys or for object-based operations (optional).
- Current working key—used online by the file system manager as a basis for capacity generation, and optionally for object-based operations.
- Previous working key—used online by the file system manager as a basis for capabilities that were generated under the previous working key.

The top key, that is, the master key, is the longest-lived secret. For highly secure models, the master key once set remains unchallengeable. It is not recorded online outside of the NASD drive. This key is used only to establish a new drive key in the event of failures or desynchronization.

Fast Forward

By employing more powerful processors with features such as block allocation (also called space management), a more abstract interface of reading and writing bytes to flexible data containers could then be enabled.

The most active work (ca. 2002) was at the Parallel Data Lab at Carnegie Mellon University (http://www.pdl.cmu.edu) originally under the direction of Garth Gibson. Development was related to the work associated with NASD and Active Disks. Additional work during this time period was done at the University of California at Berkeley, the University of California, Santa Barbara, and the University of Maryland, as well as Hewlett Packard Labs, Seagate Technology, and Intel Labs.

Storage Interface Progression

Change is inevitable, especially in the area of storage. Earlier in this book, we introduced you to the infancy of storage and discussed how it progressed in the early days of the original Shugart Technologies model ST-506. These technologies then lead to the "data separator" era outlined by the Enhanced Small Disk Interface (ESDI) and the Storage Module Device (SMD) developments of the 1980s.

The physical sector interface utilizing sector buffering (e.g., IPI-2) led to the logical block interface with error correcting code (ECC) and geometry mapping (e.g., in SCSI). This evolution has moved on to the byte string interface, where space management is one of the primary objectives and is governed by the development found in OSD.

Intelligent Storage Interface

OSD is the interface to intelligent storage. In SCSI hard drive implementation, each 512-byte sector is equivalent. In the OSD basic objects implementation, the system is "structure-aware." OSD will take control of space management, determine where to put the file data, and become completely aware of where the free space is, and if continued, can move the file data around based upon its needs and control.

As the types of data become more varied, the system control can become even more complicated. In the case of ordered sequential files, such as motion video (e.g., MPEG, JPEG, etc.), the internal structure becomes more complete. The additional functionality of "structure-aware" and "data-aware" storage (see Fig. 11.5) found in object-based storage thus aids in enabling

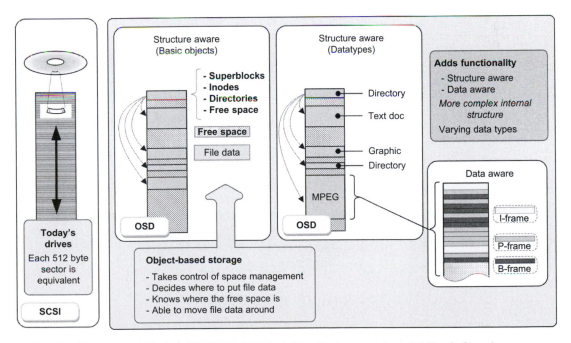

Figure 11.5 OSD as an interface to intelligent storage enables sharing, security, reliability, QoS, performance, and structure awareness as basic objects and as datatypes.

improved sharing, security, and reliability. QoS, indexing, and searching are all improved as well.

Data Objects

Data objects will have both data and metadata. An object's data is an uninterpreted sequence of bytes. The metadata associated with that object is the extensible set of attributes that describes the object.

Contained in OSDs, there will be one or more logical units that are comprised of the following types of stored data objects:

- Root object—each OSD logical unit contains one and only one root object. The root object attributes contain global characteristics for the OSD logical unit. These may include the total capacity of the logical unit, the number of partitions that it contains, and a list of Partition_IDs for the partitions in the logical unit. The root object is the starting point for navigation of the structure on an OSD logical unit. It does not contain a read/write data area.
- Partition—an OSD object created by specific commands from an application client that contains a set of collections and user objects that share common security requirements and attributes. These attributes could include, at least, the prescribed default security method and other information such as a capacity quota. User objects are collected into partitions that are represented by partition OSD objects. There may be any number of partitions, up to a specified quota or the capacity of the OSD logical unit. A partition does not contain a read/write data area.
- Collection—an OSD object created by commands from an application client, which is used for the fast indexing of user objects. A collection is contained within one partition, and a partition may contain zero or more collections. The support for collections is optional.
- User object—an OSD object containing end-user data such as a file or a database. Attributes associated with the user object may include the logical size of the user data and the time stamps for creation, access, or modification of any end-user data. A user object may be a member of zero or more collections concurrently.

Object-Based Data Access

The object-based data access model is analogous to a logical unit, which is usually addressed as a LUN. In current SCSI protocol, the LUN is a 64-bit identifier generally divided into four 16-bit pieces used to reflect a multilevel addressing scheme.

The object store in OSD allows access to data by means of storage objects. Again, the object is a virtual entity that groups data together in a means determined by the user and whose grouping is generally logically related. OSD is usually deployed as a device-oriented system that is based on data objects that encapsulate user data, including user attributes and user metadata.

As mentioned previously, the OSD then manages all the essential low-level storage, drive space management, and security functions.

Data Layout with QoS

An underlying principle in object-based storage is that it allows for the combination of data, attributes, and metadata to set up and, in turn, determines the data layout and the quality of service (QoS) for the system on a per-object basis. Thus, OSD improves manageability and flexibility for all of the data sets in a system. To place OSD into perspective, we need to look at the differences in block-based versus file-based methods of traditional storage system architectures.

Block-Based Methods

Storage area networks (SANs) will use the SCSI block I/O command set that provides high random I/O and data throughput performance using direct access to the data at the level of the disk drive or Fibre Channel. Block-based methods of storage include parallel-SCSI, SAS, FCP, PATA/ATA, and SATA.

File-Based Methods

Network-attached storage (NAS) systems use Network File System (NFS) or Common Internet File System (CIFS) command sets for accessing data. Multiple nodes can access the data because the metadata on the media is shared.

Parallel Heading

The principles of a NFS were developed by Sun Microsystems (Sun) in the 1980s, where it later became an open standard that allowed files on the network to be available anywhere. Today, the Internet Engineering Task Force (IETF) is the body responsible for NFS standards and revisions. As higher speeds for data transfers and networks placed new demands on systems, work began (ca. 2002–2003) on the development of a parallel version of NFS, which would enable much higher speeds. This work would become pNFS.

Typical NFS Servers

Standard NFS file servers function much like a conventional PC workstation does. Files that land on local disks are tracked by the computer's file system through processes that manage the location, name, creation and modification dates, attributes, permissions, size, etc. Metadata, the data about the data, is used to track these parameters, such as the location, size, and date. The metadata can be contained locally through the file system or separately.

When a file is requested, the file server receives the request, looks up the metadata, and converts that information into disk input/output (I/O) requests, where the process then collects the data and sends it over the network to the requested destination. Much of the time in this process is spent simply collecting the data. The time adds up quickly when a number of small file requests continually recur, as in database or transactional applications.

In the case where the files are quite large, as in media clips or large contiguous segments, it is the data transmission time that becomes the limiting factor. If you could segment a large file into smaller pieces and send those pieces in parallel to a compute server, ideally it would be faster than sending a single file to a single location. With several parallel connections, that time is reduced substantially.

These concepts and desires promoted the development of the parallel file system and multi-threaded computing and would be an enabling factor for accessing the storage subsystems through more efficient means and without taxing the CPU management processes attached to the file system.

Parallel NFS

Parallel NFS (pNFS) is a standards-based parallel file system serving the NFS protocol. pNFS divides the NFS file server into two types: the first is the metadata and control server and the second is one to as many storage servers as the budget (and physical space) can tolerate (see Fig. 11.6). When aligned together, the control server and the storage servers form a single logical NFS server with a plethora of network connections. The compute server, likely to be a multinode cluster, will employ a

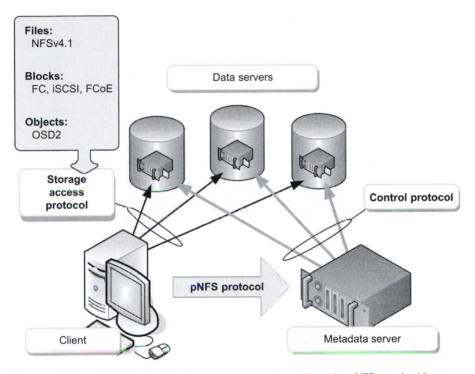

Figure 11.6 Parallel NFS using the storage access protocols from the pNFS standard from the IETF work. Note that the control protocol is outside of the pNFS standard.

large number of Ethernet ports that provision the network transfers. Large parallel, high-performance clusters have been built out of inexpensive PC-like hardware and are sometimes known as a Beowulf cluster, which might run a Free and Open Source Software (FOSS) operating system, such as Solaris, GNU/Linux, or the BSD (Berkeley Software Distribution) descendents, which form a Unix-like OS family.

Operationally, the compute server requests a file using the NFSv4.1 client (final draft produced ca. 2007–2008). The NFS control server then receives the request and then searches the location of the file chunks on the various storage servers. The information, called a layout, is sent back to the NFSv4.1 client, which tells its cluster members where to retrieve the data. Cluster members will use the layout information and request the data directly from the storage servers. Security components further provide for data integrity (explained later) through a series of secret keys and messaging. The processing, transfer, and handling speeds increase proportionally to the number of storage servers in the cluster.

Version Compatibility

pNFS is backwards-compatible with existing NFS implementations. When a previous client (e.g., NFS v3 client) wishes to access data from a pNFS-enabled cluster, it will mount the pNFS cluster like another ordinary NFS filer. Migration to pNFS v4.1 is designed to be straightforward and easy.

Applications

Parallel path processing and cluster computing is being applied to applications such as finite analysis and financial risk analysis, and it is extensively applied in 3D animation and rendering space for motion picture production. Video editing, collaborative workflows, and high-performance streaming video all could take good advantage of the features in pNFS, especially the improved data transfer times.

Concurrent user support is ideal for pNFS where multiple sets of disks can respond, thus spreading the workload across many storage servers. This improves scaling of storage requirements easily and consistently. pNFS may be implemented using Fibre Channel or block-based iSCSI on GigE file storage or object-based storage (OBS).

pNFS with OSD Protocols

When employed with object-based storage, the files are broken into smaller chunks, referred to as objects, which are uniquely identified by numbers as opposed to the traditional path names in block file storage methods. Objects use extensible metadata that enables a more refined, lower overhead security technique.

Object servers will not accept data or commands unless so authorized by the metadata server. This capability-based security scheme prevents malicious, accidental, or unauthorized access or changes to be made.

Operations that are part of the OSD protocols include the following:

READ, WRITE, FLUSH,
GET ATTRIBUTES, SET ATTRIBUTES,
CREATE, and DELETE.

When using the object-based layout, a client may only use the READ, WRITE, GET ATTRIBUTES, and FLUSH commands. All other commands are only allowed to be used by the pNFS server. An object-based layout for pNFS includes object identifiers, capabilities that allow clients to READ or WRITE those objects, and various parameters that control how file data is striped across their component objects.

Linux pNFS

Although there is a tight integration of control and data protocols for parallel file systems, the control and data flows are separate. By using pNFS as a universal metadata protocol, applications can fulfill a consistent set of file system semantics across data repositories. By providing a framework for the coexistence of the NFSv4.1 control protocol, the Linux pNFS implementation facilitates interoperability with all storage protocols. This is seen as a major departure from current file systems, which support only a single storage protocol such as OSD.

Figure 11.7 depicts the architecture of pNFS on the Linux OS. Through the added layout and transport drivers, the standard NFS v4 architecture interprets and utilizes opaque layout information that is returned from the pNFS server. The layout contains the information required to access any byte range of a file, and it may contain file system–specific access information. In the case of OSD, the object-based layout driver requires the use of OSD's access control capabilities.

To perform direct and parallel I/O, a pNFS client first requests layout information from the pNFS server, which the layout driver

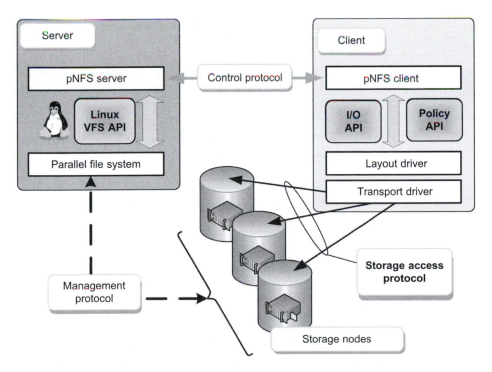

Figure 11.7 The pNFS implementation on a Linux operating system.

uses to translate read and write requests from the pNFS client into I/O requests directed to storage devices. The NFSv4.1 file-based storage protocol stripes files across NFSv4.1 data servers (storage devices). In this mode, only READ, WRITE, COMMIT, and session operations are used on the data path. The pNFS server is able to generate layout information by itself or requests assistance from the underlying file system.

Layout drivers use a standard set of interfaces for all storage protocols and are pluggable. A "policy interface" is used to inform pNFS clients of the policies that are specific to the file system and the storage system. To facilitate the management of the layout information and in performing I/O with storage, an "I/O interface" is used. Layout driver functionality can depend on the application, the supported storage protocol, and the core of the parallel file system.

The last layer between the client and storage is the transport driver, which is used to perform those input and output functions, such as iSCSI or Open Network Computing Remote Procedure Calls (ONC RPC), on the storage nodes, through the instructions and policies control described.

IETF Standards for NFSv4.1/pNFS

The IETF working groups that lead the standardization of the parallel implementation of NFS, what is now NFSv4.1, published several RFC documents related to the standardization of a suite of capabilities. At the time, the OSD standard was only at Version 1.0, but work continued with the anticipation of Version 2.0 as SNIA T10/1729-D would be forthcoming.

This second-generation OSD protocol has additional proposed features that will support more robust error recovery, snapshots, and byte-range capabilities. Therefore, the OSD version must be explicitly called out in the information returned in the layout. The IETF documents related mostly to parallel NFS are shown in Table 11.1.

OSD Management Structure

In OSD, there is a differing management structure than that of the traditional SCSI-3 Block Commands (SBC) structure defined in the references under development as ISO/IEC 14776-323, SCSI Block Commands-3 (SBC-3) [T10/1799-D]. The principle differences are at the file system storage management level, which is replaced by the OSD interface and OSD storage management (refer back to Fig. 11.4). Subsequently, the traditional sector or logical block addressing scheme is transformed and is

Table 11.1 IETF Standards for Parallel NFS (pNFS)

Implementation as NFS V 4.1		
IETF RFC Number	*Revision and Date*	*Description*
RFC 5661	Rev 29 - December 16, 2008	NFSv4.1/pNFS/file layout minor Version 1
RFC 5662	Rev 12 - December 16, 2008	NFSv4.1 Protocol description for IDL (RPCGEN) compiler
RFC 5663	Rev 12 - December 23, 2008	pNFS extensions of data structures block- and volume-based storage (layout)
RFC 5664	Rev 12 - December 15, 2008	Object-based pNFS layout type
RFC 5665	RFC 5665 Status as of January 2010	Netid specification for transport protocol independence (IPv4, IPv6, RDMA)—updates RFC 1833

now located just ahead of the block I/O manager for the storage (drive or tape) device itself.

SCSI Architecture Model

The original third-generation SCSI standards used the name SCSI-3 to distinguish them from SCSI-2. To lessen confusion, succeeding SCSI standards dropped the "-3" from their names. When the SCSI-3 architecture model (SAM) was revised, the nomenclature was simply shorted to "SAM-2" (SCSI Architecture Model - 2).

Although the individual components of the SCSI family continue to evolve, there was no SCSI-4 project envisioned. The fifth generation and current SCSI Architectural Model - 5 (SAM-5) has a INCITS T10 committee status date of May 2011 listed as T10 Project Number 2104-D, Revision 05.

As of December 2010, OSD-3 (T10 Project Number 2128-D, Revision 02) is still in development with a target date of November 2011.

Security Mechanisms

OSD implements a mechanism that provides per-object and per-command access control as its security feature. The T10 OSD security working group sets the following goals for the OSD security protocol: it would prevent against attacks on individual objects, including intentional and inadvertent nonauthorized access;

prevent the illegal use of credentials beyond their original scope and lifespan; protect against the forging or theft of credentials; and preclude the use of malformed and misshapen credentials.

Furthermore, the protocol would enable protection against network attacks, such as the so-called "man-in-the-middle" attacks on the network, network errors, malicious message modifications, and message replay attacks. The OSD security protocol must allow for low-cost implementation of the critical path for commodity devices and should enable efficient implementation on existing network transports.

The security flow follows a series of protocols and processes that allow for the goals mentioned previously to be achieved. When a client wishes to access an object, it requests a capability from the security manager. The request must specify the OSD name, partition ID, and object ID to fully identify the object. Any secondary authentication processes for the client are outside the scope of the OSD security protocol. Once the security manager has determined that the client is authorized to perform the requested operation on the specified object, the security manager generates a cryptographically secured credential that includes the requested capability. The secured credential is validated by a shared secret between the security manager and the OSD.

The credential is then sent to the client. The channel for this credential exchange should provide privacy, through encryption, so as to protect the capability key used by the client to authenticate that it legitimately obtained a capability. The client is required to present a capability on each OSD command; and before processing can continue, the OSD verifies that the capability has not been modified in any way, and that the capability permits the requested operation against the specified object. Once both tests are passed, the OSD permits the specific operation based upon the rights encoded in the capability.

It is possible that a client would request a credential that permits multiple types of operation (e.g., Read + Write + Delete), allowing the client to aggressively cache and reuse credentials. This in turn minimizes the volume of like messages between the security manager and the client.

The OSD is a trusted component, providing integrity for the data while stored. The protocol and the OSD insure that a proper following of the protocols will be controlled and not be controlled by an adversary. The security manager for its part is a component that is trusted to safely store the master/long-lived keys after authentication and follows all protocols so as not to be controlled by an adversary.

The depths of how the credentials, capability arguments, and capability keys are managed and secured are beyond the scope of these OSD discussions.

Applications of OSD

As depicted in Fig. 11.5, OSD enables intelligent, data-aware and structure-aware storage. OSD provides many new opportunities for large-scale archives and high-density storage applications. It enables scalability, increased performance, reliability, and a new, higher level of security. This is why many organizations look to OSD to support their assets at levels heretofore reserved to proprietary asset management systems.

Content Aware Storage

The archive market is already using object storage that may be found in multiple proprietary systems with application-based APIs. In an effort to promote a standardized interface with interoperability between object storage devices (OSDs) and applications, SNIA christened (in late 2005) what is called a "contributed specification," which would be called the eXensible Access Method (XAM). XAM is characterized as a Content Aware Storage (CAS) system. The contributed specification efforts were initiated by EMC and IBM in joint cooperation with HP, Hitachi Data Systems (HDS), and at that time Sun (now Oracle).

The goal for fixed content (which usually has a lengthy shelf life) is to enable self-describing data and standard metadata semantics as a methodology for consistent naming and searching. XAM, as a storage interface at the application layer, can be built on storage objects and can provide those services to or from object-storage devices.

eXensible Access Method

XAM is an open-source application to storage interface for file sharing similar to NFS on Unix-like systems and CIFS on Microsoft platforms. However, unlike file sharing protocols, XAM also provides applications and storage systems with an expanded "metadata container," giving rise to powerful information and retention management capabilities. The XAM standard promotes an interface specification that defines an access method (API) between Consumers (application and management software) and Providers (storage systems) with its capability to manage fixed content reference information storage services.

XAM includes those metadata definitions needed to accompany data so as to achieve application interoperability, storage transparency, and automation for information life cycle management (ILM) and tiered storage practices, long-term records retention, and information security.

XAM is intended to be expanded over time so as to include other data types and support additional implementations based on the XAM API to XAM conformant storage systems. The XAM specification is published in three parts as follows:

XAM–Part 1: Architecture

This is intended to be used by two broad audiences, that is, those application programmers who wish to use the XAM Application Programmers Interface (API) to create, access, manage, and query reference content through standardized XAM and those storage system vendors who are creating vendor interface modules (VIMs).

XAM–Part 2: C API

The complete reference document for C application development using the XAM API, intended for experienced programmers, for those developing applications that interface with storage systems and support the XAM API, and for those developing components of the XAM Library itself.

XAM–Part 3: JAVA API

A complete reference document for Java application development using the XAM API, intended for experienced programmers, for those developing applications that interface with storage systems that support the XAM API, and for those developing components of the XAM Library itself.

File System Differentials

The key difference between XAM and a file system is that XAM is implemented as an API, similar to block file system APIs, except with a focus on storage interface and access methods.

First, XAM abstracts the access method from the storage, a capability necessary to create location independence, policy-based automation, and portability.

Second, XAM wraps the data into what is called an "XSet" (object wrapper). This is similar to an XML wrapper, from the "physical" perspective. As files or data are written to storage media, they are placed into an information object with rich, extended metadata fields incorporated into the object (see Fig. 11.8).

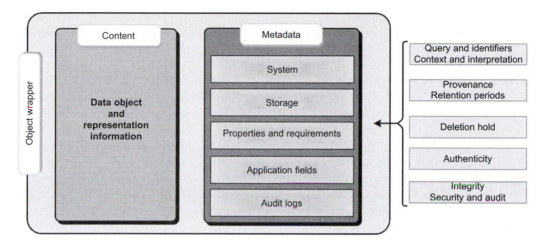

Figure 11.8 The XAM object wrapper containing content and metadata, with examples of potential metadata fields shown on the right side.

The fields will accommodate other metadata standards and application-specific requirements that are deemed necessary for retention and for information management services in most or any environment.

The 5-year activities associated with XAM (within SNIA) culminated with its release in July 2008. ANSI standardization for the XAM v1.0.1 specification, as a SNIA Architecture, was underway at the time of this publication.

Extensions

Object-based storage devices (under the OSD-2 version) enable "snap-shotting" of storage systems to occur. Snapshots are a point-in-time copy of all the objects in a partition. Each snapshot can be placed into a new partition, moved to a central store or replicated to another site.

By using copy-on-write techniques, a space-efficient duplicate of the data set is created in a way that allows two partitions to share objects that are unchanged between the snapshots. By using OSD, it could in turn physically copy the data to a new partition. However, the OSD standard also has a section that defines clones, a writeable snapshot that is created as a read-only partition and would be used in data protection functions.

A "collection" is yet another application for OSD often used for error reporting. The collection is a specific type of object that contains the identifiers of the other objects. If an object were damaged due to a software error (within the OSD environment) or a media defect, its identifier would be placed into a separate error collection, which is quarantined and then would later be independently queried for further corrective action.

Emerging and evolving technologies continue to produce documented changes to current implementations. The current status level of the standards development for object-based storage devices, at the T10 Working Group in INCITS, is "OSD-3" (a document titled "Object-Based Storage Device Commands-3"). As of July 17, 2010, the work was at revision-02 at the development status as Project 2128-D. OSD-3 will define a third-generation command set for devices that store data as objects instead of blocks of data. This version's purpose is an abstraction to assign to the storage device more responsibility for managing the location of the data.

Embedding OSD

In the consumer space, storage is becoming embedded in more devices all the time. Consequently, we are seeing "intelligent stand-alone devices" already emerging. Devices from iPods and PDAs to smart phones and iPads use intelligent, market-specific OSDs. Flash memory cards can already be considered object-based storage and are readily accepted primarily because consumers do not really care or need to know about the file system, sectors, or mount points and they care first and foremost about their pictures or music files.

File attribute changes are quite common, especially at the consumer level. OSD offers a capability to alter or change a file attribute (e.g., the artist name in an MP3 file) without having to rewrite the entire file. Extending that concept to large media files, not having to rewrite the entire file just to replace a single 500-Mbyte video clip in a 100-Gbyte set of clips adds great value to how those files are stored and their subsequent accessibility for future purposes.

Refresh Cycles

Standardized data formats may be made necessary by the continued technological advancements in data storage hardware and applications. Each time this occurs, a plan to migrate the data to the next environment must be assessed. When this need occurs, having an object-based storage system and/or a parallel file system allows the object archive to horizontally scale using third-party applications.

Further Readings

OSD: A Tutorial on Object Storage Devices. Thomas M. Ruwart, Advanced Concepts, Ciprico, Inc.

OSD DISC/Industry Collaboration.
http://www.dtc.umn.edu/disc/osd.shtml

SNIA Object-Based Storage Device TWG: OSD Technical Working Group (TWG) enables the creation of self-managed, heterogeneous, shared storage by moving low-level storage functions into the storage device itself and accessing the device through a standard object interface rather than a traditional block-based interface such as SCSI or IDE. The OSD TWG develops models and guidelines, requirement statements, preliminary standards definitions, reference code, and prototype demonstrations for OSD storage subsystems.

Open OSD Development: Includes information on the ratification of OSD-2, open source targets, pNFS over OSD, etc.
http://www.open-osd.org/bin/view

Credit is given to Oracle for a detailed, tutorial-like article regarding object-based storage devices, which provided the depth and direction for this chapter. The full article is available online at
http://developers.sun.com/solaris/articles/osd.html.

Drafts of the various INCITS T10 documents can be found at
http://www.t10.org/drafts.htm.

Credit and contributions to the XAM topics include: SNIA-XAM:
Storage Developers - It is Time to Adopt XAM (February 2010)
The Power of XAM (July 2006)

Additional information and white papers on the SNIA XAM Initiative can be found at:
www.snia.org/forums/xam/resources/publications/

12

ARCHIVES, BACKUPS, AND LINEAR TAPE

Backing up data and archiving data are frequent activities that occur in operations where information is stored on magnetic spinning disk media or solid state drives. At the enterprise level, these processes need to occur for protective reasons, for legal verification reasons, and for the long-term preservation of assets. Backing up data versus archiving data are two separate functions and the terms are not synonymous. Backing up data is a protective action, usually the process of making a temporary copy of a file, record, or data set that is intended for recovery in the event the data are corrupted, the media itself is lost or destroyed, or for use in a disaster recovery or data protection model.

Archiving involves the long-term preservation of data. An archive is a permanent copy of the file for the purpose of satisfying data records management or for future, long-term library functions intended for the repurposing, repackaging, or reuse of the information at a later date.

Backing up and archiving involve two distinct processes with succinctly different purposes. Many do not understand the differences, and even today, the terminologies and practices are sometimes used interchangeably. Many enterprises would use their backup copies for both DR and archive purposes, a practice that is risky at best and costly at worst.

A library is a physical or virtual representation of the assets that the enterprise has in its possession. The physical library may consist of the original material as captured (film, videotape, or files); and the virtual library may be the database that describes the material with a pointer to where it is physically stored in either the digital data archive, the vault, or in a remote secure site.

This chapter looks into the various physical and logical applications of archiving and backing up digital files to physical media such as tape, optical media such as DVD or Blu-ray Disc, or on magnetic spinning disk both active and inactive. How the organization addresses these options, and what steps they should take to mitigate risk and reduce cost, while at the same time developing a strategy for file management that is usable, reliable, and extensible are the topics to be covered in this chapter.

KEY CHAPTER POINTS

- The requirements of the organization, how its users need to address protective storage, and how often it plays a key part in determining how content is stored for short term, for disaster, or for long-term archive
- Differentiating a backup from an archive
- Determining when the archive is better served on tape or disk media
- Components of the archive, what is a datamover, and how data are moved between active storage and inactive storage
- Archive management
- Digital tape and tape libraries, previous versions and workflows, how it works today, and what is the roadmap to the future
- What to be looking for in choosing an archive or backup solution, and what is on the horizon for standards in archive interchange

Organizational Requirements for Data

In looking to establish an archive and backup process, the organization first needs to define their business activity, which then helps determine the user needs and accessibility requirements for its digital assets. The fundamental backup/archive activities for business data compliance will use an approach that differs from those activities that are strictly media-centric in nature. These approaches are determined by many factors, some of which include the duration of retention, the accessibility and security of the information, the dynamics of the data, and who needs to use that data and when.

The organization, as expressed early in this chapter, must recognize that simply "backing up to a tape" does not make an archive. The use of data tape brings comparatively higher time and costs associated with it; thus, the use of data tape for short-term business data compliance purposes is not as practical as employing spinning disks. When the organization has insufficient active storage capacity on spinning disks, it may turn to tape as its alternative. In routine daily uses, it can take an excessive amount of time for the users to find, examine, and recover (or retrieve) needed information. These are activities better suited for spinning disks used as near-line/near-term storage.

However, for a broadcaster with a large long-form program library that is accessed only occasionally, as in one episode a day from a library of hundreds of programs or thousands of clips or episodes, retaining that content on data tape makes better economic and protective sense than keeping it only on spinning disk.

Legal Requirements for Archive or Backup

Organizations that present material in the public interest, such as television news, have different policies pertaining to what is kept and for how long. Businesses that produce content for the Web, for their own internal training, or for the training of others, most likely have a data retention policy for moving media applications and content.

IT departments have developed their own policies and practices for the retention (archive) and the protection (backup) of data files such as email, databases, intercompany communications, etc. However, with multimedia becoming more a part of everyday operations, there may be only a small number of corporate retention policies in place due to the sophistication of cataloging moving media, the sheer size of the files themselves, and the unfamiliarity of the files, formats, and methods to preserve anything from the raw media files, to proxies, and to the varying release packages.

Broadcasters retain many of their key news and program pieces in physical libraries, on shelves, and in the master control operations area. The days of the company librarian have long gone and electronic data records seem to be the trend since its metadata can be linked to proxies, masters, and air checks. How the "legal-side" requirements for content retention at these kinds of operations works is a subject much broader than can be covered by these few chapters. Yet, more products are coming of age that do this automatically, and include such features as speech-to-text conversion, scene change detection, and on-screen character and facial recognition (such as "LIVE" or "LATE BREAKING" text indicating an important feature), in addition to more traditional segment logging and closed caption detection.

Air checks or logging can require enormous amounts of space if they use full bandwidth recording; so many of these activities have converted to lower bit rate encoding techniques that produce a proxy capable of being called up from a Web browser, or archived as MPEG-1 or MPEG-4 at a fraction of the space the original material would consume.

Repacking and Repurposing

The archive libraries carry untold amounts of information that organizations and enterprises have elected to retain for their or another's future. In many cases, the uses for these libraries have yet to be determined, and for others there are very succinct purposes for retaining the data contents. Over time, archives will become the principle repository for housing historical information in all forms, especially moving media. We will find the content linked into massively intelligent databases that will become the resource catalog that is driven by enterprise-class search engines strategically linked to third-party services such as Bing, Google, Amazon.com, and others we have not seen yet.

Repackaging is the process of taking existing content and making it available in a different venue or on a different platform. With the proliferation of mobile technologies, the repackaging of full length features into shorter "episode"-like programs is an opportunity waiting for an audience. An archive that is the central repository for such content that is upstream of the secondary post-production process will obtain good value for those businesses that have the magic and the insight to develop these potential new revenue generating opportunities.

Repurposing is much like repackaging, except that it includes legacy content that is then re-cut (re-edited) or shaped to a different length, for a different audience or purpose. Such businesses as stock footage library resale, links into electronic publications referenced from mobile readers or Internet connections, downloadable content for on demand, etc., all can make good use from archives that they may own themselves or have contracted access to.

For the media and entertainment industry, ongoing directives to provide new revenues driven from existing content will be enabled by many of those archive platforms under their control. Multi-channel video program distributors (MVPD) continually find new methods to utilize their owned content in ways that would not have been cost effective in the past. Content management, like its close relative broadcasting, will become a growing venture as the population continues down the "any content—at any time—and anywhere" direction.

A look at activities related to program production that will utilize a combination of media asset management applications in conjunction with archive systems includes

• Versioning (language related)—the adaptation of one set of video media by marrying it with different foreign languages and captioning (open and closed) services, in order to produce a new set of programs.

- Versioning (program length)—the creation of different programs aimed at differing delivery platforms, for example, short form for Web or mobile devices, long form for paid video-on-demand, etc.
- Versioning (audience ratings)—producing versions for children's audiences, mature or adults-only audiences, or broadcast versus cable/satellite purposes.
- Automated assembly—using the asset library to reconstruct full length day part programs from short clips, such as is done on the Cartoon Network where segments (cartoons) are already prepared in the library (archive), and then called for assembly to a server for playback.
- Advertising directed—specific programs that accentuate a particular brand or manufacturer that is produced for that advertiser's channel or program segment.

Preparing content for video-on-demand is a common activity for most MVPDs. Today, these processes are highly transcoder-centric, as different delivery service providers might require different encoding methods. The content, however, is kept on the archive in a master format at a high resolution, and then is called out to a server cache where it is then prepared for the service using a massive transcode farm that can simultaneously make multiple (compressed) versions and deliver them over content delivery networks (CDNs) to the end users and service providers.

Added Operational Requirements

An archive becomes both the protective copy and the master version when duplicate sets of the data are stored in different geographic locations. Protection copies may be seen as short-term backups and become part of an organization's disaster recovery plan. In the event that the master library is compromised, the protective copies become the new master, and the organization then renews the process of creating another protective duplicate from the new master.

When integrated with an asset management plan that includes the replication of all content and the distribution to other sites for protective purposes, the archive may be the best solution short of physically duplicating the media over a network to another near- or on-line spinning disk storage center. Cloud storage is surfacing as a modern means for archiving or protecting data because it is now in "virtual" storage, which by its very nature has a fundamental ability to have its own "one-to-many" replications of the stored data.

Backup or Archive: There are Differences

The main differences between data backups and data archives were introduced earlier, but only at a high level. This next section delves into the topic as it applies to the both the individual and the enterprise.

First and foremost, the purpose of a data backup is for disaster recovery (DR). For data archives, its principle use is for preservation. The differences in the two activities are based upon purpose, and that is what makes them really different from each other.

Backups

A data backup will be used for the recovery or restoration of lost or corrupted files. The highest use of the backup is to recover an accidentally deleted file or an entire drive of files because you had a laptop fail or it was stolen, or there was a double disk failure in a RAID 5 array that requires a complete restoration of the file sets to what they looked like previously.

Backups should be made when the equipment used to store those files is frequently moved or when it is routinely accessed by many users in any uncontrolled environment. Backups should be made immediately for content that is at risk of loss or has a value so high (as in a "once in a lifetime occurrence") that losing it would be more than just disastrous.

Backups are preventative in nature. For example, if something bad happened to a user's files yesterday, having a backup from a day ago might allow you to at least restore them to the point of a day or two or three ago. This is of course better than never finding even a trace of the file.

Backup software applications allow you to set up many different operating models, that is, what is backed up, how often, and under what circumstances. In media production, backups are usually made at the onset of a new version of a project. Material is transferred from the reusable in-field capturing media (e.g., XDCAM, P2, or a transportable disc) to a nearline/near-term store as it is ingested and before it is used on the nonlinear editing platform. This is in reality a transfer and not a backup, as the original content on the original media becomes the backup until a successful copy or editing session is completed.

Backups will help to support the user in obtaining a version of a file from a few weeks or months prior, provided the backups are not purged or removed from access. Recordings or media should never be erased or destroyed until after a bona fide duplicate or backup is verified.

Acting like Archives

Data archives generally will show a history of files, where they existed, when they existed, potentially who accessed them and when, and who modified them in any way. Backup systems generally are not sufficient to perform these kinds of tasks, and they will frequently only "restore" the files to a previous location or to a local desktop application. It is possible to obtain these features in some backup applications, but is probably much more difficult or costly.

Some backup applications state they are able to create an archive version, but those claims should be thoroughly understood and tested before assuming the backup and the archive could be one and the same.

Data Backups—Not Archives

Backups are essentially considered to be short term and dynamic. They are performed incrementally and append only data that have "changed" since the previous full backup. Backups do not easily allow access to individual files, instead they are highly compressed and complex to restore if and when needed. Backup processes may be placed into these general categories.

Full

A full backup is where every file or folder selected is duplicated to another location on physical media such as a DVD, Blu-ray, a portable or external hard disk drive, or a data tape (e.g., Linear Tape Open (LTO)).

Incremental

In an incremental backup, only those files that have changed since the last backup of any kind are updated. The process also resets the archive flag to indicate that the file has been saved. Incremental backups do not delete the older version of a previous version of the backed up file(s); it simply adds a copy of the newest version.

Differential

Backs up all changed files and deletes the files that are missing plus the older versions of files currently to be backed up.

If all the attributes of the old files completely match the current version of what will be the new archive files, then it is included in this differential backup process.

"Mirror"

A mirror is where the set of backup folders is continuously synchronized with the source set of folders. When a source file changes in any way, there is a copy of that change placed into the backup. This process usually happens immediately, similar in function to a RAID-mirror (RAID 1), but it will place all the backup files in a separate location on a separate set of media.

Snapshot

A snapshot is an instant capture in time of the current files, the same as a full backup, but without marking the files as saved. High performance intelligent storage systems are enabled to take recursive snapshots of the file systems so as to maintain as current an image of the overall system as possible. Most backup applications are not that sophisticated.

Internal Application-Specific Backups

Individual media software applications frequently have their own versions of backups that are used to return a set of functions to their previous state, usually called the "undo" function. In non-linear editing (NLE) platforms, production bins which contain raw material, in-production segments, and associated metadata are retained until the final composition is committed to rendering. Once the finished piece is rendered, some or all of the elements plus the history of those operations may be pushed off to an archive as permanent storage. The more sophisticated platforms may boil all the backed up individual steps from the time line and retain them so that segments of the work in process can be recovered for future use.

Some applications have plug-ins that link to third-party applications that manage the migration of these files, elements, and metadata to a tape or disk (disc)-based archive. If all the elements are migrated to the archive, recovery of the entire production process is possible. However, once a file is "flattened" and the timeline information is purged, the historical information surrounding the editing process is most likely lost forever. A representation of how one product line from Avid Technology has bridged the integration gaps in third-party archive solutions follows next.

Archive and Transfer Management— Nonlinear Editing

The Avid TransferManager "Dynamically Extensible Transfer" (TM-DET) is part of their tool kit that migrates OMF-wrapped media files (JFIF, DV, I-frame MPEG) to third-party destinations such as a central archive. DET further enables a vendor to restore previously transferred media files back into Avid Unity ("DET Pull") with Interplay Transfer or TransferManager performing an Interplay Engine or MediaManager check-in (essentially, logging media metadata into the centralized database).

DET is the appropriate API to use when the target file is already an Avid media file wrapped with MXF or OMF metadata. To allow native editing, the media files must be wrapped in MXF or OMF by an Avid editor, by the ingest platform or through the Avid TransferManager.

The Avid TransferManager "Data Handling Module" (TM-DHM) tool kit enables vendors to create a plug-in that works with Interplay Transfer and TransferManager to perform playback and ingest transfers. Playback and ingest transfers are distinct from standard file transfers in that they first convert a sequence to or from a stream of video frames and audio samples that are then transferred over an IP network.

During an ingest session, the Transfer application accepts a multiplexed stream of video and audio frames, and then converts the audio and video stream into an Avid-compatible clip by wrapping them in MXF or OMF format and checking the associated metadata into the Interplay Engine or MediaManager system. When incorporated with third-party archive applications, these solutions provide an integrated approach to media production, protection, and extensibility as production requirements change and the need to reconstruct the post-production processes surface.

Differentiation

Differentiating between how the archive stores the data and what data the archive stores is fundamental to understanding backup and archive functionality. If we look deeper into archives, especially those which are moving media process oriented, one may find there are subsets of processes related to archiving: those that occur in real time during capture or ingest; and those that happen at the conclusion of a production process or asset management routine.

In e-discovery (also "eDiscovery"), the data archive process watches the system and archives its data as it is created and in real time. On the other hand, the data backup routine runs as a batch process at prescribed intervals, usually nightly.

Another difference between the backup and the archive processes is the level of detail that the archive will store. Data archives will store all of the supplemental information associated with a file, both as structural metadata about the file and descriptive metadata about the content. For example, when email is archived, the data archiving software product stores information such as the subject line, the sender, and the receiver or it may look into the body and attachments for key words. Google Desktop is an example of the depths that an archive might take for what are purely "search" functions, and what can be done with that data from an extensibility perspective.

Archives store this information in a linked database, as well as the document and email attachments, in a similar way that a data backup system would. Archives take this data, create metatags and other relevant statistics, and then put it into a searchable database that is accessible to users and search engines. In contrast, a backup system is data that are simply stored on a tape or an external drive, without the tagging or the search integration; it is essentially a file system record without search capabilities.

Archiving for Discovery

A backup application would not be used for e-discovery or for determining which references are to be used as discovery in civil litigation dealing with the exchange of information in electronic format. These data, which are also referred to as Electronically Stored Information (ESI), are usually (but not always) an element of one of the processes of digital forensics analysis that is performed to recover evidence. The people involved in these processes include forensic investigators, lawyers, and IT managers. All these differences lead to problems with confusing terminology.

Data that are identified as relevant by attorneys is then placed on "legal hold," thus forcing the archive (and sometimes temporary backups performed prior to archive) to be put into suspension, excluding the system from further use until properly collected as evidence. This evidence, once secured, is extracted and analyzed using digital forensic procedures, and is often converted into a paper format or equivalent electronic files (as PDF or TIFF) for use in the legal proceedings or court trials.

If data are put on hold because you are being sued or investigated by a legal entity, you will most likely not be asked to restore things to the way they looked in the past. Instead, a snapshot of the entire data system is made or the entire storage system is archived so that no loss or corruption of the data/information (e.g., all emails with specific keywords in them between one person and another, company to company, or intra-company files in a particular directory) can occur.

The time, sequence, and who created or modified the content is the prime requirement to be preserved in this kind of data recovery and collection.

Data Archiving

The process of moving data that are no longer actively used to a separate data storage device for long-term retention is called "data archiving." The material in data archives consists of older data that are still important and necessary for future reference, as well as data that must be retained for regulatory compliance. Data archives are indexed and have search capabilities so that files and parts of files can be easily located and retrieved.

Data archives are often confused with data backups, which are copies of data. This distinction is not wise and, for the reasons discussed earlier, is risky and not recommended. To review, data backups are used to restore data in case it is corrupted or destroyed. In contrast, data archives protect older information that is not needed for everyday operations but may occasionally need to be accessed.

Data may be archived to physical media and to virtual space such as "the cloud." Physical media includes spinning magnetic disks, optical media, holographic media, and solid state memory platforms. Virtual space is where media is sent and managed by another entity, one who has taken sufficient precautions to duplicate, backup, and store into other forms of physical media, all of which are probably unknown to the user who contracts for this virtual storage or archive space.

The evolution of tape storage management began with simple, direct attached storage (DAS) devices and has grown steadily into the storage area network (SAN) domains. Tape, while looked upon as more than just a solution that addresses the demands for increased storage capacity, has followed in lock step with the developments of disk drive storage applications. Figure 12.1 shows three hierarchical variances of storage management using server centric storage, local area network storage and storage area network (SAN) approaches.

The next sections of this chapter will open the door to the two foremost methods of storing digital media in the archive: disk-based and tape-based physical media.

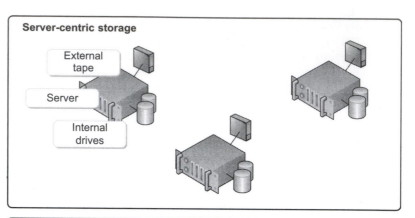

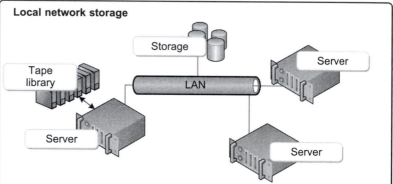

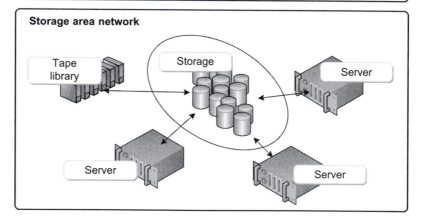

Figure 12.1 Storage management hierarchy.

Tape or Disk

The vital process of archiving moving media data is important for several reasons. Archiving data, whether for the long term or the short term, allows the organization to retrieve that data for alternative uses while simultaneously preserving the aesthetics of that time and place in history for an eternity. Government regulations are driving the retention of data, which must now be kept for a specific number of years. With these perspectives, companies will look to data archiving strategies that allow them to fulfill the government regulations, and their own internal policies.

Three principle archiving storage methods are available today. The organization may select either disk-based archiving, tape-based archiving, or a combination of both. Although there was an interest in looking beyond these two, specifically to holographic solid state archiving, those hopes seemed to peak in around the 2005 time period and have slowly disappeared from the landscape in recent years.

Pros and Cons

Marketing has a wonderful way of making one product, technology or implementation a whole lot better than its opposing counterpart. The end user is forever challenged by the means used to represent the performance, reliability, and longevity of the two primary alternatives—tape and disk—for archiving purposes.

There are several advantages and disadvantages to disk archiving and tape archiving. Organizations often choose a hybrid mix of disk and tape, using disk for short-term archives that require a high volume of data exchanges, which are termed "near-line" or "near-term" storage. Once the necessity for rapid access diminishes significantly, the data are then transferred, i.e., "archived" to data tape for long-term retention.

Access requirements are going to vary depending upon your workflow and your mission. In the first few years of any retention period, keeping your active data highly accessible so that you can get them back quickly is critical. The content that you just need to keep around and do not need access to is the first reason to port the data to tape. Ultimately, at least for this period in technology, tape becomes the most logical choice for long-term archives, regardless of the capabilities you might have or desire in a disk platform.

For short-term archives of databases, i.e., files not containing moving media, metadata, or search engine data sets, etc., users could employ technologies such as Oracle's Sun Storage Archive Manager (SAM) to move data to disk. This software provides data classification, centralized metadata management, policy-based data placement, protection, migration, long-term retention, and recovery to help enterprise-class entities to effectively manage and utilize data according to business requirements.

Self-Protecting Storage Systems

The Oracle SAM uses a self-protecting file system that offers continuous backup and fast recovery methods to aid in productivity and improve the utilization of data and system resources.

One of the patented methods that is used to monitor attempts to access protected information, called a self-protecting storage system, allows access for authorized host systems and devices while unauthorized access is prevented. In this process, authorization includes a forensic means for tracking that involves inserting a watermark into access commands, such as I/O requests, that are sent to the storage device itself. These access commands are then verified before access is permitted.

Passwords are certainly the most frequently used methods for protecting access to data; however, in one embodiment, the block addresses in I/O requests are encrypted at the host device and decrypted at the self-protecting storage device. Decrypted block addresses are compared to an expected referencing pattern. Should a sufficient match be determined, access to the stored information is provided.

Self-protection can be provided to a range of storage devices including, for example, SD flash memory, USB thumb drives, computer hard drives, and network storage devices. A variety of host devices can be used with the self-protecting storage devices, such as cell phones and digital cameras. This methodology could be added to tape archive systems, such as LTO, which could embed metadata and track location identifiers into the physical properties of the cassette itself. It could also be added to all camcorders or solid state media storage subsystems at the time of image capture, allowing that means of access control to be carried forward throughout the production and post-production stages and on through release and archive.

Disk Archiving Pluses

Disk archiving has several advantages. Disks will provide a much faster means to archive and to restore data than tape. Disks are easier to index and to search than tape archives. Users wanting to locate and recover a single file will only take a short time with disk. However, the storing of large files as archives on disk will consume a lot of unnecessary storage, not to mention floor space and energy. For a large scale, occasionally accessed archive, the exclusive use of disk storage is a costly process.

Tape Archiving Pluses

Many organizations archive huge amounts of data on tape for long-term storage. This method requires less floor space, less energy, and less cooling capacity when compared with comparable storage capacities on spinning disks.

Using tape for archiving purpose can provide better security, especially when the files are encrypted. Leaving any system online and connected over any network is an opportunity waiting for a hacker. Although IT-administrators hope not to have to go through and search individual tapes for information, which is not particularly complex if managed by an asset management system directly coupled to the archive platform, they know the option is there should it be necessary.

The scale of the storage requirement is a prime reason for using a tape-based archive system. Density-wise, tape will most likely always have an edge versus tape. If you are looking at tape because you have more than 100 TB of data, that is a good benchmark for today. However, if your needs are for less than 50 TB of data, you should evaluate the requirements for a tape library solution. It could be that a single transport application-specific tape system might serve the organization well.

Storage Retention Period

When the organization intends to store its data for 10–15 years, the total cost of ownership (TOC) for a tape-based solution will be less than a disk-based solution even with the prices for disks continuing to slide downward as capacities move upward. With tape, you do not have to go through migration; and if it is not spinning, then you are not paying for the energy, maintenance, or replacements of costly individual components.

Disadvantages of Tape

Tape has significant disadvantages that many organizations will struggle with. Those that use a mix of disk and tape to archive data say they still run into trouble when trying to restore from older tape media. Tape cartridges can become corrupted over time; they may be found unreadable, and the transport devices as well as the physical media become aged. Older formats are most likely no longer supported, meaning users may not be able to recover data that have been sitting on older tapes when they need to. Tape formats are often proprietary and can only be recovered on the same transports with the same software (especially if encrypted). This is one of the means that vendors will use to lock the user into their format until that equipment is discarded or abandoned for another.

For legal activities (such as e-discovery), the indexing and search capabilities on tape systems without an external metadata or asset management system are time consuming and frustrating. When the tape library of 9 years ago was archived using a different backup software or operating system than what is currently in place, users may be in for a long process of restoration and searching just to try and extract one or a few files from the library.

The importance of a secondary tracking system mitigates the considerable amount of time required to identify the right tapes and the right place on the tapes where the data are located. Without this kind of third-party application support, a user might end up literally restoring as many tapes as they can, only hoping that they will find the missing needle in the haystack.

Legacy Tape Archive Problems

For those organizations that feel tape is the best method for archiving, third-party solutions are available that aid in making search and indexing easier. Tape backup programs have useful lives built around the operating system that was the most prominent at the time the company wrote the application. As time marches on, those programs become obsolete, cease to be supported, or worse yet, the company that provided the software simply evaporates.

This makes the selection process for both the tape library and the software applications that support the backup or archive all the more complicated. There are programs available that are designed to search and extract files that are stored on tape archives without a secondary asset management routine or application. These "tape assessment programs" are able to search old tape libraries for a specific file, or set of files, and once found, can extract them without having to use the original backup software that was used to create those files.

Standards-Based Archive Approaches

For the moving media industries (film and television), there are new developments that help in the support of mitigating legacy format issues like those expressed previously. Part of the efforts put forth into designing the Material eXchange Format (MXF), by SMPTE, has been added to the latest releases of LTO-5. This application-specific technology is discussed later in this chapter in the section on LTO. There is also work underway for an open archive protocol.

Common Backup Formats

Common backup formats for the data side of the enterprise include:
- CA Technology's "ARCServe"
- CommVault's "Simpana"
- EMC's "NetWorker"
- IBM's "Tivoli Storage Manager" (TSM)
- Symantec's "Backup Exec" and "NetBackup"

According to storage and archive reports (2009), 90% of the marketplace uses these platforms for backup protection.

As for physical tape, Digital Linear Tape (DLT) and LTO seem to be the remaining leading players. For the purposes of recovering legacy data on older formats or media, anything that can attach to a SCSI connection should be recoverable using alternative third-party resources or applications. It is a matter of how often, and under what time constraints, the organization wants to experience the pain of recovering data from a poorly kept or mismanaged archive.

Determining the Right Archiving Method

Today companies will set their overall data archiving strategy and choose their archive systems based upon storage requirements, business activities, and sometimes legal policies. When your need is only to store data for a short period of time, if you are not going to be storing hundreds of terabytes, and you would not (or do not) have long-term retention requirements, archiving to a disk-based platform is the better solution.

If your requirements are to store a large amount of data long term that the organization does not need to access (at least in a relatively short time frame), but your organization needs to keep the content around for litigation purposes, archiving to tape is the easier and less costly option. Nonetheless, many companies are made to lean toward using both tape and disk methods for archiving. This, at least for the present, is often the better way to go.

Cloud Data Protection

An up and coming alternative that makes the financial side of operations pleased is the employment of the "cloud"—the ubiquitous virtual place in the sky that you cannot touch, see, or feel. Enterprises that protect their data through exclusive use of on-premises data storage, backup, or archive systems face potential challenges associated with complexities of implementation, capital and operational total costs of ownership, and capacity shortfalls.

The infrastructure necessary for sufficient protection of the enterprise's digital assets represent a substantial capital investment and must factor in a continual investment over time. Even after acquiring the hardware and software, the enterprise must deal with the networking subsystems and the headache of maintenance including the responsibility for a complex and burdensome disk and/or tape management process—the story does not end there.

The ongoing "lights-on" expenses and resource commitments place continued burdens that might prevent you from using the limited resources available on more strategic projects that are paramount to your actual business. Spending time monitoring the progress of backups and finding answers to troublesome problems is counterproductive to meeting the mandate of doing more with less.

Organizations, given the current economic climate of the years surrounding 2010, are turning to cloud-based data protection as a solution to their unforeseen problems. Cloud solutions are growing, with a nearly 40% expansion in the use of third-party cloud storage for off-site copies expected by 2012 (reference: "Data Protection Trends," ESG, April 2010).

Cloud Benefits

Data protection (not necessarily archiving) is an ideal application that can be moved to the cloud. For most companies, data protection is not a strategic part of their core operation; it is more a task that is necessary because of policies that are both legal and financial in structure.

It is relatively easy to buy, deploy, and manage cloud-based data protection. Cloud-based solutions avoid the upfront capital investments and the costly requirement of continued upgrades to networks, tape, disk, and server infrastructures. Relieving this burden enables the enterprise to remain agile and to provide a competitive edge without having to support, train, replace, manage, and handle the ongoing issues of data backup and/or archive. This storage solution also becomes an OpEx instead of a CapEx commitment.

Scaling

When capacity requirements are unknown, such as when a business acquisition requires a new structure in data retention, cloud-based storage capacity can scale effortlessly to meet the dynamics of the enterprise with regard to backup and archive.

Services Provided

When looking to the cloud for backup or archive support, look at features such as advanced encryption and other security technologies that are aimed at safeguarding your data during the transmission, storage, and recovery processes. A cloud-based service should be able to provide built in deduplication for capacity and bandwidth optimization. The service should employ underground data storage facilities that can satisfy the strictest security standards.

Insist that all data are replicated to a second geographically separate fully redundant data center. There should be a proactive administration and monitoring of the data as an automated, standard service. Continuous backups should cover open files and databases. For media assets, the system's network access points must be able to handle the requirements of jumbo frames and multi-gigabyte sized files.

For operational activities and for disaster recovery, the cloud should provide appliances that are capable of a fast recovery for large amounts of data, especially when deadlines loom or when collaborative post-production processes span continents.

The connections into a content delivery network suited to the business practices and requirements of your organization should also be considered. The gateway into the cloud-storage protective service should be capable of optimizing network traffic without necessarily depending upon a private network.

Holographic Storage for the Archive

Holographic storage is truly a form of solid state storage. Making use of the same principles as those in producing holograms, laser beams are employed to record and read back computer-generated data that are stored in three dimensions on a durable physical piece of plastic, glass, or polymer type media. The target for this technology is to store enormous amounts of data in a tiny amount of space.

Although not yet successfully mass-commercialized, there have been many vendors who have worked on it, including (in 2002) Polaroid spinoff Aprilis, and Optware (Japan). The best known of these vendors is InPhase Technologies. Originally

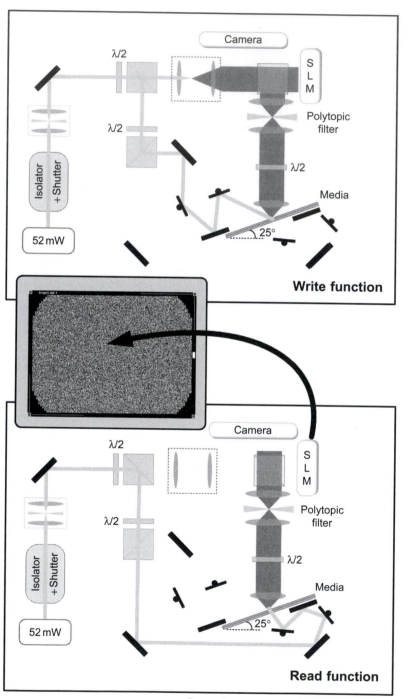

Figure 12.2 System architecture for holographic data storage.

Concepts courtesy of InPhase Technologies

founded in December 2000 as a Lucent Technologies venture that spun out of Bell Labs research, InPhase worked on a holographic storage product line capable of storing in excess of 200 gigabytes of data, written four times faster than the speed of current DVD drives. InPhase ceased doing business in February 2010, yet it was quickly reacquired in March 2010 by Signal Lake, a leading investor in next-generation technology and computer communications companies, who was also responsible for the original spinoff from Bell in late 2000. Figure 12.2 shows the fundamental read and write processes employed in holographic storage.

Holography breaks through the density limits of conventional storage by recording through the full depth of the storage medium. Unlike other technologies that record one data bit at a time, holography records and reads over a million bits of data with a single flash of laser light. This produces transfer rates significantly higher than current optical storage devices. Holographic storage combines high-storage densities and fast transfer rates with a durable low cost media at a much lower price point that comparable physical storage materials.

The flexibility of the technology allows for the development of a wide variety of holographic storage products that range from consumer handheld devices to storage products for the enterprise. Holographic storage could offer 50 hours of high definition video on a single disk; 50,000 songs held on media the size of a postage stamp, or half a million medical X-rays on a credit card.

For permanent archiving, the holographic storage medium is a technology with tremendous potential since the life expectancy of the media and the data could be centuries in duration. The advantage of holography over tape storage then becomes increased density, higher durability, and less subjectivity to destruction by electromagnetics, water, or the environment in general.

The first demonstrations of products aimed at the broadcast industry were at the National Association of Broadcasters (NAB) 2005 convention held annually in Las Vegas. The prototype was shown at the Maxell Corporation of America booth. In April 2009, GE Global Research demonstrated its own holographic storage material that employed discs, which would utilize similar read mechanisms as those found on Blu-ray Disc players. The disc was to reportedly store upwards of 500 Gbytes of data.

RAIT

Introduced in the late 1990s and early part of 2000, Redundant Array of Inexpensive Tapes (RAIT) is a means of storing data as a collection of N+1 tapes that are aggregated to act as a single virtual tape. Typically, data files are simultaneously written in blocks to N tapes in stripes, with parity information written in bit wise exclusive-OR fashion stored on from one to many additional tapes. A RAIT system will have higher performance compared to systems that only store duplicate copies of information. The drawback is that because data are striped across multiple tapes, to read a particular set of data requires that all the tapes storing that data must be mounted and then simultaneously and synchronously read in order to reconstruct any of the files stored on the tape.

Even though the system utilizes parity information for the benefit of reconstructing data lost because a tape has gone missing or has unrecoverable data, should one or more tapes be found unreadable, the system must wait until all of the remaining tapes can be read and parity information can be used to reconstruct the data set.

Since their introduction, manufacturers of tape-based storage systems looked at means to protect tape-based information in archives and backup systems in a similar fashion to RAID protection for disks. The concepts included extending high data rate throughput, robustness, and virtualization. Through the use of striping, the quality of service (QoS) would be improved by combining the number of data stripes (N) with the number

Table 12.1 Redundant Array of Independent Tapes (RAIT) Protection Schemes

	Virtual-Volume READS		
	Based Upon the Number of 160-Gbyte Virtual-Volume READS Before Data Loss Occurs		
Protection Scheme	Total Tapes	Number of Missing Tapes		
		0 Missing	1 Missing	2 Missing
None	8	10^2	1	1
1 Parity	8 + 1	109	10^2	1
2 Parity	8 + 2	10^2	10^2	10^2
3 Parity	8 + 3	10^2	10^2	10^2
4 Parity	8 + 4	10^2	10^2	10^2
Mirroring	8 + 8	10^2	10^2	15

of parity stripes (P). Defined as "scratch mount time," N+P sets would define the QoS for a particular configuration.

By implementing parity, much like that in a disk RAID set (e.g., RAID 5), the number of virtual-volume reads before data loss is mitigated. For example, by prescribing an array of striped tapes in an RAIT configuration, composed of a set of eight striped tapes plus from one to four parity tapes, the tolerance profile for the number of virtual-volume reads before data loss when one or two tapes go missing out of the set is elevated according to Table 12.1.

RAIT works essentially the same way as RAID, but with data tape instead of spinning media. RAIT is ranked by six increasing levels of protection (or security) ranging from RAIT Level 0 to RAIT Level 5.

Mirroring—Level 1 RAIT

Known as disk mirroring or disk duplexing; it is where all data are written to two separate drives simultaneously. Should a drive fail for any reason, the other drive continues operation unaffected.

Data Striping—Level 3 RAIT

Level 3 RAIT employs data striping, in which the data stream is divided into equal parts, depending on how many drives there are in the array. In Level 3 RAIT, there is a drive dedicated to maintaining parity. A parity drive can potentially cause a bottleneck because all the Read-write requests must first go through the parity drive. In the event a drive should fail, the parity information is then used to reconstruct the lost data.

Data Striping—Level 5 RAIT

The parity information is divided equally among all drives. Level 5 RAIT provides maximum data integrity, however, often at the expense of data throughput.

Not for Random Access

RAIT technologies are not a substitute for random access to data, and have not been widely accepted in the data archiving or backup circles. Although StorageTek stated a commitment to COTS RAIT in 2001, the development of virtual tape library technologies seem to have taken the marketing side of RAIT and put it on the back burner. As of this writing, there has been only a marginal commitment to RAIT at either the network or the architectural level.

Automated Tape Libraries (ATL)

In the era before file-based workflow was an everyday term, the broadcast media industry faced a challenge of how to manage both their expanding off-line and near-line digital storage requirements. Initially, the solution was the integration of a data cassette storage library coupled with their videoserver systems. That began in the mid-1990s with both dedicated single drives and with multiple drive robotic libraries using tape formats designed exclusively for data libraries, such as the Exabyte platform. This method was not widely accepted as a solution for extending the storage capacities for video media, and drove the implementation of other alternatives.

In those early years for broadcast media, those "near-line" and "long-term" archives consisted of a robotics-based automated tape library (ATL) built around a specific digital tape media format, and controlled by a data management software system generally coupled with the facility automation system. An ATL for data purposes is somewhat of a descendant of the videotape-based library cart systems from the Sony Betacart and Library Management System (LMS), the Panasonic MII-Marc, or the Ampex ACR-25 and ACR-225 eras of the 1990s. Yet the ATL is a different breed closely aligned with the computer-centric data tape management systems for transaction processing and database server systems employed by the financial records departments of banks and the medical records industry.

ATLs for broadcast and media delivery systems could not stand by themselves. They required a third-party interface placed between the tape-based (or disk-based) storage system and the server to effectively do their job on a routine operational basis. In this infant world of digital media data archiving, it was the tape format that had as much to do with the amount of data that could be stored as it did with how that data moved between the servers, the near-line, and the online systems. Automated tape libraries would not be purchased solely for the purpose of removing the burden from the videoserver. The ATL was expected to become the tool that would change the way the facility operates in total.

The selection of an ATL was based upon how that tool could create significant operational cost savings both initially and over the life of the system. Choosing an ATL was no easy matter, as the hardware and software together formed the basis for a new foundational model for broadcasting or content delivery. That model has evolved significantly since the introductory days of broadcast servers attached to automated tape libraries.

Stackers, Autoloaders, or Libraries

The distinction among tape automation systems is in the way they handle data backup and physical media access management. Stackers, sometimes referred to as autoloaders, were the first tape automation products for small and mid-size information systems operations. Typically, these systems had just one drive, with the tapes being inserted and removed by the system's mechanical picker, sometimes called an elevator, in sequential order. Operationally, if a stacker is configured to perform a full database backup, the system would begin with tape "0" and continue inserting and removing tapes until the backup was completed, or the supply of cartridges is exhausted.

An autoloader, still with only one drive, has the added capability of providing accessibility to any tape in its magazine upon request. This ability to randomly select tapes makes autoloaders appropriate for small scale network backup and near on-line storage applications.

Libraries offer the same type of functionality as autoloaders, but are generally equipped with multiple drives for handling large-scale backups, near on-line access, user-initiated file recovery, and the ability to serve multiple users and multiple hosts simultaneously. On those larger libraries, multiple robotic mechanisms may also be employed to improve data throughput and system response time.

Server and Archive Components

The dedicated videoserver archive systems consists of three fundamental entities. First is the physical tape drive (or drives); second is the library mechanism (the robot) that moves the tapes to and from the drives; and third is the software that manages the library/tape interface between the server, the datamover systems, and the facility's automation systems. Among other functions, it is the archive software that contains the interface that enables the historical media's data library and the physical archive library databases.

This portion will focus on the first of three entities, the tape drive, which consists primarily of two different technologies: helical scan technology and linear tape technology. The latter, developed by Digital Equipment Corporation as a backup media, is commonly referred to as digital linear tape or DLT.

Throughout the evolution of tape-based storage for digital assets, we have seen various products come and go. Digital tape drives and formats have spanned a tape technology evolution that has included Exabyte Corporation (acquired by Tandberg Data on November 20, 2006) with its 8 mm, Quantum, which produces DLT (ranging from the TK50 in 1984 to SuperDLT in 2001), DAT/DDS and Travan-based technologies, Ampex with its DST products, and Sony's AIT and DTF formats on their Petasite platform.

Evolution in Digital Tape Archives

Tape storage technology for broadcast-centric media archiving has its roots in the IT domain of computer science. The original concept of tape storage stems from a need to backup data from what at one time were fragile, prone to catastrophic failure devices known all too well as hard disk drives. Today, with high reliability, low cost drives—coupled with RAID technology—the need for protecting the archive takes on a different perspective. It is not the active RAID protected data that concerns us, it is inactive data that have consumed the majority of the storage capacity on the server or render farm that needs migration to another platform so that new work may continue.

Modern videoservers are built with hardware elements that can be upgraded or retrofitted without undue restructuring or destruction of the media library. Unlike the disk drive upgrades in the videoserver, which can be replaced or expanded when new capacities are required, the tape system will most likely not be changed for quite some time. While it is simply not feasible to replace the entire library of tapes or the tape drive transports, manufacturers of tape systems have recognized there are paths to upgrades for the archive in much the same manner as videoservers are upgraded.

Those who have experienced the evolution of videotape technologies should heed this strong advice. The selection of a tape storage platform is an important one. The process should involve selecting a technology that permits a smooth transition to next-generation devices that will not let the owner head down a dead end street at an unknown point several years down the road—a difficult challenge in today's rapidly advancing technological revolution.

Information technology has provided a lot of good insight into videoserver technologies. With respect to data backup in IT, the information systems manager typically looks for short run-time backup solutions that can be executed during fixed time periods and are designed to perform an incremental update of a constantly evolving database. These backups must have a high degree of data integrity, should run reliably, and generally with minimal human intervention. For the data sets captured, error-detection and correction is essential, with the name of the game being "write-the-data-once" and "read it many times thereafter."

In contrast, the video/media server model can operate in a variety of perspectives, depending upon the amount of online disk storage in service, the volume and type of material in the system, and the formats being stored on those systems. Variables such as the degree of media protection and the comfort level of the on-air facility overall make management of the archive a customizable solution with paths to the future. Thus, making the choice in a tape media for archive or backup becomes a horse of a different color—even though the industry consensus leans toward the LTO and DLT formats so prominent in data circles.

Tape Technology Basics

Historically, when tape was first used as a backup solution, helical scan technology was an acceptable, relatively inexpensive way to meet the goal of secondary storage for protection, backup, and expanded off-line storage. Linear tape technologies, with or without fixed position heads, were developed later, offering alternatives that over time have allowed a viable competition to develop between both physical tape methodologies.

Tape Metrics

Factors that users should be aware of and contribute to the selection of a tape technology (whether for broadcast or IT solutions) include the following.
- Average access time—the average time it takes to locate a file that is halfway into the tape; it assumes this is the first access requested from this specific tape, so the drive is starting to seek the file from the beginning of the tape.
- Transfer rate (effective)—the average number of units of data (expressed as bits, characters, blocks, or frames) transferred per unit time from a source. This is usually stated in terms of megabytes per second (Mbytes/second) of uncompressed

data, or when applicable, compressed data at an understood, specified compression ratio (e.g., 2:1 compression).

- Data integrity (error correction)—the uncorrected bit error rate, sometimes referred to as the hard error rate, the number of erroneous bits that cannot be corrected by error correction algorithms.
- Data throughput (system or aggregate)—the sum of all the data rates delivered to all the terminals (devices) in a network or through a delivery channel. Usually expressed in terms of megabytes per second (Mbytes/second) of uncompressed data, or when applicable, compressed data at an understood, specified compression ratio (e.g., 2:1 compression).
- Durability (media)—measured in tape passes, i.e., how many times can the tape be run through the unit before it wears out.
- Load time—the time from when a cartridge is inserted into the drive, until the cartridge is ready to read or write the data.
- Seek time—the total time it takes from the time a command is issued to the time the data actually start to be recovered or delivered. This metric is on the order of milliseconds for a spinning disk, but is in seconds for linear tape cassettes.
- Reposition time—the time for a linear tape to move from its current position to the position that it is instructed to move to, usually the place where the start of the delivery of the requested data begins.
- Head life—the period in time (days, months, years) that a recording and reproducing head on a tape transport (or equivalent) can reliably produce meaningful information (data) 100% of the time.
- Error detection—the recognition of errors caused by disturbances, noise, or other impairments during the transmission from the source (transmitter) to the destination (receiver).
- Error correction—the recognition of errors and the subsequent reconstruction of the original data/information that is error-free.
- Peak transfer or burst—usually referring to the maximum transfer rate of the bus; it is faster than sustained transfer rates and is occasional (i.e., "bursty").
- Tape life cycle—the total period of time from first use to retirement of a magnetic data recording material, specifically linear tape based.

Linear Serpentine

This recording technology uses a non-rotating (fixed) head assembly, with the media paths segmented into parallel horizontal tracks that can be read at much higher speeds during search, scan, or shuttle modes. The longitudinal principle allows for multiple heads aligned for read and write operations on each head grouping. The head will be positioned so that it can move perpendicularly to the direction of the tape path allowing it to be precisely aligned over the data tracks, which run longitudinally. The technology will simultaneously record and read multiple channels, or tracks, effectively increasing transfer rates for a given tape speed and recording density.

Note further that there are read and write heads in line with the tape blocks, which allows a "read immediately after write" for data integrity purposes. Digital linear tape is not required to "wrap" a rotating head drum assembly, as is the case with its counterpart helical scan recording.

Helical Scan Recording

Helical scan recording places data in diagonal stripes across the tape, allowing for overlapping data, which results in higher data density. Helical recording uses a spinning drum assembly with tiny heads attached to the edge of the drum that contact the tape as it is wrapped around the drum and travels linearly. The wrapping process, in the shape of the Greek letter "omega," allows for a nearly continuous contact between tape and heads as the tape moves past it.

Figures 12.3 and 12.4 depict the differences in the two technologies, showing the block data layouts on each tape format.

Historical Development of Data Tape

Helical scan tape technology was first developed as an inexpensive way to store data, with roots in the mid-1980s. At that time, manufacturers of home videotape saw 8 mm tape, a helical scan technology, as a potential high-capacity method in which to store computer data for mid- and low-end systems. Over the years, 4 mm DAT (digital audio tape) and QIC (quarter-inch cartridge) linear tape had replaced most of the early 8 mm systems. While smaller systems still relied on these technologies, many felt that DLT was the right solution (at that time) for servers, data storage, or network backup systems because of its reliability and higher performance.

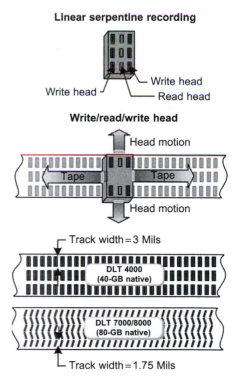

Figure 12.3 Linear tape profile using a serpentine recording method.

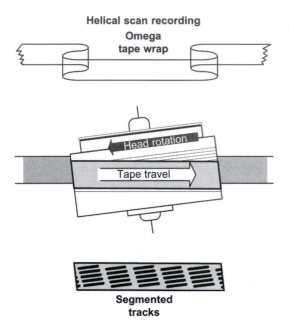

Figure 12.4 Helical scan recording with segmented blocks and tape, which wraps a rotating head drum assembly.

QIC and DAT

Introduced by the 3M Company in 1972, long before the personal computer, QIC was then used to store acquisition data and telecommunications data. QIC did not employ helical scan recording. It came in form factors including 5.25-inch data cartridges and a mini-cartridge of 3.5 inches. Tape width is either quarter-inch or in the Travan model 0.315 inches in width. QIC uses two reels in an audio-cassette style physical cartridge construction. Pinch rollers hold tape against a metal capstan rod. Opponents of this technology touted that this capstan-based method produced the highest point of wear to the physical tape media.

QIC, like DLT, which would follow almost 10 years later, used serpentine recording principles mainly in a single channel Read-write configuration. The industry eventually moved away from QIC, which was hindered by evolving standards and a steady movement toward the Travan TR-4 format.

Travan

This medium is an 8 mm magnetic tape cartridge design that was developed by the 3M Company. The format was used for backup and mass data storage in early computer systems between the years of 1995 and 2002. Over time, versions of Travan cartridges and drives were developed that provided greater data capacity, while retaining the standard 8 mm width and 750-inch length. Travan is standardized under the QIC body, and it competed with the DDS, AIT, and VXA formats.

The Travan tape hierarchy is shown in Table 12.2. Note that an 800-Mbyte native capacity, 0.25 Mbytes/second version called "TR-2" was designed by 3M, but never marketed.

8 mm Recording Technologies

Popularly referred to as "Exabyte" (the amount equivalent to 1000 petabytes), this nearly generic product line was named after the company that made it most popular, Exabyte Corporation. 8 mm tape drive technologies founded much of what we know

two CRC values is not zero), a "rewrite-necessary" command is issued and the process is repeated. Once this logical block passes all the tests, the buffer is flushed and the next group of data are processed.

Tape Media Formats and Fabrication Parameters

Items including areal data density, coefficient of friction and stiction, output levels, and drop-out characteristics are parameters that affect the longevity and performance of one form of media versus another. The tape wear specification has a dependency based upon the type of transport employed and the number of cycles that the tape must go through over its life cycle. Media bases and tape construction technologies contribute to variances in life cycle expectancy.

Metal Particle to Advanced Metal Evaporated

Newer technologies continue to emerge as the demand for storage increases. The move from metal particle (MP) media to advanced metal evaporated (AME) media is one principle used to increase capacity, especially at high bit densities. Often, as is the case with the Exabyte helical scan Mammoth 2 technology, the media and the transport system are developed in harmony where the transport is matched to the tape base, and in turn to system storage capacities. These manufacturing and research practices continue today.

The AME process was relatively new in 1998, employing two magnetic layers, which are applied by evaporating the magnetic material onto the base layers in a vacuum chamber. The magnetic recording layer of the AME media contains a pure evaporated cobalt doping that is sealed with a diamond-like carbon (DLC) coating and lubricant. AME contains 80–100% magnetic recording media that results in a 5-dB increase in short wavelength read back output compared to conventional metal evaporated tape. The average life of the tape allows for 30,000 end-to-end passes.

The 100% cobalt magnetic material is evaporated using an electron beam, which creates a much thinner, pure magnetic layer free of any binders or lubricants. The use of two magnetic layers improves the total output and frequency response while improving the signal-to-noise ratio of the media. Exabyte, at the time of its release to production, stated that their AME media is expected to withstand 20,000 passes.

Only AME media can be used on AIT drives.

Advanced Intelligent Tape (AIT)

Introduced in 1996, developed by Sony, and since licensed by Seagate, AIT was the next generation in 8 mm tape format. The new AIT drives, with increased capacity and throughput, were a significant improvement over other 8 mm products.

Sony solved the reliability problems with a redesigned tape-to-head interface. AIT uses a binderless, evaporative metal media that virtually ends the particle shedding debris deposit problems of older 8 mm drives and significantly decreases the drive failures so often experienced in 8 mm as a result of contaminants clogging the mechanisms.

One of the complaints with predecessor tape storage systems is in accessing of files and/or data directories. Legacy model tape systems use a beginning of the tape indexing structure that must be written to each time data are appended or eliminated from the tape. This requires that the tape's indexing headers be read every time the tape is loaded and then written to every time it has completed any form of data modification.

When this header is located at the beginning (or sometimes at the end) of the media, the tape must therefore be rewound to the header, advanced for the first reading of the header, then written to and reread for verification. Changing tapes was further compounded by this concept, which lay in the data-tracking mechanism. Besides taking the additional time for cycling media, any errors in this process would render the entire data tape useless, as this became the principal metadata location that contained the data about the data that were stored on the tape.

Sony, possibly from its experiences in some of the company's broadcast tape applications, took to task another method of storing the bits about the bits. Instead of just writing on the header, Sony placed header information at a location that does not require the tape be mounted in order to be read. Sony introduced its Memory-in-Cassette (MIC), which is a small 16 kbit chip (64 kbit on AIT-2) that keeps the metadata stored on the physical cassette, and not on the actual media. This reduces file access location time, and searches can be achieved in 27 seconds (for 25/50-Gbyte data tapes) and 37 seconds for the larger cassette format. Sony claimed a nearly 50% reduction in search time compared with DLT of the same generation.

One consequential advantage to the MIC concept is the "mid-tape-load" principle, whereby the transport can park the tape in up to 256 on-tape partitions instead of rewinding to the beginning before ejecting. When the tape is mounted, you are a theoretical average of 50% closer to any location on the tape than a non-mid-tape load DLT, and the time involved with reading directories in headers is gone. MIC improves media data access time, with AIT-2's built-in 64 kilobyte EEPROM to store TOC and file location information.

This concept has been extended to many other products, tape, and other forms of storage ever since.

AIT-1 technology employs a 4800 RPM helical scan head, with the AIT-2 version spinning at 6400 RPM. Higher-density data are written at an angle relative to the tape's edge. A closed-loop, self-adjusting tape path provides for highly accurate tape tracking. The AIT transport features an "auto-tracking/following" (ATF) system whereby the servo adjusts for tape flutter, which lets data be written with much closer spacing between tracks.

A redesigned metal-in-gap (MIG) tape head puts head life at an average of 50,000 h. Combining their tension control mechanism, which maintains tape tension at one-half that of other helical scan tape technologies, and Sony's unique head geometry, head-to-media pressure is reduced even further. This servo system senses and controls tension fluctuations and in turn helps to reduce tape and head wear. In addition, Sony's cooling design and Active Head Cleaner result in a mean time between failures (MTBF) of 200,000 hours for the drive itself.

AIT-5 media has a 400-Gbyte native (1040-Gbyte compressed) capacity and a transfer rate of 24 Mbytes/second. The media is only compatible with AIT-5 platforms and is available in WORM format.

Super and Turbo AIT

Sony also produced an updated format, called Super AIT (SAIT), around the 2003–2004 time frame. Their "Super Advanced Intelligent Tape" (SAIT) half-inch format utilizes advanced features in helical-scan recording technology and AME media to achieve a 500-Gbyte native (up to 1.3 TB compressed) storage capacity, within a half-inch, SAIT 1500 single-reel tape cartridge.

The SAIT format provides for a sustained data transfer rate of 30-Mbytes/second native and 78 Mbytes/second compressed. The maximum burst transfer rate is dependent upon the interface, which is 160 Mbytes/second (for Ultra 160 SCSI LVD/SE) and 2 Gbits/second on Fibre Channel. Sony's Remote-Sensing Memory-in-Cassette (R-MIC) continued to provide sophisticated and rapid data access capabilities, high-speed file search, and access. An automatic head cleaning system coupled with AME media, their "leader block" tape threading system, and a sealed deck design with simplified tape load path, results in enterprise-class reliability of 500,000 POH with 100% duty cycle.

AIT Turbo (T-AIT) is another enhancement in both capacity and speed over earlier generations of the 8 mm AIT format and technology. The AIT Turbo series provides capacities from 20 to 40-Gbyte native (52–104-Gbyte compressed) .

Despite all their technical advancements, in March 2010 Sony formally announced that it had discontinued sales of AIT drives and the AIT library and automation systems.

Digital Data Storage (DDS)

Digital Data Storage (DDS) is a format for data storage that came from the 4 mm DAT technology and was developed by Sony and Hewlett-Packard. DDS products include DDS-1 through DDS-5, and DAT 160.

DDS-5 tape was launched in 2003, but the product name was changed from DDS to Digital Audio Tape (DAT) as DAT-72. Used as a backup solution, DDS-5 media provides a storage capacity of 36-Gbyte native (72-Gbyte compressed), which is double the capacity of its predecessor DDS-3 and DDS-4 tapes. The DDS-5 transfers data at more than 3 Mbytes/second (compressed data at 6.4 Mbytes/second), with a tape length for DDS-5 of 170 m.

DDS-5 drives were made by Hewlett-Packard (HP) in alliance with tape drive manufacturer Certance, which was acquired by Quantum in 2005. DDS-3 and DDS-4 media is backwards compatible with the DDS-5. The DDS-5 tape media uses ATTOM technology to create an extremely smooth tape surface.

Data Storage Technology (DST)

Another contender in the digital tape playing field was Ampex Data Systems. The Ampex DST product was created in 1992. The format was a high speed, DDT 19 mm helical scan tape format supporting a drive search speed of 1600 Mbytes/second. Ampex drives were typically integrated with their DST series Automated Cartridge Library (ACL), a mass data storage system that contains hundreds of small to large cassettes per cabinet.

The Ampex Data Systems drive technology is founded on the same concepts and similar construction to their professional broadcast series digital videotape transport architectures. The DST tape drive interface is via the company's cartridge handling system (CHS) control via dual 16-bit fast differential SCSI-2 or single-ended 8-bit SCSI-2 (Ultra SCSI).

Error rates are specified at 1×10^{e17} with transfer rates between 15 Mbytes/second on the DST 15 series drives to 20 Mbytes/second on the DST 20 transports. Ampex also manufactured a line of instrumentation drives (DIS series) that support 120–160 Mbytes/second over a serial instrumentation and UltraSCSI interface.

With its DST products, Ampex offered the highest transfer rate of any digital tape products currently in production (1992). While their transports were physically the largest and they had the widest tape width (19 mm), at 20 Mbytes/second (160 Mbits/second), program transfers between videoservers with MPEG-2 compression ratios of 10 Mbits/second could occur at up to 16 times real-time speed (provided other portions of the system and the interfaces were capable of sustaining those rates).

In 1996, Ampex offered a double density version of the DST tape with 50 Gbytes (small cassette), 150 Gbytes (medium cassette), and 330 Gbytes (large cassette). This capacity was doubled again in 2000 to quad density.

Digital Tape Format (DTF)

Following the introduction of DTF-1, Sony introduced the second generation GY-8240 series, which supports the DTF-2 tape format, providing five times more storage than DTF-1, at 200-Gbytes native capacity (518 Gbytes with ALDC compression) on a single L-cassette. DTF is a 1/2-inch metal particle tape in two sizes: L (large), and a S (small) cassette with 60-Gbyte native capacity (155 Gbytes with 2.59:1 compression). Tape reliability is 20,000 passes and drive MTBF is 200,000 hours (roughly 22.8 sustained years).

DTF-2 supports a native data rate of 24 Mbytes/second, the fastest sustained native rate of any industry streaming tape product at that time. Designed for applications in broadcast and post production, the DTF-2 drives are also read tape compatible with the first generation DTF-1. Error correction capability is very low at 1×10^{e17}, achieved by a double Reed-Solomon error correction scheme coupled with a data buffer memory. The physical interface to the GY-8240 series drives are Ultra Wide Differential SCSI or Fibre Channel. Search speeds are up to 1.4 Gbytes/second.

Utilizing a take-off concept from the R-MIC (Remote-Memory-in-Cassette), a flash memory label is attached to the cassette, which can be read from memory instead of from the tape. When there is a large amount of information in the directory, then the information must be read from the tape.

The roadmap for the DTF format was to have included a DTF-3 drive with 400-Gbyte native capacity, a sustained data transfer rate of 48 Mbytes/second (expected in 2002) to be followed by the DTF-4 with 800-Gbyte native capacity with 96 Mbytes/second transfer (due in 2005).

The DTF format was supported on Sony's PetaSite series digital media storage automated tape library system. The PetaSite library now promotes SAIT-1 as a 500-Gbyte WORM cartridge.

Advanced Tape Materials

Employing nanotechnologies, researchers at IBM's Zurich Research Laboratories (Switzerland) developed a new magnetic media material for linear tape, alongside a novel tape-reading technology. The combination has a storage density of 29.5 billion bits per square inch (b/inch), translating to a tape cartridge capable of holding around 35 Tbytes of data. This revolution is more than 40 times the capacity of LTO Generation 4 Ultrium data cartridges and several times more than a hard disk of comparable size.

The new magnetic medium is called barium ferrite (BaFe) and is part of the advanced Nanocubic technology from Fujifilm's researchers. In cooperation with researchers from Fujifilm's labs in Japan, IBM and Fujifilm have been able to orient the barium ferrite magnetic particles such that their magnetic fields protrude perpendicularly from the tape, instead of lengthways. This advancement yields many times more bits that can be packed into a given area; plus the research has found that the magnetic fields are now significantly stronger. These new particles allow for thinner tape to be used, resulting is as much as 12% more tape, which can be stored on a single spooled cartridge.

In applications needing higher density packing with increased areal density, the data stored on the tape become more difficult to read reliably. Coupled with the close proximity and potential for electromagnetic interference, the heads themselves will retain a certain amount of residual magnetism from readings. To overcome this problem, the IBM group developed new signal processing algorithms that simultaneously process data and then predict the effect that any electromagnetic noise will have on subsequent readings.

This next generation version of Nanocubic technology uses the new ultra-fine, perpendicularly-oriented barium-ferrite magnetic medium without using expensive metal sputtering or evaporation coating methods. The combination of perpendicular oriented particles and the controlled disposition at nanometer levels has also improved the tape's running stability.

IBM's new servo format pattern, new signal processing technology, and low-friction head technology have improved the running stability of the tape overall.

Digital Linear Tape (DLT)

One of the two remaining principle and more prominent formats of magnetic data tape storage technologies was originally introduced by Digital Equipment Corporation (DEC) in the early 1980s. The technology was acquired in 1994 by Quantum Corporation who licenses the technology and retains the DLT trademark.

DLT uses linear serpentine recording with multiple tracks on half-inch (12.7 mm) wide tape. Each cartridge contain a single reel of media. The tape is pulled out of the cartridge by means of a leader tape attached to the take-up reel inside the tape drive. This leader tape is buckled to the cartridge leader during the load process.

Tape speed and tension are controlled electronically via the reel motors, eliminating the need for a capstan, which places undue wear on the tape surface. DLT tape is guided by 4–6 rollers that only contact the backing side of the tape, which is made through the process of metal particle (MP/AMP) adhesion.

Error Detection

One quarter of the data on a DLT tape cartridge is dedicated to error detection and correction. An application-specific integrated circuit (ASIC) chip containing a custom Reed-Solomon error-correction code (ECC) maintains unfailing data security. For every 64 kilobytes of user data, there are 16 kilobytes of ECC added. For every 4 kilobytes of user data, a 64-bit cyclic redundancy code (CRC) and a 16-bit error detection code (EDC) are also added. In addition, each user record is tagged with an overlapping 16-bit CRC. All DLT tape drives perform a read-after-each-write command, and will automatically re-record data on a parallel channel.

This Parallel Channel Architecture (PCA) maximizes rewrite efficiency. Even with one or more channels inoperative due to bad blocks, four-channel DLT 7000 and DLT 8000 drives can continue to write data on a parallel channel. The dual channel DLT 4000 drive also uses the PCA block structure and can continue operation even with one channel blocked.

With these multiple levels of error detection and correction, DLT tape drives offer an exceptional level of data integrity.

Adaptive Cache Buffering

DLT tape drives employ a feature called adaptive cache buffering, designed to reduce stops and starts, thus reducing drive wear and tear. Adaptive techniques enable the DLT tape system to adjust block sizes to match the host data rate. With compression turned on, data are compacted as it enters the cache buffer at a rate that closely matches the rate at which they are being written to tape. While the total throughput rate is dependent on the speed at which the host supplies data to the drive, adaptive cache buffering aids in keeping the drive in its native streaming modes, reducing delays due to repositioning.

Through this process, and additional algorithms, parity is maintained between the host system and the drive over the interface.

Compression Algorithms

Data compression is handled by the tape drive itself, with several different compression technologies employed. Quantum DLT systems will use the Lempel Ziv (LZ) compression algorithm commonly used by many systems that employ data compression because it is the most effective across the most types of data. Compression ratios of 4:1 can be achieved routinely, and in specific instances ratios as high as 25:1 are possible, but to maintain industry consistency, most DLT tape systems will conservatively use the industry standard 2:1 compression factor when specifying data density with compression turned on.

Duty Cycle

Most drive makers base their performance and reliability figures on drive utilization (duty cycle) as low as 10%. That means that in a 7×24 operation, the reliability figures are based upon as little as 2.5 hours of use during any 24-hour period. When calculating true reliability, the figure of merit should be based on 100% usage, also called the "duty cycle." MTBF should be expressed in terms of duty cycle, and for real metrics should be at the full 100% usage rate.

In real operational modes, few drives will ever be subjected to full time non-stop operation.

DLT1 Drive

Early in 2001, Quantum introduced the first DLT1 drive, delivering 40 Gbytes per cartridge native capacity (80-Gbyte compressed), with a native transfer rate of 3 Mbytes/second (6 Mbytes/second compressed). The drives are available for internal installation and as a free-standing, tabletop unit. DLT1 was designed primarily for stand-alone applications. This drive uses the same DLT IV tape cartridge that is standard for the DLT 4000 drive. This lets users of small and medium-size storage devices and workstations enjoy a migration path to future storage strategies using next-generation DLT tape formats.

DLT tape drives read and write data in a linear pattern on the tape. Each data track runs the entire length of the tape (about 1800 feet for DLT IV and Super DLT I media). During data recording, the first set of tracks is recorded on the whole length of the tape. Once at the end of the tape, the heads are repositioned to record a new set of tracks with the tape running in the other direction. This process continues until all the tracks are written to the whole length of the tape in alternating directions of tape travel. DLT drives record either 128 tracks (for DLT 4000 drives), 168 tracks (for DLT1 drives), 208 tracks (for DLT 7000 and DLT 8000 drives), or 448 tracks (for Super DLT drives) on half-inch tape.

Depending upon which generation of tape drive, the recording may be vertically aligned or diagonally angled depending upon the track record direction. For compatibility issues, when reading DLT tape cartridges recorded on earlier DLT transports, the DLT 7000 and DLT 8000 Read-write heads will automatically shift to a vertical orientation.

Super DLT

In response to the developments in LTO (Linear Tape Open) promoted by IBM, Hewlett-Packard, and Seagate, the Quantum organization remains focused on the extension of DLT. The statement that "SDLT will read well over 80% of the install base of DLT" provides a suitable migration path in the minds of many.

With the key to efficiency being the ability to increase capacity and transfer rates, the previous methods were to increase tape record density and add more tracks on the tape. SDLT accomplishes this by committing 100% of the recording area of the tape for data storage. SDLT is based upon Laser Guided Magnetic Recording (LGMR) whereby an optical encoded guide track is printed into the non-recording side of the tape during manufacture.

The advanced technologies in SDLT include LGMR coupled to a Pivoting Optical Servo that follows a guide track. This eliminates the need to pre-format the tape or to provide a pre-alignment sequence prior to reading usable data. Magneto-Resistive Cluster (MRC) heads made using a thin-film process work in conjunction with a high-efficiency PRML (positive response-maximum likelihood) channel to enable the higher data-transfer rates and capacity. PRML encoding, instituted for disk drive recording, is now in tape technology as a means to control error correction.

Advanced Metal Powder (AMP) media for extremely high densities and a robust tape-leader-buckling mechanism, called Positive Engagement, add to the high-duty cycle capabilities of the tape. AMP provides for up to 97% efficiency for greater tape recording density.

Roadmaps for SDLT

SuperDLT, when in its first generation (January 2001), was expected to have a complete roadmap of compatible products in drives and tape cartridges. The technology offers up to 160 Gbytes of storage capacity and a 16 Mbytes/second sustained data transfer rate (native mode). Second generation, Super DLT II 600-Gbyte data cartridges offer high capacity and low cost per gigabyte for customers with prior investments in DLT backup technology. The transfer rate for Super DLT II is 72 Mbytes/second (32 Mbytes/second compressed), with support for up to 320-Gbyte storage capacity per tape.

Super DLTtape II cartridges support DLTSage for improved media and drive diagnostics. This generation uses a new Super PET (S-PET) base film enabling an overall thickness reduction of 10%; resulting in a longer tape with more capacity than the previous Super DLTtape I cartridge.

A technology unique to SDLT is having the optical servo guide information coded on the rear of the media. This increases the number of recording tracks on the data-bearing media surface and allows for higher capacity tape cartridges.

Linear Tape Open (LTO)

Linear Tape Open (LTO) technology was developed jointly by Certance (now Quantum), HP, and IBM. These three companies set out to develop an "open format" technology, each providing expert knowledge of customer needs and complementary technology for the delivery of a best-of-breed technology that promotes a strong foundation for data interchange. As an open tape format specification, it is readily available to all potential manufacturers and offers licenses for the intellectual property at a reasonable investment.

LTO technology assembles the combined advantages of those linear multi-channel bi-directional tape formats in common usage today with the added enhancements of a timing-based servo, hardware data compression, optimized track layouts, and high-efficiency error correction code, which in turn maximizes capacity and performance.

The name "Ultrium" is the market name applied to the LTO tape drives and systems and is the conduit for the licensing of the tape mechanisms and the tape cartridge interchange specifications.

Genealogy

Unveiled in April 1998 by HP, IBM, and Seagate, the LTO technology raised the eyebrows of the competing tape manufacturing companies. LTO is about the implementation of linear serpentine technology for higher density recordings, concurrent data channels (eight initially with sixteen to follow), enhanced servo and head designs, and timing-based servo monitors that control the position of the tape head to avoid overwrites due to tape inaccuracies.

Many of the best features in DLT are retained in LTO. The plan was to have two flavors offered. The first, and the winner overall, is a high capacity/high reliability design, which would be called Ultrium. Ultrium would be modeled after the DLT with the tape drawn out of a single reel cartridge and attaching to a drive reel. The other, designed for high-speed access, would be called Accelis and this was to be modeled after the familiar two-reel 8 mm cassette. The Accelis concept was developed in 1997; however, because of technological developments that have occurred since it was first developed, coupled with the fact that customers have demonstrated strong satisfaction with the attributes of the LTO Ultrium tape format, there has been no significant demand for Accelis.

Accelis has essentially vanished from the radar screen, and a Google search will find it the name of a weight loss pill for dietary purposes.

LTO drives use at least four heads up to a maximum of eight. Each write head has a matching read head to allow for an immediate read-after-write. Two servo tracks per data band are recorded onto the tape media during manufacture. Precise positioning and tight control of the vertical head distances will aid in maintaining alignment and cross compatibility. Each of the 384 tracks, arranged as a set of four bands with 96 tracks each, can be recorded on the Ultrium media (the Accelis would have had two sets of bands with 128 tracks per band for a total of 256 tracks.)

Ultrium—First Generation

In September 2000, IBM brought out the first generation of Ultrium. Available in native storage capacities of 100 Gbytes, with transfer rates in the 10 to 20 Mbytes/second range, the drives use RLL 1,7 data recording. Future generations would employ PRML (positive response-maximum likelihood) recording and increase storage to 200 Gbytes with 20 to 40 Mbytes/second data transfer rates expected.

LTO Generation 1

First licensed in 1998, with product appearing in 2000, Ultrium format Generation 1 provides cartridge capacities of up to 100-Gbyte native (up to 200 Gbytes with 2:1 compression), and data transfer rates of up to 20 Mbytes/second native (40 Mbytes/second with 2:1 compression).

LTO Generation 2

Ultrium format Generation 2 provides data transfer rates of up to 80 Mbytes/second (2:1 compression) and a cartridge capacity of up to 200-Gbyte native (400 Gbytes with 2:1 compression). Licenses for Generation 2 became available in April 2002 with products appearing in late 2002.

LTO Generation 3

Featuring capacities of up to 400-Gbyte native (800 Gbytes with 2:1 compression) per cartridge, Ultrium format Generation 3 provides data transfer rates of up to 80-Mbytes/second native or

160 Mbytes/second with 2:1 compression for the third generation of the 8-channel version. Generation 3 licenses became available on July 26, 2004 with products appearing in late 2004.

LTO Generation 4

Delivering up to 800-Gbyte native (1.6 Tbytes with 2:1 compression) per cartridge, Ultrium format Generation 4 provides data transfer rates of up to 120 Mbytes/second native or 240 Mbytes/second with 2:1 compression. This LTO Ultrium format generation specification was made available to licensees in late December 2006.

LTO Generation 5

The current (2010) version features a capacity of 1.5 TB native (3 TB assuming a 2:1 compression). This, the latest generation in the LTO family, provides data transfer speed of up to 140 Mbytes/second (or 280 Mbytes/second assuming a 2:1 compression) and adds a new partitioning feature plus the new Linear Tape File System (LTFS) specification to provide enhanced file control and data management. The LTO Ultrium format Generation 5 specifications were made available to licensees in January 2010.

LTFS

LTO-5 also introduced a format for storing data that is extensible and suits the needs of the media and entertainment industry by incorporating the Material eXchange Format (MXF) standards. Known as Linear Tape File System (LTFS), it has a dual function in that it not only is a format of data recording, but also an implementation of software that provides a file system for magnetic tape data storage.

The LTO-5 specification allows for two media partitions with independent accessibility that provides for faster data access and improved data management. LTFS, developed specifically for the LTO-5 generation of digital tape (and going forward), employs one partition that holds the content and a second partition that can hold the content's index. In effect, the tape can now be classed as self-describing.

The feature sets of LTO-5 and LTFS allow for

- The capability to manage files directly on tape
- Easier sharing of the tape cartridge with others (no longer format specific or necessarily proprietary)

- File system access at the operating system level
- The enabling of viewing and accessibility to the files on the tape in "disk-like" (although linear) fashion or as would be available from other types of removable media utilizing a directory tree structure

The LTFS format is designed to address the growing needs of the media and entertainment, medical, and digital surveillance industries, plus any of those segments that deal with rich media.

IBM's Implementation

IBM has also created its own implementation, called "Long Term File System" (LTFS), which is their concept of the first file system to work in conjunction with LTO Generation 5 tape. According to IBM, this "...storage software helps reduce complexity in data management and access time through the enablement of a self describing tape..." with its own built-in file index. As a promoter and developer of the LTFS (as in Linear Tape File System), it is unclear why IBM has seemed to create its own "version," if you will, of the work developed openly by the LTO technology groups. Hopefully this differentiation is only marketing directed and not something that keeps the formats of data on those tapes continually independent.

LTO Program Roadmap

The LTO program endeavors to expand the capacity of the format and increase the data transfer speed with a steady agenda of upgrades. The LTO websites calls for the following guidelines for future generations:

LTO Generation 6 (Future)

Capacity: 8 TB (assuming 2.5:1 compression).

Data transfer speed: up to 525 Mbytes/second (assuming 2.5:1 compression).

LTO Generation 7 (Future)

Capacity: 16 TB (assuming 2.5:1 compression).

Data transfer speed: up to 788 Mbyte/second (assuming 2.5:1 compression).

LTO Generation 8 (Future)

Capacity: 32 TB (assuming 2.5:1 compression).

Data transfer speed: up to 1180 Mbytes/second (assuming 2.5:1 compression).

Security WORM

Regulatory compliance with federal and/or international financial records keeping, including the Sarbanes-Oxley Act of 2002, the Health Insurance Portability and Accountability Act of 1996 (HIPAA), and the Requirements for Brokers and Dealers (SEC Rule 17-a-4(f))—directed a requirement for a cost-effective storage medium that can definitely without question preserve corporate data in a non-rewriteable, non-erasable, and unalterable format.

The newest technologies implement LTO WORM (Write Once, Read Many), which is really an old, silicon-based firmware solution, to provide the functionality that will help address the ever-growing business compliance and regulatory requirements.

WORM security measures are found in LTO Generation 3, 4, and 5 formats, and are on the roadmap for all future planned Generation 6, 7, and 8 products. The LTO Program WORM implementation is designed to provide users with a very cost-effective means of storing data to a non-rewriteable format that meets the compliance regulations requirements.

These robust algorithms use Cartridge Memory (CM) features in conjunction with low level encoding that is mastered on the tape media at the time of manufacture and designed to prevent tampering. The LTO Ultrium format Generation 3, 4, and 5 specifications include the ability for WORM-enabled and non-WORM-enabled drives to coexist. Appending data to the end of a WORM cartridge that has been previously written to is supported, allowing users to take full advantage of the high-capacity tape media.

Why Use Tape?

With the random-access nature value of spinning disk storage, the ability to leverage local and remote replication, or mirroring for near-instant recovery, the question always arises, "Why backup to tape?" With other processes, such as data deduplication, the space occupied by data on disk can be reduced, making disk storage an even more appealing media format.

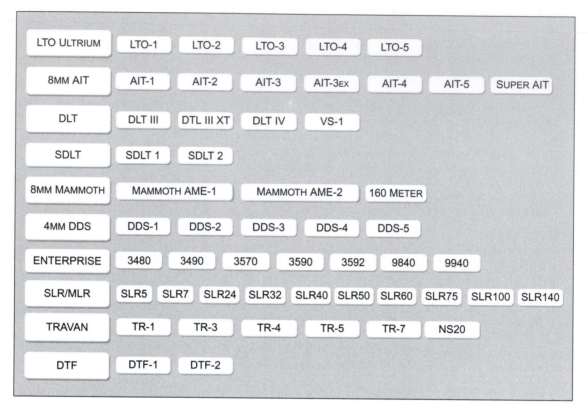

Figure 12.6 Tape media formats for digital linear data archives.

The reason promoted by the providers of tape and drives for digital tape products remains relatively simple. As data ages, their value to the business becomes intangible, and will slowly decline forcing the goal of proving the lowest possible cost for that storage. Many data protection environments are now tiered, leveraging replication technologies (e.g., snapshot, mirror, remote copies, etc.) for critical data with tight recovery time objectives (RTOs) and recovery point objectives (RPO). For cost reasons, the first tier storage practice typically applies only to specific data sets, where copies are kept for only a limited number of days. The second tier consists of disk arrays with lower performance, high-capacity drives that are employed for less critical or aging data sets. Typically, this is where deduplication is implemented with those data copies being kept for months.

With businesses now facing numerous regulatory compliance issues that can be difficult to understand, legal representatives are suggesting that companies archive data for periods as long as 5, 7, or even 10 years. The volume of archived data could easily exceed the amount of the current data used daily as "production data" by a factor of between 10 and 20 times or more.

Retaining all this archive data on disk can be costly, whether it is managed in house or is outsourced to a data warehousing company, which is why tape remains a formidable media for the immediate to long term.

Data Archiving and Tape Storage

Tape is still an excellent choice for data archiving and long-term storage, especially when looking at the operational costs of maintaining an all-disk storage environment. A tape that is not mounted in a drive consumes no energy. Although there are disk drives that can be powered down when not in use, from a cost perspective, if the data will most likely not be accessed unless there is a legal request for it, why leave them on disk? Tape storage is certainly a lower cost per unit physical location than disk-based data center space with its ongoing operational cooling, floor space, maintenance, redundancy requirements, and power costs.

Over the years, many businesses (including most SMBs) have selected a tape storage infrastructure which includes a wide variety of tape formats and recording technologies (see Fig. 12.6) to support the majority of their backup and archive needs. Tape technology still offers customary performance for most of the business retention applications due to smaller amounts of data and fewer critical servers that might need to be recovered within a given time frame.

Unless the business activity requires an unpredictable amount of continual access to all the material data it has in its control, tape (coupled with short-term disk) storage is the more cost effective way to manage your data storage requirements.

The reasons for tape and/or disk storage become obvious when you look first at past trends, then at current growth. According to data storage industry reports, unstructured data continue to grow at an explosive pace. Companies are having a difficult time trying to manage and contain all that information. In a 2008 report named the "Enterprise Disk Storage Consumption Model," IDC predicts a compounded annual growth rate (CAGR) of 21.8% of normal transactional data and as much as a 61.7% compounded annual growth for structured data.

Addressing the storage, preservation, and cataloguing of thousands of petabytes of data globally will remain an unfathomable task for generations to come. With this unfortunate spin on a multi-dimensional perspective, it is essential that content owners and creators find the means to manage and handle their most precious assets through an archive and/or backup system that is extensible to the future.

Preparing for the Archive

Planning a storage strategy can start with determining your organization's data retention period. How long will the organization want to retain the digital content? Will this period increase as time goes on? With retention periods approaching decades, this can have huge implications in long-term storage management and establishing storage capacity requirements. A thorough analysis to avoid painting oneself into a corner that could become irreversible is essential.

Consider technology obsolescence. As the actual age of the media increases, and the period for retention is extended, there is a likelihood that both the transports and the physical media formats will become obsolete, not to mention the changes in the technology (for example, holography). Migrating your data from one archive platform to another with reasonable certainty that it will be readable in the future is the only alternative. Long-term migration strategies should not be simply estimated or done manually; use the intelligence built into the archive solution's hardware and software systems to manage this process automatically and incrementally.

Organizations should be prepared for an ongoing update of their tape, disk, and archive management platforms both financially and administratively. By not addressing an update policy at the onset of establishing a media management strategy, the organization will inevitably find itself in the same situation it had previously with videotape, one where either the transports become unusable or the media is unrecoverable.

Another thought to consider, one that is being addressed by broadcast networks and motion picture content owners, is the sheer volume of material still held in libraries, vaults, and underground storage environments. Will there ever be sufficient time to convert those assets into a self-managing, digital archive platform? If there were the time available, what would that look like in terms of cost and future value? The question always looms, "Is this really worth all the effort and investment?"

In concluding this chapter on archive and backup, which turns out to be as much about process as about technology, it goes without saying that at some point a human must ultimately determine the value of the content and weigh it against the cost of keeping it. Some believe the "keep it all forever perspective" is an unrealistic concept given the growth of data is exceeding exponential rates and that it is unlikely to change (i.e., diminish) as time marches on. Archive practices and preservation still command an overwhelming percentage of the total storage volume as depicted in

Fig. 12.7. With a properly engineered archive and associated backup strategy, coupled with tiered storage and automated asset management, the enterprise can control this huge volume while achieving a balance between performance and costs overall.

Future Standards

The Society of Motion Picture and Television Engineers (SMPTE), through its standards community, have been in the throes of developing a protocol for the interchange of archive-intended material on an open and standardized platform. The committee, which is part of SMPTE TC-10E30, is a Working Group (WG) comprised of industry professionals (users and engineers) that is tasked with developing the presentation of a set of documents as a potential standard, recommended practice (RP), or engineering guideline (EG)—or combinations thereof—under the title of "Archive eXchange Format (AXF)."

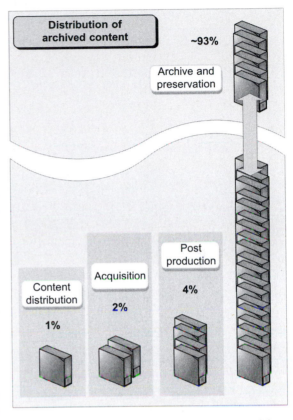

Figure 12.7 Perspective of the volume of archived content and how it is distributed across the media industry.

The proposed structural elements of the AXF protocol will be expressed as eXtensible Markup Language (XML) documents. Among the facilities that are proposed to be provided is the ability to span objects across multiple media. Further intent includes enabling and accommodating objects that are greater than the physical media on which they are stored; the inclusion of indexes of the content of the objects (internal and external), and providing for location of individual items within the objects that are stored on the medium (which does not necessarily have to be only linear digital tape). Additional needs to be considered would include the easy movement or copying of objects between differing media types, and to facilitate recovery of content from damaged media or spanned sets.

The work of AXF has resumed after a hiatus of several months and the WG hopes to present its proposals in 2011. The goal is not to supplant the efforts of LTFS (the LTO-5 implementation of a file system for linear tape), but to have AXF become an umbrella-like standard for the migration of all forms of archive intended media between platforms, media types and the like. This would include linear and non-linear media, with or without a file system; and potentially provide for extensions into the cloud.

13

METADATA AND MEDIA ASSET MANAGEMENT

Since the advent of videotape, broadcasters and enterprise class media organizations using audio, video, and rich-media have employed Media Asset Management (MAM) systems to aid in the storage, cataloging, and retrieval of static and moving media assets. Those MAM systems have typically remained a comparatively separate function from the production, playout, and distribution sides of operations. More often than not, only individual tasks such as simple cataloging have been integrated into the many OEM systems that include some degree of MAM. Serving devices, such as videoservers or library management systems (LMS), like Sony Broadcast's LMS product line, needed these features to manage the videotape or digital files contained on them. Given the uniqueness of these early requirements for MAM, the OEMs would typically write their own software and integrate it directly into their products. This practice changed once videoserver systems emerged.

Broadcast television automation systems have also carried MAM components in their program and commercial playout platform, up through and including the current evolution of videoservers. Newer "digital broadcasting" platforms that run on commercial IT-type hardware (e.g., the Omnibus iTX platform) would also manage these assets with their own flavor of MAM.

Until recent times, with the proliferation of file-based workflows and the growing scale of storage systems, what has been missing in a MAM infrastructure is the ability to fully integrate media asset management across the entire production workflow from planning, to scheduling and acquisition, through broadcast release, packaging, distribution, and archiving. New dimensions in information technology now make it possible to gain a much richer degree of integration, one that marries media and management into a harmonious operating environment across the enterprise.

This chapter will look at the fundamentals of media asset management as it applies to moving media platforms and digital storage systems utilized in the production, play to air, library, and archive processes.

KEY CHAPTER POINTS

- Identifying the terminologies associated with the management of various forms of moving media
- Defining how systems control or process information about assets that are media centric (i.e., contain audio or video), and describing their differences
- Metadata—what they are, the types of metadata, and why metadata are an essential element in media asset management systems
- How collaboration, workflow, and interoperability are affected by media asset management systems and their implementation
- Overview of Web-based and other media-based asset management services, for example, Dublin Core, PBCore, SOAP, REST
- Intelligent integrated media asset management, gluing the entire ecosystem together
- Assessing how storage systems for media asset management are deploying, including archive

Media Management Systems

Exploring the topics related to managing media centric assets, one finds there have been a number of similar terms applied to essentially a common category of topics. The terminologies have emerged from various segments of cataloging, searching, and retrieval-related activities, such as libraries, print-based publishing, and the Web:

Media Asset Management (MAM)
Content Management Systems (CM or CMS)
Production Asset Management (PAM)
Digital Asset Management (DAM)
Asset Management Systems (ASM)

For clarity, this chapter will focus mainly on media file types, which generally include audio, video, and images; in other words "media" asset management (MAM) in a digital environment. We will touch upon the parallels found in Web systems, but that topic is a much broader one that will not be addressed in depth.

Media Assets and Content

In its most fundamental form, a media asset is a form of content. Content can be information that is found in unstructured, weakly structured, and highly structured forms. These forms of information, as content or media assets, are made available to users through the physical components of electronic storage, networking, and serving systems. These assets may be used by both humans and machine-based entities.

Media assets consist of multimedia-based unstructured information objects such as pictures, diagrams, presentations, and other rich-media such as those comprised of audio and video essence. Before information becomes an asset, it may be referred to as a media information object, a component that only presents information, and that becomes more valuable when structured metadata are linked with that object (see Fig. 13.1). Once metadata are included, the media asset becomes more available, is searchable, able to be repackaged, and can be associated with databases that allow integration of the metadata records for secondary, extensible purposes.

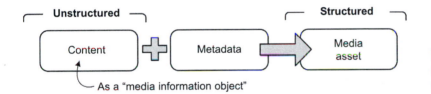

Figure 13.1 Content plus metadata creates a media asset.

Content Management System

The content management system (CMS) is a collection of procedures that will be used to manage workflow in a collaborative environment. While CMS is not necessarily specific to any particular environment, in recent times, CMS has gained more use in Web-based applications than in enterprise database-like systems. This set of procedures could be manual or computer-based, and will allow accessibility for the purpose of contributing to and sharing stored data across the enterprise or across the Internet.

In a CMS, data may be defined as documents, rich-media, movies, images, graphics, phone numbers, scientific data, etc. CMSs are frequently employed in the processes of storing, controlling, revising, enriching, and publishing that data or documentation. For closed environments (such as a corporate intranet), the CMS controls access to stored data based on user roles and permissions, aimed at defining what information each user may be permitted to view, copy, download, or edit. The CMS further supports the processes of storing and retrieving data so as to reduce repetitive or duplicative inputs.

Web-Based CMS

With the prolific use of the Web for information search and retrieval, the terms content management and content management system have in recent years become much more focused on Web-based information management. When viewed from this perspective, a content management system is designed so that it becomes the control element for Web-based content. The CMS in turn is the support conduit for the Web master or website's content contributors.

Digital Asset Management

The management tasks, decisions, and processes surrounding the ingest, annotation, cataloguing, storing, retrieval, and distribution of digital assets is referred to as digital asset management (DAM). Media asset management (MAM), which works primarily with digital images (photographs), animations, audio (music or speech), and video, is a subcategory of DAM (see Fig. 13.2). The term DAM also references those protocols used for the

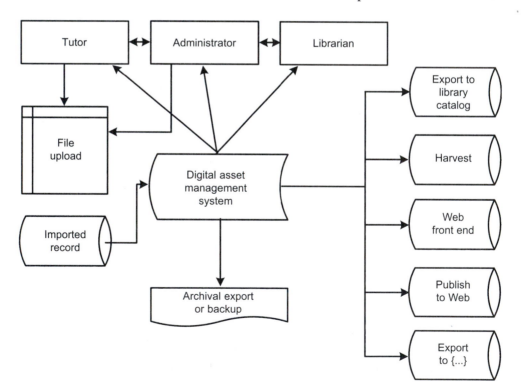

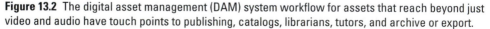

Figure 13.2 The digital asset management (DAM) system workflow for assets that reach beyond just video and audio have touch points to publishing, catalogs, librarians, tutors, and archive or export.

downloading, renaming, backing up, rating, grouping, archiving, optimizing, maintaining, thinning, and exporting of digital files.

The makeup of a DAM system will consist of the computer hardware and software applications that support the process of managing the digital assets. With certain exceptions, such as specific video or audio codecs, and the abilities to process at other than real time, the physical components of a MAM can be quite similar to those used in a DAM system.

Asset Management System

This term is sometimes used in conjunction with MAM or DAM, but should generally be thought of as pertaining to physical assets (such as property or goods). Asset management is

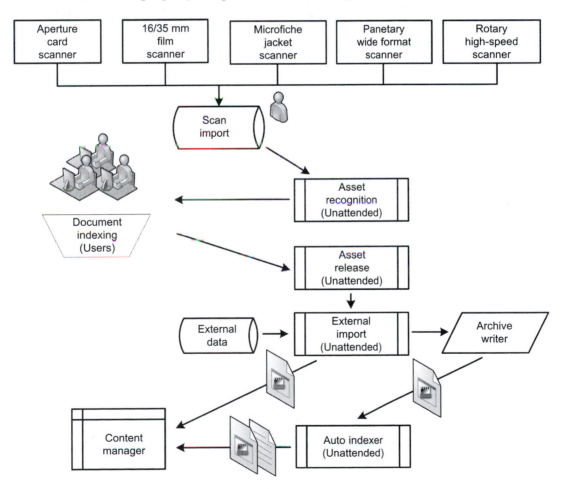

Figure 13.3 A sample workflow for static media and document (asset) recognition including processing, with scanning, indexing, and content management.

the process of maintaining, upgrading, and operating physical assets. An asset management system is a framework that provides a measure of organization performance, which is tied to short-term and long-term planning. Figure 13.3 shows a sample workflow for an asset management system that might be used in document management for static images and information in a library or non-moving media content application.

This chapter does not delve into the topic of asset management from the perspective of digital or media assets.

Media Asset Management

As the first word implies, this is the management of assets specific to media. The media may be digital or analog; however, for the purposes of refining what is a huge territory, this book will relate media asset management to only digital assets that would more traditionally be stored on a digital file server tailored for video, audio, and images.

Historically, MAM systems have focused more on providing storage management and were not involved with workflow or operations. The MAM would be that instrument that connected the files on a storage platform with a database-driven application that looked up certain tags, i.e., information provided by the user at the time the media was ingested to the storage system. The simple MAM allowed for the rudimentary searching of the media based upon that user generated information. The extremely simplistic approach was at best the electronic equivalent of a label placed on a videotape cassette or the 3×5 card stuck in the container that housed that tape.

Two of the more traditional approaches to MAM implementation employed early on were in tape-based systems and digital videoserver systems.

Tape-Based MAM

MAM solutions for videotape typically involved media assets stored in a robotic library with supporting information about those tapes kept in a data library housed on a dedicated computer system. Software cataloged the library based upon the tags (records) that were entered into that application by the user, usually at the time of ingesting the material into the tape library.

Solutions like these have been around since the mid-1980s. At the most basic level, at least for broadcast applications, the library catalog data would contain a house number that was paired against information contained in the broadcast traffic system that described that asset. This house number was the database key link between what was in the videotape library's database and what was contained in the traffic system's database. Traffic systems held the contractual information about the content, but had no network or other connection to the robotic library. It essentially knew nothing about what actually resided on the physical tape media.

In the early days prior to automated or robotic tape-based play-to-air systems (see the workflow example in Figure 13.4), the tapes (or films) on the broadcast library shelf would be manually collected according to instructions from the traffic department, moved to the dubbing/transfer area where an operator would load the tape (or film) and cue it, then either electronically dub each tape to a master commercial reel or ready videotape transports (or film projectors) for playback by an operator or other triggering mechanism associated with the station's master control play-to-air operations.

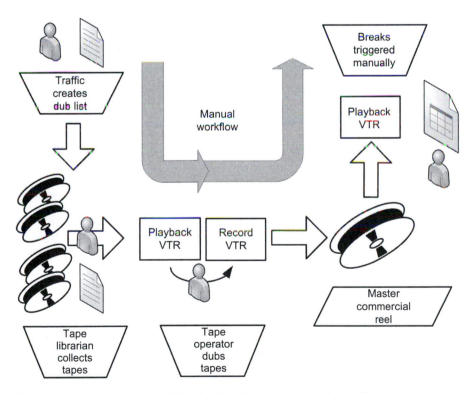

Figure 13.4 Legacy, manual workflow in a broadcast or content play-to-air environment.

Once automated tape-based play-to-air libraries were put into use by broadcasters, an operator would load the tapes into the play-to-air robotic library and enable applications that were built into this robotic system's control system (referred to as a library management system or LMS), which would be triggered by the station's external automation interfaces at the appropriate point in time based upon the station's program schedule. This was essentially the entire sum and substance of the "media asset management" process prior to the era of videoservers.

Drawbacks to Tape-Based Systems

The principle drawbacks to this type of MAM was that there was no integration or interaction between the asset management, in general, and operations. Tape was a one-function/one-action-at-a-time instrument of physical media. Tape offered no collaboration, that is, when a tape is in use, no one else could have access to that material except as linear video on a routable video transport system (a coaxial cable with BNCs on the ends). Work would be limited to just one individual, working on one specific task and only with that specific tape.

To use that asset for any other task (play-to-air, editing, or copying), a person would have to physically retrieve the tape from a shelf or library, take that tape to a location with equipment (a VTR) capable of playing that tape, load the tape, and then play the tape. No integration between the media asset management system and the playout equipment was possible.

Because assets were stored on tape and the metadata about those assets would be stored separately in a computer, users could perform searches on that metadata, but the physical retrieval process would be manual. It would take considerable time to locate and transport the assets, resulting in a risk that those assets could be lost or unavailable because they were already being used by others. The simplest functions of browsing could be quite time consuming, requiring handling the physical asset, usually in its original form.

Physical media is subject to use degradation each time the tape is played or handled. When the asset was stored on analog videotape, duplications would always be of poorer quality than the original. Even with digital videotape, the cloning process would have to be manually managed, had to occur in real time, and should any updates to the metadata be necessary, the accuracy of that update could be compromised by the user improperly recording that updated information or forgetting to make the update all together. Seldom would these systems account for usage counts or changes in media quality.

All of these disadvantages would directly translate into poor productivity. Mistakes would occur due to inefficient collaboration, introducing significant delays into the production and broadcast processes.

MAM for Videoserver Implementations

The introduction of videoservers as a buffer between tape-based libraries and play-to-air operations helped alleviate a portion of the manual processes of asset management—but not many of them. With a videoserver implementation, each videotape would be physically transferred from the tape media to the digital storage platform, where certain data about that asset would be entered and communicated to a basic media asset management program resident on the videoserver. If the transfer was part of the broadcast station's play-to-air automation, that information was collected in that platform as well as the automation program. Due to the proprietary nature of each of these variant platforms, the information on one system was seldom replicated in its entirety on another. Certain systems needed certain information while other systems might need that same information or would require a different set of data.

Videoservers with their associated storage platforms would maintain their own database populated with information that the user would enter during the ingest process. Such information, or metadata, would basically instruct the videoserver on where to begin the playout through metadata called the start of message (SOM), and when to stop the playout of that media, which in turn would trigger the next clip in a sequence of files to be played back during a commercial station break. This later metadata element, called the end of message (EOM), would set the point where playout of active video would cease. The EOM would sometimes trigger the next SOM to roll if the clip was not the last event in the sequence of a station break.

Other videoserver specific information would be more structural in nature, such as the location of the clip on the actual hard disk or storage platform, the codec, the time vcode or frame count of the clip, the number of audio channels, and other technical information. The videoserver's internal database would be application specific to that videoserver. The videoserver would tie the data to a clip identification number, which the videoserver would associate with an external database contained on the station play-to-air automation system, or, if the playout program was self contained on the videoserver, with its resident application.

For the most part, the videoserver's storage, search, and retrieval functions had several disadvantages stemming from the fact that there was no integration between asset management and operations. Any outside interaction would be contained to the station automation system, or depending upon the video-server, possibly a simple clip playback program resident to the videoserver.

Lack of Media Asset Integration

Digital storage systems might include tool sets integrated into nonlinear editors or the traffic or scheduling programs, or as a part of the media ingest or acquisition applications that provided some level of MAM. When these tool sets were integrated with a storage platform, they could offer the advantage of having immediate access to those media assets contained on that specific storage platform. These tools would usually be incompatible with other platforms and would be unable to access them without special customization for the MAM.

Metadata that was entered into one system would only reside within that system, and would not be capable of exchange throughout the MAM. This interoperability issue leaves each of the systems isolated from one another, requiring users to open specific applications on each platform that would be unable to be cross-linked into the principle MAM system.

Collaboration Issues

Carrying on work among multiple users would be complicated under these scenarios. Although tool set integration might make it possible for multiple users to employ the same tools for simultaneous access to the same material, it might not be possible for users of different tool sets to gain a comparable level of access. Since most of these early MAM systems were designed just for storage management, they would neither typically facilitate collaboration nor directly handle any rights access. Without active collaboration, these storage solutions could then have no involvement with workflow.

Metadata

Metadata are used to describe information about specific data. Often referred to as "the bits about the bits," metadata (whose genealogy is believed to begin circa 1982) provide information about a certain item's content. Another name for metadata is "metalanguage."

When a document, image, or other type of data are created, certain parameters should be added with the item as part of the complete file. Such elements, otherwise called attributes, include items such as a file name, the size or type of file, the date it was created, etc. These metadata are called structural—and generally will not change.

Additional forms of metadata may also describe the location or ownership of the file among other information considered "necessary" to be noted about the contents of the data. These are called descriptive metadata. These metadata types are explained in more detail later in the chapter.

For picture-based assets, the image may include metadata describing the pixel dimensions (how large the picture is), the color depth (e.g., 24-bit), the image resolution (e.g., 300 pixels per inch), when the image was created, and other data. A text-based asset would likely include metadata containing information about the number of words or characters in the document, who the author is, when the document was created, and potentially a short summary of the document.

Web pages often include metadata in the form of meta tags. Description and keyword meta tags are commonly used to describe the Web page's content, which enables third-party search engines to use this metadata when adding those Web pages to their search index.

This metalanguage or metadata aid in speeding up searches, allow for the creation of catalogs, can be created automatically by the encoding platform, and can be added to by the user, author, or owner.

Media-Centric Metadata

Metadata, in a digital media environment, are used to manage the file system information. They describe, at their highest level of importance, where the files are kept so that other subsystems may search for them, retrieve them, update or process them, and the like.

There are two general categories of metadata for media systems, called structural metadata and descriptive metadata. The example of Figure 13.5 shows a typical set of metadata screen shots where users or machines enter or display the respective forms of metadata fields.

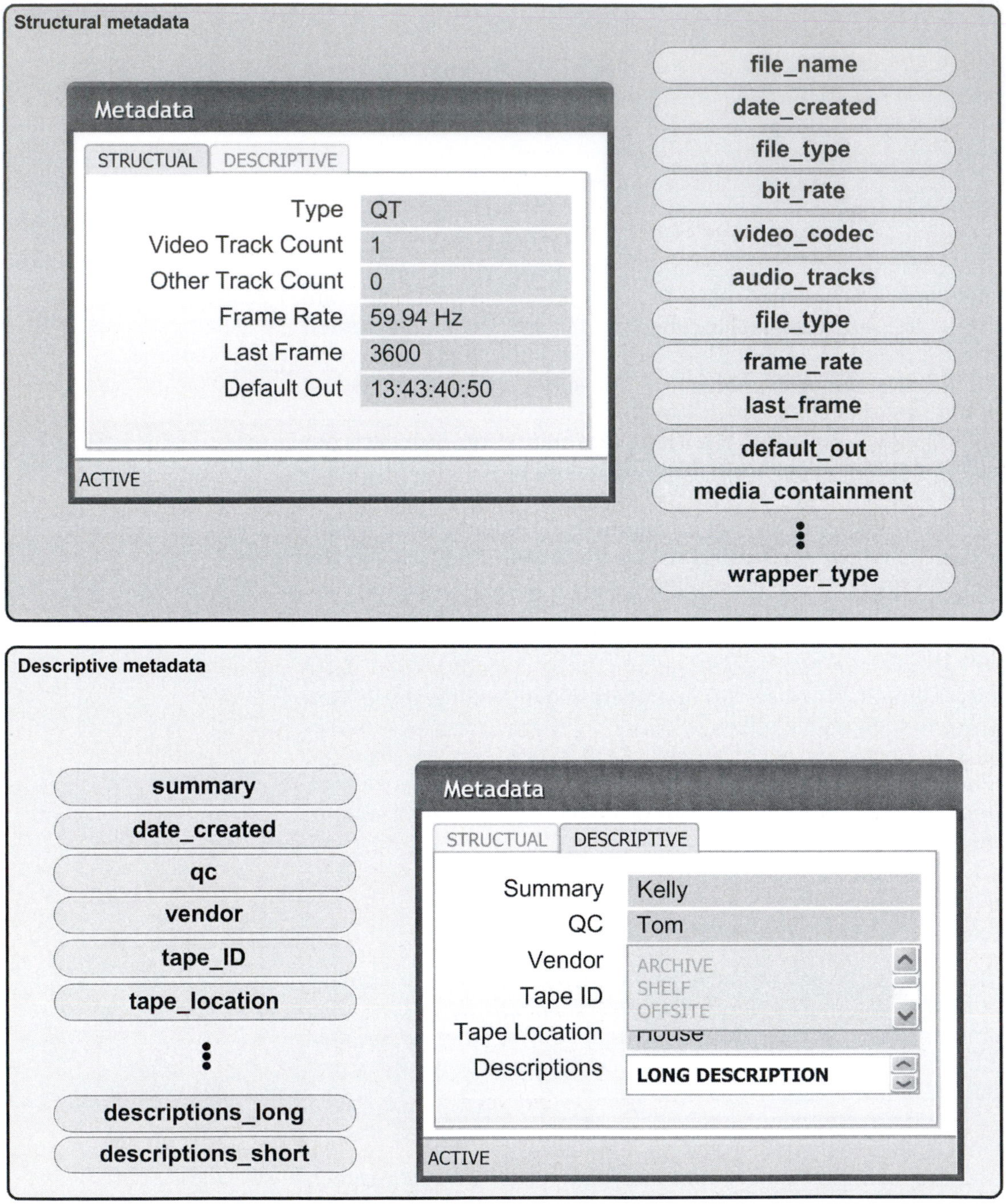

Structural metadata

Metadata

| STRUCTURAL | DESCRIPTIVE |

Type	QT
Video Track Count	1
Other Track Count	0
Frame Rate	59.94 Hz
Last Frame	3600
Default Out	13:43:40:50

ACTIVE

file_name
date_created
file_type
bit_rate
video_codec
audio_tracks
file_type
frame_rate
last_frame
default_out
media_containment
⋮
wrapper_type

Descriptive metadata

summary
date_created
qc
vendor
tape_ID
tape_location
⋮
descriptions_long
descriptions_short

Metadata

| STRUCTURAL | DESCRIPTIVE |

Summary	Kelly
QC	Tom
Vendor	ARCHIVE
Tape ID	SHELF
	OFFSITE
Tape Location	House
Descriptions	**LONG DESCRIPTION**

ACTIVE

Figure 13.5 Sample elements of structural and descriptive metadata, with sample input screen for manually entering data into the database.

Structural Metadata

These are the data used to describe the physical attributes of a file. For video assets (video essence), they will include such information as the format of the video file, their bit rate, the resolution, and the container (i.e., wrapper) type.

The overall media asset management system, and its peripheral components, depends upon the integrity of the structural metadata associated with each independent file. It is for this reason that users should never forcefully change the attributes or tags in this important set of data. The result of modifying structural metadata would be the disastrous equivalent of changing the file extension on a computer file. In a more global sense, structural metadata are as important to the MAM as the file allocation table (FAT) is to the hard disk drive.

The Society of Motion Picture and Television Engineers (SMPTE) has standardized the Structural Metadata of the MXF file format as SMPTE 380M, which contains the technical parameters of the stored material, defines how the material is played out, and provides a plug-in mechanism for a Descriptive Metadata scheme (DMS-1).

Descriptive Metadata

This information may be generated either by the system or by the operator/user. Descriptive metadata examples include shot logging, track naming, availability (allowed dates of usage), and rights or permissions. Depending upon the organization, descriptive metadata may very simple (10–20 fixed terms) or very complex (hundreds of elements or fields).

Descriptive metadata may be very selective so as to limit the number of variances that a user might enter. For example, in a baseball game, some of these entries might be limited to the number of possible play combinations, the number of batters, the players names, and what occurred with each batter at the plate (strike out, walk, fouled out, run, hit, error). These incidents may be logged using a specific application that is constructed from a tool set by the user or administrator. It is important tagging information that supports search and retrieval of media from the MAM system.

SMPTE, as part of their standards and practices documents, provides a Recommended Practice (as of this writing, version RP210-11-2008) that includes the framework for a deep set of terminologies contained in a user addressable online instrument built on a node and leaf structure (see Fig. 13.6). The SMPTE Data

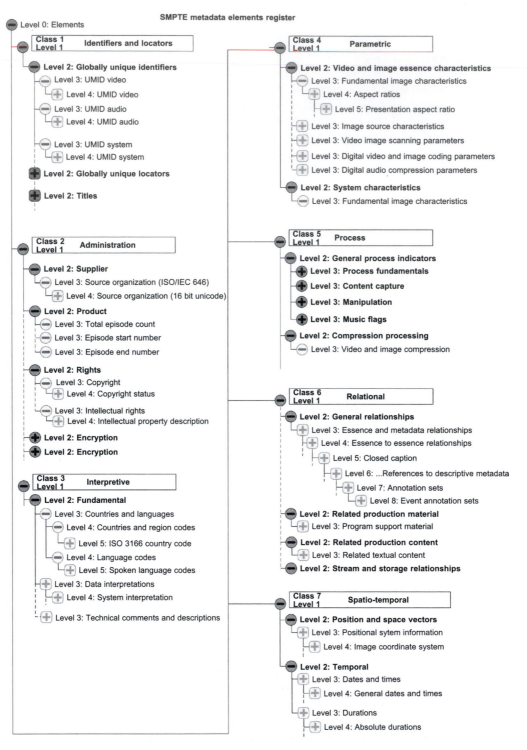

SMPTE metadata elements register

Level 0: Elements

Class 1 Level 1 — Identifiers and locators
- Level 2: Globally unique identifiers
  - Level 3: UMID video
    - Level 4: UMID video
  - Level 3: UMID audio
    - Level 4: UMID audio
  - Level 3: UMID system
    - Level 4: UMID system
- Level 2: Globally unique locators
- Level 2: Titles

Class 2 Level 1 — Administration
- Level 2: Supplier
  - Level 3: Source organization (ISO/IEC 646)
    - Level 4: Source organization (16 bit unicode)
- Level 2: Product
  - Level 3: Total episode count
  - Level 3: Episode start number
  - Level 3: Episode end number
- Level 2: Rights
  - Level 3: Copyright
    - Level 4: Copyright status
  - Level 3: Intellectual rights
    - Level 4: Intellectual property description
- Level 2: Encryption
- Level 2: Encryption

Class 3 Level 1 — Interpretive
- Level 2: Fundamental
  - Level 3: Countries and languages
    - Level 4: Countries and region codes
      - Level 5: ISO 3166 country code
    - Level 4: Language codes
      - Level 5: Spoken language codes
  - Level 3: Data interpretations
    - Level 4: System interpretation
  - Level 3: Technical comments and descriptions

Class 4 Level 1 — Parametric
- Level 2: Video and image essence characteristics
  - Level 3: Fundamental image characteristics
    - Level 4: Aspect ratios
      - Level 5: Presentation aspect ratio
  - Level 3: Image source characteristics
  - Level 3: Video image scanning parameters
  - Level 3: Digital video and image coding parameters
  - Level 3: Digital audio compression parameters
- Level 2: System characteristics
  - Level 3: Fundamental image characteristics

Class 5 Level 1 — Process
- Level 2: General process indicators
  - Level 3: Process fundamentals
  - Level 3: Content capture
  - Level 3: Manipulation
  - Level 3: Music flags
- Level 2: Compression processing
  - Level 3: Video and image compression

Class 6 Level 1 — Relational
- Level 2: General relationships
  - Level 3: Essence and metadata relationships
    - Level 4: Essence to essence relationships
      - Level 5: Closed caption
        - Level 6: ...References to descriptive metadata
          - Level 7: Annotation sets
            - Level 8: Event annotation sets
- Level 2: Related production material
  - Level 3: Program support material
- Level 2: Related production content
  - Level 3: Related textual content
- Level 2: Stream and storage relationships

Class 7 Level 1 — Spatio-temporal
- Level 2: Position and space vectors
  - Level 3: Positional sytem information
    - Level 4: Image coordinate system
- Level 2: Temporal
  - Level 3: Dates and times
    - Level 4: General dates and times
  - Level 3: Durations
    - Level 4: Absolute durations

Figure 13.6 Partial segment of the node and leaf structure used in the metadata dictionary [extracted in part from the SMPTE RP210 online registry].

Element Dictionary (formerly called the Metadata Dictionary) is a data element register that defines data elements, including their names, descriptions, and identifiers, for association with essence or other metadata. A full explanation is contained in SMPTE 335M. The spreadsheet form details can be found at www.smpte-ra.org/ under the file RP210.11.XLS. One can see the depth that such metadata can take, as it begins at the administrative levels and goes well beyond the coding levels for media-related files and essence descriptions.

Interoperability

Interoperability is a key component of any metadata strategy. Elaborate systems that are independently devised for only one archival repository will be a recipe for low productivity and high costs, and will have minimal impact. Richard Gabriel's maxim "Worse is better," which originated from when he was comparing two programming languages, one elegant but complex, the other awkward but simple, correctly predicted that the simpler language would spread faster, and thus more people would come to care about improving the simple language than otherwise improving the complex one.

Gabriel's prediction was found to be correct, as is demonstrated by the widespread adoption and success of Dublin Core (DC), which was initially regarded as an unlikely solution by the professionals on account of its rigorous simplicity.

Dublin Core

Now one of the more recognized initiatives related to metadata, this work dates back to 2000 when, at that time, the Dublin Core community focused on "application profiles" as a type of metadata schema. Application profiles, as schemas, consist of data elements that are drawn from one or more namespaces, combined together by implementers, and then optimized for a particular local application. In the application profile concept, metadata records would use Dublin Core together with other specialized vocabularies to meet particular implementation requirements.

The motivation for the work on the Dublin Core was to develop a set of 15 simple data elements (see Table 13.1) that could be used to describe document-like networked information objects in support of discovery (i.e., searching) activities. The

Table 13.1 Dublin Core Data Elements

Title	Format
Creator (Author)	Resource identifier
Subject and Keywords	Source
Description	Language
Publisher	Relation
Other contributor	Coverage
Data	Rights management
Resource type	

Dublin Core data elements consist of the following: title; creator (author); subject and keywords; description; publisher; other contributor; date; resource type; format; resource identifier; source; language; relation; coverage; and rights management.

The Dublin Core achieved wide dissemination as part of the Open Archives Initiative Protocol for Metadata Harvesting (OAI-PMH) and was ratified as IETF RFC 5013, ANSI/NISO Standard Z39.85-2007, and ISO Standard 15836:2009. Since 1997, the Dublin Core data model has evolved alongside the World Wide Web Consortium's (www.w3c.org) work on a generic data model for metadata, known as the Resource Description Framework (RDF). As part of an extended set of DCMI Metadata Terms, Dublin Core ultimately became one of most popular vocabularies for use with RDF, most recently in the context of the Linked Data movement.

PBCore

Developed by the Public Broadcasting Service (PBS) with development funding from the Corporation for Public Broadcasting (CPB), the project, which was initially published in 2005, provides a common set of terms and capabilities that address metadata and associated media asset management activities for use specifically by many public broadcasting stations, organizations, and information systems (see Fig. 13.7). These entities use this 48-element core document to describe the intellectual content, property rights, and instantiations/formats of their media items.

The PBCore project has been finalizing its XML Schema Definition (XSD) as the main framework upon which all the PBCore elements, their relationships, vocabulary pick-lists, and

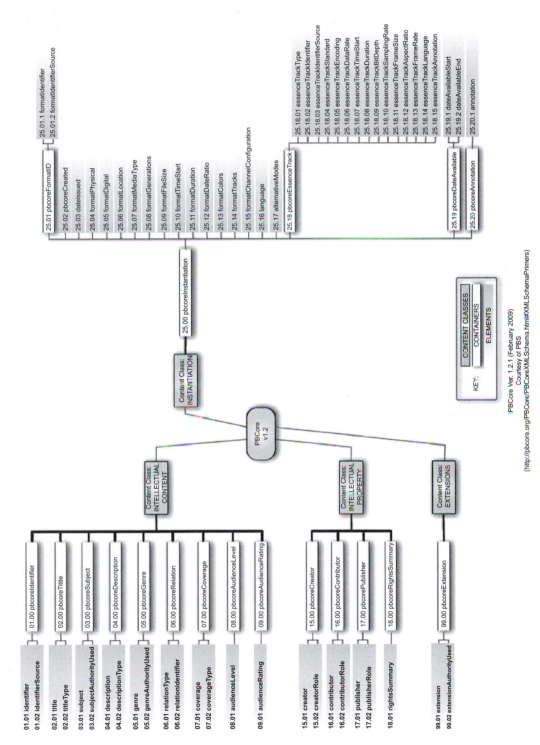

Figure 13.7 The PBCore and XML schema, and XSD (XML Schema Definition) layout utilized by PBS for metadata.

395

data types are organized and defined. PBS is building an accurate and meticulous XSD to ensure that when PBCore compliant metadata descriptions are shared between data systems, the contributing system and the receiving system are both able to "machine read" and faultlessly interpret and display these descriptions.

Formally known as the Public Broadcasting Metadata Dictionary Project, PBCore is designed to provide, for television, radio, and Web activities, a standard way of describing and using this data, allowing content to be more easily retrieved and shared among colleagues, software systems, institutions, community and production partners, private citizens, and educators. PBCore can also be used as a guide for the onset of an archival or asset management process at an individual broadcast station or institution.

PBS sees this as a standard pivotal to applying the power of digital technology to meet the mission of public broadcasting. In the process of creating the PBCore XSD, they determined enhancements to the underlying structure of PBCore were necessary. These enhancements aid in the binding together of related metadata elements (for example "Title" and "TitleType") into new element containers. The original 48 PBCore elements are now becoming a more structured hierarchical model consisting of 53 elements arranged in 15 containers and 3 sub-containers, all organized under 4 content classes.

Usage Metadata

Usage metadata is yet another form of descriptive metadata. Typically a subset of descriptive metadata, usage metadata describes life-cycle information about a video clip or file such as when the camcorder actually first captured the content. Depending upon how the metadata schema is implemented, this might include the time of day, the shooter (if the camcorder logs that information), and the MAC address of the recording equipment or the name associated with the physical recording media.

Schemas

Defined basically as a protocol that describes how one collects all these data sets together, schemas have different meanings depending upon the systems they are associated with. For example, in computer science, an XML (extensible markup language) schema is a way to define the structure, content and, to some extent, the semantics of XML documents. Since XML has becoming the de facto standard of writing code for media asset systems, particularly one that is human understandable, many of the metadata systems are being written (or translated into) XML.

Standards, Practices, and Policies for Metadata

Much of the work published on metadata, in general, comes out of the professional library (librarian) space. Setting policies that cover the endless possibilities for metadata applications is beyond comprehension, but there are still several efforts (as previously described) that continue in that domain.

Diane Hillman's (Cornell University) infamous statement, "There are no metadata police," elevated awareness of standards, practices, and policies. There are indeed prescribed standards and practices that can be observed and followed when designing a usable and extensible metadata platform. Some of these have emerged from the work in MPEG-7, and in various other global activities by standards committees and their study groups. It would be nearly impossible to present all of these, but the "Further Readings" section at the conclusion of this chapter will provide some links to current and previous activities.

Storing Metadata

There are two principle philosophies associated with where metadata are stored for media-centric applications. One belief is to associate metadata to the file in an external database housed on a separate server platform. The alternative is to embed the metadata with the actual file. Both have their pros and cons.

Metadata, particularly descriptive metadata, are quite dynamic. The size of the metadata file, that is, the byte count of the XML-based information, continues to grow as the file (content) moves through the production, distribution, and archiving processes. It is for this reason, and the risks associated with the loss of the metadata embedded in a file, that many MAM systems will employ a discrete server platform that isolates the actual essence of the file from the descriptive metadata.

Structural metadata are almost always carried with the file itself. These metadata do not necessarily follow XML formats as structural metadata are most useful to devices, such as decoders and videoservers, when the file is first presented to the playback system of root level server platforms.

Descriptive metadata would not necessarily be carried or contained (wrapped) within the essence portions of a media file. Given the dynamic nature of descriptive metadata during production and other workflows, this would potentially require that a new version of each file would be created every time that a new element is added to the metadata. This would require a continual growth in storage systems for what would be highly duplicative information.

Organizations like the Advanced Media Workflow Association (AMWA) are working on schemas that can link the metadata with the essence elements through versioning methods. It is beyond the scope of this book to delve into this topic, but expect to see continued adoption of these methods through the advancements in the MXF standards and practices.

Metadata Services

Any complete media asset management system must be able to communicate with several different elements and components when utilized in an enterprise-wide implementation. We use the term "services" to describe "code that can be called by other code," and extend that to include metadata services that can easily be handed off from one subsystem to another.

Metadata services are an object-oriented repository technology that may be integrated with enterprise-class information systems or with other "third party" applications that process metadata.

In the past, managing metadata has been as much an operational hazard as a realistic feature. In an enterprise-wide media management environment that has many sets of content collection points, editorial work stations, storage platforms (local and shared), and content databases, providing a unified set of metadata is essential to a successful implementation.

MAM products are migrating to, or are being written as, Web-based applications and technologies, using what are referred to as "messaging technologies." These messaging services transfer and interchange metadata and metadata services among the supporting hardware and software platforms.

Media Application Services

Media application services are those elements that perform tasks related to the content presented to them throughout the life cycle of that content. A content life cycle begins at the capture point, moves through ingest and interim storage, and then on through the production, distribution, and archive phases.

Table 13.2 Media Application Services Categorized by Functionality and Service Tiers

Fundamental Services	Secondary Services	Optional/Other Services
Search service	Browse service	Captioning service
Organize service	Transcode service	Quality control service
Transfer service	Distribution service	Archive service
Media service	Future service(s)	Other third-party service
Rules service		

A MAM system needs to employ various services that will allow the user to intelligently and efficiently manipulate the media files using the associated metadata collected throughout the MAM system. These services call code from other subsystems in the enterprise system and then react accordingly based upon the service functions.

Certain services (see Table 13.2) are essential to any MAM implementation and may be referred to as "fundamental services." Companies that manufacturer media server systems, such as in the case of Omneon, may offer a product specific server (Omneon calls theirs a "Media Application Server" or MAS), which is a foundation for the development and deployment of media-centric applications. The Omneon MAS enables a single virtualized view of the content across managed systems and fundamental media processing services, thus minimizing the complexities of media management.

Sophisticated MAM systems generally build in similar functions to their products, which are then configured (or customized) to the third-party serving products they integrate with. Regardless of where these services are placed in the product portfolio, these fundamental services will most likely consist of the following.

Search Services

Using both structural and descriptive metadata, these services will provide the capability to search across multiple file systems. Information may be retrieved from records of previously saved searches and can be used to populate folders dynamically.

Organizational Services

Content relationships may be created and maintained irrespective of the data types. These services will allow other services to treat these collections of relationships as single objects.

Transfer Services

Transfer services are involved with managing content movement per user requests or rule-sets defined by those users. The transfer service may be configured to automatically sense growing or static files, and then prescribe the most appropriate transfer method to move those files to locations either local to the server/ storage platform or to other third-party applications.

Media Services

Media services are those services specifically related to the media essence. Such services could be the purging of that data, the segmentation of the data, the duplication of the essence, etc.

Rules Services

Rules service allow users to develop workflow and processing rules to perform tasks or call other services based on system state, time, or manual parameters.

Additional services may be added to the pool to further support MAM functionality. A browse service will enable the generation of proxies either internally or through the calling of services from an external transcoding engine. Distribution services create the channel for distributing media files either as completed clips of media to the end user (sometimes through a content distribution network or content delivery network (CDN)), or sometimes to third-party products that prepare them for the application or service that will receive them.

Services including quality control, archive, captioning, and transcoding all become segments of the MAM system in its totality. Such services often become the "options" that are added to the base MAM system to fulfill business or operational needs. Services can be quite automated, taking those tasks away from error prone humans, while providing a justifiable validation that the proper quality control has been put into the delivery of the final product packages.

Messaging Services for MAM

Any use of proprietary messaging services in an enterprise-wide MAM implementation should be discouraged if there is to be continued flexibility in the system. Having to supply translators that remap or exchange and recode metadata between the variant other subsystems in the overall media production, storage, or operations environment spells certain disaster. When any one of the other subsystems changes their platform architecture or schemas, it will most certainly require new configurations or re-customization of the principle MAM system just to regain the previous ability to interchange your metadata.

Today, stemming from the tremendous developments in Web-based technologies, there is no reason not to develop messaging services using industry standard, open source practices for the exchange of information among platforms. These may include Web service standards such as SOAP or REST.

REpresentational State Transfer (REST) is an architectural style and not a toolkit. In REST, resources are identified by uniform resource identifiers (URIs). These resources are manipulated through their representations, with messages that are self-descriptive and stateless. REST permits multiple representations to be accepted or sent. REST has gained widespread acceptance across the Web as a simpler alternative to Simple Object Access Protocol (SOAP) and Web Services Description Language (WSDL)-based services.

SOAP was created to accomplish a better way to communicate between applications. At the time of SOAP development, it used hyper-text transfer protocol (HTTP), which was being supported by all Internet browsers and servers. SOAP provides a means to communicate between applications running on different operating systems, with different technologies and programming languages. SOAP became a W3C Recommendation on June 24, 2003.

Intelligent Integrated MAM

The current thinking in managing media assets is that systems must now be "media aware," that is, there must be intelligence integrated into the MAM that understands what the particular media is, what can be done with or done to that media, and how that media should be handled during ingest, processing, storage, distribution, and archive. This intelligence goes beyond just the elements of digital storage. The concept of the intelligent integrated MAM binds the entire production chain and multi-platform delivery into a single complete solution.

Intelligent integrated MAM pulls together the elements of business goals with the operational needs, the functionality of the systems, and the technical requirements necessary to fulfill those target goals. A system would include workflow management, tool set integration, metadata and metadata services, and collaboration among multiple users. Furthermore, the elements of centralized databases and a multi-tiered architecture are necessary to achieve a fully integrated MAM system.

Workflow Management

The MAM system must be capable of incorporating the operations side of the organization so as to manage user workflows that include scheduling, acquisition, and production; distribution and repacking; and archiving. A unified MAM system will achieve maximum benefit when it is configured to the many roles and corresponding responsibilities that any user will execute as part of their particular production workflow needs. Workflow designs will include the establishment of permissions, reporting paths for the status of jobs and their approval processes, any points where metadata are entered or altered in the MAM databases, and other essential background operational tasks and requirements.

Collaboration among Multiple Users

Given that the MAM system with its intelligent integrated components will be utilized by the entire enterprise, the elements that make up the MAM must be easily addressable by multiple users who may perform varying tasks simultaneously. These collaborative components allow users to interact and share information (content and metadata) with each other. These activities must extend across the entire organization before an effective MAM solution is realized.

At the same time, the system must include the capabilities to regulate and manage access to certain material, metadata, tool sets, and operations based upon permissions and IT-security policies. The system must also characterize priorities such as multiple or simultaneous requests for the same material so as to manage and restrict unqualified write functions that could destroy or render that material useless. This process is referred to as "access management" and is a key capability in any MAM system.

Tool Set Integration

Each step of the media production workflow will utilize tool sets that integrate operations such as metadata services, business processes, and media exchanges. These tool sets in turn must be able to directly access the storage systems and the asset catalogs (or databases). As previously discussed, these tools should be built around open standards so as to more easily work with the software and hardware in current systems and those that will emerge in the future.

The framework of the MAM system, overall, will be far more extensible when it is built around open standards. Thus, users should be discouraged from building their MAM system around dedicated or proprietary protocols or API components that require detailed or complex customization for functionality.

Centralized Database

When the media database is centralized, it becomes part of a unified depository for all media assets. Users are afforded the ability to quickly share material among each other easily and on a nearly instantaneous basis. Handing off of material from one user to another is simplified, and late breaking changes can be immediately propagated through the system.

Centralized databases are tightly coupled to the centralized storage components, and more loosely coupled to the local disks or storage found on isolated, non-integrated workstations. Proxy browsing and editing is one means to isolate the common connections of the storage and database systems and allow work to proceed without a full-time network connection. Proxy editing may be accomplished on unconnected laptops, but must be fully synchronized with the centralized MAM systems once reconnected or before any actual conforming is started. These are complex tasks that require a deep understanding of system architectures and are generally only successful on full scale media asset management platforms.

Multi-Tier Architecture

From a generalized perspective, a tightly coupled system means that the services, applications, and interfaces are assembled such that they share a common set of information. This is best accomplished with a centralized storage platform for media assets and associated databases. Critics of tightly coupled systems, those that couple workflow and assets with limited flexibility, say this architecture comes with increased risks in the long term.

For these and other reasons, enterprise MAM systems will utilize a multi-tiered architecture (see Fig. 13.8), which incorporates redundancy in both the hardware and software components. Most MAM systems will employ at least a main and a backup database. This upper tier, in the higher class systems, will include at least two database servers each with a protected (RAID) storage system and mirrored databases on separate hardware.

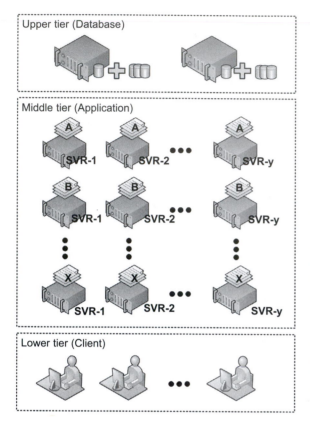

Upper tier (Database)

Middle tier (Application)

A
SVR-1
A
SVR-2
• • •
A
SVR-y

B
SVR-1
B
SVR-2
• • •
B
SVR-y

• • •

X
SVR-1
X
SVR-2
• • •
X
SVR-y

Lower tier (Client)

• • •

Figure 13.8 The multi-tiered architecture using multiple servers to process and manage the databases for services or tasks (applications) that are requested by clients.

In the middle tier, where the applications are housed, each grouping of applications will be contained on multiple servers. The application servers each perform tasks or provide services as requested by the clients. These services or tasks may include file conversion, ingesting, cataloging, search, etc. By spreading the same applications out across redundant servers, a grid of protection is built such that the applications are protected and the bandwidth accessibility is improved as more and more users gain access to the system. A load balancing application spreads those tasks out among the various servers and aids in managing the replication of the data (metadata and reporting data) across the database servers and the user/client applications.

The lower tier, at the client level, will have multiple workstations for users that are bandwidth allocated across the mid-tier applications. The applications may be called by any user, with access limited only by software licensing.

Architectures of this type mitigate the possibility of a single point of failure. Should discontinuity or failure occur, the client is transferred to another application server. Should the main database fail, the database information is immediately moved to the backup.

Scalability

Using the multi-tiered architecture approach, growing the MAM system becomes a straightforward process. Should the loads increase, additional servers can be added. Scalability is generally designed into all elements of media asset management and encompasses the storage platforms, database servers, applications servers, and clients.

Storage for MAM

How and where to storing the application databases, media content, and metadata for the components of a media asset management system is no trivial matter. The factors that govern this are driven by the providers of the MAM, and by the manufacturers of the software and hardware platforms that interact with the MAM.

It goes without saying that the important elements of these systems should be contained on protected storage that is either replication based or based on mathematical protection (RAID). Given that many of the MAM software components can be implemented on commercial off the shelf (COTS) server products, the storage elements associated with those servers are generally of a class and service level that can support the kinds of activities and workflows necessary for media asset management.

Specialty platforms, designed for mission critical applications and those that support continuous duty cycles, such as dedicated videoservers for broadcast applications, will suit the playback and/or ingest functions of a MAM. Some integrated, enterprise-class MAM systems, however, will require that IT-class servers and high-performance storage be augmented by third-party base-band video/audio ingest codecs in order to capture into storage and create those proxies and structural metadata necessary for their functionality.

Other MAM systems will provide their own serving and storage platforms, on which they have specifically developed their products. Care should be taken with this form of product line as it infers you must return to this vendor for all future updates when and if more performance-driven servers are available.

Latency

Any delay in obtaining access to material is considered latency. In the serving platforms used for MAM, latency is an important consideration, especially when content is to be shared among multiple users or across many workflows. Most MAM system providers will go through extensive planning to mitigate the impacts of latency on their systems.

Interfacing with Production Storage

Specifying how the MAM system performs with third-party storage components is sometimes called "benchmarking." This process requires a thorough understanding of the devices that the MAM must interface with.

Many assumptions will be made during the pre-design and proposal stages of defining a complete MAM system. If the MAM is to operate only within the workflow or framework of a post-production facility, that will require a set of specifications that would be different from when the MAM is working in a live or news environment.

The activities expected during ingest are more linear or real time in nature and somewhat easier to navigate versus when a dozen or more nonlinear editing platforms of various formats need access to the same content share. Activities that FTP content directly into servers can be regulated by the engines and software on both the servers and/or the CDN. Streaming media that must be captured upon presentation must have sufficient buffering to ensure no packets or video frames will be lost.

Design development will require a thorough validation of the production storage systems' capability to sustain a significantly higher number of "read-while-write" operations. IT-centric storage systems may lack this capability, so a complete understanding, and in some cases actual benchmark testing, is necessary.

For example, in applications where live ingest, live playback, streamed playback, and craft editing is required, defined as "peak usage of a system," there will be a number of read-while-write operations that occur simultaneously. These activities may include proxy generations of every image file while those high-resolution images are also being recorded, downloaded, or rendered. Further activities might include users that have to browse through these same proxies while they are being generated, and when editors are accessing high resolution while they are also being recorded (or downloaded or rendered).

The previous example is typical of a production environment for live broadcasts including sports and news. In most cases, the MAM system will be managing peripheral activities that migrate files from one platform to another. This requires not only a network architecture that can support the file sizes, bandwidth, and overhead, but it requires that media-aware and high-bandwidth (e.g., fibre channel SAN) storage systems be employed to avoid bottlenecks that will appear to be a MAM control related issue.

When third-party storage systems are employed in a facility, such as in an Avid or Final Cut Pro editing environment, it is important to understand and determine where the active files will reside and what entity controls those activities during the editorial, ingest, cataloging, and release processes. Should all assets be stored on the centralized content store, this will require that the supporting applications be capable of interfacing to and from that store. More often than not, at least in many current operations, users still prefer to work on their local (dedicated) storage. While it is possible to achieve higher local performance in this model, it encumbers the MAM system in its abilities to provide a shared-storage, collaborative workflow environment.

There are no hard-fast or concrete rules for addressing these issues. As manufacturers of editing products develop and release new capabilities (such as improved storage subsystems), the ability to reconfigure or customize the current MAM implementation grows more complex. Often, the race to keep up with all these advancements is one that is not necessarily pleasant for any of the stakeholders—and the user plays a "wait-and-see" game until the design development and update cycles are complete.

Archive

With the understanding that a MAM will be expected to work with all elements of the enterprise's workflow, its interoperability with an archive is paramount to the continuous availability of the assets under its management and control. Much like what was previously described in the section on "Interfacing with Production Storage," communicating and sharing media files with the archive requires a very tight integration between both the archive manager and the MAM system.

Archive platforms typically include elements consisting of an archive manager, the "data-mover," which handles the actual files between storage systems, and the storage system itself (e.g., data tape, optical disk, or spinning disk). Considerable effort is put into managing the handoffs between the MAM and the archive solution. The archive manager must track its assets on its platform much like the disk file system does on a spinning disk platform. The MAM must pass certain metadata elements to the archive manager who then interrogates the source end (the production storage elements) and the target end (the data mover or tape system) to keep the locations properly synchronized in their respective databases. Some of this information is never passed between the MAM and the other systems; yet tracking information such as "who has the file now," requires that the MAM must be continuously aware of all the file locations in order to support requests from the various users on the system.

Files that move from local or production storage to the archive may remain on both systems until actually purged from one or more of the respective systems. The MAM must become the traffic cop for these processes. Manually overriding the process becomes a violation of the workflow policies that can have severe negative impacts on the system and ultimately may result in the loss of the file, location data, or other pertinent information.

The archive system must therefore work integrally with the MAM system. It is not possible to specify the functionality of one without knowledge of the other.

Further Readings

A complete book on descriptive metadata for television applications is "Descriptive Metadata for Television: An Ennd-to-End Introduction," Mike Cox, Ellen Mulder, Linda Tadic. Focal Press (1st edition April 10, 2006).

Tutorials on first and second generation Web services technologies can be found at www.ws-standards.com or www.soaspecs.com.

Information about PBCore can be found at http://pbcore.org/PBCore/.

Information about Dublin Core Media Initiative (DCMI) can be found at http://dublincore.org/.

Information about XML and other Web-services can be found at the World Wide Web Consortium (W3C) at http://www.w3.org/XML/.

Information on the BBC's "Standard Media Exchange Framework" (SMEF) can be found at http://www.bbc.co.uk/guidelines/smef/.

Information on the European Broadcast Union (EBU) project group P/META, whose work is based on an extension of the BBC's SMEF, can be found at http://www.ebu.ch/en/technical/trev/trev_290-hopper.pdf.

Information on the Institute fur Rundfunktechnik (IRT) XML mapping of the MXF metadata structures (DMS-1) can be found at http://mxf.irt.de/activities/2004-02_dms_workshop.php.

14

CLUSTERING

Traditionally, storage systems were designed for structured data where the file sizes were small, and the systems, such as databases or email servers, could be optimized for high levels of transactional processes. With the growth in unstructured content, certainly for motion imaging, motion picture production, and multimedia applications, traditional storage systems can no longer address the demanding issues arising as media files have exploded in size, volume, and complexity.

Storing unstructured media data requires some fundamental changes to storage systems due to larger file sizes and data volumes, higher throughput requirements, high concurrent file access, and read-intensive access patterns. Solutions developed to address these differences grew out of the concepts of clustered servers.

Clustered architectures, including storage and servers, have changed the rules of how data is stored, accessed, and processed. This chapter is about those changes and how the requirements for the storage of unstructured data, especially media files, might be met through clustering.

KEY CHAPTER POINTS

- Defining distinctions between grids and clusters from the storage perspective and the computer/server perspective
- Looking at the various "sharing" architectures such as shared nothing, shared everything, and mirroring
- Qualifying, selecting, and managing grids and/or clusters
- Common scaling characteristics for clusters and grids

Why Use Clusters?

The enterprise has continually been driven to address the growing needs for increased compute power and enhanced storage capacity. During this evolution, it was not uncommon for the

IT managers to employ multiple sets of discrete workstations or servers to address the ever increasing scaling of processes. Managing the proliferation of individual devices and dedicated storage increased the time and risk associated with data and information services.

IT system administrators began to adopt clustered server architectures as a means to handle these requirements without having to displace an already hefty investment in existing servers, workstations, and other storage components. By aggregating standard industry grade servers, systems would achieve higher levels of performance, reliability, and scalability. Concurrently, overall workload management also improved. Through the employment of clustering, systems could be expanded and the performance of the systems increased at a fraction of the cost of the traditional "big iron" single-box solutions with their complex multiprocessor subsystems and file management architectures.

Clustering may be looked at as a solution to protection against failures. It can also provide an avenue for load distribution. It can be used as a means to extend the useful life of legacy servers or storage components. Regardless of how and under what kind of architecture it is implemented, clustering seems like a valuable direction to go in when existing solutions and components fall short.

However, clustering of servers brought on new issues for storage management. Administrators would have to respond to the islands of storage that were now dedicated to each of the server/ cluster functions. Virtualization was certainly one possibility; cloud storage seems to be becoming another. Nonetheless, seeming to solve one problem unfortunately created an entirely new one. Industries, even before the growth in unstructured data, were in search of a different solution that could handle the integration of SAN, NAS, and DAS storage systems.

Defining clustered storage can be difficult, because although it is similar in concept to clustered servers, it can have several different meanings and implementations. Depending upon the application and business requirements in which clustered storage is applied, the sharing and consolidation of storage-centric activities can yield significant cost reductions, performance increases, and manageability of both growth and obsolescence.

Clustering is, in fact, one of the oldest types of storage because of its appealing abilities to scale out (horizontally) in terms of capacity well beyond the limits of a stand-alone storage implementation. Clustering is not bound by geographic regions and can be implemented over great distances adding to versatility, performance, and resilience.

Clustering may be tightly coupled or loosely coupled. Solutions from vendors are available in either method. Clustering can be applied in file, block, or object based configurations; with the latter being the most distinctive. Clustering offers the advantage of managing a single namespace instead of multiple servers, each with their own.

Clustering aids in mitigating single points of failure (SPOF) by providing multiple paths and components that can keep the system working even if one of the segments or elements is unavailable.

Physical Components

Traditionally, storage systems are bound by the physical components of their respective configurations. Some of those elements include the following:

- Number of disk drives
- Number of attached servers
- Cache size
- Disk and/or storage controller performance

It is given that storage systems never seem to be static. The dynamic nature of the applications, users, and implementations forces varying changes in storage architectures, capacities, performance, addressability, and redundancy. When expanding these storage systems, administrators must address both functional and logical constraints. A portion of these issues may include items such as the number of file systems supported, the number of snapshots or replications of the data sets, and others, which are outlined in this book.

Solution sets may be predefined with real and/or artificial boundaries that force the users into decisions that can involve upgrades to a larger storage system and/or the necessity for an increased storage management tool set as the storage system limits are approached.

For the traditional storage systems deployed throughout the enterprise, there have been typically three principle storage architectures, which are as follows:

- Direct-attached storage (DAS)
- Storage area networks (SANs)
- Network-attached storage (NAS)

These architectures are described in detail in various chapters of this book.

Clustered storage is the fourth principle of storage architecture. Clustering enables the pulling together of two or more storage systems, which then behave as a single entity.

Capabilities and Types of Clustering

The capabilities of clustered storage vary in terms of their ability to scale capacity, performance, and accessibility at the block or file level, including availability and ease of use. Clustered storage is categorized in types, each with different characteristics or "architectures":

- Two-way simple failover
- Namespace aggregation
- Clustered storage with a distributed file system (DFS)

Two-Way Simple Failover

Protected storage systems have traditionally employed both a primary and a redundant node-based architecture. In this model, each node, defined as a combination of server or controller head and a hard disk drive or disk drive array, can be configured to stand on its own. This protected node concept, when design is appropriated, provides for more than just a means to mitigate the risks of having all your (storage) eggs in one basket. Adding multiple nodes can provide for increased bandwidth (throughput), but this configuration was not typically managed for this purpose.

When configured to operate in only a simple protection mode, if one of the nodes failed, the system entered into a process called "failing over" whereby the redundant node would take over the entire responsibilities of storage system until the failed node could be repaired. This simple failover concept should not be defined as a true clustering technique but more properly described as a redundancy technique.

The NAS community would refer to this as "two-way clustering," which evolved out of the need to improve both fault tolerance and redundancy for those legacy or traditional single-head storage architectures (see Fig. 14.1). This mode enables one controller head to assume the identity of the failing controller head, allowing the failed controller's data volumes to continue to be accessed or written to by the new controller head. The main limiting factor of this approach was its inherent limited performance and scalability. This model worked best on small file system sizes, but it increased management complexity and had a relative high cost to achieve the high availability of the file data.

As the growth of unstructured data exploded, it became evident that this type of solution would not meet the future needs of the enterprise.

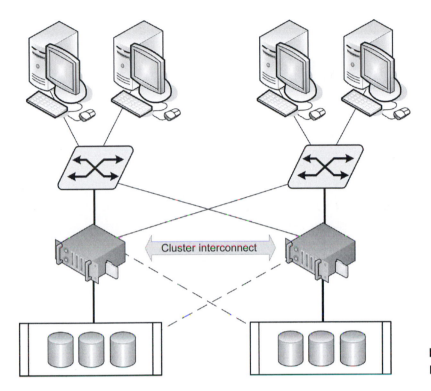

Figure 14.1 Two-way failover protected by clustering.

Namespace Aggregation

This form of clustered storage solution essentially presents a single pane of glass, a veneer that pulls the elements of storage management together. Such solutions can be purely software-based (i.e., software virtualization) or can be a combination of software and hardware (i.e., appliance and switch). It creates a single namespace and cluster of storage resources that appear as one large pool of data management (see Fig. 14.2). Typically, these solutions enable "synthetic trees" that encompass a cluster of NAS servers or storage devices, present the silos to a network user as one (unified) namespace, and store the data on any given silo. In other words, they create gateways through which data from several different files and heterogeneous systems is redirected to be accessed from a common point.

Solutions in this class control laying out a file (i.e., striping data) across disk volumes to a specific silo—but not across the silos that make up the cluster—and they still allow data movement between tiers of storage with limited client interruption. Although this approach can be attractive on the surface from

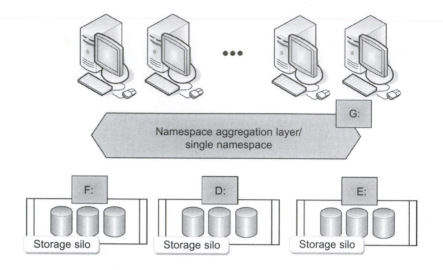

Figure 14.2 Namespace aggregation as a type of clustered storage.

an initial cost standpoint, the IT administrator is still managing, growing, and configuring these islands of storage (i.e., heterogeneous silos of storage), but now with an additional virtualization layer. This approach creates more complexity, higher management burden, and greater long-term operational costs.

Clustered Storage with a Distributed File System

Evolution extended the two previously described types of clustering, "two-way simple clustering" and "namespace aggregation," into distributed clustered storage as a network storage system that allows users to combine and add storage nodes, which all access the same data pool. This solution resides on the storage layer and utilizes one or more distributed file systems that span across any number of nodes or storage controllers.

Generally, a software system resides at the storage layer, providing the ability to completely control the layout of data (through "data striping") across all the storage nodes that make up the cluster. Access goes all the way down to the error correction and concealment (ECC) level at every element of the data pool. This is in contrast to namespace aggregation (such as in virtualization products) that only directs the specific storage silo to which data is written.

This system has the intelligence to make the nodes both symmetric and distributed. The cluster in turn works as an intelligent and unified system, allowing each node the capability of running

Table 14.1 Clustered Storage Data Striping and File Layout

Forms of Clustered Storage		
Cluster Type	Data Striping	File Layout
Simple two-way failover cluster	Within a specific silo, data blocks are stripped across a RAID group.	Files are stored on one of the silos. During failover, the remaining controllers assume the duties of the failed head.
Namespace aggregation	Data blocks striped within specific silos make up a cluster.	Controls which storage silos receive which files. Presents and aggregates all namespaces of file locations.
Clustered storage with distributed file system (DFS)	Files are broken into data blocks that are striped across all storage nodes and disks comprising a cluster.	Uses a single global namespace. Distributes file layout across all storage nodes and disks. Presents a single unified view of all files from every node.

on its own and communicating with the other nodes to deliver files in response to the needs of the hosts and users. In this way, each node knows everything about the other nodes. Thus, each node in the cluster is a "coherent peer" to the other.

Distributed clustered storage in turn provides the highest levels of availability, scalability, aggregate throughput, reliability, and ease of management when compared to the solutions of "two-way failover" and "namespace aggregation" described (see Table 14.1).

Cluster Scaling Characteristics

As mentioned, clustering allows systems to scale more easily. The complicated or cumbersome issues related to increasing performance, availability, and accessibility can now be more easily and effectively improved as the storage capacity requirements increase and unstructured storage architectures expand. These improvements include the following:

- Performance—optimization and increases in bandwidth, IOPs, or a combination of both are tuned for large, sequential read or write operations such as those found in moving media applications or time-sensitive, random reads and writes such as those in transaction-oriented operations.

- Availability—including the elimination of single points of failure, the capability to implement transparent failover, and the ability to achieve self-healing processes.
- Capacity and connectivity—the implementation of Fibre Channel, Ethernet, or InfiniBand ports that can support significantly larger storage capacities, increased server access, and extended connectivity.
- Accessibility—enabling block access like that used in iSCSI, Fibre Channel, or InfiniBand; or for network-attached storage (NAS) file systems such as NFS, CIFS, or proprietary; or for data sharing.
- Recoverability—the ability for the system to return to normal operations after some level of failure.
- Sharing—including shared-nothing, shared-something, or shared-everything architectures; may be based upon open or proprietary hardware and software using tightly or loosely coupled interconnects.

Shared Structures

The sharing of data (as information) among machines, users, and environments is a key element that allows effective collaboration, distribution, and aggregation of content; whether that content is multimedia, moving images, linked metadata, or transactional databases. Much has been written about the various methodologies that surround sharing. Sharing can mean shared storage, shared projects, and/or shared resources. Regardless of whether the architecture is clustered, the structures of these sharing architectures become the secret sauce of the systems in which they are deployed.

Sharing structures include (but are not necessarily limited to) the following:
- Shared-nothing (SN) clusters
- Shared-disk clusters
- Mirrored-disk clusters
- Shared something
- Shared-partial model
- Shared everything (SE)

Each of these has different, sometimes overlapping, meanings. Some of the terms were created for marketing or coined to convey a slightly different perspective on a quite similar alternative. Where possible, these systems will be described in the context of what the industry has accepted the terms to mean.

Shared-Nothing Clusters

A shared-nothing architecture (SN) was initially employed in a distributed computing architecture, characterized by each node being independent and self-sufficient. Michale Stonebraker (UC Berkeley) identified shared nothing in the context, "neither memory nor peripheral storage is shared among processors," in his paper (1986) that describes the three dominant themes in building high transaction rate multiprocessor systems. A shared-nothing cluster is sometimes referred to as a "federated system."

In distributed data storage, such as in a clustered environment, shared nothing means there is no single point of contention across any portion of the system. Data in a SN-computing system is partitioned in some manner and then spreads across a set of machines with each machine having sole access, and hence sole responsibility, for the data it holds.

The industry contrasts shared nothing with systems that maintain a large amount of centrally-stored state information, whether in a database, an application server, or any other similar single point of contention.

The value of shared nothing is in its scalability, making SN popular for Web development. Google has demonstrated that a pure SN system can scale almost infinitely simply by adding nodes in the form of inexpensive computers, and hence calls this "sharding."

Shared-nothing architectures are prevalent in data warehousing, despite the debate as to whether a shared-nothing approach is superior to a shared-disk application. Shared nothing does not involve concurrent disk accesses from multiple nodes; that is, the clusters do not require a distributed lock manager (explained shortly). Shared-nothing cluster solutions are found in Microsoft Cluster Server (MSCS), a suite of software applications that allow servers to work together as a computer cluster, providing failover, network, and component load balancing; and increased availability of applications or parallel computational power as in the case of supercomputing or high-performance computing (HPC) clusters.

Shared-Disk Clusters

A shared-disk (SD) architecture is a comparable architecture popular in clustered data systems, where the disk itself is accessible from all cluster nodes. In shared disk, any node can access any data element, and any single data element has no dedicated owner.

Shared-disk clusters rely on a common I/O bus for disk access; however, they do not require shared memory. In SD, all nodes may concurrently write to or cache data from the central disks by way of a synchronization mechanism that is used to preserve coherence of data within the system. Cluster software, called the "distributed lock manager," takes on the role of managing this synchronization.

An SD cluster will support much higher levels of system availability; that is, if one node fails, the other nodes should not be affected. Nonetheless, high availability comes at the cost of a modest amount of reduced performance that occurs due to the overhead of using the distributed lock manager, as well as the potential bottlenecks that occur whenever hardware is shared. The SD cluster makes up for this with relatively good scaling properties, such as those cluster technologies employed in Oracle Parallel Server (OPS), a version of the Oracle database system designed for massively parallel processors (MPPs) that allows multiple CPUs to access a single database, or in IBM High Availability Cluster Multiprocessing (HACMP).

The shared file system is available with shared-disk clustering. Multiple systems are also attached to the same disk. All nodes in the cluster must then have access to the shared disk, but only one node has ownership of the disk; that is, there is only one database instance. In this application, if one node fails, the other takes over.

Mirrored-Disk Clusters

Mirroring is the replication of all application data from the primary storage components to a secondary or backup storage system. Often, the backup system resides at a remote location or for availability purposes may be immediately adjacent to the primary system. The replication function generally occurs while the primary system is active. A mirrored backup system, as in a software mirroring application, may not typically perform any work outside of its role as a passive standby.

Should a failure occur in the primary storage system, the failover process transfers control to the secondary (backup) system. Depending upon the scale of failure, this process can take some time. During this critical period, applications may lose some state information when they are reset; however, mirroring does enable a reasonably fast recovery scheme, requiring little administrative or human intervention.

Mirrored-disk clusters will typically include only two nodes. The configurations will usually self-monitor those applications, networks, servers, and storage components on the system.

These combined processes automate application restarts on an alternate (local or remote) server should there be a planned or unplanned service outage. Additional functionality includes the failback of services, applications, and data in a rapid and efficient method to ensure business continuity with a minimal amount of interruption.

Shared-Something Clusters

Worth mentioning, but rather vague in meaning and rarely publicized, the Oracle Real Application Cluster (RAC) database might be defined as a shared-something (SS) cluster. Oracle RAC uses multiple computers to run the Oracle Relational Database Management System (RDBMS). In their configuration, there is shared data access plus some application-level memory sharing. This definition gets fuzzy once you get into RDMA-based architectures like those found in InfiniBand, where nodes are actually granting direct memory access to other nodes within a cluster.

With all these shared architecture terminologies, it is not a surprise to find a "shared kind-of-something-but-not-really" (SKS-BNR) concept because it had not been thought of quite yet.

Shared-Partial Model

These instances of data and storage sets share some resources and cooperate in a limited way. In this configuration, a portion of the system memory is designated as shared memory in which each instance can then be accessed. Both the code and the data for each instance are stored in private memory. Data that is shared by applications in several instances is stored in the shared memory.

In this shared-partial model the instances are not clustered.

Shared-Everything Clusters

Commercially available in some databases, the idea of a shared-everything (SE) cluster is that it behaves like a single big box built from multiple smaller boxes.

To give an abbreviated perspective of an application, a systems complex or "Sysplex" is a single logical system that runs on one or more physical systems. This design drives the requirements of a shared-everything storage concept. In IBM mainframes, Sysplex joins multiple processors into a single unit, sharing the same logical devices often isolated within a single system. Parallel Sysplex technology allows multiple mainframes to perform as one.

In the shared-everything cluster, parts of applications may be spread among different cluster nodes in order to take advantage of additional CPUs, memory, and I/O when available on other nodes. In terms of workload processing, multiple instances of applications in a hierarchy of dependent resources per cluster running will handle each of the particular duties and resources that come from the hierarchy of dependent resources, but would be running on different nodes.

Although shared nothing (SN) is considered to be the most scalable, it is sensitive to the problems of data skew, which is the difference in the arrival time of a data set at two different registers. Conversely, SE allows the collaborating processors to share the workload more efficiently; however, SE suffers from the limitation of memory and disk I/O bandwidth. A potentially better approach would be a hybrid architecture in which SE clusters are interconnected through a communication network to form a SN structure at the inter-cluster level. In such a hybrid approach, the processing elements are clustered into SE systems to minimize any skew effect. Each cluster would be kept small within the limitation of the memory and I/O technology in order to avoid the data access bottleneck.

Managing Storage Clusters for Scalability

The management of the cluster itself is yet another element in the overall storage clustering system. Tool sets can provide for management of the many elements of the cluster components, but they may not necessarily manage the scalability or performance of the cluster.

The goal of cluster management is to simplify the management of the overall system, which is certainly useful. However, usually these tools would not provide the linear scalable performance of a true cluster.

Approaches to scaling a cluster include the combining of two controller nodes that are actually an active–active cluster and then connecting this controller node pair to other pairs. There is no aggregation of performance with the other pairs.

In managing scalability, one should look at complete node protection for high availability, which aims at eliminating all single points of failure, including the failure of an entire distributed controller node. The RAID architecture should be distributed RAID, which allows for capacity efficiency. A clustered storage system that uses distributed RAID protects the distributed controller nodes and can provide up to double the usable capacity of a clustered system that only copies (or mirrors) data between nodes.

To obtain a maximized bandwidth to performance ratio, clustered systems should eliminate a master controller and aggregate the network ports to provide the highest bandwidth. For media installations, this allows for the support of more workstations without necessarily requiring expensive proprietary Fibre Channel or even 10 Gbit Ethernet.

Deployment

Prior to the deployment of a clustered solution, engineers should look for potential SPOFs, as well as additional design features including N+1 redundancy, and systems incorporating hot-swappable component design with self-healing capabilities that can identify, isolate, and contain faults before they can turn into problems. Although there is plenty of opportunity to prevent failures because of the multiplicity of the systems in a cluster, there are always points in a system that, if they should fault, may bring down a system completely.

Tight or Loose

Tightly coupled clustered storage divides the data between nodes in the cluster at a level of granularity smaller than a file and typically at the block or subblock level. In a typical dual-controller architecture, performance will peak at around 50% of drive capacity, after which it actually declines. In tightly coupled clusters, users should see an improvement in performance as drives and nodes are added to the environment.

Tightly coupled storage clusters tend to be focused on primary storage. You may find archives and some disk-to-disk backup systems that may employ tightly coupled storage. The downside to tight coupling is that the components of the cluster are stricter, seldom will use heterogeneous subsystems, will most always come from a single supplier, and are weaker on flexibility.

Loosely coupled clusters are essentially dual-controller standalone systems that use a global namespace to reduce management requirements over the entire environment. Although this achieves greater flexibility in the members of the cluster and the cluster can start with just one member, the entirety of the file must be on a single node. This is the opposite of a tightly coupled cluster where the data is stored across nodes in the cluster.

However, the data can be mirrored to other nodes for redundancy, with some software solutions providing the capability to use the secondary copy as a backup, automatically. The downside of loosely coupled clusters comes from the fact that the node housing the data limits the maximum performance and capacity of the cluster. Performance will not scale-up as nodes are added, a feature reserved for a tightly coupled cluster environment. Therefore, loosely coupled clusters tend to be deployed where performance is still important, but the costs for increasing the storage capacity have more impact.

Tightly coupled and loosely coupled clustered storage can both address the issues of expandability, capacity and performance scale, and I/O. Caution is urged because the differences between the two can be camouflaged by driving up the performance side of the dual controller and then driving down the impacts of storage costs.

Support and Growth

If selecting a solution from a storage vendor, look to how they intend to support and manage the growth over the next 5 years. Understand what the costs, service requirements, and extensibility of the solution will be over both the financial lifetime and the practical lifetime of the solution. Look for barriers to expansion. And then, before making the choice, check if there is still another alternative, such as grid storage, that might be an equally good or a potentially better implementation.

Grid Computing

Grids are usually computer clusters that are focused more on throughput like a computing utility, rather than running fewer, tightly coupled jobs. Often, grids will incorporate heterogeneous collections of computers. The sets may be distributed geographically, and they may be administered by unrelated organizations.

Grid computing is optimized for workloads that consist of multiple independent jobs. These jobs are sometimes referred to as "packets of work" or just packets. Packets do not need to share data between the other independent jobs during the computation process. Grids are not essentially an entity, but they are designed to serve and manage the allocation of other jobs to computers that will perform the work independently of the rest of the grid cluster.

Resources such as storage may be shared by all the nodes on the grid. Intermediate results of one job do not affect other jobs in progress on other nodes of the grid. Grid computing is excellent for handling applications that have large bandwidth requirements.

Grids and clusters are frequently lumped together into the same category, but there are differences in the two architectures.

Grids and Nodes

A grid is an approach to storing data that employs multiple self-contained storage nodes that are interconnected such that any node is able to communicate with any other node through means that do not require the data to pass through a centralized switch.

Storage nodes each contain their own storage medium, a microprocessor, a management layer, and a means to index the storage. In more typical applications, multiple nodes may share a common switch; however, each node must also be connected to at least one other node in the cluster. Grid topologies are found to have many layouts, including the interconnection of nodes in an n-dimensional hypercube configuration, similar to how nodes are interconnected in a mesh network.

Grid storage provides advantages over older storage methods. Grid storage also introduces another level of redundancy and fault tolerance. Should one storage node fail, or the pathway between nodes be interrupted, the grid can automatically reroute access to a secondary path or to a redundant node. The obvious impact is that online maintenance is reduced and downtime is alleviated, potentially all together. Furthermore, using multiple paths between each node pair ensures that the storage grid will maintain optimum performance even under conditions of fluctuating or unbalanced loads.

Grid storage is easily scalable and reduces the need for expensive hardware upgrades that require significant downtime. When a new storage node is added, software will automatically recognize it and configure it so that it integrates with the rest of the grid as a normal, essentially background task.

Grid or Cluster

So the question looms: "Is a cluster a grid?" The answer depends in part on what the user (or the vendor) sees in the definition of a grid. One might consider a grid to be a service or an architecture, which could be both hardware and/or software based. The solution may be spanning distance, or it could be providing some other set of capabilities. As a consequence of the variety of applications or definitions, there exist many different vendor, industry, and technological definitions and opinions as to what constitutes either a grid or a cluster for the server or the storage environments where they will play a role.

Often missing in the "what constitutes a grid" discussion is what few exploit as an essential component. This element is one that on the surface seems straightforward, but in context is just as hard to define. Supervisory control and data acquisition

(SCADA) is the term applied to the command and control functionality of a system. The concept is applicable to all forms of industry. A facility that has a lights-out work environment still requires some form of SCADA. A computer system and a storage system both need this kind of management to provide efficiency and predictability as the system is used in normal and abnormal workflows.

To add just one more tangent to the discussion, another variable in the grid versus cluster determination is what kind of SCADA functionality is available for "transparent" command and control of a storage system. By this, we mean self-monitoring, self–healing, and self-reporting subsystems that intelligently perform multiple threads of background tasks that help to optimize the systems for bandwidth, resiliency, and other provisions. The further chapters on storage networking, high performance, and shared storage cover several elements of what can be—and often is—provided for in a clustered storage environment.

Mitigating SPOF

Eliminating single points of failure (SPOF) is central to enhancing data availability, accessibility, and reliability. When looking at cluster solutions, candidates should be evaluated for potential areas where if one component failed it would bring the entire system down. Features that include N+1 redundancy, multiple pathing, and hot-swappable component design with self-healing capabilities are aids to identifying, isolating, and containing faults before they can turn into problems.

N+1 Architecture

Another class of storage solution that is present in the grey area as to whether it is a cluster is the proverbial "N+1 architecture." This class of storage is intended to provide the faithful level of redundancy that most seem to feel they require. An N+1 model uses two or more (N) primary I/O nodes or controllers, generally configured as NAS heads. A secondary on-standby or failover node, in either an active or inactive mode, provides the "+1" component.

What can make an N+1 model most confusing is how the vendor views the architecture for the components they supply. Some find that by positioning dual-controller RAID arrays or dual NAS head solutions as clusters for availability, they have achieved this "N+1" redundancy.

Differentiators

Items that separate one form of clustered storage solution from another include the following:

- How nodes of the cluster are interconnected: loosely or tightly coupled, open, or proprietary
- Input/output affinity
- Performance load balancing across nodes
- Hardware choices—open propriety, commercial off-the-shelf (COTS), or heterogeneous (different sets of third-party components) versus homogeneous (provided by a single source/vendor) servers and storage
- File sharing capabilities and methods—clustered file system software, host-based agents, or drivers
- Duplication, replication, and mirroring: local and/or remote mirroring, degrees or levels of replication, point-in-time (PIT) copy, and snapshotting
- Growth of the storage—modular storage with virtualization, automated load balancing, chassis/array or crate additions, and knowing the limitations of each form or level of expansion
- Performance tuning—capabilities for adjusting sequential read and write parameters and random updates
- Security and protection—concepts of distributed lock management and cluster coherency

Clustered storage can be a good fit for diverse environments of all sizes. When the need to grow demands that the user enable a "just-in-time storage acquisition" mentality, they do not need the complexity of disruptive upgrades or added management complexities. Clustered storage can provide those solutions.

Single Logical Storage System

A cluster will provide a single logical storage system regardless of the number of nodes in the system. This means that any application can access any element of data stored on it through any storage controller in the cluster. A cluster thus provides for the aggregation of all the hardware resources as a single system.

A clustered storage system will greatly improve performance while providing a single level of management when additional storage controllers are added to the cluster, regardless of how big the cluster might become. An inherent property of the cluster is that when a new node is added, the data is then automatically redistributed to that new node. This process is referred to as "load balancing", a function which is then applied across the entire cluster.

Input/Output Operations Per Second (IOPS)

IOPS is a common benchmark for hard disk drives and computer storage media. A numerical benchmark is often published by SAN and drive manufacturers. These numbers can be misleading and may not actually guarantee a real-world performance metric.

Performance benchmarks for clustered storage systems are metrics that have relevance to the overall system. Metrics, such as random IOPS numbers, are primarily dependent upon the storage device's random seek time. Sequential IOPS numbers, especially when considered for large block sizes, typically indicate the maximum bandwidth that a storage device can handle. You may find that sequential IOPS numbers are often replaced by a simpler specification that describes bandwidth in terms of a Mbytes/second metric.

Third-party software vendors can supply tool sets that are used to measure IOPS. Some of the recognized applications include Iometer (originally developed by Intel), IOzone, and FIO. These tools are used primarily with servers in support of finding the best storage configuration for the given server applications.

The achievable IOPS numbers for a given server configuration may vary greatly depending upon the variables utilized when the analyst enters those numbers into the applications. Such values may include the balance of read and write operations, the mix of random or sequential access patterns, the number of worker threads and queue depth, and the data block sizes.

In large systems, the tools available for monitoring performance metrics are particularly useful in tuning the systems for applications that change during workflows. For example, toward the end of a production, when editorial elements are combined with special effects, a significant amount of computer-intensive rendering will be necessary. These are usually pure number-crunching activities, which have little interaction with users, and can occur during "lights-out" operations. If the storage system had been tuned mostly for collaborative editing and the interaction with humans making choices with less intense activity, the system may not perform well for rendering if it remains in that configuration.

Tool sets that watch IOPS also monitor trends that occur during normal activities. The watchdog monitors network traffic, access and response times, and general bandwidth utilization. The tools may also probe the storage system resources and track the individual drive or RAID controller performance and carry that data into their own tracking systems. Benchmarking the system performance allows you see if that level of performance is degraded because of a particular drive that has too many read-repeats or write errors. Storage technicians can find and replace those degraded elements so as to improve performance and to head off an unexpected failure before it occurs.

Provisioning

Storage systems of today usually support some degree of clustering solution. Leading suppliers will support dual-controller node configurations with active–active or active–passive architectures. Storage systems that support N-way active architectures will scale far beyond dual-controller/dual-node systems. Theoretically, there is no real limit to how far a storage system can scale. Some systems have 80 or more controller nodes in just a single cluster.

In summary, storage clustering offers the following features and capabilities which, to some degree, are configurable and selectable on a varying set of levels:

- Single-level management—when adding more physical resources to a cluster, there is still only one logical system to manage. The cluster remains a single system regardless of its scale or geographic location.
- Just-in-time scalability—where nodes are added to achieve additional processing capacity, cache memory, and bandwidth as needed. It has the ability to add those resources when demand requires it, and it has the ability to avoid making those choices up front.
- Performance protection—the capability to add nodes levels the protection equation but also heightens performance. Storage systems that are only in a dual-node mode are at risk if one of the nodes fails. Failure of one node decreases performance and will slow it down by at least 50%. With a three-node controller cluster, the performance hit drops to 33%, with four nodes, it is 25%, and so on.
- Lower cost—for those already possessing a system, the addition of another controller node is significantly less costly than buying a completely new storage system. Some updates may be only for hardware, with software charges already covered.
- Easy to add on—additional node extensions to existing storage clusters is far less complicated than implementing and transitioning to a whole new storage system. Certainly, this depends on the particular product (or the vendor), but usually the addition of a new node to a storage cluster is an online and often transparent process to the user, which requires a minimum level of planning.

Summary

Grids and clusters have concepts that overlap and principles that are differentiating. Throughout this book, many of the storage concepts, approaches, and technologies are found in stand-alone configurations. Most of these technologies can become elements in a grid or cluster topology. Some of the media technology vendors, providing videoservers, storage systems, and content management solutions, provide elements of grid computing, grid storage, and clustering within their product lines.

These products and others are application-specific implementations; they may or may not actually utilize the grid or clustering storage technologies as described in this chapter. However, when you see vendors claim these implementations make up a heterogeneous storage solution, make sure that you understand all of the underlying implications of that solution, whether or not they use the terms "grid" or "cluster" outright.

Further Readings

An example of test results, which also depict configurations and benchmarks of various intelligent storage system providers, that covers the period from 2001 through 2008 can be found at:
http://www.spec.org/sfs97r1/results/sfs97r1.html.

15

NETWORKED STORAGE

The key to successful modern storage implementations is in assembling a system of components that interoperate well, can be cost effective, are easily managed, are able to expand to meet capacity demands, and have sufficient bandwidth so as to not become the bottleneck when placed into an enterprise-level storage environment. And by the way, the system must operate $24 \times 7 \times 365$, be reliable and inexpensive, and must provide levels of protection including redundancy so as not to be a risk to the myriad assets it will handle.

The role of storage systems continues to evolve. The explosion in the volume of media assets that need to be managed, coupled with how businesses must now operate to meet their objectives, has given way to new sets of requirements and expectations. In Chapter 1, we discussed the notion of data and information, but we have only touched upon how those entities are stored and managed, each of which are important elements that return value from any system.

In a storage network for computer systems, the bits and bytes that make up the data sets can reside most anywhere on the storage devices. Data is turned into information by applications that address the meaning of the bits and bytes. However, in a media-based system, storage systems need to take on different roles. Storage systems designed for media applications must operate like transaction-based systems in the financial world, as in if they cannot respond to the user's needs immediately when called (i.e., demanded) upon, then their value reduces to a near-zero level.

In later chapters, we will explore intelligent storage and virtualization, and how they help support users that deal with different storage platforms being accessed by an increasing number of servers and applications; additionally, we will look at storage is managed.

This chapter discusses the concepts of storage networking as applied to both computer data and media systems. We will look into Fibre Channel and "networked" storage systems, not just the specifics related to storage area networks (SAN) or network-attached storage (NAS), which are elements of an overall networked storage solution.

KEY CHAPTER POINTS

- Networking concepts applicable to storage technologies, the OSI model, and the Fibre Channel protocol stack are introduced.

- Data networks, communications, and voice and storage networks are compared.

- Filing systems and block-level and file-level functionalities are applied to storage networking.

- Direct-attached storage (DAS), network-attached storage (NAS), and storage area networking (SAN) are defined and compared.

- SAN architectures, and the planning and scaling of SANs for new and legacy systems are discussed.

Networked Storage—Fundamentals

Storage networks consist of elements that when efficiently combined will form a system that can fulfill the needs of the devices that must store data, interchange data, and retrieve that data for those applications that the data supports. In addition to these requirements, networked storage systems must further provide flexibility, adaptability, maintainability, resilience, and fault tolerance.

Storage System Environment

The highest level components that make up the environment of a storage system consist of the host, its connectivity, and the associated storage. In a host, which is the entity that contains the applications and runs those applications, usually the physical components include the central processing unit (CPU), the storage devices including internal memory and disk drives, and the input/output devices.

The storage medium that stores the data can be subdivided into temporary (cache) and persistent (long term). Memory in the host can be random access in nature, such as RAM; or nonvolatile read-only memory such as ROM. Semiconductor memory, such as RAM or ROM, once a premium for host devices, is no longer a cost factor. It is common to find workstations with as much RAM as most computer disk drives held a few short years ago. The physical media used for the long-term storage of persistent data generally resides on hard disk drives, optical (CD, DVD, and Blu-ray Disc), or magnetic tape media (LTO or DLT).

Communication Channels

The physical components that enable the sending or retrieval of data to or from a host communicate by using basic input/output (I/O) human interface devices (HID) such as a monitor, a mouse, and a keyboard (see Fig. 15.1). For host-to-host communications, a network device such as a modem or network interface card (NIC) is required. For a host to a storage device, a port will provide connectivity through an adapter, such as a host bus adapter (HBA) that is designed to be an application-specific purpose-built device to address the interfaces and protocols of the storage system. The HBA relieves the CPU from I/O processing workloads that would otherwise contribute to system bottlenecks or reduced throughput.

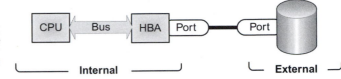

Figure 15.1 Components for physical connectivity.

Logical and Physical Connectivity

Networking has depended upon the Open Systems Interconnections (OSI) model for decades, even before the Internet and long before high-speed systems such as GigE (Gigabit Ethernet) came into existence. The OSI model has two major components: an abstract model of networking, called the Basic Reference Model, better known as the seven-layer model, and a set of specific protocols.

Open Systems Interconnection Model

The OSI model was originally developed in the late 1970s under the auspices of the ISO and became a framework for modern day implementation between various elements in a network. The depth of this model is beyond the topics in this book as there are many written dissertations about what this architecture is, and how it is utilized. Nonetheless, it is good to know some of the basic concepts so as to understand statements such as "layer 2 switching" in a switched network topology.

The basic overview of the OSI model follows, with references to Figure 15.2.

Layer 1: Physical

This layer defines the physical and the electrical requirements for devices. It includes the relationship between the physical transmission medium such as copper or fiber optic cable and the device itself.

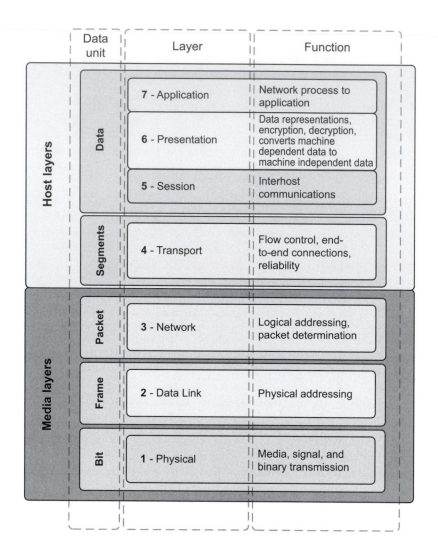

Data unit	Layer	Function
Data	7 - Application	Network process to application
	6 - Presentation	Data representations, encryption, decryption, converts machine dependent data to machine independent data
	5 - Session	Interhost communications
Segments	4 - Transport	Flow control, end-to-end connections, reliability
Packet	3 - Network	Logical addressing, packet determination
Frame	2 - Data Link	Physical addressing
Bit	1 - Physical	Media, signal, and binary transmission

Host layers: 7, 6, 5, 4
Media layers: 3, 2, 1

Figure 15.2 Open Systems Interconnection (OSI) model.

When two computers are connected together, they require a physical connection, connectors, and a wiring or transmission method such that data can flow from one device to another. Layer 1 is where raw, unstructured bits move from the connector through some form of media (fiber, twisted pair, coax, and even the air) to the other connector. Layer 1 also describes how media are connected to a NIC. It includes information about connector pinouts, electrical or optical levels, and functional characteristics about the media connection methods.

Layer 1 is concerned only with raw bits that have no specific meaning when compared with the original application. Layer 1, however, is also responsible for ensuring that if a bit was sent out as a "1," it is received as a "1." Further information is also represented, including data encoding, synchronization, length, and electrical characteristics of the bit and its type or form, for example, if the pulse is negative going, balanced, or differential.

To compare this in video technology, Layer 1 might be equated to the BNC connector on the back of the distribution amplifier. In video, it must be a true 75-ohm connector that meets a specification of particular size, electrical specificity, and material.

Layer 2: Data Link

This layer provides the functionality and procedures necessary to transfer data between network entities, and to detect and potentially correct any errors that may have occurred in Layer 1.

Layer 2 interfaces data from the lower Physical Layer to the layer above it, the Network Layer. Layer 2 translates the raw bit stream into data frames or packets that make sense out of the bit stream before it is acted upon by the Layer 3. A data frame consists of the elements shown in Figure 15.3. The forward most portion of the data frame is called the header. Just like the information on the envelope of a letter, there is a sender ID and a destination ID. A control ID is added as a guide for functions such as synchronization, routing, or frame type. The bulk of the data frame is the actual data (the meaningful information that needs to find its path to the Application Layer). Finally, a trailer or cyclic redundancy code (CRC) is attached for error correction and frame verification.

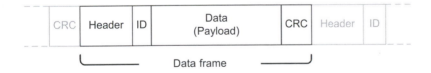

Data frame

Figure 15.3 Basic data frame construction.

At each of the layers, this root process is ordered, defined, and adhered to so that the interchange between the layer below it and layer above it is consistent regardless of where the hardware or software resides. Enough information is contained in each data frame so there is certainty that data from a word processing document will end up as a word processing document, although many more functions occur before the data really "appears" as a word processing document.

Layer 3: Network

Aimed at maintaining the quality of service requested by the Transport Layer (above it), Layer 3 provides the functional and procedural requirements for transferring variable length data sequences from the source through the networks. This layer performs routing functions in a logical addressing scheme so that data may be sent throughout extended networks.

This is the upper level for network services. Layer 3 addresses packet or data frame switching and is where the virtual circuit is established, that is, the translating of logical names and addresses into physical addresses associated with the connection method. The Network Layer determines the data path within the network based upon network traffic and congestion.

Another function of Layer 3 is to resize the data so that it fits within the confines of the router. Should data be too large to squeeze into the space defined by the Data Link Layer below it, the Network Layer will break data into smaller units and send it on. At the other end of the virtual connection, the information sent along from this layer enables reassembly of the packets into meaningful data as it passes up through the network layers and on to the application.

Layer 4: Transport

This layer effectively provides a transparent interchange of data between end users, including reliable data transfer services to the layers above it. Through flow control, segmentation and desegmentation, and error control, this layer controls the reliability of a given link within the network architecture.

The barrier between the Network Layer and the Transport Layer is a zone where many anomalies must be accounted for. Packet orders may be wrong, bit errors must be accounted for (and corrected), and even the multiplexing or demultiplexing of several messages on the same bit stream must be accomplished.

Layer 4 manages these functions. Here, another piece of header information is added to the packet that identifies it to the Transport Layer when it is received on the other end. This layer regulates data flow by controlling the message based upon the priority that it received. Layer 4 also resolves receiver and transmitter problems associated with all the packets that pass through its layer. This layer is responsible for sending acknowledgments forward or backward through the network stating that the data is either okay or needs to be resent because errors that it detected were unrecoverable.

Still left to discuss are the three remaining layers, Session, Presentation, and Application. From now on, the tasks become more complex and more information is added to (or stripped from) the overall data frame or packet as you move through the OSI model.

Layer 5: Session

Connections, known also as dialogs, between computers are managed and/or terminated between the local and remote applications.

Up to this point in the OSI model, the emphasis has been on bits and messages within the bit stream. The user on the network has been of no concern so far. Layer 5 is that portion of the network model that establishes when the two computers begin, use, and end this virtual connection. As the name implies, this period of use is called a "session." When a session is started, whether for simplex (one way), duplex (two way), or half-duplex (both directions on the same link, but reversing), this layer sets the checkpointing, any restart procedures, and the adjournment (termination) of that particular session.

You can think of a session on a network connection like a video editing session. Similar types of events happen. For example, a client books a session with the editor, who allocates either directly or indirectly the edit suite and associated equipment, and then requests the use of certain pooled resources for that particular edit session. Then the editor initiates the edit session by creating a name for the session. Starting with "edit#1," then "edit-#2," and so on, a number of active elements in each edit (or event) are arranged to create an overall flow to the program. The edit listing might not be in sequential order in the edit decision list or on the working screen. That is left to other tasks, but the process where these tasks are grouped is called a session. The session therefore becomes the binder of the processes.

Layer 5 also places markers that act as checkpoints in the data stream. These markers provide synchronization that in turn allows the session to resume, from that point forward, should a failure occur that temporarily interrupts that session. A network failure may be catastrophic or completely transparent to the user. Something as simple as a continuous collision of data or a hiccup on a router might signify a millisecond pause in the session and may not be visible without a network analyzer. However, these are things that slow down performance and become part of the software tuning that network LAN engineers and specialists look for in peaking up a network's overall throughput.

Layer 5 goes a few steps further. Its traffic control function determines when transmissions can occur, who goes first, and how long they will have to transmit. These sessions are virtual in nature and occur continuously with numerous other activities on the network overall.

Layer 6: Presentation

Layer 6 is the network's translator. It formats the data to and from the previous Session Layer so that it can be interpreted and utilized properly at the final stop, the Application Layer.

In Layer 6, protocols are converted, for example, from "terminal protocol" or "transmission protocol" into another protocol. This is where encryption and decryption occur, and where character sets (ASCII or EBCDIC) are managed. Data compression is also managed at Layer 6, and a function called redirection (which relates to server I/O operations) also occurs.

Layer 7: Application

As the topmost layer, Layer 7 acts as the gateway to the actual user-specified applications such as higher-level applications, email, and multimedia. Layer 7 is responsible for remote log-ins and the statistics of network management. This is the layer that is adjusted to fit specific industry needs. As such, and because different user programs have different requirements, it is difficult to describe the details of the protocols found at this level.

Layer 7 determines the identity and availability of communication partners for an application with data to transmit. For resource availability, Layer 7 decides whether there are sufficient network resources or the requested communication exists. Synchronizing communication between applications requires cooperation that is managed by Layer 7. Implementations handled by this Application Layer include Hypertext Transfer Protocol (HTTP), File Transfer Protocol (FTP), and Simple Mail Transfer Protocol (SMTP).

Networks

To set storage networks into perspective, we need to differentiate the types of communication networks as to their functionality.

Voice Networks

This was once the preeminent network before the generalization of the term network was commonplace. This, obviously, is the ever familiar telephony systems that at one time were managed by a human operator who literally plugged connections between one or more parties together. The voice network continued, albeit aided by analog switching technologies, up through the era of the digital switch. Today, the digital telephone network dwarfs the capabilities of the early analog connectivity and employs far more sophistication than ever before given the multidimensional services that voice communication systems have evolved to.

The integration of voice into data networks has become a reality. Packetized voice communications have enabled the transport of voice over the same networks that transport data now.

Data Networks

At its most simplistic level, a data network is an electronic communication process that allows for the orderly transmission and reception of data. The data may be files containing video and audio essence or metadata, email communications, or documents such as letters or spreadsheets. A primary difference that sets the data network apart from other forms of communication, such as an audio network, is that the data network is configured to transmit only data. It may be a simplex (one-way) or duplex (two-way) network. In contrast, the voice network, often employed for both voice communications and the transmission of data such as a facsimile transmission, is designed as a two-way system, that is, it must receive and transmit data.

Two basic types of data networks are in operation today—private and public. A private data network is essentially a local network designed for the transmission of data between the various groups or departments within a given entity, typically a business or a household. All the locations in that business may be included as nodes on the network. They communicate through a common server that functions as the repository for all data files that are used throughout the business. Private data networks may allow for data sharing between several geographic companies that are part of the same enterprise organization, usually on a closed basis. Connections made on this type of network are achieved through a virtual private network (VPN) that is resident on the primary network server or through connections provisioned by a communication carrier.

By contrast, a public data network is widely accessible to both residential and corporate clients on a given carrier network. Public networks may involve the utilization of multiple servers and connection to the network through several different processes. Public data networks involving a carrier are usually fee based. Through a subscription, the service provider creates a set of access credentials that permit the consumer to access authorized portions of the network and engage in functions commonly involved with data.

Public networks, such as those provisioned by a cable company, become a gateway to the Internet, a global system of interconnected networks that use the standard Internet Protocol Suite (TCP/IP) to serve users worldwide. The Internet has become a network of networks consisting of millions of private, public, academic, business, and government networks interconnected by a growing array of electronic and optical networking technologies. The public Internet is employed to carry information resources and services, best known as the interlinked hypertext documents of the World Wide Web (WWW). The "net" also has enabled the global infrastructure to support electronic mail.

Introducing Storage Networks

It was not long ago that data was stored on disk and data tape drives that were directly connected to the serving platform. Storage was seen as a peripheral to a computer and later on a server. Storage of media resources has similar parallels, stored first on videotape, and then as digital video emerged, that content was stored to disks on editing systems or on digital disk recorders (DDRs) for the short term.

In the data world, functions including access rights, security, virus protection, etc., were performed on the server. In the videotape-based media world, there were no security rights, no electronic access control, and no "requirement" for virus protection. Content would be physically contained on a videotape, protected only by the holder of that tape, a vault or a lock drawer. Once digital nonlinear editing was introduced, the potential for storage grew with the transport being either real-time video (over a broadcast centric infrastructure) or via a point-to-point interconnection over Ethernet. Nonlinear editing rapidly changed the video paradigm as it moved from tape ingest/tape output to the all digital file-based infrastructure, which we are familiar with today.

Storage networks are the extension of these models. For data, servers can be added with or without sufficient disk storage to manage the information sets it will process. For media, multiple sets of editing and processing hardware (servers and computers) can be added, but the storage requirements for these activities can be quite different than those for conventional data storage.

For these applications, there were growing needs to interconnect servers, computers, and islands of storage that for the most part remained as locally isolated platforms interconnected by conventional networking components such as NICs, twisted pair cables, and switches. The storage network began from a desire to serve those needs and has since become its own entity with choices including network-attached storage (NAS), storage area networks (SAN), and others.

Storage networks have become a fundamental technology just like local area networks and databases. They have opened up a wealth of new opportunities for the management of data as information. Storage networks have different requirements to fulfill, as with server-centric IT architectures.

Direct-Attached Storage

When storage is attached directly to the server or the host computer, this is referred to as "direct-attached storage" (DAS). DAS may be classified by the location where that storage resides, with respect to the host. For the purpose of continuity, we may assume that a host might be a server, a computer, or a device that performs services as applications.

DAS may be classified as either internal DAS or external DAS. Applications access DAS at block-level protocols.

Internal DAS

When the storage is physically located within the perimeter boundaries of the host and generally connected either by a parallel or a serial connection, it is considered internal direct-attached storage. Internal DAS is usually distance restricted to allow for high-speed connectivity. The internal bus architecture is limited to a finite number of devices that can be connected to the bus.

External DAS

When the host connects directly to storage via a protocol such as SCSI or Fibre Channel (FC), it is considered external storage. Again, these are one-to-one to one-to-a-few connections that still remain relatively close, physically, but are generally found to utilize much larger volumes of disk storage and, therefore, do not generally remain inside the host chassis. Figure 15.4 shows an example of how clients and servers would use external DAS.

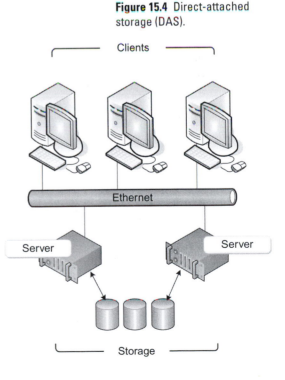

Figure 15.4 Direct-attached storage (DAS).

Interfaces for DAS

DAS, which was the original form of storage for host communications, requires a relatively low level of interface at a substantially less costly amount of investment. DAS, however, is limited in terms of scalability. Disk utilization is governed by the performance of DAS. Its throughput, cache memory, and lack of virtualization capabilities limit the implementation of DAS to all but a few applications.

Host and storage devices communicate with each other through predefined protocols that have been standardized and implemented on the disk drive controller. Chapter 5 covers the details of how the buses, ports and interfaces for DAS (and other disk systems) are interconnected to computers and hosts through various protocols which have continued to evolve through modern times.

Parallel SCSI and IDE/ATA specifications were the predominant interfaces when disk drives became more closely associated with PCs and local workstations. The PC world used IDE/ATA, and the Mac world seemed to go the SCSI route. The limitations of SCSI and IDE/ATA parallel cabling forced the migration to serial interfaces of the same or quite similar protocols on twisted pairs or sets of cables.

Filing Systems

The filing system and the storage system typically function in a master/slave relationship. The storage devices are typically slaved to the filing systems that write data into and read data from them. Filing systems may be either file systems or database systems.

File systems include the following:
- NTFS (Windows XP, 2000, NT, Vista, Windows 7)
- CDFS (Linux virtual file system)
- exFAT/FAT64
- UDFS (user defined file system)
- FAT and FAT32
- Unix file system (UFS) with its variants
  Database systems include the following:
- Sybase databases
- SQL databases
- Oracle databases
- Informix databases
- Veritas file system (VxFS)

Filing System Functions

In a broad view, there are two functions that filing systems will do: represent data to users and applications, and organize where that data is in storage. Data is typically organized in directories or folders in some hierarchical fashion. It depends upon whether that data is structured or unstructured as to how that data is actually organized.

Block Level

Filing systems organize where that data is placed in storage. Because of the drive architecture of most storage systems and to obtain reasonable access performance, the filing systems will scatter the data throughout the storage container (system) as part of its policies to make sure that all data can be accessed with a minimal impact to the users and applications. The structuring of this data is achieved by using the storage block addresses to determine where the data is placed. Because the disk drives maintain their own block translation tables, these storage block addresses are actually logical block addresses that point to the disk drive tables, which are the real knowledge base of where the data can be found on a block-by-block basis.

To summarize, block-level storage refers to the filing system sending commands to slave storage that instructs the storage on how to write and retrieve data from certain blocks.

File Level

Filing systems may be called upon to request data using what is called file-level storage. Here, the user-level data representation interface is done by the client using the data's filename. The name may be a directory location, a uniform resource locator (URL), or another data naming or locating principle. This methodology is referred to as the client/server communication model.

Functionally, the server receives a filing request, it looks up the data storage locations where the data is stored, and then it retrieves the data using block-level storage functions. The server sends this file as bytes, not as blocks because file-level protocols lack the ability to understand block-level commands. In contrast, block protocols are unable to convey file access requests or responses.

Filing and storing are tightly coupled, meaning that one cannot work without the other. The functions can exist on the same network; however, storing and filing traffic are transferred over a bus or a network independent of the physical connection or wiring used in support of the communications. It is the storage application protocols that differentiate the file-level from the block-level storage methodologies.

Network-Attached Storage

With the previous discussion on filers or filing systems, the next logical progression in storage is network-attached storage (NAS), the name for a preconfigured file server. The most elemental form for a NAS server is a set of components that are wrapped together and include one or two servers, some capacity of preconfigured storage, and a rudimentary special operating system (OS). Figure 15.5 shows a NAS server, where the server and the storage are integral components. The alternative is a NAS gateway, where the server appliance is placed external to the storage and interface components.

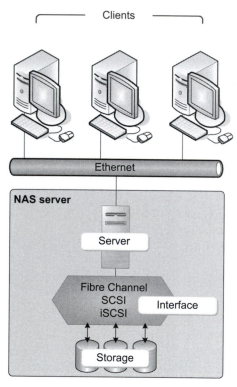

Figure 15.5 NAS server with the storage and interface preconfigured and integrated into a single package.

When the storage is external, a preconfigured server, called a NAS gateway, becomes the interface between the clients on the network and the storage interface (e.g., Fibre Channel, SCSI, or iSCSI). This configuration is shown in Figure 15.6 where a server with a scaled down operating system becomes a mid-level storage interface controller/file server.

NAS servers are specifically designed for file sharing, which allows the integrated and optimized operating system to focus on just those activities associated with receiving and delivering files over the network. This distinguishes the NAS server from the file server by allowing it to operate faster and be installed and configured quicker. This also allows for the NAS server to be very scalable.

In an organization, a NAS server could be dedicated for every project, for each editing group, or for individual departments. If an editing project or a feature production needed more storage, simply add it onto that network segment and work continues.

One caution: NAS server upgrade paths may be unclear and are limited to what the manufacturer has provided. Adding a server with better performance may not be possible without adding an entire new NAS system. NAS servers are not particularly well suited for intensive operations, such as databases, backups, or batch processes. Certainly some NAS products have been fully optimized for these kinds of activities or specifically for media-centric applications (such as scale-out NAS from Isilon (now a part of EMC) or from NetApp's unified storage architecture), but the more generic NAS products have much broader service applications, such as for email or websites.

Multiple Protocol Support

NAS servers often support multiple protocols, such as the older AppleTalk (since displaced with Mac OS X), the Server Message Block (SMB) or Common Internet File System (CIFS), and common network protocols such as Network File System (NFS), File Transfer Protocol (FTP), and Hypertext Transfer Protocol (HTTP). These protocols may not have sufficient performance for I/O-intensive operations even though they are designed for traditional file sharing activities. Note that I/O-intensive operations typically employ disk storage subsystems, not file servers, from which to draw their storage.

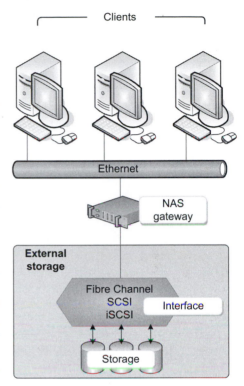

Figure 15.6 NAS gateway configuration with external storage.

Acceleration

Manufacturers that provide NAS solutions may build accelerators into their platforms that support specific performance functions and high availability. When file sizes get very large, typical to media operations such as high-definition video or Digital Picture Exchange (DPX) files used in the preparation of digital intermediaries or digital cinema releases, disk bandwidth becomes a governing factor that most storage architectures ignore. A high-performance NAS system must be capable of operating with a wide variety of file sizes. The environments found in motion picture productions, effects, and editing require massively concurrent access to many small files (metadata files, short clip segments, or graphics); but must also provide for high-throughput sequential data access to single large files.

File Size Optimization

NAS, when used in node or clustered configurations, allows the disk side of the storage platform to be optimized for a variety of file sizes. The operating system associated with the NAS can use different approaches in handling smaller files versus handling large files. Such an OS must be adaptive and leverage the CPU power against the I/O disk in order to increase performance for all file configurations.

Direct Access File System

Similar to NFS and CIFS, Direct Access File System (DAFS) allows applications to transfer data while bypassing operating system control, buffering, and network protocol operations that can bottleneck throughput.

DAFS Protocol

Remote file-access protocols have been in widespread use for more than 15 years for workgroup data sharing. Advantages have increasingly made DAFS attractive to the data center for use in database and local file-sharing applications.

DAFS is designed to take advantage of direct access transports (DATs) to achieve remote file access at CPU overheads that are as good as or better than what is achieved through block access, while retaining the advantages of the shared file-access paradigm.

The transport mechanism used by DAFS is the Virtual Interface (VI), a hardware application that transfers data to and from application buffers without using the operating system. This concept frees up the processor and operating system to perform other processes, allowing files to be accessed by servers using different operating systems. DAFS, a remote file-access protocol that uses a request-response protocol (like that in NFS), was designed for optimized clustered, shared-file network environments, for Internet, e-commerce, and database applications. It is also optimized for high-bandwidth InfiniBand networks and works with any interconnection that supports VI including Fibre Channel and Ethernet.

NetApp (Network Appliance) and Intel formed the DAFS Collaborative, an industry group of more than 85 companies whose target is to specify and promote DAFS. In 2001, SNIA (the Storage Networking Industry Association) took over that work.

Recent developments (2008) in system area networks have produced a new networking paradigm, that is, direct access transports (DATs). DATs exploit the remote direct memory access (RDMA) suite of capabilities that will enable enormous improvements in the performance, scalability, and reliability of data centers.

Examples of networks that support direct access include Virtual Interface on Fibre Channel (FC-VI), InfiniBand (http://www.ibta.org/), and the Remote Direct Data Placement (RDDP) protocol for the Internet (http://www.ietf.org/html.charters/rddp-charter.html and http://www.rdmaconsortium.org/).

Storage Area Network

A storage area network (SAN) is a high-speed dedicated network of shared storage devices and servers that is traditionally connected over Fibre Channel networks. It carries data between servers and to storage devices through switches specifically designed to carry the Fibre Channel (FC) protocols.

Before one looks at the SAN, an understanding of Fibre Channel is necessary, given that the concepts and functionality of a SAN grew out of the efforts of Fibre Channel technologies. The following sections provide an introductory thumbnail overview of Fibre Channel. This technology is one of the faster growing segments of networking architectures with multiple technical committees inside of INCITS continuing to provide many extensions to FC.

Fibre Channel Networks

Standardization and adoption of FC began in the 1988 time frame when it was introduced through the chartered efforts of the Fibre Channel Working Group to the American National Standards Group (ANSI). FC developed as an extension of work on the Intelligent Peripheral Interface (IPI) Enhanced Physical standard. FC was originally designed as a backbone technology for LAN connections. It would be six full years later before the interconnection standard would be adopted, and the Fibre Channel Association (FCA) would be founded.

As a high-speed network technology, FC initially had a throughput of 100 Mbytes/second, a much improved implementation over the 20 Mbytes/second speed of its closest competitor, Ultra SCSI, which at the time was the state-of-the-art for DAS. When configured in full duplex mode, FC can sustain a throughput of 200 Mbytes/second, with the latest improvements hitting 8 Gbits/second (in 8 GFC) for 1600 Mbytes/second, and product announcements (by QLogic in September 2010) for the 16 Gbits/second standard ratified by 16-Gbits Fibre Channel standard ratified by the ANSI INCITS T11.2 Technical Committee and announced by the Fibre Channel Industry Association (FCIA).

Channels and Networks

Fibre Channel combined two opposing methods of communications, channels, and networks to create the best of both worlds.

Channels operate in a closed master-slave environment. Channels are used for transferring data with error-free delivery and a lessened concern over transfer delays. Networks operate in an open, peer-to-peer, and unstructured environment. Networks transfer both data and media-related information that is time dependent—where error-free delivery is secondary.

Network communications offer more flexibility than channel communication technologies. Networks provide for greater geographic separation, and they are less encumbered by the effects of distance. For PCs, networks provide connectivity to, for example, servers and server-based applications, file and print services, and internal or dedicated intranets. This kind of network provides shared bandwidth and the capability to communicate with different systems. Network technologies also have the characteristics of lower performance than a channel, a high-protocol overhead, and a dynamic configuration.

Fibre Channel captures many of the benefits of both networks and channels. Before undertaking the design of a fabric, an understanding of Fibre Channel is essential. Going from DAS-attached SCSI to Fibre Channel—as SCSI over Fibre Channel—allows one to overcome the distance issues associated with SCSI and the scalability and accessibility issues of DAS, and allows for dynamic flexibility; all of the latter being better suited to FC than DAS or even NAS.

Fibre or Fiber

The spelling of Fibre Channel was chosen ("Fibre" as opposed to "fiber") because the physical serial media can be copper wire, coaxial cable, or fiber optic cable. The word "Channel" in this case does not refer to the channel protocol as described above.

Initiators and Targets

One of the terminology pairs found in describing data interchange grew out of the work on SCSI. Here devices identify themselves using a SCSI ID, a unique number that addresses each unique device on the bus. By itself, the SCSI bus can address up to eight logical units (LUNs). Typically, the numerical ordering for the LUNs is from 0 to 7, and each LUN can play the role of either a target or an initiator.

The "initiator" will generally issue a command or request, and the "target" will execute that request. SCSI, by design, must consist of at least one initiator and one target device, although some SCSI devices can act as both initiator and target.

Topologies

Three topologies are provided in the FC standard: point-to-point, a bidirectional connection between two devices; arbitrated loop (AL), a unidirectional ring whereby only two devices can ever exchange data between one another at a time; and fabric (sometimes capitalized as Fabric), a network that permits multiple devices to exchange information simultaneously without additional bandwidth restrictions. Arbitrated loop and fabric topologies are incompatible with each other due to the differences in their protocols.

Common to each of these topologies are the storage devices, servers, and switches. The fabric topology is the most common as it utilizes the best performance advantages of FC. Core-edge fabric is a popular design topology with multiple variations; mesh being one that is commonly deployed in SAN implementations.

Fibre Channel is not bound by dependency upon any one topology. This differs from what many were used to in network topologies such as token ring (IEEE 802.5), Ethernet (IEEE 802.3), and FDDI. Nearly all network transports are prohibited from sharing the same physical media because their access protocols were constructed strictly for only one use.

Fibre Channel was intentionally designed to support multiple topologies. Inherently a closed system, Fibre Channel relies on ports logging in with each other. If the topology is a fabric, it must trade information on characteristics and attributes so a harmony exists from the start of the session.

The important principle to realize is that management issues related to the topology have no bearing on Fibre Channel. Whether the fabric is a switch, a hub, a LAN/WAN, or a combination of the above, Fibre Channel expects the management to be handled externally from the process of configuring and moving frames and sequences around the connected network.

The selection of a topology for Fibre Channel is based upon system performance, budget, extensibility (growth), and hardware packaging.

Nodes, Links, and Ports

"Nodes" are Fibre Channel devices, each of which has at least one port. Workstations, disk arrays, disk drives, scanners, etc., can all be nodes. Ports provide access to other ports on other nodes. A "port" generally consists of an adapter and a certain level of software. When there is more than one port on a host node (i.e., a primary CPU or server), the software may be shared across all the ports—making the distinction between port and node somewhat fuzzy.

"Links" are pairs of signal-carrying media (two fibers, a pair of twisted copper wires, or two coaxial cables) that attach to the node ports. One carries data into the port, and the other carries data out. The topology of the Fibre Channel system consists of the physical media, transceivers, and the connectors that connect two or more node ports, which are interfaced through a global link module (GLM), an avenue that easily converts between fiber optic cable and copper wire as a connection medium.

FC Protocol Stack

The FC protocol stack is divided into four lower layers that describe the transmission technology (FC-0 through FC-3), and the upper layer (FC-4) that defines how the applications' (e.g., SCSI and IP) protocols are mapped onto the FC network.

The layering model for Fibre Channel is shown in Figure 15.7. The interface connection enters at the Physical portion (FC-0) of the model, shown at the bottom, and moves upward through the various levels until routed to appropriate other channels or networks. These levels are bidirectional, with each successive handoff from one level to the next having introduced all the necessary information to make flow possible, regardless of the connection on either side of the level boundaries.

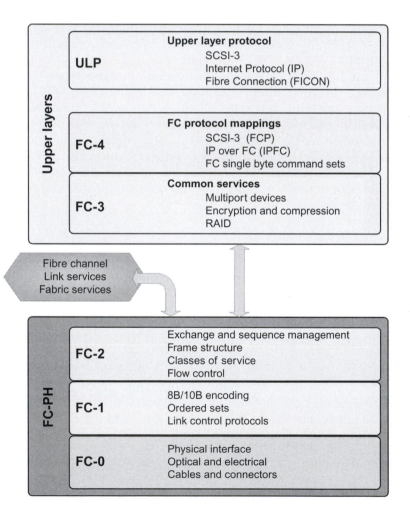

Figure 15.7 Fibre Channel protocol stack.

Physical Layer

The Fibre Channel Physical (FC-PH) interface, layers 0 through 2, was the first to be standardized. Historically, the first review of FC-PH was in January 1993, and the second review began in October 1993. FC-0 accepts the physical media input; at the time of the standardization, at specific speeds from 131 Mbits/second through 1 Gbit/second. Since then, this growth has now reached 8 Gbits/second.

The layering model for Fibre Channel is shown in Figure 15.7. Although the model continues to evolve, from a standard point, the FC protocol stack is like the OSI model for networking familiar to most IT-network technologists.

The interface connection enters at the Physical portion of the model, shown at the bottom, and moves upward through the various levels until it is sent to appropriate other channels or networks. The principle in these levels is that the signal path becomes bidirectional. Each successive hand-off from one level to the next has introduced all the necessary information to make flow possible, regardless of the connection on either side of the level boundaries.

From this point, the system makes the proper translation into the FC-1 level where the transmission protocol is defined. At the FC-1 level, 8B/10B encoding, error detection, and order of word transmission are set up. From here, in FC-2, the signaling protocol and framing, sequences, and exchanges are established.

FC-2 manages the exchange and sequence of data, the frame structure, the classes of service, and flow control. Once the properly configured data leaves the FC-PH standard, it enters the common services level, which is considered the entry point to the upper layers and upper layer protocols (ULPs) of the Fibre Channel stack.

Upper Layers

Fibre Channel's level FC-3 and level FC-4 are the two top levels of the Fibre Channel architectural model.

Level FC-3 is the level intended to provide common services and those necessary for advanced features. Striping is one of these proposed features. The intent in striping is to multiply bandwidth using multiple N_Ports in parallel to transmit a single information unit across multiple links.

Hunt groups, another of the common services in FC-3, are a set of associated N_Ports attached to a single node. When assigned a special identifier, any frame containing that identifier can be routed to any available N_Port within the set. This effectively permits more than a single N_Port to respond to the same alias address. By decreasing the chance of reaching a busy N_Port (one that has already been connected to another port), efficiency will be improved.

Multicasting is the delivery of a single transmission to multiple destination ports. This includes broadcasting to all N_Ports on a fabric or to a subset of the N_Ports on a fabric.

The highest level in the Fibre Channel stack is FC-4. This, like the highest layer in the OSI model, defines the application interfaces that can execute over Fibre Channel. Here, mapping rules for the upper layer protocols are defined so that they may be properly used on the levels below. Because Fibre Channel is capable of transporting both network and channel information, concurrently, this makes it possible to address a variety of existing protocols.

Above FC-4 is where additional ULPs are defined, such as how Internet Protocol (IP), the balance of the SCSI interfaces, and Fibre Connection (FICON) are enabled.

Both FC-4 and ULPs are considered application protocols. These layers map the application protocols on the underlying FC network. Protocol "mappings" define how these FC mechanisms are used in the applications.

Fiber Channel Ports, Links, and Fabric

The port is the fundamental building block of the FC network. Fibre Channel defines several types of ports and may be grouped in differing ways.

N_Port

Any port on a node device, e.g., a workstation, hard drive in an array, or a single disk, is an N_Port. Also known as the "node port," this is the end point in the fabric. This port is physically a host port (i.e., a host bus adapter—HBA) or a storage port that is connected to the FC switch, which becomes a part of the fabric.

NL_Port

In support of the Fibre Channel-Arbitrated Loop (FC-AL) topology, this port is also known as the "node port loop."

F_Port

The port on a switch that connects to the N_Port is also known as the "fabric port." This port cannot connect to an NL_Port because it cannot participate in FC-AL.

FL_Port

This port does participate in FC-AL and can connect to NL_Ports on the loop. Furthermore, this is the topology interface that connects a loop into a switch in a switched fabric.

Private and Public Loops

A "public loop" is where NL_Ports in the FC-AL participate in Fibre Channel-Switched Fabric (FC-SW). By contrast, an arbitrated loop without any switches (it may use a simple hub) is called a "private loop." Although a private loop contains nodes with NL_Ports, it does not contain any FL_Ports.

E_Port

Ports that connect switches are called E_Ports. They are also known as "expansion ports" and generally do not need to follow Fibre Channel protocols. E_Ports connect to other E_Ports through a link known as an inter-switch link (ISL).

Inter-Switch Link

The entity that typically connects Fibre Channel switches to one another.

Fabric

This topology is used to connect as many as 2^{24} devices in a cross point switch configuration. This topology allows many devices to communicate at the same time without the need to share the same media. It almost certainly requires the more expensive FC switches for implementation. Fabric technology, like advanced FC, is a very deep topic that is beyond the basic context of this thumbnail Fibre Channel overview.

G_Port

A port that acts as either an E_Port or an F_Port is called a G_Port. Its functionality is determined automatically during initialization.

GL_Port

A G_Port with loop capabilities.

Media

Despite the misconceptions in the name, Fibre Channel (not "fiber channel") can run over both copper and fiber optic (FO) media. Longer distances can be achieved with fiber, and although more expensive can be far more reliable. Fiber-optic implementations are on the rise and may overtake copper media in the next few years. Up to 100 Mbytes/second data rates can run on both copper and fiber (distance limited in some cases), but rates in excess of 200 Mbytes/second and 400 Mbytes/second require fiber optic media.

For copper, acceptable cable types include shielded, high-performance video cable, and shielded twisted pair (STP); with the most common implementation as STP using a D-subminiature 9-pin connector (sometimes abbreviated DB-9).

For fiber optic media, choices include 62.5-mm multimode, 50-mm multimode, and single mode. Typically, an SC connector is used, but that becomes manufacturer/interface vendor specific.

FC Frame

The frame is block of bytes packaged together that includes control information similar to addressing. A Fibre Channel frame, as shown in Figure 15.8, consists of multiple transmission words. The length of the frame may be up to 2148 bytes—with the payload from 0–2112 bytes.

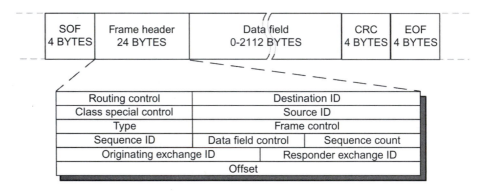

Figure 15.8 Fibre Channel frame with header details.

A frame header is 24-bytes long and is used at the transport level (FC-2) to carry control information. Inside this header is data that identifies the sender, the destination, the protocol, and the type of information.

- Source ID (S_ID)
- Destination ID (D_ID) (standard FC addresses for the source and destination ports)
- Sequence ID (SEQ_ID)
- Originating Exchange ID (OX_ID) (identifies the frame as a component of a sequence or an exchange)

- Sequence Count (SEQ_CNT)
- Responder Exchange ID (RX_ID)
- Additional control fields

The "start of frame" (SOF) and the "end of frame" (EOF), each 4-bytes long, become the frame boundary limiter. A 4-byte cyclic redundancy check (CRC), generated for each frame, follows the data payload.

Fibre Channel frames are grouped into sequences, and then sequences are grouped into exchanges.

Figure 15.9 Fibre Channel point-to-point topology.

Fibre Channel Point-to-Point

The simplest of the suite of Fibre Channel connectivity, this mode allows for only two devices to be connected in a one-to-one operational configuration (Fig. 15.9). It offers only limited connectivity and cannot be scaled to large numbers of network devices. DAS will utilize point-to-point connectivity.

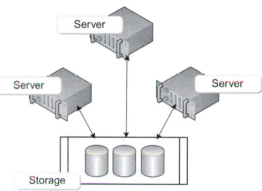

Fibre Channel Arbitrated Loop

Using a shared loop, this implementation is similar to the token ring topology with the physical arrangement of a star. FC-AL must arbitrate for its attention, with the highest priority winning. Only a single device can perform I/O operations on the loop at any given time. Figure 15.10 shows the FC-AL connection topology for servers and external storage.

Figure 15.10 Fibre Channel-Arbitrated Loop (FC-AL) topology.

This technology was used in the earliest implementations of FC on videoserver platforms. It worked well until it could no longer be scaled any further. A simple FC hub (not necessarily a switch) can be used to tie the devices together.

FC-AL must share the bandwidth throughout the entire loop. Data having to wait their turn while others get attention results in lower data transmission throughput.

FC-AL only allows for 8-bit addressing and supports not more than 127 devices on a loop. Adding or removing a device results in having to reinitialize the loop, which disrupts data traffic until completed.

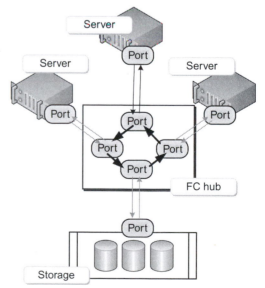

Fibre Channel Switched Fabric

Abandoning the loop and point-to-point limitations required the creation of what has become

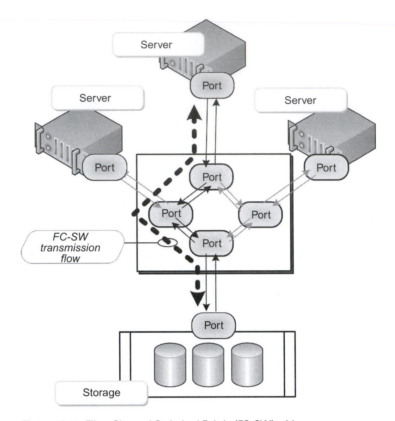

Figure 15.11 Fibre Channel Switched Fabric (FC-SW) with one transmission path shown.

the primary reason for utilizing Fibre Channel in SANs. A FC switched fabric network (see Fig. 15.11) provides for dedicated bandwidth allocation and a high degree of scalability. The fabric is a logical space where all nodes can communicate among each other in the network. This space can be created with a single switch or a network of switches.

As part of the fabric addressing scheme in a FC-SW environment, each switch is provided a unique domain identifier. The nodes in a switched fabric do not share a loop, but data is transferred through dedicated node paths.

The intelligence in a FC-SW topology is significant. The switch handles the data traffic (frame routing) from an initiator node to a target node directly through its switch ports. Using the same log-in procedures, traffic can be isolated from other node paths, thus preventing latencies in delivering data to the other ports.

Zoning

A switch function in FC, zoning enables the logical segmentation of nodes within the fabric. Through the log-in procedures, when a host device or storage array logs into the fabric, it becomes registered with the name server. When a port logs in, it goes through the discover process based upon those devices registered in the name server. Zoning allows only the members of the same zone to establish services as the link level.

There may be multiple zones defined in a fabric, but only a single zone can be active at a given time. Members may be associated with more than one zone and are defined in a zone hierarchy during configuration. A port or a node may be a member of more than one zone as well.

Zone sets, also known as zone configurations, are the makeup of the groupings of zones that can be enabled (activated) or disabled (deactivated) at any time by a single fabric entity. Like before, only one zone set per fabric is allowed to be active at the same time.

Naming Zones and Devices

The preferred means of naming these zones is through the 64-bit unique identifier called the World Wide Name (WWN). FC uses the World Wide Node Name (WWNN) or the World Wide Port Name (WWPN), which are assigned dynamically (unlike the FC address) in a similar fashion to how Media Access Control (MAC) addresses are used in IP networking. It is the name server in the FC environment that tracks the association of the WWNs to the dynamically assigned FC addresses for nodes.

Fibre Channel Class Support

Fibre Channel uses the term "class of service" to describe communication strategies for making connections or conveying information for a wide range of needs. Some of the classes, Classes 1–3, are routinely used in FC services; with other classes (Classes 4 and 5) not employed as often.

FC Class 1

Based on hard, circuit-switched connections where the complete path is established before data transfer begins. When a host and a device are linked, that path is not available to other hosts. Connection time is short, and this method is used for rapid, high-rate high-volume data transmission.

FC Class 2

A frame-switched service does not have a dedicated connection. Delivery is guaranteed, and a receipt (or acknowledgment) is returned. If data cannot be delivered, a "busy signal" is returned, and the transmission must be retried.

An optional mode, called Intermix, can be selected. Intermix reserves the full bandwidth as a dedicated connection—but allows excess bandwidth, idle Class 1 time, to be allocated for connectionless traffic. This is an efficiency plus in Fibre Channel and maximizes the use of links for more than one class of service. This class will confirm delivery of data.

Intermix

Intermix is an option of FC Class 1 whereby FC Class 2 and FC Class 3 frames may be transmitted at times when FC Class 1 frames are not being transmitted. Both N_Ports and the fabric must support Intermix for it to be utilized.

FC Class 3

Also called datagram service, Class 3 is similar to Class 2, but is connectionless. By eliminating the requirement for confirmation of received data, delivery can be made to several devices attached to the fabric. This one-to-many form of transmission does provide notification to the sender that data has been received. If one or more of the user's links are busy, the system cannot know to retransmit the data. Datagram delivery is not confirmed.

Delivery time for these services is a key factor in deciding which class of service to employ. When the transmission distance is a factor, and time is a key, it may be prudent to determine which service is best for the application required. This is where the final class of service, Class 4, fits in.

FC Class 4

These upper classes are less used and not as well published compared with the lower three. FC Class 4 uses virtual connections (or virtual circuits [VCs]) rather than dedicated connections. It is still a connection-oriented type of service, but Class 4 distributes the bandwidth of a port among several destinations. This class will confirm delivery.

Class 4 provides fractional bandwidth allocation of the resources of a path through a fabric that connects two N_Ports. Class 4 can be used only with the pure fabric topology. One N_Port will set up a VC by sending a request to the fabric indicating the remote N_Port as well as quality of service parameters. The resulting Class 4 circuit will consist of two unidirectional VCs between the two N_Ports. The VCs need not necessarily be at the same speed.

Like the Class 1 dedicated connection, Class 4 circuits will guarantee frames arrive in the order they were transmitted and will provide acknowledgement of delivered frames (Class 4 end-to-end credit). The major difference is that an N_Port may have more than one Class 4 circuit, possibly with more than one other N_Port at the same time. In a Class 1 connection, all the resources are dedicated to the two N_Ports; however, in Class 4, the resources are divided up into potentially many circuits. The fabric in turn regulates traffic and manages buffer-to-buffer flow control for each VC separately.

FC Class 5

This class is not described in the FC-PH documents. Class 5 involves isochronous, just-in-time service and is still undefined, or may possibly be abandoned altogether.

FC Class 6

FC Class 6 provides support for multicast service through a fabric and is similar to Class 1. Procedurally, a device that needs to transmit frames to more than one N_Port at a time sets up a Class 1 dedicated connection with the multicast server within the fabric. The multicast server then sets up individual dedicated connections between the original N_Port and all the destination N_Ports. The multicast server carries the responsibility for replicating and forwarding the frame to all other N_Ports in the multicast group. N_Ports become members of a multicast group by registering with the Alias Server at the same well-known address.

FC Class Commonalities

FC classes 1 through 3 are the three most popular in use for SANs in a Fibre Channel fabric. FC Class 1 and FC Class 4 employ fixed routing, are circuit switched, and require a setup and a tear down. FC Class 2 and FC Class 3 utilize adaptive routing, frame-switched service and may encounter routing delay and potential out-of-order delivery.

Flow Control

When a device receives data (or frames) at a rate faster than it can process them, bottlenecks occur, and failures in the transmission will happen. Flow control is intended to mitigate these problems before they occur. Without flow control, a device is forced to drop some of the frames. Fibre Channel uses a built-in flow control mechanism as its solution to this problem.

Flow control functionality works as follows: a device can transmit frames to another device only when the other device is ready to accept them. Ahead of the devices sending data to each other, they will login to each other. The login administration processes establish a "credit," which refers to the number of frames a device can receive at a time. This value is exchanged with the other device during login, for approval and to alert both of how many frames the other can receive. As the data flow continues, and once enough frames have been transmitted, i.e., "credit runs out," no more frames can be transmitted until the destination device indicates it has processed one or more frames and is ready to receive new ones. The intent is to prevent any device to be overrun with frames.

Fibre Channel uses two types of flow control: buffer-to-buffer and end-to-end.

Buffer-to-Buffer

This form of flow control deals only with the link between an N_Port and an F_Port or between two N_Ports. Both ports on the link can exchange values of how many frames they are willing to receive at a time from the other port. This value becomes the other port's BB_Credit value, which remains constant for as long as the ports are logged in. For example, when ports A and B log into each other, A may report that it is willing to handle 4 frames from B; B might report that it will accept 8 frames from A. Thus, B's BB_Credit is set to 4, and A's is set to 8.

Each port will keep track of the respective credit, which is called BB_Credit_CNT. It is first initialized to zero, then as each frame is transmitted, BB_Credit_CNT will be incremented by one. In return, the value is decremented by 1 for each R_RDY Primitive Signal received from the other port.

Transmission of an R_RDY indicates the port has processed a frame, freed up a received buffer, and is ready for another. Once the BB_Credit_CNT reaches BB_Credit, the port cannot transmit another frame until it receives an R_RDY.

End-to-End

End-to-end flow control is not concerned with individual links; instead, it deals with the source and destination N_Ports. While similar to buffer-to-buffer flow control, the difference is when the two N_Ports log into each other, they report how many receive buffers are available for the other port. This value becomes

EE_Credit. Like buffer-to-buffer, EE_Credit_CNT is set to zero after login and increments by one for each frame transmitted to the other port. Upon reception of an ACK Link Control frame from that port, it is decremented. ACK frames can indicate that the port has received and processed one frame, N frames, or an entire sequence of frames.

Fibre Channel over Ethernet

Fibre Channel over Ethernet (FCoE) enables the convergence of Fibre Channel-based storage and Ethernet-based data traffic onto an enhanced 10-Gbit Ethernet (10 GbitE) network. FCoE is a standard of mapping of Fibre Channel frames over selected full duplex IEEE 802.3 networks and is the name given to a technology being developed (in 2010) within INCITS Technical Committee T11 as part of the FC-BB-5 (Fibre Channel Backbone) project. The mapping allows Fibre Channel to leverage 10-Gbit Ethernet networks while still preserving the Fibre Channel protocol. FCoE essentially maps Fibre Channel natively over Ethernet while being independent of the Ethernet forwarding scheme.

The FCoE protocol specification replaces the FC-0 and FC-1 layers of the Fibre Channel stack with Ethernet, and retains the native Fibre Channel constructs for a seamless integration with existing Fibre Channel networks and management software.

Those that use Ethernet for TCP/IP networks and Fibre Channel for storage area networks (SANs) now have the option of another network protocol that runs on Ethernet, alongside traditional Internet Protocol (IP) traffic. The difference with FCoE is that it runs alongside IP on Ethernet, unlike iSCSI, which runs on top of IP using TCP.

FCoE does not use IP (Layer 3) and is not routable at the IP layer, thus it will not work across routed IP networks.

FCoE requires three specific modifications to Ethernet in order to deliver the capabilities of Fibre Channel in SANs:
- Encapsulation of the native Fibre Channel frame into an Ethernet Frame
- Extensions to the Ethernet protocol to enable a lossless Ethernet fabric
- Replacing the Fibre Channel link with MAC addresses in a lossless Ethernet

The Converged Network

Computers employing FCoE now use a Converged Network Adapter (CNA), which is both a Fibre Channel host bus adapter (HBA) and an Ethernet network interface card (NIC) to the server, yet it appears as a single Ethernet NIC to the network. The CNA essentially provides a new approach to consolidation of server I/Os over a single Ethernet network, thus reducing network complexity.

With FCoE, network (IP) and storage (SAN) data traffic can essentially be consolidated with a single switch. The ability to combine Fibre Channel with 10-Gbit Ethernet (GigE), so that the the enterprise can consolidate I/O, is referred to as "unified I/O." The value in this implementation is that it reduces the number of NICs required to connect to disparate storage and IP networks, decreases the number of cables and adapters, lowers the overall power and cooling costs, and increases utilization of the servers through server virtualization technologies.

Fibre Channel SAN Components

Up to this point in this chapter, we have looked at network storage technologies that include direct-attached storage (DAS), network-attached storage (NAS), and the roots of Fibre Channel (FC). With this background and its perspectives on applications and technology, it is time to introduce the concepts of the storage area network (SAN).

In actuality, many of the protocols upon which a FC-SAN is built were covered in the previous sections on Fibre Channel. To paraphrase again, a storage area network is provisioned to use Fibre Channel switches to carry (transmit and receive) data between servers (or hosts) and storage devices. The SAN provides the roadmap for the consolidation of storage by allowing it to be shared across multiple servers and across other networks.

Fibre Channel storage area networks use Fibre Channel exclusively for the transport of the commands, data, and status information. Originally, the SAN was implemented on a local basis and to a relatively discrete set of servers and storage systems. Many were purpose built to serve a particular storage requirement, to extend bandwidth on a platform, or as a specific solution to a sprawl of computers, servers, and islands of storage that collectively drew down on the overall computer power of the system as a whole.

These early systems would use a hub as the center of the spokes connecting storage and servers together. Those applications utilitzed less costly peripheral products, such as fabric switches, and for many satisfied the requirements of adding capacity and increasing bandwidth simultaneously. Videoserver platforms that began looking at external storage quickly jumped on the Fibre Channel bandwagon.

Elements of the SAN

Three fundamental components make up the SAN at its highest level (see Fig. 15.12):
- Network infrastructure
- Servers
- Storage

Another level of granularity of components for the SAN breaks these primary components down slightly further into:
- Storage arrays
- Cabling (copper or fiber optic)
- Node ports
- Software (for the management of the SAN)

Storage systems may include intelligent storage systems (discussed in a later chapter); arrays comprised of disks in RAID configuration and specifically Fibre Channel disk drives that primarily employ SCSI protocols; tape library or virtual tape library (VTL) storage systems; or a combination of some or all of these elements.

Management software are both those embedded into the FC switches, nodes, and storage systems; and those loaded onto the host devices that support the applications through terminals that can configure and manage the data flow parameters. This software will further control the logical partitioning, called zoning, described earlier. This software also provides for the management of the HBAs, storage components, and associated interconnecting devices or subsystems.

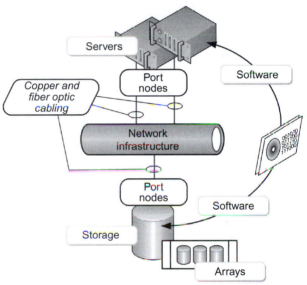

Figure 15.12 Elements of a SAN.

Topologies or Architectures

A defining element of the SAN is its "topology" through which the SAN connects to devices on the network. The word "architecture" is also tightly coupled with the topology. Much like the term when it is applied to buildings, the "architecture" of any system is comprised principally of a formal description that defines the properties of that system, and how it "appears" to the other associated elements within that system.

Topology is a somewhat more ambiguous term depending upon what it refers to and in what context it is placed. A topology might be expressed as a layout or pattern of interconnections for various elements within a system, typically in this discussion, a network. It may be virtual, physical, or structural. Although it is a graphical map of the connectivity of a network, while it describes how the cables are connected to devices, it lacks in defining the functionality of how those devices interact or influence one another.

Topologies may be both physical and logical, and they may be identical or indifferent to each other on that same network. This chapter has already discussed the topologies of a networked storage system, in terms of switches, for example if the system is point-to-point connected, if it is on a switched architecture, and the like.

Homogeneous or Heterogeneous

Often used to describe storage and storage networking environments, homogenous is an environment where the components are provided by the same vendor directly or via a partner relationship. Heterogeneous is a mixture of technologies from multiple vendors, provided as an environment with interoperable components. For example, a heterogeneous SAN would likely include switches running in interoperability mode.

The homogenous environment will most likely be a proprietary or vendor-specific implementation where all the system components are provided by a single company that makes all the elements under their own brand (e.g., Brocade, Cisco, or QLogic SAN). A storage vendor-specific SAN that pairs switches and adapters from a partner with specific storage solutions would be another example of a homogeneous design.

Even though another vendor may use the same partner switches and adapters, the storage vendor might not provide support for that certain other vendors' storage—thus, this becomes a heterogeneous "storage environment."

Prominent Fibre Channel Topologies

At this juncture, we will focus attention on the more prominent topologies in Fibre Channel: island, mesh, collated, and core-edge fabric. Although each topology serves a particular niche, of the groups described, core-edge fabric is the most scalable and widely deployed in SAN implementations.

Designing any scale of a SAN core-edge fabric can be a complicated process. A Fibre Channel SAN may consist mainly of an individual fabric or multiple sets of fabrics that are connected through a FC routing function. At an enterprise level such a SAN might have the architectural look shown in Figure 15.13.

Island SAN

When the SAN exists as a discrete, isolated entity within a larger SAN, it is called an "island SAN." The components are usually located all within the same building or a single room.

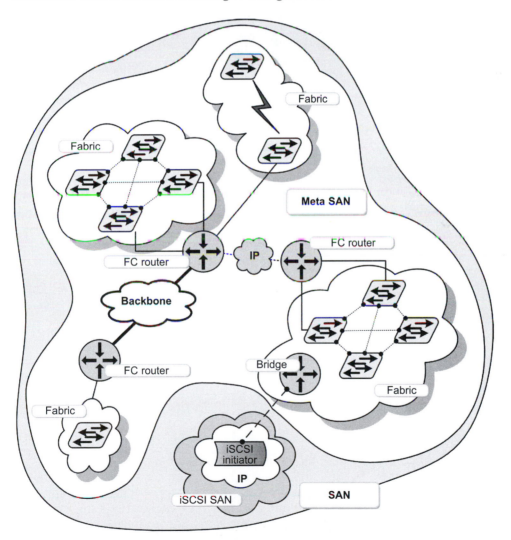

Figure 15.13 A complete storage area network (SAN) schematic.

SAN islands will typically evolve as the organization grows. When a large SAN consists of several islands, those individual islands may be interconnected and are enabled so as to share data collectively. There are several ways in which SAN island interconnection can be accomplished, although they each carry their own challenges (see Fig. 15.14).

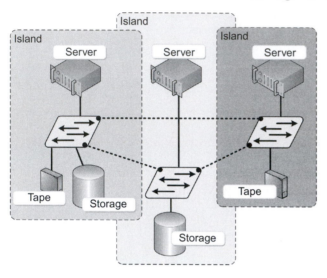

Figure 15.14 Three SAN islands set into a meshed SAN.

Even though a SAN island may be physically located to a specific site, it may be used for many applications, by more than a single department within that organization, or by multiple organizations within the enterprise. If necessary, an administrator may elect to allocate all of a SAN island's resources to a single critical application.

Drive sharing and data copying are a common activity among SAN islands. Data redundancy, where important files or folders are duplicated, and then contained on multiple SAN islands, is not uncommon.

Island SANs that are connected together through inter-switch links (ISLs) become a "meshed SAN." The drawback is when interconnecting these smaller switches into a meshed fabric, the number of required ISLs quickly grows per the number of included switches. This limits the number of ports available on the fabric.

Collocated SAN

When the approach blends storage devices and host connections on the edge switches while keeping paired devices as close together as possible, this is referred to as a "collocated SAN." With this structure, as depicted in Figure 15.15, scalability is much like that of a pure core-edge design. In a collocated SAN, none of the devices are placed on the core; in turn, this allows for much better performance since the resources are kept close to their users.

Over the long term, the maintenance of a collocated SAN grows in difficulty. Edge switches are not usually expandable. To allow for future growth, ports on every edge will need to be reserved, burdening the size of the switches from the first level of implementation. As time goes on, connections to devices that are distant from its user tend to stay put for the long term. This inherently reintroduces latency and ISL congestion

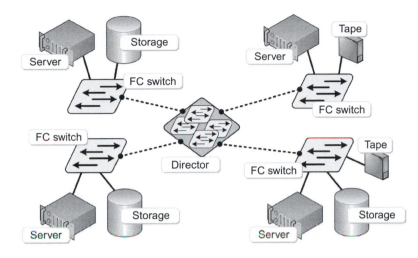

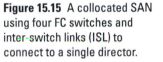

Figure 15.15 A collocated SAN using four FC switches and inter-switch links (ISL) to connect to a single director.

concerns that the collocated design concept was supposed to mitigate.

A real benefit of a collocated design is that SAN islands are already collocated. Adding a director to interconnect the outlying fabrics instantly transforms it into a collocated SAN.

Fabric Protection

An element that is critical to any design and should always be in place is that of dual redundant fabrics. At the enterprise level, an interconnected SAN is the seawall around the entire organization's data. Should an island SAN sink, it then only takes out a few applications. One method to protect the enterprise from a complete collapse is to implement two mirror-image fabrics and connect every host and storage system to each. Pathing software is then used to maintain connectivity should one SAN fails.

Even though virtual SAN technologies provide extra protection from a fabric failure, never rely on a single piece of hardware to provide both paths; instead separate the fabrics with a physical "air-gap" between the two.

Core-Edge

Usually comprised of switches, this is a relatively inexpensive means to add more hosts in a fabric. Best practice core-edge SAN designs can be built out gradually over time. Such a design is allowed to evolve from a chain of isolated SAN islands to a completely unified, large-scale SAN (see Fig. 15.16).

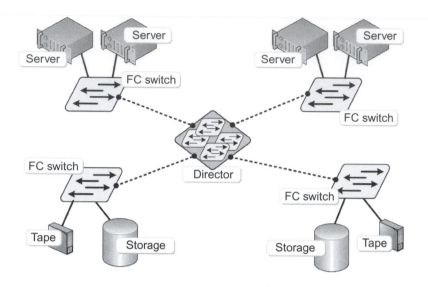

Figure 15.16 A core-edge SAN configuration.

Scaling the SAN

It goes without saying, again, that growth is inevitable. Going back to the well for new equipment, especially those intangible items that accountants see little to no ROI from, is a task most of us do not enjoy going through. Careful planning and the appropriate reuse of components can make scaling for the future a productive process.

Most sites would not have the luxury of director-class hardware, so determining where to relocate the current switches into a new topology can be remedied by having those legacy switches become the edge switches in the new environment. One of the front end postures you should take includes upgrading to newer switches if you have products that are more than a year old. If you are currently using FC hubs, for example in an arbitrated loop (FC-AL), and you do not need that kind of connectivity, this would be a good time to retire them.

Avoid heterogeneous SANs. Pick a single vendor for the new SAN, and swap out other equipment where appropriate.

Be sure to understand, and evaluate, the compatibility of firmware revisions running on the new (and existing) switches being consolidated. There may be special compatibility mode settings necessary to make the different switch types work together.

To avoid SAN segmentation, make sure the identifiers (such as domain IDs and zone names) are unique on all the switches. Implementing a segregated core-edge design requires that the storage and servers be reconnected to their respective sides of the director. Collocated SANs will require little reconnection; however, port reservation for the future is a necessity for growth.

Next Generation SANs

In the following chapter, the concepts of intelligent storage will be developed. The advancements since the introduction of 1 Gbit/second Fibre Channel have extended well into the 8 Gbits/second range and are headed toward 16 Gbits/second; with expectations far beyond that. However, the increased development of Ethernet added to the other advancements such as Fibre Channel over Ethernet, Fiber Channel over IP, and other converged network infrastructures brings another added dimension to storage at a network level.

Further Readings

Gupta, M. (2002). *Storage Area Network fundamentals*. Cisco Press.

Thornburgh, R. H., & Schoenborn, B. J. (2001). *Storage Area Networks - designing and implementing a mass storage system*. Hewlett-Packard Professional Books.

InterNational Committee for Information Technology Standards (INCITS) on storage, and their associated Technical Committees (TC):
http://www.incits.org/

T10 - SCSI Storage Interfaces technical committee
T11 - Fibre Channel Interfaces technical committee
T13 - ATA Storage Interfaces technical committee

Fibre Channel Industry Association.
http://www.fibrechannel.org/

Storage Networking Industry Association.
http://www.snia.org

16

HIGH-PERFORMANCE AND SHARED STORAGE

Scaling your storage system without having to engage a forklift upgrade is a challenge that will haunt IT administrators, managers, and the finance department of organizations throughout the life of any system. As the demands for capacity increase and throughput continues to grow, eventually one of many situations will negatively expose decisions that were made early in the deployment of the current "legacy" storage system in use today. Some of these situations are unavoidable, as they are a product of the normal and expected course of business activities and were financially impractical to address at the time. Other practices that can be employed today may reduce the impact of major changes that will naturally occur as technology advances.

This chapter looks at the causes and effects of these situations, in hopes of preparing the user for the growth they will have to address in the future. The topics that follow should help to expose the various solutions and guide the users to a properly crafted storage solution for today and tomorrow.

In the concluding portion of this chapter, a deeper look into shared storage is taken where many of the elements previously discussed in the chapter will be applied to considerations for core shared storage platforms that must be designed to live in the real world of progressively adding storage (and client workstations) to a legacy environment.

KEY CHAPTER POINTS

- How to employ the concepts of a SAN storage accelerator appliance to improve overall performance in a file-sharing environment
- Issues in production and postproduction workflows that develop when certain forms of storage (DAS, NAS, or SAN) architectures are utilized to solve short-term issues, but with long-term impacts

- What intelligent, adaptive storage means and how is it applied to systems that must handle large file sizes in real time and in concurrent collaborative work environments such as those in postproduction

- How extreme performance, scalability, and advanced data management can aid in supporting SAN, NAS, and combinations of the two

- Storage consolidation for smaller SANs, and issues of contention, cache coherency, latency, and load balancing; plus the impacts on I/O block size requests and file-sharing SANs

- Scaling of NAS systems, including topics regarding limitations, management, and latency

- Scale-up and scale-out systems, what they are, and their advantages and disadvantages

- Considerations for constructing, upgrading, and using a shared storage environment; and how resiliency, performance, connectivity, and expansion are so interrelated

Applications for High-Performance Storage

High performance intelligent storage platforms continue their advancement as they are deployed within media organizations and service providers at an astounding rate. Such storage systems are now far more prevalent in companies that develop and produce content, that distribute content to users, and that provide the production platforms for the gaming, motion picture production, postproduction, and broadcast entertainment businesses. These storage platforms are now integral components in the workflow. They provide the scalability, performance, density, and power efficiency necessary to store and manage the enormous amounts of unstructured data that power the digital entertainment world.

The entertainment industry has moved deep into the entire digital world. Although today's content is created and stored digitally, there has become a growing fundamental migration in how that content is not only produced but also distributed; one that leverages high-bandwidth distribution via the Internet at a level of consumer quality equal to or better than broadcast high-definition television and video. This migration is taking place across the entire industry from broadcast television stations to film studios, to production houses, and to digital intermediate (DI) facilities.

The industries have all witnessed an extremely rapid growth in very large media files. These digital images, video, and audio account for 85% of total storage capacity; material that consists of unstructured data as opposed to the transaction-based data that dominated many organizations in recent times.

Traditional storage architectures that were optimized for transactional data are not well suited for this evolving digital world. Storage systems must now employ technologies capable of handling very large files in real time. The platforms must be able to expedite workflows, while providing the paths to stay ahead of this exponential capacity growth that requires supporting millions of users, storing billions of images, videos, and music files, and delivering these files to other systems with submillisecond response times. All the while, these systems must continually provide the ability to stream massive amounts of high-definition content without ever missing a single frame. Storage platforms must be capable of delivering write performance that equals system read performance. The systems must be able to provide a guaranteed quality of service with predictable performance on large files while simultaneously ingesting multiple sets of data streams.

Postproduction

Motion picture and digital media content creation are made possible by the collaboration of teams that comprise a massive mix of production activities. Those activities include the creation of visual effects, 2D and 3D animation, main titles, and trailers, and mixing sound. The releases consist of feature films, television, advertising, interactive visual media, and video games. Today's postproduction houses and boutiques feature many subsets of the same digital capabilities; some offering end-to-end solutions and others only providing a specific, usually specialized activity.

In order to meet the often stringent deadlines, real-time collaborative workflow is required. Collaboration is essential to a successful postproduction process, no matter if the company offers the full end-to-end solution or is simply a segment of the overall production process. These operations cannot tolerate system downtime, inaccessible data, or reduced throughput because of data transfer bottlenecks.

Today's workflows must now create content of increasing complexity for a distributed environment and at a mix of resolutions ranging from HD (1K) to 2K, 4K, and 8K (UHDTV) formats. Most organizations are finding that they are technically challenged when it comes to supporting a mixture of real-time workflows, including concurrent multiuser editing and colorists and growing file sizes that begin at ingestion station and then continue to expand throughout the postproduction process or through multiple releases of the content that must be packaged per the contractual requirements from the marketing side of the organization. Conventional storage systems are often found to be inadequate for this level of postproduction, so they turn to highly intelligent, high-performance storage solution platforms and subsystems for their answers.

In a working postproduction environment, a central storage system may be called upon to support edit-in-place functionality for dozens of Apple Final Cut Pro uncompressed HD workstations while at the same time streaming four sets of uncompressed 4K content streams for the editing processes of a feature film. Such extreme performance might require as much as 240 GBytes/second of scalable storage capacity, which then must support open systems consisting of multiple CPUs, operating systems, and file systems; all in a collaborative file-sharing environment.

Broadcast

Broadcast entities now find themselves developing content, preparing content in multiple formats, and then distributing multiple streams in support of consumer demands for on air services, online streaming for mobile phones and media players, and delivery to Web portals for distribution over the Internet. In an environment that thrives on competition comprised of a mixture of hundreds of cable channels, satellite broadcast, plus YouTube, Netflix, and video-on-demand, the activities supporting content production and delivery are growing at an alarming rate.

These expanding activities require another breed of high throughput and scalable storage systems that not only are able to support real-time collaborative workflows but also must be able to store the billions of files that make up the unstructured data found in static images, videos, and music.

This caliber of storage system must be designed to specifically handle extremely large files at very high throughput. On a daily basis, the volume of new content can easily exceed multiple terabytes, which can only be enabled through concurrent digitization on multiple ingest stations.

All the while, this same storage platform must be capable of concurrently delivering multiple gigabytes of data to editing stations, playout servers, transcode farms, render farms, and content distribution networks. Video playout depends upon the flawless streaming of video, so the storage platforms must deliver real-time performance with uncompromising reliability.

Graphics and effects have historically operated in a parallel job task fashion, but usually on silos of individual stores that are either locally attached to the workstation or contained in small NAS (occasionally SAN) systems optimized for the types

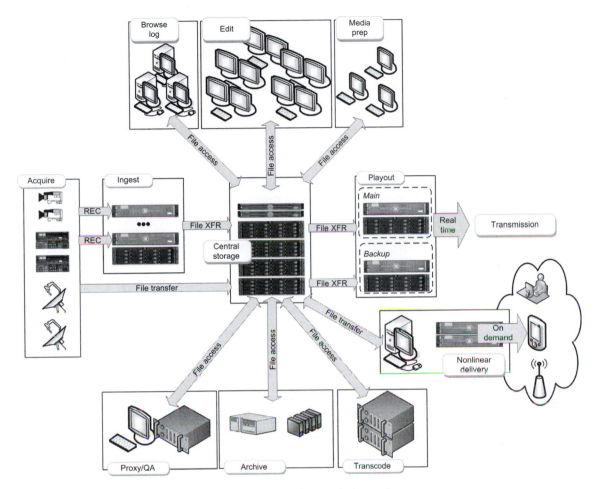

Figure 16.1 A typical large-scale broadcast production and transmission environment.

of workflow suited to their needs. In contrast, news editing environments have traditionally found their staff doing most of their operational duties sequentially, rather than in parallel. Intelligent storage systems offer parallel storage solutions that are changing the news and graphics/effects models by enabling a centralized repository of managed files with performance equaling and usually exceeding earlier archaic solutions.

Video Gaming

Game makers continually must address the challenges of producing highly successful upcoming products in shorter release cycles. The games must now be tailored with heightened sophistication and expectations are higher for both physical media releases and the growing number of online multiplayer gamers. Although gaming on physical media continues to enjoy growth, the new contender has become distribution platforms that rely on the Internet for both content and live gaming, both of which are providing new revenue streams for video game companies.

New intelligence must now be built into storage systems so as to handle the large multimedia files and high-performance requirements found in collaborative workflows that are a critical part of the game developers' production processes. Games must now be capable of reacting to users at submillisecond response times; employing multiple streams in a single session; and dealing with millions of users that are accessing multiplayer games over the Internet at unpredictable time intervals.

This expanding reach requires that current storage platforms be able to power two kinds of environments—the production development environment and the provisioning of live interactive services for real-time gaming. These necessitate that multiple applications must now run simultaneously in parallel, while still providing tremendous performance and capacity. Storage density increases now find that users are managing 2 or 3 Pbytes of storage capacity in only a couple of floor tiles of data center real estate all the while delivering sustained throughput at upwards of six or more gigabytes per second for both writes and reads. And all this must be deployed repeatedly for every new title that is produced.

Roots of Intelligence

Intelligent storage solutions first became evident in the early part of 2000; however, as is typical to all technologies, such solutions have since expanded in lock step with industry needs, storage densities, and performance requirements. Once video compression, high-resolution and high-definition images, and techniques for larger format and digital cinema production began, it became more apparent that size did matter and the industry would need to address the scaling requirements for storage in earnest.

The remainder of this chapter explores solutions that support the interests and changes experienced in collaborative workflows and those environments that depend upon an all-digital production and distribution model.

Size Matters

The media and entertainment industry has gone through significant and rapid changes in recent times. With higher resolution content (HD, 2K, and 4K), file sizes are growing to incredible proportions requiring the implementation of intelligent systems that can manage high-performance storage with highly scalable capacities. As desirable as high-performance SAN storage and infrastructures are for real-time data capture, they can be equally undesirable for postproduction work. In general, SANs can be far too expensive and much too difficult to scale for workload sharing.

NAS has been a formidable answer for postproduction, with its built-in collaboration and workload sharing. The storage cost advantage of NAS over SAN makes NAS more attractive, and simpler to implement, operate, manage, and use. Regrettably, many NAS systems have not coped with the rapidly changing realities of the 21st-century media and entertainment (M&E) market space. As a consequence, we find that many users wrongly deploy their multiple sets of NAS, generating what is referred to as "NAS sprawl." Once users adopt NAS for their solution, they find it proliferates more rapidly than expected, creating management, operational, and real estate headaches such as excess power consumption and cooling problems of huge proportions.

Intelligent Adaptive Storage

Storage systems need to be engineered so they can adapt easily and adjust on the fly to the ever-increasing performance and scalability requirements of media production and postproduction workflows. An adaptive environment with the means to scale only as required eliminates the problems of system proliferation. For the artistic and creative world made up of animators or special effect designers, one should look to intelligent adaptive storage platforms that can address the needs of their workflow and in turn eliminate both the short-term and long-term storage crisis.

In many segments of this industry, collaboration is an important requirement for the successful use of what is now a global workforce. Collaboration has never been more important for the world of digital postproduction editing, compositing, animation, special effects, color grading, mastering, and archiving. With this need expanding, we find that native SAN storage is less effective at providing collaborative workload sharing.

SAN and NAS Workload Sharing

To run workload sharing on a small, high-performance SAN environment, there needs to be a shared SAN file system. The problem is that when shared SAN file systems are scaled vertically or horizontally, system performance usually degenerates quickly. Production processes are routinely required to quickly push real-time content from SAN storage onto lower-cost mid-level performance NAS for their postproduction work. Although a NAS implementation may greatly reduce collaborative storage costs, most NAS systems are unable to meet the demands of larger scale postproduction activities. As a result, users find they cannot effectively scale performance or capacity and thus experience serious performance and operational bottlenecks.

The end result becomes a postproduction storage crisis. However, in recent times, there have been many supplemental additions that support scaled-up, scaled-out, and collaborative low-latency high-performance solutions to aid in mitigating the storage crisis.

Storage Accelerators

Users working in an all-digital production environment depend upon several media-savvy systems that are capable of simultaneously managing the intake of rich media, providing for the various craft editorial and graphics applications, and distributing the media throughout the enterprise and to other users in a variety of formats and resolutions.

To support these various activities, many users are moving toward a single, centralized storage network that is capable of providing significant productivity gains while at the same time dramatically lowering storage acquisition and operating costs. Any networked storage solution needs to meet the demanding quality of service (QoS) requirements of an often complex digital media production and delivery environment. Such environments require that their storage system delivers data at high speeds to often hundreds of servers and workstations simultaneously, reliably, and without content degradation.

Of the needed solutions that support this environment, one of them is concurrent access to consolidated content with a QoS level that remains sufficient enough to meet the demands of digital broadcast workflow, often both in real-time and faster than real time. Given that broadcast and content professionals are usually required to ingest, create, and deliver content simultaneously and in parallel, performance is extremely important to the storage and server system. When maintained at a high level, workflow efficiencies are improved, increased productivity is realized, and the total cost of ownership (TCO) is lowered.

Storage Appliance Technologies

To accelerate application performance, simplify information management, and to establish an intelligent platform for deploying application-specific storage software, appliance technology (introduced in the 2000–2001 time frame) is used as a far more advanced approach to data access than NAS or nonappliance SAN solutions. By coupling storage appliance technologies with file-based storage intelligence, the combined architecture increases manageability, performance, and reduces I/O bottlenecks more than was possible when using conventional "preappliance" Fibre Channel SAN technologies.

An appliance is a device or system that manages and accelerates the delivery of data to or from storage subsystems and hosts. Prior to these appliance-like technologies, so called "first generation" storage area networks (SANs) were found to impose several limitations and restrictions to systems that were trying to move data. One of the options employed by users was to create multiple SANs and then overlay a software layer that would transfer data from one SAN to another SAN. Besides being a costly measure, it was realized that this approach did not scale well and was profoundly difficult to manage.

An alternative option for first generation SANs was to stripe the content across several RAID controllers. However, this practice introduced latencies and contention (collisions) within the overall storage architecture that reduced the QoS desired. Furthermore, this practice still did not mitigate the system constraints in scalability, configuration, and management found in either option.

Fault Tolerance

Activities that occur during video postproduction may be called "video transactions." These activities support the processes surrounding editing, color grading, animation wire-frame creation, and rendering and effects compositing. In the digital domain, most of these activities happen at high definition (1K) and above resolutions (e.g., 2K and 4K) and will routinely employ data rates that are in the hundreds of megabytes per second. Whether working at lower bit rates (using compressed 20–50 Mbits/second data rates), or with these very large files, there will always be a continual stream of video transactions and consequently, there remains a very high requirement to provide for fault tolerance while at the same time maintaining high availability. Along with the total bandwidth requirements for a storage system comes the demand for handling multiple sets of parallel transactions; something most conventional SAN architectures were unable to achieve using the technologies available during the early times of high capacity and high bandwidth storage system development.

SAN adaptations can deliver less performance and reliability and are often plagued by the complications associated with expanding or growing the SAN at an economical price tag. Delivering a guaranteed bandwidth to the production environment is essential when editing is to be carried out directly on shared storage. This model does not allow for file transfers to local storage, and thus, some SAN implementations must be further supplemented in order to help ensure maximum accuracy, efficiency, and consistency for all the hosts that attach to the store.

Figure 16.2 shows a conventional approach to a storage network with redundant servers cross feeding multiple RAID controllers. To address the complications of media-centric operations, devices including grid storage, large SAN architectures, and massively parallel compute systems have been modified to support the jumbo files associated with moving media storage technologies. New storage networking appliance technologies are available that have overcome many of the limitations in those first generation SANs, leading to the development of advanced acceleration components that aggregate the many legacy components of the conventional approach (see Fig. 16.3).

Figure 16.2 Typical high-performance network.

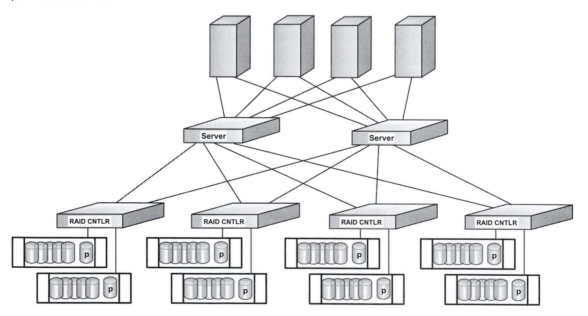

File-Sharing SANs

File-sharing SANs present special challenges for high-performance environments, among which are the performance and scalability issues that are common to rich-media environments. Extremely high performance and tremendous scalability in both connectivity and capacity present complex configuration issues for SANs.

SAN file systems that are often found in fairly large-scale deployments include systems with 40 hosts or greater or bandwidths in the hundreds of megabytes per second region. Significant challenges exist in scaling to that level particularly when each host demands such high levels of throughput; for example, when the systems reach a high-proportionate fraction of a full Fibre Channel connection.

Typical challenges include contention and switching latencies, which are exacerbated by the creation of high-speed volumes through striping by the host computers. Figure 16.4(A) illustrates a SAN configuration using eight typical RAID systems (or alternatively four dual-controller RAIDs) plus a Fibre Channel switch. Figure 16.4(B) shows a similar configuration, but with a storage appliance comprised of equivalent single (or multiple) RAID-controller functionality coupled with silicon (solid state)-based caches in a dual protection mode.

Several issues are immediately apparent in the configuration of Figure 16.4(A). First, note that each disk array has a dedicated RAID controller. In this mode, operationally, every storage access by any host might result in eight distinct transactions, one to every RAID system (or in pairs when configured in dual sets of RAID arrays). What this means is that there will be eight (or alternatively four) switching latency occurrences that could potentially reduce performance.

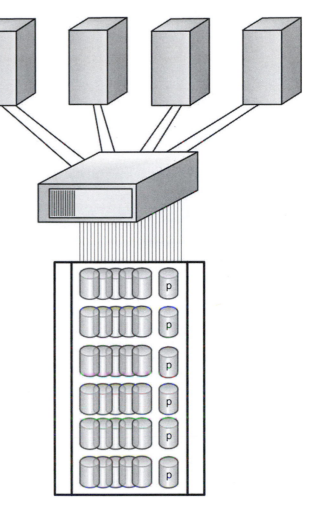

Figure 16.3 Complex high-performance network using a common accelerator appliance in place of discrete storage controller nodes.

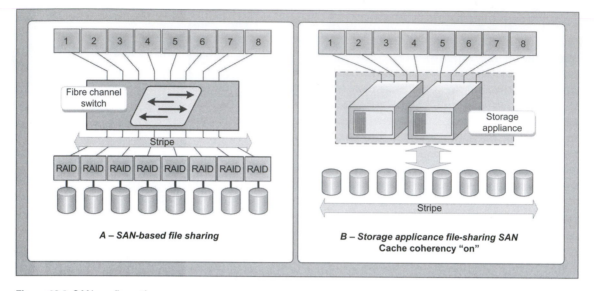

Figure 16.4 SAN configurations with discrete Fibre Channel controllers to RAID (A), compared with file sharing with an appliance-based SAN configuration (B).

Of greater impact is the effect of multiple hosts making I/O requests concurrently. Not only are there switching latencies to contend with, but far worse are the number of collisions present when trying to access switch ports attached to the individual RAID systems. Referred to as "contention," this issue can severely limit the aggregate throughput provided through the Fiber Channel switch.

The combination of switching latencies and contention can degrade the actual aggregate throughput in a high-bandwidth environment by up to one-half of what the RAID systems might theoretically provide. The effects of switching latency and contention continue to worsen as both the number of hosts and the complexity of the switching fabric increase.

Consolidation Using Smaller Storage SANs

Production facilities often will employ RAID sets or small SANs that are attached to a group of edit workstations (e.g., Final Cut Pro HD). A media director is used to allocate system, bandwidth and the interfaces to or from the file system, which sits over the top of the storage platform. As growth is experienced, the enterprise finds that the storage system has reached its limitations in capacity or performance, driving it to find alternative storage profiles or to consolidate the existing islands into something that is more productive for the whole of the organization. Eventually this scenario exhausts its options and the enterprise determines that the consolidation process is unproductive. These circumstances become elevated to the point that some other means to resolve the storage dilemma is necessary.

In those applications where it is desirable to apply consolidation methods to group sets of smaller storage sets, the performance or capacity of multiple RAID systems becomes impractical or insufficient. However, when higher performance is needed, and/or greater capacity storage is necessary, multiple RAID systems may still be required. This form of application is a potential candidate for virtualization through the deployment of a storage appliance. The advantages found in virtualization are such that it allows the disk pool resources to be allocated to any host, at the highest levels of performance.

This is more difficult with SANs where disks and associated data are captured behind individual RAIDs (see Fig. 16.5A and Fig. 16.5B).

In a small SAN it is possible that simple Fibre Channel switches may provide sufficient parallelism to ensure good performance to each host. This is the case where individual hosts "own" all of the storage behind a particular RAID controller. However, if multiple hosts access the storage behind a shared RAID controller, contention of the switch port to that controller will occur, which then degrades performance. This degradation is particularly punitive when moving large files that tend to monopolize port access and demand greater throughput from the RAID engine.

For instances where the user has employed smaller SANs, but still desires consolidation, there are further issues that must be considered. Some storage consolidation SANs may not achieve

Figure 16.5 SAN consolidation using traditional discrete components (A); and consolidation using a dual, protected SAN storage appliance (B).

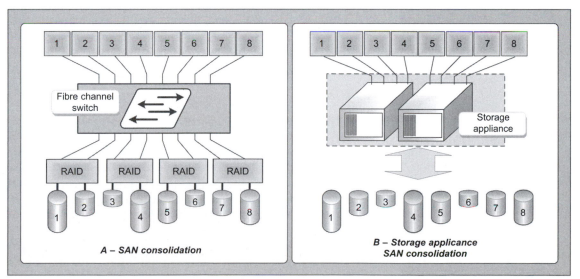

A – SAN consolidation

B – Storage applicance
SAN consolidation

the performance benefits or capacity increases available from multiple RAID-based systems. However, one can use a storage acceleration appliance that is capable of providing more raw performance and scalability than many of the more capable dual-controller RAID systems.

The point here is that users planning expansion through consolidation need to understand the impacts of moving from an overtaxed small SAN to the next level of storage. They should be certain that they would not paint themselves into the same corner they had by employing multiple smaller SAN islands.

Contention and Latency

The storage acceleration appliance can greatly reduce or potentially eliminate the contention and latency problems associated with a switch fabric. Host ports in the accelerator each provide collective parallel access to all storage resources without having to incur the punitive consequences of contention or switching latency. The concept is analogous to having multiple pipes leaving a reservoir of water; there is no need to wait for any pipe to provide water, and none of the pipes will interfere with each other—the result is that the downstream user can take as much as they need from any single pipe regardless of what is happening to the pipes next to or surrounding it. This is especially important when all the edit seats attached to the storage pool want access to many sets of files simultaneously.

Parallel host port capabilities in accelerators are a major differentiating factor for this kind of architecture when compared against straight traditional switching fabrics or other storage configurations. Parallel access not only improves fault tolerance, also provides for additional resiliency and bandwidth while simultaneously reducing latency.

Implications of Striping on I/O Block Request Sizes

Another limitation caused by striping that can limit performance in a file-sharing SAN is the reduction in I/O block size requested by each storage unit. When the host application makes an I/O request to a volume, it makes a request of a particular I/O block size. Block sizes typically will range from several hundred bytes (e.g., 512 Kbytes in a standard TAR) up through several megabytes or more when high bandwidth applications are employed.

Large block size requests are generated by applications that transfer huge amounts of data typical to video or imaging, or for applications in data mining or computational supercomputing. Disk storage systems, in order to achieve high throughput for rich-media applications, prefer to receive as large an I/O block size request as possible. For these applications, storage systems will attempt to maximize their throughput by requesting block sizes in excess of 512 Kbytes or more. The shortcoming is that most applications (and file systems) will limit the I/O block request size to a storage volume to the 1 Mbytes range; although in large super computers where there is a tremendous amount of real memory, or where block sizes may range well above these figures, the requirements scale differently.

Even for an example with an 8-way stripe, if the storage volume received a 512 Kbytes I/O block size request, it would still result in each individual storage unit only seeing 512 Kbytes divided by the 8-way stripe, or in essence only a 64 Kbytes I/O block size request. Such a 64 Kbytes block size would not come close to maximizing a storage unit's throughput.

The storage accelerator appliance (with a solid state cache) provides simultaneous full-bandwidth access from each host port to individual data or to the same data in a shared disk pool configuration. Such an implementation enables very high-performance volumes to multiple hosts without the impediments of host-based striping (see Fig. 16.6).

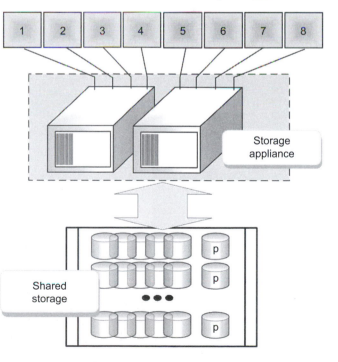

Figure 16.6 Single-LUN virtualization in cache coherency ON mode.

To obtain full-bandwidth access from a single shared storage pool requires that the shared LUN be of very high speed. By RAID characteristics that allow a single LUN to be spread across an arbitrary number of parity group "tiers," a single LUN can be constructed that can sustain in the range of 650–700 MBytes/second, provided that 512 Kbytes or greater I/O block size requests are possible.

A high-speed LUN of this type is created without the necessity of striping at the host or the SAN file system level. This results in three benefits being created: first is that large I/O block size requests may be realized at the storage unit; second is that the contention and switching latency "chatter" present in a switched fabric are reduced (should one be employed); and third, there is a reduction in CPU utilization that striping through the host computer burns up.

Media Directors

One of the components of storage accelerator appliances may be the "media director." These units, which function like a server might, manage the activities between the hosts and the caches that are placed ahead of the storage disk arrays themselves. For protection, redundancy, and for enabling a smooth failover in the case of link losses, host bus adapter (HBA) failures, or even physical cabling issues, there will usually be two fully redundant media directors to act as the traffic cops for the flow of data between hosts and drives.

Media directors have multiple host ports and will include their own local cache often in RAM or as a solid state drive (SSD). Each of the host ports provide access to any LUN "owned" by that media director. Access to LUNs owned by the other media director may not be accessed unless cache coherency is enabled; this allows all ports from both media directors to access all the storage resources simultaneously.

Cache Coherency

Cache coherence is a special case of memory coherence. Also known as cache coherency, this functionality refers to the maintenance of the consistency of data that is stored in local caches of a shared resource.

In a system where clients maintain caches of a common memory resource, problems may arise with data that is inconsistent. This can occur in CPUs of a multiprocessing system or in memory storage systems with parallel ports from hosts acting to improve bandwidth or throughput. Figure 16.7 shows that if Client 1 has a copy of a memory block from a previous read, and Client 2 changes that memory block, then Client 1 could be left with an invalid cache of memory without any notification of the change. Cache coherence manages such conflicts and maintains consistency between cache and memory.

The behavior of reads and writes to the same memory location is called "coherence." Cache coherence

Figure 16.7 Cache coherency in a shared memory resource application.

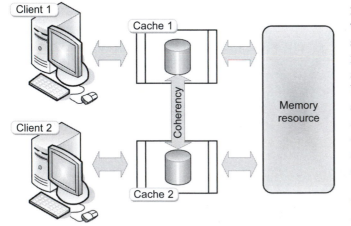

(related to program order preservation) is obtained when the following conditions are met:

- When a READ made by Processor-P to Location-X follows a WRITE by the same Processor-P to Location-X, with no WRITES to Location-X by another processor occurring between the WRITE and the READ instructions made by Processor-P, then, Location-X must always return the value written by Processor-P.
- A READ made by Processor-P1 to Location-X that follows a WRITE by another Processor-P2 to Location-X must return the written value made by Processor-P2 if no other WRITES to Location-X made by any processor occur between the two accesses. This is a condition that defines the concept of a "coherent view of memory." If the processors can READ the same old value after the WRITE is made by Processor-P2, then that memory is considered "incoherent."
- WRITES to the same location must be sequenced. That is, if Location-X received two different values A and B (in that order) from any two processors, the processors can never read Location-X as B and then read it again as A. To paraphrase this, Location-X must be seen with values A and B and only in that order.

These conditions are defined with the supposition of instantaneous READ and WRITE operations happening precisely simultaneous with each other, an occurrence that is not possible given memory latency or other aspects of any compute or storage architecture. A WRITE by Processor-P1 may not be seen by a READ from Processor-P2 if the READ is made within a tiny period following when the WRITE was made. Such a memory consistency model defines when the written value must be seen by the following READ instruction ordered by the other processor(s).

Accessing Fresh Data

With cache coherency enabled, the hosts always access "fresh" data with no risk to file or file system integrity. Enabling cache coherency will have performance impacts whenever WRITE operations occur. This is because a WRITE's data will be present only in the media director whose cache is attached to the host that performed the operation. When cache coherency is enabled, the system makes sure that a subsequent request for that data through a host attached to the other media director supplies only fresh data.

Such a validation process requires a period of time to perform; thus, a high-WRITE environment will degrade overall performance, whereas a high-READ environment will have little to no degradation since most data in this case is static. When dealing with load-balanced server forms such as with Web servers, media servers, ingest or download servers—or in other environments where there is a high ratio of READs to WRITEs—this is ideal.

Should a system desire a high-READ-WRITE performance, then cache coherency should be disabled. In such a high-WRITE environment, a configuration would be made that allows the host computers to attach to both media directors when required. Through the use of dual-pathing and through a switched fabric with one or more switches for redundancy (as shown in Fig. 16.8), or alternatively by using two Fibre-Channel Host-Bus Adapters in each host, which then dual-attaches each host to a separate media director/storage-appliance (as seen in Fig. 16.9).

Load Balancing for High Availability

To improve performance and utility, storage accelerators may use multiple ports that operate in parallel. This methodology provides for extremely efficient high-availability failover, as well

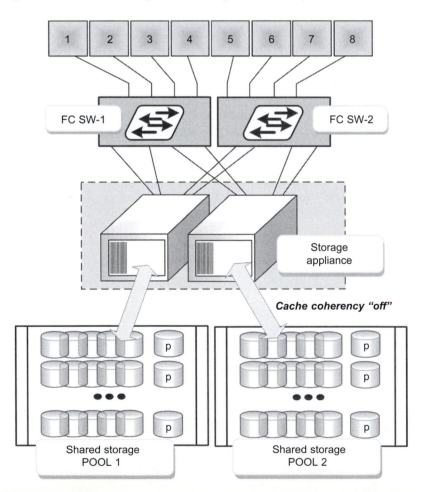

Figure 16.8 Silicon storage appliance fabric multipathing (cache coherency OFF).

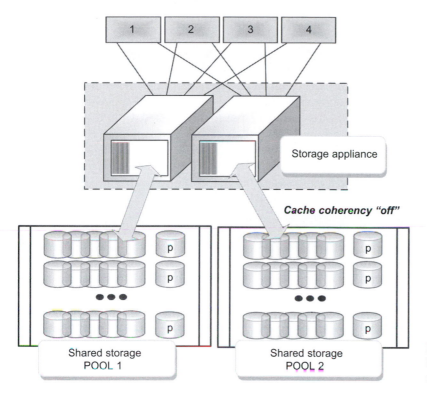

Figure 16.9 Local multipathing in the cache coherency OFF mode.

as efficiency in load balancing capabilities. Configurations utilizing switched fabric should use care when implementing switch zoning to ensure that data transfers are evenly distributed across the accelerators' parallel host ports. Under normal conditions, switch routing requests will go to the lowest numbered port that can provide access to a storage resource. When the storage accelerator has parallel host ports and if zoning is not used, it is possible that all data transfers could be directed through a single accelerator host port, creating an imbalance that is essentially the opposite of load balancing.

Failover

High-availability environments can be categorized into either of two failover scenarios. Generally these failover modes will fall into either a "local storage failover" scenario or a "host-to-host failover" cluster.

Local Storage Failover

A local storage failover scenario will be concerned with only a single host computer and is considered the simplest case. In a mode like that of a direct-attached dual-controller RAID configuration, if a path to either RAID controller is lost, the host may access the storage behind the RAID controller through the remaining RAID controller. This access redirection requires that a process on the RAID system reassigns all of the LUNs to the remaining active controller. It must further redirect data access to the HBA that is connected to the currently active controller.

A local storage failover could be caused by a failure in the interface cable, the HBA, or the RAID controller itself. In normal RAID systems, the LUNs generally must be accessed only through the controller that "owns" them. In the example of a local storage failover mode, only one controller remains active, so it is not possible to load balance the RAID systems.

The storage accelerator appliance, by virtue of its own parallelism, enables a much faster and more elegant failover operation and further permits a load balancing capability unavailable

Figure 16.10 Dual storage accelerator appliance provisioned for local failover and load balancing.

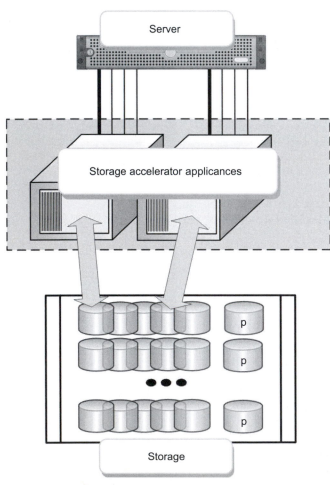

Server

Storage accelerator applicances

p

p

p

Storage

with other storage infrastructure devices. In the dual storage accelerator example shown in Figure 16.10, a single host server is configured with multiple alternate paths to two storage accelerator appliances. This arrangement demonstrates that when there is a minimum of two ports available (shown by the thick lines) and a pair of four port appliances, that up to eight native ports (the combination of both the thicker and the thinner lines) are available for the continued flow of data between the server and storage. Operations will continue even when more than two connections are disabled or are reduced in throughput.

In storage accelerator appliances, it may be beneficial to allow the user or the program to turn cache coherency either on or off. In the case where cache coherency is on, all ports may access all of the LUNs. If a host fails, the intelligent storage appliance looks for an alternate path. This path could be to the same media director or through another alternative media director. In an intelligent storage accelerator, there are no failover events that would require the accelerator itself to reassign LUNs. There is no latency in the system because no time is wasted as the alternate path is instantly available.

Alternative Pathing

Alternate pathing software during a failover event may be provided by the host manufacturers themselves or through third party software vendors. These applications are provided at the driver level and allow for extremely fast failover events. The software applications may further continue to permit load balancing should alternate paths to the storage be available.

In telecommunications, this capability is known as "bonding" or "trunking," a model analogous to disk striping except that it does not require separate LUNs to stripe against. Instead, the host transfers the data as fast as possible using all the available paths, or through the ability to route around a failure using any of the available paths.

Inactive Cache Coherency

If cache coherency is disabled, some software solutions may allow the configuration of a predetermined alternate path should connectivity be lost. For some of the selective operating systems, vendors may provide this functionality in their HBA driver. Should a media director failure occurs, a storage accelerator could automatically reassign LUNs to the alternate media director, creating a completely automated failover.

Host-to-Host Failover Cluster

In the failover of a cluster, the host-to-host failover mode provides for similar local failover capabilities, but further provides support for redundant hosts in the case where there is a catastrophic host failure. In this mode, both hosts require access to the same LUNs, although typically a LUN is "owned" by an active host, with the other host supporting it in a passive mode. The hosts are continually monitored through a heartbeat signal that connects to the redundant host(s). Should the heartbeat disappear, then the passive host takes ownership of all LUNs and it becomes active. When a parallel system is comprised of two storage accelerator platforms, and when media directors are configured, any failover should occur quickly and in a nearly transparent fashion like that of the local failover mode described previously.

A host-to-host failover cluster is shown in Figure 16.11. In this model, load balancing is still employed (shown by the thinner lines). Should increased port connectivity be required, Fibre Channel switches may be added.

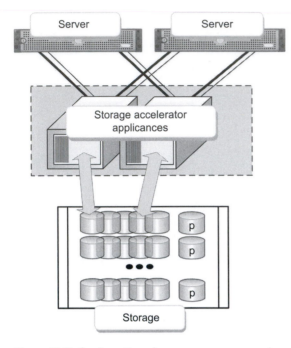

Figure 16.11 Configuration of a storage appliance as a host-to-host failover cluster with high availability (HA) and load balancing.

Workflow Improvement

These new classes of intelligent storage infrastructures provide capabilities that were not available in previous storage architectures. Storage accelerator appliances, which are often modeled with silicon (solid state) disk or RAM architectures, are easily managed, become less complicated, and provide for high-performing and more robust SANs.

Storage accelerator appliances are equally adept at simple storage consolidation, file sharing and highly available fault tolerant environments. Through their parallelism and virtualization capabilities, benefits are achieved that were not previously possible when amalgamating discrete storage devices. Parallelism further enhances the switched fabric by reducing performance obstacles found as a result of switching latency and contention.

The storage accelerator platform can simplify the workflow by providing a single instance of digital content that is accessible by many users simultaneously. An intelligent storage accelerator enables the storage platform to make data writes happen as fast as data reads.

Such implementations streamline the production pipeline as they significantly reduce errors, shorten production time, and enable faster creativity in content development. Combining all these elements in turn reduces both complexities and administrative overhead challenges.

Real-World Performance

Employing high performance storage with a high QoS factor is an absolute requirement when working with real time, high-bit rate video or digital film. Such storage systems, in SAN configurations, now operate at 4-Gbit/second and 8-Gbit/second Fibre Channel; and 10-Gbit/second or 20-Gbit/second InfiniBand. These implementations are critical when operating in high throughput, high-data volume environments such as those found in production or postproduction workflows.

Users should be cautioned that employing high-performance SAN storage and the supporting infrastructure that these systems require can be expensive. Consideration must also be given to scaling limitations associated with concurrent shared workloads that may be accessing. Understanding the QoS of the system and knowing that it can be guaranteed for the workflows desired are crucial in selecting the switches, storage components, and RAID controllers.

Guaranteed Delivery

In real-time delivery workflows, it is not enough to know that a system will deliver say 90% of the I/O requests in less than 400 ms, but the remaining 10% are completely unpredictable— unless you are willing to tolerate dropped frames or periods of black in the video stream. A guaranteed QoS means that a system will never exceed a specified time for a request, regardless of the stream's content or system loading.

Postproduction editing, compositing, animation, special effects, color grading, mastering, and archiving can be highly collaborative processes. As discussed earlier, improperly configured SAN storage may lack the ability to provide native collaborative workload sharing. Thus, workload sharing is often confined to a smaller high-performance SAN environment when there is a shared SAN file system.

Scaling for Shared SAN File Systems

Shared SAN file systems are typically available from the leading providers of editing platforms. When users scale these shared SAN file systems to mid- or large-sized SANs, there is a potential for the overall system performance to decline rapidly. Performance degradation may be caused in part by the increased load on the metadata controller. In this scenario, the metadata controller becomes incapable of providing the necessary resources to guarantee the data stream for video/film real-time streaming. In order to effectively scale these levels of SAN systems, users must provide dedicated systems to smaller groups.

Systems that are specifically designed to integrate the various server functions with the switches and the storage media, including the metadata server and media directors, can be configured to provide a guaranteed QoS—but these systems will not be "commercially available" off-the-shelf components with random performance specifications. Such systems will need enterprise-class drives, performance-driven RAID controllers, and managed switches (gigabit Ethernet and Fibre Channel) designed to meet continuous 100% duty cycle operations in harsh, demanding environments.

NAS Solutions

A NAS solution can reduce the costs for collaborative postproduction storage. NAS solutions allow the postproduction storage fulfillment to reach around 80% of the necessary capacity for as much as half the cost of an equivalent storage budget in a SAN. Unfortunately, many NAS systems are still unable to meet the demands of rich-media postproduction for digital film or real-time video. Many traditional NAS systems are incapable or cannot effectively scale in performance or capacity. This results in perplexed operators who must then seek alternative means to complete their work on smaller systems. That work must then later be migrated and merged into other platforms, often continuously throughout the postproduction processes.

Tradition NAS and even some of the clustered NAS solutions are not designed to handle the performance requirements of postproduction. These systems typically must provide both high input/output operations per second (IOPS) and high throughput concurrently, something the majority of standalone NAS systems do not provide. Although it is certainly possible to tune the NAS system for one metric or two metrics, providing the proper balance for all services, at a QoS that can support the production demands, will often come up short of the enterprise's critical needs and expectations.

As an example, NAS systems tend to have extremely long rendering times with read access times that are much too slow. Write outs also become slower following the completion of rendering, creating bottlenecks that force production workflows to crawl. Another concern is that these storage systems are unable to provide backup services concurrently with production access throughout the day. Prioritization policies fail and the backups move into the off hours further degrading rendering time, which is traditionally done overnight when other activities are subdued. Frequently, the ability to combine rendering and workstation creative activities concurrently causes delays in obtaining approvals or in completing other tasks during the work day, forcing yet another bottleneck into the workflow. The domino effect becomes obvious.

Such performance constraints, caused by the storage system throughput, can lead to application failures or crashes, a direct result of such I/O timeouts.

NAS Performance Scaling

Scaling the performance of a NAS system is yet another critical system issue. While reading the next sections on scalability, keep

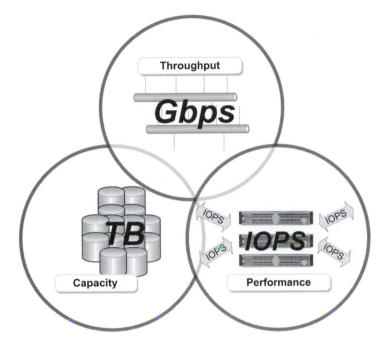

Figure 16.12 Three axes of scalability.

in mind the three axes of scalability (shown in Fig. 16.12) that need to be balanced both functionally and economically.

When the systems add more clients (workstations), traditional NAS systems tend to experience acute limitations in performance. Growing the number of clients attached to a NAS causes desktop response times to slow to a crawl when opening or saving a project. These performance issues only get worse when meeting the demands of HD (6 Mbytes), 2K (12 Mbytes) and 4K (49 Mbytes) file sizes.

When a NAS system approaches its maximum performance or maximum file capacity, the system often becomes unresponsive. If the system crashes, then the support team has to address a system restart and in the worst case, the recovery of lost or "suspended" data. Should the data be unrecoverable under conventional restart means, then the system must be rebuilt. Any of these tasks can be a painstakingly lengthy process.

At this point of frustration, users often take the approach of implementing more NAS systems. While a potentially suitable short-term fix, it is not a particularly good work-around; it really does not solve the scalability or the capacity problem, and never addresses the bandwidth (throughput) problem. In fact, it simply defers it, creating other problems of its own—known as "NAS sprawl."

NAS Management

The issues of NAS management do not increase in linear proportion to the size or capacities of the systems—it, in fact, increases exponentially. The management is both physical (e.g., increase in size, space, and cooling) and virtual (i.e., data wrangling). One of the biggest constraints becomes the continual manual, hands-on data migration between systems. The next big headache comes from the continuous recalculations needed for the efficient utilization of the assets, sometimes improperly called "load balancing."

Low Latency Solutions

An intelligent storage system for postproduction should be designed from the ground up so as to meet the demands and requirements of these forms of workflows. Such systems must further allow for scalable collaboration, high-speed low-latency performance, and the expectations for increased storage capacity.

The intelligent storage platform should be capable of offloading from RAID or other disk management systems some of the performance draining functions found in CIFS or NFS. With the advent of field-programmable gate arrays (FPGA), and solid state disks or RAM caches that are implemented into the silicon, an ultra-low latency for server I/O request handling can be achieved. In this case, latency is defined as the measurement of how quickly a server responds to the clients' requests; i.e., the lower the latency, the greater number of clients and I/O that can be handled.

Low-latency capability enables the storage platform to be concurrently combined with ingest, rendering, and other workstation activities in support of the overall workflow. These architectures allow systems to handle maximum loads simultaneously through the use of distributed memory, state engines, and parallel pipelines. Parallelism permits systems to process I/O requests at maximum performance limits without service degradation. These high-performance architectures are designed to remove data-flow constraints and eliminate performance bottlenecks especially when employed in large and powerful render farms. The results are faster rendering times with fewer dropped frames and far less rework for the data wranglers.

Scale-Up and Scale-Out

Two terms often associated separately and distinctly are phrases that have as much marketing spin as performance spec. "Scale-up" refers to the scaling capacity within the NAS filer. "Scale-out," also called horizontal scaling, at a simple level, refers to the clustering of more than two heads in a single image.

Scale-out storage enables commodity storage components to be combined with multiple small, low cost computers either to (a) create an aggregate storage pool or to (b) increase computing power. Both scenarios exploit the traditional models of storage and computer power with the intention that when configured they will exceed the capabilities and performance of single traditional storage arrays or single, high-performance workstations or servers. As the demand increases for storage virtualization, for shared data storage, or for expanded data protection services, this commodity-based scale-out model is being offered by many vendors and is becoming increasingly more popular.

Clusters and grids are both examples of scale-out systems. However, the concept of "scale-out" can apply equally as well to the SAN as it does to those NAS environments from which the advantages of scale-out are more commonly associated.

Scaling Storage Topologies

Scale-out is a term often assumed to be synonymous with NAS. Scale-up is often assumed to be synonymous with SANs. The fact is that scalability is not necessarily a direct function of the storage architecture. Thus, scale-out could apply to all the major storage topologies, as follows:

DAS Scale-Out

The simpler of the storage technologies to manage, direct-attached storage (DAS) can scale-out to a limited degree such that it increases performance and capacity by simply increasing the HDD count or by adding larger or faster drives. DAS scale-out may be further accomplished by cascading additional control units that can in turn increase the HDD count. However, the drawback is that DAS lacks the ability to provide many of the efficiencies and/or advanced functionalities that make the management efforts simpler or add operational advantage as the storage pool grows.

NAS Scale-Out

Network attached storage (NAS) is the architecture comprised of servers, disks, and storage management software that is dedicated to serving files over a network. Scale-out storage is frequently associated with NAS systems because of their ability to scale to a cluster of NAS nodes. The crucial point here is that the nodes can scale in terms of capacity and performance, either in combinations or as independents, and still maintain a single-system image.

Unstructured data, usually in "file format," is a huge segment of all the digital storage that is mostly stored on NAS. Unstructured data has outpaced structured data growth, and as a result, has increased the demand for low-cost scale-out storage.

Scale-Out SANs

Scale-out in storage area networking is achieved by creating a scale-out SAN fabric, usually through the addition of more SAN switches and drive arrays. This approach allows users to achieve both increased performance horsepower and storage capacity in linear steps.

For the enterprise, SANs provide excellent scale-out capability that can address their anticipated growth in information storage requirements. Unlike DAS, any excess capacity in the SAN can be pooled to provide for higher utilization of resources as well as advanced functionalities. SAN topologies are implemented to meet differing needs in scaling. They can scale-out through the connection of SAN islands that were built around individual switches to form larger single fabrics. They can use routers to physically connect the switches while logically isolating the

Table 16.1 Comparative Strengths and Weaknesses of Scale-Up (Vertical) versus Scale-Out (Horizontal) Storage for NAS, SAN, and DAS

Scaling Factor	Scale-Out (SAN/NAS)	Scale-Up (DAS/SAN/NAS)
Hardware scaling	Addition of more commodity devices	Addition of faster and larger devices
Hardware limits	Scale beyond limits of devices	Scale-up to limits of device(s)
Level of disruption	Less disruptive	More disruptive
Resiliency and availability	Generally higher	Generally lower
Complexity of storage management	Higher volume of resources to manage usually requires virtualization software	Less resources to manage
Geographic spanning across multiple locations	Yes	No
NAS	Yes (common for NAS)	Yes
SAN	Yes (adds more switches or directors)	Yes
DAS	Limited	Yes

fabrics. For virtualized storage, the scale-out principle will often be employed using SANs.

Scale-Up

When a system scales up vertically, it adds resources to a single node in a system. This may involve the addition of CPUs or memory (or both) to a single computer. Scale-up can apply to servers, individual workstations, or storage subsystems.

Such vertical scaling of existing systems also enables them to use virtualization technology more effectively, as it provides more resources for the hosted set of operating system and application modules to share. Scale-up means that processors, connectivity, and capacity can be dynamically added in a single unit, and that there can be support for page-level tiering. Often scale-up will intermingle with scale-out, meaning that individual units can be dynamically combined into a single logical system with shared resources, and the storage needs of the servers can then be prioritized and provisioned to form a common pool of storage resources. Table 16.1 places scale-up and scale-out systems in perspective to the various storage architectures of SAN, NAS and DAS.

Page-Level Tiering

The relatively new terminology of page-level tiering lets the organization break up storage data at the page level, rather than at the logical unit number (LUN) level. It moves the data to the storage media that best matches the data's requirements.

With the ability for a LUN to span multiple tiers of pages, typically when databases grow, there would be tendencies for large amounts of data that would not have been touched in a long time to stay in tier one or tier two storage where the fastest drives are. With this new page-level tiering hierarchy, some pages can now drop to the lowest tier, letting the system match data, at a more granular level, to a particular tier of storage.

Another term, "scale-deep," is applied when the platform lets organizations dynamically virtualize new and existing external storage systems.

Backend RAID Scale-Up

Scale-up storage can be achieved by employing backend RAID storage. This is where controllers and drives are attached (or added) to the storage subsystem and then virtualized into a single pool or multiple pools. By adding both controllers and storage, capacity scaling results in more processing power for the storage subsystem, which allows for the linear scaling of performance (bandwidth) as well as capacity.

Many NAS filers do not scale the backend RAID processing side of the equation. Hence, without increasing both the RAID controllers and the drives there becomes a point at which there are only marginal returns and where the actual performance declines as the storage capacity increases.

Shared Storage Implementations

This chapter, so far, has looked quite deeply into storage technologies that have helped to support the consolidation of smaller islands of storage, or where the proliferation of NAS or smaller SANs has reached a point where something major needed to be done. In very large, complex data centers and in production facilities that have ebbed and flowed with the demands for creating more with less, these forms of storage solutions make practical sense. In many of the smaller scale facilities, there has been a continuing trend to manage workflows with the same kind of structure as, say, a Windows Workgroup. Every solution has its place, but in the final section of this chapter we will look at how shared storage fits into the workspace and see just how one can make intelligent, cost-effective solutions that solve the issues of storage islands, consolidation, and collaborative workflow.

Examining the Current State of Affairs

As users go out to look for solutions that can fulfill their organization's needs for storage, and having read or examined as much as possible about NAS, SAN, or DAS architectures, an approach that seems to make a significant amount of practical sense is the deployment of a shared storage platform. In Fig. 16.13, a number of storage subsystems are shown orbiting around a centralized storage system that feeds to or receives from the entities around that center blob.

Around this core you find ingest and playout devices that may input directly to the shared storage or may be used to stage content to or from the other storage devices. The core further supports the preparation of content for the delivery formats needed, including the transcoding operations necessary to present content from the system to the outside.

In a production environment, many of the accesses to or from core shared storage tend to occur when the nonlinear editors are conforming production segments (which are also stored on the core) into finished work. The balance of the peripheral access is

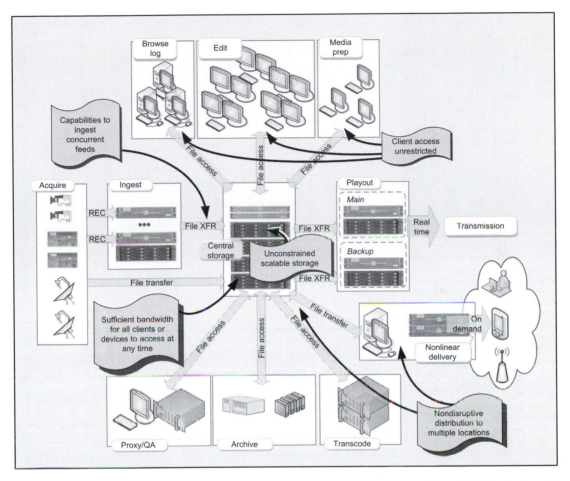

Figure 16.13 Typical broadcast and/or production environment with annotations describing key concerns when building out a core shared storage system.

focused on ingest, playout, proxy generation, transcoding services, archive, or replication for disaster recovery applications.

Legacy Status Quo

Many who are reading this book have most likely already gone through round one or round two of file-based workflow implementations. At this stage, the users are probably looking at how to optimize their organization's workflows. In some cases, there may already be some level of shared storage in place, but they have worked around certain performance metrics by having separate islands of storage that are application specific.

The reasons for these work-arounds often stem from the inability to connect subsystems together because, for example, there was not a file system driver for a particular application, or

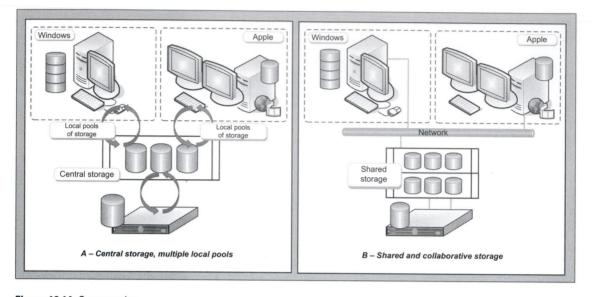

Figure 16.14 Comparative differences between pools of storage connected to a central store (A) versus shared storage connected in a collaborative network-based configuration (B).

the file formats were incompatible with one another. Another drawback to having multiple pools of existing storage is discovered when the users outgrow the local storage capacity and must expand the system; this often brings roadblocks that were not recognized when the original systems were installed.

Expansion can be a costly experience, exacerbated by having to backup all the existing data, wipe all the storage pools, and then rebuild them with the newer, larger storage systems. The various storage subsystems may have indeed reached their design capacity, limiting the ability to grow the current storage any further and resulting in a "forklift" upgrade with the disposition of all the current storage subsystems.

Workstation performance may also limit the ability to grow the local storage islands (or "pools"). In this case, the avenues available get quite limited. The replacement of the workstation and/or the storage may not yield any further performance improvements and may indeed hinder collaborate workflows altogether. In this case, a solution that improves storage capacity, bandwidth, resilience, and collaboration is in order (see Fig. 16.14).

Benefits to Collaborative Storage

Having everything under a single file system makes a huge improvement in overall system performance. In most first or second generation file-based workflow implementations, many of the tool sets operating on the files were addressed through "watch folders." This is the place where users magically drop a file into a designated folder and then some other device grabs the file to perform some action on it. Once that task is completed, the file is returned to yet another watch folder where a signal is given to retrieve that file for other uses. Sometimes this watch folder workflow is required only because there is no common single file system available; while for others it is the only way that the third party application will work.

All of this file movement costs something. It may be time, storage space, or a utility that must be purchased. In terms of space, whenever you move a file to a folder you are required to have a duplicate amount of storage space (provided—and recommended—that you want to keep the original file as a protective backup). The more the users can consolidate files into a single central location, the less duplication there is, and the faster and more efficient the workflow becomes. Furthermore, there will be less management of the system when the architecture is based upon a collaborative, centralized storage environment.

In order to achieve true collaborative storage, there will be challenges.

Challenges to Collaborative Workflow

The main challenges in getting the most out of a collaborative storage model is getting all the devices connected, achieving sufficient bandwidth with the least amount of latency with regard to performance, and addressing expansion or growth in the system. Each of these challenges play off of each other. Conversely, there may be trade-offs necessary to reach one goal that are offset by the capabilities remaining in another.

For example, you may want more bandwidth in the system but it may have to be paid for by a modest increase in latency. Or if an expansion of capacity is a target goal, you may not be able to expand performance at the same time or perhaps even independently.

The center of the thought process on shared storage is not to look at trade-offs, but to look deeper into creative ways to find solutions that deal with the linkage of the systems so that what is achieved in the end is not a compromise, but is something that fits and optimizes for the different categories as shown in Fig. 16.15.

Resilient Storage

The method to accomplish resiliency in a system is one of the big factors in optimizing data availability throughout the workflow. The way that you can achieve this is through arithmetic recovery

Figure 16.15 The four categories required for building a collaborative and shared storage environment.

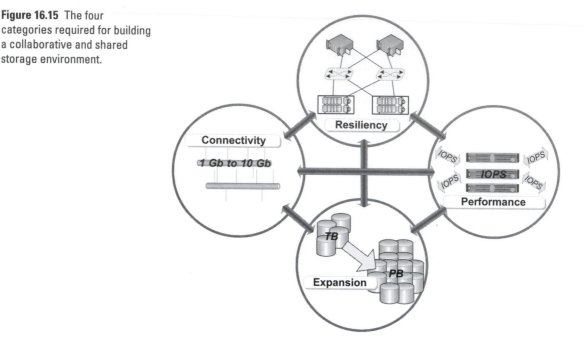

(as in RAID), or through replication as in duplicated slices of files spread across a high-availability (HA) storage system. In arithmetic recovery, there is not an exact duplicate of the data in the system, but there is a way to recover the data through parity or other means. In replication, the system relies on another set of the data located somewhere on the system that can be used to reconstruct the data set in another portion of the system. The system, in either case, may be a local core shared storage platform or a remote located system or disaster recovery site.

Chapter 19 is devoted to resilience and fault tolerance in storage systems and goes into greater depth on those topics as well as virtualization.

Data Access, Repair, and Vulnerability

Users will need access to the data not just when everything in the system is running fine, but also when something has been compromised. This ties in with the discussion about connectivity, whereby more than one data path is available by employing dual network interfaces or redundant switches in a system. Data in the system must have the ability to be accessed constantly.

Additionally, repairing of the data should occur transparently in the background and without user intervention. At the core of any storage system will be spinning disks. These are mechanical devices, and the question is not if they will fail—but when. If a failure occurs in a drive, especially after hours or on weekends when critical "number crunching" typically happens, it should not require an operator or technician to come in and do something just to resume normal operations. Having repairs happen automatically with a "self-healing" system reduces vulnerability by not having to enlist a human to find, diagnosis, and correct by trial and error.

If the system has been optimized for performance and not just for the clients doing their routine day-to-day work, the performance of that repair function will occur in isolation from the user or the workflow. By having the system optimized for resiliency, the organization has reduced the risk of vulnerability.

The key differentiator in a highly resilient, core shared storage environment is being able to keep doing your work without compromise no matter what is happening with the system, and without having to experience any downtime.

Reducing Risk

A means to reduce the impact of a compromise in the systems, whether unintentional or as a result of a planned outage (temporary repair or update), is through the practice of distributing the data across a grouping of storage components that mitigates the risk of a failure or reduction in performance. In this example, when data is ingested into the system, it is first spread across the storage platform such that if any portion of the system fails, the balance of the data is not compromised, and all of the data is recoverable. The diagram (Fig. 16.16) shows a replication scenario, which has then been bisected such that if a section loses connectivity or an element in one slice needs attention, the remainder of the system can pick up the balance of the workflow until connectivity is restored or repairs are completed.

Connectivity

Having the ability to interface between all the subsystems is essential to the successful implementation of a core shared storage platform. If each of the systems are unable to easily and efficiently exchange data, the entire purpose of implementing a shared storage environment is negated.

The system, as a whole, should provide for sufficient network and storage connectivity to allow it to fail over to an auxiliary path. Should any part of a system fail, the question becomes, "What sort of access is available so that each of the clients attached to the system do not lose their ability to continue doing their work?" Of course, in this case, resilience is not the only factor to contend with, but system performance now also plays

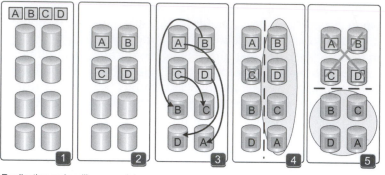

Replication and resiliency model

(1) Contains an empty store plus data sets A-B-C-D. This data is written into four sectors of the store as shown in (2).

(3) Depicts the previously written data sets replicated to another area of the store, giving a complete duplicate set of data from which a full set of the data could then be reconstructed if any section of the store failed.

(4) Shows what happens if data "C" is compromised. In this situation, the data could be completely reconstructed from the primary and the replicated sets – shown by the oval on the right side of (4). Should a serious defect cause the entire top section of the store to fail (5), the replicated section could be used either to deliver data or to aid in reconstructing the data once the top portion is restored.

In normal operation, the replicated data provides for increased bandwidth and performance.

Figure 16.16 Resiliency through division and distribution of a shared storage environment that maintains access in the event of a failure or when a portion of the storage system must be maintained or updated.

a role in terms of fulfilling the expectations that the system will continue to meet its target objectives. This can be achieved by building in redundant fabrics to interconnect the storage components, which also are connected redundantly to each of the clients attached to the system.

This kind of configuration not only provides for resiliency in terms of connectivity but also improves performance by allowing parallel access to two halves of the system continuously when it is in full 100% operational mode. Furthermore, any design should allow for the use of all of the tools in the system, regardless of if those tools are part Windows-based and part Mac-based or even Linux-based.

When planning the system design be certain that all of the foreseeable needs can be met, especially now that the application world is so multiOS centric. This investigation includes looking beyond just the applications you are using in house today; it also means addressing both 32-bit and 64-bit apps as well.

Fabric or Network?

Not long ago the means to performance, bandwidth, and reduced latency dictated the deployment of a Fibre Channel–based storage architecture. In nonlinear editing systems, this belief still exists. That is not necessarily the case any longer. Having an infrastructure that is based around network protocols, such as Ethernet, is essential to make today's evolving file-based workflow and shared storage environments practical and economical.

This is not just 1 Gbit Ethernet connectivity; it goes well into ranges above and below that data rate. Wireless connectivity to iPads, for example, helps allow users to work in a multiplatform, nonfixed base environment. Building around a network-based infrastructure allows the organization to have more clients connected and to work in ranges from wireless to multiple 10 Gigabit data ranges. Having a sufficient backbone with enterprise-class switching or routing as the foundation will be money well spent from the beginning. Replacing a backbone mid-operation is simply not an option.

The cost versus performance trends are clearly headed in the direction of Ethernet (or IP) connectivity. The sheer volume of Ethernet-based equipment being manufactured and installed today versus Fibre Channel offsets any hope for reducing the cost of even an equivalent smaller scale Fibre Channel storage infrastructure. Faster drives coupled with technologies that ride over or under the Fibre Channel banner are making it very practical to build out on alternative topologies.

Bandwidth

Bandwidth, in the perspective of collaborative shared storage, really should be separated from the topic of latency. In this discussion, bandwidth may pertain to the ability to sustain high-data transfer rates. From another standpoint, there are fundamental needs to get data from point A to point B and if sufficient bandwidth is not supplied then the ability to get work accomplished could be severely impacted. At this point, these decisions really become ones that are more business-related than equipment selection-related. Although most of the issues can be solved through technology-related solutions, the organization's capital should be utilized first and foremost is in support of the business and productivity requirements.

In the world of file-based workflow, the discussion can quickly turn to "How fast can I get a file to a given point?" and "What am I willing to pay?" to accomplish a certain task in a certain period of time. In these situations, it may be practical to increase connectivity by adding a second network interface card (NIC) to a compositing station and connect it to shared storage because by doing so "Bob" gets his work done twice as fast.

The capacity solution may not be as simple as just adding another NAS head to the system, a solution deemed to be less costly than building out a shared storage system. Adding a NAS head solves a short-term issue, but in terms of performance (led by bandwidth), it turns out to be rather limiting unless the NAS head is a performance-based, intelligent storage subsystem like those discussed much earlier in this chapter. In many areas, adding a NAS head for the purpose of gaining additional access (i.e., bandwidth) is not necessarily the suggested solution for something that is performance sensitive; but it also is not the only way to go.

Leaving the NAS head in as an optional solution for an access point, such as in legacy architectures, has its own potential set of values. It could indeed be more practical to utilize the additional storage as an access point for FTP, NFS, Apple Filing Protocol (AFP), or Samba. The NAS solution may further open the door to a shared storage system for those in-place legacy systems, acting more like a gateway than it does a storage island. This is not to suggest that subsystems be added such that more bottlenecks are created; however, the concepts are certainly worthy of consideration from a flexibility standpoint.

Direct Access

What is really desired is the ability to have direct access to the files, content, data, and others in the workgroups so that you mitigate latency while also gaining parallel access to the shared storage elements. Of course, this requires that the system components have the capability to take advantage of parallel access so that the additional layer of latency is constrained. This is akin to the earlier discussion about adding a second NIC to the workstation, or the redundant Ethernet switch to improve throughput by means of channeling data directly from a workstation to shared storage.

From a latency perspective, we are now switching away from the "How much raw throughput can I get?" question to a scenario that matters much more to those nonlinear editing platforms that are connected to a central store for the purpose of edit-in-place. Nonlinear editors (NLEs), by the functional nature of their workflow, are not moving through large sequential files (like an ingest point or playout server does), but rather the NLEs are "cutting" together multiple elements that involve taking small bits from one area of the store and then more from another part and assembling them into a single contiguous file that will be sequential in nature at the time the editing is concluded.

To exemplify the complexities of enabling a collaborative workflow, there have been applications from some vendors that have actually not allowed both SD and HD files on the same RAID structure because it impaired the performance of the opposite format from which it was working in. Such vendors were obviously not too cognizant of the practical aspects of shared storage environments and would actually force the take down of the RAID system and require it to be reformatted in order to meet the required workflow objectives specific to their applications and the format of the files (resolution and compression format wise).

In any system that requires the interplay of various file formats and structures, it would be entirely impractical to force the reconfiguration of the storage system just to address an application inconsistency. In a large system, you certainly do not want to be restriping or relaying your data on a file system. The system must be content media aware so as to mitigate the configuration issues that eat away at productivity while simultaneously reducing performance.

In today's world, constraining the storage platform would be almost unheard of. However, looking forward, if your organization has any potential to do 1080p60 production, or stereoscopic (3D) or even 2K or 4K postproduction, then not having the capability to scale-out the storage could limit the overall system functionality and prohibit working in those larger dimensions.

Media Affinity

Digital video and audio likes to be handled in the domain that it is most accustomed to work in. A/V content by its very nature has an affinity to being recorded or played back at its real-time rate. If you can identify what the particular data structure is, then when it is written into the system or copied or moved, you can arrange the data so that it is laid out with certain chunk sizes. Later, when you access that data in the file system, it has already been optimized for the way the system will be reading or writing it, based upon the data's affinity for real-time use.

What the system is actually being optimized for is I/O operations per second (IOPS). This is the real battleground that is shaping up in media operations, that is, the system must be tuned up to address the number of IOPS needed for the application, which the storage system must support. In terms of current technology, this is where the solid state drive (SSD) is becoming more applicable in that it allows short-term data to be moved very quickly to storage where it will be repeatedly accessed in smaller chunks during the production workflow process (for more about SSD technologies, refer to Chapter 7).

These kinds of applications must be handled quite differently from large bulk transfers of sequential data, like when a system is in a playout-only mode.

Performance Tuning

Storage system architectures need to posses content awareness capabilities. By this, we mean that through the use of structural metadata (explained in Chapter 13) the chunks of data can be categorized so that they may be placed onto optimized storage sets that best address the IOPS requirements.

Storage systems will be "tuned" to meet the various media read and write affinities. If your system is agile enough to address the placement of data based upon the structural metadata it reads, then the hidden management of the data types can be optimized without the user or the administrator continually shuffling the data between storage containers.

Having a system that allows for striping and parallel access to the storage systems helps to address the performance tuning equation. Through the use of buffering and IOPS tuning, controlled from the structural metadata information obtained by the file system, the organization can adjust the performance of the system to meet either the workgroups that need the access or to allow for changes to be made in bandwidth or latency based upon what the organization requires for its current workflow.

As an example, looking at three file types of A/V media, one can see that these have three distinct and radically different dimensions:

- Video: .MOV at 220 Mbits/second, ProRes/DNxHD, file size = 1.5 Gbytes, slice size = 2 to 8 Mbytes/slice
- Graphics: .PSD image size 4K × 2K, 16 bits per channel, file size = 100 Mbytes, slice size = 1 to 2 Mbytes/slice
- Audio: .AIFF at 24 bit, 48 kHz sampling, file size = 50 Mbytes, slice size = 256 to 512 Kbits/slice

Placing all of these files into the same, highest-sized storage would not be optimizing the system performance based upon the media type. Instead, the storage architecture and the system IOPS would be arranged so as to meet the requirements of each media type, allowing the specifics of each file type to be optimized for the workflow it needs. This means the audio files would be segmented to the digital audio workstation (DAW) clients possibly on their own VLAN so that these smaller slices are not bogged down by, for example, the 2–8 MByte slices of full motion video. The same goes for the graphics system, where access is far less frequent, so the Mac workstations outfitted with Adobe Photoshop can get the best IOPS performance when needed.

Expansion

Consideration must be given, at the onset, to the requirements of growing the shared storage environment. When getting a quote for a shared storage system, do not just stop with the cost question. Understand what the long-term implications of starting with that particular solution and then having to grow it over time actually means. Know what the support costs will be over five years, and how the supplier intends to support the system once the initial technology becomes "legacy" technology.

Look closely at the options for expansion. Ask the vendor what the limitations are and in what increments can expansion occur. Will there be a brick wall whereby no more storage can be added without a forklift upgrade being required? Know if the drives in the system can be upgraded, or if you want to upgrade them, can you mix drive sizes without having to offload all your data and then reformat the arrays.

Flexibility and options are the keys to a cost-effective long-term growth option. It may seem impressive to have saved 30% on a system price at the time it was first implemented only to find you need to spend all that, and more, just to expand to the next plateau of capacity or performance. This may even mean the freedom of switching from rotating media to solid state media without necessarily having to replace or abandon the existing drive chassis.

Users should be able to add capacity but not be bound to use a particular increment of size. If you want to add a single unit of storage, you should not be forced to double the size of the entire system because of some unforeseen issue or ill-conceived architecture that kept incremental growth from occurring. When you add volumes to the system, you do not want that to sit empty while you gain no bandwidth performance increases. What is desired is a system that will redistribute all data in the background when new volumes are added to balance out the new capacities and spread the data across all of the shared storage. This alone will allow for increased performance through the effects of increased bandwidth and/or parallel access. Furthermore, by distributing the data across more capacity, this increases the number of responders that can handle more requests for access, in parallel, which in turn reduces latency while increasing bandwidth.

Storage Scaling and Management

As you move onto the next chapters, it will become evident that the management of storage, especially for media content, is becoming a science that goes well beyond traditional IT technologies. Vertical and horizontal scaling for capacity and performance are being addressed by the higher end specialty storage manufacturers that provide solutions to the massive file sizes and collaborative working environments found in the production of modern digital media films, videos, and effects.

Further Readings

An example of test results, which also depict configurations and benchmarks of various intelligent storage system providers, and covers the period beginning around 2001 through 2008 can be found at http://www.spec.org/sfs97r1/results/sfs97r1.html.

Selected providers of intelligent, high performance storage include:
NetApp (http://www.netapp.com)
Quantum StorNext (http://www.quantum.com/)
Data Direct Networks (http://www.datadirectnet.com/)
Isilon (now part of EMC) (http://www.isilon.com/ and http://www.emc.com/)
Hitachi Data Systems (http://www.hds.com/)

Selected providers of shared storage architectures for broadcast and production media operations include:
Omneon (part of Harmonic) (http://www.omneon.com/)
Grass Valley (http://www.grassvalley.com/)
Harris (http://www.broadcast.harris.com/productsandsolutions/Servers/)
Seachange (http://www.schange.com/)

Further industry information and comparative analysis regarding scale-up and scale-out storage can be found at http://www.enterprisestrategygroup.com/2010/06/scale-out-storage/.

17

SCALABILITY, EXTENSIBILITY, AND INTEROPERABILITY

Storage networking grew out of the need to scale storage capacity and increase performance over conventional direct-attached storage (DAS) systems. Network-attached storage (NAS) and storage area networks (SANs) provide the avenues to extend the practicality, usage, and reach of storage systems, as well as to enable the interchange of information between similar and/or dissimilar platforms through interoperability. The three terms that head this chapter, "scalability," "extensibility," and "interoperability," impart a number of concepts and definitions related to storage, systems, and performance.

Accompanying these three major headings are additional prerequisites that round out the considerations for storage networking: flexibility, reliability, availability, and accessibility. When these are harmonized with the first three characteristics, a set of requirements necessary to support storage networking is created.

This chapter defines their meanings, how and why they are important, and what their impacts are on networked storage systems.

KEY CHAPTER POINTS

- Defining scalability, interoperability, and extensibility as they apply to storage and the interchange of media-centric data
- How open standards versus formalized standards impact implementations of storage systems
- How networked storage systems can scale
- How performance metrics (e.g., MTBF) for mechanical disk drives and flash-based solid state drives are derived

Scalability

Growth is the most common way that a system changes. When growth can no longer be achieved either practically or economically, the system becomes unusable or obsolete. Factors that limit the growth potential in a storage environment include the ability to record and process all of the information desired. Providing a suitable and economical means to hold the vast and ever increasing collection of digital information that an organization creates is more than just a matter of adding storage capacity. The other end of the storage chain requires that these collections must also be accessible.

Scalable solutions that allow for the expansion of data repositories without interruptions to the services they provide are essential in a storage networking environment.

Performance

Providing for a system that is scalable also implies that the system's performance will scale accordingly. The advent of 1, 2, 4 and 8 Gbit/second Fibre Channel (FC) and the deployment of 10 Gbit/second Fibre Channel over Ethernet (FCoE) have shown that storage area networks (SANs) can intrinsically be designed to scale in the data transfer, performance, and capacity domains.

Integrating the lower speeds with the higher speeds not only extends the performance of existing data storage infrastructures but also permits the entire system to scale as new technologies and increased storage requirements demand. One of the emerging areas that is allowing scalability and performance increases to happen is the combining of multiple switches, routers, or fabrics to permit a wider throughput of data, but in a means that reduces traffic congestion in storage networks.

Inter-Switch Links and Trunking

Fibre Channel networking uses a component called an inter-switch link (ISL) to add extensible and scalable performance increases to the SAN fabric.

In the late 1990s, ISL was introduced as a method of encapsulating tagged local area network (LAN) frames and then transporting them over a full-duplex, point-to-point Ethernet link. At that time, the encapsulated frames would be token-ring or Fast Ethernet. The frames were carried unchanged from transmitter to receiver.

ISL carries data "hop-by-hop" as compared with "point-to-point" links, thus neither the Fast Ethernet nor Gigabit Ethernet constraints of 1,500-byte data frame size are applicable. In this application, ISL may be used to transport the far-larger 18 Kbyte token-ring frames (or alternatively, 100-byte packets). Ethernet-based ISL may be carried as Fast Ethernet on Category 5 (or 5e) copper cabling or fiber-optic cabling as its transport medium, allowing 100 Mbit/second to GigE speeds between switches and servers.

ISLs join FC switches through their E_Ports, which are similar in purpose to the uplink channel in an Ethernet switch.

Cisco Systems employs a proprietary Cisco Inter-Switch Link protocol that maintains VLAN information as traffic flows between switches and routers, or between different switches. ISL is Cisco's VLAN encapsulation method, which is supported only on Cisco's equipment through Fast and Gigabit Ethernet links. The size of an Ethernet-encapsulated ISL frame may start from 94 bytes and increase up to 1548 bytes through the additional fields (overhead) that the protocol creates via encapsulation. This implementation of ISL adds a 26-byte header that contains a 15-bit VLAN identifier and a 4-byte CRC trailer to the frame.

ISL functions at Layer 2 (the Data Link Layer) of the OSI model and is used in maintaining redundant links. For the SAN, ISL technology optimizes performance and simplifies the management of multiswitch SAN fabrics.

ISL Trunking

Combining multiple ISLs in a logic group is called ISL Trunking (see Fig. 17.1). These are generally software applications that simplify fabric design, lower provisioning time, and extend the growth of the storage platform for data replication or remote backup sites by enabling 10 Gbit/second Fibre Channel transfer speeds over dark fiber using dense wave division multiplexing (DWDM).

Brocade employs its version, which they call "ISL Trunking" as an optional system for small- to mid-size data centers whereby when two or more ISLs are used to connect two switches, the switches then automatically group to form a single logical ISL. This application is designed to significantly reduce traffic congestion by combining ISLs in 1, 2 and 4-Gbit/second switches (with the appropriate directors), providing a trunking throughput from 4 Gbit/second to as much as 32 Gbit/second. Using fiber optic transmission, similar forms of technology allowed multi-lane 10-Gbit/second fiber optic transmission to scale upwards from 40 to 100 Gbit/second through the utilization of IEEE Standard 802.3ba-2010.

To balance workloads across all of the ISLs in the trunk, each incoming frame is sent across the first available physical ISL in the trunk, preventing transient workload peaks, which would otherwise impact the performance of other portions of the SAN fabric. Through a technique called Dynamic Path Selection (DPS), fabric-wide performance is automatically optimized (i.e., load balanced) to find the most effective path through the switching network. Thus, ISL Trunking reduces bandwidth that might otherwise be wasted by inefficient traffic routing.

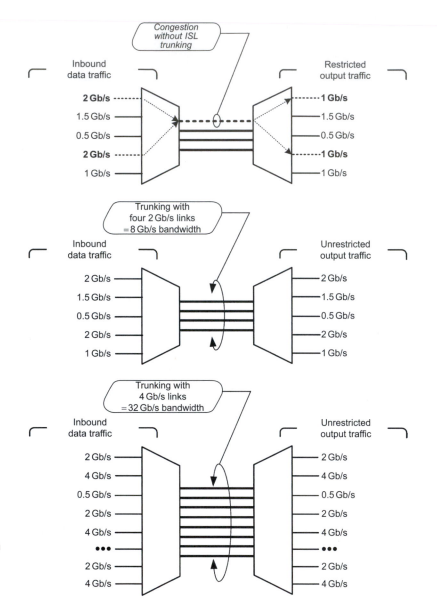

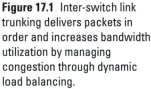

Figure 17.1 Inter-switch link trunking delivers packets in order and increases bandwidth utilization by managing congestion through dynamic load balancing.

Dynamic Load Balancing

Management processes must ensure that delivery of the data is "in order," so that the system is reliable even if a line in the trunk fails. The system is dynamically load balanced when there are significant differences in the amount of data handled through a lower speed switch versus a higher speed channel. Dynamic load balancing, used in clustering, ensures that the system bandwidth is not wasted.

Backbone Fabric

Fabric backbones, also called backbone fabric (BB-fabric), are highly robust network-switching platforms that are designed for the scaling of the enterprise-level data center. When machines are employed in systems that operate on a fabric backbone, each machine will be comprised of components that combine performance, scalability, and energy efficiency to ensure system reliability and performance while protecting the investment made by the enterprise.

The backbone fabric enables scalable Meta SANs by the networking of multiprotocol routers that connect to the backbone fabric via the E_Port interfaces, a standard Fibre Channel mechanism that enables switches to network to each other.

Multifabric Communications

A collection of all devices, switches, edge and backbone fabrics, logical SANs (LSANs), and multiprotocol routers that make up a physically connected but logically partitioned storage network is called a Meta SAN. In a data network, one would simply call this "the network"; however, additional terms are required to specify the differences between a SAN as a single-fabric network; as a multifabric network without cross-fabric connectivity, as in a "dual-redundant fabric SAN"; and as a multifabric network with connectivity or Meta SAN. Additional information about Fibre Channel and fabric communications can be found in the Appendices on the companion website for this book.

Logical Storage Area Network

Another concept that enables scalability is a logical storage area network that spans multiple fabrics, called an LSAN. The LSAN, along with LSAN zoning, was introduced as a trade name implementation by Brocade in the mid-2000s. The path between the devices in an LSAN can be local to an edge fabric or cross one or more multiprotocol routers and up to one intermediate backbone fabric. LSANs are administered through LSAN zones in each edge fabric. An LSAN zone is a mechanism by which the LSAN is administered where a multiprotocol router listens to the two attached fabrics for the creation of matching LSAN zones on both of those fabrics. When it occurs, a phantom domain is created, and the appropriate Fibre Channel Network Address Translation (FC-NAT) entries are inserted into the name servers on the fabrics. LSAN zones are compatible with standard zoning mechanisms.

Virtual Storage Area Network (VSAN)

The VSAN is a dedicated network of isolated devices, physically connected to the same fabric, yet appearing to be an independent fabric. The VSAN promotes improved availability, scalability, and security. A VSAN creates independently managed groups of fabric resources within the broader fabric, thus reducing cost by eliminating stranded resources. VSANs increase administrative scalability, while reducing risk through the limitation of access to specific VSANs.

A VSAN may have access control to other fabric resources, such as access to remote storage or shared network facilities. From a protocol perspective, the VSAN can actually appear independent through the creation of multiple processes tuned to particular needs—a function not possible in the LSAN.

The VSAN will use an independent management domain within the broader fabric that includes an externally assigned subset of the fabric's physical resources. The approach is used by Cisco Systems and allows traffic isolation within designated portions of the network. The subscribers to that particular portion of the network may be added, removed, or relocated without the need to physically change the network layout.

Flexibility

There are differing ends of the spectrum that defines storage flexibility. Each segment of that scale is dependent upon the size of the organization, the growth expectations near term and long term, the applications for the storage, and the level of financial commitment the organization has at the initial deployment and further on during the life of that storage system.

Flexibility is somewhat of an intangible requirement that is an offshoot driven by many of the topics discussed in this chapter. As for the categories of storage, when the organization is large, it might take an "enterprise storage" approach. If it is a small boutique using individual "PC-based" storage with internal drives, a small NAS or possibly something as simple as an external USB or Firewire-attached drive is sufficient for their expansion. If the growth expectation is uncertain, then "cloud storage" might be applicable (see Fig. 17.2). And of course, the public cloud storage services that have emerged are built on scale-out platforms, and only a selected group offers the enterprise features needed for growth and performance.

When the organization operates in a shared file structure where many need access to any or all of the data at any time, a

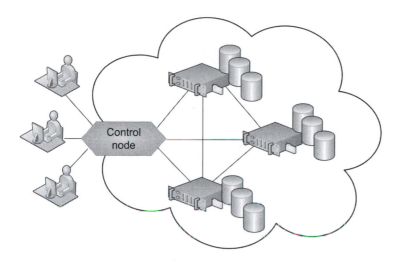

Figure 17.2 The basic "cloud" storage solution for databases and other file storage applications.

shared-disk cluster configuration or high-end enterprise-class storage like a NAS or a SAN may be required. When databases or rich-multimedia applications require constant access, then the requirements would include high performance and highly available storage that allows for multi-attached data sharing from a single volume of LUN across multiple nodes in a cluster.

This latter example would justify the up-front costs of a highly expandable, single file system–based architecture, which provides the flexibility to add storage or rearrange the configuration almost on the fly.

Shared-Disk Clustering

Smaller offices or independent boutique media companies who are unwilling to pay for high-end storage may rely on PC-based storage or a small-scale NAS array to satisfy their applications. An approach that does not involve cloud storage but could be applicable to these small- or medium-sized operations and provide a reasonable amount of scalability is shared-disk clustering. Clustering has many dimensions and many meanings but generally may be associated with three configurations called shared disk, mirrored disk, and shared nothing (refer to Chapter 18 for a thorough look at clustering).

In the broadest sense, network clustering connects otherwise independent computers and allows them to work together in a coordinated fashion. The hardware configuration of clusters varies substantially depending on the networking technologies chosen and the intended purposes of the system.

One approach to clustering utilizes central I/O devices accessible to all nodes within the cluster. These systems are called shared-disk clusters and will utilize central I/O devices that are accessible to all the nodes (i.e., the computers) within the cluster. The I/O involved is typically disk storage utilized for normal files or databases. A shared-disk cluster relies on this common I/O bus for disk access but does not require shared memory. Since all nodes may concurrently write to or cache data from the central disks, a synchronization mechanism is employed to preserve coherence of the system. The mechanism uses an independent piece of cluster software known as the "distributed lock manager" to achieve consistency and to prevent random file associations and orphans that might be assumed as the correct file but in fact may be a broken or incomplete version that is unknowingly wrong.

Shared-disk clusters (see the example in Fig. 17.3) support high levels of system availability. Should one node fail, the other nodes need not be affected. Higher availability comes at the cost of a somewhat reduced performance factor due to the overhead required in using a lock manager. There are also opportunities for potential bottlenecks when employing shared hardware in all cases, but shared-disk clusters compensate for this shortcoming by providing relatively good scaling properties.

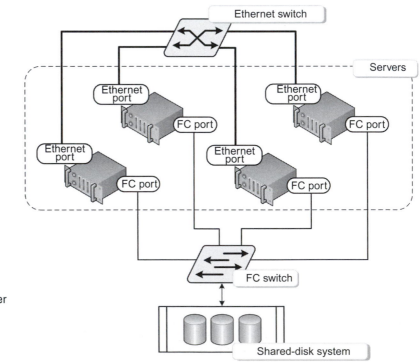

Figure 17.3 Shared-disk cluster using Fibre Channel for the shared storage portion and an Ethernet switch with NICs for server connectivity.

Accelerators

Today, storage solutions can come in many flavors. This book discusses many of those systems, and with technology what it is, we see there are new approaches to storage functionality being developed all the time. When users of storage systems begin to see performance deficiencies due to excessive access, reduced availability, or limited capacity, they are faced with making some choices. One of those is to replace the storage platform entirely; another is to augment it with capacity, convert DAS to NAS, or implement a SAN solution.

Another option is to employ an accelerator cache. These outboard server-like additions function as an I/O throttle that manages the bottlenecks that conventional disk drive controllers cannot. By removing I/O bottlenecks, system performance is increased, which in turn reduces the notion that the storage system is slow.

Accelerators may come in the form of card-based additions to servers, but today they are typically external self-contained units that employ solid state disk (SSD) devices that are capable of delivering data upwards of 3 Gbytes/second. SSD devices (see Chapter 7) reduce the latency impacts associated with head positioning or seek times. The resulting read-write operations are hundreds of times faster than conventional spinning disks. Although such stand-alone accelerator devices are well suited for small capacity databases or email queues, they are not necessarily appropriate for applications that continually require shared access such as those of an editing or graphics platform that uses rich media.

However, for high performance and highly available intelligent storage platforms, sophisticated accelerators are often directly built in to the product.

Array Accelerator

An array accelerator uses an intelligent read-ahead algorithm that anticipates data requests and reduces wait time. The algorithm detects sequential read activity on single or multiple I/O threads and then predicts which requests will follow next. The data is then gathered and stored in the high-speed cache of the array accelerator. As soon as the data is requested by the operating system, it is delivered at as much as 100 times faster than a disk can deliver the data.

An array accelerator cache capacity is by default divided equally between reads and writes. To improve performance, the storage system administrator can balance or tune up the cache if the applications have significantly more reads than writes or more writes than reads. The optimal ratio is application dependant, which is sometimes the reason why separate servers may be employed with separate I/O functions, especially in enterprise-wide media management operations.

As a preventative measure, when a random access pattern is detected, the read-ahead algorithm is disabled. Using the read-ahead algorithm with random I/O will slow a system down, effectively rendering the value of cache detrimental instead of making the storage processing faster.

Accelerators will throttle according to the system data flow. When the disks are busy, new writes are stored in the cache and then written to the disk later when there is less activity. This feature is called "write-back" or "copy-back" cache. Some of the smaller blocks can usually be combined into larger blocks, resulting in fewer but larger blocks being written to the disk, thus improving performance.

Accelerators also optimize the storage system by improving latency and throughput, which can lead to reduction in the number of disk spindles or shelves required and reduces cooling, power, and rack space as well.

The take-home point about flexibility is that the storage systems of today are far more adaptable to users' needs than a decade ago. Going beyond the elementary plug-n-play concept at the interface level, it means, for example, that if a storage system employed just two years ago seems like it has run out of horsepower, there may be alternatives such as accelerators or repurposing that can help ease the financial impact of a wholesale replacement or retirement.

Reliability

As per the definition provided in IEEE 90 (Standard 610.12-1990), "reliability" is the ability of a system or component to perform its required functions under stated conditions for a specified period of time. There are no specific definitions for "high reliability" because it becomes more relative to the parameters of "time period" and "required functions."

Developing highly reliable high-performance storage architectures requires consideration of both the performance and the reliability characteristics of each storage type or element in the overall solution. Manufacturer specifications will report reliability data for all their respective devices. These include mean time to failure/mean time to replacement (MTTF/MTTR) and drive life estimates. Most of these reports cannot be faithfully applied to determining failure modes or failure rates in high-performance storage systems.

A more meaningful perspective would be to consider the true reliability of a system when looking at real-world failure rates with weighting factors including the age of the product and the operating conditions, such as OPS (operations per second) and the randomness of those operations.

Mechanical or Solid State Devices

Memory and storage components can be divided among a sample of mechanical devices (hard disk drives, CD, DVD, and Blu-ray drives) and solid state devices (flash-based and DRAM-based solid state drives). For the highest performance applications, the use of DRAM-based SSD can provide the lowest cost and highest reliability.

Although the reliability continues to improve with spinning magnetic disk technologies, the question is not about if it will fail, but when will it fail. Mechanical devices will inevitably reach a point where one of the components will fail, rendering it useless.

Optical-based drives, though their media is more tangible than magnetic-based storage, have physical limitations that follow the same story as their magnetic counterparts. With that, the care of the optical media once out of the drive environment becomes the relative factor in determining the life and reliability of the storage medium.

Data tapes, such as Linear Tape Open (LTO) and other legacy linear tape formats, have a twofold risk not unlike that of the optical-based medium. If properly maintained, both physically and logically, the linear digital data tape formats can be very reliable long term.

Optimization Using a Tiered Approach

Today, the better solution to overall media management reliability from the storage perspective involves a hybrid mixture of both magnetic spinning disk and solid-state/flash-based storage. By tiered approach, we mean the distribution of the data is spread among a variety of systems based upon access requirements, security, redundancy, longevity, and performance.

The ultimate goal of any solution targets an objective of best reliability coupled with the highest performance and the lowest total cost of ownership (TCO). The TCO must consider costs of maintenance and ongoing support including the routine replacement of media or components over the expected financial and technological lifetime of the storage system.

Mean Time Between Failure

The life expectancy of any product is often considered of paramount importance to its value in a system. Hard disk drives have always been classified as a component with a long life cycle when used properly and in a consistent manner. A frequently cited reliability term used to classify hard drives is the "mean time between failure" (MTBF), also called "mean time before failure." Ironically, MTBF becomes a nearly unrealistic statistic when applied to hard disk drives (HDD). Even the idea of a mean time "between" a failure is nearly ridiculous because once a hard drive fails, it is nearly 100% certain it will not fail again; thus, there is no "between" the first and second failure.

Nonetheless, typical MTBF specifications will be in the 1 million hours range (give or take a hundred thousand). This, even at 75% run time, approaches between 80 and 90 years before a drive fails. The hard drive has only been in existence (commercially) for about half a century, so this statistic is about as applicable as predicting the number of drops in the ocean at any given instant (and maybe as valuable).

In all fairness, most storage experts will admit these values are only theoretical and will not provide a true indicator of the life expectancy of the HDD. In reality, for a large population of a given particular drive, this value is used to determine the expectation for an annual failure rate, also known as the annual replacement rate (ARR) in percent, based upon 8760 hours in a year divided by the specified MTBF:

$$8760/MTBF = ARR\%$$

For the HDD with the median 1 million hour MTBF (at a 75% run time), this becomes a 1.2% nominal annual failure rate. A flash-based solid state drive (F-SSD) will have an MTBF of 5 million hours, but given they are powered up at all times, their run rate is 100% and their ARR would be 0.18%. It must be noted that both F-SSD and HDD will have known "wear-affected" failure modes that will seriously alter the ARR, and there are plenty of real-world statistics available to validate this.

Failure Classification

MTBF is often quoted without providing a definition of failure. Even when defined, the relative impact to an overall system makes the failure postulation ambiguous. To address this ambiguity, it can be argued there are two basic postulates of a failure:
- Postulate one—the termination of the ability of the device, as a whole, to perform its required function constitutes a failure of that device.

- Postulate two—the termination of the ability of any single component to perform its required function, but not the termination of the overall capabilities of the device, as a whole system.

For decades, disk drive arrays have been constructed in such a way that if a redundant disk (RAID—redundant array of independent disk) in that array fails, the failure will not prevent the entire array from performing its required function, that is, the supply of data at any time. However, the disk failure does prevent a component of the disk array from performing its required function of supplying storage capacity. Therefore, according to the first postulate, this is not a failure; but according to the second, it is a failure.

The same could be said about the power supplies in a main and redundant operation, a mirrored set of RAID arrays, or a local and remote disaster recovery site. Nonetheless, on an individual basis, the HDD failed, rendering that particular device useless and thus a failure.

Environmental Impacts on Reliability

One must consider the applications for which his/her devices are used in and the environments in which they are placed, in order to account for the true failure rate of the device. One must consider the length of time the device has been in service and the usage properties for that device in that environment.

Secondarily, once must also account for the quantities of devices in that application and the type(s) of storage configurations. Then, equate that to the entire solution to extrapolate the probability of a data loss in the storage array based upon empirical reliability data.

It goes without surprise that there can be a comparatively high replacement rate for those storage devices that are not kept in a clean room environment or in the case where the vendors do not test their products in a real-life world such as those found in a data center, where heat, dust, vibration, or noise are real factors.

Failure Rates over Time

When looking at a large sample of HDDs over the course of many varying applications in an approximately equal number of differing locations, you begin to see that HDD reliability curves take on a rather consistent form. During the initial period of the sample set, a certain number of devices will exhibit an early failure mode (infant mortality). A high number of drives in this sample set will perform consistently and reliably over the full life of the sample set. Toward the end of the statistical life of this set, drives will begin to wear out and show higher failure modes until all but a few of the samples eventually quit functioning.

Thus, in the real world, the failure rates of the HDD are mostly related to the age of the drive.

Workload Impacts

How a storage system is utilized is one of the factors not typically considered in developing a particular storage system. Without evaluating the real-world failure rates based upon age and workload, any storage system design may incur a high degree of risk to data loss. Thus, most systems that are sold by the premier storage industry manufacturers will carefully select the components in their systems and analyze the real-world applications for those components before signing on to a system deployment contract.

Accelerated Life Testing

Stress testing is a method of checking, statistically and actually, how or when a device might fail. When a drive system is put into consistently high rates of random access, such as in a nonlinear video editing (NLE) platform, the drives' mechanical systems are subject to stresses that are quite different from those of lighter IT-based, transactional database, or structured data applications. High-performance computing environments will have a similar effect to that of a NLE-based operational pattern. In the NLE or high-performance world, the life of the drives is shortened considerably versus the IT-based environments.

Accelerated life testing (ALT) is necessary because of the product development and market life cycle typical to high technology products. ALT involves the acceleration of failures with the single purpose of quantification of the life characteristics of the product at normal use conditions. ALT can be divided into two areas: qualitative accelerated testing and quantitative accelerated life testing.

Qualitative accelerated testing involves the engineer identifying failures and failure modes without attempting to make any predictions as to the product's life under normal use conditions. Quantitative accelerated life testing (QALT) finds the engineer interested in predicting the life of the product using life characteristics such as MTTF or B(10) life at normal use conditions, from data obtained in an accelerated life test. QALT consists of tests designed to quantify the life characteristics of the product, component, or system under normal use conditions. Accelerated life test stresses and stress levels are chosen such that they accelerate the failure modes under consideration but do not introduce failure modes that would never occur under use conditions. These stress levels normally fall outside the product specification limits but inside the design limits. Figure 17.4 shows a generic stress testing model whereby the device under test (DUT) is cycled through design up to destruct levels at both ends of its range of performance.

QALT thereby provides reliability information about the product and can take the form of usage rate acceleration or overstress acceleration. Because usage rate acceleration test data can be analyzed with typical life data analysis methods, the overstress acceleration method is the testing method relevant to accelerated life testing analysis (ALTA).

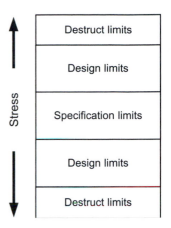

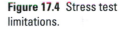

Figure 17.4 Stress test limitations.

Constant Stress versus Random/Inconsistent Operations

The transmission videoserver that plays back long program segments from start to finish over and over again, day in and day out, creates far less stress on its systems than those of a nonlinear editor system. Designing a storage system for high reliability with high performance must take into consideration the amount and kinds of stress that will be placed on its components.

The random access nature of a constant calling from different short segment (short duration) locations on a disk drive array keeps the armatures, heads, and other mechanics (besides the platter drive motor) in constant step. The same drive when used for a contiguous long form program playback from linear tracks on a hard drive's platter will not exhibit the same random access actions, and thus its life span will naturally be increased.

Drive arrays would be heavily challenged if they were required to perform both long form and nonlinear editing-like functions on a constantly changing basis. It is for this reason that vendors providing storage platforms for moving media will fully qualify their products offerings and seldom allow for the end user to specify their own sources of drive arrays for those videoserver/editing applications.

Performance Effects on Reliability

High-performance applications typically require large numbers of drives to meet the high IOPS requirements. Array controllers and the drive chassis components required to house those drives, including the power supplies and cooling fans, must endure greater demands. This aspect of the system design will multiply the failure rates overall, thus reducing the system reliability and risk of data loss.

Other protective measures that help the system survive the impacts of failures include hot-swap capability of critical components, RAID drive and parity redundancy, and hot-standby/cold spares, which all extend the reliability and therefore increase overall system performance.

Durability and Endurance

Reliability factors also take into account additional elements including durability and endurance. In a flash-SSD-based memory system, these become the vulnerability points, along with another factor, data retention, that is, the amount of time that the flash cell will remain programmed. Generally, data retention can be estimated as the inverse of the number of write–erase cycles. For F-SSD, when the drives have a minimal write–erase cycle count, the retention rate of data can be as much as 10 years. However, when the drives are operated at the other extreme, that is, at the maximum write–erase cycle count, the data retention capability may be reduced to 1 year.

The limitation of write–erase cycles becomes a key constraint for flash memory cells. For the two different types of flash technologies, the single level cell (SLC) supports up to 100,000 write–erase cycles, whereas the multilevel cell (MLC) version will support about 10,000 cycles, that is, a 10:1 differential.

Accessibility and Availability

An often overlooked metric in analyzing storage system performance is how quickly data is made available to the requesting device. This metric is generally classified by both the accessibility and the availability of the device, system, or environment that it supports or works within.

Stored data is requested by users at virtually anytime. Regardless of the type of data being requested, each user believes their level of importance is highest among all those that may desire access to the stored information. The classification of "availability" is described by the IEEE as "the degree to which a system or component is operational and accessible when required for use."

In support of that statement, intelligently designed and implemented storage networks must be able to provide access to data and manage or control potential threats to that access, at any time. Sometimes this requires rerouting of the services to secondary or remote locations where data has been replicated or stored as a backup to the primary storage systems.

Accessibility is a measure of the degree to which a device or services can be utilized. The term should not be confused with "usability" that is used to describe the extent to which a device, service, or environment may be used by specified users to achieve specified goals with effectiveness, efficiency, and sufficient satisfaction when put into a specified context of use.

Data Handling and Validation

The process of ensuring whether data is stored or archived in a secure manner, and in a safe location, is one component of the management side of accessibility. Ensuring that the integrity of the data has not been compromised or altered in an unauthorized way, whether intentionally or unintentionally, by a person or by a machine involves the process known as data validation access.

Many storage systems provide their own levels of security, data integrity management, and accessibility permissions. When a RAID volume error is detected, sophisticated data validation software routines are run, which check many parameters that can indicate if the data is compromised. In a RAID-1 storage protection scheme, the ability to compare drive 0 against the data on drive 1 for consistency is fairly straightforward. When the RAID storage is at a level 3 or 5 or combination of another RAID format, the systems get a little more complicated than when the data is directly mirrored on one drive against another.

During time periods when RAID volumes are being checked, performance and even accessibility may be reduced until all of the data is validated by the independent controller system of the storage array.

Availability

Storage manufacturers and storage service providers (SSPs) use the term "availability" to describe products and services that ensure data continues to be available (or accessible) at a prescribed performance level in conditions ranging from routine (normal) through disastrous. One of the means by which data availability is achieved is through redundancy.

Where data is stored and how it can be accessed are important elements in the requirement sets for any storage system. There are varying philosophies on how this can be achieved and in what structure. One method describes having a combined data center and a storage-centric solution, whereas another method looks at the solution as a server-centric philosophy and environment.

The architecture of the storage solution depends heavily upon the size or scale of the facility, the enterprise, or the geographic reach of the users who need access to the data. The approach taken in a smaller single-site facility would be different from the approach taken by a campus-wide facility. Furthermore, a closed campus model would differ from a global enterprise-level corporation.

Regardless of the scale of the facility, users will undoubtedly want continued access to their data. They will grow to expect the concept of "any data, anytime, anywhere," leading to the need for swift availability at high bandwidths that are unencumbered by the number of users requesting that data.

In the data-centric world of business/finance, large enterprise computer systems will typically access data over high-speed optical fiber connections between storage systems. Early examples of these access systems include ESCON (Enterprise Systems Connection), Fibre Channel, and more recent implementations include 10-Gbit/second or greater Ethernet and high-speed, high-capacity SAS drives. ESCON is a data connection interface specification created by IBM in the 1990s, and later through the management of the ANSI X3T1 committee, it became the Single-Byte Command Code Sets Connection architecture (SBCON) standard in 1996 (see Fig. 17.5). It is commonly used to connect IBM mainframe computers to peripheral devices such as disk storage and tape drives. ESCON is an optical fiber, half duplex,

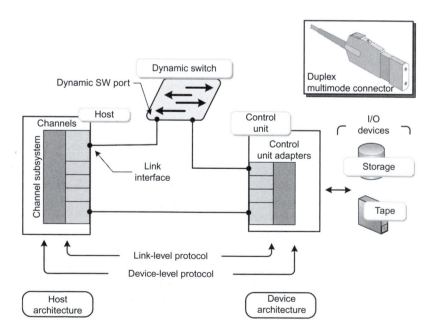

Figure 17.5 System architectural example of Single-Byte Command Code Sets Connection architecture (SBCON) Rev 2.3 adapted from ANSI documents (X3T11/95-469 1996).

serial interface, originally operating at a data rate of 10 Mbytes/second and later increased to 17 Mbytes/second.

The figure and example connector is provided as an historical example of how I/O and interconnection architectures were defined for fiber optic links, switched point-to-point, and I/O protocols for high bandwidth, high performance and long-distance exchanges of information. The developments since that time are enormous, with fiber optic media growing in acceptance and usability globally.

Redundancy

The level of redundancy will promote the quality of a system; it may be advantageous or superfluous as an extra or unnecessary item of information, or it may be a bit or set of bits that aid in the delivery of data from one point to another. The most familiar methodology for promoting protection in computers, servers, and storage systems is to have a fully functioning identical copy of the hardware and software that a system can fail over to when the primary system no longer functions properly.

Mirroring

The complete duplication of a system or component in a system is referred to as "mirroring." This technique is often utilized in mission critical operations models, especially in videoserver applications for television program transmission. Mirroring will often include a redundant server system complete with input/output codecs and/or a redundant storage system, which is usually additionally protected through a RAID-controlled storage platform.

Mirroring is costly as all the components in a system are essentially completely duplicated. However, mirroring will aid in the support of maintenance, upgrades, and protection, which allows business operations to continue on one system while the secondary system is offline.

Systems

Computer or network system components that are usually made redundant include fans, hard disk drives, servers, operating systems, switches, and telecommunication links. These systems may be entirely or partially duplicated. Often subsets of these components are duplicated, for example a network switch in an enterprise-level organization may be redundant (mirrored), but other components may not. How a system is designed, that is, the "architecture" of the system, depends upon the level of critical protection deemed necessary by the user organization.

Duplicated Information

Redundant information is another, sometime unnecessary form of duplicity. In a video editorial environment, clips or entire segments of content are often duplicated on various workstations, in various storage systems, and even in various locations. Sometimes this duplication is intentional, more often it is not. The administrative efforts necessary to control duplicated information can be enormous and often go unaddressed until storage capacities are reached and "something must be done."

Mismanagement of duplicated information (data) can cause performance issues and reduce availability of other data. The control of duplicated data is especially important when storage is limited or when the storage system approaches capacity. To address the management of redundant information, intelligent storage systems will utilize special software systems and processes (e.g., deduplication) to ensure that storage availability is maximized and that user data, regardless of where it is stored, is protected.

Parity and Error Correction

Data systems and transmission systems generate extra bits that aid in validating the integrity of the data being transferred from one system to another, especially when that data traverses numerous touch points within a network.

Extra bits will be generated in a RAID system, which are called parity bits, and they are either interleaved into a data set and spread across the disk stripes or stored on a separate dedicated parity disk drive. These bits help in the regeneration or reconstruction of data should a single drive fail or if a data inconsistency error is detected. A deeper discussion of RAID and parity is found in Chapter 6.

Digital communication systems need to employ error correction (added bits of information injected to its signals) when transmitting information between the sender and the user. The added bits help the receiving end to correct any noise that is added to the system during the channel (transport) portion of the link. All communication systems, whether over the radio waves or point-to-point, must provide a system to compensate for these anomalies that are generated throughout the system.

The fundamentals of a digital communication system, as shown at a conceptually high level in Figure 17.6, are the following:

Encoder and Decoder

The encoder adds redundant bits to the sender's bit stream to create a code word. The decoder uses the redundant bits to

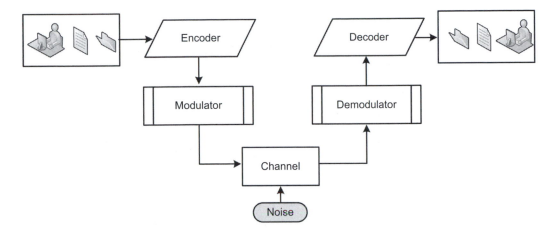

Figure 17.6 Basics of a digital communication system.

detect and/or correct as many bit errors as the particular error-control code will allow.

Modulator and Demodulator

The modulator transforms the output of the digital encoder into a format suitable for the channel. The demodulator attempts to recover the correct channel symbol in the presence of noise. When the wrong symbol is selected, the decoder tries to correct any errors that result.

Channel

The channel is the medium that transmits or transports the signal. It is where errors are introduced. The medium may be radio, twisted wire pair, coaxial cable, fiber optic cable, magnetic tape, optical discs, or any noisy medium.

Error correction (EC) is used to ensure that the data is proper and completely received at the receiving end of the link. The science of EC is applied to all forms of data, including compressed video, audio, and telephony, and mobile communications.

Forward error correction (FEC), also called channel coding, is accomplished by adding redundancy to the transmitted information using a predetermined algorithm. Such additional bits will add "overhead" to the transmission link but are often essential to making certain that the data can be properly reassembled further downstream in a system. FEC is generally applied when there is no handshaking capability between the source and destination, as in a single (unidirectional) transmission. Serial communication protocols will utilize both scrambling and FEC to aid in the delivery of data over various link formats.

Digital encoding for compressed or uncompressed media will almost always use EC in the processes of encoding. When those signals are carried over unidirectional links (as in a serial transport), the application of FEC is highly likely.

High Availability

When a system is designed with specific protocols and their associated implementations are engineered to ensure a certain degree of operational continuity during a given measurement period, the system may be referred to as a high-availability system. High-availability storage systems provide a high level of service to their users. These systems will be designed to incorporate sufficient system overhead to handle peak periods of demand, that is, when data access to and from the stores is at full throttle, and then more requests are added.

High-availability systems will incorporate varying sets of background tasks that aid in keeping data integrity at its highest level. One of these is a provision that increases the availability of the data by delivering real-time replicas of as many copies as are needed to virtually any location.

High availability may be accomplished by the provisioning of two or more servers: one as a production (source) server and the other a standby (target) server. The same application may be considered for the storage components. Virtualization allows these servers to be configured for several purposes and automatically provisioned to address peak demands or failover modes of operation. This concept keeps these servers active until called upon for a service, mitigating idle time and preserving the investment of the organization.

No matter how much "protection" is put into a system, sometimes it must be taken down. Planned and unplanned downtime definitely impacts accessibility and availability. Many a user on a corporate network has seen the message "it has become necessary to reboot the xyz-server…please save your work and log off immediately." When this occurs, the access to data becomes zero, the availability of the data or the systems goes to zero, and the productivity of the corporation goes to zero.

Determining the degree of availability requires significant background research that analyzes workflow, data throughput, protection, and a time/value equation that assesses the cost of downtime and many more conditions. Most providers of high-end and intelligent storage platforms have the tool sets to help the user understand the cost and performance impacts, at various degrees, of implementing a high-availability system.

High-availability solutions can be physically extended to both local and remote server/storage configurations, used for disaster recovery, or employed globally to geographically isolated locations.

Extensibility

By definition, in the information technology world, extensible describes something that is "designed so that users or developers can expand or add to its capabilities." A typical well-known programming language example is the Extensible Markup Language (XML), which was designed to be added to by the users through the following of more formalized or accepted approaches versus those found, for example, in HTTP. Lesser examples, such as those used in software applications, are colloquially called "hooks," that is, a provision or capability for a user that allows a system to be amended or modified to suit a particular feature, application, need, or use.

Storage systems, by nature, must be extensible but not necessarily by the same constructs as in software or programming languages. The addition of storage as disk drives, complete arrays, entire SANs, or NAS attachments should be straightforward and easily accomplished if a storage platform is said to be extensible. The degree of that extensibility is what sets one system apart from another. The level to which you can expand that system is also of key importance, one that would prevent the necessity for a "forklift upgrade" just to gain additional storage or performance.

Videoserver platforms should be extensible. For the most part, the architecture of the codec and server components should be such that as new codecs come to market, they can easily be added to the server system without unduly disrupting the remainder of the server's functionality and certainly without a forklift upgrade.

Frameworks

Extensible designs are also called frameworks, as they set the boundaries and the targets by which a system performs or grows. However, extensibility, in the previous and following examples, can be as much a marketing term as it is an application of technology.

A framework can be a real or a conceptual structure that is intended to serve as a support or guide for the building of something that expands the structure into something useful.

A framework may be a layered structure indicating what kind of programs (in a computer system) can or should be built. The framework should describe how the structures or programs interrelate. A framework may

- be defined for a set of functions within a system
- describe how those systems interrelate
- be the layers of an operating system
- be the layers of an application subsystem
- represent how communication should be standardized at some level of a network

Computer system frameworks may include the actual program applications, or may specify programming interfaces, and may offer programming tools for using the frameworks. In general, a framework will be more comprehensive than a protocol and more prescriptive than a structure.

Extensible Storage Engine

Searching on the term "extensible" reveals a Microsoft core component formerly known as Joint Engine Technology (JET), often used interchangeably with the term Extensible Storage Engine (ESE), as in "JET Blue" or just simply "JET" (also "JET Red," a database engine that is used by Microsoft Access). Both JET implementations are completely different with vastly dissimilar feature sets.

Indexed and Sequential Access Method

ESE, a Windows component introduced first in Windows 2000, is an advanced indexed [and] sequential access method (ISAM) storage technology that enables applications to store and retrieve data from tables using indexed or sequential cursor navigation. The ISAM product was originally developed by IBM for mainframe computers and had many related concepts specific to product names. ISAM was introduced as a database system API for search indices, or more commonly as any index for a database, relational or otherwise. The original ISAM product was replaced with a methodology called Virtual Storage Access Method (VSAM), which later became DB2, the primary database management system (ca. 2004). Today, ISAM-like implementations extend to products from MySQL, Paradox, and other database managers.

ESE supports and provides a crash recovery mechanism so that data consistency is maintained even in the event of a system crash. It provides Atomic Consistent Isolated Durable (ACID) transactions over data and schema by way of a "write-ahead log" and a "snapshot isolation model." ESE transactions are highly concurrent, making it useful for server applications by caching data so as to maximize high-performance access to that data.

Note that ESE is for use in applications that emphasize a need for fast and/or light-structured data storage, where raw file access (or the registry) does not support the application's indexing or data size requirements. It is used by applications that never store more than 1 Mbyte of data, but it has been used in extreme cases for applications with databases in excess of 1 Tbyte and commonly over 50 Gbytes. Not all these features or APIs are available in all versions of the Windows operating systems.

Atomic Consistent Isolated Durable (ACID)

The changes that occur in a database or transaction-based environment must be processed reliably. Applications for media workflow, such those used in editing, metadata management, and asset management, depend upon multiple levels of interlinked databases. The idea of ACID is a little hard to grasp, unless one puts himself/herself in the actual procedural steps that occur during a database transaction, and then suddenly there is any level or form of departure from that orderly process. Such things occur when there are outside influences such as a momentary power glitch, an unexpected software routine that stalls the completion of the transaction, an interruption in the network connection, or a host of other hiccups that may never even be noticed on the outside.

Databases and transaction processing are essential to operational models in file-based workflows. Metadata and the servers that support that data are essentially relational database systems that hold the keys to the assets in terms of structural and descriptive information. Metadata servers will constantly change, not unlike what occurs in transaction-based processing. Keeping the metadata and the metadata servers aligned requires that a consistent set of procedures and parameters are maintained. This is where the term ACID comes in play.

The acronym ACID means the following:
- Atomic—all changes are made (committed) or none are made (rolled back).
- Consistent—the transaction will not violate declared system integrity constraints and the rules of the database.
- Isolated—the results are independent of the concurrent transactions.
- Durable—any committed changes must survive various classes or levels of hardware failure.

Atomic

The meaning of atomic is that all the changes or none of the changes that occur by a transaction are recorded for posterity. This is the property where clients will see all or nothing is Isolation.

If your application or the database server crashes in the middle of the transaction, then none of your changes will "take." If the database is volatile, it becomes trivial, but if it is "durable," then the transaction, that is, all of the changes, will be rolled back; essentially the changes are discarded.

On the outside, this may seem a poor idea; however, it is generally better than committing an unpredictable or incorrect action that is really only a partial product of the production database.

Consistent

All transactions maintain data integrity constraints. When a data set meets integrity constraints, it can be called consistent. A transaction maintains data integrity constraints if, when starting with a consistent data set, the transaction will result in a consistent data set.

A database management system (DBMS) can maintain consistency by aborting transactions that would cause inconsistency. To make this clear, consistency does not require correctness. Consistency with regard to database systems does not refer to the sort of cache consistency issues seen in distributed computation; in this scenario the issues would be handled by what is called "isolation."

Consistency will not apply to the intermediate stages of a transaction. The transaction must be completed, without interruption, before it can be considered consistent.

Isolation

In database management systems, isolation is a property that defines how or when the changes made by one operation become visible to another concurrent operation. In other words, in successful transactions, the reads and writes of one transaction will not be affected by reads and writes of any other transaction, whether or not those other transactions were or are successful.

Isolated transactions are ordered and considered "serializable," that is, they occur one after another without deviation. The final state of the system can be reached by placing any of the system transactions in a global order where each transaction occurs one at a time without any concurrency.

It is said that the isolation property is the most often relaxed ACID property in a database management system.

When discussing implementations of transactional systems, one might hear about "optimistic transactions" and "pessimistic transactions." These two terms describe how isolation is achieved.

In optimistic transactions, the transaction management application generally assumes the other transactions will complete and further assumes they will not read or write to the same place twice. It allows reads and writes to data accessed by other transactions; however, should it turn out that the other transaction is aborted, or that an ordering conflict occurred (such as a transaction actually hitting the same place twice), then both transactions will be aborted and retried. There is the potential for a live lock, which would give no guarantee of progress.

In a pessimistic transaction, resources are effectively locked until they are committed. This guarantees that nothing else can interfere with transaction, yet if one transaction needs the resources in use by another, it will wait, often unnecessarily, which can hurt performance.

If the other transaction needs the resources of the first, then this results in a deadlock. Such a deadlock can be broken by first detecting it and then selectively aborting just that one transaction. This action allows progress to be guaranteed.

Many hybrid approaches to these actions may exist; for example, optimistic at first, less optimistic on retries, with the aim being to achieve the typically greater performance of optimistic transactions while sustaining the ability to guarantee progress from the pessimistic approach.

Relaxing this isolation property generally occurs for the same reasons that those hybrid models vacillate between optimistic and pessimistic: to improve performance and guarantee progress.

The ANSI/ISO SQL standard defines these isolation levels as follows:

- SERIALIZABLE
- REPEATABLE READ
- READ COMMITTED
- READ UNCOMMITTED

Durable

Sometimes viewed as the easiest requirement to meet, what it really means is that a committed change makes a permanent change to the data. Usually, a database client initiates a transaction, performs some operations on data, and then issues a commit.

Until that point occurs, the client should not assume anything about the outcome of the operation, even if the client application allows the user to see some kind of success in each operation.

Once the DBMS responded with an authorization to forward and to commit, the DBMS must make sure that anything that happens to the database once the modifications are issued will persist virtually forever. This does not necessarily mean that the data itself is physically changed (there are reasons for the "undo" command), it provides for an option by another client to modify the change again in the future, insuring the logical effects of modified data on future transactions.

Simply writing modified data to the disk is not enough to achieve durability. It is still possible that the disk may crash (however, there are other means to reduce the likelihood of this and the resultant impact). What happens on the protection side is that the database manager will keep logs about the changes it makes, and will first make sure that the logs are permanent. Usually, these logs need to be redundant, and only after the logs are validated and the software flushes the operating system buffers can the DBMS issue the command to commit the operation, assuming that the remainder of the conditions are properly met.

Despite the intent to follow the properties of ACID, sometimes for either efficiency or speed one may selectively sacrifice certain aspects of ACID.

Extensible Metadata Platform

Another example of extensibility, one that is more relevant to the rich-media world, is the Extensible Metadata Platform (XMP), developed by Adobe. XMP provides users with a common XML framework that standardizes the creation, processing, and interchange of document metadata across publishing workflows. Encompassing framework, schema, XMP packet technology, and an XMP Software Development Kit, XMP is available as an open-source license based on the World Wide Web Consortium's open standard for metadata, known as the Resource Description Framework (RDF).

The embedded metadata can include any XML schema, provided it is described in RDF syntax.

Resource Description Framework (RDF)

A standard model for data interchange on the Web, RDF has features that facilitate data merging even if the underlying schemas differ. The RDF specification consists of a suite of recommendations from the World Wide Web Consortium (W3C), which were published in 2004.

RDF specifically supports the evolution of schemas over time without requiring all the data consumers to be changed. It extends the linking structure of the Web to use Uniform Resource Identifiers (URIs) to name the relationship between things, as well as the two ends of the link, usually referred to as a "triple." URI is a string of characters used to identify a name or a resource on the Internet, which enables interaction with representations of the resource over a network using specific protocols. Schemes specifying a concrete syntax and associated protocols define each URI.

Using this simple model, it allows structured and semistructured data to be mixed, exposed, and shared across different applications. The linking structure forms a directed, labeled graph, in which the edges represent the named link between two resources, represented by the graph nodes.

Interoperability

The ability of a set of diverse systems or organizations to work together is the fundamental meaning behind "interoperability," that is, to interoperate. When initially defined for information technology systems or services, the intent was to make sure that the interfaces employed were thoroughly understood, so that they would work with other systems and products, and that they would endure without restriction to access or implementation for the present and the future. In short, to be interoperable means the product's interface has no encumbrances to working with other products.

When reflected in a technical systems engineering perspective, a similar definition can be applied.

Open Standards

For a system to be interoperable, it is often referred to as employing "open standards." An open standard is one that was designed by an open process. They are generally publicly available but may also have various rights-to-use associated with it. Even though it is deemed "open," there may be various properties relating to how it was designed or how it might be implemented.

The terms "open" and "standard" have a wide range of meanings associated with their usage. There are number of definitions of open standards, which emphasize different aspects of openness, including of the resulting specification, the openness of the drafting process, and the ownership of rights in the standard.

Standards are established documents, recommendations, or practices that are applicable to technologies and are approved by formalized committees recognized as standards developing organizations (SDO). Internationally recognized organizations include the IEC, ANSI, ISO, ITU-T, IETF, and SMPTE. These committees are open to participation by all interested parties and operate on a consensus basis. As noted above, the term "open" may have a wide range of meanings. For example, openness may be the way the drafting process occurred; it may be the ownership rights associated with the adoption of the specification or any combination of many other representations. Industry sanctioned organizations or associations that are specifically focused on certain technologies but are not formal SDOs contribute heavily to the concept of "open" standards development. These independent trade associations have participation (often on a membership/fee basis) from industry manufacturers or technology companies that seek recognition and compatibility in the devices they manufacture, promote, or design.

These trade organizations include the following:

- Storage Networking Industry Association (SNIA)
- Optical Storage Technology Association (OSTA)
- SCSI Trade Association (STA)
- Fibre Channel Industry Association (FCIA)

Best Intentions

Returning to the interoperability topic, most will agree open standards facilitate interoperability and data exchange among different products or services and are intended for widespread adoption. Taking that concept almost literally, if one designs and builds a truly interoperable system, then the exchange of information between those devices should be consistent, openly available, and without restriction.

Of course that is the target intention, but as with most technologies, slight modifications aimed at improving a product's functionality to make it more marketable or to solve a specifically identified problem leads to standards drift. In file-based media formats, including codec development, companies have sought to find a compromise between a standard and a proprietary implementation. This has led to consternation among how valid or appropriate a particular open standard really is.

It has been the goal of many industry manufacturers to find a means to be fully interoperable yet maintain a performance edge in their products. One such effort is in the establishment of a meaningful and useful interchange of media-centric files (audio, video, data, and metadata) between operating platforms.

Media-Related Interoperability

The Material eXchange Format (MXF), a flexible open file format that was developed during the 1990s by the ProMPEG Forum and standardized by the Society of Motion Picture and Television Engineers (SMPTE), allows for the interchange of file-based media between platforms. MXF is the most commonly recognized wrapper standard in the television industry (next to SMPTE time code). The acceptance by the video industry has helped to promote interoperability between moving media serving platforms.

The MXF standard is not a codec format, but it is an open file format conceived to act as a wrapper of audio–visual content (including associated data and metadata). Designed to promote interoperability, MXF is extensible, which has been demonstrated in the years that have followed since its adoption.

MXF is an extensible format that continues to be developed for many forms of applications and advancements in the moving media industry. The SMPTE standards community has developed many extensions to the standard that integrate with all forms of file-based workflows. The Advanced Media Workflow Association (AMWA) provides the vision to applying the MXF standards as a platform for the industry from which application-specific uses can be uniformly applied to real working situations.

AMWA is developing constrained specifications of MXF to ease interoperability in media workflows. The Application Specifications AS-02 and AS-03, for media versioning and program delivery, meet vital needs for AMWA members and the working industry as a whole.

A detailed look into MXF can be found in Chapter 9.

Science and Technology

Media storage system technologies have followed the paths of IT, data servers, PC workstations, and mainframe computers in developing and adopting the systems necessary for continued success, practicality, and implementation. As a direct result of decades of development, storage system designs have become a science and a technology unto themselves. Although the meanings of the terms may be somewhat different when applied to the technologies they are used in, the concepts remain essentially the same.

Further Readings

Storage and networking trade organizations actively involved in their respective segments include:
Storage Networking Industry Association (SNIA).
   http://www.snia.org/

Optical Storage Technology Association (OSTA).
http://www.osta.org/

SCSI Trade Association (STA).
http://www.scsita.org/

Fibre Channel Industry Association (FCIA).
http://www.fibrechannel.org/

Advanced Media Workflow Association – originally founded in January 2000 as the AAF Association for Advanced Authoring Format, became AMWA in May 2007. It is an open, community-driven forum focused on the creation of timely, innovative, business-driven specifications and technologies for networked media workflows.
http://www.aafassociation.org/

Material eXchange Format (MXF) is a suite of SMPTE standards employed in modern file-based workflows and for the interchange of media related content between devices and systems such as videoservers, compression systems, transcode engines and other electronic AV media engines. The MXF suite of standards includes:

MXF Base Documents

SMPTE 377M: The MXF File Format Specification (overall master document)
SMPTE EG41: MXF Engineering Guide (guide explaining how to use MXF)
SMPTE EG42: MXF Descriptive Metadata (guide explaining how to use descriptive metadata in MXF)

MXF Operational Patterns

SMPTE 390M: OP-Atom (simple, highly constrained layout for simple MXF files)
SMPTE 378M: OP-1a (layout options for a minimal MXF file)
SMPTE 391M: OP-1b
SMPTE 392M: OP-2a
SMPTE 393M: OP-2b
SMPTE 407M: OP-3a, OP-3b
SMPTE 408M: OP-1c, OP-2c, OP-3c

Generic Containers

SMPTE 379M: Generic Container (how essence is stored in MXF files)
SMPTE 381M: GC-MPEG (Generic Container) (MPEG essence data in MXF using the Generic Container)
SMPTE 383M: GC-DV (Generic Container for DV) (DV essence data in MXF using the Generic Container)
SMPTE 385M: GC-CP (Generic Container for Content Packages) (SDTI-CP essence data in MXF using the Generic Container)
SMPTE 386M: GC-D10 (Generic Container for D10) (SMPTE D10 essence data in MXF using the Generic Container)
SMPTE 387M: GC-D11 (Generic Container for D11) (SMPTE D11 essence data in MXF using the Generic Container)
SMPTE 382M: GC-AESBWF (Generic Container – AES/Broadcast Wave) (AES/EBU and Broadcast Wave audio essence data in MXF)

SMPTE 384M: GC-UP (Generic Container – Uncompressed Picture) (Uncompressed Picture essence data in MXF using Generic Containers)
SMPTE 388M: GC-AA (Generic Container – A-law Audio) (A-law coded audio essence in MXF using the Generic Container)
SMPTE 389M: Generic Container Reverse Play System Element
SMPTE 394M: System Item Scheme-1 for Generic Container
SMPTE 405M: Elements and Individual Data Items for GC SI Scheme 1

Metadata, Dictionaries, and Registries

SMPTE 380M: DMS1 (Descriptive Metadata 1) (standard set of descriptive metadata for use with MXF files)
SMPTE 436M: MXF Mappings for VBI Lines and Ancillary Data Packets
SMPTE RP210: SMPTE Metadata Dictionary (current version online at http://www.smpte-ra.org/mdd/index.html)
SMPTE RP224: Registry of SMPTE Universal Labels

18

STORAGE MANAGEMENT

Simply having storage available and in sufficient capacity with adequate bandwidth is only part of an overall system reliability and performance equation. If one assumes, wrongly, that the system would never grow, that users would never increase, that every rule in the book would be followed, and that all users would cooperate equally, then there would be no requirements for "storage management." With that kind of criteria not on your agenda, then this chapter could be passed over completely.

However, this is never the case for a network or a computer system. Nor is this the case in dealing with unstructured, digital media storage. Storage management is a requirement regardless of the scale of the system, the size of the storage array, or the number of users.

There are obvious elements of storage management, and there are others not so obvious. In a system, we find there are applications that handle certain functions of storage management routinely and sufficiently, and there are other elements or subsystems that must be routinely administered.

Storage management is becoming a segment of the security and auditing processes that ensure copyrighted intellectual property (IP) is not compromised. When services such as digital color timing, online assembly, digital opticals (fades, dissolves, etc.), titles, digital cinema, as well as film and video output, depend upon advanced, highly intelligent active storage platforms for continued business activities, the ability to manage the stores that support those activities becomes a routine and indispensible activity.

This chapter now takes a look into the topics associated with the management of storage systems from background-related tasks to the more complex processes that involve NAS and SAN consolidation, monitoring, and performance tuning.

KEY CHAPTER POINTS

- Computers and networks—an overview and review of the fundamental elements that comprise the services and applications now generally accepted as routine in digital media infrastructures

- An introduction to what storage management is, and why it is important to control at the early stages of implementing a storage platform
- Life expectancy, including the caring for physical media assets, storage, protection, and preventative measures that will aid in extending the life and value of the media
- Managing file-based assets, and the impacts and effects of disk and file fragmentation
- Practical monitoring and management of a SAN environment using tools that capture traffic flow and other metrics continuously and in real time for the purpose of tuning the SAN or observing the impacts that applications have on performance
- Using root cause analysis to ascertain performance values in a storage system
- NAS consolidation methodologies that include NAS gateways and other nontraditional approaches such as file system clustering, parallel file systems, and NAS aggregators
- Snapshots of data volumes and how they are used to protect, audit, and provide an avenue for user restoration in real time
- Backup and data replication technologies aimed at reducing or managing storage capacity that include data deduplication, compression, and delta differencing
- Storage capacity management for media-centric operations; there is a time and place for everything—are the techniques for structured data the same as for unstructured data?

Storage System Dependencies

Two elements that depend upon storage systems, whether large or small, are computers and servers. We will begin the introduction to storage management with a review of these two fundamental elements in computing and networking.

Computers

Computers and servers depend upon storage, and thus they become important elements in the storage management chain. From a definition perspective, we will represent a computer as an electronic machine used in making calculations, which supports storing and analyzing information it receives from peripheral sources including storage systems (i.e., disk drives, optical media, etc); networks (i.e., local and Internet); and other devices such as displays, sound reproduction devices, and image processors.

Computers do not think, they merely process data and control (directly or indirectly) a seemingly endless set of input and output parameters through applications (software), sending that information to and from devices including storage systems.

Servers

A sometimes misunderstood or misrepresented term, a server (when referred to in computer networking) is a program that operates as a socket listener. We tend to associate servers with physical hardware, for example, a videoserver. We further associated server(s) with prefixes, such as a Web server or file server.

The term server is also generalized to describe a host that is deployed to execute one or more programs. These terms are all relative to each other and to computers, but they are generally not directly associated with physical hardware such as the computer/CPU, and its memory, peripherals, or storage components. The server, thus, remains simply a program that can be installed on application-specific hardware, embedded into a silicon-based programmable device, or in a virtual space such as in the "cloud."

Server Applications

To provide a contrast to how a particular server may be deployed, we look at some examples of what server applications are and where they might be routinely applied.

One server application will use what is called a server socket listener, an app that is created in software and monitors the traffic on a particular port. This process, called polling, involves an application that looks for a form of service, for example, one that is trying to make a TCP connection to the server program. Extensions to this type of socket application may be created to see if the server actually responds to a request with some form of valid data (i.e., the TCP connection is up and the application is running). This may further extend the protocol to allow the server to return detailed status information about the system in response to a "status" type of message.

Media Servers

A media server may be either a dedicated computer appliance or a specialized application in software. This device simply stores and shares media. Media servers may range from enterprise-class machines providing video-on-demand or broadcast transmission services to small personal computers that utilize network-attached storage (NAS) for the home that is dedicated to storing digital video clips, long-form movies, music, and picture files.

In the world of telephony, the computing component that processes audio and/or video streams associated with telephone calls or connections is also called a media server. When used in conference services, a special "engine" is necessary that can mix audio streams together, so that participants can hear from all the other participants.

Streaming Servers

Media streamed over a network to a receiver that buffers and decodes the media for display or viewing on a constantly received basis requires a serving platform that can manage either the incoming signal (for live, linear video and audio) or the pulling of media files (from storage, cache or a library) through its server and on to distribution/transmission to one or more network addresses and users. Media is generally presented in a linear fashion and without interruption, as though it were a television broadcast signal emanating from a local television station. Additional network requirements, such as a multicasting-enabled network, require special considerations tailored to streamed media.

The following section contrasts the two main methods of delivering media over the Internet. The first method using a standard Web server to transmit the file is sometimes called "progressive download." The other method is a streaming media server. As you will see, the server and network transportation method is the substantial differentiator between the two methodologies.

Web Servers

A computer with high-speed access to the Internet that is customized for sending Web pages and images to a Web browser is called a Web server. The computer will often run Web server software, such as Microsoft Internet Information Services (IIS) or the Apache Foundation's Apache HTTP Server ("Apache"). The same technologies will often be used to host computer files and executable programs or to distribute media files containing video and audio.

Player software installed on the client or user's computer is used to access media files from a Web server. Player applications, such as Windows Media Player or RealPlayer, will utilize a technology called "progressive download" to receive and play out those files. Addresses would be like those found in your browser window:

http:// (for general, open communications)

or

https:// (for secure communications)

For streaming media applications, the server (like the Web server) is connected to a high speed Internet connection. However in this case, the computer would be running streaming media server software such as Windows Media Services (WMS from Microsoft) or Helix Server (from RealNetworks).

To contrast the two, streaming media versus progressive download, the differences are the server software and corresponding network protocol used to transmit the media file.

Streaming media files would have an address something like the following:

mms://x.x.x.x/streaming_media_file_directory/media_file_name.wmv

or

rtsp://x.x.x.x/directory/filename.rm

Sometimes streaming media addresses are embedded inside a text file that is downloaded from a Web server and then opened by the media player. Such a file might end in the .asx (Windows Media) or .rm (Real) file extensions.

Files downloaded over the Web generally cannot be viewed until the entire file is downloaded. Files delivered to the server using streaming media technology are buffered and playable shortly after they are received by the computer they are being viewed on.

The streaming server works in concert with the client to send audio and/or video over the Internet or intranet for nearly immediate playback. Features include real-time broadcasting of live events, plus the ability to control the playback of on-demand content. Viewers are able to skip to a point part way through a clip without needing to download the beginning. When the download speeds are inadequate to deliver the data in time for real-time playout, the streamed Web cast sacrifices image quality, so that the viewing can remain synchronized as close to real time as possible.

Storage Management Concepts

As previously mentioned, storage systems are the platforms that support the processors and processes associated with computers and servers. Storage may appear as RAM (memory on silicon, including flash) and as mechanical or optical storage media (CDs, DVDs, hard disk drives).

Regardless of how or where that storage exists, the management or handling of the media before, during, and after is an important and sometimes overlooked process.

Caring for Media

It comes as no surprise that preventative care for your media assets is something that should happen, but is often overlooked. Understanding what the media can tolerate and still produce reliable data requires a commitment to processes not generally viewed as important to many organizations, both large and small.

Life Expectancy

For most users, the length of time for which the disc remains usable is considered its "life expectancy" (LE). The media's LE assumes some implied or acceptable amount of degradation. What type and how much degradation is acceptable?

Some physical media can tolerate certain levels of abuse and still reproduce some or all of the digital or image content contained on the media. Others, for a multitude of reasons, may not reproduce any information when subjected to abuse due to storage, handling, or uncontrollable environmental impacts. Data, when recorded to physical media (such as a removable disc), has been captured with certain additional bits of information that are used to properly reconstruct the data should it be incorrectly recovered by the read mechanisms employed by the storage platform.

The classes of error correction can be divided between electronic data correction and physical data correction. The latter, referred to as "end-of-life," is far more complicated to address than the former.

Correcting Data Errors

Most systems that playback media (audio and/or video) have correction capabilities built in that correct a certain number of errors. Referred to as "error detection and correction," the playback systems will adjust or augment data errors up to the point when the error correction coding is unable to fully correct those errors. At this point, many differing anomalies will develop depending upon how the media was coded and the sophistication of the playback systems that reproduce the data.

When determining whether data correction is achievable, one of the classifications that hopefully can be avoided is the media's "end-of-life" (EOL). One means of determining EOL for a disc is based on a count of the number of errors on the disc ahead of or before error correction occurs. Disc failure chances increase with the number of errors. It is impossible to specify that number in relation to a performance problem, that is, either a "minor glitch" or a "catastrophic failure." Failure modes depend on the number of errors remaining after error correction and where those errors are distributed within the data. Once the number of errors (prior to error correction) increases to a certain level, the likelihood of any form of disc failure, even if small, might indeed be unacceptable, at which time the disc is considered EOL.

CD and DVD Life Expectancy

The consensus among manufacturers that have done extensive testing is that under recommended storage conditions, CD-R, DVD-R, and DVD+R discs should have a life expectancy of 100 to 200 years or more; CD-RW, DVD-RW, DVD+RW, and DVD-RAM discs should have a life expectancy of 25 years or more.

The information available about life expectancy for CD-ROM and DVD-ROM discs (including audio and video) is sparse, resulting in an increased level of uncertainty for their LE. Still, expectations vary from 20 to 100 years for these disc types. Through an accelerated aging study conducted by at the National Institute of Standards and Technology (NIST), the estimated life expectancy of one type of DVD-R disc used for authoring is 30 years if stored at 25 °C (77 °F) and 50% relative humidity.

Blu-Ray Life Expectancy Testing

Experiments by Panasonic engineers with regard to life expectancy and durability examined the symbol error rates (SER) rather than the jitter during data recovery mainly because jitter is more affected by environmental conditions such as dust or erosion. Using 50-Gbyte Blu-ray (BD-R), both the high (36 Mbits/second, 4.92 m/s at 1X) and low (72 Mbits/second, 9.84 m/second at 2X) recording rates were employed in the evaluation. SER is more directly connected with the playability, so it is the "write power" (in the recording process) that is judged during the first practical use of the recording.

To confirm the stability of the recorded data, dependencies on SER read cycles with high-frequency modulation were measured and recorded. Lastly, an acceleration test confirmed the reliability of the disc from an archival stability perspective using a number of prescribed stress tests. The data sets were compared against the Blu-ray Disc specifications when each sample disc was exposed under each condition.

From the inorganic tests conducted by engineers at Matsushita (Panasonic) and reported in the IEEE report (see Further Readings at the end of this chapter), it was concluded that the lifetime of the dual-layer Blu-ray Disc using Te-O-Pd inorganic recording material would exceed 500 years.

Preserving Digital Media

When it comes to the preservation of digital media, particularly physical media (including tape or film-based materials, plastic CD/DVD/BD media, and when portable, media such as XDCAM discs), there are three general categories of environmentally induced deterioration that impact the life expectancy and performance of the media: biological, chemical, and physical (or mechanical).

Biological Decay

This factor includes living organisms that may harm the media. Mold, insects, rodents, bacteria, and algae all have a strong dependence on temperature and relative humidity (RH). Mold and mildew are serious threats to media collections. Any sustained high RH at or above 70% for more than a few days should be avoided.

Chemical Decay

Chemical decay is a result of a spontaneous chemical change to the storage or operational environment. Fading of color dyes in photographs and degradation of binder layers in magnetic tape are examples of decay caused by chemical reactions occurring within the materials themselves. The rate of deterioration depends primarily on temperature; however, moisture will also impact the rate as well. As the temperature of the storage area increases, and as the RH rises, chemical decay will occur at a more exaggerated rate. Chemical decay is a major threat to media that have color dyes and/or nitrate or acetate plastic supports. Cold storage is recommended for film-based materials, and a frozen storage environment is recommended when there are signs of deterioration.

Solid and Gaseous Contaminants

For the successful storage of media collections, users should include a means to control solid and gaseous contaminants that are present in the atmosphere.

Particulates

Particulates are very small-diameter solids that settle on surfaces in storage spaces, which come from outside, when no filtration is provided, or may be produced inside from the debris that results from deteriorating materials or even human activity. Any particulates that come in the form of dust or grit will cause surface abrasion. For tape, images, or plastic media (DVD, Blu-ray), the negative impact from particulates can be quite reactive toward images or data.

Gaseous Pollutants

Such pollutants will arise mostly from outside sources, with the media hampered by air quality, automotive exhaust, and other industrial processes. However, gaseous pollutants can also be produced inside, as a consequence of deteriorating materials or poor-quality enclosures. When pollutants are released by a degrading material, they may affect adjacent materials contained in the same storage area. Many routine activities such as photocopying, general maintenance, or construction can introduce ozone, form-aldehydes, ammonia, or other pollutants.

Ozone and nitrogen dioxide are high-level oxidizing pollutants that can be damaging to organic dyes, silver images, and image binders. Plastic-based media that utilize organic dyes in some of their processes are equally vulnerable to gaseous pollutants.

Protecting against Pollutants

Large commercial buildings often used cloth (or "bag") filters to capture particulates as they enter the building. Internally produced particulates are further reduced by filters as the air is recirculated inside the building. Filters aimed at removing gaseous pollutants that enter from the outside are far less common in conventional building environments. Although charcoal filters can remove ozone and some other gaseous pollutants fairly efficiently, they are less effective with nitrogen dioxide (NO_2). Although potassium permanganate media can remove NO_2, this method is rarely found to be used in conventional buildings, except in more highly controlled environments such as clean rooms.

Generally as a precaution, when bag filters are employed, they should be cleaned and/or changed regularly. Gaseous pollutant filters should be handled by trained, experienced professionals.

Electronic Media Management

There is a lot more to managing and handling of these precious digital media assets than meets the eye. Quite often, the extent of the physical handling of the storage mediums (discs, hard drives, tapes) is limited to the occasional dusting or cleaning of the filtration systems that draw air into or through the chassis. In the case of tapes (videotape or data tape), in general, there is more care given to the operational environment than the storage environment that contains these assets.

There are many ways to protect and/or handle the physical environments in which the media is stored or used. We have covered some of the impacts on the physical handling of the media in previous sections, and any further deliberation would be outside the scope of this book. What we will look at now is how the digital assets (the files and such) are managed by both automated and manual methods.

Let us start first with a foundation definition of the file.

What's a File

Any collection of data that is treated as a single unit on a storage medium (such as a disk) is referred to as a computer file or simply a "file." The analogy, in fact the actual term, came from the precomputer office model associated with the filing cabinet. In similar fashion to the manila folder (the file) that holds sheets of paper (the elements of the file) in a filing cabinet, a computer stores files in a disk, with the disk acting as a filing cabinet.

A file can be found and retrieved (accessed), changed in some way (modified), and stored again back on the disk. Multiple hundreds of thousands of pieces of information can be stored on a physically small hard disk drive, far more than can be stored in any regular office filing cabinet.

Files accumulate extremely rapidly when looking at computer systems, laptops, workstations, and servers. They often plague the storage platforms at levels of indescribable proportions, especially when large storage arrays are employed.

One of the management areas that greatly concerns users and affects performance of any storage system is fragmentation.

Fragmentation

Fragmentation is the process of splitting up elements into smaller segments (fragments) and having them scattered randomly all over the storage medium. Files are ideally recorded contiguously, that is, each element is sequentially adjacent to each other.

Disk fragmentation has affected every operating system (OS) throughout history. The root cause of this is based upon several factors, and for the OS, it may reach a magnitude that can severely curtail performance. The OS is often a dynamic instrument, which is constantly updated to protect against viruses, to correct software interdependency issues, to improve performance, and to patch previous versions when anomalies are discovered by the developer. With the propensity to engage a fallback mechanism such as restore points that enable the OS to return to a previous state should it be corrupted, the number of files that get scattered all over the drive increases in untold proportions.

In computer workstations, PCs, or other similar devices, the continual changes that are made when applications are added, updated, or removed will often augment the negative impacts that occur during those processes, resulting in what is commonly referred to as "fragmentation."

Types of Fragmentation

There are two types of fragmentation that affect storage and computer system performance: file fragmentation and free space fragmentation.

File fragmentation (see Fig. 18.1) refers to computer files that are no longer contiguously spaced in a sequential matter. This creates problems with file access.

Free space fragmentation (see Fig. 18.2) refers to when the empty space on a disk is broken into small sets of scattered segments that are randomly distributed over the medium. Writing to this space is inhibited because this empty space scattering forces the drive electronics and mechanical components to randomly place each of the new file elements into various noncontiguous tracks and blocks that are no longer sequentially accessible.

Ideally, free space would all be located in sets of big open spaces on the disk drive; and files should ideally be contiguously recorded onto the disk surface, so they can be sequentially and rapidly accessed and read without having the mechanical latencies of the head arm and

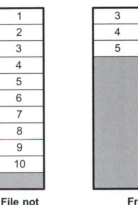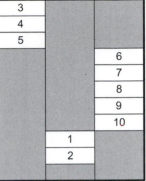

File not fragmented   **Fragmented file**

Figure 18.1 File fragmentation.

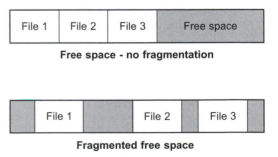

Figure 18.2 Fragmented free space.

rotational wait times of the spinning platters detract from access and read functions.

File fragmentation will cause problems when accessing data stored in computer disk files. Free space fragmentation causes problems when creating new data files or extending (i.e., adding to) old ones. Together, these two types of fragmentation are generally referred to as "disk fragmentation."

One point that is important to understand when speaking about fragmentation is we are referring to the file as a "container" for data. This is not about the contents (i.e., the "data") of the file itself. Sometimes the term fragmentation is also used to describe a condition whereby a file has its records (i.e., its "contents") scattered about within the file, which may be separated by numerous small gaps. Fragmentation of this type may be the results of a problem with an application that maintains the file, but it is not something that is inherent in the operating system or disk file structure itself.

File Fragmentation

When the data associated with a single file is not contiguously located in the same location, that is, it is scattered around on the drive or array, then file fragmentation occurs. File fragmentation can become a real problem as the capacity limits are reached on a single disk, for example, direct-attached storage (DAS).

Temporary files are constantly being created by applications. Every time an application calls upon a file to be opened or created, additional information is created and stored somewhere on the disk drive. Most notable are the files that a word processor creates for backup protection should the app freeze or the user (or some external force) inadvertently force the improper closure of the file or the application, which would also include a crash. These files are usually purged by the application, except in the case of an abnormal or improper closing, as in a crash or write hiccup.

Graphics, CAD programs, and various multimedia or editing programs also create temporary files that allow for repetitive "undo" operations to occur. And of course, the Internet is renowned for creating an incorrigible number of temporary files that are often never cleaned up unless through the conscious management of all the directories, folders, and applications (both internal and external) of the programs resident on the workstation or server.

The proliferation of temp files can sometimes be controlled by the user, and at other times, the user has no control. Third party or integral operating system housekeeping programs can be configured to clean up these leftovers, but they will seldom take the next needed step in storage management, that is, defragmentation.

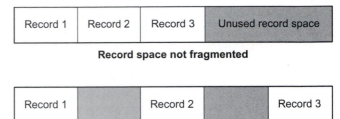

Record space not fragmented

Record Space Fragmentation

In the case of recording, fragmentation may occur at the time an application directs the I/O system to write to the disk. In the example of Figure 18.3, three records are arranged first contiguously and then again with the records separated by empty record space. In the first arrangement, the record space is not fragmented and the files are consolidated into one large area. This provides for good read access and mitigates latencies when the drive heads are instructed to recover the data.

Fragmented record space

Figure 18.3 Fragmented record space.

In the second arrangement, the record space is fragmented. This can occur because of improperly synchronized write activities, interruptions in the write processes, or other factors.

Since record space fragmentation is the concern of how the applications are written and not necessarily of the operating or file system(s), this section need not address the topic any further.

Master File Table Fragmentation

The Master File Table (MFT) is a fundamental component of the NT file system (NTFS). The MFT is the master index or lookup point for all the files on an NTFS volume. The MFT maintains a reference to all file names, file attributes, and pointers to the files themselves. In other words, the MFT is that element that keeps track of all the files on a disk.

When the file system needs access to a file, it first must go through the MFT to obtain the file's location. When the file has been scattered (i.e., fragmented) all over the disk, the MFT must then provide the direction to each file fragment and to all those attributes associated with those fragments. Under a high percentage of fragmentation, tracking this data can be an enormous task. MFT fragmentation is complicated and time consuming to manage; and when uncontrolled, it leads to disk performance degradation during read activities.

There will be one MFT for every NTFS disk. Because the operating system has to go through the MFT to retrieve any file on the disk, fragmentation of the MFT can seriously impact performance. In the Microsoft Windows 7 operating system, the size of the MFT can be reallocated to prevent fragmentation and in turn preserve performance. These topics and work-around remedies should be left to the IT professional, especially when working with media applications from third parties.

Note that in Microsoft's Windows 7 operating system, the term "MFT" is used in another context. In this domain, the term then means "Media Foundation Transform," and it refers to a processing model for streaming media and other media-related activities.

System Fragmentation

System fragmentation is another extension of file fragmentation. In this perspective, one would consider the entire system, including a file-level perspective, a disk-level perspective, a volume set-level perspective, and a complete system-level perspective.

Disk-Level Fragmentation

Many of the previously discussed defragmentation level activities are nonintrusive, that is, they will not (usually) cause harm to the data and do not necessarily require backing up the HDD data prior to execution; however, this is not the case for activities that are designed to "condense" a disk drive.

When it is necessary to perform disk-level defragmentation, this is considered an activity that is "intrusive" in nature. It could be harmful to the data if the application aborts or fails mid-process. The disk-level defragmentation process may be issued on a disk-by-disk basis or on a system-wide basis. You should always have a backup before you perform data intrusive activities such as a disk-level defragmentation command.

Free Space Fragmentation

Free space fragmentation can become a problem when you approach a low capacity level on the hard drive. When there is a small percentage of disk available (free), and one frequently uses this space and follows it up with the deletion of temporary files, then one would be likely to have a high free space fragmentation percentage. What this means is that any remaining free space is scattered all over the hard drive in tiny amounts and in noncontiguous segments.

Ultimately, this impacts any OS's ability to control file fragmentation. The system then loses the ability to rewrite large growing files into contiguous empty space because there is none. New, large files that are written are now fragmented because of the same issues.

When space is fragmented, any system or application caching files also get spread around all over the disk drive. Many operating systems (even Apple's OS X) will use file caching heavily. The drawback to having only a minor amount of cache free space is latency, that is, I/O access times are increased as the files and cache spaces are continually exercised at every read or write command. The ability to write and access caches from the same physical area produces a very noticeable increase in speed. Rebuilding the caches after defragmenting can be highly advantageous.

Apple's HFS+ Approach to Fragmentation

The Apple Mac operating system OS X manages file fragmentation by rewriting files into a contiguous space when a file is opened. The triggers for this are when the file is under 20 Mbytes and when it contains more than eight fragments. This preventative, background task is a standard measure aimed at preventing any heavy file fragmentation, but it does not prevent free space fragmentation.

OS X implements Hot File "Adaptive" Clustering in its HFS+ file system (originally introduced with Mac OS Version 8.1 in 1998), which monitors frequently accessed files that are essentially read only and are not changed. The OS then moves these often accessed files to a special hot zone on the hard drive. When the files are moved, OS X automatically defragments them and then places them into an area of the hard drive that allows for the fastest access.

Hot File Clustering is a multistaged clustering scheme that records "hot" files (except journal files, and ideally quota files) on a volume and moves them to the "hot space" on the volume. The hot space on a volume is a small percentage of the file system and is located at the end of the default metadata zone (which is located at the start of the volume).

Defragmenting Solid State Drives

Defragmentation is not recommended for solid state drives (SSDs) of flash memory–based construction. To review, the main reasons for defragging a disk are the following: (1) to limit the amount of times the drive heads must move to a different section of the disk to read the data and (2) to place the majority of your data on the outer edge of the disk where read and write speeds are fastest.

SSDs eliminate both of these reasons. The SSD's seek times are almost immeasurable compared with mechanical drives, thus moving data to a different section of the flash memory disk is of no value. On an SSD, files need not be placed sequentially on the disk, as there is no degradation in performance over the entire size of the flash memory disk. Defragmentation on an SSD will actually decrease the life expectancy on the drive, as there are a finite number of writes per cell before failure.

SAN Management

The management and administration of storage area networks (SANs) include the configuration of the RAID systems, drive capacity management, and SAN optimization, performance, and troubleshooting. Many of the SANs used in both structured and unstructured data environments are deployed in a virtual machine environment. Figure 18.4 compares a traditional application/operating system to a virtual machine implementation. Note that multiple operating systems (OS) may be integrated through the concepts of the virtual machine layer between physical hardware and applications.

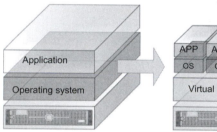

Virtual machine configuration remains the same regardless of the physical hardware.

Servers are encapsulated in a set of files.

Virtualization layer abstracts the virtual machine from the physical hardware.

Figure 18.4 Traditional versus virtual architecture.

Complete tool sets that are essential to the management of SANs are available, which can provide real-time, continuous SAN monitoring through the gathering of detailed virtual machine (VM) to logical unit number (LUN) statistics that transact among high-traffic fabric links. Management systems should be able to visualize all the host-VM-LUN conversations and allow for the accurate measurement of application transaction times within the virtualized environment. System monitoring allows for the highlighting of SAN-induced latency issues that can impact service level agreements (SLA) in a commercial activity.

Caution should be raised when looking into system managers, particularly when addressing the multiple elements that the SAN is composed of. Often, these tools are "manager of managers." They simply collect information from other monitoring tools and then provide a "topology view" that aids in provisioning or capacity planning.

Enterprise-class tool sets, known as Storage Resource Management (SRM) tools, support to a limited extent a heterogeneous SAN environment. SRM tools promote a "single pane of glass" view for most of the administrative functions of SAN management. As information is collected from SAN switch fabric managers, and storage array monitoring tools and hosts, the SRM tools typically may not provide any additional SAN performance or health information beyond what the component element managers themselves may provide. However, they may provide more complete and aggregated reporting, including topology rendering.

When applied to the area of SAN troubleshooting, SRM tools will usually identify those failed components or the data paths that are affected by the failed component, up to and even including the application itself. However, this is just the first step in optimizing how specific applications perform in a virtualized storage or shared environment.

SRM tool products will support a number of services or aids across several dimensions. The broader services will define the degree of heterogeneous device support, how agents are being used on the system, application awareness, recording and reporting on change management, provisioning and configuration, and others.

Using Agents

Software agents are often employed into the systems so as to enable storage resource management, switch management, and monitoring. These tools may utilize software APIs that poll the system and then collect metrics at specified intervals. These pre-scribed "out-of-band" agents are used to minimize the actual effect of performance measurement on the SAN being measured. They observe and report on the data path and unfortunately may not look at nonperformance-oriented functions like capacity management. Thus, the out-of-band process does not affect capacity reporting, but it does affect performance reporting in an inaccurate way.

By design and function, SANs are optimized for two primary tasks: one is to move the data through a system to its destination at the fastest possible interval and the other is to ensure the integrity of the data as it traverses the systems. When the traffic load on the network is at its highest, this software agent's priority will adjust (i.e., fall) in an effort to allow for the SAN primary functionality, that is, rapid data movement, data integrity, and maintainability.

Some agents will take inquiry cycles no matter what the current application or transaction load may be. This invokes impertinent data that then skews the actual meaning of the information obtained. The agent may then either ignore the cycle or provide a reading at a time that is irrelevant to the performance of the SAN at that instant when the readings were taken. What is needed most is a 24×7 monitoring process that ignores nothing and invokes triggers based on real-time events that can be used to affect the overall performance of the system at the application and the storage level.

Application and Virtual Machine Monitoring

These monitoring tools are used for optimizing the server environment. Most are inadequate for network monitoring and analysis or are incapable of finding root cause performance bottlenecks. Knowing that the biggest cause of application latency is in I/O, some tools in this category lack the ability to tune the overall environment so as to obtain a higher application performance and higher server consolidation ratio.

SAN Switch Fabric Management

SAN switch fabric managers (switch monitoring tools) are primarily designed to enable proper switch provisioning, zoning, and capacity management. These tools manage and secure the flow of data across single-vendor supplied multiple fabrics at the level of a central view. The management tool set is used to measure, monitor, and achieve the goals related to SLAs, and aid in promoting security and compliance while containing operating expenses.

Storage Virtualization Monitors

The aim of storage virtualization is to manage storage as a single resource. Virtualization combines storage capacity from multiple, often heterogeneous disk systems into a single reservoir of sufficient capacity, which can be managed as a business resource. The components of a virtual storage platform will include the host, switches, appliances, and array-based storage. In order to increase storage utilization, the storage virtualization monitor will provide the host applications with more efficient access to capacity through flexible provisioning.

Today's practices include the configuration of storage solutions into tiers, which are comprised of varying forms of storage components, such as Fibre Channel drives, SATA or SAS drives, and associated switches. This process mandates the processes of data migration in order to balance capacity against the required bandwidths per the applications that they address. The managers then match the application to the SLA and migrate the data to the proper storage tier.

These tools may further support advanced copy or snapshot services to enhance data protection and further provide varying levels of management reports. However, many of the tools, like the others described previously, make little attempt to specialize in performance measurement or analysis.

Real-Time Reporting and Monitoring

When optimizing SAN performance, whether for a VM or when the SAN is the principal platform for media-centric file interchanges, a tool set that allows for real-time monitoring and filtering and will calculate statistics based on checking all of the Fibre Channel frames traveling through the VM infrastructure and the Fibre Channel SAN is important.

Traditionally, most of the SRM and switch monitoring solutions will take SAN statistics only at a set of preset intervals. In this case, the metrics are only sampled or averaged and do not provide a sense of how the SAN is performing on an instantaneous or a continuous basis. Detailed performance information is usually not captured especially when there is a burst of data or when a large amount of traffic passes through the system between the sample intervals. Once these statistics are aggregated, important instantaneous data such as the total capacity on a particular port is no longer visible. Furthermore, this practice of interval monitoring cannot convey how the individual application transactions or traffic flow is handled on any particular port at any particular time.

This is analogous to what happens when watching a video stream where there are thousands of frames being presented to the storage system or the decoder. Most of the video is seen as unimpaired, but the one or two frames that get skipped or dropped are not noticed, and the system does not report any problems because from an "average" perspective, nothing was "visibly" lost.

Application Latency

SANs are often blamed for problems that occur as a result of an application hiccup. With today's SAN management tools, any root cause analysis could take weeks of time to analyze or diagnose. By having a tool set that utilizes advanced filtering or alerting mechanisms, the number of false positives is reduced and the administrator is allowed to concentrate on real issues affecting SAN performance.

Through historical trending, the administrator can use the tool sets to help identify when a problem manifested itself and then employ various metrics that can capture in precise time what happened. Such tools often can automatically trigger a protocol analyzer that can capture the relevant data and speed up the process of root cause analysis.

The best performance metric is knowing what effect the SAN has on an application's response time when it is captured or recorded at every transaction. This diagnostic then determines what is referred to as "application latency." To get a perspective on this encumbrance, many analysis tools will be looking only at I/O operations per second (IOPS) or data throughput in Mbytes/ second to come up with an overall performance number. This is akin to watching a speedometer and then equating that observation to predict how long it takes to go to a location on a highway that might be congested due to an unforeseen automobile accident. If you extend that analogy and look at a number of trips along this corridor and then equate that to confirm your average speed, you would never know (i.e., when statistically averaged) if one of the excursions took longer than another or if you were diverted or stalled because of that unforeseen complication.

Finding what the effects of application latency are is like using a stopwatch to report just exactly how long each trip took down a highway during a certain road condition and at a known traffic volume. With this type of latency measurement diagnostics, one will know in real time if any one of those trips might have taken longer than it might otherwise normally have taken.

Data movement when in a storage environment must overcome many obstacles as it moves through servers, switches, physical interfaces (cabling, converters, etc.) and onto or away from the storage medium. The proper management of these systems during peak load times (e.g., rendering or collaborative editing) and the ability to reconfigure the SAN for specific workflows can be accomplished with the appropriate tool sets in place.

Furthermore, when changing configurations such as when adding more storage or consolidating SAN islands, performance metrics can be captured and compared so as to apply the right functions and applications to satisfy demands from the users or associated other systems.

NAS Management

Like the SAN, a NAS environment can provide needed storage solutions with respect to capacity while controlling costs within the parameters defined by the organization's workflows or activities. There are numerous configurations and solutions that can aid in handling issues that affect capacity, growth, consolidation, control, and cost.

Integrated NAS Boxes

Traditionally, NAS boxes have come as either gateways or integrated boxed solutions. The NAS gateway will use a front-end file server with external back-end storage attached via Fibre Channel (FC). The integrated NAS box will use a front-end file server with back-end storage integrated into a single storage subsystem. The number of options available in an integrated box solution is limited from the back-end storage side, whereas a NAS gateway can potentially provide support for storage from many manufacturers.

NAS Consolidation

The need for consolidation of NAS storage components arises when the overall system performance can no longer be effectively scaled or when the limits on capacity are reached beyond which another resolution is necessary. It may also be used when organizations already have a SAN solution in place and want to mitigate the number of discrete NAS implementations (i.e., curb "NAS sprawl") throughout the enterprise.

There are at least four basic ways to consolidate NAS data:
- Acquiring more, larger, or better versions of those NAS gateways or integrated NAS filers that are already in use
- Clustering of the file systems (where large computer clusters already exist) to provide high-performance access to file system data
- Employing parallel file systems, similar to those of clustered file systems, which can provide concurrent access to a single file across a number of nodes that are operating in parallel
- Using a set of NAS aggregators that consolidate data across a number of distinct NAS filers, both as gateways and integrated NASs.

Table 18.1 summarizes many of the differences associated with NAS consolidation.

NAS Gateways

When organizations are significantly vested with NAS storage, and they already utilize a SAN infrastructure independently, the NAS gateway is a means for consolidating their NAS data onto SAN storage. The major NAS vendors all provide tools for data migration from their NAS storage to their representative gateway products. Support is also available for all the NAS protocols and most of the operating system environments.

Although gateway performance and capacity are quite good, the NAS gateway approach falls short when compared with other

Table 18.1 Alternatives and Value in NAS Consolidations

NAS Consolidation Comparisions			
Approach	Pros	Cons	Best Fit
NAS gateways	Available SAN storage can be used Easy single-vendor migration tool sets Upgrades back-end or front-end storage separately	Capacity and performance limited to what is available behind a gateway	Large enterprise-class users already employing a SAN Single-vendor consolidation
Integrated NAS	No SAN requirement Simpler configuration Single-vendor migration is easy	Compared with gateways, it has limited file system, performance, and capacity All or nothing upgrades	Small enterprise-class users not already using a SAN Single-vendor consolidation
Cluster file systems	Able to scale out Server performance can be tuned to whatever is necessary	Some vendors may have only limited or no support for CIFS	Large compute cluster users that require high-performance access to file data
Parallel file systems	Able to scale out Improved throughput and performance with parallel file system	Some vendors may not support CIFS Some may have limited NFS support Parallel file access only available on limited clients Requires special client software	Large compute cluster users that require high-performance access to file data Those needing parallel access to file data
NAS aggregators	Heterogeneous box consolidation Single namespace over multiple NAS boxes	Added overhead Additional hardware required Added installation and maintenance	Multibox and multivendor environment Single namespace configurability and usability

available nontraditional alternatives. Gateways tend to provide for more flexibility and scalability when compared with integrated NAS boxes. If the requirement is only to upgrade back-end storage performance, the NAS gateway allows you to do that separately from the NAS front end.

NAS gateways are often configured as blades in a high-performance storage subsystem. Blades are available that include local storage. These types of blade sets may be combined into a single chassis, up to the limits of the slots in the blade chassis.

Users should understand the constraints of this kind of blade architecture. Blades may support one or more file systems; however, be sure to understand if files can or cannot be shared across blades.

The operating environment needs to be determined to complete interoperability. The gateway may also include high-end capabilities such as sophisticated file replication and mirroring, or automatic volume management, which lets administrators increase file-system space without client intervention. Consider whether the blade or NAS gateway will support alternative back-end storage.

NAS storage providers offer NAS gateway products based on Windows Storage Server (WSS) software. Most WSS products are configured as gateways that provide similar base functionality. Client support on Windows platforms using WSS is very tight and allows for easy deployment. When using CIFS or NFS and Windows Distributed File System (DFS), WSS in turn provides for a clustered file system that is accessible across all active nodes and configures nodes as active for servicing data or as passive for cluster failover.

Some NAS gateways may offer both file and block access through one system. Others may employ block access that goes directly to back-end storage and bypasses the filer altogether. In this application, both the filer front-end and back-end storage can be expanded transparently to client access, making storage provisioning easier. This concept lets the nodes act as a cluster, providing file access to the shared back-end storage. File systems should be capable of being updated a node at a time and be able to be read by multiple nodes.

In a node failover mode, any active node should be capable of picking up the file services of the failing node. Additional services such as snapshot, asynchronous local data mirroring, virtual servers, and full Network Data Management Protocol (NDMP) support may also be desired.

NAS gateways should seamlessly integrate into mission-critical enterprise-class SAN infrastructures. They should allow users to deliver NAS and block solutions, while also dramatically increasing utilization of the current infrastructure. Organizations can gain the advantages of enterprise-class Fibre Channel storage connectivity without incurring the costs of physically connecting each host to the SAN infrastructure. This optimizes storage usage and preserves future scalability.

Nontraditional Approaches

Of the many secret sauces employed in NAS gateways, vendors often tout their products as a means to achieve independent performance scaling for both the back-end and front-end storage.

Alternative, nontraditional implementations go a step further by not only allowing a scale-up (vertical growth) of performance in the front end achieved by increasing node horsepower but also providing a scale-out (horizontal growth) of the front end by adding multiple independent nodes that can access the same single namespace.

The following sections discuss three nontraditional approaches to NAS consolidation.

Clustered File Systems

For operating across multiple nodes, usually at least eight or more, clustered file systems can be deployed using commercial off-the-shelf (COTS) hardware and standard operating system software. Nodes may be metadata nodes, storage nodes, or hybrid (supporting both metadata and storage services).

The performance of a cluster file system can be throttled up to mostly any degree desired by adding additional nodes to the cluster.

NAS box clusters make a claim of high availability; however, the box cluster implementations are not quite up to the performance available from a clustered or parallel file system product. True clustered (or parallel) file systems will scale performance linearly in proportion to the number of nodes and still provide access to the same data across all the added nodes.

Clustered file systems are used when large compute clusters need high-performance access to file system data. The downside is that clustered file system products may not be as useful for Windows users, as some systems offer little to no support for CIFS, noting further that this may be a vendor-specific condition that warrants closer examination.

Parallel File Systems

Similar in construct to clustered file systems, a parallel file system implementation provides concurrent access to a single file across a number of nodes that operate in parallel. Parallel file systems require that the file data be striped across multiple nodes, as well as any client-specific software needed to process all the file parts simultaneously.

Those that employ large compute clusters are offered the advantage of massive performance scalability, which is inherent in parallel file system products. Nonetheless, it is always important to check if a parallel file system will support the intended operating systems, as there may be some limitations, for example, outside of Linux.

A common feature of the nontraditional approaches to NAS consolidation is a global namespace (GNS). A GNS enables a single mount point or share for a number of file systems. By providing a single share for a number of file systems, GNS presents a central management point for the files under its domain. WSS along with other products may use Windows DFS to provide a GNS across several CIFS servers.

NAS Aggregators

A tool or system that provides support to NAS architectures is called a NAS aggregator. In appearance, the NAS aggregator acts as a gateway for a series of NAS devices or NAS head gateways. The aggregator allows you to consolidate those files stored on NAS devices into a single domain, enabling the user to add more NAS storage and to then manage those files that are stored on the NAS.

Installation of a NAS aggregator is really no more complicated than adding a NAS gateway. However, the user needs to make some decisions about the structure of the new NAS storage environment, including how it will function before beginning the installation. The following sections are aids to determining how, why, and what to do when selecting and installing a NAS aggregator.

Need for NAS Aggregators

When looking to storage system consolidation, particularly when there are multiple NAS systems from differing vendors, users may want to consider a NAS aggregator. In such cases, a NAS aggregator can be very useful and may actually result in saving costs, as well as being an aid to mitigating management headaches. A word of caution is urged; the more one departs from the consolidation picture, the more the problems inherent in NAS aggregators are likely to affect the operation.

NAS aggregators are not inexpensive. They may be found in hardware and some in software. Regardless, they will all have to be managed. Whether in hardware or software, aggregators will add another layer of complexity to the storage system; and depending upon the configuration, they may limit the NAS bandwidth (especially in-band versions).

A stand-alone aggregator, especially one of the hardware-based versions, will introduce a single point of failure into the NAS system. Most aggregators will be employed in pairs at which time they may also be used to provide failover.

Before deciding on an aggregator, one should consider other options. If the consolidation needs are moderate, one might be better off simply moving up to a larger NAS appliance or gateway.

NAS Aggregator Planning

NAS aggregators will introduce major changes into the storage architecture. At the virtual level, by combining the view of files stored on various NAS file systems, the aggregator then requires the storage administrator to reexamine how this new storage platform will be organized. This is beyond the physical changing of the locations of the files in storage; the aggregator now reorganizes the storage architecture so that there is a new view of the file system that both administrators and users can work with.

Making optimal use of this capability requires careful and precise planning. The administrator should map out any new structure before selecting an NAS aggregator and then choose one that will best support the file views that he or she wants to use in the environment where it is applied.

Remote Mirroring of NAS Aggregators

Support for remote mirroring, which is the duplication of data between sites, is yet another consideration for NAS aggregators. If remote mirroring is part of your organization's data protection scheme, you should take this into account prior to committing to any hardware selections.

Remote site replication across heterogeneous NAS boxes is a protection scheme that provides for quick access to remote data if the primary site's data services should failover. High-availability capabilities will include the option of two boxes configured as an active/active or active/passive pair.

There are three different levels of performance available in varying product lines. Bandwidth requirements, as with any in-band appliance, are important considerations that must be analyzed for any deployment. Some remote mirroring applications will provide for policy-based migration of files between the primary and remote sites. Policy scripts are used to migrate files from an active box to a less active one to level performance and free up the high-performance storage assets. In provisioning file-level migration and so as to retain quick global name access to both systems, some vendors will duplicate all the file directory information at its appliance.

Other software-only implementations may use out-of-band scenarios such as those employed using Windows Active Directory, which fulfill the GNS requirement. Such an out-of-band appliance should not hinder file read-write operations, but users may find it inhibits fully transparent migration of data from one NAS box to another. In these models, much of the manual work required to migrate data from one share to another is eliminated through automation.

Migration Policy Planning

Most aggregators will allow the users to automatically migrate files between aggregators. Through the use of sophisticated policy management, load balancing is achieved and those heretofore manual file migration tasks can become almost fully automated. Such policy-based migration requires that a thorough plan be developed for data migration, something that users need to explore before selecting the support hardware for any proposed configuration.

NAS Aggregator: In-Band versus Out-of-Band

Aggregators may be in-band, out-of-band, or even hybrid in nature. With an in-band aggregator, reads and writes flow through the appliance on the way to and from the storage. This form of aggregator is likely to create a bandwidth problem, as well as adding overhead to current storage operations.

Out-of-band aggregators need not require reads and writes to go through the aggregator. They instead rely on a file system service (such as Windows Active Directory) to provide the GNS necessary to consolidate files. This mode prevents bandwidth limitations for storage operations. However, these out-of-band products do not see as deeply into the data and typically are incapable of automatically migrating files from one NAS system to another. In this model, a "system" may be either a stand-alone NAS appliance or a NAS gateway.

Hybrid products are thought of as out-of-band appliances, but in fact, they will use in-band techniques to migrate files. It is more complicated to automate file migration with a true hybrid implementation, so users should thoroughly investigate the plans and techniques for hybrid systems.

Snapshots

Functionally, a "snapshot" is a point-in-time copy that enables users to protect their data without any performance impact and through a minimal expenditure of storage space. The technology enables a point-in-time replication of the file systems ranging from a single file to a complete data capture for disaster recovery purposes. Vendors providing snapshot capabilities state they can make copies in less than one second, regardless of volume size or level of activity on the system; with as many as 255 snapshot copies per volume, which instantly creates online backups for user-driven file or system recovery.

A snapshot is a locally retained point-in-time image of the data presented on a system at the time of capture. Several companies employ snapshots as part of their data security, protection, or recovery schemes. NetApp uses their snapshot technology as a feature of their Write Anywhere File Layout (WAFL®) storage virtualization technology, which is a part of the microkernel that ships with each NetApp storage system.

Snapshots are used by system administrators to enable frequent, low-impact, user-recoverable backups that are "frozen-in-time," usually read-only views, of a volume that provide an easy access point for older versions of directory hierarchies, files, or LUNs. A snapshot will greatly improve the reliability of a backup and will generally incur only a minimal hit to performance overhead. Snapshots can be safely created on a running system, providing near-instantaneous, secure, user-managed restores of data should a write failure occur or a storage system become temporarily disabled.

Users should be able to directly access replication copies that allow them to recover from accidental deletions, corruptions, or modifications of their data. The security of each file is retained in the snapshot copy, and the restoration is both secure and simple. Snapshots further aid in meeting MPAA usage audits, security, and forensic analysis.

Virtual Snapshots

When used in conjunction with a virtual machine infrastructure, storage array–based snapshots are touted for business continuity, disaster recovery, and backups because of their ability to create these "point-in-time" images of virtual machines (VMs). It is important to understand how virtualization affects storage array snapshot use, as incorrect usage could render storage array snapshots unreliable or valueless.

In this case, the snapshots to which we refer are not VMware-like virtual machine snapshots; rather, they are the snapshots provided by the storage array directly. These snapshots are, by default, not integrated in any way with VMware serving platforms, so a few extra steps are necessary to ensure reliability, consistency, and usability.

VM-level file system consistency is the key to ensuring consistent and usable snapshots. Users need to understand that there are multiple levels of operations that will continually occur simultaneously.

There are three types of snapshots that can be created in a VMware environment:

Hot Snapshots

These will require no downtime, yet they run the risk of proliferating inconsistent data. In a hot snapshot, the virtual machine is live at the time when the snapshot is taken. The guest operating system will be given no warning or direction to flush the I/O buffers, nor is the host given time to commit writes to the storage array. This results in a high risk level in file system inconsistency for the guest OS, which will then force a file system check upon reboot. Although the file system may recover, applications running in the guest OS (such as databases and e-mail systems) may not recover. This is where there is a risk that data loss may result should the storage array snapshot not be restored. The use of hot snapshots should be avoided in order to alleviate potential problems with VM-level file system inconsistency.

Cold Snapshots

They require the most downtime yet provide the greatest guarantee of VM-level file system consistency. To obtain a cold snapshot, one must shut down the virtual machine, take a snapshot, and then restart the virtual machine. Although this can be scripted, it still requires downtime that operations must take into consideration.

Warm Snapshots

This snapshot mode will require less downtime but will require a virtual machine–level file system check (i.e., "chkdsk" or "fsck"), once the virtual machine has recovered from the warm snapshot capture. In most cases, the NTFS or EXT3 file system journaling will prevent data corruption, but because the VM is paused or suspended while the snapshot is taken and resumed after the snapshot is complete, file system recovery techniques are required to ensure that no data corruption has taken place.

Scripts are generally used in these instances, and they will generally invoke the use of the sync driver that helps to flush the virtual machine file system buffers to the disk as a support method to ensure file system consistency.

In general, the use of cold and warm snapshots introduces varying degrees of downtime and service interruption for virtual machine applications. These interruptions may be intolerable to the organization.

Combining Snapshots

One way to mitigate the data inconsistency risks associated with snapshots is to combine storage array snapshots with virtual machine snapshots. Products from VMware, which are initiated through and managed with the VirtualCenter application, employ a differencing disk where all the changes to the virtual machine's file system are cached. Storage array snapshots taken in conjunction with a VMware snapshot will behave much like the warm snapshots described in this section. Under this operation, the virtual machine initiates a file system check, but in this implementation, there should be no service interruption or downtime incurred.

When these solutions are used in conjunction with the published best practices from the SAN supplier, they can help to ensure that the storage array–based snapshots of the virtual machines remain usable in the event they are called upon.

Data Deduplication

With the global extension of collaborative workflows, data is routinely and continuously replicated to multiple locations that are geographically separated from one another. The result is an enormous amount of redundant data creation, much of which is unnecessary once the principle activities associated with those files are complete.

Data deduplication is a method for mitigating storage capacity limitations by eliminating all redundant data in a storage system. In this practice, there becomes only a single unique instance of the data that is actually retained on storage media. The storage platform may be either disk or tape based.

Any instances in the applications that will access the redundant data will be replaced with a pointer that targets the location of the unique data instance. In e-mail, for example, a typical system could contain multiple instances of the same 1-Mbyte file attachment. When the e-mail platform is archived or backed up, all of these instances are saved, which, if there are a hundred instances of each attachment, could end up consuming 100 Mbytes of storage space.

Through the application of data deduplication, only a single instance of the attachment is actually stored. Then, for each subsequent instance, a reference is made back to that single saved copy. Thus, the 100 Mbytes of storage consumed would be reduced to only a single 1-Mbyte instance, saving 99 Mbytes of storage space.

Data deduplication is often called "intelligent compression" or "single-instance storage." It offers other benefits, including the more efficient use of disk space, an allowance for longer disk retention periods, and an easier approach to better recovery time objectives (RTO) for a longer time. Data deduplication further reduces the need for extensive overburdening tape backups.

The data deduplication process can occur at any point in the backup path, including at the client (the source system), the backup media server, or at the backup target. When employed for remote site mirroring, replication, or off-site archiving/disaster recovery applications, data deduplication can further reduce the amount of data that is sent across a WAN.

File- or Block-Level Deduplication

Data deduplication operates at either the file or the block level. Block deduplication looks within a file and saves unique iterations of each block. File deduplication eliminates duplicate files, but this is not a very efficient means of deduplication.

Each chunk of data is processed using a hash algorithm such as MD5 or SHA-1 (or later). These two commonly used hash algorithms are described next.

Message Digest 5 (MD5)

Message digest functions, also called "hash functions" are used to produce digital summaries of information called "message digests" (MD), which are also known as "hashes." The MDs are commonly 128 bits to 160 bits in length and provide a digital identifier for each digital file or document. MD functions are mathematical functions that process information so as to produce a different message digest for each unique document. Identical documents should have the same message digest; however, if even one of the bits for the document changes (called "bit flipping"), the message digest changes.

Cryptographic hash functions are deterministic procedures or algorithms that take an arbitrary block of data and return a fixed-size bit string that is known as the "hash value." This "message digest" serves as a means of reliably identifying a file.

MD5 is the most recent of the message digests in use today. MD5 is a widely used 128-bit cryptographic hash function, which is specified in RFC 1321, and it is typically expressed as a 32-digit hexadecimal number. MD5 is employed in a variety of security applications but is commonly used to check the integrity of files. However, MD5 has been shown not to be particularly collision resistant, making MD5 unsuitable for applications such as SSL certificates or digital signatures (which rely on this property). In applications where security and reliability of the data is extremely important, use of alternative cryptographic methods should be considered.

Secure Hash Algorithm

SHA-1 (for Secure Hash Algorithm), is a hash function developed by the National Security Agency (NSA) and published by the National Institute of Standards and Technology (NIST),

Information Technology Laboratory, as a U.S. Federal Information Processing Standard (FIPS).

A hash function takes binary data, called the message, and produces a condensed representation, called the message digest. A cryptographic hash function is a hash function designed to achieve certain security properties. SHA-1 is the most widely used of the existing SHA hash functions and is employed in several widely used security applications and protocols.

According to NIST, research by Professor Xiaoyun Wang in 2005 announced a differential attack on the SHA-1 hash function, which claimed to identify a potential mathematical weakness in SHA-1. The attack primarily affects some digital signature applications, including time stamping and certificate signing operations where one party prepares a message for the generation of a digital signature by a second party, and third parties then verify the signature. There are many applications of hash functions, and many do not require strong collision resistance. Keyed hash applications, such as Hash-based Message Authentication Code (HMAC) or key derivation applications of hash functions, do not seem to be affected.

Nonetheless, this potential attack led to the development of SHA-2, which is algorithmically similar to SHA-1 but includes a family of hash functions, namely SHA-224, SHA-256, SHA-384, and SHA-512, which are used in digital signature applications. As of this writing, there is a yet another new hash algorithm, to be called SHA-3, which will augment the hash algorithms currently specified in FIPS 180-2, the "Secure Hash Standard." SHA-3 intends to convert a variable length message into a short message digest (MD) that can be used for digital signatures, message authentication, and other applications.

NIST has decided to develop one or more additional hash functions through a public competition, similar to the development process of the Advanced Encryption Standard (AES). The NIST "hash function competition" is scheduled to end with the selection of a winning function in 2012.

Identifying Files

This hashing process generates a unique number for each part which is stored in an index. When any file is updated, only the changed data itself is saved. If only a few bytes of a document or presentation are changed, then only those blocks that were altered are saved. This eliminates the requirement to save the entire file again, plus retain the original, as the changes to just this one segment would not constitute an entirely new file. This behavior makes block deduplication far more efficient. The downsize is that block deduplication takes more processing power and requires a much larger index to track the individual pieces.

Hash Collisions

When a piece of data receives a hash number, that number is compared with the index of other existing hash numbers. If that hash number is already in the index, the piece of data is considered a duplicate and does not need to be stored again. If the hash number is unique, the new hash number is added to the index and the new data is stored.

In rare cases, the hash algorithm could produce the same hash number for two different chunks of data. This is known as a "hash collision" and is the reason that this method causes a potential problem with deduplication. When a hash collision does occur, the system will not store the new data because it checks that its hash number already exists in the index; this is known as a "false positive" and results in a loss of that data.

Some products will use a combination of hash algorithms to reduce the possibility of a hash collision; and others are examining metadata to identify data and prevent collisions.

Delta Differencing

Also known as "delta differential," this is a technique used to make the backup processes more efficient. Delta differencing involves examining a backup file set and locating the blocks or bytes that have changed since the last backup period. In similar fashion to data deduplication, any changed data is sent to the backup target locally via the local area network (LAN) or to a virtual tape library (VTL), or to even a remote storage location via a wide area network (WAN).

Delta differencing is a time-saving function. Enterprise data sets generally change by only a small percentage each day. The complete backup is essential when it is the initial duplicate of the data set; but to routinely do a full or partial/incremental backup is cumbersome and time consuming. For these reasons, organizations often defer complete backups to the weekends, which lead to an unacceptably large recovery point objective (RPO).

The delta differencing approach gathers and saves only the changed data. With this technique, it is possible to perform faster and more frequent backup cycles without monopolizing the LAN or WAN bandwidth. The smaller backup segments use available storage space far more efficiently and forego the many file duplications that result in wasted space in repeated full backups.

A facility with several hundred terabytes of storage may only change by a few hundred gigabytes each day. A complete backup of the storage could take many hours (or even days), whereas a delta differencing backup can update the complete backup with any "daily changes" in only a few minutes or hours.

Replication

Data replication is yet another practice that protects the stored information by making a complete duplicate copy of the data and storing it in another location. In grid storage, this information is "sliced" into segments and then placed into another location on the storage platform so that it can be either used by others (which increases bandwidth) or used as a redundant set of data in the event the primary set is compromised.

Many different approaches to replication are employed by vendors and by users. Replication is an alternative to RAID, although in some perspectives, replication is a close cousin to mirroring. The differences are that in replication, there is a full 1:1 hit for each duplicated set of data. If the replication factor is 2, then it requires twice as much storage to achieve that level of protection (which is a 50% hit in capacity). The counterpoint to that is in replication, the drives employed usually cost less than for high-performance, mission-critical applications; and the need for RAID controllers is preempted by the software applications that manage the placement and tracking of the data slices.

In the video media domain, Omneon (now a part of Harmonic), has built a series of products around this replication concept, which they call "MediaGrid." The storage principles employed in Avid Technology's Unity "ISIS" (Infinitely Scalable Intelligent Storage) platform take a similar approach to replication, but it is referred to as redistribution.

Time and Place

The continued growth of data storage is becoming almost unmanageable. Recently, in a survey of users conducted by Enterprise Storage Group (ESG), users stated that they expected their annual storage growth to be between 11% and 30%. An additional 28% of those respondents are expecting their storage growth to be greater than 30% annually.

The price of storage is not limited to just the hardware. Escalating power and cooling costs and scarce floor space pose a serious challenge to the "just buy more disks" or "we'll wait for the 2-TB drive" approaches. In practice, data deduplication is often used in conjunction with other forms of data reduction including compression and delta differencing. Collectively, these technologies can enhance a well-designed storage plan, one that is coupled with increasing disk/platter densities, larger disk drives, and faster performing drives such as solid state disks.

Media Production Deduplication

It is unclear, as of this writing, if there is a place for deduplication in the media-centric storage environments, especially on the postproduction side. Compression technologies for video media when the images must be retained in 1K to 4K resolutions are not acceptable, except during the previewing or off-line editing functions where proxies or acceptance dailies are involved. Thus, the storage demands remain quite high throughout the postproduction workflows and processes.

The concept of data deduplication is potentially practical when considering backups; however, when looking at routine daily production operations, it is the individual applications such as editing, compositing, and rendering that manage their data sets independently from the central storage. This brings challenges to identifying what is duplicated data and what is duplicated "scratch" data. Backups, in this environment, are used mainly for protective purposes, whereas the "scratch data" are caches that allow the applications to function rapidly and efficiently.

Many in the media and entertainment space are still debating the value or requirements for data deduplication. The argument is expected to continue and may become the responsibility of those who manage cloud-based storage solutions.

Further Readings

Comer, D. E., & Stevens, D. L. (1993). *Vol. III: Client-server programming and applications*. Internetworking with TCP/IP. Department of Computer Sciences, Purdue University. (pp. 11. ISBN 0134742222). West Lafayette, IN 47907: Prentice Hall.
http://www.diskeeper.com/fragbook/intro.htm

A collaboration between the National Institute of Standards and Technology (NIST) and the Library of Congress (LC) on Optical Media Longevity.
http://www.itl.nist.gov/iad/894.05/loc/index.html

Further information about the testing of BD-R life expectancy can be found in the referenced document:
Miyagawa, N., Kitaura, H., Takahashi, K., Doi, Y., Habuta, H., Furumiya, S., Nishiuchi, K., & Yamada, N. (2006). *Over 500 years lifetime dual-layer blu-ray*

disc recordable based on Te-O-Pd recording material. Montreal, Canada: AV Core Technology Center, Matsushita Electronic Industrial Co., Ltd., as it appeared in Optical Data Storage 23–26 April 2006.

Further information on the NIST cryptographic competition for SHA-3 can be found at the following website:
http://csrc.nist.gov/groups/ST/hash/index.html

RESILIENCE, FAULT TOLERANCE, AND VIRTUALIZATION

Resilience and fault tolerance are subjective terms from any perspective, just like virtualization. As in most technologies, the terms can take on many different meanings, especially when used in varying contexts and for diverse applications. The technologies used in attaining high degrees of resilience, fault tolerance, and virtualization may be applied to disk drives, clusters, storage area networks (SANs), tape libraries, computers, etc.

This chapter explores regions of storage management that lacked the technology and that needed to be addressed until shortly after the beginning of the new millennium. Ironically, as we have seen the desktop computer just about peak in performance with the laptop not far behind, we now find that manufacturers of chips and operating systems are focusing on mobility. This means transportability and virtualization of nonlocation-based computing through the deployment of processors, displays, and applications at a level not seen, nor probably expected, until recently.

As such, many new issues ranging from collaboration through security are surfacing. This is challenging for IT managers at corporate levels and in turn has seen the launch (and the roots of acceptance) of storage in the cloud and software as a service. However, we are only scratching the surface of the future for the media and entertainment industry when it comes to storing the assets associated with moving media.

KEY CHAPTER POINTS

- Techniques and practices for achieving high levels of resiliency for storage platforms and their associated systems
- Storage tiering, the layers, and levels of how storage can be managed using automated policy-based storage tiering, hierarchical storage management (HSM), and virtualization

- Defining operational objectives and applying storage performance metrics, such as recovery time objective (RTO) and recovery point objective (RPO), to classify storage systems and service level agreements (SLAs)

- Working with legacy or existing storage components in a heterogeneous environment

- Proactive techniques to prevent corruption of data at the disk level employing RAID scrubs, checksums, checkpoints, snapshots, lost write protection, and early detection technologies

- Virtual file systems, virtual server, and virtual storage

- Approaches to obtaining high accessibility (HA) and fault tolerance for simple or complex storage and server systems

Resilience

Data can have varying degrees of value based upon the user's perspective. Information, the meaningful part of data, can have even greater value not only to those that are directly affected by it but also to those who have no idea of whether the information exists. This means that data, once it becomes meaningful information, needs to be both accessible and resilient to the many influences it may come in contact with.

The value and importance of data may not be uniform across the domain of information technologies. However, most information will generally be treated equally in the way it is managed and in the way it may be stored. Nonetheless, there will be conditions where the information (as data) can be at risk. It is the task of designers, engineers, system architects, and IT professionals to reduce the risks associated with data/information storage and management by carefully weighing and analyzing the many options and paths available in storage technologies.

The Merriam-Webster online dictionary defines "resilient" to mean "capable of withstanding shock without permanent deformation or rupture" and "tending to recover from or adjust easily to misfortune or change." With this context, we will explore how storage can be designed to protect and to correct for anomalies that often occur when moving, replicating, or manipulating data, which is a routine part of operations and workflow.

The challenges of building storage networks and systems that are resilient is a science that continues to be developed. If you place yourself in the perspective of a few of the high profile, highly active online environments, you might have a better understanding of the degree of resilience that a system must have in order to be highly accessible and "ready to action" at anytime.

If you look at six-year-old Facebook, now with some 500 million active users, 50% of them log on everyday and they collectively spend over 700 billion minutes/month online (per the statistics from the Press Room at Facebook.com on November 23, 2010); you can see that this platform must be one of, if not the most, active information systems on the planet.

The network and storage systems that support this global endeavor must continue to be resilient to attacks, responsive to all its users, and fault tolerant to all potential thwarts at all levels and at all times. Furthermore, these systems must be flexible and scalable so as to adapt to changes and demands without warning.

Storage Tiering

Assigning data to an appropriate type of storage is just one of the methods for achieving system resiliency. Where data is placed and onto what type of storage it is contained is a management process that is generally supported by specific applications such as automation, production asset management (PAM), or enterprise-wide media asset management (MAM). Such applications may be enough to control where the data resides and for how long it is at a particular storage location based upon workflow, needs for accessibility, and usage policies.

Storage tiering is the process of introducing data onto appropriate levels or types of storage inside an overall enterprise-wide storage pool. The general rule of thumb for employing tiered storage is that only active and dynamic data is kept on primary storage. Fixed or static data, known as persistent (i.e., nontransactional or posttransactional) data, does not belong to primary storage. Users will gain increased accessibility to active or dynamic data when persistent data is moved away from primary to secondary storage.

In its most elemental form, storage tiering is the segregating of a storage environment into two or more different types of storage. Each type of storage is optimized for specific characteristics, for example, performance, availability, or cost. Storage tiering matches files with the most appropriate type of storage, depending on the needs or requirements of a user.

There are no "standardized" industry schemes used in segmenting, restricting, classifying, or numerically assigning tiers. Organizations are not restricted on establishing how they structure or into what segments they introduce their data, but there are some guidelines to storage tiering that an organization can employ.

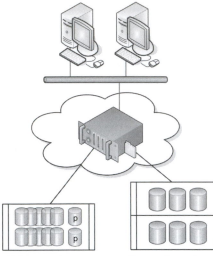

Users and applications

Primary storage
(Availability and
performance)

Secondary storage
(Capacity and cost)

Figure 19.1 The two-tier storage approach is suitable for most organizations.

Most organizations can meet their goals for storage management by employing two storage tiers. A typical two-tiered storage environment (as shown in Fig. 19.1) adds data into an environment that is optimized as primary storage for performance and availability, with a secondary tier aimed at storage capacity and cost.

However, a two-tier storage approach may not be sufficient for some organizations. Certain business requirements and diversification may make it necessary to expand beyond the simple "primary" and "secondary" storage analogies, so intermediary or tertiary platforms may need to be implemented that fulfill these additional requirements. By dividing storage into multiple tiers, other advantages are realized, such as options, configurations, and feature sets that can be provisioned and managed more easily.

Assigning your data to an appropriate type of storage is just one of the methods for achieving overall system resiliency. We will first look at a two-tier approach to managing storage, given that this is the most common and convenient method.

Two-Tier Approach

When business activities do not command more aggressive multitier approaches to storage, alternatives are available to mediate the dynamics of the storage requirements. A two-tiered approach has the opportunity to use all or some of the applications, approaches, and technologies that will be discussed throughout this chapter and aggregate them to one of the two tiers: one for high production and high availability and the other for long-term preservation, archive, or business continuity.

One of the solutions that storage professionals may employ, regardless of the tier level, is automation. Higher end multitier solutions will use automation and data traffic flow analysis to ensure that their assets are placed on the right tier and can be accessible for the needs of the operation when demanded. These systems monitor various data activities and may utilize technologies such as snapshots and deduplication to support the storage systems' performance and requirements on an ongoing basis. Long-standing technologies, like hierarchical storage management (HSM), are solutions that automatically move data from high cost storage to less cost storage based upon usage or demand for those assets and historical trends or policies set by the users or administrators.

Hierarchical Storage Management

HSM provides an automatic way of managing and distributing data between the different storage tiers (or layers) to meet user needs for accessing data, while minimizing the overall cost. The concept of hierarchical storage management involves the placement of data items in such a way as to minimize the cost of data storage, while maximizing the accessibility.

The principal features that hierarchical storage management provides include the following:

- A reduced total cost of storage—data that is accessed less frequently will be moved to and reside on lower cost storage.
- Performance benefits—freeing up costly, high-performance storage when less frequently utilized data resides on a lower tier, less costly, level of storage. This strategy has the potential to increase overall system performance.
- Utilizing tape automation—when an automated tape library is employed, there are further opportunities to reduce operating costs. For backup recovery and media services, automated tape systems reduce operational costs by mitigating manual intervention. Because most tape operations are unattended, the chances for human errors are substantially reduced. Using a hands-off approach assures that all the proper data is moved to backup or archive without prompting.
- Improved system availability—historical data is not repeatedly saved. The number of instances of the same data are reduced. Active data stays on high-performance online storage, whereas inactive data is moved to near line or archive under a rules- or policy-based model.
- Transparent to applications—no application changes are required as data is moved to a different storage technology.
- New applications are enabled—printed information, information in file drawers, and information that is not presently managed can be stored inexpensively when enabled on an HSM.

When asset management, content management, or other forms of media management are integrated with hierarchical storage management applications, the features embedded in each of these data management systems collectively give rise to significant cost savings and revenue opportunities throughout the business. Users will find a reduction in the total costs of disk and tape hardware derived from the more effective use of expensive "high-performance" disk storage as opposed to less expensive tape storage.

Benefits are further realized by reducing the costs of labor derived from those skills that were previously required to manage the assets. A one-time savings area is that those previously allocated tasks involved in the management and cleanup of system disk space, as maximum storage capacities were reached, are now transformed because automation can carry those services. Another cost reduction is that the systems now respond faster to requests for archive data, and the deliveries are more error free.

HSM can be integrated with any of the subtiers associated with the storage solution, including near line and archive. HSM may be deployed in a disk-to-disk (D2D), a disk-to-tape (D2T), or a disk-to-disk-to-tape (D2D2T) environment, providing efficiency and rapid response to user requests.

Either in a two-tiered or in a multitiered approach, the principles of HSM can be applied to migration, archive, and storage management systems as part of the asset management system or as an application layer in an overall storage management architecture.

Policy-Based Automated Storage Tiering

Attempting to manually manage data between two (or more) tiers of storage is an ill-advised practice; hence, the practice known as "policy-based management" was created. Some vendors and systems will utilize an "over-the-top" approach to automate policy-based storage management. This practice may be used when the storage management system needs to touch several vendors' hardware or software, such as in the case of an asset management system. Another approach is to employ an "in-line" solution that works across all the storage tiers.

Utilizing an in-line, policy-based solution to automate storage management practices is a much more practical approach. One of the architectures employed by those systems with only two tiers is an in-line device that is logically situated between clients and file storage. This device acts as a proxy for all file accesses. By employing an in-line technology, the system can respond dynamically to changes in storage system requirements.

When taking a two-layer approach, the data management on two tiers of storage is simplified and requires little human intervention. Companies that provide this form of two-layer management may offer a stand-alone "box" solution and applications set between the client and the storage platforms, or they may provide a similar set of services bundled into a larger set of services including HSM, deduplication, snapshotting, accelerators, and the like.

We will first look at the two-layer management approach and examine the multitier alternatives. Later, we will diversify the discussion into the associated services and technologies that may be applied in either a two-tier or a multitier storage management implementation.

File Virtualization Layer

The first of the two layers, referred to as "file virtualization," allows enterprises to build storage environments that are comprised of different storage devices, platforms, vendors, and technologies. This process decouples the logical access to a file from its physical location on back-end storage.

Through these principles of file virtualization, the system federates multiple physical storage resources into a single virtual pool. In this simplified model, a virtual share is comprised of the total capacity that is found on two separate storage resources, a primary storage unit and a secondary storage unit. The first storage unit provides the online, mission-critical file storage. The second storage unit is used for less often accessed storage and may provide other services, such as deduplication, to keep storage capacities maximized. Using this approach, user/clients see a logical view of a single virtual share instead of two physical shares. The user/clients obtain "logical access" to files through the virtual share, and administrators (or third party applications) can move files between the two physical shares without impacting user/client access.

As the logical file mapping does not change, the file migrations never require any user/client reconfiguration.

Automation Layer

The second of the two layers, the automation layer, provides the necessary intelligence to ensure that all files are located on the appropriate storage tier. Data management policies are configured so that the system determines not only when and where to move existing files but also where to place newly created files. Policies are based on a number of considerations, including a file's age, type, location, access rights, project status, etc. The automation engine consists of several components, the filesets, and placement rules. Figure 19.2 shows how the two tiers of storage are migrated using automation and file-virtualization layer technologies.

A fileset informs the storage management controller to which collection of data it should apply a policy. It defines a group of files based on a shared attribute or collection of attributes. Filesets can be created based on any portion of a file's name, including its path or extension, size, or age based on last accessed or last modified date. Filesets can also be combined in unions or intersections to create more sophisticated policies.

For example, an aging policy can target MP3 files that have not been modified in the last 30 days, or all MP3 files that have not been accessed in the last 30 days. A "placement rule" then instructs the storage management system where to place a file

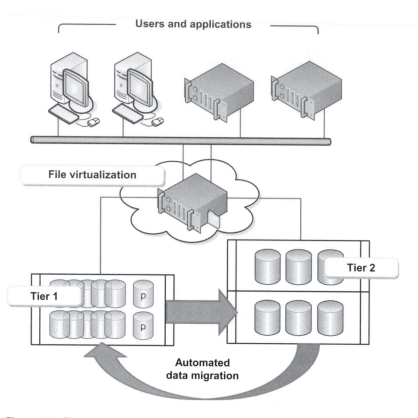

Figure 19.2 Two-tier automated storage using file virtualization.

that was matched by a fileset. Placement rules can be set up to target a specific share or, on a broader basis, a collection of shares as either the source or the target for data migration.

To ascertain the scale of the storage management platform, one must consider the flow of data through the system at average and peak times. Configured in part like a Gigabit Ethernet switch with channelized control to manage throughput, the storage management system is built around both hardware and software. The hardware components are basically Gigabit Ethernet ports that are sized to the maximum throughput requirements of the data flows. Dedicated policy-based file virtualization systems (consisting of both hardware and software) take the place of the traditional multiport Ethernet switches that cross connect each user or server to a large pool of individual storage subsystems.

In summary, file virtualization systems simplify many of the traditional storage management tasks that would normally have been addressed individually on a platform by platform basis.

Multitiered Storage

Some organizations, especially larger enterprises and businesses that provide for several kinds of service, may wish to depart from the simpler two-tiered storage approach, even with the several value-added capabilities the more confined architecture may provide. When this is the objective, the storage solution moves into a multitiered configuration, often through the means of a "highly resilient storage environment."

In this alternative, enterprise-wide storage data is then shifted so as to map the many elements of storage management into different tiers, also called "service levels," depending upon the value of the data (information) to the enterprise as a whole. With this perspective, the easiest method to ascertain which data is assigned to which service level (tier) is to consider the value of that data to the enterprise relative to each working environment and each workflow. This will obviously vary with the business and the structure of the organization, so, for example, we will segment the storage tier architectures into the following four tiers:

Tier 1—where mission-critical, online data are maintained

Tier 2—where business critical information is kept

Tier 3—where workgroup and distributed enterprise data are placed

Tier 4—where reference, archival, and business compliance data are kept

The highest tier will be assigned the highest level of resiliency. As the service levels move to the lower tiers, the resiliency options can be selected appropriately. Regardless of the tier level, even for the lowest tiers (where archive, reference, or business compliance data is stored), there are inherent cost-effective and value-driven features available to increase storage resiliency for those purposes.

Before looking into what options and practices could be applied to which tier or service level, it might be advisable to understand how the industry looks at ascertaining or measuring recovery when an event, small or large, occurs that disrupts operations. An event could be anything from an outage on the network, to a loss of data accessibility, to a complete disaster when multiple systems or the entire site fails.

Recovery Parameters

Reducing the impact to the business in the event of failures and recovery times is a prime objective that is essential to establishing the degree of resiliency that a system must have. Every consideration will add to the overall cost of the storage system, so establishing the business value of each data class will more than likely involve certain trade-offs.

The industry uses two metrics to associate the performance of a storage tier and for setting a range of boundaries for acceptability: they are "recovery point objective" (RPO) and "recovery time objective" (RTO). Also note that these two metrics are used in establishing parameters for a disaster recovery (DR) solution.

- Recovery time objective (RTO)—The length of time it takes to return to normal or near normal operations in the event of an outage where accessibility to data is lost.
- Recovery point objective (RPO)—The amount of data, measured in time, that you can lose from the outage event.

These two primary considerations should be used in establishing the appropriate storage tier level for your data. These metrics are business-driven and set the stage for the following: whether you recover from disk or tape; where you recover to; and the size of the recovery infrastructure and staff needed to manage your systems. The RTO metric is relatively straightforward to understand, but RPO is a little more complex as it includes describing an "acceptable level of data loss"; that is, the tolerance level when data is inaccessible. RPO can vary, for example, from hours for reference data to zero data loss for compliance data.

Once in a situation where data is unavailable to those applications that expect the data to be present in order to function, the nonproductivity clock begins to run. As a result, when the recovered data is made available again to the application and what time it is available may be especially important, as only the end users and owners of the critical applications affected by any outage can understand (and pay for) the RPO and RTO specific to the "usability of the application." The additional indicators that you may want to implement and/or account for are called "RPO-Data" and "RTO-Data" and may apply to situations where service contracts or internal financial accountability metrics influence the scale of the resiliency and how that scale affects budgets.

Operational Objectives

It is important to understand, especially when trying to design a solution that fits all the possible instances or implications, that RTO and RPO both by name infer that they are "objectives," which by definition is effectively a target. If an RPO is eight hours, then the design solution architecture must ensure data loss of eight hours or less. Thus, when testing performance, or actually recovering from an event (i.e., a "disaster"), be sure to track and document the actual thresholds that are achieved, which will include recovery "point" and recovery "time."

From the operational perspective, all too often, the time to recover does not meet the objective due to unconsidered "overhead" time. Overhead time needs to be accounted for when the organization needs to make considerations for items such as the selection of DR teams and if they can be fulfilled with the "available staff" as opposed to outsourcing the services as in a vendor-provided service contract or other outside entity. When disaster strikes, you need to understand when the actual declaration is made and mark the time for getting to the recovery site from that point. Finally, it is important to know and accept that this could be a massive undertaking and that the overall bedlam involved in initiating a recovery from a disaster is not something that occurs in everyday operations and is difficult to replicate, just as a fire drill does not exactly replicate the actual fire "event" or its aftermath.

Through the efforts of tracking and documenting actual versus objective (especially during acceptance, compliance, or routine testing), the organization will understand what is being accomplished in a given period of time. The value being that you will ultimately defend future investments by honing the recovery methodologies and processes to better meet or exceed those objectives.

When Disaster Strikes

In any form of disaster recovery, whether short term with minimal intervention or long term with deeper impacts, the recovery teams will be looking at all elements of the production and storage chain: servers, networks, and storage. Each of these areas have both interrelated and isolated roles that pertain to getting the system back online from a disaster. For this reason, organizations must routinely test the procedures and document the findings.

Depending upon the scale of the disaster, once the infrastructure is recovered and the associated application data is again available to users, there will typically be several other tasks that are necessary to make the application usable and presentable to end users. For example, if there is a suspicion that databases were corrupted, the analysts will need to evaluate what impact the outage had on lost data or unrecoverable information. These people need to do to the databases what the application and software teams needed to do to validate system functionality.

Having the metrics of your system available, because they were documented against actual test runs, will aid in assessing the short- and long-term impacts of how well the resiliency factors, which were designed into the system originally, performed. Briefly, it may not be fully possible to assess how well the design worked until it failed over and recovered back.

With these perspectives in mind, the context of tiers begins to make better sense.

Tier Classification Ranges

Whether in an enterprise-class data center or in the central nerve centers of a broadcast program distributor, mission-critical data (your product in the case of a broadcaster) typically demands no unplanned outages and a zero tolerance for data loss (i.e., no "off-air or black time" for the broadcaster). These requirements place this level of data and the systems that support it into the tier 1 service classes for storage.

The requirements of other departments (such as news production or postproduction) typically have lower service levels and for the most part may be able to withstand longer unplanned downtime and minutes of lost data. This does not mean their data is anymore or less important; it is that the costs involved in supporting the equipments and values that these services have to the organization or product are not like those associated with mission-critical operations.

For other operations, such as long-term promotional services, Web design, or for smaller remote offices without shared storage, these workgroups could withstand as much as a day's worth of data loss or inaccessibility, with outages resolved in hours instead of minutes.

As discussed earlier in this chapter, data storage can be segmented into different tiers or service levels for activities that occur and influence the productivity and performance of the enterprise. We will now look at some of the components and rationale for the multitier classifications outlined earlier.

Tier 1: Mission-Critical, Online Data

Mission-critical data has the highest value to the organization and by necessity requires the highest tier of storage resiliency. Data segmented to this tier is intolerable to any amount of lost data. Rarely, an occasional few moments of unplanned downtime will be withstood without directly impacting the front-facing product or the top line of revenue generation. In order to meet this level of storage resiliency, the enterprise needs to implement a set of features and guidelines and a set of options that result in a resiliency target with the following metrics:

- Recovery point objective (RPO)—zero data loss
- Recovery time objective (RTO)—zero downtime to recovery in minutes

Not only online applications will need sufficient protection but a scheme to migrate critical data to and from secondary storage (tier 2 or tier 3) should also be planned for. For broadcast on-air operations, the videoserver platform will generally have RAID drives, often RAID 6 or RAID 60, and occasionally RAID 5 for budget conscious operations. High profile program channels will usually use two identical server and storage platforms, called main and protect, with the protect being a 100% mirror of the main system.

For a production environment that works with digital intermediates (DIs) and visual effects for digital film production (i.e., "digital cinema"), tier 1 storage implementation could span the range from modest to high-end storage management. This workflow does not have the equivalent constraints of commercial on-the-air or program content distribution broadcasting, so a different approach is taken. However, the deadlines imposed on these activities are every bit as crucial to the organization as is getting a broadcaster's program and its commercials on the air and on time.

For motion picture or high-end national advertising productions, seldom is the original material exposed to the risks of the postproduction processes and storage platforms until the rendering or final assembly process. For this working environment, the original material is often transferred to an uncompressed data library with a high-resolution (high definition or equivalent) digital proxy created. Once the proxy is created, the production community only works with these proxy-based assets.

One of the differences in motion picture production is that the size of the data sets and the number of elements involved in a production (especially with effects) can be orders of magnitude larger in size compared with broadcast or program playback. With that in mind, the complications of handling these data sets or with migrating them to secondary storage or to backup protection present an entirely different set of issues.

For a data center or business operations' environment, storage should be protected from any local storage-related issues through mirroring, the replicating of high value data to remote locations, and the use of nonsynchronized snapshots to mirror sites or vaults using a high-speed, long-distance interconnection. For reconstruction, to speed the process and to reduce the risks during reconstruction, the number of loops should be maximized. The size of the RAID groups should be smaller to support faster reconstruction, and also because of the reduced risks in the event of a smaller RAID set failure versus a large set with significantly larger single-drive capacities.

Tier 2: Business Critical Data

Here the target is minimization of disruptive activities. At this level, a business will typically be processing high value data. The loss of data or its unavailability for more than a few minutes is to be avoided. Higher value data classes are generally placed on storage systems with a resiliency level not unlike that of mission-critical systems but potentially with a reduction in the number of mirrored servers and storage set combinations.

Storage clustering may be employed when the organization is geographically dispersed or when several smaller offices are routinely connected into another set of regional offices. Clustering does not necessarily require that the drive components be physically adjacent to each other, and in some cases for data protection, they are allocated across more than one location.

- Recovery point objective (RPO)—from zero lost data up to minutes of lost data
- Recovery time objective (RTO)—recovery can take minutes (but not hours)

Tier 3: Distributed Environments and Workgroups

Some segments of the organization's structure, which might include localized workgroups and workgroups that are geographically distributed across an enterprise environment, are often able to tolerate longer unplanned outages and some level of data loss. These types of deployments, at these lower service levels, can employ lower cost storage solutions that leverage the reduced costs associated with these lower tiers of functionality or performance.

Storage resiliency options are available when this class of storage is utilized in an active–active configuration.

- Recovery point objective (RPO)—data loss of minutes to hours for local workgroups, possibly up to a day for remote offices
- Recovery time objective (RTO)—recovery can take minutes to hours

Tier 4: Reference, Archive, and Compliance Data

This tier of storage is typically implemented as near-line storage using lower cost media, such as SATA disks in "just a bunch of disks" (JBOD) or simple array configurations. The data stored on this tier is seldom active and infrequently accessed for reads; so this environment is tolerant of longer downtime. For write activities, most archival applications will buffer the write data for hours, but are capable of queuing up the data for much longer should the tape or disk library be temporarily unavailable, out of operation for maintenance or for other uncontrollable reasons.

Tier 4 storage may include disk-to-disk (D2D), disk-to-tape (D2T), or even disk-to-disk-to-tape (D2D2T) methods for archive or data compliance applications. Which of these profiles are selected depends upon the need for accessibility, the volume of data, and the degree of protection required by the organization.

- Recovery point objective (RPO)—ranging from a few minutes up to a day of lost data acceptability, with no acceptable loss of data for compliance archiving (business data compliance is now critical in terms of legal protection and corporate records associated with Sarbanes-Oxley regulations).
- Recovery time objective (RTO)—recovery can take minutes to hours. If the data is stored in a protected vault off-site, the RTO could become a day or more.

From the loss of data perspective, a high degree of resiliency is still expected. Reference data accessibility can usually tolerate hours of inaccessibility, whereas any business compliance data loss is totally unacceptable.

Protecting Data and Storage

Data can be protected in various ways and by differing configurations. Based upon the needs, performance, and values that the storage contributes to the organization, a storage device hierarchy can potentially incorporate many layers of both physical (drives, controllers, and other hardware) and logical (software, virtualization, and replication) subsystems. The architecture of the storage solution affects the levels of protection and performance that can be achieved. Looking from a global perspective, the concept of a "storage triangle" (shown in Fig. 19.3), reveals three axes of storage that could be employed from one to many regions of the organization. The triangle graphically describes three differing configurations based upon capacity, bandwidth, or resiliency.

Capacity

If the goal is to achieve maximum capacity without worrying too much about bandwidth or resiliency, then the upper point of the triangle is one of the more straightforward approaches. In the "capacity" model, a massive number of inexpensive (e.g., SATA) drives could be strung together to form a JBOD configuration that holds oodles of gigabytes of data. The drawback of this course is that there is no protection, no integrated backup, and no resiliency in the case of having any one single drive in the JBOD group fail.

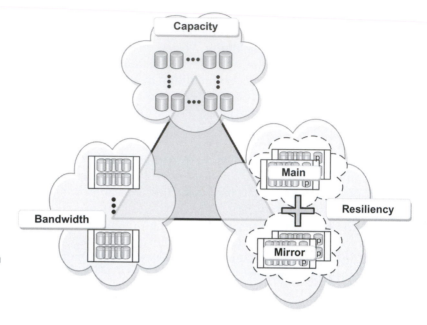

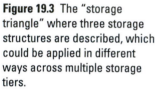

Figure 19.3 The "storage triangle" where three storage structures are described, which could be applied in different ways across multiple storage tiers.

This JBOD approach is not the recommended solution for a wide-scale, single-only storage implementation. However, this solution is not without amendments, as it could involve a mirrored (RAID 1) set of JBOD, or utilize a tape storage system for backup (not shown in the figure). This solution also has finite performance limitations and will only suffice as a second tier (or higher) solution without much online performance. Nonetheless, this is how the majority of PC workstations are configured, and reliance on other means of protection is becoming the norm (e.g., online Internet-connected storage backup in the cloud).

Bandwidth

The left lower corner of the triangle is where sets of striped RAID arrays (usually RAID 3 or RAID 5) could be used to provide both protection and bandwidth. Such a solution could be augmented with extensions using, for example, RAID 6 or RAID 53, RAID 10, etc. The significance here is that the data is protected at the block level, the drives are protected at the RAID-array level, and the system gets an additional benefit in that throughput (bandwidth) performance specs increase exponentially as more RAID sets are added. However, one of the today's drawbacks is with drive capacities increasing through the 1-TB boundary and headed toward 2-TB boundary, and beyond in short order, the number of drives needed in an array to achieve needed capacity goes down, but the time to rebuild a drive during a failover increases horribly. This is why many storage vendors are finding that for bandwidth and RAID-striped protection, it is almost better to use more of the subterabyte-sized drives and gain the performance by other means.

Resiliency

The ultimate in storage protection and resiliency is achieved when there is a MAIN storage subsystem and MIRROR backup, as depicted in the "storage triangle" of Figure 19.3. Here, one finds an exotic array of RAID 6 protected LUNs grouped into primary (or primary plus backup) and then a complete mirror of the same set of storage arrays is placed either adjacent to the main array or in a remote location for added protection. RAID 6 provides two levels of parity protection, often with another "hot spare" included. In this model, the data is striped across additional RAID 6 arrays (or LUNs), all of which collectively provide bandwidth and protection. Mirrored drives provide resiliency by allowing for a 100% failover to the other system without a loss of productivity or performance.

Dynamic Capacity Balancing

Balancing policies help enable the enterprise to create a larger pool of "virtual file servers" composed of existing file storage devices. When coupled with "file virtualization," a process that makes the physical location of the file immaterial, it is possible to aggregate various storage resources into a single pool. Completely utilizing a pool of storage resources falls on the shoulders of what is referred to as "dynamic capacity balancing."

Beyond getting the best economic value out of any existing storage resources, the capacity, bandwidth, (throughput), and processing power for these physical devices can be optimized for application performance using virtualization techniques. Grouping all the storage resources together under a common set of storage management policies allows administrators to perform data management tasks, such as load balancing and provisioning without disrupting users or applications, and it can be accomplished in real time.

Additional value is obtained because backups can be optimized by splitting the virtual file system into multiple physical ones and then by performing smaller backups in parallel to mitigate the complications and the time involved with a single, large backup. Restoration activities are then shortened as well. And with a single virtual file server, performance hot spots are eliminated because those individual devices are now aggregated and controlled by a single server instead of individually managed.

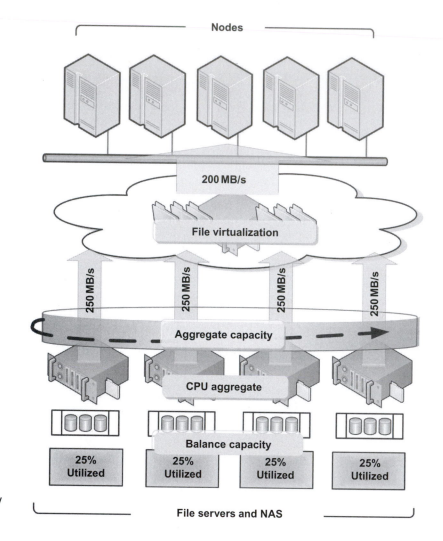
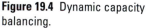

Figure 19.4 Dynamic capacity balancing.

Figure 19.4 depicts how minimally used resources are aggregated through the virtualization process to obtain more usability than when the individual resources are discretely addressed. The aggregation process, consisting of intelligent file virtualization, improves bandwidth and system-wide efficiency.

The depths and topics of overall load balancing at a system level involve several areas, not the least of which are network-based, and must certainly include all the elements of hosts, nodes, members of groups, servers, and the like. Load balancing, in theory, allows the distribution of inbound traffic across multiple back-end destinations, thus forcing the concept of a collection of back-end destinations. Clusters (also called pools or farms) are collections of similar "services" that are available on any number of hosts.

In moving media applications, services that provide for the transcoding of all video and audio streams throughout the organization would be housed onto what might be called the "transcode farm." Quality control and file-syntax compliance checking are a processing service that might be clustered to the "QC pool" and so on. The fundamental concept here is that all these systems have a collective object that refers to "all similar services." The task then becomes to make the best use of each of the services, without having to know (and independently control) the physical devices that provide the services.

The same applies to storage utilization, with the best use approach then being managed through the concepts of dynamic (load) capacity balancing.

Heterogeneous Environments

Influenced by an emphasis on cost control, much has been made on the value of heterogeneous storage architectures where storage elements from different vendors can be installed that are able to interoperate and still meet organizations' storage demands. Common to any "best-of-breed" IT purchase argument, the benefits cited in this philosophy are lower product acquisition costs due to price competition, potential decreases in total storage costs, and avoidance of proprietary solutions provided only with vendor lock-in.

Coupled with the slow progress perceived by the storage industry toward a more unified storage management environment, the lack of emerging storage management standards, or the consolidation of storage management tools, external third party solutions are coming of age as a centerpiece in resolving such issues as NAS sprawl, variances in performance across the overall enterprise-wide storage solutions' package, and a preponderance of individuals aimed at using departmental budgets to solve their own problems with little concern for the overall long-term enterprise storage management objectives.

Island Management

The time and effort it takes to manage islands of storage across a large enterprise are growing in proportion to the amount of storage added, which we all know is continuous. The complexity of employing storage components from diverse numbers of vendors necessitates developing compatibility matrices that must be matched and adhered to retain peak operational performance. This alone can grow exponentially with the increasing number of vendors that all too often provide a low-bid solution to an enterprise-level problem. So, these services must be outsourced, which also adds to the cost of operations and induces risk if or when failures occur.

Managing the different versions of embedded code, software, and driver interfaces can be even more complex, usually outside the expertise of most IT departments, especially those who have "help desk" oversaturation at much lower levels.

Storage management solutions that integrate multiple sets of heterogenic storage products need to provide user-transparent functionality through the employment of hidden, almost sideline, tool sets that effectively manage data tranformation from a virtual storage pool to the user/client platforms, and vice versa, regardless of whether the assets are stored on primary and secondary storage components. Storage management needs to enable flexibility and compatibility with network-attached storage (NAS) and storage area network (SAN) devices and servers in order to enjoy the benefits of virtualization across a heterogeneous infrastructure. By employing an intelligent in-line storage management solution that virtualizes the individual storage components, one can prevent the need for forklift upgrades of hardware, the replacement of existing file systems, or the installation of software agents across the enterprise.

Storage management solutions should use industry-standard file access protocols to communicate with clients and servers; for example, CIFS for Windows devices and NFS for Unix or Linux devices. The solution should not need to introduce a new file system and instead should only act as a proxy to those file systems that are already in place.

Employing RAID

The predominant method for data and storage protection comes from the multiple choices available when employing RAID technologies for resiliency and bandwidth. Using RAID to protect data on the hard disks reduces the risk that data will be lost should a drive fail, while at the same time improving data throughput and the bandwidth of the overall storage picture. In Chapter 6, the depths and dimensions of the various RAID levels are covered in much greater detail.

In platforms that require all three elements of the storage triangle, that is, capacity, bandwidth, and resiliency, it is important to select a RAID level that supports redundant parity and hot spares as an aid to maintain the responsiveness of the storage system. In the unfortunate event that a drive in an array (or LUN) fails, having the additional readiness of an extra parity drive will help maintain the operation of that segment of storage.

Yet RAID protection, mirroring, and remote extensions for disaster protection are only a part of the resiliency equation. We have explored storage tiering and other elements aimed at assuring "nondrive related" anomalies will not affect operations. Even with automation or storage management subsystems, we need to be even more certain that the storage platforms can address the answers to the resiliency questions with instruments that also focus directly on the physical disk media used in the storage subsystems.

Lost Write Protection

Other than during a complete disk failure, a write operation disk malfunction will rarely occur where a block of data is silently dropped or lost, but the disk is unable to detect the write failure, and it still signals a successful write action status (a false positive reporting). If no detection and correction mechanism are in place, this "lost write" event causes silent data corruption.

Checksums, used for data integrity (explained below) will not protect against a lost write event. By employing a "write signature" feature implemented in storage virtualization technology that aligns closely with RAID integration, this type of failure can be identified and will be detected upon the next read, and the data is then re-created using RAID. Such an implementation is available on systems from vendors, in particular NetApp, in conjunction with their Write Anywhere File Layout (WAFL) storage virtualization technology, where even block-oriented, SAN installations can have this level of protection.

Note that this is not the same as a "lost delayed-write data" error message that might have been received under extremely heavy file system stress activities (an occurrence in Windows 2000).

RAID Checksums for Data Integrity

High-performance, resilient storage solutions will frequently offer additional drive data protection schemes beyond those already implemented in the RAID controller. One of these methods generates a checksum for each block of data that is stored as part of that block's metadata. To ensure data accuracy, when that block is later read back, a new checksum is calculated from that read data and is then compared against the metadata originally stored for that block. Should the metadata differ, the data read back is presumed invalid; therefore, the requested data is then recreated from the parity information on the RAID set, and the data is rewritten to the original block. The entire check is re-created to validate the second (replaced) data set that can be properly recovered with valid data.

For active data sets, where reads and/or writes occur frequently, the checksum provides another avenue to data integrity. This form of resiliency is referred to as a "self-healing" storage activity and is used to proactively protect data path and other disk drive errors. In systems that employ this degree of self-preservation, the functions are usually turned on and remain on at all times.

RAID Scrubs

Ensuring drive reliability improves accessibility and in turn increases system resiliency. Enterprise drives, which are bound by compliance requirements, normally develop fewer errors than standard drives (e.g., SATA) found in home computers and PC workstations or used in secondary storage arrays. However, any drive may develop errors for a variety of reasons that can be both age- and usage-related. The unsuspected damage may occur from microscopic particles that have become lodged in the media, or frequently accessed areas of a drive may simply wear out and become corrupted. This kind of damage is called a "latent sector error" (LSE), because there is no routine way to detect the error until a request to read the data is made.

Another anomaly that can occur is from those files that are located in home directories, which tend not to be accessed nearly as often as active data, mainly because of the age of those files. While RAID checksums ensure that data read from the drive is accurate before it is offered out to the user (i.e., application) as "requested data," it may not be the full answer to ensuring disk drive integrity.

A process referred to as "scrubbing" improves data availability by finding and correcting media and checksum errors while a drive or RAID group is in its normal state. The activities may be run manually or assigned to a schedule, usually once a week for high-performance, high-availability systems.

Many current systems will perform sequential disk scrubbing, which is checking disk sectors sequentially at a constant rate, and is employed to detect LSEs in a timely fashion. Some storage system providers (such as EMC Corporation in cooperation with RSA) are looking at a different approach where rather than using the sequential method of scrubbing they will vary the scrubbing rate over a number of sectors in a given time period. Utilizing the fact that LSEs tend to arise in clusters, a repeated sampling of a region will identify LSEs faster than when scanned using a sequential process; this staggered adaptive strategy in theory makes sense.

Determining an optimal scrubbing strategy for a given disk configuration may in turn lead to a way to automatically engage a recovery operation when errors are detected. The results of the scrub could be transformed into the solid state/flash memory domain (as in SSDs) to predict errors in memory before they affect other cache implementations.

Ideally, both the scrubbing and checksum methods will help improve the reliability of storage systems and the availability of the information contained on those storage systems. While adaptive scrubbing algorithm technologies are still in their infancy, researchers further feel that these technologies will lead to better-designed algorithms that will significantly improve existing storage and data integrity technologies.

Predicted Errors

Enterprise disk systems and high-performance, intelligent storage platforms all employ levels of predictive diagnostics that aid in supporting advanced notifications of eminent drive failures. Some of these systems use the reporting features of the drives, plus their own data collection routines and algorithms, to signal that a drive may be failing or is about to fail. These systems will then jump into a routine that tries to read and then write as much as possible from the affected disk into a cache or hot standby disk, with the balance of the corrupted or missing data generated from parity.

Again this is a practice that is widely deployed by storage management systems and can routinely be found in professional broadcast videoserver systems, news-editing platforms, and purpose-built storage systems used in mission-critical applications.

Historical File Tracking

When automated storage tiering is employed, physical media consumption should theoretically be reduced. The added benefit in reduced storage consumption management is that the time required to support both backup and recovery periods is also decreased. These objectives are beneficial to controlling the physical costs of the media that include not only the capital costs of the hardware but also the operational costs of power, cooling, and data center or central equipment room real estate. In addition, automated tiering storage should offset the lost productivity time during the recovery periods. However, automation can also make it more difficult to locate and restore individual files from the backup media, unless other levels of system management are included.

Given that storage management is now more virtual in nature, a means to simplify file recovery is necessary. One of those methods is "historical file tracking," a method by which administrators can use elements of the storage management solution to identify the physical location of the individual files at any point in time. With file versioning, coupled with virtualization, it is now all the more important to know not only the name of the file but also the version of the file (usually chronologically categorized) so that time is not lost having to analyze the file content after the file or files have been located, restored, and prepared for usage.

Checkpoints and Snapshots

When integrating or combining heterogeneous storage environments into a virtual environment, for example, in the concepts described earlier, the potential for data corruption as a result of moving data between the storage tiers is always possible. The risks associated with data interchanges between disparate storage platforms, such as false writes or reporting of false writes, require an alternate means for ensuring data accuracy. One of the concepts developed to aid in validating that write actions to drives indeed occurred and that the data was properly recorded is referred to as "snapshotting."

Snapshots

Snapshots are used to capture an instance in time where all the states of the most recent read or write activities are recorded to a secondary protective storage subsystem. This procedure is a cache-based activity that quickly captures the changes in a data set, stores it into another location, and then uses it to match the present datasets to the data that was properly written to or read from main storage memory. The technology is used in support of coordinating physical snapshots across multiple NAS devices and file systems, even those from different vendors within the same virtual namespace. The snapshot is navigable in the same manner as the virtual file system from which it was created, giving users the ability to recover their files in a virtual environment.

Snapshots are useful for storing the state of the system so that an administrator could return to that state repeatedly. A virtual machine snapshot is a file-based representation of the state of a virtual machine at a given time. The snapshot will generally include both configuration and disk data.

In these highly active environments, snapshots will consume significant amounts of storage space over time, unless they are purged after backups or file audit/reconciliation. Snapshots are often contained to solid state (ram-disk like) devices, or similar short-term storage caches that are based on technology that can rapidly write data to the store, then hold it there while checks are made, and then purge it quickly in preparation for the next capture.

Checkpoint

A checkpoint, in a virtualization context, is a snapshot of the state of a virtual machine. Like a restore point in the Windows operating system, a checkpoint allows the administrator to return the virtual machine to a previous state.

Checkpoints are most commonly used to create backups before conducting updates. Should an update fail or cause problems, the administrator can return the virtual machine to its state prior to the update. The recover action is used to return the system to the checkpoint state.

Virtualization in File-Based Storage

Virtualization is not new to most computing environments. Parenthetically, any technology that is camouflaged behind an interface that masks the details of how that technology is actually implemented could be called virtual.

Virtualization, from the perspective of a server needing to address the storage systems, is used to abstract a view of the storage, its locations, and its resources.

Needs and Wants for Next Generation Storage

Driven by the enormous growth in file-based information and the critical needs to more reliably and cost-effectively manage these information assets, organizations from small offices through production boutiques to enterprise-size IT-centric corporations and motion picture production studios are implementing new strategies for building and managing file-based storage solutions. These appropriately called next generation ("NextGen") solutions must now meet prescribed business and technical requirements to be successful and to provide value to the organization. Corporations and businesses are now compelled to retain significantly more information, electronic and otherwise, than in the past.

These NextGen solutions now allow enterprises to deploy and consistently manage services across a wide range of disk- and tape-based storage tiers with different performances, capacities, availabilities, and cost characteristics. The challenge is that they must attempt to do this without having to make a forklift level, wholesale displacement of their existing assets. NextGen systems now enable a common set of scalable and highly available global namespaces that support data migration, data life-cycle management, and data protection services across multiple storage tiers.

Virtualization, in concert with cloud-based storage technology, is a widely discussed trend throughout the IT industry. For traditional workstation and certain server implementations, the IT managers may be consolidating many x86-based applications onto a single server.

Storage Virtualization

Virtualization has become an equally important trend in the storage market. Yet, the focus is almost exactly the opposite. Rather than consolidating multiple servers onto one piece of hardware (as in the traditional virtualization sense), network-based storage virtualization is frequently about allowing storage professionals to manage multiple storage systems (e.g., NAS- and SAN-attached arrays) into a centralized pool of storage capacity. These next generation storage systems will allow IT managers to more straightforwardly and nondisruptively migrate data between storage platforms, heighten the utilization of installed capacity, scale data protection and security processes, and implement tiered storage policies to control costs.

The following sections will explore the elements of file virtualization, and the techniques and technologies that once lived entirely in the data center but are now migrating to the cloud as we search for improvements in storage and data management.

File Virtualization at a Network Level

Determining objectives and considering what elements to address when looking at network-based file virtualization can be approached by examining some general cases and practices that IT administrators are faced with when looking for solutions to this global explosion of data. Three of those areas will be looked at in the following sections:
- File migration and consolidation
- Dynamic storage tiering
- File sharing on a global dimension

File Migration and Consolidation

In order to boost utilization of NAS systems, consider the consolidation of dispersed file servers or legacy NAS systems onto a smaller number of NAS systems. This opportunity enables greater data sharing and improves both backup and data retention processes. The challenge to this is that the migration time for even a small set of file servers can take upwards of a year to plan, implement, and complete. It can take a huge number of resources away from the IT-management side and be quite disruptive to users, limiting productivity and forcing continual incremental workflow adjustments.

Of course, these numbers grow continually, especially when organizations of any scale might be adding a terabyte or more of data per week to their NAS systems. By changing to a file virtualization approach, organizations are able to reduce all the elements that would have been involved with migration, including the time associated with planning and mostly if not all of the downtime. In some cases, this implementation methodology dropped from 1 year to less than 1 month and radically reduced the amount of disruption to users and productivity.

Dynamic Storage Tiering

Optimizing capacity of NAS systems so as to control cost and NAS sprawl can be resolved by deploying a solution that moves old, stale, and infrequently accessed data and the associated backup copies of that data to a storage tier that focuses on capacity and low cost (refer again to the "storage triangle" of Fig. 19.3). End users will typically refuse to eliminate old files from networked drives, dispersed production editing platforms, e-mail systems, and other departmentally isolated storage platforms. These islanders further refuse to manually move data to separate archival drives, elevating the risk factor to enormous proportions. Most use cases will find that as much as 60–80% of this stored data is infrequently accessed. So, the time and capacity management issue becomes even greater because backing up all this infrequently used data now increases the backup times, makes data more complicated to locate when or if it must be restored, and leads to massive duplication of data on tapes. Given that most tape backup libraries charge by the volume of tape being administered, the cost impacts to the bottom line are massive.

By employing the techniques of network-based file virtualization, case studies in as recent as the 2007 time frame (about the time when file virtualization emerged to the forefront) showed that organizations were able to reduce spending on disk storage hardware by around 40–60%. In IT-based organizations, some found that they reduced the recovery times for files and e-mail from days to hours and further reduced the time and costs of backup to tape by 50–80%.

By shifting the data from high-performance NAS-head configured storage to less costly SATA drives (an average cost reduction of around 75% only for the drives), and by employing an auto-mated data migration system using virtualized files, case studies showed that the frequency of backing up older files (e.g., spread sheets, e-mail, general office documents) decreased from once a week to once a month.

For media organizations, such as content owners that produce their own original programming with hundreds to thousands of "legacy" or archived clips or program segments, which could be located all over the enterprise, these activities could be greatly reduced once a file-virtualization program with automated data migration is set in place. Media asset and content management solutions generally provide some of this functionality, but more is necessary if consolidation and protection of assets are to be achieved.

File Sharing on a Global Dimension

Dedicated content production systems have been wrangling their own data on their own platform for ages. With the trend continu-ing, whereby isolated companies work on different platforms and with various applications, sharing the content during the pro-gram or production development processes is a growing concern. Not only are there connectivity issues to be dealt with but also file versioning, security, and true collaboration are all high on the agenda.

When the organizations are geographically separated, this problem increases geometrically. To facilitate collaboration on projects or program production, all these users need a reliable, easy to manage, and secure means of sharing files across diverse geographically separated locations in order to boost productivity and, more importantly, to minimize version control issues. The challenges are raised when considering that each department, location, or independent contractor has its own file namespace, so sharing either requires opening up access to all potential users (posing major security risks) or necessitates the continual repli-cation of files over long distances.

File virtualization can improve productivity by allowing users in multiple workgroups and remote locations to collaborate more effectively through a common access platform that allows them to share files transparently between them. Using an automated migration and file management platform will aid these processes in a global sense because new workgroups and users no longer need to know what the other workgroups or locations' particular file naming requirements are. They simply work as usual, and in the background, the file management system handles all the "under the hood" storage, backup, duplication, or replication activities, improving productivity and minimizing risks due to security flaws or lost data.

Storage Resource Virtualization

Virtualized storage resources are becoming part of the new "converged infrastructure" (Fig. 19.5). In order to realize the true benefits of convergence, storage solutions are needed that will easily accommodate data growth and align strongly to business applications. A converged infrastructure will use its storage resources to be virtualized, which then allows for the dynamic provisioning of resources to support applications when capacity (or bandwidth) is needed most. This enables capacity optimized with lower cost components to be used effectively. It will reduce management complexities as the organization reacts to the explosive growth is data.

One of the principle concepts behind storage virtualization is its ability to address the three dimensions of storage system demands, while maintaining a single environment that is transparent to the user and easily administered throughout the enterprise storage life cycle. For this, all the following elements of scaling are required:

- Scale-up—addresses increased system demands through the dynamic addition of virtual storage directors, ports, caches, and storage capacity. Such scaling activities aid in managing storage growth, while continuing to provide the highest performance for the environment.

- Scale-out—meets the multiple demands by dynamically combining multiple devices into a logical system with shared resources to support the increased demand in virtualized server environments and to ensure the quality of service expected through the partitioning of cache, ports, and access control based on resource groupings.

- Scale-deep—extends the storage value by virtualizing new, existing external storage systems on a dynamic basis, even with storage provided by different vendors. Scale-deep enables the off-loading of less demanding data to lower (external) tiers so as to optimize the high availability (HA) of tier 1 resources.

Figure 19.5 A virtualized storage infrastructure.

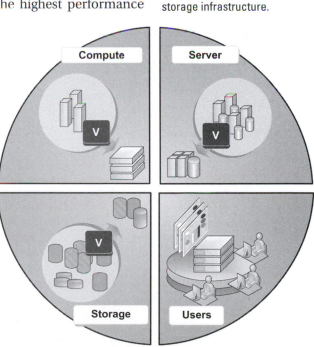

When and How Much

Even though virtualization is now showing up in all the segments of the storage infrastructure, there still remains some misunderstanding on when to use it and even where to embed it. Administrators see control and visibility of virtualization as key elements in obtaining the maximum benefits possible from this technology. When to use it depends in part on the physical and logical sizes of the storage infrastructure, the locations that will be consolidated, and the type of applications running on the platforms.

Storage managers will need to balance the benefits of virtualization against the complexity it brings. They need to match the intelligence of the existing SAN or NAS components to the levels of (file) server and degree of storage virtualization. Through partitioning, the process of assigning each layer of storage virtualization its own administration, bandwidth, and processing, the storage manager can determine how best to satisfy the requirements at each layer. This prevents applications in one partition from impacting the productive aspects of another.

The degree of virtualization needs to be analyzed and tested. Sometimes it is more appropriate to use less virtualization for performance-intensive applications. For example, a GPU processor component may be better suited to one layer of storage versus a render farm engine that needs a different layer to achieve its throughput targets. This concept can be applied to "edit in place" functionality for nonlinear editorial production versus art-intensive graphics composition. Both need highly available and independently addressable workspaces to accomplish their tasks due in part to the fine-tuning of the applications running on the workstations. However, with file format interchange capabilities, such as in the MXF format, this hurdle is getting lower to cross as time moves on.

Scaling into virtualized storage or servers begin with the low performance services or the less utilized segments of the environment. This is because low performing servers will see the highest performance returns when moved to a virtual environment. High-performance, high-utilization components are already finely tuned to achieve maximum throughput and may only realize a modest gain in performance.

Table 19.1 shows the comparison of legacy solutions with the NextGen storage management solutions.

Fault Tolerance

Designing a system that has no "single point of failure" (SPOF) is a common issue facing most engineering teams when answering Requests for Proposals (RFPs) related to media storage

Table 19.1 Next Generation Storage Management Solutions Comparisons

Function or Feature	Next Generation Storage Management	Legacy Storage Management
Data reduction	Progressive and incremental selections	Full + incremental and Full + differential
Deduplication	Integrated across all elements	Duplicate backup and infrastructure
Load balancing	Transfer workloads easily	None
Tiered storage	Flexible, automated ability to use all media forms (tape-to-disk, optical)	Limited, individually applied per storage type or media
Data recovery	Rapid, near-instant restore	Restore to disk required before migration
Server recovery	Integrated basic/bare machine recovery	None

Source: Information and concepts are derived in part from IBM's "Tivoli" storage management products

technologies. Improperly judging what has become a mostly generalized "no-SPOF" requirement often leads to over engineering the solution. However, if the system is under engineered the approach leads to potential liabilities should their "low bid" be awarded and the provider is forced to design a system that fails. When confronted with designing or providing for a fault tolerant system, the better statement would be one that the end user sees as livable and more in tune with real-life operations. So the question that needs to be answered becomes "explain how your system will be fault tolerant using the components provided for in your design." Answering this question correctly requires that the vendor have a true and fundamental understanding of what fault tolerance really means and systems in your design." To answer that statement, fundamental understanding of what fault tolerance really means is required.

Fault tolerance is the property that enables a system to continue operating properly in the event of the failure of one or more components within the system. Sometimes called "graceful degradation," the concept to understand is that if the operating quality of a system decreases at all, the decrease is proportional to the severity of the failure of the component. These components could be the network, the transmission protocol, the protection scheme for the disk arrays, the software applications, etc.

Fault tolerance can be achieved by recognizing and anticipating conditions that are well outside the routine expectations and performance of a system (when functioning properly) and then designing the system to handle them. It could be that the systems either will muddle through the fault with transparent but reduced performance or will survive the problem by switching over to a completely redundant parallel system that simply waits in the wings to be called to duty.

Fault-Tolerance Characteristics

Systems that are designed for high availability and high reliability are built so that they are resilient to all conditions related to failover. Fault-tolerant systems are characterized into two classifications: planned service outages and unplanned service outages. The services are measured at the application level because, for the most part, the hardware level (when it fails) will more than likely be realized first at the application level.

Fault tolerance is, in a sense, the opposite of scalability. A system is considered scalable when its ability as an application or a product to continue to function well is changed in size or volume according to a user's need. With this, it is the ability not only to function well in the rescaled situation but also to actually take full advantage of it. A system's fault-tolerance factor is considered high when, as the system begins to scale down due to an issue in any one or more of its components (or subsystems), it will continue to work but with elements of performance degradation that do not significantly impact the user's needs.

There is obviously a point where fault tolerance moves to the stage of failover, but if the system was designed with sufficient protective measures, then it will failover seamlessly and operations will continue undisrupted.

To meet these objectives, the basic characteristics required are:

- No single point of repair—that is, all components must be either replaceable or repairable without risk to terminating operational services.
- Fault isolation—a failing component can be detected and quarantined (isolated) from the rest of the system to enable diagnostics or repairs to occur.
- Fault containment—the potential for a failing component to continue to affect other components must be alleviated so that propagation of the failure does not escalate to the level of a system failover or disaster.
- Ability and availability of reversion—the ability of a system to return to normal operations once the failed components or issues have been rectified.

Fault tolerance is particularly sought after in high-availability or life-critical systems. However, in the context of storage systems, a precursor to fault tolerance is high availability leading to systems or components that will be in continuous operation for a long duration of time.

Availability is measured relative to a figure of 100% operational; that is, a "never failing" condition. This is a widely held and yet extremely difficult to achieve standard often known by the vernacular of "five 9s" (99.999%) availability. This level of service, often used in statements described in "service level agreements" (SLAs), is equivalent to only 5.26 min/year of outage (6.05 seconds of downtime in a 1-week period). It is also a statement that requires a substantial amount of definition as to just what downtime, failure, or reduced performance mean. In many cases, especially for SLAs, this becomes an answerable and defendable question only by attorneys.

Complex Systems

By nature, systems with a high degree of complexity are generally composed of multiple parts that when properly combined take advantage of their respective strengths to build a value that is much greater than the sum of their individual parts. If there are many parts in the systems, then it makes sense to have some of those "mission-critical" parts far more fault tolerant than others. This brings in the concept of multipathing and how it helps to achieve the effective implementation of complex systems.

Multipathing

Simply stated, when there is more than one means to get to the same physical device, then the system is built with multipathing.

Multipathing can be achieved by using several adapters in a server that is assigned to the same logical unit (LUN) or volume in a storage platform. Multipathing may be implemented through additional ports in an enterprise class switch or storage subsystem (see Fig. 19.6), or by a combination of both. In complex systems (see Fig. 19.7), this happens with multiple NICs, dual redundant switches, two or more media directors, and split storage arrays with sufficient capacity and availability to service the entire system on their own (i.e., stand-alone).

Bottlenecking

The previous examples are more physical in nature than logical, although the processes that manage the path that is in command are essentially software related. Performance in an application

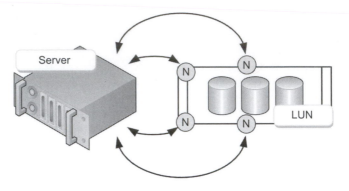

Figure 19.6 Multipathing by providing more than a single adapter between a server and a storage device.

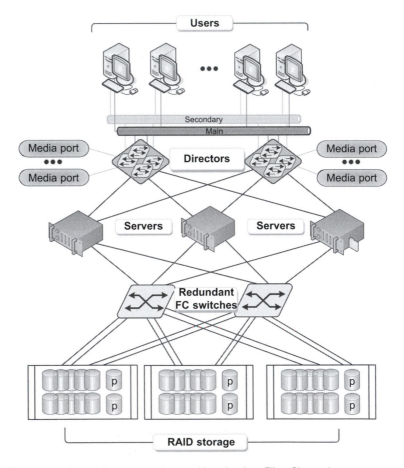

Figure 19.7 A complex server system with redundant Fibre Channel storage switches, media directors, LAN switches, NICs, and media ports.

depends upon several physical components (e.g., the memory, disk, or CPU), such as the speed of the network and disk I/O and the associated parameters of the application servicing the user.

One means to increase performance, and thus build resiliency and fault tolerance, is to remove bottlenecks in the servers, storage systems, and networks. Multipathing can help alleviate bottlenecks in the following ways:

- Add additional I/O adapters to the server—they increase the I/O rate of the server.
- Use or add additional host adapters on the enterprise storage system—this allows for more throughput (bandwidth) provided the controllers can address the increased I/O cycles.
- Add more CPU horsepower or data flow management capabilities—systems can add more compute power or prioritize data activities on an application-specific basis.
- Add multipathing software—increases the systems' abilities to handle multiple streams simultaneously, as in render farm engines or content distribution platforms.

Disk mirroring, explained in Chapter 6 as RAID 1, places two copies of all the data on two drives. This is accomplished either in hardware or software by the RAID controller. Software mirroring accomplishes the same function but does not employ an outboard hardware controller, instead one or more applications create the duplicate content and manage its distribution to and from the two (or more) mirrored disk drives. Hardware controllers manage these activities without CPU intervention.

Multipathing is ideal when there is a nonmirrored environment or when mirroring is not an option. Although mirroring protects against data loss by a disk failure, if the mirror ends up with the same errors as the primary, nothing has been resolved.

Clustering

The grouping of servers and/or other resources so as to provide a set of network resources to a client as a single system, which enables high availability (HA), parallel processing, and/or load balancing, is called "clustering." Chapter 14 discusses clustering in greater depth, so this section will focus more on the fault-tolerance aspects in storage systems.

Clustering groups multiple workstations and servers, multiple storage devices, and redundant interconnections to form what appears to the outside user as a single highly-available system. Clustering may be used to flatten out application or storage hot spots, called "load balancing," so as to achieve maximum utilization of the resources. Advocates suggest that an enterprise can reach 99.999% availability by employing cluster technologies, yet these numbers must consider all the influences across the entire organization.

Load balancing will divide the amount of work that a compute system is assigned to do among two or more compute platforms (e.g., individual workstations) so that more work is accomplished in the same period of time. Load balancing can be implemented with a combination of hardware and software, similar in function to what modern CPUs with multicore processors might do instead of having multiple fully fledged chassis-like workstations employed. Load balancing is typically the chief reason for computer server clustering.

An alternative to load balancing is parallel processing whereby program execution is accelerated by dividing the instructions and activities among multiple processors (CPUs typically) with the objective of running a program in less time.

Clustering further protects the client from changes to the physical hardware, which brings a number of benefits, especially in terms of high availability. Resources on clustered servers act as highly available versions of heretofore unclustered resources.

Nondisruptive Operations

Administrators have the availability to employ any number of policies that are useful for the tasks of data migration, upgrades, and preserving fault tolerance. Regardless of whether the tasks are quite simple, such as migrating from one RAID set to another or larger, more complex activities that involve moving entire sets of individual files to one file system, all these activities must appear nondisruptive or fault-tolerance sustainability is not achieved.

When performing activities such as data migration or upgrades, especially between heterogeneous storage devices (e.g., both NFS- and CIFS-oriented data),they should be scheduled so as to avoid peak traffic times or system backup windows. Migrations should also be performed without changes to mount points or drive mappings so as to eliminate outages and mitigate business disruption that might have been previously associated with other data migrations.

Upgrades, if at all possible, should be implemented on redundant hardware before committing them to the system full time. Versioning of all software and hardware should be well documented and validated against conflicts with legacy versions of any components in the enterprise system, unless of course those other systems will never interact with each other in any form (something that is highly unlikely in today's technology wrapped world).

Key sets of considerations should be understood and planned to avoid disrupting business activities that would otherwise impact users or halt applications. High-performance HA systems will usually allow administrators to perform data migrations for any reason at anytime. This class of system will support the completion of data migrations in less time and with no need to schedule downtime with business groups or users. When performed properly under the control of automated policies, data migration will use fewer resources and eliminate the requirements for reconfiguration of individual clients.

Conclusion

Resilient systems, high-availability systems, and fault-tolerance systems, including those using virtualized components, are now all a part of the "expected performance criteria" that we have grown to depend upon for e-commerce, homeland security, banking, and even simple everyday social networking.

The media and entertainment industry has grown into the same mold as it produces more content in shorter time frames, with less people and declining budgets. By providing a service-oriented architecture (SOA) that is composed of resilient HA systems that users can depend upon to accomplish their work—even in times when certain fault-tolerance systems have moved into backup mode or are recovering from a failover—we can obtain a much greater value from both our legacy existing systems and any new systems that we add to the enterprise working environment.

Further Readings

"Fault Tolerant Storage Multipathing and Clustering Solutions for Open Systems for the IBM ESS," IBM Redbooks, April 2002

White papers, product design literature, and other resources from storage providers including Network Appliance (NetApp), EMC Corporation, F5, Hitachi Data Systems, and IBM are available at the following websites:

http://www.netapp.com

http://www.emc.com

http://www.f5.com

http://www.hds.com

http://www.ibm.com

INDEX

Page numbers followed by *f* indicates a figure and *t* indicates a table.

NAS (*continued*)
nontraditional approaches,
567–571
scale out, 494–496
scale up, 494–495
scaling, 492–493, 493*f*
storage topologies, 495–496
secure disks, 309–310
servers, 442, 442*f*, 443*f*
solutions, 492
sprawl, 493
workload sharing, 475–476
Networked services, 27–28
Networked storage
logical and physical
connectivity
application layer, 436
data link layer, 433–434, 433*f*
network layer, 434
physical layer, 431–433
presentation layer, 436
session layer, 435–436
transport layer, 434–435
storage system environment,
430–431
Networks, 445
block level, 441
DAS, 439–442, 439*f*
data networks, 437–438
file level, 441
storage networks, 438–439
voice networks, 436–437
Next generation storage, 611*t*
needs and wants for, 605–606
NIC, *see* Network interface card
NIST, *see* National Institute of
Standards and Technology
NLE, *see* Nonlinear editing;
Nonlinear video editing
NL_Port, 450
Nodes, 447
No-ID recording, 102
Nondisruptive operations,
616–617
Nonlinear editing (NLE), 46, 65,
214, 334, 335
definition of, 215
implementations, 216
platform, 18

Nonlinear video editing (NLE),
524
Non-real time, 214–216
computerized editing, 216
offline editing, 215
Non-return-to-zero inverted
(NRZI), encoding, 191
Non-volatile memory (NVM),
167
NOR, 169
cell structures, 172*f*
flash memory, 169–170
vs. NAND, 171
N_Port, 450
NRZI, *see* Non-return-to-zero
inverted
N-Step-SCAN, 91
NTSC, *see* National Television
Systems Committee
Numbers, RAID by, 140–141

Object based storage devices
(OBSD), 303–304, 312
access control and security,
309–310
applications of, 321–324
attributes, 305–307
categories, 307–310
command interface, 305
disk structures, 303*f*
management structure,
318–319
OSD command set, 305
OSD versions, 307
security mechanisms,
319–321
types of, 304
versions, 307
Object identifier (OID), 302
OBSD, *see* Object based storage
devices
Obstacles, 96–97
OEM systems, 379
Offline editing, 215
Off-line transcoding, 250
Onetime pad (OTP) protection
registers, 179
OP-Atom, *see* Operational
Pattern Atom

Open Systems Interconnection
(OSI), 256
model, 68, 432*f*
application layer, 436
data link layer, 433*f*,
433–434
network layer, 434
physical layer, 431–433
presentation layer, 436
session layer, 435–436
transport layer, 434–435
Operational objectives, 590–592
Operational pattern (OP), 233
generalized, 236, 236*f*
Operational Pattern Atom (OP-
Atom) in MXF, 234–235, 235*t*
OPS, *see* Oracle Parallel Server
Optical media
care and handling, 210–211
definitions, 188–195
format for recording, 200*t*
terminologies with
misconceptions, 189–195
Optical-based drives, 521
Optimistic transactions, 537
Optimization using tiered
approach, 521
Oracle Parallel Server (OPS), 418
Oracle Videoserver, 42
Organizational requirements,
328–329
Organizational services, 399
OSI, *see* Open Systems
Interconnection
Out-of-band
agents, 561
aggregators, 571

Package Complexity axis, 237
Page-level tiering, 497
Pages, arrays of cells, 173–174
PAL, *see* Phase Alternating Line
Parallel ATA (PATA), 110*f*,
116–117, 137
Parallel buses, 110–111
Parallel file systems, 568–569
Parallel heading
NFS servers, 314
parallel NFS, 314–318